# Understanding
# CURRENT PROCEDURAL
# TERMINOLOGY & HCPCS
## Coding Systems

**2023**

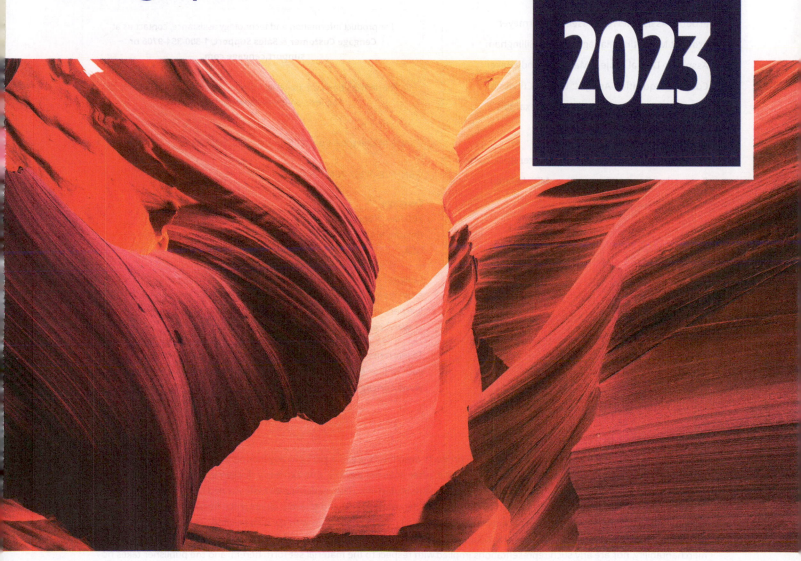

## Mary Jo Bowie
### MS, BS, AAS, RHIA

Cengage

Australia • Brazil • Canada • Mexico • Singapore • United Kingdom • United States

**Understanding Current Procedural Terminology & HCPCS Coding Systems, 2023 edition**
**Mary Jo Bowie**

SVP, Product: Erin Joyner

VP, Product: Thais Alencar

Associate Portfolio Product Manager: Laura Stewart

Sr. Portfolio Product Manager: Stephen G. Smith

Learning Designer: Jarmila Sawicka

Content Manager: Mark Peplowski

Product Assistant: Tennessee Sundermeyer

Product Marketing Manager: Annie Gillingham

Associate Digital Project Manager: Andy Baker

Content Acquisition Analyst: Erin McCullough

Sr. Manager, Content Acquisition: Alexandra Ricciardi

Designer: Gaby McCracken

Cover Image Source: antishock/Shutterstock.com

Production Service/Compositor: MPS Limited

Library of Congress Control Number: 2022920916

ISBN: 978-0-357-76430-5

**Cengage**
200 Pier 4 Boulevard
Boston, MA 02210
USA

Cengage is a leading provider of customized learning solutions. Our employees reside in nearly 40 different countries and serve digital learners in 165 countries around the world. Find your local representative at **www.cengage.com.**

To learn more about Cengage platforms and services, register or access your online learning solution, or purchase materials for your course, visit **www.cengage.com.**

**Notice to the Reader**

Printed in Mexico
Print Number: 1     Print Year: 2022

# TABLE OF CONTENTS

Preface ............................... ix

How to Use the Textbook ............. xiii

**Chapter 1: Introduction to Current Procedural Terminology          1**

**Introduction** . . . . . . . . . . . . . . . . . . . .1

**History of Current Procedural Terminology** . . . . . . . . . . . . . . . . . . .2

**The Structure and Design of CPT** . .2

The Introduction . . . . . . . . . . . . . . . . .3

Symbols . . . . . . . . . . . . . . . . . . . . .3

Sections, Subsections, Categories, Subcategories, and Headings of the CPT Manual . . . . . . . . . . . . . . .6

Guidelines . . . . . . . . . . . . . . . . . . . .7

Index . . . . . . . . . . . . . . . . . . . . . . . .8

Appendices . . . . . . . . . . . . . . . . . . . .8

**CPT as Part of HCPCS** . . . . . . . . .10

HCPCS . . . . . . . . . . . . . . . . . . . . . .10

**Summary** . . . . . . . . . . . . . . . . . . . . .11

**Internet Links** . . . . . . . . . . . . . . . . .11

**Chapter Review** . . . . . . . . . . . . . . . .11

**Coding Assignments** . . . . . . . . . . .12

**Short Answer** . . . . . . . . . . . . . . . . .12

**Chapter 2: Modifiers          14**

**Introduction** . . . . . . . . . . . . . . . . . .15

**Definition and Purposes of Modifiers** . . . . . . . . . . . . . . . . . . .15

**Use of Modifiers for Various Procedures and Service Locations** . . . . . . . . . . . . . . . . . . .16

Modifiers Used with Physician Services . . . . . . . . . . . . . . . . . . . .16

Use of Multiple Modifiers— Modifier 99 . . . . . . . . . . . . . . . . . .17

**Modifiers Used for Hospital Outpatient Services** . . . . . . . . . .18

Modifiers Approved for Ambulatory Surgery Center Hospital Outpatient Use . . . . . . . . . . . . . .18

**CPT Level I Modifiers** . . . . . . . . . .19

Increased Procedural Services— Modifier 22 . . . . . . . . . . . . . . . . . .19

Unusual Anesthesia—Modifier 23 . . .19

Unrelated Evaluation and Management Service by the Same Physician or Other Qualified Health Care Professional During Postoperative Period—Modifier 24 . . . . . . . . . . .19

Significant, Separately Identifiable Evaluation and Management Service by the Same Physician or Other Qualified Health Care Professional on the Same Day of the Procedure or Other Service—Modifier 25 . . . .20

Professional Component— Modifier 26 . . . . . . . . . . . . . . . . . .20

Multiple Outpatient Hospital E/M Encounters on the Same Date—Modifier 27 . . . . . . . . . . . .20

Mandated Services—Modifier 32 . . .21

Preventive Service—Modifier 33 . . .21

Anesthesia by Surgeon— Modifier 47 . . . . . . . . . . . . . . . . . .21

Bilateral Procedure—Modifier 50 . . .21

Multiple Procedures—Modifier 51 . . .22

Reduced Services—Modifier 52 . . .22

Discontinued Procedure— Modifier 53 . . . . . . . . . . . . . . . . . .22

Surgical Care Only—Modifier 54 . . .23

Postoperative Management Only—Modifier 55 . . . . . . . . . . . .23

Preoperative Management Only—Modifier 56 . . . . . . . . . . . .23

Decision for Surgery—Modifier 57 . . .23

Staged or Related Procedure or Service by the Same Physician or Other Qualified Health Care Professional During the Postoperative Period—Modifier 58 . . . . . . . . . . .24

Distinct Procedural Service— Modifier 59 . . . . . . . . . . . . . . . . . .24

Two Surgeons—Modifier 62 . . . . . .25

Procedure Performed on Infants Less Than 4 kg—Modifier 63 . . . .25

Surgical Team—Modifier 66 . . . . . .25

Discontinued Outpatient Hospital/ Ambulatory Surgery Center (ASC) Procedure Prior to the Administration of Anesthesia—Modifier 73 . . . . . .26

Discontinued Outpatient Hospital/ Ambulatory Surgery Center (ASC) Procedure After Administration of Anesthesia—Modifier 74 . . . . . . . .26

Repeat Procedure or Service by Same Physician or Other Qualified Health Care Professional— Modifier 76 . . . . . . . . . . . . . . . . . .26

Repeat Procedure or Service by Another Physician or Other Qualified Health Care Professional— Modifier 77 . . . . . . . . . . . . . . . . . .26

Unplanned Return to the Operating/ Procedure Room by the Same Physician or Other Qualified Health Care Professional Following Initial Procedure for a Related Procedure During the Postoperative Period— Modifier 78 . . . . . . . . . . . . . . . . . .27

Unrelated Procedure or Service by the Same Physician or Other Qualified Health Care Professional During the Postoperative Period— Modifier 79 . . . . . . . . . . . . . . . . . .27

Assistant Surgeon—Modifier 80 . . .27

Minimum Assistant Surgeon— Modifier 81 . . . . . . . . . . . . . . . . . .27

Assistant Surgeon (When Qualified Resident Surgeon Is Not Available in a Teaching Facility)— Modifier 82 . . . . . . . . . . . . . . . . . .28

Reference (Outside) Laboratory— Modifier 90 . . . . . . . . . . . . . . . . . .28

Repeat Clinical Diagnostic Laboratory Test—Modifier 91 . . . .28

Alternative Laboratory Platform Testing—Modifier 92 . . . . . . . . . . .28

Synchronous Telemedicine Service Rendered Via Telephone or Other Real-Time Interactive Audio-Only Telecommunications System—Modifier 93 . . . . . . . . . . .29

Synchronous Telemedicine Service Rendered Via a Real-Time Interactive Audio and Video Telecommunications System—Modifier 95 . . . . . . . . . . .29

Habilitative Services—Modifier 96 . . . 29

Rehabilitative Services— Modifier 97 . . . . . . . . . . . . . . . . . .30

Multiple Modifiers—Modifier 99 . . .30

**HCPCS Level II Modifiers** . . . . . . 30

Level II—HCPCS Alphanumeric Modifiers . . . . . . . . . . . . . . . . . . . .30

Additional Modifiers F to G9 . . . . . .32

G Modifiers . . . . . . . . . . . . . . . . . . .33

Modifiers J through V . . . . . . . . . . .33

Ambulance Origin and Destination Modifiers . . . . . . . . . . . . . . . . . . . .35

**Summary** . . . . . . . . . . . . . . . . . . . . 35

**Internet Links** . . . . . . . . . . . . . . . . .36

**Chapter Review** . . . . . . . . . . . . . . .36

**Case Studies** . . . . . . . . . . . . . . . . .37

**Chapter 3: Evaluation and Management          40**

**Introduction** . . . . . . . . . . . . . . . . . .41

**Documentation Guidelines for Evaluation and Management Services** . . . . . . . . . . . . . . . . . . . .41

**Overview of the Evaluation and Management Section** . . . . . . . . . .42

**Evaluation and Management Coding** . . . . . . . . . . . . . . . . . . . . 43

New Patients versus Established Patients . . . . . . . . . . . . . . . . . . . . .43

Location of the Service Provided . .45

Office or Other Outpatient Services (99202–99215) . . . . . . . . . . . . . . .47

Documentation of Patient's History and Examination . . . . . . . . . . . . . .51

Hospital Inpatient and Observation Care Services Coding . . . . . . . . . .59

Consultations . . . . . . . . . . . . . . . . .61

Emergency Department Services
(99281–99288). . . . . . . . . . . . . .63

Critical Care Services (99291 and
99292) . . . . . . . . . . . . . . . . . . . . .64

Nursing Facility Services
(99304–99316). . . . . . . . . . . . . .68

Home or Residence Services
(99341–99350). . . . . . . . . . . . . .70

Preventive Medicine Services
(99381–99429). . . . . . . .73

Non-Face-to-Face Services (99091,
99421–99423, 99441–99458, 99473,
99474) . . . . . . . . . . . . . . . . . . . .75

Special Evaluation and Management
Services (99450–99456) . . . . . . .75

Newborn Care (99460–99463) . . . .75

Delivery/Birthing Room Attendance
and Resuscitation Services
(99464, 99465). . . . . . . . . . . . .76

Care Management Services (99424-
99427, 99437, 99487, 99489, 99490,
99491, 99439). . . . . . . . . . . . .76

Transitional Care Management
Services (99495, 99496) . . . . . . .77

Advance Care Planning
(99497, 99498) . . . . . . . . . . . .77

Other Evaluation and Management
Services (99499) . . . . . . . . . . . .77

**Summary**. . . . . . . . . . . . . . . . . . .**77**

**Internet Links**. . . . . . . . . . . . . . .**78**

**Chapter Review**. . . . . . . . . . . . . .**78**

**Case Studies**. . . . . . . . . . . . . . **80**

**Chapter 4: Anesthesia           85**

**Introduction** . . . . . . . . . . . . . . . **86**

**Guidelines Related to the National
Correct Coding Initiative (NCCI)**. . .**86**

**Abbreviations Relating to
Anesthesia** . . . . . . . . . . . . . . . . . **86**

**What Is Anesthesia, and How Is It
Administered?**. . . . . . . . . . . . . . .**87**

Types of Anesthesia. . . . . . . . . . . .87

**Coding and Billing Anesthesia
Services** . . . . . . . . . . . . . . . . . . . **88**

Arrangement of the Anesthesia
Section. . . . . . . . . . . . . . . . . . . .88

Locating Anesthesia Procedure
Codes . . . . . . . . . . . . . . . . . . . .88

Anesthesia Modifiers . . . . . . . . . . .89

**Calculating Anesthesia
Charges**. . . . . . . . . . . . . . . . . . **90**

Basic Value. . . . . . . . . . . . . . . . . .91

Time Units . . . . . . . . . . . . . . . . . . .91

Modifying Units . . . . . . . . . . . . . . .91

**Special Billing Consideration—
Anesthetic Administered by
Physician**. . . . . . . . . . . . . . . . . . .**93**

Moderate or Conscious Sedation. . . 94

**Billing Concerns** . . . . . . . . . . . . .**94**

**Summary**. . . . . . . . . . . . . . . . . . .**94**

**Internet Links**. . . . . . . . . . . . . . .**94**

**Chapter Review**. . . . . . . . . . . . . **95**

**Coding Assignments**. . . . . . . . . **95**

**Case Studies**. . . . . . . . . . . . . . **96**

**Chapter 5: Surgery and the
Integumentary System           100**

**Introduction** . . . . . . . . . . . . . .**101**

**Surgery Guidelines**. . . . . . . . . .**102**

Services . . . . . . . . . . . . . . . . . . .102

Surgical Package. . . . . . . . . . . . .102

Follow-Up Care for Diagnostic
and Therapeutic Surgical
Procedures . . . . . . . . . . . . . . . .104

Supplied Materials. . . . . . . . . . . .104

Reporting More Than One
Procedure/Service . . . . . . . . . .104

Separate Procedure. . . . . . . . . . .104

Unlisted Service or Procedure and
Special Reports. . . . . . . . . . . . .104

Imaging Guidance . . . . . . . . . . . .104

Surgical Destruction . . . . . . . . . .104

Foreign Body/Implant Definition. . .104

**The National Correct Coding
Initiative (NCCI)**. . . . . . . . . . . . .**105**

**Guidelines Related to the
National Correct Coding Initiative
(NCCI)** . . . . . . . . . . . . . . . . . . . .**106**

Unbundling. . . . . . . . . . . . . . . . . .106

**Abbreviations Related to the
Integumentary System** . . . . . . .**107**

**Anatomy of the Integumentary
System**. . . . . . . . . . . . . . . . . . . .**104**

**Procedures Performed on the
Integumentary System** . . . . . . .**109**

General (10004–10021) . . . . . . . . .109

Paring or Cutting (11055–11057). . . 111

Routine Foot Care . . . . . . . . . . . . 111

Pilonidal Cyst (11770–11772) . . . . .116

Introduction (11900–11983) . . . . . .116

Other Procedures (15780–15879). . 126

Pressure Ulcers (Decubitus Ulcers)
(15920–15999) . . . . . . . . . . . . . .126

Burns, Local Treatment
(16000–16036). . . . . . . . . . . . . .126

Destruction (17000–17286) . . . . . .127

Other Procedures (17340–17999). . 129

Breast (19000–19499) . . . . . . . . . .129

**Summary**. . . . . . . . . . . . . . . . . .**130**

**Internet Links**. . . . . . . . . . . . . .**130**

**Chapter Review**. . . . . . . . . . . . .**131**

**Coding Assignments**. . . . . . . . .**131**

**Case Studies**. . . . . . . . . . . . . . .**132**

**Chapter 6: Musculoskeletal
System           137**

**Introduction** . . . . . . . . . . . . . . .**138**

**Guidelines Related to the National
Correct Coding Initiative (NCCI)**. . **139**

**Abbreviations Related to the
Musculoskeletal System**. . . . . . .**139**

**Anatomy of the Musculoskeletal
System**. . . . . . . . . . . . . . . . . . . .**140**

**General Procedures
(20100–20999)**. . . . . . . . . . . . . .**141**

Wound Exploration—Trauma
(20100–20103) . . . . . . . . . . . . . .141

Excisions (20150–20251) . . . . . . . .142

Introduction or Removal
(20500–20705). . . . . . . . . . . . . .143

Replantation (20802–20838) . . . . .144

Grafts or Implants
(20900–20939). . . . . . . . . . . . . .146

Other Procedures
(20950–20999). . . . . . . . . . . . . .147

**Procedures for Musculoskeletal
System by Body Site** . . . . . . . . .**148**

Incision. . . . . . . . . . . . . . . . . . . . .149

Excision . . . . . . . . . . . . . . . . . . . .150

Introduction and Removal . . . . . . .150

Repair, Revision, and
Reconstruction . . . . . . . . . . . . .151

Fracture/Dislocation. . . . . . . . . . .154

**Arthrodesis** . . . . . . . . . . . . . . . .**157**

**Application of Casts and
Strapping (29000–29799)** . . . . . .**157**

Cast Removals or Repairs
(29700–29750) . . . . . . . . . . . . . .158

**Endoscopy/Arthroscopy
(29800–29999)** . . . . . . . . . . . . .**159**

**Summary**. . . . . . . . . . . . . . . . . .**160**

**Internet Links**. . . . . . . . . . . . . .**160**

**Chapter Review**. . . . . . . . . . . . .**161**

**Coding Assignments**. . . . . . . . .**161**

**Case Studies**. . . . . . . . . . . . . . .**162**

**Chapter 7: Respiratory
System           167**

**Introduction** . . . . . . . . . . . . . . .**168**

**Guidelines Related to the National
Correct Coding Initiative
(NCCI)** . . . . . . . . . . . . . . . . . . . .**168**

**Abbreviations Related to the
Respiratory System**. . . . . . . . . . .**168**

**Anatomy of the Respiratory
System**. . . . . . . . . . . . . . . . . . . .**169**

**Procedures Completed on the
Nose (30000–30999)**. . . . . . . . . .**171**

Incision (30000, 30020) . . . . . . . . .171

Excisions (30100–30160). . . . . . . .171

Introduction (30200–30220) . . . . .172

Removal of Foreign Body
(30300–30320). . . . . . . . . . . . . .172

Repair (30400–30630) . . . . . . . . . .173

Destruction and Other Procedures
(30801–30999). . . . . . . . . . . . . .174

**Procedures Completed on the
Accessory Sinuses
(31000–31299)**. . . . . . . . . . . . . .**175**

Incisions (31000–31090) . . . . . . . .176

Excisions (31200–31230) . . . . . . . .177

Endoscopy (31231–31298). . . . . . .177

**Procedures Completed on the
Larynx (31300–31599)**. . . . . . . . .**178**

Excision and Introduction
(31300–31502) . . . . . . . . . . . . . .178

Endoscopy of the Larynx
(31505–31579) . . . . . . . . . . . . . .179

Repair and Other Procedures
Completed on the Larynx
(31580–31599) . . . . . . . . . . . . . .180

**Procedures Completed on the Trachea and Bronchi (31600–31899)** . . . . . . . . . . . . . .180

Incision (31600–31614) . . . . . . . . .181

Endoscopy of Trachea and Bronchi (31615–31654) . . . . . . . . . . . . . .181

Bronchial Thermoplasty (31660–31661) . . . . . . . . . . . . . .182

Introduction, Excision Repair, and Other Procedures Completed on the Trachea and Bronchi (31717–31899) . . . . . . . . . . . . . .182

**Procedures Completed on the Lungs and Pleura (32035–32999)** . . . . . . . . . . . . .183

Incision (32035–32225) . . . . . . . . .183

Excision/Resection, Removal, Introduction and Removal, and Destruction (32310–32562) . . .184

Thoracoscopy (Video-Assisted Thoracic Surgery [VATS]) (32601–32674) . . . . . . . . . . . . . .185

Stereotactic Radiation Therapy (32701) . . . . . . . . . . . . . . . . . . .185

Repair (32800–32820) . . . . . . . . .186

Lung Transplantation (32850–32856) . . . . . . . . . . . . . .186

Surgical Collapse Therapy, Thoracoplasty, and Other Procedures (32900–32999) . . . . .186

**Summary** . . . . . . . . . . . . . . . . . . . .187

**Internet Links** . . . . . . . . . . . . . . .188

**Chapter Review** . . . . . . . . . . . . . .188

**Coding Assignments** . . . . . . . . .189

**Case Studies** . . . . . . . . . . . . . . . .190

**Chapter 8: Cardiovascular System    194**

**Introduction** . . . . . . . . . . . . . . . . .195

**Guidelines Related to the National Correct Coding Initiative (NCCI)** . . . . . . . . . . . . . . . . . . . . .195

**Abbreviations Relating to the Cardiovascular System** . . . . . . . .195

**Anatomy of the Cardiovascular System** . . . . . . . . . . . . . . . . . . . .196

**Coding Cardiovascular Procedures** . . . . . . . . . . . . . . . . .198

Pericardium, Cardiac Tumor, and Transmyocardial Revascularization (33016–33141) . . . . . . . . . . . . . . .198

Pacemaker or Pacing Cardioverter-Defibrillator (33202–33275) . . . . .199

Electrophysiologic Operative Procedures, Subcutaneous Cardiac Rhythm Monitor, Implantable Hemodynamic Monitors, and Wounds of the Heart (Including Valves) and Great Vessels (33250–33340) . . . . . . . . . . . . . . .202

Cardiac Valve Procedures (33361–33496) . . . . . . . . . . . . . .203

Coronary Artery Anomalies and Endoscopy (33500–33509) . . . . .204

**Coronary Artery Bypass Grafts Procedures** . . . . . . . . . . . . . . . . . 205

Venous Grafting Only for Coronary Artery Bypass (33510–33516) . . . . . . . . . . . . . .205

Combined Arterial-Venous Grafting for Coronary Bypass (33517–33530) . . . . . . . . . . . . . .206

Arterial Grafting and Code for Coronary Artery Bypass (33533–33548) . . . . . . . . . . . . . . . . . . .206

Anomaly Repair and Other Procedures (33600–33926) . . . . .206

Heart/Lung Transplantation (33927–33945) . . . . . . . . . . . . . .207

Extracorporeal Membrane Oxygenation or Extracorporeal Life Support Services (33946–33989) . . . . . . . . . . . . . .209

Cardiac Assist (33967–33997) and Other Procedures (33999) . . . . . .209

**Arteries and Veins** . . . . . . . . . . . .210

Embolectomy/Thrombectomy (34001–34490) . . . . . . . . . . . . . 210

Venous Reconstruction (34501–34530) . . . . . . . . . . . . . .211

Endovascular Repair of Abdominal Aortic and/or Iliac Arteries (34701–34834) and Fenestrated Endovascular Repair of the Visceral and Inferenal Aorta (34839–34848) . . . . . . . . . . . . . .212

Direct Repair of Aneurysm or Excision (Partial or Total) and Graft Insertion for Aneurysm, Pseudoaneurysm, Ruptured Aneurysm, and Associated Occlusive Disease (35001–35152) . . . . . . . . . . . . . .215

Repair of Arteriovenous Fistula (35180–35190) . . . . . . . . . . . . . .215

Repair of a Blood Vessel for Reasons Other Than Fistula (35201–35286) . . . . . . . . . . . . . .215

Thromboendarterectomy (35301–35390) . . . . . . . . . . . . . .215

Angioscopy (35400) . . . . . . . . . . .215

Bypass Graft—Vein (35500–35572) and In-Situ Vein (35583–35587) . . . . . . 216

Bypass Graft—Other Than Vein (35600–35671) . . . . . . . . . . . . . .216

Composite Grafts, Adjuvant Techniques, and Arterial Transposition (35681–35697) . . .216

Excision, Exploration, Repair, and Revision (35700–35907) . . . . . . .216

**Vascular Injection Procedures (36000–36598)** . . . . . . . . . . . . . .217

**Arterial and Arteriovenous Procedures (36600–37799)** . . . . .217

Arterial and Intraosseous Codes (36600–36680) . . . . . . . . . . . . . .217

Hemodialysis Access, Intervascular Cannulation for Extracorporeal Circulation or Shunt Insertion (36800–36861) . . . . . . . . . . . . . .218

Dialysis Circuit (36901–36909) . . .218

Portal Decompression Procedures (37140–37183) . . . . . . . . . . . . . .218

Transcatheter Procedures (37184–37218) . . . . . . . . . . . . . .218

Endovascular Revascularization (Open or Percutaneous, Transcatheter) (37220–37239) . . .219

Vascular Embolization and Occlusion (37241–37244) and Intravascular Ultrasound Services (37252–37253) . . . . . . . . . . . . . .219

Endoscopy (37500–37501) . . . . . . .219

Ligation and Other Procedures (37565–37799) . . . . . . . . . . . . . .220

**Summary** . . . . . . . . . . . . . . . . . . . 220

**Internet Links** . . . . . . . . . . . . . . 220

**Chapter Review** . . . . . . . . . . . . . 220

**Coding Assignments** . . . . . . . . . .221

**Case Studies** . . . . . . . . . . . . . . . . 222

**Chapter 9: Hemic and Lymphatic Systems    226**

**Introduction** . . . . . . . . . . . . . . . . 227

**Guidelines Related to the National Correct Coding Initiative (NCCI)** . . . . . . . . . . . . . . . . . . . . 227

**Structures of the Hemic and Lymphatic Systems** . . . . . . . . . . 227

**Procedures Completed on the Spleen (38100–38200)** . . . . . . . 227

Excisions (38100–38102) . . . . . . . .227

Repair (38115) . . . . . . . . . . . . . . . .228

Laparoscopy of the Spleen (38120 and 38129) . . . . . . . . . . . .229

Introduction (38200) . . . . . . . . . . .229

**General Procedures (38204–38232) and Transplantation and Post-Transplantation Cellular Infusions (38240–38243)** . . . . . 229

**Procedures Performed on the Lymph Nodes and Lymphatic Channels (38300–38999)** . . . . . 230

Incision (38300–38382) . . . . . . . . .231

Excisions (38500–38555) . . . . . . . .231

Limited Lymphadenectomy for Staging (38562, 38564) . . . . . . . .232

Laparoscopy (38570–38589) . . . . .232

Radical Lymphadenectomy (Radical Resection of Lymph Nodes) (38700–38780) . . . . . . . . . . . . . .232

Introduction and Other Procedures (38790–38999) . . . . . . . . . . . . . .233

**Summary** . . . . . . . . . . . . . . . . . . . 234

**Internet Links** . . . . . . . . . . . . . . 234

**Chapter Review** . . . . . . . . . . . . . 234

**Coding Assignments** . . . . . . . . . 235

**Case Studies** . . . . . . . . . . . . . . . . 235

**Chapter 10: Mediastinum and Diaphragm    238**

**Introduction** . . . . . . . . . . . . . . . . 238

**Guidelines Related to the National Correct Coding Initiative (NCCI)** . . . . . . . . . . . . . . . . . . . . 239

**Procedures Completed in the Mediastinum (39000–39499)** . . . 239

**Procedures Completed on the Diaphragm (39501–39599)** . . . . 240

Summary....................241
Internet Links..............241
Chapter Review..............241
Coding Assignments........242
Case Studies...............242

**Chapter 11: Digestive System  244**
Introduction ...............245
Guidelines Related to the National Correct Coding Initiative (NCCI) ...................246
Abbreviations Related to the Digestive System ...........247
Procedures Completed on the Lips, Mouth, Tongue, Teeth, Palate, Uvula, and Salivary Glands and Ducts (40490–42699) ........247
  Lips (40490–40799) ...........247
  Vestibule of the Mouth (40800–40899) ............249
  Tongue and Floor of Mouth (41000–41599) ............249
  Dentoalveolar Structures (41800–41899) .............250
  Palate and Uvula (42000–42299)..251
  Salivary Glands and Ducts (42300–42699)..............251
Procedures Completed on the Pharynx, Adenoids, and Tonsils (42700–42999) .............252
Procedures Completed on the Esophagus (43020–43499)....253
  Endoscopy Procedures (43180–43278) .............254
  Repairs (43300–43425) ........256
  Manipulation Codes and Other Procedures (43450–43499).....256
Stomach (43500–43999).......257
  Incision (43500–43520) ........257
  Excision (43605–43641)........258
  Laparoscopy (43644–43659).....259
  Introduction (43752–43763)......259
  Bariatric Surgery (43770–43775)..259
  Other Procedures Completed on the Stomach (43800–43999) .............259
Intestines, Except Rectum (44005–44799) .............260
  Incision (44005–44055) ........262
  Excision (44100–44160)........262
  Laparoscopy (44180–44238).....262
  Enterostomy—External Fistulization of Intestines (44300–44346) ....264
  Endoscopy, Small Intestine, and Stomal (44360–44408) ........264
  Codes 44500 to 44799.........264
Meckel's Diverticulum and the Mesentery (44800–44899) ....265
Appendix (44900–44979) .....265
Colon and Rectum (45000–45999)..............265
Anus (46020–46999) ........266
Liver (47000–47399) ........268

Biliary Tract (47400–47999) ... 268
Pancreas (48000–48999) ......270
Abdomen, Peritoneum, and Omentum (49000–49999) ......271
  Repair—Hernioplasty, Herniorrhaphy, Herniotomy, Suture, and Other Procedures (49491–49999).....271
Summary....................272
Internet Links..............272
Chapter Review..............272
Coding Assignments..........273
Case Studies...............274

**Chapter 12: Urinary System  280**
Introduction ...............281
Guidelines Related to the National Correct Coding Initiative (NCCI) .....................281
Abbreviations Related to the Urinary System ..............281
Anatomy of the Urinary System.....................282
Procedures Completed on the Kidneys (50010–50593) ......284
  Incision (50010–50135) ........284
  Excision (50200–50290)........284
  Renal Transplantation (50300–50380) .............286
  Introduction (50382–50396 and 50430–50437) ...............287
  Repair (50400–50540)..........287
  Laparoscopy (50541–50549).....287
  Endoscopy (50551–50580) ......288
  Other Procedures (50590–50593)...............288
Procedures Completed on the Ureter (50600–50980).........289
  Incision, Excision, and Introduction (50600–50695) ...............289
  Repair (50700–50940) .........290
  Laparoscopy and Endoscopy Procedures (50945–50980).....290
Procedures Completed on the Bladder (51020–52700).......290
  Incision, Removal, Excision, and Introduction (51020–51720).....291
  Urodynamics (51725–51798) .....292
  Repair (51800–51980) .........292
  Laparoscopy and Endoscopy (51990–52010) ...............293
  Transurethral Surgery (52204–52356)...............294
  Vesical Neck and Prostate (52400–52700)...............294
Procedures Completed on the Urethra (53000–53899)........295
  Incision, Excision, and Repair (53000–53520)...............295
  Manipulation and Other Procedures (53600–53899) .............295
Summary....................295
Internet Links ............296
Chapter Review............296

Coding Assignments.........296
Case Studies................297

**Chapter 13: Male Genital System  302**
Introduction ...............303
Guidelines Related to the National Correct Coding Initiative (NCCI) .....................303
Abbreviations Related to the Male Genital System........303
Procedures Completed on the Penis (54000–54450)........304
Procedures Completed on the Testis (54500–54699) ........305
Procedures Completed on the Epididymis and Tunica Vaginalis (54700–55060) ...........305
Procedures Completed on the Scrotum, Vas Deferens, Spermatic Cord, and Seminal Vesicles (55100–55680) .............306
  Scrotum (55100–55180)........307
  Vas Deferens (55200–55400)....307
  Spermatic Cord and Seminal Vesicles (55500–55680) .......307
Procedures Completed on the Prostate (55700–55899) ......307
Reproductive System Procedures (55920) and Intersex Surgery (55970–55980) .............308
Summary....................308
Internet Links .............309
Chapter Review............309
Coding Assignments.........309
Case Studies................310

**Chapter 14: Female Genital System  315**
Introduction .................316
Guidelines Related to the National Correct Coding Initiative (NCCI) .....................316
Abbreviations Associated with the Female Genital System.....317
Vulva, Perineum, and Introitus (56405–56821) .............317
Procedures Completed on the Vagina (57000–57426)........320
Procedures Completed on the Cervix Uteri (57452–57800) ...322
Procedures Completed on the Corpus Uteri (58100–58540)...323
Laparoscopy and Hysteroscopy (58541–58579 and 58674).....324
Procedures Completed on the Oviduct and Ovary (58600–58960) ...........324
In Vitro Fertilization (58970–58976) and Other Procedures (58999) ..326
Summary....................326
Internet Links ..............326

Chapter Review. . . . . . . . . . . . .327
Coding Assignments. . . . . . . . .327
Case Studies. . . . . . . . . . . . . . 328

## Chapter 15: Maternity Care and Delivery    332

Introduction . . . . . . . . . . . . . . 333
Guidelines Related to the National Correct Coding Initiative (NCCI) . . . . . . . . . . . . . . . . . 333
Abbreviations Associated with Maternity Care and Delivery. . . 333
Antepartum and Fetal Invasive Services (59000–59350) . . . . . . 334
Vaginal Delivery, Antepartum and Postpartum Care (59400–59430), and Cesarean Delivery (59510–59525). . . . . . . . . . . . . .337
Delivery after Previous Cesarean Delivery (59610–59622) . . . . . . 338
Abortion and Other Procedures (59812–59899) . . . . . . . . . . . . 339
Summary. . . . . . . . . . . . . . . . . 339
Internet Links . . . . . . . . . . . . . 340
Chapter Review. . . . . . . . . . . . . 340
Coding Assignments. . . . . . . . . 340
Case Studies. . . . . . . . . . . . . . . 341

## Chapter 16: Endocrine System    345

Introduction . . . . . . . . . . . . . . 345
Guidelines Related to the National Correct Coding Initiative (NCCI) . . . . . . . . . . . . . . . . . .347
Abbreviations Associated with the Endocrine System. . . . . . . . 348
Thyroid Gland (60000–60300). . . 348
Parathyroid, Thymus, Adrenal Glands, Pancreas, and Carotid Body (60500–60605) . . . . . . . . 349
Laparoscopy and Other Procedures (60650–60699) . . . . . . . . . . . . 350
Summary. . . . . . . . . . . . . . . . . 350
Internet Links . . . . . . . . . . . . . 350
Chapter Review. . . . . . . . . . . . . 350
Coding Assignments. . . . . . . . . .351
Case Studies. . . . . . . . . . . . . . .351

## Chapter 17: Nervous System    355

Introduction . . . . . . . . . . . . . . 356
Guidelines Related to the National Correct Coding Initiative (NCCI) . . . . . . . . . . . . . . . . . 356
Abbreviations Associated with the Nervous System . . . . . . . . 356
Anatomy of the Nervous System. . . . . . . . . . . . . . . . . . 356
Procedures Completed on the Nervous System (61000–64999) . 361
Skull, Meninges, and Brain (61000–62258). . . . . . . . . . . . .361

Spine and Spinal Cord (62263–63746) . . . . . . . . . . . . . 365
Extracranial Nerves, Peripheral Nerves, and Autonomic Nervous System (64400–64999) . . . . . . . .365
Summary. . . . . . . . . . . . . . . . . .367
Internet Links . . . . . . . . . . . . . 368
Chapter Review. . . . . . . . . . . . . 368
Coding Assignments. . . . . . . . . 368
Case Studies. . . . . . . . . . . . . . . 369

## Chapter 18: Eye and Ocular Adnexa    373

Introduction . . . . . . . . . . . . . . .374
Guidelines Related to the National Correct Coding Initiative (NCCI) . . . . . . . . . . . . . . . . . .374
Abbreviations Relating to the Eye and Ocular Adnexa . . . . . . . . . .374
Anatomy of the Eye . . . . . . . . . 375
Procedures Completed on the Eyeball (65091–65290) . . . . . . . .376
Procedures Completed on the Anterior Segment (65400–66999) . . . . . . . . . . . . .378
Procedures Completed on the Posterior Segment (67005–67299) . . . . . . . . . . . . 380
Procedures Completed on the Ocular Adnexa (67311–67999) . . . . . . . . . . . . 382
Procedures Completed on the Conjunctiva (68020–68899) . . . 383
Summary. . . . . . . . . . . . . . . . . 383
Internet Links . . . . . . . . . . . . . 384
Chapter Review. . . . . . . . . . . . . 384
Coding Assignments. . . . . . . . . 385
Case Studies. . . . . . . . . . . . . . . 386

## Chapter 19: Auditory System and Operating Microscope    389

Introduction . . . . . . . . . . . . . . 390
Guidelines Related to the National Correct Coding Initiative (NCCI) . . . . . . . . . . . . . . . . . 390
Abbreviations Associated with the Auditory System . . . . . . . . 390
Anatomy of the Auditory System. . . . . . . . . . . . . . . . . . .391
Procedures Completed on the External Ear (69000–69399) . . . 392
Incision (69000–69090) . . . . . . . .393
Excision (69100–69155) . . . . . . . 393
Removal (69200–69222) . . . 393
Repairs and Other Procedures (69300–69399) . . . . . . . . . . . .393
Procedures Completed on the Middle Ear (69420–69799) . . . . 394
Incision (69420–69450) . . . . . . .394
Excision (69501–69554) . . . . . . .394
Repair (69601–69676) . . . . . . .394

Osseointegrated Implants (69714–69719, 69726, 69727). . . . 395
Other Procedures (69700–69799). . . 395
Procedures Completed on the Inner Ear and the Temporal Bone, Middle Fossa Approach (69801–69979). . . . . . . . . . . . . 396
Operating Microscope . . . . . . . 396
Summary. . . . . . . . . . . . . . . . . .397
Internet Links . . . . . . . . . . . . . .397
Chapter Review. . . . . . . . . . . . . .397
Coding Assignments. . . . . . . . . .397
Case Studies. . . . . . . . . . . . . . . 398

## Chapter 20: Radiology    401

Introduction . . . . . . . . . . . . . . 402
Guidelines Related to the National Correct Coding Initiative (NCCI). . . . . . . . . . . . 402
Terminology Associated with Radiology. . . . . . . . . . . . . . . . 402
Abbreviations Associated with Radiology. . . . . . . . . . . . . . . . 405
Coding for Radiology. . . . . . . . . 405
Diagnostic Radiology (70010–76499) . . . . . . . . . . . . . 405
Vascular Procedures (75600–75893) . . . . . . . . . . . . . 406
Transcatheter Procedures (75894–75989) . . . . . . . . . . . . .408
Other Procedures (76000–76499) . . 408
Diagnostic Ultrasound (76506–76999) . . . . . . . . . . . . . 409
Radiologic Guidance (77001–77022) . . . . . . . . . . . . . .410
Breast Mammography (77046–77067) . . . . . . . . . . . . . 410
Bone/Joint Studies (77071–77092) . . . . . . . . . . . . . .411
Radiation Oncology (77261–77799) . . . . . . . . . . . . . .411
Nuclear Medicine (78012–79999) . . . . . . . . . . . . . .414
Summary. . . . . . . . . . . . . . . . . 415
Internet Links . . . . . . . . . . . . . .415
Chapter Review. . . . . . . . . . . . . .415
Coding Assignments. . . . . . . . . .416
Case Studies. . . . . . . . . . . . . . . .417

## Chapter 21: Pathology and Laboratory    422

Introduction . . . . . . . . . . . . . . 422
Guidelines Related to the National Correct Coding Initiative (NCCI) . . . . . . . . . . . . . . . . . .423
Coding for Pathology and Laboratory Services . . . . . . . . .423
Abbreviations Associated with Laboratory Coding . . . . . . . . . 424
Sections . . . . . . . . . . . . . . . . . 424
Organ or Disease-Oriented Panel (80047–80081) . . . . . . . . . . . . .424

**Drug Procedures** . . . . . . . . . . . . .426
   Drug Assay (80305–80377
    and 83992) . . . . . . . . . . . . . . . . .426
   Therapeutic Drug Assays
    (80143–80299) . . . . . . . . . . . . . .426
   Evocative/Suppression Testing
    (80400–80439) . . . . . . . . . . . . .426
   Pathology Clinical Consultations
    (80503–80506) . . . . . . . . . . . . .427
   Urinalysis (81000–81099) . . . . . . .427
   Molecular Pathology
    (81105–81408 and 81479) . . . . . .427
   Genomic Sequencing Procedures
    and Other Molecular Multianalyte
    Assays (81410–81471) . . . . . . . . .427
   Multianalyte Assays with Algorithmic
    Analyses (81490–81599) . . . . . . .427
   Chemistry (82009–84999) . . . . . . .427
   Hematology and Coagulation
    (85002–85999) . . . . . . . . . . . . . .427
   Immunology (86000–86849) . . . . .428
   Transfusion Medicine
    (86850–86999) . . . . . . . . . . . . . .428
   Microbiology (87003–87999) . . . . .428
   Anatomic Pathology
    (88000–88099) . . . . . . . . . . . . . .428
   Cytopathology (88104–88199) . . . .428
   Cytogenetic Studies
    (88230–88299) . . . . . . . . . . . . . .428
   Surgical Pathology
    (88300–88399) . . . . . . . . . . . . . .428
   In Vivo (e.g., Transcutaneous)
    Laboratory Procedures
    (88720–88749) . . . . . . . . . . . . . .428
   Other Procedures and Reproductive
    Medicine Procedures
    (89049–89398) . . . . . . . . . . . . . .429
   Proprietary Laboratory Analyses
    (0001U–0354U) . . . . . . . . . . . . . .429
  **Summary** . . . . . . . . . . . . . . . . . . . 429
  **Internet Links** . . . . . . . . . . . . . . . 429
  **Chapter Review** . . . . . . . . . . . . . . 429
  **Coding Assignments** . . . . . . . . . 430

**Chapter 22: Medicine**    **431**
  **Introduction** . . . . . . . . . . . . . . . . 433
  **Guidelines Related to the National
  Correct Coding Initiative (NCCI)** . . 433
  **Immune Globulins
  (90281–90399)** . . . . . . . . . . . . . . 433
  **Immunization Administration
  for Vaccines and Toxoids
  (90460–90474) and
  (0001A–0112A)** . . . . . . . . . . . 433
  **Vaccines and Toxoids
  (90476–90756) and
  (91300–91311)** . . . . . . . . . . . . . 434
  **Psychiatry (90785–90899)** . . . . 435
  **Biofeedback (90901–90913)** . . . .437
  **Dialysis (90935–90999)** . . . . . . .437

   Hemodialysis (90935–90940) . . . .437
   Miscellaneous Dialysis Procedures
    (90945–90947) and Other Dialysis
    Procedures (90989–90999) . . . .438
   End-Stage Renal Disease Services
    (90951–90970) . . . . . . . . . . . . . . 438
  **Gastroenterology
  (91010–91299)** . . . . . . . . . . . . . . 439
  **Ophthalmology (92002–92499)** . 439
   Other Specialized Services . . . . . .440
  **Special Otorhinolaryngologic
  Services (92502–92700)** . . . . . . 440
  **Cardiovascular (92920–93799)** . . 440
  **Noninvasive Vascular Diagnostic
  Studies (93880–93998)** . . . . . . . .441
  **Pulmonary (94002–94799)** . . . . 442
  **Allergy and Clinical Immunology
  (95004–95199)** . . . . . . . . . . . . . . 442
  **Endocrinology (95249–95251)** . 442
  **Neurology and Neuromuscular
  Procedures (95700–96020)** . . . . 442
  **Medical Genetics and Genetic
  Counseling Services (96040) and
  Adaptive Behavior Services
  (97151–97158)** . . . . . . . . . . . . . 443
  **Central Nervous System
  Assessments and Tests
  (96105–96146), Health Behavior
  Assessment and Intervention
  (96156–96171), and Behavioral
  Management Services (96202–
  96203)** . . . . . . . . . . . . . . . . . . . . 443
  **Hydration, Therapeutic, Prophylactic,
  Diagnostic Injections and Infusions,
  and Chemotherapy and Other Highly
  Complex Drug or Highly Complex
  Biologic Agent Administration
  (96360–96549)** . . . . . . . . . . . . . 444
  **Photodynamic Therapy
  (96567–96574)** . . . . . . . . . . . . . 445
  **Special Dermatological Procedures
  (96900–96999)** . . . . . . . . . . . . . 445
  **Physical Medicine and Rehabilitation
  (97010–97799)** . . . . . . . . . . . . . . 445
  **Additional Procedures
  (97802–99607)** . . . . . . . . . . . . . 446
  **Summary** . . . . . . . . . . . . . . . . . . . 446
  **Internet Links** . . . . . . . . . . . . . . . 446
  **Chapter Review** . . . . . . . . . . . . . . 446
  **Coding Assignments** . . . . . . . . . .447
  **Case Studies** . . . . . . . . . . . . . . . 448

**Chapter 23: HCPCS Codes**   **449**
  **Introduction** . . . . . . . . . . . . . . . . 449
  **Certificate of Medical Necessity
  for DME Items and Advance
  Beneficiary Notice** . . . . . . . . . . 450
  **Organization and Use of HCPCS
  Level II Codes** . . . . . . . . . . . . . . .451

**HCPCS Sections** . . . . . . . . . . . . **453**
  A Codes—Transportation Services
   Including Ambulance, Medical
   and Surgical Supplies . . . . . . . . .453
  B Codes—Enteral and Parental
   Therapy . . . . . . . . . . . . . . . . . . . .454
  C Codes—HCPCS Outpatient
   PPS . . . . . . . . . . . . . . . . . . . . . . .454
  D Codes—Dental Procedures . . . .455
  E Codes—Durable Medical
   Equipment . . . . . . . . . . . . . . . . . .455
  G Codes—Temporary Procedures/
   Professional Services . . . . . . . . . .455
  H Codes—Behavioral Health and/
   or Substance Abuse Treatment
   Services . . . . . . . . . . . . . . . . . . . .456
  J Codes—Drugs Administered
   Other Than Oral Method . . . . . . . .456
  K Codes—Temporary Codes
   Assigned to DME Regional
   Carriers . . . . . . . . . . . . . . . . . . . .456
  L Codes—Orthotic and Prosthetic
   Procedures and Devices . . . . . . . .456
  M Codes—Medical Services
   and Quality Measures . . . . . . . . .457
  P Codes—Pathology and
   Laboratory Services . . . . . . . . . . .457
  Q Codes—Temporary Codes . . . . .457
  R Codes—Diagnostic Radiology
   Services . . . . . . . . . . . . . . . . . . . .457
  S Codes—Temporary National
   Codes . . . . . . . . . . . . . . . . . . . . .457
  T Codes—Temporary National
   Codes Established for State
   Medicaid Agencies . . . . . . . . . . .458
  U Codes—Other . . . . . . . . . . . . . .458
  V Codes—Vision Services and
   Hearing Services . . . . . . . . . . . . .458
  **Appendices** . . . . . . . . . . . . . . . . **458**
  **Summary** . . . . . . . . . . . . . . . . . . . 459
  **Internet Links** . . . . . . . . . . . . . . . 460
  **Chapter Review** . . . . . . . . . . . . . . 460
  **Coding Assignments** . . . . . . . . . 460
  **Case Studies** . . . . . . . . . . . . . . . .461

**Appendix I: Billing Forms
(CMS-1500 and UB-04)**    463
**Appendix II: Surgical Positions**   465
**Appendix III: Abdominopelvic
Divisions**    466
**Appendix IV: 2023 Anesthesia
Code Base Units**    467
**Appendix V: Locality-Adjusted
Anesthesia Conversion
Factors as a Result of the
CY 2023 Final Rule**    470
**Appendix VI: Case Studies**    474
**Glossary**    492
**Index**    506

*Understanding Current Procedural Terminology and HCPCS Coding Systems* represents a comprehensive approach to learning and mastering procedural coding. This book provides detailed instruction for CPT coding as well as additional resource information that is essential for coders. This book can be used in an academic setting and also as a reference in a working environment. Space has been provided in the text for the learner to work on exercises to promote a hands-on approach to coding.

This book approaches procedural coding in a fresh and innovative manner. Many clinical examples are used throughout the text to provide the student with real-life coding examples and practice. The book also provides a review of human anatomy that is relevant to selecting procedural codes. Learning is reinforced by the use of illustrations of anatomy and operative procedures.

# New to the 2023 Edition

- The textbook, MindTap, and Instructor's Manual have been updated to include the most current code sets available at the time of publication.
- Explanation of new symbol impacting Telemedicine
- Review of new S and T Appendices
- Information on new modifier 93
- Overview of new guidelines for E/M coding
- Additional information about instructional notations and out of sequence codes found in various subsections of CPT manual
- COVID-19 resoruces update

# Organization of the Text

*Understanding Current Procedural Terminology and HCPCS Coding Systems* has 23 chapters, which present an introduction to CPT coding and detail on all of the main sections of CPT. Each chapter contains Internet links, a summary, and a chapter review to facilitate learning. Case studies are used throughout the text to enrich the learning process.

# Special Features of the Text

Several features are incorporated into the chapters to facilitate learning:

- **Chapter outlines** located at the beginning of each chapter help organize the material.
- **Learning objectives** establish goals for each chapter and can be used as a checklist for reviewing concepts.
- **Key terms** are identified at the beginning of the chapter, are boldfaced throughout the chapter, and appear in the glossary to assist readers in learning the technical vocabulary associated with coding.
- **Exercises** challenge the learner's knowledge and reinforce understanding of presented materials.
- **Examples** illustrate key concepts to promote understanding.
- **Illustrations** of human anatomy and procedures appear throughout the book. These help the student visualize operative procedures and are a valuable resource for coders.

- **Internet links** encourage users to expand their knowledge and stay current with the most up-to-the-minute information.
- **Coding assignments** require learners to assign codes using coding manuals.
- **Case studies** encourage readers to apply concepts taught within the text to actual clinical scenarios.

# Instructor and Student Resources

Additional instructor and student resources for this product are available online. Instructor assets include an Instructor's Manual, Solution and Answer Guide, MindTap Educator's Guide, Transition Guide, PowerPoint® slides, and a test bank powered by Cognero. To provide maximum pedagogical value, the 2023 edition PowerPoints have been updated to include additional interactive activities. Student assets include additional Peer Coding Audit Activities. Sign up or sign in at www.cengage.com to search for and access this product and its online resources.

## MindTap

MindTap is a fully online, interactive learning experience built upon authoritative Cengage content. By combining readings, multimedia activities, and assessments into a singular learning path, MindTap elevates learning by providing real-world application to better engage students. Instructors customize the learning path by selecting Cengage resources and adding their own content via apps that integrate into the MindTap framework seamlessly with many learning management systems.

The MindTap includes:

- Auto-graded Exercises, Chapter Review, Coding Assignments, and Case Studies from the textbook
- Video Quizzes that walk students step-by-step through coding patient cases
- Chapter Quizzes
- Medical Coding Trainer which presents learners with realistic, multi-page patient records to code

The 2023 edition has been updated to include automated feedback explaining the correct answers for Coding Assignments, in addition to feedback already provided for Exercises, Chapter Reviews, Case Studies, and Video Quizzes.

To learn more, visit www.cengage.com/training/mindtap.

# Optum360® EncoderPro.com

Enhance your course with Cengage learning materials and online coding tools from Optum360®. *EncoderPro.com Expert* is an online coding and reference tool designed to enhance your coding capabilities.

- Using online coding tools can help by: saving you time and money;
- increasing accuracy, reducing denials, and ensuring you receive complete reimbursement; and
- reducing required storage space and paper.

Features of EncoderPro.com Expert include:

- ICD-10-CM code content search
- ICD-10 mapping tools
- Coders' Desk Reference
- Complete code history
- Local Coverage Determinations (LCDs) and Medicare Pub. 100 access
- Medicare CCI edits
- Modifier crosswalk

- Enhanced compliance editor
- Enhanced LCD/NCD policy searching
- Cross-coder relationships from seven coding and billing specialty reference books

To make the switch and start saving on coding materials with Cengage and Optum360®, contact your Cengage Learning Consultant today at cengage.com/repfinder.

# About the Author

## Mary Jo Bowie, MS, BS, AAS, RHIA

Consultant and Owner, Health Information Professional Services, Binghamton, New York. Active member, American Health Information Management Association (AHIMA). Mary Jo has over 40 years experience in the health information and coding profession. Professionally she has served the New York State Health Information Management Association as Education Director and was a member of the Board of Directors, 1989–1991; Ambulatory Care Coding Guidelines (ACGC) Committee, 1995–2001; and was Chairperson of the ACGC Committee, 1993–1995. She was the New York State Nominee for the American Health Information Management Association National Award for Literary Contribution to Profession, 1993 and 1994. Mary Jo has completed numerous national professional seminars on ICD-9-CM, ICD-10-CM, and CPT coding. She was the lead trainer for Cengage Learning's ICD-10-CM Peer-to-Peer Training. She is an AHIMA-approved trainer for ICD-10-CM/PCS.

# Dedication

To my husband Bill, who is always by my side no matter what we face together, you are my motivation for all I do. To my daughter Sarah, and daughter Bethannie, son-in-law Jesse, and grandchildren Isabella, Jesse, Adelyn, and Deklyn and others yet to come. My love is always with you. To my parents, who showed our family the manner in which to navigate life by their strong and consistent faith.

In memory of Ted Bowie, who taught us all to fight until we hear the referee blow the whistle.

A special thanks to Mark Peplowski, who keeps me on track and make authoring a joy. Mark's dedication to assisting me in completing revisions is surpassed by none. To my extended Cengage family, thanks for all the work you do in marketing and promoting my books. A very special thanks to Lou Ann Decker for her time and work reviewing these pages and attaching the hot pink notes! You are a joy to work with.

—Mary Jo Bowie

# Acknowledgments

A special thank you is extended to the reviewers who have provided recommendations to enhance the content of this work.

**Misty Green, CPC**
Department Head, Medical Billing & Coding Program
Community Care College
Tulsa, OK

**NaTunya Davis Johnson, Ed.S.**
Professor and District Department Chair
Holmes Community College
Ridgeland, MS

**Marilyn A. Martin, DBA, MBA, CPC**

Chair, Medical Office Administration and Office Administration

Central Piedmont Community College

Charlotte, NC

**Michelle Ruggiero, MsED, CPC, CCS-P**

Instructor

Bryant & Stratton College

Buffalo, NY

**Tracy Smith, MBA**

Department Chair

Hinds Community College

Pearl, MS

# Technical Reviewer

Both Mary Jo and the Cengage team offer their profound thanks to Lou Ann Decker for her significant technical review efforts. Your efforts were invaluable on this revision. Many thanks for all that you do!

**Lou Ann Decker, AAS, RHIT**

## Chapter Outline

At the beginning of each chapter, you will find an outline of all major headings. Review these headings of topic areas before you study the chapter. They are a road map.

## Learning Objectives

Learning Objectives provide a framework for study of the chapter content.

## Key Terms

Key Terms represent new vocabulary that is highlighted within the chapter at first usage. Use the end-of-book Glossary to study definitions of all key terms.

### Chapter Outline

Introduction
History of Current Procedural Terminology
The Structure and Design of CPT
CPT as Part of HCPCS
Summary

Internet Links
Chapter Review
Coding Assignments
Short Answer

### Learning Objectives

**At the conclusion of this chapter, you should be able to:**

1. Explain the purpose of Current Procedural Terminology (CPT).
2. Identify key parties and dates in the development and revision of CPT.
3. Summarize the format and contents of the sections of the CPT code manual.
4. Interpret the symbols and punctuation used in CPT.
5. Locate a CPT code in the CPT code manual.
6. Differentiate between Level I and Level II codes in HCPCS.

### Key Terms

add-on code symbol (+)
audio-only telemedicine services symbol ◄
bullet symbol (●)
category I proprietary laboratory analyses (PLA) tests symbol (↑↓)
Category II

Current Procedural Terminology (CPT)
flash symbol (↗)
forbidden symbol (⊘)
guidelines
Healthcare Common Procedure Coding System (HCPCS)

horizontal triangles symbol (►◄)
Level I codes
Level II codes
National Codes
number symbol (#)

prohibitory symbol (⊘)
proprietary laboratory analyses (PLA) tests symbol (Ж)
star symbol (★)
triangle symbol (▲)

## Exercises

Sprinkled throughout the chapters, Exercises encourage readers to stop periodically and apply critical thinking skills to solve coding challenges.

### Exercise 2.1—Check Your Understanding

List the modifiers given in the series in the proper order. If the order does not make a difference, indicate this with ND.

1. 62, 22 _____
2. GW, US _____
3. 56, T2 _____

4. AA, 47 _____
5. 59, 51 _____

## Coding Assignments

For each code listed, note the main section of the CPT manual in which you would find the code. The first one is done for you.

1. 00142   Anesthesia
2. 23076   _____
3. 88348

11. 64400   _____
12. 77003   _____
13. 30520

## Coding Assignments

Coding Assignments invite you to use CPT and HCPCS coding manuals to identify proper procedural codes.

## Internet Links

For more information about CMS and the HCPCS coding system, visit **http://www.cms.gov**.

## Chapter Review

### True/False

**Instructions:** Indicate whether the following statements are true (T) or false (F).

1. _____ CPT codes tell the insurance carrier what brought the patient to the physician's office.
2. _____ Text, symbols, and the history of CPT are found in the introduction of the code book.
3. _____ The CPT code book is updated annually on July 1.
4. _____ The Surgery section of codes begins with code 10001 and goes through code 69999.
5. _____ ▲ is the symbol for a revised code.

### Fill in the Blank

**Instructions:** Fill in the blanks in the statements that follow.

6. The CPT coding system was first published in 1966 by _____.
7. A complete and detailed description of all modifiers used in CPT is found in _____.
8. The CPT manual contains _____ main sections.
9. The _____ separates the common portion of the code description from additional portions of the code.
10. The _____ is organized by main terms.

## Internet Links

Internet Links encourage you to expand your knowledge base with the most up-to-date information available on the Web.

## Chapter Review

Chapter Review sections appear in every chapter, and test your understanding of the material through questions in varying formats.

## Case Studies

**Instructions:** Review each case and indicate the correct code(s).

### Case 1

**Preoperative diagnosis:** Carcinoma of the mediastinum
**Postoperative diagnosis:** Tumor of mediastinum, carcinoma
**Reason for procedure:** Two weeks ago, the patient had a biopsy of a mass found in the mediastinum. Pathology confirmed that the mass was a carcinoma of the mediastinum.

## Case Studies

Case Studies challenge you to carefully select codes appropriate to the scenarios described.

# Introduction to Current Procedural Terminology

## CHAPTER 1

## Chapter Outline

Introduction

History of Current Procedural Terminology

The Structure and Design of CPT

CPT as Part of HCPCS

Summary

Internet Links

Chapter Review

Coding Assignments

Short Answer

## Learning Objectives

**At the conclusion of this chapter, you should be able to:**

1. Explain the purpose of Current Procedural Terminology (CPT).
2. Identify key parties and dates in the development and revision of CPT.
3. Summarize the format and contents of the sections of the CPT code manual.
4. Interpret the symbols and punctuation used in CPT.
5. Locate a CPT code in the CPT code manual.
6. Differentiate between Level I and Level II codes in HCPCS.

## Key Terms

add-on code symbol (+)

audio-only telemedicine services symbol ◀

bullet symbol (●)

category I proprietary laboratory analyses (PLA) tests symbol (↑↓)

Category II

Category III

Current Procedural Terminology (CPT)

flash symbol (↗)

forbidden symbol (⊘)

guidelines

Healthcare Common Procedure Coding System (HCPCS)

hollow circle symbol (o)

horizontal triangles symbol (►◄)

Level I codes

Level II codes

National Codes

number symbol (#)

prohibitory symbol (⊘)

proprietary laboratory analyses (PLA) tests symbol (⊁)

star symbol (★)

triangle symbol (▲)

## Introduction

The coding system known as **CPT**, or **Current Procedural Terminology**, was developed by the American Medical Association (AMA). The AMA annually updates the code sets within CPT, and the new codes become effective on January 1 of each year. These five-digit codes are part of the language used by physicians and insurance companies to convey the services provided to a patient during an encounter. Just as the ICD-10-CM diagnostic codes explain what brought the patient to the provider for the encounter, CPT tells the insurance carrier what service or services were provided to the patient during that encounter.

The biggest hurdle that a coder might have with CPT coding is translating the physician's terminology or documentation into a billable service. Physicians communicate in medical terminology, whereas insurance carriers communicate in reimbursement language. For this reason, a working knowledge of CPT coding is necessary for the correct coding of procedures and services. Insurance carriers require that CPT codes be submitted on claims to determine the appropriate payment for the services rendered.

This chapter will provide an overview of the CPT manual as well as the terms and symbols used to guide coders to the proper selection of CPT codes. The CPT manual is officially titled Current Procedural Terminology Codebook. However, it is commonly known as the CPT manual or the CPT code book.

# History of Current Procedural Terminology

The CPT coding system was first published in 1966 by the AMA. The system provided uniform reporting of physician services performed in the outpatient setting. The first CPT manual was pocket sized and contained only 163 pages. It contained four-digit codes, along with brief descriptions.

The CPT manual has grown in size and descriptions since 1966. The CPT manual now contains six main sections, which are divided into subsections, and then further divided into subcategories and headings. It now contains thousands of codes, which continue to be revised and updated annually.

# The Structure and Design of CPT

The CPT update notifications are released in early fall to allow time for providers to become educated and update their systems to be in compliance with the January 1 code changes. Coding changes that are announced include additions, deletions, and code revisions from the previous year. Coders need to review the annual updates in CPT so that they have an understanding of the most current codes; therefore, submitted claims will not be rejected because of invalid or outdated codes.

The CPT manual consists of an introduction, the main body of the book, the appendices, and the index. To locate a procedure completed during an encounter, the coder may need to look for the service in several different ways. Becoming familiar with the layout and format of the book will help the coder to better locate a code.

In order to become familiar with the contents of the CPT manual, you should use your CPT manual and locate the following (the table of contents for CPT is found at the front of the manual):

- Introduction
- Evaluation and Management Services Guidelines
- Evaluation and Management
- Anesthesia Guidelines
- Anesthesia
- Surgery Guidelines
- Surgery
- Radiology Guidelines (Including Nuclear Medicine and Diagnostic Ultrasound)
- Radiology
- Pathology and Laboratory Guidelines
- Pathology and Laboratory
- Medicine Guidelines
- Medicine

- Category II Codes
- Category III Codes
- Appendices
- Index

## The Introduction

The introduction to the CPT manual contains valuable information that will help you navigate through the manual. Text, symbols, history, and how to use the book are all explained within the introduction section of the manual.

Also found in the introduction is a breakdown of the section numbers and their sequence, instructions for using the CPT manual and for formatting, and an explanation of guidelines, add-on codes, and modifiers. To become familiar with the information found within the introduction, read the introduction contained within the CPT manual.

## Symbols

Various symbols are used to alert the coder to unique features of the CPT manual. Symbols that are included in the CPT manual are discussed below. The symbols are located in front of the code numbers within the various sections to denote that the symbol applies to a specific code.

### Triangle Symbol ▲

The **triangle symbol** is used to denote that a code has been revised from the previous edition of CPT with a substantial change in the CPT description of the procedure or service. Appendix B contains a summary of codes that have been revised, as well as additional and deleted codes. When a code is revised, the triangle symbol will appear before the code number in the main body of the CPT manual. In Appendix B, the triangle symbol will appear before the code number, and the deleted language in the code description will be noted with a strikethrough. The newly added information will be underlined.

In the 2023 edition of CPT, for example, code number 15851 was revised.

> **EXAMPLE:** In 2022, the code descriptor stated:
>
> 15851    Removal of sutures under anesthesia (other than local), same surgeon
>
> In 2023, the code descriptor was revised as follows:
>
> 15851    Removal of sutures or staples requiring anesthesia (ie, general anesthesia, moderate sedation)

Reference code 15851 in the CPT manual and in Appendix B to note how this symbol is used.

### Bullet Symbol ●

The **bullet symbol** is used to denote a new code that has been added since the previous edition of CPT. In the body of the CPT manual, the bullet symbol will appear before the code number. A summary of these newly added codes appears in Appendix B of the CPT manual. In Appendix B, the bullet symbol appears next to the new code number with the phrase "Code added." The full description of the new code does not appear in Appendix B.

In the 2023 edition of CPT, the following appeared as a new code:

> **EXAMPLE:**
>
> 30469    Repair of nasal valve collapse with low energy, temperature-controlled (ie, radiofrequency) subcutaneous/submucosal remodeling

Review this code addition in both Appendix B and in the CPT manual Surgery code section and note how the bullet symbol is used.

## Horizontal Triangles Symbol ►◄

The **horizontal triangles symbol** is used to indicate new or revised text in the CPT manual. When the horizontal triangle symbol appears, the coder must note the information that has been added or revised from the previous edition of the CPT manual.

> **EXAMPLE:** In the 2023 edition of CPT, revised text appears after code 44705. Reference this section in the CPT manual to review the revised information, and note the location of the horizontal triangles that appear around the phrase that states "(Do not report 44705 in conjunction with 74283, 0780T)."

## Add-on Code Symbol +

The **add-on code symbol** is used within CPT to list procedures that are completed in addition to the primary procedure or service performed. Appendix D in the CPT manual lists these codes, and they are denoted in the body of the CPT manual when the add-on code symbol appears before the code number. Add-on codes must be reported in addition to the primary procedure or service code and can never be reported alone. In addition, they are to be reported by the same provider of the service. Additional information on add-on codes is located in the Introduction of the CPT manual under the heading of "Add-on Codes."

> **EXAMPLE:** 11000 Debridement of extensive eczematous or infected skin; up to 10% of body surface +11001 each additional 10% of the body surface, or part thereof (List separately in addition to code for primary procedure)

The placement of the symbol alerts the coder that code 11001 is an add-on code and can be used only in conjunction with code 11000.

## Number Symbol #

The **number symbol** indicates codes that are out of numerical sequence. As CPT codes have been added over the years, codes have been listed out of numerical order to allow the placement of procedures with related concepts within code families, regardless of the availability of sequential numerical code numbers. The number symbol is used in the body of the CPT manual to indicate a code that is out of numerical order. The symbol will precede other symbols that have been assigned to a code.

> **EXAMPLE:**
>
> Excision
>
> ```
>          (For bone biopsy, see 20220-20251)
>   21550  Biopsy, soft tissue of neck or thorax
>          (For needle biopsy of soft tissue, use 20206)
>   21552  Code is out of numerical sequence. See 21550-21558
>   21554  Code is out of numerical sequence. See 21550-21558
>   21555  Excision, tumor, soft tissue of neck or anterior thorax,
>          subcutaneous; less than 3 cm
> # 21552  3 cm or greater
> ```

Code 21552 is the code that is out of numerical sequence. Appendix N lists a summary of resequenced CPT codes, thus indicating the codes that do not appear in the body of the CPT manual in numerical order.

## Forbidden or Prohibitory Symbol ⊘

The **forbidden or prohibitory symbol** indicates that a code is exempt from modifier –51 and also has not been denoted as a CPT add-on code. Modifier –51 indicates that multiple procedures have been performed. The use of modifiers will be discussed later in the textbook. Appendix E of the CPT manual lists the summary of CPT codes that are exempt from modifier –51. Review Appendix E for the complete list of codes that are exempt from the use of modifier –51.

> ⊘ **20974**    Electrical stimulation to aid bone healing; noninvasive (nonoperative)

## Hollow Circle Symbol ○

The **hollow circle symbol** indicates a reinstated or recycled code in CPT. This symbol is used in the CPT manual only if a code has been reinstated. In those years in which no codes are reinstated or recycled, the hollow circle symbol will not appear in the code book.

In 2010, code 1127F was deleted, and then it was reinstated in 2012. Thus, the following example appeared in the 2012 edition of CPT:

> **EXAMPLE:**
> ○**1127F**    New episode for condition (NMA—No Measure Associated)

This symbol only appears the year it has been reinstated, therefore, the 2022 edition of CPT does not have the hollow circle symbol next to this code.

## Flash Symbol ⚡

The **flash symbol** indicates codes for vaccines that are pending FDA approval. To see examples of vaccines awaiting FDA approval, reference Appendix K in the CPT manual.

## Proprietary Laboratory Analyses (PLA) Tests Symbol ⵠ

The **proprietary laboratory analyses (PLA) tests symbol**, ⵠ, is used to denote duplicate proprietary laboratory analyses (PLA) tests. The PLA codes define proprietary clinical laboratory analyses. Appendix O, of the CPT manual, includes all codes that are included in the Proprietary Laboratory Analyses subsection of the Pathology and Laboratory Section of the CPT manual. PLA test codes will be further defined in the Pathology and Laboratory chapter of this textbook. **The Category I proprietary laboratory analyses (PLA) tests symbol ⇅** is used to identify Category I PLA codes. For a full explanation of PLA codes and the use of symbols that relate to PLA, reference the information found in the CPT manual prior to code 0001U found at the end of the Pathology and Laboratory section of the coding manual.

## Star Symbol ★

The **star symbol** was added in the 2017 edition of CPT to denote codes that may be used to report synchronous (real-time) telemedicine services when modifier –95 is appended to the code. Telemedicine services are services that are rendered using electronic communication and encompasses interactive telecommunications, which, at a minimum, includes video and audio communication between the patient and the provider. The star symbol is listed in the CPT manual preceding the code number. Appendix P of the CPT manual lists the CPT codes that can be used as telemedicine codes. In 2020 as the United States faced the COVID-19 pandemic the country saw an increase in telemedicine services. Telemedicine is a safe manner in which patients could "see" their providers without having to leave their homes and face the possibility of being exposed to COVID-19.

> **EXAMPLE:** Dr. Jones treats patients with a diagnosis of Parkinson's Disease who reside in a nursing home facility via telemedicine services to evaluate the progression of the disease. Dr. Jones selects the evaluation and management code 99309 to report the subsequent nursing facility care services. Code 99309-95 is used to report this service since this is performed via telemedicine.

Reference code 99309 in the evaluation and management section of the CPT manual and note that the star symbol appears before the code to indicate that this service can be provided via telemedicine. Further explanation of the use of modifier –95 will be explained in Chapter 2 of this textbook.

## Audio-only Telemedicine Services symbol ◀

The audio-only telemedicine services symbol placed next to a code identifies codes that may be used to report audio-only telemedicine services when appended by modifier 93. The use of the 93 modifier will be discussed in greater detail in Chapter 2 of this textbook.

## Sections, Subsections, Categories, Subcategories, and Headings of the CPT Manual

There are six main sections in CPT. These main sections are as follows. (Note that the sections do not appear in numerical order within the CPT manual.)

| Section Title | Code Range |
|---|---|
| Evaluation and Management | 99202–99499 |
| Anesthesia | 00100–01999, 99100–99140 |
| Surgery | 10004–69990 |
| Radiology | 70010–79999 |
| Pathology and Laboratory | 80047–89398, 0001U–0354U |
| Medicine | 90281–99199, 99500–99607 |

Each main section is divided further into subsections arranged by anatomic site, procedure, descriptors, or condition subheadings.

**EXAMPLE:** Referencing the Surgery section of the CPT manual you will see the following arrangement for codes that relate to incision and drainage procedures of the integumentary system. I have selected the specific code 10080 for this illustration:

```
(Section) Surgery
   (Subsection) Integumentary System
      (Subcategory) Skin, Subcutaneous, and Accessory Structures
         (Heading) Incision and Drainage
            (Procedure) 10080 Incision and drainage of pilonidal cyst; simple
```

The coder should keep in mind that the CPT manual is also arranged from head to toe and from the trunk outward. The Surgery section illustrates this clearly with the procedures for the Musculoskeletal System.

**EXAMPLE:**

```
(Section) Surgery
   (Subsection) Musculoskeletal System
      (Subcategory) Head
         (Heading) Incision
            (Procedure) 21010 Arthrotomy, temporomandibular joint
```

The next subcategory is the Neck (Soft Tissues) and Thorax, with the heading of "Incision," starting with procedure code 21501. Then the code subcategories move on to the Back and Flank, Spine (Vertebral Column), Abdomen, Shoulder, Humerus (Upper Arm) and Elbow, Forearm and Wrist, and Hand and Fingers. The subcategories continue in the same manner, beginning with the Pelvis and Hip Joint and moving the rest of the way down the body.

The codes are in numeric order within each section of the code manual, except for those cases when codes have been added out of sequence. These out-of-sequence codes are identified by the number symbol (#), as discussed earlier in this chapter. Locating specific codes will be discussed later in this chapter.

When a code is located in the main section of the CPT manual, please be aware of semicolon (;) use within the code descriptions. The semicolon is a very important symbol in CPT; it is the key to making proper code selections. The semicolon separates the common portion of the procedure description from the unique portion of the procedure description.

**EXAMPLE:** The provider documentation states, "I&D of a pilonidal cyst was performed today. Extensive amounts of pus were exudated. Patient tolerated procedure well. This is considered a complicated I&D because of the presence of infection."

The procedure codes for this case are found in the Surgery section and read as follows:

```
10080    Incision and drainage of pilonidal cyst; simple
10081        complicated
```

The code 10081 would be selected to report this procedure.

The way to read the code description for code 10081 properly is, "Incision and drainage of pilonidal cyst; complicated." The indentation indicates that after the semicolon, the term "complicated" is used for code 10081.

## Exercise 1.1—Check Your Understanding

**For the codes given, indicate the section and subsection where the code is found. The first one is done for you.**

| | Code | Section/Subsection | | Code | Section/Subsection |
|---|---|---|---|---|---|
| 1. | 70300 | Radiology/Diagnostic Radiology (Diagnostic Imaging) | 10. | 65112 | |
| | | | 11. | 90371 | |
| | | | 12. | 99203 | |
| 2. | 60220 | | 13. | 10160 | |
| 3. | 26034 | | 14. | 33120 | |
| 4. | 88036 | | 15. | 50100 | |
| 5. | 43651 | | 16. | 21811 | |
| 6. | 38115 | | 17. | 66184 | |
| 7. | 99304 | | 18. | 52441 | |
| 8. | 97010 | | 19. | 61000 | |
| 9. | 77021 | | 20. | 59074 | |

## Guidelines

At the start of each of the CPT main sections, section-specific guidelines are presented. **Guidelines** define items that are necessary for appropriately interpreting and reporting the procedures and services contained within that section of the CPT manual. The guidelines specific to each section of CPT codes are strictly followed. Guidelines are provided at the start of each main section, but guidelines, or notes, may also appear at the beginning of a subsection.

**EXAMPLE:** In the Surgery section, prior to the description for code 11200, the following note appears after the heading "Removal of Skin Tags":

Removal by scissoring or any sharp method, ligature strangulation, electrosurgical destruction, or combination of treatment modalities, including chemical destruction or electrocauterization of wound, with or without local anesthesia.

This note further explains that if the skin tag was removed by any method listed, it would be proper to assign the appropriate CPT code from this subsection.

Coders should read and review each of the guideline sections at the start of each year for any noted changes that may have been made from the prior year's guidelines. As discussed earlier in this chapter, when text changes are made the revised text will appear within the horizontal triangles symbol.

## Index

The Index is located in the back of the CPT manual. Instructions for the use of the CPT Index appear in the back of the CPT manual prior to the Index. The Index is organized by main terms. The main terms, which are in bold print, are organized by one of the following:

1. Procedure or Service
2. Organ or other Anatomic Site
3. Condition
4. Synonyms, Eponyms, and Abbreviations

When locating a term in the index, always follow this order. First, attempt to locate the main term by the name of the procedure or service, then attempt to identify it by organ or anatomic site, then by condition, and last by synonyms, eponyms, or abbreviations.

Main terms in the Index can be followed by a series of subterms that modify the main term. Subterms further define or clarify the main term. The coder must review the subterms because they have an effect on the selection of the appropriate code for the procedure. Some entries in the Index will have more than one code that applies to a given index entry; a range of codes will be listed. You will notice a comma separating the two codes. If more than two codes in a series apply, they will be separated by a hyphen. The coder must reference all the codes listed in the Index in the main section of the CPT manual. The coder should select the code after referencing the main sections. Always verify codes in the main text of CPT.

## Appendices

The appendices are located in the back of the CPT manual, before the Index. Locate the appendices in the CPT manual and review the content found in each appendix of the manual. The appendices in CPT can be summarized as follows.

| Appendix | Description |
|---|---|
| Appendix A—Modifiers | Detailed description of each of the modifiers used with CPT codes. |
| Appendix B—Summary of Additions, Deletions, and Revisions | Additions, deletions, and revised CPT codes for the current edition of CPT. This is a good reference at the beginning of the year when a new edition of CPT is published as it can be referenced for updating billing sheets and code summary sheets used by clinical staff. The appendix shows the actual changes that have been made to the code descriptions, new codes that have been added and deleted codes. In Appendix B of the CPT manual, read through the paragraph following the heading for additional information about how the symbols are used in this appendix. |
| Appendix C—Clinical Examples | In the 2023 edition of CPT the clinical examples, formerly known as Appendix C, have been removed from the manual. |
| Appendix D—Summary of CPT Add-on Codes | List of add-on codes found throughout CPT. Add-on codes can be recognized within the sections of the CPT manual because preceding the code number the + symbol is listed in the CPT manual. |
| Appendix E—Summary of CPT Codes Exempt from Modifier 51 | The codes listed here are exempt from use of a −51 modifier. |
| Appendix F—Summary of CPT Codes Exempt from Modifier 63 | The codes listed here are exempt from use of a −63 modifier. |

(continues)

*(continued)*

| Appendix | Description |
|---|---|
| Appendix G—Summary of CPT Codes That Include Moderate (Conscious) Sedation | On January 1, 2017, the summary of CPT codes that include moderate (conscious) sedation, Appendix G, was removed from the CPT appendices. Appendix G now states that for information and guidance on reporting moderate sedation services the coder should reference the guidelines for codes 99151, 99152, 99153, 99155, 99156, and 99157. |
| Appendix H—Alphabetical Clinical Topics Listing (AKA, Alphabetical Listing) | This appendix, which included the Alphabetical Clinical Topics Listing, has been removed from the CPT manual. The appendix now lists the AMA website for obtaining this information. |
| Appendix I—Genetic Testing Code Modifiers | Genetic testing code modifiers have been removed from the CPT manual. The appendix now lists a website to reference for up-to-date information. |
| Appendix J—Electrodiagnostic Medicine Listing of Sensory, Motor, and Mixed Nerves | This appendix contains a listing of sensory, motor, and mixed nerves and the appropriate nerve conduction study code that is used. This should be referenced when selecting codes 95907–95913. |
| Appendix K—Product Pending FDA Approval | This appendix contains a listing of vaccines pending FDA approval. |
| Appendix L—Vascular Families | Appendix L contains a listing of vascular families, the branch order, and those families commonly reported during arteriographic procedures. |
| Appendix M—Renumbered CPT Codes–Citations Crosswalk | This appendix contains a listing of renumbered and crosswalked codes and their descriptions. |
| Appendix N—Summary of Resequenced CPT Codes | Appendix N contains a listing of the CPT codes that are not in numerical order in the CPT manual. This appendix can be referenced to identify the codes out of numerical order. |
| Appendix O—Multianalyte Assays with Algorithmic Analyses and Proprietary Laboratory Analyses | This appendix lists codes that are unique to a single clinical laboratory or manufacturer. |
| Appendix P—CPT Codes That May Be Used for Synchronous Telemedicine Services | This appendix is a summary of the CPT codes that may be used to report real-time telemedicine services. |
| Appendix Q—Severe Acute Respiratory Syndrome Coronavirus 2 (SARS-CoV-2) (coronavirus disease [COVID-19]) Vaccines | This appendix can be used to identify the individual severe acute respiratory syndrome coronavirus vaccine product codes and the associated immunization administration codes, the name of the vaccine manufacturer, the specific vaccine name, the National Drug Code (NDC) product ID, and the dosing interval for the vaccine. |
| Appendix R—Digital Medicine-Services Taxonomy | This appendix contains a listing of digital medicine services and it classifies CPT codes into categories related to digital medicine services. The categories are: clinician-to-patient services, clinician-to-clinician services, patient monitoring services and digital diagnostic services. The appendix defines each of these categories and provides additional information about the use and purpose of Appendix R. Locate Appendix R in the CPT coding manual and read all of the notes that pertain to this appendix. Also review the information in the table that is present in the appendix. |
| Appendix S—Artificial Intelligence Taxonomy for Medical Services and Procedures | The definitions and taxonomy, in Appendix S, provides guidance for classifying various types of artificial intelligence (AI) applications used in medical services and procedures. The three categories of AI are: assistive, augmentative, and autonomous. Locate Appendix S in the CPT manual and review all of the information that appears in the appendix. |
| Appendix T—CPT Codes That May Be Used For Synchronous Real-Time Interactive Audio-Only Telemedicine Services | Appendix T is a listing of CPT codes that may be used to report audio-only services. The audio-only service is reported by adding modifier 93 to the code. Review Appendix T in the CPT manual. |

Become familiar with the contents of the appendices because they provide an excellent source for reference information. Please note that the information in Appendix Q—SARS-CoV-2 Vaccines will continue to be updated as additional booster doses of vaccines are approved and administered.

# CPT as Part of HCPCS

Until 1983, CPT codes were recognized only by private insurance companies. After that time, the Healthcare Financing Administration developed the **Healthcare Common Procedure Coding System (HCPCS)**, using CPT codes as part of the HCPCS system for reporting Medicare services. The Healthcare Financing Administration is now known as the Centers for Medicare & Medicaid Services (CMS). The CPT codes that were already in use became the Level I or Category I codes of the new HCPCS coding system for the Medicare program. Some third-party payers also recognize the additional codes in HCPCS.

## HCPCS

The Healthcare Common Procedure Coding System, commonly referred to as HCPCS (pronounced "hicpics"), is divided into Level I and Level II.

### HCPCS Level I

The CPT codes are **Level I codes**. These codes are divided into Category I, Category II, and Category III. **Category I** codes are the codes from the main sections of CPT:

- Evaluation and Management
- Anesthesia
- Surgery
- Radiology
- Pathology and Laboratory
- Medicine

These codes are used to report services rendered by providers. They are mandatory.

**Category II** codes are not mandatory and are considered tracking codes. In the CPT manual, following the Medicine section, Category II codes can be located. Category II codes should never be used as a primary procedure code.

> **EXAMPLE:** The following code represents a Category II code:
>
> **1005F**   Asthma symptoms evaluated (includes documentation of numeric frequency of symptoms or patient completion of an asthma assessment tool/survey/questionnaire) (NMA-No Measure Associated)

**Category III** codes, located in the CPT codebook after the Category II codes, are temporary codes for emerging technologies, services, procedures, and service paradigms, and are used for the collection of statistical data. With the creation of new procedures and technologies, these temporary codes can be assigned as additional codes to track their use. To become familiar with the reporting guidelines for Category III codes, reference the Category III code listing in the CPT manual. (The Category Code listing is found in the section prior to the start of the Appendices in the CPT manual.) As stated in this section of the CPT manual, if a Category III code is available, the Category III code must be reported instead of a Category I unlisted code. This will be discussed further later in the textbook.

> **EXAMPLE:** The following represents a Category III code:
>
> **0208T**   Pure tome audiometry (threshold), automated; air only

## HCPCS Level II

HCPCS **Level II codes** are commonly referred to as **National Codes**. These codes are published annually by the Medicare program and are used to bill for services and procedures that are not included in the Level I codes. These codes can be obtained on the Centers for Medicare & Medicaid Services (CMS) website and from the published annual edition of the codes. HCPCS Level II codes consist of one alpha character (A through V) followed by four digits. HCPCS Level II codes are discussed in Chapter 23 of this textbook.

# Summary

- Current Procedural Terminology (CPT) comprises codes and guidelines used by the medical profession to report procedures and services provided to a patient during an encounter.
- The introduction of CPT contains explanations of the symbols used, how to maneuver through the book, and instructions for using the book.
- The main sections of CPT contain the codes used to report procedures to the insurance company/payer.
- The index helps the coder find the service that needs to be reported.
- The appendices further assist the coder with quick references to modifiers and coding changes.

# Internet Links

For more information about CMS and the HCPCS coding system, visit ***http://www.cms.gov***.

# Chapter Review

## True/False

**Instructions:** Indicate whether the following statements are true (T) or false (F).

1. _____ CPT codes tell the insurance carrier what brought the patient to the physician's office.

2. _____ Text, symbols, and the history of CPT are found in the introduction of the code book.

3. _____ The CPT code book is updated annually on July 1.

4. _____ The Surgery section of codes begins with code 10001 and goes through code 69999.

5. _____ ▲ is the symbol for a revised code.

## Fill in the Blank

**Instructions:** Fill in the blanks in the statements that follow.

6. The CPT coding system was first published in 1966 by _____.

7. A complete and detailed description of all modifiers used in CPT is found in _____.

8. The CPT manual contains _____ main sections.

9. The _____ separates the common portion of the code description from additional portions of the code.

10. The _____ is organized by main terms.

# Coding Assignments

For each code listed, note the main section of the CPT manual in which you would find the code.
The first one is done for you.

1. 00142    Anesthesia _____
2. 23076    _____
3. 88348    _____
4. 62281    _____
5. 65091    _____
6. 90935    _____
7. 99456    _____
8. 75810    _____
9. 37766    _____
10. 93283   _____

11. 64400   _____
12. 77003   _____
13. 30520   _____
14. 89264   _____
15. 92326   _____
16. 90651   _____
17. 80345   _____
18. 77307   _____
19. 33955   _____
20. 99188   _____

# Short Answer

Using the introduction to the CPT manual as a reference, define the following.

1. Unlisted procedure or service

_____
_____
_____

2. Add-on codes

_____
_____
_____

3. Modifiers

_____
_____
_____

4. Special Report

_____
_____
_____

5. Alphabetical Reference Index

_____
_____
_____

6. Section Numbers and Their Sequences

   _____

   _____

   _____

7. Using Appendix D of the CPT manual, review the following codes to determine if the code listed is an add-on code.

   Next to the code, write "Yes" if the code is an add-on code or "No" if the code is not an add-on code.

   | Code | Is this an add-on code? | Code | Is this an add-on code? |
   |------|------------------------|------|------------------------|
   | 11047 | _____ | 63082 | _____ |
   | 60540 | _____ | 81416 | _____ |
   | 36100 | _____ | | |

8. Using Appendix E of the CPT manual, review the following codes to determine if the code listed is exempt from modifier –51 use.

   Next to the code, write "Yes" if the code is exempt or "No" if the code is not exempt.

   | Code | Is this code exempt from the use of modifier –51? | Code | Is this code exempt from the use of modifier –51? |
   |------|--------------------------------------------------|------|--------------------------------------------------|
   | 99202 | _____ | 93618 | _____ |
   | 20975 | _____ | 36620 | _____ |
   | 97535 | _____ | | |

9. Differentiate between Level I and Level II codes in HCPCS.

10. Reference Appendix Q in the CPT coding manual. For the vaccine code listed state the vaccine administration code(s) that are reported with the vaccine code listed according to the table. List the codes for the first and second dose. If only one dose is given list only one code.

    | Vaccine Code | Vaccine Administration Code(s) |
    |--------------|-------------------------------|
    | 91302 | |
    | 91304 | |
    | 91303 | |

# 2 Modifiers

## Chapter Outline

Introduction

Definition and Purposes of Modifiers

Use of Modifiers for Various Procedures
    and Service Locations

Modifiers Used for Hospital
    Outpatient Services

CPT Level I Modifiers

HCPCS Level II Modifiers

Summary

Internet Links

Chapter Review

Case Studies

## Learning Objectives

### At the conclusion of this chapter, you should be able to:

1. Identify where a list of CPT modifiers can be found in the CPT manual.
2. Sequence pricing and statistical modifiers in the proper order.
3. Differentiate between pricing and statistical modifiers.
4. Define the various CPT modifiers used.
5. Identify modifiers approved for hospital outpatient services.
6. Define the various HCPCS Level II modifiers used.
7. Assign CPT and HCPCS Level II modifiers to procedural statements.
8. Identify where modifiers are listed on the CMS-1500 form.

## Key Terms

alternative laboratory
    platform testing—
    modifier 92

anesthesia by surgeon—
    modifier 47

assistant surgeon—
    modifier 80

assistant surgeon (when
    qualified resident
    surgeon is not
    available)—modifier 82

bilateral procedure—
    modifier 50

CPT modifier

decision for surgery—
    modifier 57

discontinued outpatient
    hospital/ambulatory
    surgery center (ASC)
    procedure after
    administration of
    anesthesia—modifier 74

discontinued outpatient
    hospital/ambulatory
    surgery center (ASC)
    procedure prior to
    the administration of
    anesthesia—modifier 73

discontinued
    procedure—modifier 53

distinct procedural service—modifier 59

habilitative services—modifier 96

increased procedural services—modifier 22

informational modifiers

Level I (CPT) modifiers

Level II (HCPCS/National) modifiers

mandated services—modifier 32

minimum assistant surgeon—modifier 81

multiple modifiers—modifier 99

multiple outpatient hospital E/M encounters on the same date—modifier 27

multiple procedures—modifier 51

postoperative management only—modifier 55

preoperative management only—modifier 56

preventive service—modifier 33

pricing modifiers

procedure performed on infants less than 4 kg—modifier 63

professional component—modifier 26

reduced services—modifier 52

reference (outside) laboratory—modifier 90

rehabilitative services—modifier 97

repeat clinical diagnostic laboratory test—modifier 91

repeat procedure or service by another physician or other qualified health care professional—modifier 77

repeat procedure or service by same physician or other qualified health care professional—modifier 76

significant, separately identifiable E/M service by the same physician or other qualified health care professional on the same day of the procedure or other service—modifier 25

staged procedure

staged or related procedure or service by the same physician or other qualified health care professional during the postoperative period—modifier 58

statistical modifiers

surgical care only—modifier 54

surgical team—modifier 66

synchronous telemedicine service rendered via a real-time interactive audio and video telecommunications system—modifier 95

synchronous telemedicine service rendered via telephone

or other real-time interactive audio-only telecommunications system—modifier 93

two surgeons—modifier 62

unplanned return to the operating/procedure room by the same physician or other qualified health care professional for a related procedure during the postoperative period—modifier 78

unrelated E/M service by the same physician or other qualified health care professional during postoperative period—modifier 24

unrelated procedure or service by the same physician or other qualified health care professional during the postoperative period—modifier 79

unusual anesthesia—modifier 23

# Introduction

At times, a CPT code needs to be reported with the addition of a modifier. Modifiers give additional information, when necessary, about the CPT code to a third-party payer to ensure that claims are paid correctly.

# Definition and Purposes of Modifiers

A **CPT modifier** is a two-digit code that is appended to the CPT code to indicate that a service or procedure has been altered for some reason, but it does not change the main definition of the code. The modifier further describes the service performed. Two types of modifiers are used with CPT codes: **Level I (CPT) modifiers** are two-digit numeric codes, whereas **Level II (HCPCS/National) modifiers** are two-digit alphanumeric modifiers. A complete listing of Level I modifiers is contained in Appendix A of the CPT manual. To become familiar with the modifier codes and descriptions, review Appendix A of the CPT manual.

Modifiers are used for various reasons, including the following:

- A service or procedure has both a technical and professional component.
- A service or procedure was performed by more than one physician.
- A service or procedure was performed in more than one location.

- A service or procedure has taken more time to complete than routinely would occur.
- A service or procedure was reduced or increased.
- Only part of a procedure was completed.
- A bilateral procedure was performed.
- A service or procedure was completed multiple times.
- An unusual event occurred during the procedure.
- An accompanying or adjunctive procedure was performed.

# Use of Modifiers for Various Procedures and Service Locations

As mentioned earlier in this chapter, Appendix A of the CPT manual lists the Level I modifiers. It should be noted that instruction is also given as to which modifiers are used for physician services and which modifiers are appropriate for ambulatory surgery center hospital outpatient use.

## Modifiers Used with Physician Services

When billing physician services, place modifiers in item 24d of the CMS-1500 form, following the CPT code. Appendix I of this textbook provides an example of the CMS-1500 form. Reference Appendix I, Figure A1-1, of this textbook to see where to place the modifier on the CMS-1500 form.

When reporting modifiers for Medicare claims, the CPT code is followed by the modifier. It should be noted that some third-party payers use different instructions for reporting modifiers. It is important to review the modifier instructions for the payer you are billing. This will be explained further when we discuss the various modifiers.

The CMS-1500 claim form contains modifier fields. For Medicare claims, when you enter only one modifier, enter it in the first modifier field. When more than one modifier is submitted, the modifiers must be ranked according to whether the modifier will affect the fee for the service. Modifiers that affect pricing are listed in Table 2-1 and should be reported in the first modifier field because they directly affect the fee for a service. The modifiers listed in Table 2-1 are often referred to as **pricing modifiers**, and they either increase or decrease the fee for the service.

The remaining modifiers, often referred to as **statistical modifiers** or **informational modifiers**, are used for informational purposes and have an impact on the processing or payment of the code billed but do not affect the fee. Table 2-2 lists the statistical/informational modifiers.

It is important for the coder to also enter the pricing modifier in the first modifier field.

> **EXAMPLE:** Ranking of Two Modifiers—One pricing modifier and one statistical modifier.
>
> Assume that Dr. Smith performed an open incision and drainage of an appendiceal abscess and reported code 44900. Two days later, Dr. Smith repeated the same procedure on the same patient. During this episode of care, he only performed the surgical care; therefore, modifier 54, surgical care only, would be appended to the code 44900. Because this is a repeat procedure by the same physician, modifier 76 also would have to be reported. Therefore, modifier 54 should be reported in the first modifier field, because it affects pricing, and modifier 76 would be entered in the second modifier field, because it does not affect pricing.

**TABLE 2-1**  Pricing Modifiers That Affect Fees

| AA | AD | AH | AJ | AS | GM | QB | QK | QU | QX | QY | QZ |
|----|----|----|----|----|----|----|----|----|----|----|----|
| SG | TC | UN | UP | UQ | UR | US | 22 | 26 | 50 | 51 | 52 |
| 53 | 54 | 55 | 56 | 62 | 66 | 73 | 74 | 78 | 80 | 82 | 99 |

**TABLE 2-2** Statistical and Informational Modifiers

| AE | AF | AG | AK | AR | AT | AM | CC | CG | E1 | E2 | E3 |
|----|----|----|----|----|----|----|----|----|----|----|----|
| E4 | EJ | EM | EP | ET | F1 | F2 | F3 | F4 | F5 | F6 | F7 |
| F8 | F9 | FA | FP | G1 | G2 | G3 | G4 | G5 | G6 | G7 | G8 |
| G9 | GA | GB | GC | GE | GG | GH | GJ | GN | G0 | GP | GQ |
| GT | GV | GW | GY | GZ | K0 | KP | KQ | KX | LC | LD | LR |
| LS | LT | Q3 | Q4 | Q5 | Q6 | Q7 | Q8 | Q9 | QA | QC | QD |
| QL | QM | QN | QP | QQ | QS | QT | QV | QW | RC | RD | RP |
| RT | SF | SW | SY | T1 | T2 | T3 | T4 | T5 | T6 | T7 | T8 |
| T9 | TA | VP | 23 | 24 | 25 | 32 | 47 | 57 | 58 | 59 | 76 |
| 77 | 79 | 90 | 91 | 95 | | | | | | | |

When reporting more than one statistical or informational modifier with no other pricing modifiers, you can report the statistical or information modifiers in any order, with the exception of the QT, QW, and SF modifiers. These three modifiers are valid for use only in the first modifier field. Assume that modifiers T7 and 58 are being reported together. The modifiers can be sequenced in any order because they are both statistical modifiers.

## Exercise 2.1—Check Your Understanding

List the modifiers given in the series in the proper order. If the order does not make a difference, indicate this with ND.

1. 62, 22 _____

2. GW, US _____

3. 56, T2 _____

4. AA, 47 _____

5. 59, 51 _____

## Use of Multiple Modifiers—Modifier 99

**Modifier 99—multiple modifiers** indicates that multiple modifiers are needed for an individual CPT code. This modifier is not recognized by all insurance plans, so coders must review the coding guidelines for plans that are being billed. Medicare recognizes modifier 99, and coders should refer to Medicare administrative contractor information for instructions on reporting this modifier. Many Medicare administrative contractors require modifier 99 to be entered in the first modifier field when more than two modifiers apply. Additional information is required in the narrative field (item 19 on the claim form), listing all modifiers in the correct ranking order.

## Exercise 2.2—Check Your Understanding

Pricing and Statistical/Informational Modifiers

For the following modifiers, state whether the modifier is a pricing modifier or a statistical/informational modifier.

| Modifier | Type | Modifier | Type |
|----------|------|----------|------|
| 1. 52 | _____ | 6. 23 | _____ |
| 2. E3 | _____ | 7. 59 | _____ |
| 3. 82 | _____ | 8. 50 | _____ |
| 4. 78 | _____ | 9. 77 | _____ |
| 5. GN | _____ | 10. QD | _____ |

# Modifiers Used for Hospital Outpatient Services

Hospital outpatient services are reported on the UB-04 form, also known as the CMS-1450 form. When modifiers are reported for these services, they should be placed in field 44 of that form. Reference Appendix I, Figure A1-2, of this textbook to determine where modifiers should be placed on a UB-04/CMS-1450 form.

## Modifiers Approved for Ambulatory Surgery Center Hospital Outpatient Use

Not all modifiers are approved for use on ambulatory surgery claims. The list of approved modifiers is reviewed annually. Table 2-3 lists the currently approved modifiers. Appendix A of the CPT manual also lists the modifiers that are approved for the ambulatory surgery setting. Familiarize yourself with the modifiers used in this setting by reading the listing and the modifiers' descriptions in Appendix A of the CPT manual.

**TABLE 2-3** Modifiers Approved for Ambulatory Surgery Center Hospital Outpatient Use

| Level I Modifiers | | | | | | | | | | | | |
|---|---|---|---|---|---|---|---|---|---|---|---|---|
| 25 | 27 | 33 | 50 | 52 | 58 | 59 | 73 | 74 | 76 | 77 | 78 | 79 | 91 |
| **Level II Modifiers** | | | | | | | | | | | | |
| LT | RT | E1 | E2 | E3 | E4 | FA | F1 | F2 | F3 | F4 | F5 | F6 |
| F7 | F8 | F9 | TA | T1 | T2 | T3 | T4 | T5 | T6 | T7 | T8 | T9 |
| LC | LD | LM | RC | RI | GG | GH | QM | QN | XE | XS | XP | XU |

## Exercise 2.3—Check Your Understanding

**Modifiers Used for Ambulatory Surgery Center Hospital Outpatient Claims**

Mary Smith is an outpatient surgery coder at Sunny Valley Hospital, and she is developing a list of modifiers that can be used in this setting. Next to the modifier listed, write "Yes" if the modifier should be used in this setting or "No" if the modifier should not be used in this setting.

| Modifier | Use in Outpatient Surgery Setting? | Modifier | Use in Outpatient Surgery Setting? |
|---|---|---|---|
| **1.** 22 | _____ | **9.** E4 | _____ |
| **2.** 50 | _____ | **10.** RT | _____ |
| **3.** 53 | _____ | **11.** F3 | _____ |
| **4.** 59 | _____ | **12.** TC | _____ |
| **5.** 62 | _____ | **13.** RC | _____ |
| **6.** 66 | _____ | **14.** GG | _____ |
| **7.** 73 | _____ | **15.** T1 | _____ |
| **8.** 76 | _____ | | |

# CPT Level I Modifiers

The best way to understand how to use modifiers is to review the definition for each modifier found in Appendix A of the CPT manual. Here, we discuss the use of each modifier and give examples of cases that require modifier use. The titles of the modifiers are listed as they appear in the CPT manual.

## Increased Procedural Services—Modifier 22

Assign modifier 22 when the service provided is greater than that usually required for the listed procedure. This modifier should not be appended to an Evaluation and Management code.

> **EXAMPLE:** A radical abdominal hysterectomy with bilateral total pelvic lymphadenectomy and para-aortic lymph node biopsy was performed on Peg Smith. The procedure took 50 minutes longer than normal because, during the surgery, the patient experienced prolonged bleeding.

The code to report would be 58210-22 because of the unusual amount of time that it took to complete the procedure.

The use of modifier 22 is tracked by insurance companies. This should be used only for cases that are truly unusual and for which documentation of the case can justify the unusual aspect of the service. The surgeon needs to identify the additional work, such as technical difficulties during the procedure, or an increased intensity and/or time, just to name a few items. When this modifier is reported, an operative note will be requested and a special report may be requested, which would require the following information:

- A complete description of the procedure performed.
- The reason the service fell outside the parameters of the CPT code description.
- The time, effort, and equipment used during the procedure.
- The complexity of the case, describing the patient's condition and symptoms that occurred during the procedure.
- The preoperative and postoperative diagnoses.
- Pertinent physical findings that influenced the case and procedure.
- Any diagnostic and therapeutic services that were rendered in association with the procedure.
- Concurrent diagnosis, symptoms, and problems that were present.
- The anticipated follow-up care.

## Unusual Anesthesia—Modifier 23

Occasionally, a procedure that routinely is not completed with any type of anesthesia or local anesthesia requires the use of general anesthesia. When this occurs, modifier 23 is appended to the CPT code.

> **EXAMPLE:** A patient with a psychiatric condition needs to undergo surgery for a simple drainage of a finger abscess. Because the patient has much anxiety about the procedure, the physician uses general anesthesia.

The code to report is 26010-23.

## Unrelated Evaluation and Management Service by the Same Physician or Other Qualified Health Care Professional During Postoperative Period—Modifier 24

For each procedure, a postoperative period is established that denotes the usual postoperative period for the condition related to the surgery. When a patient is seen for an unrelated Evaluation and Management service during a postoperative period, modifier 24 is appended to the Evaluation and Management code, abbreviated E/M code.

This would indicate that an E/M service was performed during a postoperative period for a reason or reasons unrelated to the original procedure. The diagnosis code reported for the unrelated Evaluation and Management service must reflect the reason for the unrelated service.

> **EXAMPLE:** Stella Monkowski had an open cholecystectomy and was discharged home. Five days after the surgery, she experienced chest pain and was seen by the same physician who performed the surgery. He evaluated the chest pain.

The physician reported code 99213-24 to indicate that she was seen for a condition unrelated to the surgery. The diagnosis code for this visit would be chest pain, which is a condition that is not related to the cholecystectomy.

## Significant, Separately Identifiable Evaluation and Management Service by the Same Physician or Other Qualified Health Care Professional on the Same Day of the Procedure or Other Service—Modifier 25

Modifier 25 is added to any appropriate level of an Evaluation and Management service when the physician needs to indicate that on the day a procedure or service was performed, the patient's condition required a significant, separately identifiable Evaluation and Management service that was above and beyond the other service provided or beyond the usual preoperative and postoperative care associated with the procedure that was performed.

> **EXAMPLE:** Devon presented to the doctor's office with knee pain that was a result of a sports injury. The physician examined Devon and determined that he had tendonitis. In the course of his examination, several warts were noted on the plantar side of Devon's left foot. The doctor felt that treatment should be started due to the size of two of the three warts. Devon did state that he has pain when wearing his shoe gear.

The physician reported code 99213-25 with a diagnosis of knee pain and tendonitis; in addition, he reported 17110 for cryotherapy treatment of the warts. The diagnosis code assigned to 17110 would be plantar warts. As per the definition of modifier 25, there are times when the Evaluation and Management service may be prompted by the same symptom or condition for which the procedure and/or service was provided; therefore, in these cases, different diagnoses are not required for the reporting of the E/M service on the same date.

## Professional Component—Modifier 26

A number of CPT procedures have both a professional and a technical component. Examples of codes that have both a professional and a technical component include codes in the Pathology and Radiology chapters and cardiology codes found in the Medicine chapter of CPT. When a physician is reporting only the professional component, the service is identified by adding modifier 26 to the usual procedure number.

> **EXAMPLE:** Dr. Ty, a radiologist, interprets a four-view x-ray examination of the cervical spine.

This is reported using code 72050-26.

Modifier 26 should not be appended to codes that represent a professional component but do *not* have a technical component as part of the code definition. An example of a code that represents only the professional component is code 93042—Rhythm ECG, one to three leads; interpretation and report only.

## Multiple Outpatient Hospital E/M Encounters on the Same Date—Modifier 27

Modifier 27 is appended to an E/M service code when separate and distinct E/M encounters are performed in multiple outpatient hospital settings on the same date. This modifier is not to be used for physician reporting of multiple E/M services performed by the same physician on the same day. This is to be used for the reporting of services in the Hospital Outpatient Prospective Payment System.

> **EXAMPLE:** Suni Wong is seen by Dr. Smith in the podiatry clinic at Sunny Valley Hospital, and Dr. Smith selects code 99213 to report the services provided. Later that day, Suni Wong goes to the oncology clinic at Sunny Valley Hospital, and Dr. Johnson selects code 99214.

Dr. Smith would report code 99213, and Dr. Johnson would report code 99214-27.

## Mandated Services—Modifier 32

At times, services are performed because the service is required or mandated by an insurance company or by a governmental, legislative, or regulatory agency. When this occurs, **modifier 32** is appended to the CPT code to indicate that the service was a mandated service.

> **EXAMPLE:** Joe Wenn was in an automobile accident. His auto insurance company is mandating that he be examined by Dr. Spy to determine the extent of his injuries. Joe has already been seen by his own primary care physician. Because Dr. Spy's examination of Joe is mandated by the auto insurance company, modifier 32 should be appended to the E/M code that Dr. Spy submits.

Dr. Spy submits code 99214-32.

## Preventive Service—Modifier 33

**Modifier 33** is used for the purpose of identifying the delivery of an evidence-based service in accordance with a U.S. Preventive Services Task Force A or B rating. The modifier is appended to codes representing preventive services. For separately reported services specifically identified as preventive, the modifier should not be used.

## Anesthesia by Surgeon—Modifier 47

**Modifier 47** is used by physicians or surgeons only when regional or general anesthesia is provided by the same physician or surgeon who is completing a procedure or service. This modifier is not to be used when local anesthesia is used. This modifier is appended to a procedure code or service code and is never appended to the anesthesia code.

> **EXAMPLE:** Dr. Boaz performs a dilation of the esophagus by unguided bougie under general anesthesia on patient Bobby Jones.

Dr. Boaz reports 43450-47.

## Bilateral Procedure—Modifier 50

**Modifier 50** is used by both facilities and professionals when bilateral procedures are performed in the same operative session. It is used only with codes that describe a unilateral procedure. Modifier 50 is not used on codes that describe bilateral procedures, such as code 31231—Nasal endoscopy, diagnostic, unilateral, or bilateral. It should be noted that some payers prefer RT (right) or LT (left) modifiers instead of modifier 50 and require the code to be reported twice.

> **EXAMPLE:** Dr. Sinus completed a bilateral intranasal maxillary sinusotomy on Linda New.

The code to report this procedure for Medicare patients would be 31020-50. Some insurance companies instruct providers to report the codes as follows: 31020 and 31020-50 or 31020-RT and 31020-LT.

# Multiple Procedures—Modifier 51

At times, during the same operative/procedural session, multiple procedures are performed by the same provider. When multiple procedures, other than E/M services, Physical Medicine and Rehabilitation services, or provision of supplies (e.g., vaccines), are performed at the same session by the same provider, the primary procedure or service code would be reported as listed in the CPT manual. The additional procedure(s) or service(s) would be reported by adding **modifier 51** to the additional procedure or service code(s).

> **EXAMPLE:** John Jones has a puncture aspiration of an abscess on his left shoulder. During the same session, the cutting of three benign hyperkeratotic lesions also occurred.

Code 10160 would be reported for the puncture aspiration, whereas code 11056-51 would be reported for the cutting of the lesions.

This modifier is used only by providers and is not used by facilities. It should also be noted that this modifier should not be appended to designated add-on codes or Evaluation and Management codes. Appendix E within the CPT manual contains a list of codes that are exempt from modifier 51.

# Reduced Services—Modifier 52

When a service or procedure is partially reduced or eliminated at the physician's discretion, **modifier 52** should be appended to the service or procedure code. This modifier should be used to report reduced services without changing the identification of the basic service. In other words, modifier 52 is used when part of the procedure was performed, but part of the procedure or service was not completed, at the provider's discretion. The use of modifier 52 may prompt a payer to request supporting documentation. The provider documentation should clearly state the reason for the reduced service.

> **EXAMPLE:** Kevin is 10 years old and is presenting for a physical for soccer camp. His physician reviews the camp forms and performs the required physical, but no comprehensive history is obtained. The examination is detailed but not comprehensive.

Kevin's physical is coded with a 99393—Periodic comprehensive preventive medicine; late childhood (age 5–11). A 52 modifier is appended because the history and examination do not meet the requirements for the comprehensive physical code that is used.

CMS states that for outpatient hospital reporting, modifiers 73 and 74 are used in place of modifier 52 for previously scheduled procedures/services that are partially reduced or canceled as a result of extenuating circumstances or those that threaten the well-being of the patient prior to or after administration of anesthesia. Reference the definition of modifier 52 in Appendix A of the CPT manual for additional clarification.

# Discontinued Procedure—Modifier 53

At times, the physician may terminate a surgical or diagnostic procedure because of extenuating circumstances that threaten the well-being of the patient. **Modifier 53** would be used for cases in which the surgical or diagnostic procedure was started but discontinued. However, this modifier is not used to report the elective cancelation of a procedure prior to the patient's anesthesia induction and/or surgical preparation in the operating suite.

> **EXAMPLE:** Dr. Rissen brought Danielle into the OR for an endoscopic resection of a renal tumor. Danielle was put out under general anesthesia, and the procedure was started. As Dr. Rissen moved the scope into place through the established nephrostomy and touched the tumor to prep for removal, Danielle's blood pressure dropped from 150/80 to 100/50. Dr. Rissen stopped the procedure immediately, and Danielle was sent to recovery. The surgery was rescheduled when Danielle's blood pressure was stabilized.

Dr. Rissen reported code 50562 with a 53 modifier. The code reflects the renal endoscopy through established nephrostomy with resection of tumor, and the 53 modifier indicates that the procedure was discontinued by the surgeon due to the condition of the patient. The use of the 53 modifier indicates that additional services may be provided in the future.

As noted earlier for modifier 52, modifiers 73 and 74 are required for outpatient hospital ambulatory surgery center reporting in place of modifier 53. Reference the definition of modifier 53 for further clarification on the reporting for outpatient hospital/ambulatory surgery center reporting.

## Surgical Care Only—Modifier 54

For most surgeries, the preoperative care, the surgery, and the postoperative care are completed by the same provider. However, in some cases, elements of surgical care are divided among providers. When this occurs, modifiers are used to indicate which provider performed various elements of the surgical care. **Modifier 54** is used when one physician performed the surgical procedure and another provider or providers completed the preoperative and/or postoperative management.

> **EXAMPLE:** Dr. Patel performed a repair of a ruptured spleen with a partial splenectomy. A different provider performed the pre- and postoperative care.

Because Dr. Patel did not provide the preoperative and postoperative care, the code reported by Dr. Patel would be 38115-54.

Modifier 54 is not used for any procedures that have zero global surgical days. Documentation must show transfer of care between physicians to justify the separation of the reporting of the surgical code. The pre- and postoperative services provided by the physician other than the surgeon would be coded with an appropriate E/M code.

## Postoperative Management Only—Modifier 55

**Modifier 55** indicates that one provider performed the postoperative management and another provider performed the surgical procedure.

> **EXAMPLE:** Dr. Hill performed a repair of a ruptured spleen with a partial splenectomy on Mary Smith. However, following the surgery, Dr. Cook provided the postoperative care.

Dr. Cook would report code 38115-55.

## Preoperative Management Only—Modifier 56

At times, a different provider will perform the preoperative care and evaluation, and another provider will perform the surgical procedure. When this occurs, **modifier 56** is used to report the preoperative care.

> **EXAMPLE:** Prior to surgery, Dr. House evaluated and cared for Mary Smith. Then Dr. Hill performed a repair of a ruptured spleen with a partial splenectomy on Mary Smith.

Because Dr. House performed the preoperative care, the code to report this service would be 38115-56.

## Decision for Surgery—Modifier 57

**Modifier 57** is appended to an Evaluation and Management service code when, during the service, the initial decision was made to perform surgery.

> **EXAMPLE:** Dr. Jones examined Mary Lou, a 27-year-old female patient, and determined that she needed to have a tonsillectomy and adenoidectomy. This was scheduled to occur in two weeks. Dr. Jones completed a comprehensive history and a comprehensive examination and documented medical decision making of high complexity. The encounter lasted 45 minutes.

Dr. Jones would report 99215-57.

The use of modifier 57 on a minor procedure performed on the same day as the decision for the procedure should be checked with the particular insurance carrier. Some insurance companies allow this; Medicare does not. Medicare prefers the use of a 25 modifier on the Evaluation and Management code for minor procedures with global days of 0 or 10. The coder should check with the payer to find out how they would like the decision for surgery reported.

## Staged or Related Procedure or Service by the Same Physician or Other Qualified Health Care Professional During the Postoperative Period—Modifier 58

**Modifier 58** is used during the postoperative period of a procedure when

- During the original procedure, a second procedure is planned as part of the care. (This is known as a **staged procedure**.)
- During the postoperative period, more extensive care is needed than what was rendered in the original procedure.
- During the postoperative period, therapy is required following the surgical procedure.

> **EXAMPLE:** A patient presents for insertion of Heyman capsules for clinical brachytherapy. The documentation states that this is the first of two procedures.

The code for the first treatment would be 58346, and the second time the patient presents would be recorded as 58346-58.

Although this modifier indicates that more extensive care was needed, it is not to be used to report the treatment of a problem that requires a return to the operating room. In these situations, modifier 78 is appropriate.

## Distinct Procedural Service—Modifier 59

Under certain circumstances, the physician may need to indicate that a procedure or service was independent from other non-E/M services performed on the same day. **Modifier 59** identifies procedures that are not typically reported together but are appropriate under the circumstances. Different anatomical sites or procedures that are not ordinarily encountered or performed on the same day by the same physician may require use of this modifier. It should be noted that when another, already established modifier is appropriate, it should be used rather than modifier 59.

> **EXAMPLE:** Six-year-old Elizabeth fell down in her driveway. She had a 3-cm laceration on her right arm and gravel embedded in the forearm of her left arm. There was an intermediate repair of the laceration on her right arm. There was a 10-square cm debridement of subcutaneous tissue, epidermis, and dermis of her left arm.

The intermediate repair of the laceration includes the debridement of the gravel and would be reported using code 12032. The debridement of the gravel that was embedded in the left arm would be coded 11042 with a 59 modifier. It should be noted that modifier 59 is not appended to an E/M service.

Effective January 1, 2015, four new HCPCS modifiers (XE, XP, XS, XU) were implemented to define specific subsets of modifier 59. The modifiers are collectively referred to as the −X {EPSU} modifiers. Please note that modifier 59 will continue to be used after January 1, 2015 with the new −X {EPSU} modifiers. Modifier 59 is one of the most widely used modifiers, and CMS felt that it was necessary to have more specific information from providers and facilities regarding the submission of the modifier, thus they established the −X {EPSU} modifiers to provide that information.

The −X {EPSU} modifiers are defined as follows:

- XE Separate Encounter—A service that is distinct because it occurred during a separate encounter.
- XS Separate Structure—A service that is distinct because it was performed on a separate organ/structure.

- XP Separate Practitioner—A service that is distinct because it was performed by a different practitioner.
- XU Unusual Non-Overlapping Service—The use of a service that is distinct because it does not overlap usual components of the main service.

CMS will continue to recognize the –59 modifier, but note that Current Procedural Terminology instructions indicate that modifier 59 should not be used when a more descriptive modifier is available. Therefore if an –X {EPSU} modifier is used for a code, it is incorrect to include modifier 59 as an additional modifier for the code.

## Two Surgeons—Modifier 62

**Modifier 62** is used when two primary surgeons work together to perform a distinct part(s) of a single reportable procedure. In this situation, each surgeon should report his or her own distinct operative work by adding modifier 62 to the single definitive procedure code. In addition, each surgeon should report any associated add-on codes for the procedure, as long as the two surgeons continued to work as primary surgeons, and append the add-on procedure codes with modifier 62.

> **EXAMPLE:** Mr. Pearl needed surgery to insert a pacemaker. Dr. Johnson made the incision and created the generator pocket. At this point in the procedure, Dr. Hyder inserted the atrial electrode and programmed the pacemaker. The electrode was tested, and then Dr. Johnson closed the incision.

Both surgeons in our example would document their piece of the surgery and report the surgery using 33206-62. It should also be noted that if additional procedure(s) (including add-on procedure[s]) were performed during the same surgical session and one of the surgeons acts as an assistant, those services are reported with modifier 80 or 82 added. The separate code(s) would be reported without modifier 62 added.

## Procedure Performed on Infants Less Than 4 kg—Modifier 63

**Modifier 63** reports procedures performed on neonates and infants up to a body weight of 4 kg. This modifier is not to be appended to codes from the Evaluation and Management section, Anesthesia section, Radiology section, Pathology/Laboratory section, or Medicine section. As per the definition in Appendix A of the CPT manual, this modifier is to be used on codes 20100–69990, unless otherwise designated in the manual.

> **EXAMPLE:** A 3.6-kg male infant, underwent a repair of a congenital arteriovenous fistula of the thorax and abdomen.

This procedure would be reported with code 35182-63 because of the weight of the child.

## Surgical Team—Modifier 66

Some highly complex procedures require the services of several physicians, often of different specialties, plus other highly skilled, specially trained personnel and various types of complex equipment during the operative procedure. When this occurs, it is known as the *surgical team* concept. To indicate this on the claim, each provider should append **modifier 66** to the basic procedure number used for reporting services.

> **EXAMPLE:** A patient underwent the repair of some complex cardiac anomalies by the modified Fontan procedure. It was also necessary to perform a cavopulmonary anastomosis to a second superior vena cava. It was necessary for several cardiothoracic surgeons to work together as a team to accomplish this procedure successfully.

Codes 33617 and 33768 would be used to report this procedure. A 66 modifier is appended to the services to indicate the surgery was performed by a team of surgeons, not just one or two. Each surgeon would need to document the procedure, indicating the need for a team of surgeons, unless one op note can clearly delineate each surgeon's role in the procedure.

# Discontinued Outpatient Hospital/Ambulatory Surgery Center (ASC) Procedure Prior to the Administration of Anesthesia—Modifier 73

Modifier 73 is used for outpatient or ambulatory surgery centers and is used when, due to extenuating circumstances or situations that threaten the well-being of the patient, the physician cancels a surgical or diagnostic procedure after the patient's surgical preparation. The preparation includes sedation, when provided, and being taken to the room where the procedure is to be performed; however, the surgery is canceled prior to the administration of anesthesia. Under these circumstances, the procedure code for the intended procedure is used and appended with modifier 73.

> **EXAMPLE:** Mrs. Evans was wheeled into the OR for her breast biopsy. As she was being prepped, minutes prior to the administration of the anesthesia, there was a mechanical problem with the electrical power to the operating room. The generator was not responding, and the other operating rooms were being utilized. The surgeon had to cancel the surgery until a later date.

It should be noted that modifier 73 is not used for the elective cancelation of a service prior to the administration of anesthesia and/or surgical preparation of the patient.

# Discontinued Outpatient Hospital/Ambulatory Surgery Center (ASC) Procedure After Administration of Anesthesia—Modifier 74

Like modifier 73, modifier 74 is used for outpatient or ambulatory surgery centers. Modifier 74 is used when, due to extenuating circumstances or those that threaten the well-being of the patient, the physician terminates a surgical or diagnostic procedure *after* the administration of anesthesia or after the procedure was started. Modifier 74 is appended to the usual procedure code for the intended procedure.

# Repeat Procedure or Service by Same Physician or Other Qualified Health Care Professional—Modifier 76

At times, it is necessary for a physician or other qualified health care professional to repeat a procedure or service subsequent to the original procedure or service. When this occurs, modifier 76 is used. The original procedure or service code is the same for both sessions.

> **EXAMPLE:** A patient underwent a needle thoracentesis aspiration of the pleural space by Dr. Ferrico. Later that day, another thoracentesis was necessary, and Dr. Ferrico performed it.

Dr. Ferrico reported the second procedure with code 32554-76. Note that this modifier is not to be appended to an E/M code.

# Repeat Procedure or Service by Another Physician or Other Qualified Health Care Professional—Modifier 77

Modifier 77 is used when a physician or other qualified health care professional needs to indicate that a basic procedure or service performed by another physician had to be repeated. The physician who repeated the procedure would append modifier 77 to the repeated procedure or service code, which would be the same procedure or service code as the original procedure or service code. By slightly modifying our previous example, we can see how to use modifier 77:

> **EXAMPLE:** Mrs. Roberts underwent a needle thoracentesis aspiration of the pleural space by Dr. Clark. The next day, another needle thoracentesis aspiration of the pleural space was necessary; however, Dr. Clark was not available. Dr. Lewis performed the procedure.

Dr. Lewis reported it with code 32554-77. This modifier is not be be appended to an E/M code.

# Unplanned Return to the Operating/Procedure Room by the Same Physician or Other Qualified Health Care Professional Following Initial Procedure for a Related Procedure During the Postoperative Period—Modifier 78

At times, a patient is taken back to the operating room for a *related* procedure during the postoperative period of the initial procedure. The claim would indicate that another procedure was performed during the postoperative period of the initial procedure by appending **modifier 78** to the procedure code of the subsequent procedure. It is possible that an unforeseen complication may arise from the original surgery and that the patient may need to be returned to the operating room.

> **EXAMPLE:** A patient had hip replacement surgery performed by Dr. Weiss. Two days postop, the incision developed a hematoma. This required a return trip to the OR, where Dr. Weiss performed a superficial wound dehiscence with a simple closure.

To report this service properly, you would use code 12020-78. Should documentation be requested by a payer, it needs to support the use of this modifier.

# Unrelated Procedure or Service by the Same Physician or Other Qualified Health Care Professional During the Postoperative Period—Modifier 79

During a postoperative period, it may be necessary for the performance of another procedure that was unrelated to the original procedure. When this situation occurs, **modifier 79** is used.

> **EXAMPLE:** Mr. Duncan underwent an excision of two lesions on the small intestine by Dr. Cass. Mr. Duncan was experiencing pain in the area of the diaphragm 30 days postop. Several tests were done, and a diaphragmatic hernia was diagnosed. Mr. Duncan underwent surgical repair of a paraesophageal hiatal hernia via thoracotomy.

Dr. Cass reported code 43334-79.

# Assistant Surgeon—Modifier 80

During surgery, it is not uncommon for a surgeon to assist another surgeon. To report the services of the assistant surgeon, add modifier 80 to the usual procedure code. The assistant surgeon reports the same code(s) as the primary surgeon, but a **modifier 80** is added to his or her services.

> **EXAMPLE:** Dr. Barton performed an anastomosis on the extrahepatic biliary ducts and gastrointestinal tract. Dr. Carrey assisted Dr. Barton with this procedure.

In our example, Dr. Barton would bill code 47780, whereas Dr. Carrey would report 47780-80 for his services.

It should be noted that Medicare Part B does not cover the services of an assistant surgeon for certain procedures. The physician fee schedule on the CMS Web site lists the modifier 80 exemptions. Payment cannot be collected from the patient for these services if the provider is enrolled as a participating Medicare provider.

# Minimum Assistant Surgeon—Modifier 81

**Modifier 81** would be used if the circumstances required a second surgeon for a short time, but not throughout the whole procedure. Another instance that would warrant an 81 modifier would be when a second or third assistant surgeon was needed during a procedure.

**EXAMPLE:** Dr. Grace was performing an open revision of arteriovenous fistula with an autogenous dialysis graft with thrombectomy. At one point, he required the assistance of Dr. Brown to help with some bleeding. Dr. Grace got the patient stable and finished the procedure. Dr. Brown was present only during the critical portion of the surgery and left the surgical suite after the patient stabilized.

Dr. Grace would report his services with CPT code 36833, whereas Dr. Brown would report his services with code 36833-81.

## Assistant Surgeon (When Qualified Resident Surgeon Is Not Available in a Teaching Facility)—Modifier 82

Modifier 82 is used when there is the unavailability of a qualified resident surgeon. In the teaching hospital setting, some residency programs allow their residents to participate as assistants-at-surgery. Modifier 82 is appended if a qualified resident surgeon is not available. CMS guidelines require a certification on file for each claim submitted with this modifier as part of section 1842 of the Social Security Act.

**EXAMPLE:** Dr. Evans was the surgeon on call at 3:00 a.m. when four people were brought into Mercy Hospital, a teaching facility. The four patients had been seriously injured in a motor vehicle accident. All four patients needed immediate surgical attention, which left the surgical teams shorthanded. Dr. Evans asked a colleague in his practice, Dr. Donaldson, to assist because all the surgical residents were caring for other patients.

Dr. Donaldson's services are reported with an 82 modifier to indicate that no surgical residents were available to assist Dr. Evans.

## Reference (Outside) Laboratory—Modifier 90

Modifier 90 is used on laboratory procedure codes to indicate that the laboratory procedures are performed by a party other than the treating or reporting physician.

**EXAMPLE:** Dr. McGuire ordered a urine culture to be done on a patient who he suspected had a bladder infection but who was sensitive to certain antibiotics. The culture was to be done by an outside laboratory because Dr. McGuire's lab does not perform cultures.

The urine culture would be reported with a 90 modifier to indicate that the test was sent out to be run.

## Repeat Clinical Diagnostic Laboratory Test—Modifier 91

Modifier 91 is used to indicate that the same laboratory test was repeated on the same day to obtain subsequent (multiple) test results. Problems with equipment or collected specimen, confirmation of initial test results, and the availability of an all inclusive code are *not* considered valid reasons to append this modifier.

**EXAMPLE:** Jenny presented to her physician with a blood sugar reading of 325. Jenny had a quantitative blood glucose test in the doctor's office, which confirmed her high blood sugar reading. She was given Glucophage, p.o., right then in the office. The physician asked her to wait for an hour, and the test was rerun, with results showing Jenny's blood sugar back in a more acceptable range.

The first test would be reported with code 82947, and the second with code 82947-91.

It should also be noted that this modifier is not used when the code description includes a series of test results that are run on the same day.

## Alternative Laboratory Platform Testing—Modifier 92

Modifier 92 is used when laboratory testing is performed by the use of a kit or transportable instrument for HIV testing: codes 86701–86703 and 87389. The kit's components can include a single-use, disposable analytical chamber, which can be carried or transported to the vicinity of the patient.

**EXAMPLE:** The family planning clinic of the Northeast is conducting HIV screening testing at a college campus using a transportable instrument. The staff is using a finger-stick blood sample to test for HIV-1.

The code used to report the HIV-1 test is code 86701-92.

## Synchronous Telemedicine Service Rendered Via Telephone or Other Real-Time Interactive Audio-Only Telecommunications System- Modifier 93

Modifier 93 is used to report Synchronous Telemedicine Service rendered via Telephone or Other Real-Time Interactive Audio-Only Telecommunications System. The CPT definition of synchronous telemedicine service is defined as "real-time interaction between a physician or other qualified health care professional and a patient who is located away at a distant site from the physician or other qualified health care professional". The definition also future explains that the synchronous telemedicine service must meet the key components and/or requirements of the same service if the service was performed face-to-face. Locate Appendix A of the CPT manual and review the full definition of modifier 93. Also review Appendix T to identify the CPT codes that may be used for reporting audio-only services. These codes, such as code 90785, 90791, etc., would be appended with modifier 93 to indicate that an audio-only service that was rendered.

## Synchronous Telemedicine Service Rendered Via a Real-Time Interactive Audio and Video Telecommunications System—Modifier 95

Modifier 95 is used to report synchronous telemedicine services that occur using a real-time interactive audio and video telecommunications system. This modifier can only be appended to services that are listed in Appendix P of the CPT manual. The CMS HCPCS modifier GT (defined as via interactive audio and video telecommunication systems) also currently exists to report telemedicine services to Medicare, but the GT modifier is not accepted by all payers. Modifier 95 was added to provide for the reporting of telemedicine services for payers that do not accept the GT modifier.

When using the 95 modifier the following criteria must be met:

1. The CPT code that is to be reported is listed in appendix P of the CPT manual and the telemedicine star icon appears next to the CPT code description in the CPT manual. (Reference the code description for code 99214 in the CPT manual and in Appendix P of the CPT manual to see how this displays in the CPT manual.)

2. All components of the CPT code description are completed via telemedicine and are documented by the provider of service.

3. A real-time audio and video telecommunication system is used and the provider and patient are in different locations when the service is performed.

> **EXAMPLE:** Dr. Bibbs performed services reported by code 99214 via telemedicine services. Dr. Bibbs is in his office and the patient is 5 miles from his office at a skilled nursing facility. Code 99214-95 is the correct code to report to a payer that accepts the 95 modifier but not the GT modifier.

Remember, prior to using the 95 modifier you must determine that the code may be used for synchronous telemedicine services.

## Habilitative Services—Modifier 96

There are services and procedures that are completed for either habilitative or rehabilitative purposes. For example physical or occupational therapies are such services. Modifier 96, is be used by a physician or other qualified health care professional, to denote when a service or procedure is provided for habilitative purposes.

Within the CPT manual, habilitative services are defined as services that teach an individual learned skills and functions for daily living that the individual has not yet developed. The habilitative services will then additionally help the individual to maintain and improve the learned skills or also help the individual to maintain, learn, or improve skills and functioning for daily living.

## Rehabilitative Services—Modifier 97

Modifier 97 is used to denote services or procedures that are rehabilitative in nature and can be used by a physician or other qualified health care professional. Rehabilitative services are services that occur after an individual was sick, hurt, or disabled. The purpose of the rehabilitative service is to help the individual maintain, get back, or improve skills and functions for daily living that were impaired or lost due to the sickness, injury, or a disability that the individual sustained.

## Multiple Modifiers—Modifier 99

Under certain circumstances, more than two modifiers may be necessary to delineate a service completely. When more than two are necessary, modifier 99 is used.

> **EXAMPLE:** Marty presented to Dr. Taggert for treatment of his mycotic nails. He had the great toe on both feet treated, as well as the fourth and fifth toes on the right, and the third and fourth toes on the left.

Dr. Taggert would report his treatment of mycotic nails, code 11721, with the modifiers for the toes that were treated: TA, T2, T3, T5, T8, T9. Since all these modifiers will not fit in the modifier field, the use of modifier 99 would be appropriate. To report this on a claim, most insurance companies require the 99 modifier in the first field, followed by the next three modifiers and the remaining modifiers in the narrative.

# HCPCS Level II Modifiers

HCPCS Level II modifiers accompany the HCPCS Level II codes. The Healthcare Common Procedure Coding System (HCPCS) is an alphanumeric system that describes services provided by physicians and other providers. The HCPCS system also provides codes for ambulance and durable medical equipment (DME). DME services include such things as crutches, walkers, and canes. These codes may or may not be reimbursed. The coder, as well as the providers, needs to know that just because a CPT code for a service exists does not mean that the service is reimbursable. This is something that the insurance carriers should be contacted about. More details about the HCPCS code set are explained later in this textbook.

HCPCS modifiers are assigned for the same reason that the other modifiers are assigned: the service being provided needs to be explained further. The author referenced the HCPCS Level II modifier information at *http://www.cms.gov/Medicare/Coding/MedHCPCSGenInfo/index.html.* Listed below are some of the modifiers that are used. The list is not exhaustive. Coders should use the Web sites of the various insurance carriers, as well as the CMS site for clarification on usage of these modifiers. A comprehensive list is found in Appendix 2 of the HCPCS Level II book. The purpose of the following partial listing of Level II HCPCS modifiers is to provide an overview of the use and types of Level II modifiers that are used when reporting HCPCS Level II codes.

## Level II—HCPCS Alphanumeric Modifiers

The following is a partial list of the Level II HCPCS modifiers:

**A1**—Dressing for 1 wound.

**A2**—Dressing for 2 wounds.

**A3**—Dressing for 3 wounds.

**A4**—Dressing for 4 wounds.

**A5**—Dressing for 5 wounds.

**A6**—Dressing for 6 wounds.

**A7**—Dressing for 7 wounds.

**A8**—Dressing for 8 wounds.

**A9**—Dressing for 9 or more wounds.

**AA**—Anesthesia services performed by anesthesiologist.

**AD**—Medical supervision by a physician, more than four concurrent anesthesia procedures.

**AE**—Registered Dietician.

**AF**—Specialty Physician.

**AG**—Primary Physician.

**AH**—Clinical Psychologist (CP) services. [Used when a medical group employs a CP and bills for the CP's service.]

**AI**—Principal physician of record.

**AJ**—Clinical Social Worker (CSW). [Used when a medical group employs a CSW and bills for the CSW's service.]

**AK**—Nonparticipating Physician.

**AM**—Physician, team member service.

**AP**—Determination of refractive state not performed in the course of diagnostic ophthalmological examination.

**AQ**—Physician providing a service in an unlisted health professional shortage area (HPSA).

**AR**—Physician Provider Services in a Physician Scarcity Area (PSA). [Effective for dates of service on or after January 1, 2005.]

**AS**—Physician Assistant, Nurse Practitioner, or Clinical Nurse Specialist services for assistant at surgery.

**AT**—Acute treatment. (This modifier should be used when reporting a spinal manipulation service [codes 98940, 98941, and 98942].) Effective dates of service October 1, 2004, and after.

**CC**—Procedure code changed. [This modifier is used when the submitted procedure code is changed either for administrative reasons or because an incorrect code was filed.]

**CR**—Catastrophe/disaster related.

**EJ**—Subsequent claims for a defined course of therapy (example: EPO, sodium hyaluronate).

**EM**—Emergency reserve supply (for ESRD benefit only).

**EP**—Service provided as part of Medicaid early periodic screening diagnosis and treatment (EPSDT) program.

The following modifiers are used to identify various body parts that might need to be identified when multiple procedures are reported.

**E1**—Upper Left, Eyelid.

**E2**—Lower Left, Eyelid.

**E3**—Upper Right, Eyelid.

**E4**—Lower Right, Eyelid.

**FA**—Left Hand, Thumb.

**F1**—Left Hand, Second Digit.

**F2**—Left Hand, Third Digit.

**F3**—Left Hand, Fourth Digit.

**F4**—Left Hand, Fifth Digit.

**F5**—Right Hand, Thumb.

**F6**—Right Hand, Second Digit.

**F7**—Right Hand, Third Digit.

*(continues)*

*(continued)*

**F8**—Right Hand, Fourth Digit.

**F9**—Right Hand, Fifth Digit.

**LM**—Left Main Coronary Artery.

**LT**—Left Side. [Used to identify procedures performed on the left side of the body.]

**RC**—Right Coronary Artery.

**RI**—Ramus Intermedius Coronary Artery.

**RT**—Right Side. [Used to identify procedures performed on the right side of the body.]

**TA**—Left Foot, Great Toe.

**T1**—Left Foot, Second Digit.

**T2**—Left Foot, Third Digit.

**T3**—Left Foot, Fourth Digit.

**T4**—Left Foot, Fifth Digit.

**T5**—Right Foot, Great Toe.

**T6**—Right Foot, Second Digit.

**T7**—Right Foot, Third Digit.

**T8**—Right Foot, Fourth Digit.

**T9**—Right Foot, Fifth Digit.

## Additional Modifiers F to G9

The following is a partial listing of the F to G9 modifiers. Modifiers G1 to G6 are used to report information about dialysis services. End Stage Renal Disease (ESRD) facilities report CPT code 90999 (unlisted dialysis procedure), and one of the G modifiers (G1, G2, G3, G4, and G5) on all claims for hemodialysis to reflect the most recent urea reduction ratio (URR). Medicare reviews the reported G1 to G5 modifier to determine the adequacy of dialysis to measure the quality of dialysis services. Code 90999-G6 reports to Medicare that less than six dialysis sessions have been provided in a month.

**FP**—Service provided as part of Medicaid Family Planning Program.

**FX**—X-ray taken using film.

**G1**—Most recent urea reduction ratio (URR) reading of less than 60.

**G2**—Most recent urea reduction ratio (URR) reading of 60 to 64.9.

**G3**—Most recent urea reduction ratio (URR) of 65 to 69.9.

**G4**—Most recent urea reduction ratio (URR) of 70 to 74.9.

**G5**—Most recent urea reduction ratio (URR) reading of 75 or greater.

**G6**—ESRD patient for whom less than six dialysis sessions have been provided in a month.

**G7**—Pregnancy resulted from rape or incest, or pregnancy is certified by physician as life threatening.

**G8**—Monitored Anesthesia Care (MAC) for deep complex, complicated, or markedly invasive surgical procedure.

**G9**—Monitored Anesthesia Care (MAC) for patient who has history of severe cardio-pulmonary condition.

# G Modifiers

Knowledge of the following G modifiers is important if you are reporting services for Medicare patients; use of these modifiers will help prevent Medicare payment denials and allows for the proper payment of Medicare claims.

**GA**—Waiver of Liability Statement on file. [Effective for dates of service on or after October 1, 1995, a physician or supplier should use this modifier to note that the patient has been advised of the possibility of noncoverage.]

**GC**—This service has been performed in part by a resident under the direction of a teaching physician.

**GE**—This service has been performed by a resident without the presence of a teaching physician under the primary care exception.

**GG**—Performance and payment of a screening mammogram and diagnostic mammogram on the same patient, same day.

**GH**—Diagnostic mammogram converted from screening mammogram on same day.

**GJ**—"Opt Out" physician or practitioner emergency or urgent service.

**GM**—Multiple patients on one ambulance trip.

**GN**—Services delivered under an outpatient speech language pathology plan of care.

**GO**—Services delivered under an occupational therapist plan of care.

**GP**—Services delivered under a physical therapist plan of care.

**GQ**—Via asynchronous telecommunications system.

**GT**—Via interactive audio and video telecommunication systems.

**GV**—Attending physician not employed or paid under arrangement by the patient's hospice provider.

**GW**—Service not related to the hospice patient's terminal condition.

**GY**—Item or service statutorily excluded or does not meet the definition of any Medicare benefit.

**GZ**—Item or service expected to be denied as not reasonable and necessary.

# Modifiers J Through V

The following is a partial list of modifiers J to V. A complete listing of modifiers J to V is found in the HCPCS Level II manual. This partial listing helps to outline the types of modifiers that are found in this range of modifiers.

**J1**—Competitive Acquisition Program (CAP), no-pay submission for a prescription number.

**J2**—Competitive Acquisition Program (CAP), restocking of emergency drugs after emergency administration and a prescription number.

**J3**—Competitive Acquisition Program (CAP), drug not available through CAP as written, reimbursed under average sales price (ASP) methodology.

**KL**—DMEPOS item delivered via mail.

**KO**—Single drug unit dose formulation.

**KP**—First drug of a multiple drug unit dose formulation.

**KQ**—Second or subsequent drug of a multiple drug unit dose formulation.

*(continues)*

*(continued)*

**LC**—Left circumflex coronary artery.

**LD**—Left anterior descending coronary artery.

**LR**—Laboratory round-trip.

**LS**—FDA-monitored intraocular lens implant.

**Q3**—Live kidney donor and related services.

**Q4**—Service for ordering/referring physician qualifies as a service exemption.

**Q5**—Service furnished by a substitute physician under a reciprocal billing arrangement.

**Q6**—Service furnished by a locum tenens physician.

**Q7**—One Class A finding.

**Q8**—Two Class B findings.

**Q9**—One Class B and Two Class C findings.

**QC**—Single channel monitoring.

**QD**—Recording and storage in solid-state memory by digital recorder.

**QK**—Medical direction of two, three, or four concurrent anesthesia procedures involving qualified individuals.

**QL**—Patient pronounced dead after ambulance called.

**QM**—Ambulance service provided under arrangement by a provider of services.

**QN**—Ambulance service furnished directly by a provider of services.

**QP**—Documentation is on file showing that the laboratory test(s) was ordered individually or ordered as a CPT-recognized panel other than automated profile codes 80002–80019, G0058, G0059, and G0060.

**QS**—Monitored anesthesia care service.

**QT**—Recording and storage on a tape by an analog tape recorder.

**QW**—Clinical Laboratory Improvement Amendment (CLIA) waived test. (Modifier used to identify waived tests.)

**QX**—CRNA service with medical direction by a physician.

**QY**—Anesthesiologist medically directs one CRNA.

**QZ**—CRNA service without medical direction by a physician.

**RA**—Replacement of a DME, orthotic or prosthetic item.

**RC**—Right coronary artery.

**RD**—Drug provided to beneficiary but not administered "incident to."

**SF**—Second opinion ordered by a Professional Review Organization (PRO) per Section 9401, P.L. 99-272 (100% reimbursement—no Medicare deductible or coinsurance).

**SG**—Ambulatory Surgical Center (ASC) facility service.

**SL**—State supplied vaccine.

**SW**—Services provided by a Certified Diabetic Educator.

**SY**—Persons who are in close contact with member of high-risk population (use only with codes for immunizations).

**TC**—Technical Component. Under certain circumstances, a charge may be made for the technical component alone. Under those circumstances, adding modifier TC to the usual procedure number identifies the technical component charge. **Note:** The TC modifier should not be appended to procedure codes that represent the technical component (e.g., 93005).

**TG**—Complex/higher level of care.

**UN**—Two patients served.

**UP**—Three patients served.

**UQ**—Four patients served.

**UR**—Five patients served.

**US**—Six or more patients served.

**VP**—Aphakic patient.

## Ambulance Origin and Destination Modifiers

The following modifiers are used to designate the place of origin and destination of a transport. The first position identifies the place of origin, and the second position identifies the destination.

**EXAMPLE:** A patient is picked up at the scene of an accident and transported to a hospital. Place "S" (scene of accident or acute event) in the first modifier position to indicate the place of origin. Place "H" (hospital) in the second modifier position to indicate the destination of the patient.

**D**—Diagnostic or therapeutic site other than "P" or "H" when these are used as origin codes.

**E**—Residential, domiciliary, custodial facility (other than an 1819 facility).

**G**—Hospital Based ESRD facility.

**H**—Hospital.

**I**—Site of transfer (e.g., airport or helicopter pad) between modes of ambulance transport.

**J**—Free-standing ESRD facility.

**N**—Skilled Nursing Facility.

**P**—Physician's office.

**R**—Residence.

**S**—Scene of Accident or Acute Event.

**X**—Intermediate stop at physician's office on the way to the hospital (Destination code only).

# Summary

- Modifiers offer additional information to insurance payers and Medicare to release payment for services.
- Modifiers work as adjectives in describing services provided to patients.
- Some modifiers affect payment.
- Some modifiers are for information only.
- Modifiers indicate that additional information may be found in the supporting documentation.
- The two types of modifiers are CPT Level I modifiers and HCPCS Level II modifiers.

# Internet Links

For federal regulatory information about physician billing and payment, go to **http://www.cms.gov** and search physician billing.

# Chapter Review

## Fill in the Blank

**Instructions:** Fill in the blanks in the statements that follow.

1. A CPT modifier is a(n) _____ digit modifier appended to a CPT code to indicate that a service or procedure has been altered.

2. A complete listing of Level I modifiers commonly found in the CPT coding book can be found in _____.

3. When billing physician services, place modifiers in item _____ of the CMS-1500 form.

4. Statistical modifiers, also known as _____ modifiers, are used for informational purposes and affect the processing or payment of the code billed but do not affect the fee.

5. Modifier 99 indicates that _____ modifiers are needed for an individual CPT code.

6. Modifier 56 is used only when _____ management is provided.

7. A mandated service is reported using modifier _____.

8. When a surgeon completes only the surgical care, modifier _____ should be appended to the CPT procedure code.

9. To report the services of the assistant surgeon, add modifier _____ to the procedure code.

10. Modifier 90 is used on _____ laboratory or reference laboratory procedure codes to indicate that the procedure was performed by a party other than the treating or reporting physician.

## Identify the Modifier

**Instructions:** For the following situations, list the correct modifier to use, or supply a short answer.

1. Two surgeons _____

2. Unusual anesthesia _____

3. Increased procedural services _____

4. Reduced services _____

5. Postoperative management only _____

6. Explain when modifier 26 is used. _____

7. Explain when modifier 47 is used. _____

8. When a bilateral procedure is performed in the same operative session and the CPT code describes a unilateral procedure, which modifier should be appended to the CPT code? _____

9. Which modifier is used to indicate that a different provider performed the preoperative procedure management of a patient? _____

10. Repeat procedure or service by the same physician or other qualified health care professional
_____

11. Discontinued procedure _____

12. Decision for surgery _____

13. Surgical team _____

14. Assistant surgeon _____

15. Professional component _____

16. What modifier would be added to code 90999 to indicate that a patient's most recent URR reading was 61.4? _____

17. Right hand, fourth digit _____

18. Multiple patients were transported on one ambulance trip. Which modifier should be appended to the service code? _____

19. Minimum assistant surgeon _____

20. Repeat clinical diagnostic laboratory test _____

## Case Studies

Review each case and indicate the correct code(s).

### Case 1

Marty went to the doctor's office with a sore throat and an upset stomach. The doctor performed an exam and evaluation of Marty. In the course of the evaluation, Marty mentioned he was having some back pain. The doctor also evaluated this issue and performed an osteopathic manipulation on one body region. The doctor reported a 99213 with a(n) _____ modifier and a 98925 for the OMT.

### Case 2

Dr. Albert is performing a complicated pyeloplasty on Kelly. Kelly was tolerating the procedure fairly well until her blood pressure began to drop dangerously low. After having trouble stabilizing her, Dr. Albert discontinued the procedure because he felt it would be too dangerous to continue. The doctor reported the part of the service he performed with a 50400 and a(n) _____ modifier.

## Case 3

Jamie South was out of town playing football two weeks ago, and he sustained a broken ankle. He was taken to the local hospital, and Dr. Books performed a closed treatment of trimalleolar ankle fracture with manipulation. Today he is being seen by Dr. Thompson for the postoperative care for the fracture treatment. Dr. Thompson should report code 27818 with modifier _____.

## Case 4

Aza is a 19-day-old neonate who weighs 3.2 kg and who is undergoing an arthrotomy with biopsy of the interphalangeal joint. The surgeon reports code 28054 with modifier _____.

## Case 5

Dr. Cook is performing a pulmonary valve replacement. Dr. Samson is the assistant surgeon for the case. Dr. Cook reports code 33475, whereas Dr. Samson should report _____.

## Case 6

Sam is a 10-year-old child who has had chronic ear infections for the last year. Today Dr. Abbes has decided that Sam needs to have tubes inserted into his ears. This is scheduled to occur in three weeks. Today's visit was coded with 99214 appended with modifier _____.

## Case 7

James Tree is a patient at an intermediate care facility. Today he is being seen by Dr. Rip because of a state mandate for the resident to be seen every six months. Code 99309 was reported with modifier _____ to report the mandated service.

## Case 8

Dr. Whoo interprets an MRI of the temporomandibular joint. This is reported with code 70336, appended with modifier _____.

## Case 9

Drs. Jones and Smith work as a surgical team to perform a double lung transplant with cardiopulmonary bypass. Dr Jones would report code 32854, and Dr. Smith would report code 32854-66. Is this correct? _____

## Case 10

Dr. Patel performed a therapeutic pneumothorax on Sal Desai and reported code 32960. Later that same day, the procedure was repeated by Dr. Patel. How should the second procedure be reported? _____

# 3 Evaluation and Management

## Chapter Outline

Introduction

Documentation Guidelines for Evaluation and
  Management Services

Overview of the Evaluation and Management
  Section

Evaluation and Management Coding

Summary

Internet Links

Chapter Review

Case Studies

## Learning Objectives

### At the conclusion of this chapter, you will be able to:

1. Define key terms related to evaluation and management coding.
2. Locate codes in the subsection and subcategory of the CPT Evaluation and Management section.
3. Identify the documentation needed to justify the selection of a code from the Evaluation and Management section of the CPT manual.
4. Differentiate between a new and an established patient.
5. Select place of service codes for CPT services and codes.
6. Explain the consequences of submitting an incorrect place of service code.
7. Classify parts of the patient's SOAP note.
8. State documentation requirements for the selection of a consultation code.
9. Choose the correct E/M code for services provided.
10. Explain the rules related to coding for hospital observation services, critical care services, nursing facility services, and preventive medicine services.
11. Identify and code procedures for evaluation and management from case studies.

# Key Terms

| | | | |
|---|---|---|---|
| care plan oversight | face-to-face time | past, family, and social history (PFSH) | review of systems (ROS) |
| case management | family history | past history | SOAP note |
| chief complaint (CC) | history | pertinent PFSH | social history |
| consultations | history of the present illness (HPI) | place of service (POS) | Standby Services |
| critical care | low birth weight (LBW) | preventive medicine services | very low birth weight (VLBW) |
| emergency department (ED) | new patient | psychiatric residential treatment center | |
| established patient | observation | referral | |
| Evaluation and Management (E/M) | observation status | | |

# Introduction

The first section of CPT is titled **Evaluation and Management (E/M)** and is commonly referred to as the E and M section. *Evaluation and Management* means exactly what it says. The patient is first evaluated by a physician, nurse practitioner, physician assistant, or in some cases a nurse. After the evaluation is completed, a management plan is implemented and recorded in the patient's medical record. The evaluation of the patient, along with the management plan, are considered billable services, and the CPT codes are used to delineate the type of service given to the patient, thus determining the revenue amount generated by the service provided.

# Documentation Guidelines for Evaluation and Management Services

In 1995 and 1997, the American Medical Association (AMA) and the Centers for Medicare & Medicaid Services (CMS) developed documentation guidelines for Evaluation and Management services. This was done to provide the health-care industry with a reference tool that could be used to give providers guidance in documenting and selecting Evaluation and Management codes, as well as a way to measure code selection. The documentation guidelines are very clear in stating the components that are needed to justify the selection of E/M codes. However providers found it labor intensive to document all of the components needed for code justification. Effective January 1, 2021 the AMA released new codes and guidelines for office and other outpatient evaluation and management service codes. The new codes streamlined the selection of codes for code range 99202 to 99215. Effective January 1, 2023, new guidelines were released for other codes found in the Evaluation and Management Section of the CPT manual.

Coders will need to be aware of the 1995 and 1997 guidelines as these guidelines will be used if a retrospective audit occurs that involves the time period in which the guidelines were in effective. The Internet links for both the 1995 and 1997 guidelines can be found on the CMS website at: https://www.cms.gov/Outreach -and-Education/Medicare-Learning-Network-MLN/MLNEdWebGuide/Downloads/95Docguidelines.pdf and https://www.cms.gov/Outreach-and-Education/Medicare-Learning-Network-MLN/MLNEdWebGuide /Downloads/97Docguidelines.pdf, respectively.

# Overview of the Evaluation and Management Section

The Evaluation and Management section contains categories for office visits, hospital visits, emergency room visits, preventive medicine visits, consultations, and nursing facility and other types of visits, as summarized in Table 3-1. To become familiar with the various categories within the Evaluation and Management section, simply use Table 3-1 to walk through the section by identifying the categories listed in the table.

**TABLE 3-1** Categories and Code Ranges in the Evaluation and Management Section

| Category | Code Range |
| --- | --- |
| Office and Other Outpatient Services | 99202–99215 |
| Hospital Inpatient and Observation Care Services | 99221–99239 |
| Consultations | 99242–99255 |
| Emergency Department Services | 99281–99288 |
| Critical Care Services | 99291–99292 |
| Nursing Facility Services | 99304–99316 |
| Home or Residence Services | 99341–99350 |
| Prolonged Services | 99358–99359, 99415–99418 |
| Standby Services | 99360 |
| Case Management Services | 99366–99368 |
| Care Plan Oversight Services | 99374–99380 |
| Preventive Medicine Services | 99381–99429 |
| Non-Face-to-Face Physician Services | 99421–99458 |
| Special Evaluation and Management Services | 99450–99456 |
| Newborn Care Services | 99460–99463 |
| Delivery/Birthing Room Attendance and Resuscitation Services | 99464–99465 |
| Inpatient Neonatal Intensive Care Services and Pediatric and Neonatal Critical Care Services | 99466–99486 |
| Cognitive Assessment and Care Plan Services | 99483 |
| Care Management Services | 99490–99483, 99490–99437, 99487–99489, 99424–99427 |
| Psychiatric Collaborative Care Management Services | 99492–99494 |
| Transitional Care Management Services | 99495–99496 |
| Advance Care Planning | 99497, 99498 |
| General Behavioral Health Integration Care Management | 99484 |
| Other Evaluation and Management Services | 99499 |

## Exercise 3.1—Check Your Understanding

**Subsection and Subcategories of the CPT Evaluation and Management Section**

Using a CPT manual, identify the subsection and subcategory of the CPT Evaluation and Management section for the following codes. The first two are completed for you.

| CPT Code(s) | Subsection and Subcategory of E/M Section | CPT Code(s) | Subsection and Subcategory of E/M Section |
|---|---|---|---|
| 1. 99211–99215 | Office and other outpatient services; established patient | 4. 99238–99239 | _____ |
| | | 5. 99252–99255 | _____ |
| | | 6. 99366–99367 | _____ |
| 2. 99281–99285 | Emergency department services; new or established patient | 7. 99231–99233 | _____ |
| | | 8. 99242–99245 | _____ |
| | | 9. 99497–99498 | _____ |
| 3. 99341–99345 | _____ | 10. 99360 | _____ |

# Evaluation and Management Coding

The Evaluation and Management section of CPT has some unique guidelines that coders must understand in order to code effectively within this section. In the CPT manual reference the Evaluation and Management Services Guidelines. These guidelines are located directly before the codes for the Evaluation and Management section. Read the guidelines. The guidelines define commonly used terms and instructions for selecting a level of E/M service. There are three major questions that must be asked when you are identifying an Evaluation and Management code:

1. Is the patient a new or an established patient?
2. Where was the service provided?
3. What was the level of the service rendered?

## New Patients versus Established Patients

The majority of the categories in this chapter (i.e., office visits, hospital visits, and nursing facility) are divided according to whether the patient is a new or established patient. For example, the Office or Other Outpatient Services codes, 99202–99215, are divided as follows:

New Patient codes—99202–99205

Established Patient codes—99211–99215

It should be noted, however, that not all categories within the Evaluation and Management section differentiate between new and established patients. For example, the Emergency Department Service codes do not differentiate between new and established patients. In referencing the Emergency Department Service codes, 99281–99285, it should be noted that CPT states that this range of codes is for new *or* established patients.

## New Patient

The criteria for what constitutes a new patient needs to be understood when it is time to assign a code from the Evaluation and Management section of the CPT manual. The CPT manual defines a **new patient** as a patient who has not received any professional services from the physician/qualified health care professional, or from another physician/qualified health care professional of the exact same specialty and subspeciality who belongs to the same group practice, within the past three years. Important components of the definition to be considered when you select a code include the terms

- same specialty or subspeciality,
- same group practice,
- three years.

### Same-Specialty Consideration

**EXAMPLE:** Bob Light is a patient at Troy Medical Associates, which is a multispecialty group practice. This practice includes family practice physicians and various specialists. Bob is a regular patient of Dr. Sign, who is a family practice physician. Bob is experiencing back pain, and he has made an appointment with Dr. Hey, an orthopedic surgeon who is also a physician for Troy Medical Associates.

In this case, when Bob is seen by Dr. Hey, Dr. Hey's office can bill Bob as a new patient because the physicians are of a different specialty, even though they are within the same multispecialty group. Remember, each first encounter in a different specialty can be considered new when the patient has not been seen by that specialty within the same group practice.

Another consideration you must take into account is whether the patient has been seen by different groups or by different physicians who are not in the same group practice but are of the same specialty.

### Same versus Different Group Practice Considerations

**EXAMPLE:** Mrs. Smith called Valley Medical Associates to make an appointment with internist Dr. Case. When asked if she was a patient of Dr. Case, Mrs. Smith replied that she had never seen Dr. Case. However, she had been a patient of Dr. Kelly, who was also an internist, but he was located at Hilltop Associates, another group of internists in town. Dr. Kelly had recently retired, and Mrs. Smith needed to refill her blood pressure medicine and establish herself with a new doctor.

In our example, Mrs. Smith is seen by Dr. Case, who will bill her as a new patient. Dr. Case and Dr. Kelly are both internists; however, because they do not belong to the same group practice, Dr. Case can code Mrs. Smith's visit as a new-patient visit.

Also, when determining if a patient is a new or an established patient, coders must consider the last time that a patient was seen. Remember, the definition states, "within the last three years."

### Three-Year Consideration

**EXAMPLE:** Sue Lutes lived in New York and was an established patient with Dr. Jones. In May 2016, she was seen by Dr. Jones before she moved to Florida. She lived in Florida until June 2020 and then moved back to New York. In July 2022, she was experiencing symptoms of an upper-respiratory infection and was seen by Dr. Jones.

In this example, when Sue was seen by Dr. Jones in July 2022, she can be billed as a new patient because she was not seen by Dr. Jones for more than three years. However, if she had been seen within the three-year period by Dr. Jones, she would not have been billed as a new patient.

This understanding is critical because assignment of the wrong code can result in a denial from the insurance company, stating that new-patient guidelines have not been met. Should this type of denial occur, it would be corrected by identifying the level of service for an established patient that is supported in the documentation, and by reprocessing it using the correct code.

## Established Patient

An **established patient** is a patient who has received professional services from the physician/qualified health care professional, or another physician/qualified health care professional of the same exact specialty and subspeciality, who belongs to the same group practice, within the past three years.

> **EXAMPLE:** Mike Roberts is a patient of the ABC Family Practice. Mike was ill and called the office to get an appointment with Dr. James, his primary care provider. Mike had seen Dr. James one month earlier for an annual physical. For today's visit, Dr. James was away, but Dr. Matthews (a partner in the group) had an opening in his schedule, which Mike agreed to take. This was the first time that Mike had ever seen Dr. Matthews.

In our example, Dr. James and Dr. Matthews are both family practice providers who belong to the same group practice, ABC Family Practice. Because the established patient criteria was met, Mike would be billed as an established patient, even though he was a new patient to Dr. Matthews. Remember, in cases where another physician was covering or was on call for a physician, the patient's encounter is billed as though the patient had been seen by the physician who was not available.

## Location of the Service Provided

As we noted earlier in this chapter, the Evaluation and Management section of CPT is divided into categories according to the location of the service. Therefore, in order to select a code, the coder must know where the service was provided: was the service provided in a physician's office, the hospital, or a nursing facility? When attempting to locate the correct CPT code for an Evaluation and Management service from the index, the coder can reference the location of the service to locate the correct Evaluation and Management code. For example, if the patient was seen in the hospital, the term to reference in the index would be "hospital," which would lead the coder to "Hospital Discharge Services" and "Hospital Services." To become familiar with the locations, review Table 3-1 of this chapter.

When services are billed on professional claims, the claim form requires a place-of-service code. See Appendix I for an example of a CMS-1500 professional claim form. Coders need to understand the concept of **place of service (POS)**, so we will note it here because there is a correlation between Evaluation and Management codes and place of service codes. The place of service code is a different code from the Evaluation and Management code.

A place of service code is required in box 24B of the CMS-1500 form. Place of service codes are maintained by the Centers for Medicare & Medicaid Services (CMS) and are used by payers (Medicare, Medicaid, and other private insurance companies) to specify where a service was rendered. POS is described using a numeric code that is usually listed in the beginning of the CPT manual. Table 3-2 lists POS codes.

The POS lets the payer know where care was rendered, such as the office (POS 11) or an urgent care facility (POS 20). Use of an incorrect place of service with an E/M code can result in a rejection by the insurance carrier.

> **EXAMPLE:** Dr. Calvin, an emergency-department physician, saw Matt for abdominal pain and cramping. After evaluating Matt, it was determined that he needed to be admitted under the care of a surgeon for an appendectomy.

In our example, Dr. Calvin would be submitting a code from the Emergency Department Service codes 99281–99285, because he was the emergency-department doctor. The place-of-service code that would be submitted on the claim with Dr. Calvin's charges would be 23-Emergency Room—Hospital. The POS code and Evaluation and Management code are "connected" in that they have a correlation.

Evaluation and Management coding requires attention to documentation in the patient's medical record which will justify the level of E/M code selected.

**TABLE 3-2** Place of Service Codes

| Place of Service Code(s) | Place of Service Name |
| --- | --- |
| 01 | Pharmacy |
| 02 | Telehealth Provided Other than in Patient's Home |
| 03 | School |
| 04 | Homeless Shelter |
| 05 | Indian Health Service Free-Standing Facility |
| 06 | Indian Health Service Provider-Based Facility |
| 07 | Tribal 638 Free-Standing Facility |
| 08 | Tribal 638 Provider-Based Facility |
| 09 | Prison/Correctional Facility |
| 10 | Telehealth Provided in Patient's Home |
| 11 | Office |
| 12 | Home |
| 13 | Assisted Living Facility |
| 14 | Group Home |
| 15 | Mobile Unit |
| 16 | Temporary Lodging |
| 17 | Walk-in Retail Health Clinic |
| 18 | Place of Employment/Worksite |
| 19 | Off Campus—Outpatient Hospital |
| 20 | Urgent Care Facility |
| 21 | Inpatient Hospital |
| 22 | On Campus—Outpatient Hospital |
| 23 | Emergency Room—Hospital |
| 24 | Ambulatory Surgical Center |
| 25 | Birthing Center |
| 26 | Military Treatment Facility |
| 27–30 | Unassigned |
| 31 | Skilled Nursing Facility |
| 32 | Nursing Facility |
| 33 | Custodial Care Facility |
| 34 | Hospice |
| 35–40 | Unassigned |
| 41 | Ambulance—Land |
| 42 | Ambulance—Air or Water |
| 43–48 | Unassigned |
| 49 | Independent Clinic |
| 50 | Federally Qualified Health Center |
| 51 | Inpatient Psychiatric Facility |
| 52 | Psychiatric Facility—Partial Hospitalization |
| 53 | Community Mental Health Center |

*(continues)*

**TABLE 3-2** (continued)

| Place of Service Code(s) | Place of Service Name |
|---|---|
| 54 | Intermediate Care Facility/Individuals with Intellectual Disabilities |
| 55 | Residential Substance Abuse Treatment Facility |
| 56 | Psychiatric Residential Treatment Center |
| 57 | Non-residential Substance-Abuse Treatment Facility |
| 58 | Non-residential Opioid Treatment Facility |
| 59 | Unassigned |
| 60 | Mass Immunization Center |
| 61 | Comprehensive Inpatient Rehabilitation Facility |
| 62 | Comprehensive Outpatient Rehabilitation Facility |
| 63–64 | Unassigned |
| 65 | End-Stage Renal Disease Treatment Facility |
| 66–70 | Unassigned |
| 71 | State or Local Public Health Clinic |
| 72 | Rural Health Clinic |
| 73–80 | Unassigned |
| 81 | Independent Laboratory |
| 82–98 | Unassigned |
| 99 | Other Place of Service |

## Exercise 3.2—Check Your Understanding

### POS and Evaluation and Management Codes

Using Table 3-2, select the correct POS code for the following CPT services and codes.
The first two are completed for you.

| CPT Code | POS Code | CPT Code | POS Code |
|---|---|---|---|
| 1. 99215, office visit | 11 | 6. 99307, subsequent skilled nursing facility care | _____ |
| 2. 99221, initial hospital care | 21 | 7. 99238, hospital discharge | _____ |
| 3. 99341, home visit | _____ | 8. 99205, new office visit | _____ |
| 4. 99315, skilled nursing facility visit | _____ | 9. 99384, physical exam, office | _____ |
| 5. 99252, initial inpatient consultation | _____ | 10. 99283, emergency room | _____ |

## Office or Other Outpatient Services (99202–99215)

Office or Other Outpatient Services is the first category of codes in the Evaluation and Management chapter of the CPT manual. The code range for office visits begins with 99202 and concludes with 99215. The category is further broken down into the subcategories of New Patient (99202–99205) and Established Patient (99211–99215). The note at the beginning of the category instructs the coder that codes in this subcategory are used for services provided in an outpatient setting, such as a doctor's office or an ambulatory setting.

When selecting a code for office or other outpatient services, as stated earlier in this chapter, the coder must determine if the patient is a new or established patient according the CPT definitions. If the patient is a new patient, then codes 99202 to 99205 are used for the office or other outpatient services. If the patient is an established patient then codes 99211 to 99215 are used. To assist the coder in identifying new versus established patients, a Decision Tree entitled "Decision Tree for New vs Established Patients" can be found in the CPT manual in the E/M Services Guidelines. Locate the decision tree and review the information found in the guidelines.

As stated earlier in the chapter the third question that a coder must ask is, "What was the level of the service that was rendered?" In the E/M Services Guidelines you will find a section entitled "Levels of E/M Services" Read this information that is contained in the guidelines and note that the selection of an appropriate level of E/M services is based on the level of medical decision making or the total time for the service performed. There is one code that does not use the concept of medical decision making; that is code 99211.

Code 99211 is reported for an office or outpatient visit for an established patient that does not require the presence of a physician or other qualified health care professional. Commonly this level of service is called a nurse level visit but this level is reported by all providers. Examples of this level of service are: a patient that presents for an injection, a patient that presents for a drug screen, or a patient that presents for removal of packing following surgery.

To report an office or other outpatient visit using medical decision making as the criteria, the coder must understand the guidelines that relate to the three components of medical decision making. As you read through the guidelines you will see an explanation of medical decision making. Medical decision making is the process that a provider completes as the patient's condition is being assessed, a diagnosis is being determined, and as a course of treatment is being established. In CPT there are three elements that define a level of medical decision making. The three elements are:

- The number and complexity of problems addressed at the encounter. For each encounter, the provider will assess the patient to determine a clinical impression or diagnosis, and this information will be used to determine the number of diagnoses and the complexity of the problems addressed during the encounter. The number and complexity of the diagnoses and problems should be documented in the patient's record.

- The amount and/or complexity of data reviewed and analyzed. The more information the provider reviews, the higher level of medical decision making that is justified. Providers must document that they have reviewed diagnostic findings, reports and old records to justify the amount and complexity of the data reviewed.

Important points to remember when you review the record to determine the amount and complexity of the data reviewed are as follows:

- The more tests and procedures reviewed by the provider, the higher the level of this element.

- The review of a report can be documented by the provider either in a note or by the provider initialing and dating the report of the test results.

- If a provider personally reviews an image, tracing, or specimen that she or he ordered, the complexity of the data reviewed increases.

- When documenting the complexity of the data reviewed, providers should clearly document the information obtained in order to justify the types of data reviewed.

- The risk of complications and/or morbidity or mortality of patient management.

The third factor that determines the type of medical decision making is the risk of complications and/or, morbidity or mortality of patient management. The risks are described as minimal, low, moderate, or high and are based on the risks associated with presenting problem(s), the diagnostic procedure(s), and possible management options. Table 1, found in the E/M Service Guidelines of the CPT manual, should be used to guide the coder in selecting the type of risk.

The following should be considered when selecting the type of risk:

- Comorbidities and underlying diseases increase the complexity of the risk.

- Surgical and invasive procedures performed during an encounter increase the risk. The procedures need to be documented in the record.

- Undiagnosed problems, multiple diagnoses, and acute and chronic conditions that pose a threat to life or bodily function increase risk.
- The more complex the diagnostic tests ordered are, the greater the level of risk.
- The more complex the management options ordered are (e.g., prescription medications, procedures, need to resuscitate, etc.), the greater the level of risk.

There are four types of medical decision making that are used regardless of the location of the service: straightforward, low, moderate, and high. It should be noted that the four types of medical decision making apply to various subsections of E/M codes. The E/M Services Guidelines contain a table entitled "Table 1: Levels of Medical Decision Making (MDM)" This table is to be used as a guideline when selecting codes based on medical decision making. Review this table and note that it contains each level of medical decision making in relation to the three elements of medical decision making. The table lists the specific elements that are needed for each of the types of medical decision making. When selecting a level of medical decision making only two of the three elements must be met or exceeded to qualify for a specific level of MDM. The provider's documentation in the patient's record will be the justification for the level of MDM.

## EXAMPLE:

### Patient 1:

Adebella is an established patient and is seen in follow-up for a surgical wound site. Last week the patient was seen because the wound appeared red and inflamed. She was instructed to come back to the office this week for an assessment of the wound site. At this time the wound site has healed and the sutures were removed. This level of medical decision making is straightforward because there is one self-limited problem, (the healed red and inflamed wound site) and the risk of complications is minimal. Code 99212 would be selected for this visit.

### Patient 2:

Dexter is an established patient and is seen for a cough and sore throat. Dr. Jones orders a test for strep throat and test result is positive. This level of medical decision making is low because there is one acute illness (the strep throat), one test ordered (the strep test) and one element of data to be analyzed (the results of the strep test). Code 99213 would be selected for this visit.

### Patient 3:

Theodore is an established patient and is seen for hypertension which is not controlled on his current medications. He presents today with a blood pressure of 160/95 and says he was some chest discomfort. Dr. Smyth orders an EKG and it is completed at this time. Dr. Smyth notes that the EKG is normal. Dr. Smyth reviewed an EKG report that Theodore had three months ago in the emergency department. Dr. Smyth increases Theodore's blood pressure medication, Losartan to 50 mg in the morning and 25 mg in the evening. The uncontrolled hypertension and chest discomfort represent a moderate level of complexity of problems addressed at the encounter. The amount and/or complexity of data reviewed and analyzed is also moderate because the EKG was ordered and the read and the provider reviewed the previous information from the emergency department. There is a moderate level of risk due to the prescription drug management. Therefore code 99214 would be selected for this visit.

### Patient 4:

Angelina is an established patient of Dr. Malone's. Today she is seen for confusion and numbness on the right side of her face. The patient comes to the office with her daughter and her daughter states that her mother has been confused for the last 48 hours. Today the right side of her face became numb. She is not complaining of any other symptoms at this time. Angelina is not able to give a history of the last 48 hours so the daughter is providing the information.

Dr. Malone orders an X-ray of the skull. The X-ray is completed and Dr. Malone reviews the X-ray and there is a suspicious mass. Dr. Malone calls Dr. Tyre, a neurologist, and they determine that Angelina should be sent to the hospital and Dr. Tyre will admit her for a full work-up.

The complexity of the problem for this case is high because the patient presents with an acute illness that poses a threat to life. In this case the patient may have experienced a stroke or the mass could be causing the symptoms present. The amount and/or complexity of data reviewed and analyzed is extensive because the X-ray was ordered and reviewed, and the daughter had to give the assessment. Additionally Dr. Malone spoke with Dr. Tyre to determine the management of the patient. This case also has a high level of risk because the patient is being admitted to the hospital. Therefore code 99215 would be selected for this visit.

The other method that can be used for selecting an E/M code for office or other outpatient service is the amount of time that the provider spends with the patient. The guidelines for time require a face-to-face encounter between the provider and patient. The time reported for these services is the total time on the date of the encounter. When time is being used to select a code the time should be documented in the patient's record. The use of time to select a code for other E/M services, such as hospital inpatient services, observation, consultations, etc. varies according to the services provided.

In the CPT manual locate the E/M Service Guidelines and locate the section entitled "Guidelines for Selecting Level of Service Based on Time." Read this section of information. Time alone can be used for code selection for codes: 99202, 99203, 99204, 99205, 99212, 99213, 99214, and 99215. Note that time is not included in code 99211.

When reporting an office or other outpatient service based on time, the amount of time to report is the total time that the provider spends involved in face-to-face and non-face-to face services on the day of the encounter. The guidelines clearly state what activities are included in the professional time spent by the provider. The activities include:

- Preparation to see the patient. This would include the provider reviewing test findings, reading medical reports from other providers and reviewing information from a patient's visit to the emergency room.

- Obtaining and/or reviewing a separately obtained history. When a patient is seen typically a nurse or medical office assistant obtains a chief compliant and history from the patient. The provider then reviews this information and completes a more detailed history.

- Completion of a medical examination and/or evaluation. The provider needs to document the examination of the patient and the evaluation from the findings of the exam.

- Counseling and educating the patient, family and/or caregiver. After the examination the provider will explain the findings to the patient and others and may also provide education based on the diagnosis.

- Ordering medications, tests and/or procedures. Based on the provider's assessment the ordering of medications, tests and/or procedures may occur.

- Referring and communicating with other health care professionals. Based on the findings of the exam it may be necessary to refer the patient to another provider for additional evaluation and care. If this time is not reported as a separate service it can be included in the time reported for the encounter.

- Documentation. The time the provider spends documenting the information that relates to the patient encounter can be included in the time reported in the E/M code.

- The independent interpretation of results from testing and the communication of this information to the patient or others. For example if a test is ordered and the results are not immediately available until after the patient is seen, the provider may call the patient with the results later in the day. If the provider calls the patient later in the day of the encounter the time spent may be included in the time of the E/M code.

- Coordination of care. The time spent in care coordination can be included in the time for the E/M code as long as the care coordination is not separately reported. If the provider speaks with a nursing facility to discuss the admission of a patient to the facility and this occurs on the same day as the provider sees that patient, this time can be included in the time for the E/M service code.

At times more than one person may see a patient based on the complexity of the case or other circumstances involved in the case. When a physician and other qualified health care provider, such as a nurse practitioner or physician assistant, both jointly treat the patient a shared or split visit occurs. To report the time for the encounter, the time individually spent by both individuals on the day of the encounter is summed to define the total time. However when the individuals jointly meet with the patient or discuss the patient only the time of one individual is counted in the total time.

> **EXAMPLE:** Joel, an established patient, comes to the walk-in clinic and sees Tom, a physician's assistant. Tom takes 10 minutes to obtain a history and to examine the patient. Tom is concerned about a finding and requests Dr. Jones to come into the room to examine the patient. Dr. Jones completes a 10 minute examination of the patient. Tom and Dr. Jones then spend an additional 15 minutes discussing the case and explaining the findings to the patient.
>
> The total time reported for this case is 35 minutes; Tom's time of 10 minutes, Dr. Jones' time of 10 minutes and an additional 15 minutes of shared time. Code 99214 is reported for this encounter.

## Prolonged Service Time

In some cases a provider will see a patient for an office or other outpatient service and the total time spent with the patient will exceed the time of the highest-level codes for this service type. Code 99205 and 99215 are the highest-level codes for an office or other outpatient service. Code 99205 reports a new patient visit with time between 60 to 74 minutes. Code 99215 reports an established patient visit with time between 40 to 54 minutes. Review these two codes in the CPT code book and note the instructional notation that appears after each of these codes. The notation states for services longer than the times listed for the codes the coder should use prolonged service code 99417. 99417 is an add-on code for prolonged service with or without direct patient contact on the date of an office or other outpatient service. Code 99417 is to be reported for each 15 minutes of total time that exceeds the time listed in codes 99205 or 99215. Do not report code 99417 if the prolonged time is less than 15 minutes. Locate code 99417 for the full description of the code and for additional information on the reporting of the code.

> **EXAMPLE:** Dr. Terps spent 80 minutes with a new patient. To report this service using time the coder would report codes 99205 and 99417.
>
> Dr. Terps spent 75 minutes with an established patient. To report this service using time the coder would report codes 99215, 99417, and 99417.

# Documentation of Patient's History and Examination

As previously discussed in this chapter, choosing a level of an E/M code is based on the level of medical decision making or time. Throughout the description of the E/M codes the following phrase also appears: "... which requires a medically appropriate history and/or examination..." Let's take some time to review information that could appear as part of a patient's history and examination even though the history and examination do not contain specific requirements that relate to specific codes.

Typically a provider will document a history, examination and medical decision making when seeing a patient. The treating provider determines the medically appropriate history and physical examination. In the E/M Services Guidelines, in the CPT manual, locate the heading entitled "History and/or Examination." This section delineates the guidelines that are relevant to the history and physical examination.

## History

Coders must be able to review the medical documentation and note that a history is documented.

Each **history** is based on the following element(s):

- Chief complaint (CC)
- History of presenting illness (HPI)
- Review of systems (ROS)
- Past, family, and social history (PFSH)

**Chief Complaint (CC)**  A **chief complaint (CC)**, defined as the reason for the patient encounter, should be recorded in the patient's record. In other words, why did the patient need to seek care? A chief complaint is usually stated in the patient's own words and should be recorded for each encounter.

**History of the Present Illness (HPI)**  Also typically recorded as part of the history is the **history of the present illness (HPI)**, a chronological description of the patient's present illness. The HPI is based on elements that describe the location of the problem, how long the problem has been going on, the severity, the quality, timing, context, and modifying factors, as well as the associated signs and symptoms relating to the problem.

**Review of Systems (ROS)**  The **review of systems (ROS)** is an inventory of body systems that is obtained from the patient to identify signs and/or symptoms that the patient may be experiencing or may have experienced.

Remember, the ROS is obtained by querying the patient. It is most commonly completed by a series of questions from the provider to the patient.

**Past, Family, and/or Social History (PFSH)**  The last portion of the history consists of **past, family, and social history (PFSH)**. The **past history** includes information regarding major illnesses, surgeries, injuries, and hospitalizations, as well as current medications and allergies. Past history refers to any past medical information that may affect the medical decision making process.

**Family history** includes information regarding immediate family members who suffer from a chronic or acute illness that would impact care of the patient during either the current encounter or future encounters. Typically, a complete family history is obtained during the annual physical examination or an initial visit to initiate care and is updated as needed.

**Social history** is the portion of the history that discusses the patient's marital status; use of tobacco, alcohol, and drugs; the patient's occupation; sexual history; and other social factors that would affect care of the patient or that the provider feels may be relevant to comprehensive patient care.

The past, family, and/or social history documented in the patient's record will depend on the complexity of the problem that the patient presents with. As stated earlier in this chapter, the number and complexity of problems addressed during the encounter is one of the elements that is used when selecting the level of service based on medical decision making. Therefore it is essential for the provider to completely document an accurate history to reflect the symptoms, diagnoses, comorbidities and diseases that will impact the medical decision making. In the E/M Services Guidelines, in the CPT manual, locate the heading entitled "Number and Complexity of Problems Addressed at the Encounter." This section of the guidelines explains the definitions that apply and impact the medical decision making process. Documentation plays a critical role in the justification of the level of medical decision making.

**SOAP Notes**  Many providers record encounters by using a *SOAP note*. The HPI is sometimes referred to as the "S," or subjective, portion of a SOAP note. A **SOAP note** contains a subjective portion (the history), an objective portion (the exam), an assessment portion (the diagnosis), and a plan (the plan for the patient's care). The following diagram may help you visualize how this information is connected.

| S | O | A | P |
| --- | --- | --- | --- |
| ↓ | ↓ | ↓ | ↓ |
| HPI/ROS/PFSH | EXAM | DIAGNOSIS | PLAN |

MEDICAL DECISION MAKING

The author has found that when training students and providers, this example has helped to visualize the components of an Evaluation and Management code.

Let's review some examples that show various types of histories when the patient is seen in a skilled nursing facility.

**EXAMPLE:**

**Patient 1:**

Sara, a resident of Mountain View Skilled Nursing Facility, is seen today with a sore throat and fever (chief complaint). She has had a sore throat and fever for two days (HPI).

**Patient 2:**

Sara, a resident of Mountain View Skilled Nursing Facility, is seen today with a sore throat and fever (chief complaint). She has had a sore throat and has been running a fever of 101 to 102 for the past two days (HPI). She states that she has had difficulty swallowing (a review of system related to problem—ENT).

**Patient 3:**

Sara, a resident of Mountain View Skilled Nursing Facility, is seen today with a sore throat and fever (chief complaint). She has had a sore throat and has been running a fever of 101 to 102 for the past two days. She states that she has had difficulty swallowing, but her ears do not hurt, and she has had no shortness of breath (HPI with pertinent review of systems that includes not only ENT, but also lungs). Sara's sister, who visited four days ago, has been diagnosed with strep throat (family history).

**Patient 4:**

Sara, a resident of Mountain View Skilled Nursing Facility, is seen today with a sore throat and fever (chief complaint). She has had a sore throat and has been running a fever of 101 to 102 for the past two days. She states that she has had difficulty swallowing, but her ears do not hurt, and she has had no shortness of breath, diarrhea, nausea, vomiting, or abdominal pain or cramping, and her bowel and bladder habits have not changed (HPI with pertinent review of systems in addition to other body systems—ENT, lungs, gastrointestinal, abdomen, urinary). Sara's sister, who visited four days ago, has been diagnosed with strep throat. Her sister typically tests positive for strep 4 to 5 times a year. Currently there are two other residents at the facility that have strep throat. She has not been exposed to secondhand smoke at home during her life or here at the facility. Until today, she has been very healthy with no serious illness to speak of (past, family, and social history).

An important documentation concept to remember is that the review of systems and the past, family, and social history should be reviewed and updated as needed, but they do not need to be rerecorded at each visit. However, if they directly impact the current visit, documentation needs to reflect this. Any changes should be noted, along with the date and location of the note being referenced.

**EXAMPLE:** Bobby is seen today for symptoms of a sinus infection. Review of systems as well as review of past, family, and social history were taken during the patient's annual physical dated April 12, 20XX, and are located in this record. Information was reviewed and discussed with the patient. The following changes were noted: ROS is positive for facial pain and postnasal drip. The PFSH is unchanged from the April 12, 20XX, note.

## • • • Guideline

**Locate Table 1 in the E/M Services Guidelines, in a CPT manual, and note that the level of medical decision making is based on 2 out of 3 elements of medical decision making.**

## Exercise 3.3—Check Your Understanding

**Documentation of Patient History**

The following documentation represents a history for a patient encounter. Identify the parts of the history using the terms listed. The first one is done for you.

1. Social history
2. Chief complaint
3. Past history
4. Family history
5. Review of systems
6. Associated signs and symptoms

Beth is seen today with a cough and nasal congestion (1) ___2___. She says she has an extremely painful, nonproductive cough. She has had a fever, which the patient states ran between 101 and 102 over the last few days (2) _____. Her sister is just getting over strep throat, but no other family members are ill (3) _____.

Beth says she has never been hospitalized and has no drug allergies (4) _____.

She has no ear pain, no nausea, no vomiting, and no change in bowel habits (5) _____.

Beth is not a smoker, does not consume alcohol, and is not a recreational drug user (6) _____.

## Examination

Documentation recorded for E/M services should also include an examination. The examination is also recognized as the "O," or objective, portion of the provider's note. This is the portion of the visit in which the provider conducts an examination of the patient.

There are various types of exams: general multisystem examinations and single-organ examinations. The following is a partial of the single-organ examinations:

Cardiovascular
Ear, nose, and throat
Eye
Genitourinary
Hematologic/lymphatic/immunologic
Musculoskeletal
Neurological
Psychiatric
Respiratory
Skin

Any type of exam can be performed by any physician or qualified health care professional, regardless of specialty. However, certain specialties are not paid for multisystem exams as they fall out of their particular scope of practice (e.g., podiatry—unless there is cardiovascular or neurologic involvement, the exam would focus on the area of the body from the knee down).

As stated in the E/M Service Guidelines the extent and nature of the examination is selected by the examining provider and is based on the nature of the presenting problem, the patient's history, and the physician's clinical judgment. During a multisystem exam various body systems are examined.

Table 3-3 illustrates the elements of examinations that relate to a multisystem examination according to system/body area. Coders should have an understanding of the elements that are typically found in a general multisystem exam. The length of the exam will vary depending on medical necessity and is determined by the treating provider.

**TABLE 3-3** Elements of A General Multisystem Examination

| System/Body Area | Elements of Examination |
|---|---|
| Constitutional | Measurement of *any three* of the following seven vital signs: <br> 1. sitting or standing blood pressure <br> 2. supine blood pressure <br> 3. pulse rate and regularity <br> 4. respiration <br> 5. temperature <br> 6. height <br> 7. weight <br> (Vital signs may be measured and recorded by ancillary staff.) <br> General appearance of patient (e.g., development, nutrition, body habitus, deformities, attention to grooming) |
| Eyes | Inspection of conjunctivae and lids <br> Examination of pupils and irises (e.g., reaction to light and accommodation, size, and symmetry) <br> Ophthalmoscopic examination of optic discs (e.g., size, C/D ratio, appearance) and posterior segments (e.g., vessel changes, exudates, hemorrhages) |
| Ears, Nose, Mouth, and Throat | External inspection of ears and nose (e.g., overall appearance, scars, lesions, masses) <br> Otoscopic examination of external auditory canals and tympanic membranes <br> Assessment of hearing (e.g., whispered voice, finger rub, tuning fork) <br> Inspection of nasal mucosa, septum, and turbinates <br> Inspection of lips, teeth, and gums <br> Examination of oropharynx: oral mucosa, salivary glands, hard and soft palates, tongue, tonsils, and posterior pharynx |
| Neck | Examination of neck (e.g., masses, overall appearance, symmetry, tracheal position, crepitus) <br> Examination of thyroid (e.g., enlargement, tenderness, mass) |
| Respiratory | Assessment of respiratory effort (e.g., intercostal retractions, use of accessory muscles, diaphragmatic movement) <br> Percussion of chest (e.g., dullness, flatness, hyperresonance) <br> Palpation of chest (e.g., tactile fremitus) <br> Auscultation of lungs (e.g., breath sounds, adventitious sounds, rubs) |
| Cardiovascular | Palpation of heart (e.g., location, size, thrills) <br> Auscultation of heart with notation of abnormal sounds and murmurs <br> Examination of <br> carotid arteries (e.g., pulse amplitude, bruits) <br> abdominal aorta (e.g., size, bruits) <br> femoral arteries (e.g., pulse amplitude, bruits) <br> pedal pulses (e.g., pulse amplitude) <br> extremities for edema and/or varicosities |
| Chest (Breasts) | Inspection of breasts (e.g., symmetry, nipple discharge) <br> Palpation of breasts and axillae (e.g., masses or lumps, tenderness) |

*(continues)*

**TABLE 3-3** (*continued*)

| System/Body Area | Elements of Examination |
|---|---|
| Gastrointestinal (Abdomen) | Examination of abdomen with notation of presence of masses or tenderness |
| | Examination of liver and spleen |
| | Examination for presence or absence of hernia |
| | Examination of anus, perineum, and rectum, including sphincter tone, presence of hemorrhoids, rectal masses |
| | Obtain stool sample for occult blood test when indicated |
| Genitourinary | MALE: |
| | Examination of the scrotal contents (e.g., hydrocele, spermatocele, tenderness of cord, testicular mass) |
| | Examination of the penis |
| | Digital rectal examination of prostate gland (e.g., size, symmetry, nodularity, tenderness) |
| | Examination of urethra (e.g., masses, tenderness, scarring) |
| | Examination of bladder (e.g., fullness, masses, tenderness) |
| | Cervix (e.g., general appearance, lesions, discharge) |
| | Uterus (e.g., size, contour, position, mobility, tenderness, consistency, descent or support) |
| | Adnexa/parametria (e.g., masses, tenderness, organomegaly, nodularity) |
| Lymphatic | Palpation of lymph nodes in *two or more* areas: |
| | Neck |
| | Axillae |
| | Groin |
| | Other |
| Musculoskeletal | Examination of gait and station |
| | Inspection and/or palpation of digits and nails (e.g., clubbing, cyanosis, inflammatory conditions, petechiae, ischemia, infections, nodes) |
| | Examination of joints, bones, and muscles of *one or more* of the following six areas: |
| | 1. head and neck |
| | 2. spine, rib and pelvis |
| | 3. right upper extremity |
| | 4. left upper extremity |
| | 5. right lower extremity |
| | 6. left lower extremity |
| | The examination of a given area includes |
| | Inspection and/or palpation with notation of presence of any misalignment, asymmetry, crepitation, defects, tenderness, masses, effusions |
| | Assessment of range of motion with notation of any pain, crepitation, or contracture |
| | Assessment of stability with notation of any dislocation (luxation), subluxation, or laxity |
| | Assessment of muscle strength and tone (e.g., flaccid, cog wheel, spastic) with notation of any atrophy or abnormal movements |
| Skin | Inspection of skin and subcutaneous tissue (e.g., rashes, lesions, ulcers) |
| | Palpation of skin and subcutaneous tissue (e.g., induration, subcutaneous nodules, tightening) |
| Neurologic | Test cranial nerves with notation of any deficits |
| | Examination of deep tendon reflexes with notation of pathological reflexes (e.g., Babinski) |
| | Examination of sensation (e.g., by touch, pin, vibration, proprioception) |

(*continues*)

**TABLE 3-3** (continued)

| System/Body Area | Elements of Examination |
|---|---|
| Psychiatric | Description of patient's judgment and insight |
| | Brief assessment of mental status, including |
| |     orientation to time, place, and person |
| |     recent and remote memory |
| |     mood and affect (e.g., depression, anxiety, agitation) |

The documentation *must* reflect what your provider actually did so that the most accurate level of service determination possible for the visit can be billed.

The following examples illustrate the levels of examination that are found in provider documentation for a nursing facility patient. These examples also illustrate the increasing detail that is needed to move to a comprehensive examination.

**EXAMPLE:**

**Patient 1:**

Provider documentation is as follows:

Vital signs: BP, 120/70; Weight, 120 lb; Temp, 99
HEENT: TMs clear, PND, throat is very red and tonsils swollen

**Patient 2:**

Provider documentation is as follows:

Vital signs: BP, 120/70; Weight, 120 lb; Temp, 99
GENERAL APPEARANCE: NAD
HEENT: TMs clear, PND, throat is very red and tonsils swollen; Facial pain in the sinus area
LUNGS: Clear to percussion

**Patient 3:**

Provider documentation is as follows:

Vital signs: BP, 120/70; Weight, 120 lb; Temp, 99
GENERAL APPEARANCE: NAD
HEENT: TMs clear, PND, throat is very red and tonsils swollen. Facial pain in the sinus area
LUNGS: Clear to auscultation and percussion
HEART: RRR
EXTREMITIES: No swelling; pedal pulses normal bilaterally
ABDOMEN: Soft, nontender
NECK: No mass or tenderness; thyroid appears normal

**Patient 4:**

Provider documentation is as follows:

Vital signs: BP, 120/70; Weight, 120 lb; Temp, 99

GENERAL APPEARANCE: Well-developed, well-nourished 78-year-old male who appears to show some signs of anxiety and depression. Patient is oriented to time, place, and person

HEENT: TMs clear, PND, throat is very red and tonsils swollen. Facial pain in the sinus area

LUNGS: Clear to auscultation and percussion

HEART: RRR

EXTREMITIES: No swelling; pedal pulses normal bilaterally

NEUROLOGIC: DTR normal bilaterally; patient exhibits decreased sensation to touch in the left foot

ABDOMEN: Soft, nontender, no splenomegaly or enlargement of liver

NECK: No mass or tenderness; thyroid appears normal

SKIN: No rashes noted. Palpation of skin shows subcutaneous nodule in the axillary area

The preceding examples reflect how a provider can document an examination that focuses on a problem focused examination to increasing more complex examinations including additional body systems. Remember, if it was not documented, it was not completed. Therefore it is essential for providers to document all of the body systems that are examined.

The coder's task is to review the documentation in the patient's record and to select the Evaluation and Management code that accurately reflects the services provided during the encounter.

The coder needs to keep in mind that no matter how much documentation a provider generates for a visit, the questions that need to be answered when you assign codes are "What caused the patient to be seen during this encounter?," "What service was provided when the patient was seen?," and "Is the service being billed supported by medical necessity and documentation?" Once the coder has answered these questions, a code assignment can be made with confidence. Tying all the information together becomes easier with experience and familiarity with the CPT manual. Coders may differ on how elements are looked at, but overall, the code selected needs to be supported in the documentation. *Remember:* In the eyes of a Medicare auditor or an insurance auditor, "If care is not documented, it was not done!"

# Hospital Inpatient and Observation Care Services Coding

CPT has a specific code range for hospital coding. This category of CPT is divided into initial hospital inpatient and observation care codes and subsequent hospital inpatient and observation care codes for additional visits after the admission. These categories include both new and established patients.

To have a complete understanding of the hospital inpatient and observation care service codes, coders must read the detailed notes that appear in the CPT manual under the headings "Hospital Inpatient and Observation Care Services," "Initial Hospital Inpatient or Observation Care," and "Subsequent Hospital Inpatient or Observation Care." Locate these headings in a CPT manual and read the information.

## Initial Hospital or Observation Care (99221–99223)

Initial hospital inpatient or observation care codes, 99221–99223, depend on the level of service that is rendered. These codes are used to report the first hospital inpatient or observation care encounter.

When referencing codes 99221–99223, the language used to describe the service should be noted. The term *per day* is used to describe the code. This means that only one of these codes should be reported per day. In the CPT manual, read the information that follows the heading "Hospital Inpatient and Observation Care Services." Note that the coder is instructed to report codes 99234, 99235, or 99236 for a patient that is admitted and discharged from hospital inpatient or observation on the same date. This notation also instructs the coder to report total time on the date of the encounter by calendar date, thus a continuous service that spans two calender days is considered a single service and is reported on one calendar day. Review this information in the CPT manual for more detail.

Table 3-4 lists and describes each of the initial hospital inpatient and observation care codes.

**TABLE 3-4** Initial Hospital Inpatient or Observation Care (99221–99223)

| Initial Hospital Inpatient or Observation Care Code | Description |
| --- | --- |
| 99221 | Code 99221 is considered a low level code for initial care. This code is used for a new or established patient. Prior to assigning this code the coder needs to read and reference the CPT manual for a complete listing of all the instructional notes that apply to this code as well as codes 99222 and 99223. |
| 99222 | Code 99222 reports a mid-level code for an initial visit. This code is utilized for new and established patients. Reference the CPT manual for a complete description of the code and additional information about the reporting of this code. |
| 99223 | Code 99223 is considered a high level code for initial care Code 99223 is the most comprehensive of codes 99221, 99222, and 99223. The level of medical decision making is of high complexity, therefore is it essential that the documentation in the patient's record is recorded to support the high level of medical decision making. |

Review the CPT manual and note the times that are reflected in codes 99221, 99222 and 99223. If time is used to select one of these codes it is suggested that the amount of time be reported in the patient's record.

## Exercise 3.4—Check Your Understanding

### Evaluation and Management Coding

Using a CPT manual, choose the correct code for the level of E/M service rendered (99221–99233), based on the following statement. The first one is done for you.

1. Subsequent hospital care visit with detailed examination/high level of medical decision making _____ 99233

2. Initial hospital care visit with history and examination/straightforward medical decision making _____

3. Subsequent observation care visit with medically appropriate examination/ moderate level of medical decision making _____

4. Initial hospital care visit with comprehensive history and detailed examination/ low level of medical decision making _____

5. Initial hospital care visit with comprehensive history and comprehensive examination/high level of medical decision making _____

## Subsequent Hospital Inpatient or Observation Care Visits (99231–99233)

After the initial code is used, subsequent hospital inpatient or observation visits are billed with codes from the 99231–99233 code range. These codes reflect the physician's work for subsequent days of service performed in the hospital inpatient or observation care setting. These codes are summarized in Table 3-5.

**TABLE 3-5**  Subsequent Hospital Inpatient or Observation Care Visits (99231–99233)

| Subsequent Hospital Inpatient or Observation Care Visit Code | Description |
|---|---|
| 99231 | The lowest level code for subsequent hospital inpatient or observation care is code 99231.<br><br>To review the complete description of code 99231 reference the CPT manual and note the instructional notations that appear prior to the code. The information that appears prior to code 99231 also governs codes 99232 and 99233. It should also be noted that each code contains total time that is specific to each code. |
| 99232 | Code 99232 is considered a mid-level code that reports subsequent care.<br><br>Reference the CPT manual to review the additional components for code 99232. |
| 99233 | The highest level code for a subsequent care visit is code 99233.<br><br>Please review the CPT manual for the additional components for code 99233. Remember this is the highest level code for subsequent hospital inpatient or observation care. |

## Exercise 3.5—Check Your Understanding

**Hospital Service Codes**

Select the correct hospital inpatient code based on the information given using a CPT manual.

1. Dr. Calvin admitted Ms. Jones, and, after taking a history, he completed a examination and medical decision making a moderate level. The code chosen for this visit is _____.

2. Dr. Smith saw his patient on the medical unit of the hospital. This was a follow-up visit from the day before. The history and examination were updated, and medical decision making was of a moderate level. The code chosen for this visit is _____.

3. Dr. Cary sent Ms. Kelley to the hospital from his office. He saw her later that at the hospital. The history and examination that Dr. Cary completed at the hospital was documented in the inpatient record. The medical decision making was of a high level. The level of service chosen for this hospital visit is _____.

4. Sandy was seen as a hospital inpatient on her third day of admission. The doctor completed an examination, and updated orders. He talked to her and her family about follow-up care. This all took 25 minutes. The correct code for this hospital visit is _____.

5. Mr. Alexander was admitted to the hospital two days ago by Dr. Simmons. Dr. Simmons had been seeing Mr. Alexander each day. Today, Dr. Simmons documented an updated examination. Because a new problem developed, medical decision making was of a moderate level. The level of service chosen for this hospital visit is _____.

## Hospital Inpatient or Observation Care Services (Including Admission and Discharge Services)

Codes 99234 to 99236 are used to report hospital inpatient or observation care services when the patient is admitted and discharged on the same date of service. Locate these codes in the CPT manual and review the notations that appear after the heading entitled "Hospital Inpatient or Observation Care Services (Including Admission and Discharge Services)." As stated in this section of the CPT manual, there needs to be two or more encounters on the same date. Minimally there needs to be an admission encounter and a discharge encounter to report these codes. It should also be noted that codes 99234 to 99236 are for patients that are not newborns. For discharge services for newborns admitted and discharged on the same date, code 99463 should be reported.

### Hospital Inpatient or Observation Discharge Codes (99238, 99239)

To indicate that a patient has been discharged from the hospital inpatient or observation setting, the coder would use code 99238 or 99239. These codes are time based and include all services provided to a patient on the date of discharge. Code 99238, reports "Hospital inpatient or observation discharge day management: 30 minutes or less," is the standard discharge and is used to indicate that the work involved in discharging a patient took approximately 30 minutes or less. If the provider needs to take more time in the discharge process, code 99239, "Hospital discharge day management; more than 30 minutes," would be used. It is essential that the time spent in the discharge process is documented when code 99239 is used.

## Exercise 3.6—Check Your Understanding

**Hospital Inpatient or Observation Coding**

Indicate whether the following statements are true (T) or false (F).

1. _____ Beth was admitted on August 10 at 4:30 a.m. for observation for stomach cramps. She was discharged that same day at 7:30 p.m., when she began feeling better. Based on the doctor's documentation meeting the levels of service, this visit should be coded with codes in the range 99234–99236.

2. _____ Code 99221 is a subsequent hospital inpatient or observation care code.

3. _____ For discharge services provided to newborns admitted and discharged on the same date report code 99463.

4. _____ When a doctor codes an encounter by using code 99236, there needs to be medical decision making of a high level.

5. _____ Codes 99221 to 99223 are used once per day while a patient is a hospital inpatient or in observation care for the initial care.

6. _____ Code 99239 reports 30 minutes or less of hospital inpatient or observation discharge day management.

7. _____ Code 99222 is to be used to report 30 minutes of initial hospital inpatient care.

8. _____ Code 99235 would be reported if there is medical decision making of high level.

9. _____ Code 99233 is used to report an initial observation care service.

10. _____ Code 99234 reports hospital inpatient or observation care for a patient that has been admitted and discharged on the same date of service.

## Consultations

**Consultations** are services rendered by providers when their opinion or expertise is requested by another provider or appropriate source. If you follow the rule of "3 Rs," you should be able to distinguish a consult from other Evaluation and Management services. The 3 Rs are as follows: your provider receives a *request* to *render* an opinion or give advice and, in doing so, they are *responding* to the request.

The response to the request closes the circle, and the decision can then be made as to whether this is actually a consult. The patient's medical record must reflect all three of these components before a consult code is assigned. The request can be a verbal request, but documentation by both the provider making the request and the provider rendering the opinion must reflect the fact that a request was made. See Figure 3-1 for an example of a consult circle.

For every consultation billed, the record should contain documentation stating the following:

- The request for the consultation
- A written consultation report that identifies:
  - The specific problem for which the consultation was requested
  - The extent of the history, exam, and medical decision making that occurred during the encounter
  - The consultant's findings and recommendations
- A written report of the findings that is sent to the referring provider

The consultation codes are divided according to the site of service. Code range 99242–99245 is for consultations that are performed in the office or other outpatient setting. Codes 99252–99255 are for

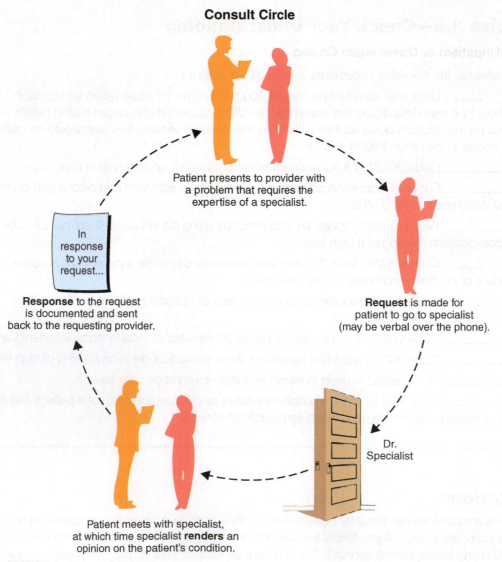

**Consult Circle**

Patient presents to provider with a problem that requires the expertise of a specialist.

**Request** is made for patient to go to specialist (may be verbal over the phone).

Dr. Specialist

Patient meets with specialist, at which time specialist **renders** an opinion on the patient's condition.

In response to your request...

**Response** to the request is documented and sent back to the requesting provider.

**FIGURE 3-1** Consult Circle

consultations that are performed when the patient is a hospital inpatient or in observation, a resident of a nursing facility, or a patient in a partial hospital setting. These code ranges are for new and established patients and can be reported only once per setting. If, after the completion of the consultation, the consultant assumes care for the management of the patient, the appropriate Evaluation and Management service code should be assigned according to the site of service in which the service was performed.

**EXAMPLE:** Dr. Jones is a cardiologist who is called into Sunny Valley Hospital for a consultation to see Ms. Brown, who is experiencing chest pain.

Depending on the level of service rendered, Dr. Jones would bill the consultation using code range 99252–99255. Dr. Jones determines that Ms. Brown has a cardiac condition that he is going to follow.

### ● ● ● Guideline

**Code range 99252–99255, Inpatient or Observation Consultations, is used to report consultations for hospital inpatients or patients in observation, residents of nursing facilities, or patients in a partial hospital setting. Only one consultation should be reported by a consultant per admission.**

Providers should not bill consult codes when the request for a second opinion comes from the patient or a family member. In these cases, the service is billed using the appropriate code from the office visit codes or other site-of-service codes.

A second opinion may be requested by an insurance company or a peer-review organization. If this is the case, modifier 32, mandated services, needs to be appended. Modifier 32 indicates that the service was mandated to be performed. If a decision for major surgery (usually surgery with 90-day global) is made at the time of the visit, modifier 57, decision for surgery, is appended to the Evaluation and Management service code.

Conditions that are diagnosed and require treatment from another provider do not constitute a consult.

**EXAMPLE:** Kevin was sent to Dr. Derm by his primary care physician in the hope that Dr. Derm would be able to treat the three plantar warts on Kevin's left foot. Dr. Derm looked at Kevin's foot and performed cryosurgery on each wart.

The example given is categorized as a referral. A **referral** is when a patient is sent, or referred, to a specialist for treatment of a condition that has been diagnosed and the specialist doesn't need to render an opinion on a patient's condition. These cases are billed using the appropriate Evaluation and Management code that depends on the site of service.

## Emergency Department Services (99281–99288)

CPT defines an **emergency department (ED)** as "an organized hospital-based facility for the provision of unscheduled episodic services to patients who present for immediate medical attention." Codes 99281–99285 are used by providers who perform services in the ED of a hospital-based facility, which is open 24 hours a day, seven days a week. Codes in the range of 99281–99285 are used by ED doctors, nurse practitioners, and physician assistants. It should be noted that code 99281 does not require the presence of a physician or other qualified health care professional. These codes are not used by other physicians who may be called into the ED to consult or admit the patient.

> **EXAMPLE:** Dr. Jones is the treating provider for the ED at ABC Hospital. Dr. Jones saw Sara Daniels regarding heartburn and pressure in her chest. Tests were run, and Dr. Jones contacted Ms. Daniels's primary care provider, Dr. Calvin. Dr. Calvin was already in the hospital rounding. He came to the ED, reviewed the test results, performed his own examination, and decided to admit Sara to the chest pain clinic for further evaluation.

Dr. Jones would bill an Emergency Department code from the 99281–99285 range for the visit because he was the treating ED provider and needs to submit a charge for the services he performed when Sara Daniels presented at the hospital. Dr. Calvin would code his part of the visit using the 99221–99223 range because he admitted Sara to the chest pain clinic for further evaluation. The fact that Dr. Calvin saw Sara in the ED does not affect the code choice.

Codes 99281–99285 are used for both new and established patients. The component of time is not established for ED service codes and, therefore, would not be considered a factor when a code is selected.

Code 99281 is the lowest level of an E/M emergency department code, and thus it does not require the presence of a physician or other qualified health care professional. Code 99282 reports straightforward medical decision making. The next higher level code is code 99283 which reports a low level of medical decision making. The medical decision-making piece is where the difference is evident when you choose between these two codes.

Codes 99284 and 99285 are the two highest level codes for the emergency department. The medical decision making for these codes is also different. For code 99284, medical decision making is of a moderate level. For code 99285, medical decision making is of a high level, thus these patients may have a significant threat to life or physiological function. When patients present to the ED, they may not be capable of giving a comprehensive history due to their state of consciousness or other modifying conditions that may prevent a patient's response to questions.

The differences noted in medical decision making are of importance in the instance of the ED because the patients are usually new to these providers and require a more extensive history and examination. Coders will encounter some difficulty when trying to educate an ED physician about levels of service due to the nature of the environment in which these doctors are practicing. Severe problems and life-threatening conditions are a daily occurrence in this setting, so the doctors' view of severity of a presenting problem may be somewhat skewed. A coder will sometimes need to reeducate a doctor on what constitutes the levels of medical decision making.

Code 99288—"Physician or other qualified health care professional direction of emergency medical systems (EMS) emergency care, advanced life support" is available to physicians or other qualified health care professionals who are communicating by two-way voice communication when a provider is located in the hospital and the patient is outside the hospital with emergency rescue personnel. The physician is giving direction on care of the patient that might include telemetry, cardiopulmonary resuscitation, intubation, and administration of fluids or drugs. This code is not used very often for some payers, because it is considered bundled into the ED code billed after the patient arrives at the hospital ED.

## Critical Care Services (99291 and 99292)

**Critical care** refers to a patient who requires constant attention by the provider due to situations related to their medical condition, and whose illness or injuries would put the patient at high risk should they not get this constant attention. Typically, there is organ system failure or the threat of organ system failure involved. The patient does not have to be admitted to the intensive care unit (ICU) or a critical care unit of a hospital to be considered as receiving critical care services. If the criteria outlined in CPT at the start of the Critical Care Service category are met, the codes can be billed. A new coder should review this information in detail.

Critical care codes (99291 and 99292) are time-based codes. It is essential that the total time billed for critical care codes reflect the time spent exclusively on care of this patient, whether the time is face to face or is spent on the floor providing services for this one patient.

The time billed can reflect the time coordinating care, discussing (with family members or other doctors) necessary information needed for treatment, or any other work directly related to the individual patient's care, which could include the following:

- Reviewing test results and radiological images
- Documenting the critical care service provided in the patient's medical record
- Time spent obtaining a medical history from the patient or other persons involved in the event that the patient's medical condition affected his or her ability to give a history.

*Remember: The time reported must be directly related to the management of one and only one patient!* If the doctor is caring for other patients during downtime while he or she is administering the critical care services to the original patient, this intermittent time *cannot* be counted.

Certain services are considered an integral part of critical care services. The CPT manual lists these services in the note preceding the codes for critical care services. If the service is not included in the list provided, it is allowed as a separately billable service.

**EXAMPLE:** Dana was admitted to ICU with severe chest pain, shortness of breath, and vomiting. The doctor ordered a pulse oximetry, EKG monitoring, blood gases, and a chest x-ray. Shortly after arrival, Dana required an emergency tracheostomy. The doctor spent 2½ hours at Dana's bedside trying to stabilize her, which he had detailed documentation to support.

In our example, Dana's doctor wanted to bill 2½ hours of critical care services. The coder would be able to bill out the following:

99291 × for the first hour and 14 minutes and a 99292 × 3

If additional services are provided that are not in the list provided in CPT, they are allowed as a separately billable service and can be submitted as a separate charge. So, going back to our example, in addition to our critical care codes, the emergency tracheostomy (code 31603) would also be coded because this procedure is not included in the critical care services. The critical care code would require a 25 modifier be appended to it to indicate that this was a separately identifiable service.

Critical care services have their own set of guidelines, which are detailed at the start of the Critical Care Services category. The coder should read and thoroughly understand these guidelines before assigning a code from this section.

Coding for critical care services requires that the documentation contain at least a sentence summarizing how much time was spent directly caring for the patient, even if the time spent was not continuous or face to face. If the time spent was less than 30 minutes another E/M code would be assigned, depending on whether the patient was an inpatient or an outpatient. An unlimited amount of time can be billed under critical care codes, but the documentation *must* support *any* time billed with critical care codes.

## Pediatric Critical Care Patient Transport (99466, 99467, 99485, and 99486)

At times, critically ill pediatric patients (*pediatric* being defined here as 24 months of age or less) are transported to facilities, accompanied by a provider. When this occurs, code range 99466–99467, Pediatric Critical Care Patient Transport, should be reported. The guidelines for these two codes are specific. The physician is required to accompany the patient during interfacility transport. Face-to-face care is required, and the time associated with the face-to-face care needs to be documented.

The coder will note the plus sign (+) attached to code 99467. This indicates that code 99467 is an add-on code and cannot be billed alone. Code 99466 is used for the first 30 to 74 minutes, adding code 99467 for each additional 30 minutes.

**EXAMPLE:** Dr. Howard wanted her 18-month-old female patient transported to a facility that specialized in pediatric heart patients. Because of the age of the patient and the severity of the heart condition, Dr. Howard decided to accompany the baby in the ambulance to be sure she remained stable during the 1-hour, 45-minute drive.

In this example, Dr. Howard is able to bill for this service. She would need to bill 99466 for the first 30 to 74 minutes and then code 99467×1 for the remainder of the time.

Codes 99485 and 99486 are used to report non-face-to-face supervision by a control physician during an interfacility transport for a critically ill or injured pediatric patient, 24 months or younger. Code 99485 reports the first 30 minutes while code 99486 reports each additional 30 minutes. Thus code 99486 must be reported following code 99485 when reported on a claim. Before reporting codes 99466, 99467, 99485, and 99486, coders should review the guidelines in the CPT manual that precede code 99466. At this time, reference the guidelines that are present in the CPT manual that pertain to codes 99466, 99467, 99485, and 99486.

## Exercise 3.7—Check Your Understanding

### Critical Care Services

Using a current CPT coding book, indicate whether each statement is true (T) or false (F).

1. _____ Codes 99291 and 99292 are used to report the total time spent by a physician providing critical care services to a critically ill or critically injured patient.
2. _____ Critical care services provided to infants 29 days through 24 months of age in an inpatient setting are reported with codes 99291 and 99292.
3. _____ The time that can be reported as critical care is the time spent engaged in work directly related to the individual patient's care.
4. _____ The physician needs to be immediately available to the patient to bill critical care services.
5. _____ Code 99291 can be used only once per date, even if time spent by the physician is not continuous on that date.
6. _____ Activities performed in the critical care unit that directly impact care of the patient can be counted as time in coding critical care services.
7. _____ Gastric intubation and ventilatory management are separately billable when performed with other critical care services.
8. _____ Physician attendance during transport of a 3-year-old is reported with codes 99466 and 99467.
9. _____ If a patient is unable to give a history, obtaining that history through discussion with family members may be reported as critical care.
10. _____ A provider may bill critical care services if he is on the floor and available for questions but is seeing other patients during the same period.

## Inpatient Neonatal and Pediatric Critical Care Services (99468–99480)

Codes 99468–99480 are for neonatal and pediatric critical care services provided in an inpatient setting. These codes require the neonate or pediatric patient to be in the hospital and include the same services noted in the guidelines at the beginning of the Critical Care code range. The guidelines at the beginning of this section of CPT, prior to code 99468, list all services bundled in the neonatal and pediatric critical care codes. Before assigning a code, in addition to the critical care codes, the coder should pay close attention to the list of bundled services.

Code range 99468–99476 is differentiated according to initial or subsequent services and the age of the patient. Neonatal critical care services, for patients 28 days or younger, are coded using 99468 for initial inpatient neonatal critical care and 99469 for subsequent visits. Code 99468 for initial inpatient neonatal critical care can be billed in addition to the following: 99464, "Attendance at delivery;" and 99465, "Newborn resuscitation," if any of these codes apply to the physician's role during delivery. Review the guidelines that appear before code 99468 and after the heading Inpatient Neonatal and Pediatric Critical Care for additional information pertaining to these codes.

Pediatric critical care services for children 29 days through 24 months of age are reported with code 99471 for initial care and code 99472 for subsequent care. For children 2 through 5 years of age, code 99475 reports the initial inpatient pediatric critical care, and code 99476 reports the subsequent inpatient pediatric critical care.

As part of critical care, the Initial and Continuing Intensive Care Services codes, 99477–99480, are found at the end of the pediatric and neonatal critical care section of CPT. These codes are used to indicate that an infant needs services that do not fall under critical care guidelines but are intensive enough to require more care than a typical hospital code. There is typically continuous monitoring and a team of healthcare professionals involved in the care of an infant, with the physician coordinating the care.

Codes 99478, 99479, and 99480 are based on present body weight. Keep in mind when you are looking at body weight, that 1,000 grams is equal to 35.27 ounces. Table 3-6 summarizes the assignment of these codes.

**TABLE 3-6** Continuing Intensive Care Services

| Instructions for Assigning Codes |
| --- |
| Prior to assigning codes 99478, 99479, and 99480 the coder must reference the CPT manual and review the information that appears prior to code 99477. Code 99478 is the lowest level of the subsequent intensive care service codes. Codes 99478, 99479, and 99480 are only reported once per day, for the evaluation and management of the recovering very low birth weight infant. A very low body weight is a weight less than 1,500 grams. The record needs to reflect the present body weight of the infant to justify the use of this code. |
| Code 99479 reports subsequent intensive care services for the evaluation and management of the recovering low birth weight infant. The present body weight for this code is from 1,500 to 2,500 grams. Reference the CPT manual for additional information that applies to this code. |
| Code 99480 is the final subsequent intensive care service code, for the evaluation and management of the recovering infant. This code is used when the present body weight of the infant is 2,501 to 5,000 grams. Documentation in the record needs to record the body weight of the infant to justify the use of this code. |

A coder may encounter abbreviations such as for **low birth weight (LBW)** and **very low birth weight (VLBW)**. Should you encounter such abbreviations when coding, be aware that to be considered VLBW, the weight of the infant would be less than 1,500 grams. LBW would be an infant with present body weight of 1,500–2,500 grams. Normal weight for a newborn would be a present body weight of 2,501–5,000 grams.

## Exercise 3.8—Check Your Understanding

**Critical Care Services**

The following questions relate only to critical care services. Please fill in the blanks in the following statements with the term(s) that correctly complete the sentences. Reference the CPT manual for the complete language used for the coding of critical care services.

1. In addition to the history, examination, and medical decision making, the physician is also required to document _____ spent in direct care of the patient to support the billing of codes 99291 and 99292.

2. When coding Pediatric Critical Care Transport, the coder needs to use code 99466 for the first 30 to 74 minutes and code _____ for each additional 30 minutes thereafter.

3. Initial inpatient neonatal critical care services are coded using code _____.

4. _____ is the abbreviation that a coder may see when coding an infant chart when the infant's present birth weight is less than 1,500 grams.

5. Mr. Mills was admitted to ICU, where Dr. Brown spent 1 hour and 20 minutes performing critical care services. Dr. Brown submitted the following code(s) for his services: _____.

6. Sandrine required constant observation by a health-care team in the neonate ICU. She is 5 days old and has been in the ICU for the past 3 days. Day 4 services in ICU are billed with code _____.

7. Critically ill or injured children over the age of _____ years of age or older would be reported with hourly critical care service codes 99291 and 99292.

8. If the same physician provides critical care services for a pediatric patient 23 months of age in an outpatient setting and an inpatient setting on the same day, critical care services would be reported using code(s) _____.

9. _____ is the direct delivery by a physician(s) of medical care for a critically ill or critically injured patient.

10. Time spent that can be reported as critical care is the time spent _____ related to the patient's care, whether it is face-to-face or floor/unit time.

# Nursing Facility Services (99304–99316)

Code range 99304–99316 is used to report evaluation and management services provided to patients in Skilled Nursing Facilities (SNF), Long Term Care Facilities (LTCF), or Intermediate Care Facilities (ICF) codes. This range of codes is referred to as Nursing Facility Services codes. If your provider refers to the place of service as any of the preceding, this is the code range you would use. Convalescent care and rehabilitative care are also provided in these facilities, and these services also fall under this code range.

In addition to these sites, patients in a psychiatric residential treatment center would have services coded from this section of CPT as well. A **psychiatric residential treatment center** provides 24-hour care that includes a therapeutically planned and professionally staffed group-living and learning environment. These codes are also used to report services provided in immediate care facilities for people with intellectual disabilities.

Physician assessment and care plans are required, and in most cases, affect the payment received by the facility. Resident Assessment Instrument (RAI), Minimum Data Set (MDS), and Resident Assessment Protocols (RAPs) are the most common assessments that are referred to in the nursing facility setting. These assessments are required at admission/readmission to a facility. Should a patient's condition substantially change, a reassessment must be completed on the patient.

There is no distinction made between new and established patients, but a distinction is made between initial and subsequent care. Initial Care codes (99304–99306) are reported once per admission per provider. Review the instructional notations, that appear in the CPT manual, under the heading "Initial Nursing Facility Care." Specific guidelines are present in relation to the use of these codes for reporting initial comprehensive visits. Review all of the information that follows the heading. Nursing facility initial care codes are noted in Table 3-7.

**TABLE 3-7** Nursing Facility Initial Care (99304–99306)

| Instructions for Use of Codes |
| --- |
| Code 99304 reports an initial nursing facility care service for the evaluation and management of a patient. This code contains medical decision making that is straightforward or of low complexity. |
| Prior to code 99304 there is an extensive notation that applies to all codes for initial nursing facility care codes. Review the CPT manual for this additional information. |
| Code 99305 reports the mid level code for an initial nursing facility care service for the evaluation and management of a patient. Medical decision making is of moderate complexity. |
| Code 99306 is considered the highest level of the initial nursing facility care service codes for the evaluation and management of a patient. As with codes 99304 and 99305, code 99306 is a "per day" code. Review the CPT manual for the full description of these codes. 99306 reports a high level of medical decision making. |

Subsequent Care codes (99307–99310) are reported once per day. Bundled into the subsequent care codes are review of the patient's medical record and review of any ancillary studies. The codes, with descriptions, are found in Table 3-8.

**TABLE 3-8** Nursing Facility Subsequent Care (99307–99310)

| Instructions for the Use of Codes |
| --- |
| The lowest level of the subsequent nursing facility care codes for evaluation and management of a patient is code 99307. Straightforward medical decision making is reported by the use of this code. |
| Reference the CPT manual for the complete code description. It should be noted that codes 99307, 99308, 99309, and 99310 are "per day" codes. |
| Code 99308 reports subsequent nursing facility care for evaluation and management of a patient. This is considered a higher level code than code 99307 the medical decision making reported with this code is of a low level. |
| Subsequent nursing facility care for evaluation and management of a patient is reported with code 99309 which identifies medical decision making of moderate level. |
| Code 99310 is the highest level code for the reporting of subsequent nursing facility care for evaluation and management of a patient. Medical decision making that is high is reported with the use of this code. This is considered the highest level code for subsequent care and therefore the medical documentation should be reviewed to ensure that the reporting of this code is justified prior to submitting a claim. |

Nursing facility discharge services are coded using codes 99315 and 99316. These codes are time based, and if code 99316 is used, documentation must be provided to substantiate why the discharge took more than 30 minutes. The codes include final examination, final instructions and prescriptions given, and any discussion of nursing facility stay, even if the time is not continuous. Table 3-9 summarizes these codes.

**TABLE 3-9** Nursing Facility Discharge Services (99315 and 99316)

| Instructions for the Use of Codes |
| --- |
| Time is a deciding factor when assigning codes for nursing facility discharge services. 99315 is used to report nursing facility discharge day management. This code is used when the management for discharge is 30 minutes or less. The best practice is to have providers record the time they spend in completing the discharge management. |
| Code 99316 reports a nursing facility discharge day management with a time of more than 30 minutes. It is essential that the provider records that more than 30 minutes is spent to justify the use of this code. |

## Exercise 3.9—Check Your Understanding

### Nursing Facility Services

Using the CPT manual, indicate whether the following statements are true (T) or false (F).

1. _____ A subsequent nursing facility visit that has a comprehensive exam and an updated history with moderate medical decision making would be coded with CPT code 99309.

2. _____ Code 99306 reports 25 minutes of total time.

3. _____ A subsequent nursing facility visit that has a medically appropriate history and examination, and straightforward medical decision making is coded with CPT code 99307.

4. _____ Code 99308 is the highest level of initial nursing facility care service codes.

5. _____ Codes 99304–99306 are billable using time as a determining element.

6. _____ Services for patients seen in an immediate care facilities for people with intellectual disabilities are reported with nursing facility service codes.

7. _____ Nursing Facility Service codes are broken down between new and established patients.

8. _____ Mr. Wallace was discharged from a nursing home. His doctor completed a final examination, discharge instructions and wrote prescriptions for the patient's pharmacy. The doctor spent 25 minutes with the patient. Code 99315 was reported. The code assignment is correct.

9. _____ Dottie was being discharged to home from her convalescent stay at Sunny Valley nursing facility. Her doctor spent 1 hour discussing discharge orders, preparing the prescriptions, and giving Dottie a comprehensive physical prior to discharge. Her doctor submitted code 99309 for these services. The code assignment is correct.

10. _____ If a patient is in a psychiatric residential treatment center and is also receiving psychotherapy, the psychotherapy is a separately billable service.

## Home or Residence Services (99341–99350)

This category is broken down into new versus established patient visits. The unique thing about home services is that the provider must document why the patient was seen at home (in a private residence) and not in the office. Home is defined as a private residence and includes temporary lodging, short-term accommodations such as a hotel, cruise ship, campground, or hotel. Review the information that follows the heading Home or Residence Services in the CPT manual. Here you will find additional information about the use of these codes for assisted living facilities, group homes, custodial care facilities and residential substance abuse treatment facilities. This series of codes should not be billed for care plan oversight. Time is allowed as an element when you are choosing a code for services rendered, but travel time is not billable, so only face-to-face time should be documented and included in code selection. Table 3-10 lists the codes and criteria associated with the new-patient home service codes.

**TABLE 3-10** Home or Residence Services—New Patients (99341–99345)

| Code(s) | Description |
| --- | --- |
| 99341, 99342, 99344, and 99345 | Codes 99341 to 99345 report home visits for the evaluation and management of a new patient. Code 99341 reports the lowest level of E/M service and includes straightforward medical decision making.<br><br>Reference the CPT manual and note that the level of E/M for the patient increases throughout the code range. When reporting these codes it is necessary to document the level of medical decision making or the total time to justify code selection. |

The Established Patient Home Visit codes are described in Table 3-11.

**TABLE 3-11** Home or Residence Services—Established Patients (99347–99350)

| Code(s) | Description |
| --- | --- |
| 99347, 99348, 99349, and 99350 | Home or residence visits for the evaluation and management of an established patient are reported with code 99347 to 99350. The codes for established patients increase in the level of medical decision making. Note that code 99350 reports high medical decision making. Reference the CPT manual for the full descriptions of the code range. |

## Prolonged Services (99358–99359, 99415–99418, 99360)

Codes 99358 and 99359 report Prolonged Service on date other than the Face-to-Face Evaluation and Management Service without Direct Patient Contact. Table 3-12 summarizes these codes.

**TABLE 3-12** Prolonged Service Without Direct Patient Contact (99358, 99359)

| Code(s) | Description |
| --- | --- |
| 99358 and 99359 | Codes 99358 and 99359 report prolonged evaluation and management service before and/or after direct patient care. It should also be noted that these codes are time based codes. Prior to code 99358 the CPT manual contains extensive information about the use of these codes. Read the information prior to code 99358 found in the CPT manual. |

The next subcategory in the Prolonged Services category of codes is entitled Prolonged Clinical Staff Services With Physician or Other Qualified Health Care Professional Supervision. This subcategory includes codes 99415 and 99416. These services are provided in the office or outpatient setting and are to be reported when a physician or qualified health care professional provided direct supervision of clinical staff that provided prolonged face-to-face services that is beyond the typical face-to-face time of the E/M service. Codes 99415 and 99416 are reported in addition to the designated E/M service code. Code 99415 reports the first hour of prolonged clinical staff service during an E/M service and code 99416 reports each additional 30 minutes. Prior to assigning these codes, coders need to read the guidelines that are found prior to code 99415 which provide detailed instructions on the use of these codes. As stated in this section of the CPT manual, code 99415, is to be reported only once per date. Reference the table that follows code 99416 in the CPT manual for further explanation of the assignment of these codes.

Codes 99417 and 99418 report Prolonged Service with or without Direct Patient Contact on the Date of an Evaluation and Management Service. Locate these codes in the CPT manual and review the information that appears before the code descriptions. This information details the use of these codes.

**Standby Services** (99360) is the last code in the Prolonged Services section. This code is used when a physician requests that another physician stand by in the event his services are needed. Standby service does not require direct patient contact. A physician cannot use this code when precepting another physician or if the standby physician performs a service that has a global period attached to it, because the standby service is considered bundled into the surgical package. Typically, this code may be used with regard to a problematic delivery. You must clearly show that the physician spent more than 30 minutes on standby. Do not report code 99360 along with 99464, "Attendance at delivery."

## Case Management Services (99366–99368)

**Case management** is a service provided by an attending physician in which the physician not only supervises but also coordinates direct care received by a patient. This category of CPT contains codes for Medical Team Conferences. Table 3-13 summarizes the code for Medical Team Conferences with direct (face-to-face) contact with the patient and/or the patient's family. Extensive notations appear in the CPT manual, which you should review before assigning codes 99366 to 99368. Locate and review the notations found in the CPT manual prior to code 99366.

**TABLE 3-13**  Medical Team Conference, Direct Contact with Patient and/or Family (99366)

| Code | Description |
|------|-------------|
| 99366 | Code 99366 is a time based code that reports a medical team conference. Review code 99366 and note the description of the code. |
|  | (Please note that an instructional notation within the CPT manual states that for team conference services less than 30 minutes, the service should not be reported separately.) |

The codes are used to report medical team conferences in which at least three qualified health-care professionals from different specialties or disciplines meet face to face to develop, revise, coordinate, or implement health-care services needed by the patient. Table 3-14 summarizes the codes that report conferences without direct contact with the patient and/or family.

**TABLE 3-14**  Medical Team Conferences Without Direct Contact with Patient and/or Family (99367–99368)

| Code(s) | Description |
|---------|-------------|
| 99367 and 99368 | Codes 99367 and 99368 report medical team conferences when the patient and/or family member is not present during the conference. These conferences must be at least 30 minutes or longer to be reported. Reference the CPT manual to review the full description of the codes and note the code differences. |

When reporting these codes, note that no more than one individual from the same specialty may report these codes at the same encounter. These codes also should not be reported when the medical team conference is part of a facility or organizational service that is contractually provided by the facility or organizational provider.

## Care Plan Oversight Services (99374–99380)

**Care plan oversight** is a service that is billed once a month and includes all care rendered to a patient over a 30-day period. These codes are billed by only one physician in a group practice over the 30-day period to reflect services coordinated or rendered by a physician. Patients in nursing facilities or under the care of a home health agency should not be billed with these codes. These codes are summarized in Table 3-15.

**TABLE 3-15** Care Plan Oversight Services (99374–99380)

| Code(s) | Description |
|---------|-------------|
| 99374 and 99375 | Supervision of a patient under care of home health agency (patient not present) in home, domiciliary, or equivalent environment is reported with codes 99374 and 99375. Reference the CPT manual and note the full description of the codes. The codes are time based and are reported based on services completed within a calendar month. Code 99374 reports 15 to 29 minutes and code 99375 reports 30 minutes or more. |
| 99377 and 99378 | Supervision of a hospice patient (patient not present) is reported with code 99377 and 99378. Review the CPT manual for the full description of these codes and note the time associated with each code. |
| 99379 and 99380 | Supervision of a nursing facility (patient not present) is reported with code 99379 and 99380. Reference the CPT manual and read the full descriptions of these codes and note the time used for each code. |

# Preventive Medicine Services (99381–99429)

**Preventive medicine services** are provided to a patient who is presenting to a medical office for a "well visit" or a "physical examination." They include a routine checkup, annual gynecologic examinations, and other examinations whose focus is promoting health, such as smoking and tobacco use cessation counseling visits and alcohol and/or substance abuse structures screening and intervention services. Because preventive services are age driven, no HPI is associated with the visit.

Preventive medicine does not typically entail problems, but it can be reported with a problem-oriented Evaluation and Management code should the occasion arise. If you find it necessary to code two levels of service, keep the following in mind:

- Modifier 25 is necessary to indicate that a separate Evaluation and Management service was rendered during the same visit.

- A separate note is needed, identifying the problem encountered along with any additional history, examination, and/or medical decision making that was deemed necessary to show how this problem was greater than the preventive service rendered.

- When the coder intends to "split bill," or break out a separate E/M service, the insurance carrier should be contacted to see if the separate service will be recognized and if any adjustment to the fee submitted needs to be made.

As you will note when reviewing the codes listed, preventive medicine codes are assigned by whether the patient is new or established, and then by the age of the patient.

## Preventive Medicine Services—New Patient (99381–99387)

Initial preventive medicine services are categorized according to age, as summarized in Table 3-16.

**TABLE 3-16** Preventive Medicine Services—New Patient (99381–99387)

| Code(s) | Description |
|---------|-------------|
| 99381 | Codes 99381 to 99387 report initial comprehensive preventive medicine evaluation and management of an individual new patient. The codes are differentiated by the age of the patient. Reference the CPT manual and note the components of the codes. Code 99381 is used for infants that are under 1 year old. |
| 99382, 99383, and 99384 | These codes report services provided to child under 17. Reference the CPT manual to identify the age range associated with each of these codes. |
| 99385, 99386, and 99387 | These codes report service provided to individuals 18 years old and over. Reference the CPT manual for the specific age ranges. |

## Preventive Medicine Services—Established Patient (99391–99397)

Preventive medicine services for established patients are categorized by age, as listed in Table 3-17.

**TABLE 3-17** Preventive Medicine Services—Established Patient (99391–99397)

| Code(s) | Description |
|---------|-------------|
| 99391 | Code 99391 reports comprehensive preventive medicine reevaluation and management of an established patient that is under 1 year of age. Reference the CPT manual and review the specific components for this code. |
| 99392, 99393, and 99394 | These codes report preventative medicine services for established patients that are 17 years or younger. Reference the CPT manual for the specific age ranges. |
| 99395, 99396, and 99397 | These codes report preventative services for an established patient that is 18 years and over. Reference the CPT manual to identify the specific age ranges. |

## Counseling Risk Factor Reduction and Behavioral Change Intervention (99401–99409)

### Preventive Medicine, Individual Counseling, and Behavior Change Interventions, Individual

Code range 99401–99409, Counseling Risk Factor Reduction and Behavior Change Intervention, Individual, is used to report counseling and/or risk-factor reduction interventions for new and established patients. The codes are organized as shown in Table 3-18.

**TABLE 3-18** Preventive Medicine, Individual Counseling, and Behavior Change Interventions, Individual (99401–99409)

| Code(s) | Description |
|---------|-------------|
| 99401–99404 | Preventive medicine counseling and/or risk-factor reduction interventions(s) provided to an individual are reported with codes 99401 to 99404. The codes are separate procedure codes and are differentiated by time. Reference the CPT manual for the specific times reported by each code. |
| 99406–99407 | Smoking and tobacco use cessation counseling visit (The codes are differentiated by the length of time spent counseling.) |
| 99408–99409 | Alcohol and/or substance (other than tobacco) abuse structured screening and brief intervention services (These codes are differentiated by the length of time.) |

**Preventive Medicine, Group Counseling**   Table 3-19 describes the codes for preventive medicine group counseling.

**TABLE 3-19** Preventive Medicine, Group Counseling (99411, 99412)

| Code(s) | Description |
|---------|-------------|
| 99411 and 99412 | Preventive medicine counseling and/or risk factor reduction intervention(s) provided to individuals in a group setting are reported with codes 99411 and 99412. These are separate procedure codes that are differentiated by time. Reference the CPT manual and note the full description of the codes and the time associated with each code. |

**Other Preventive Medicine Services**    Table 3-20 describes the code for other preventive medicine services.

**TABLE 3-20**  Other Preventive Medicine Services (99429)

| Code | Description |
|------|-------------|
| 99429 | The final code that relates to the reporting of preventative medicine services is code 99429. This code reports unlisted preventative services. |

# Non-Face-to-Face Services (99091, 99421–99423, 99441–99458, 99473, 99474)

Non-face-to-face service codes are used to report telephone services, online digital medical evaluations, and interprofessional telephone/internet consultations. During these services, the provider does not see the patient. Extensive notations appear in CPT about the use and definitions for these codes. Note that numerous codes in this subsection are time based codes.

# Special Evaluation and Management Services (99450–99456)

The next group of CPT codes in the Evaluation and Management chapter of the CPT manual is used only for evaluation services performed to gather information for insurance certificates. A separate note should be documented to support use of these codes because work done for the 99450–99456 range cannot be included in the other E/M services. Special report code 99080, found in the Medicine section of CPT, would not be billed in addition to these codes.

These codes would be used for disability insurance, life insurance, or work-related medical certifications. Insurance companies or the workers' compensation board may request these evaluations. Payment by any other carriers should be explored before a patient is seen. These codes may not be paid by the patient's carrier.

## Basic Life and/or Disability Evaluation Services (99450)

Code 99450 is used to report a basic life and/or disability examination that includes measurement of height, weight, and blood pressure; completion of a medical history following a life insurance pro forma; collection of blood sample and/or urinalysis complying with "chain of custody" protocols; and completion of necessary documentation/certificates.

## Work-Related or Medical Disability Evaluation Services (99455, 99456)

Code 99455 reports work-related or medical disability examinations by the treating physician that include completion of a medical history commensurate with the patient's condition; performance of an examination commensurate with the patient's condition; formulation of a diagnosis, assessment of capabilities and stability, and calculation of impairment; development of a future medical treatment plan; and completion of necessary documentation/certificates and reports.

Code 99456 reports a work-related or medical disability examination by someone other than the treating physician that includes completion of a medical history commensurate with the patient's condition; performance of an examination commensurate with the patient's condition; formulation of a diagnosis, assessment of capabilities and stability, and calculation of impairment; development of a future medical treatment plan; and completion of necessary documentation/certificates and reports.

These two codes are used only in the event that an insurer is asking for a work-related examination or an examination with regard to a medical disability problem.

# Newborn Care (99460–99463)

Newborn care codes from this section are used when care is provided for normal or high-risk newborns in the settings listed. Careful attention to the setting is key in assigning the correct newborn care code. Discharge services provided on the same date as assessment services should be coded using 99463. Table 3-21 lists these codes.

**TABLE 3-21** Newborn Care and Delivery/Birthing Room Attendance and Resuscitation Services (99460–99465)

| Code(s) | Description |
|---|---|
| 99460 and 99461 | Codes 99460 and 99461 report initial care for evaluation and management of normal newborn infant. Review the full descriptions of these codes in the CPT manual and note that the codes are "per day" codes and are differentiated by the site where the service is performed. |
| 99462 | Code 99462 is used to report subsequent care of a normal newborn that is provided in a hospital. Note that this code is reported per day. |
| 99463 | Code 99463 is reported for evaluation and management of normal newborn infant that was admitted and discharged on the same date. Review the CPT manual and note that the care is provided as initial care in a hospital or birthing center. |

## Delivery/Birthing Room Attendance and Resuscitation Services (99464, 99465)

Code 99464 reports an additional provider's attendance at delivery, when it is requested by the delivering provider, and the initial stabilization of the newborn. In the CPT manual an instructional notation appears that lists the codes that can be used in conjunction with code 99464. The CPT manual contains a complete listing of the codes that can be used with 99464. Here is a partial listing of some of the common codes used with code 99464:

- 99460—initial hospital or birthing center care, per day, for the evaluation and management of normal newborn infant
- 99468—initial inpatient neonatal critical care, per day, for the evaluation and management of a critically ill neonate 28 days of age or younger
- 99477—initial hospital care, per day, for the evaluation and management of the neonate, 28 days of age or younger, who requires intensive observation, frequent interventions, and other intensive care services

Code 99465, per the CPT description, "reports delivery or birthing room resuscitation, provision of positive pressure ventilation, and/or chest compressions in the presence of acute inadequate ventilation and/or cardiac output." The instructional notation that follows code 99465 in the CPT manual also states the codes that can be used in conjunction with code 99465 and states that additional procedures, such as intubation, are to be reported separately. Make note of this instructional notation found in the CPT manual following code 99465.

It should also be noted that codes 99464 and 99465 are not to be reported in conjunction with each other.

## Care Management Services (99424-99427, 99437, 99487, 99489, 99490, 99491, 99439)

Care management services codes are used to report services provided to patients who reside at home, in a domiciliary home, a rest home, or an assisted living facility who receive care management services from a physician or other qualified health care professional. These codes are time based and are used to report the management of services for specific patients that have been identified to need these services based on their continuous or episodic health conditions that are expected to be present for the next 12 months or until the death of the patient. These codes are reported only once per calendar month by a single provider who assumes the responsibility of the care management services. To become familiar with the many care management activities and office capabilities that must be present for the use of these codes, read the instructional notations that are found prior to code 99490. The notations appear after the heading of "Care Management Services." Please note that the codes for care management services contain a number of resequenced codes. Code 99490 reports chronic care management services that include at least 20 minutes of clinical staff time. Code 99439 is an add-on code this is reported with code 99490. Code 99439 reports each additional 20 minutes of time. Code 99491 reports at least 30 minutes of time. Code 99437 is a resequenced code that reports chronic care management services for each additional 30 minutes. Review code 99437 for the full code description. Code 99487 reports the first hour of complex chronic care management services. Reference this code in the CPT manual and review the required elements for this code. One of the most important elements for this code and code 99489 is that there is moderate-or high-complexity medical decision making. This must be documented in the patient's medical record. Code 99489 is an add-on code and reports each additional 30 minutes of time and is reported in conjunction with codes 99487. Codes 99424, 99425 and 99426 and 99427 are resequenced codes that report Principal Care Management Services that focus on the medical and/or psychological needs manifested by a single complex chronic condition. Review these codes in the CPT manual for the full description of the codes.

## Transitional Care Management Services (99495, 99496)

Transitional care management services are reported with codes 99495 and 99496. These codes are used when a new or an established patient is transitioning from an inpatient setting to a community setting and needs these services because of medical and/or psychosocial conditions that require moderate- or high-complexity medical decision making. In the CPT manual, extensive guidelines are written for these codes. Read the guidelines that precede code 99495. Code 99495 reports transitional care management services that include communication with the patient and/or caregiver within two business days of discharge, medical decision making of least moderate complexity during the service period, and a face-to-face visit within 14 calendar days of discharge. Code 99496 reports transitional care management services that include communication with the patient and/or caregiver within two business days of discharge, medical decision making of high complexity during the service period, and a face-to-face visit within seven calendar days of discharge. Reference the CPT manual for an extensive listing of codes that cannot be reported with codes 99495 or 99496.

## Advance Care Planning (99497, 99498)

Codes 99497 and 99498 are time-based codes and are used to report advance care planning. Advance care planning includes face-to-face services in which advance directives for health care are discussed. These services can or cannot include the completion of legal forms such as a Health Care Proxy, Durable Power of Attorney for Health Care, Living Will, and so on. Code 99497 reports the first 30 minutes of face-to-face time, and code 99498 is an add-on code that reports each additional 30 minutes. Codes 99497 and 99498 are not to be reported on the same date of service with codes:

- 99291, 99292—Critical care, evaluation and management of the critically ill or critically injured patient
- 99468, 99469, 99471, 99472, 99475, and 99476—Inpatient Neonatal and Pediatric Critical Care
- 99477, 99478, 99479, 99480, and 99483—Initial and Continuing Intensive Care Services for a child who requires intensive care services

See the instructional notation in the CPT manual that follows code 99498 that denotes these codes that cannot be used on the same date of service as codes 99497 and 99498.

## Other Evaluation and Management Services (99499)

This code is used *only* in the event that there are *no* other E/M codes that accurately reflect the service provided. This code is used very infrequently and will generate an inquiry from the insurance carrier as to the service actually provided; in other words, supporting documentation will be required.

# Summary

- When a patient comes into a physician's office, skilled nursing facility, or hospital, code assignment should begin with the Evaluation and Management chapter of the CPT manual. The patient is evaluated, and then the management or plan of care is recorded in the medical record.
- For selecting a level of service for office and other outpatient services, medical decision making or total time determine a code level.

- To assign codes properly, you should know whether a patient is new or established, whether the patient is an inpatient or an outpatient, and what the place of service was.
- Emergency Service codes are not differentiated as new and established patients.
- POS, or place of service, codes represent where the service or care was rendered.
- A new patient is a patient who has *not* received services from a provider of the same specialty, who belongs to the same group practice within the past three years.
- An established patient is a patient who *has* received services from the physician or another physician of the same specialty, who belongs to the same group practice within the past three years.
- A chief complaint (CC) is the reason the patient is seen.
- Past, family, and social history (PFSH) are recorded as part of the review of systems.
- The four levels of medical decision making are straightforward, low complexity, moderate complexity, and high complexity.
- Hospital inpatient or observation coding is divided into initial care codes, subsequent hospital care codes, and discharge services.
- Observation codes are for patients who have not been admitted as inpatients but who need to be observed for assessment of their medical condition.
- Consultations are services rendered by a provider whose opinion or advice is requested by another provider.

# Internet Links

Visit **www.cms.gov** and search the Medicare Learning Network (MLN) homepage for E/M documentation guidelines and other references that relate to billing and coding. The link for the MLN Homepage is found on the CMS homepage under the section entitled "Top 5 Resources."

# Chapter Review

## True/False

**Instructions:** Indicate whether the following statements are true (T) or false (F).

1. _____ After a patient is evaluated, a management plan is implemented and recorded in the medical record.

2. _____ A new patient is one who has not received face-to-face care from their provider within two years.

3. _____ There are seven key components to choosing a level of E/M service for codes 99304–99306.

4. _____ The lowest level of code for an office visit for a new patient is code 99211.

5. _____ The ROS is the part of the note in which the provider documents any body system(s) that might be affected by the chief complaint.

6. _____ Code 99223 requires medical decision making of high complexity.

7. _____ An incorrect place of service can result in a rejection by insurance carriers.

8. _____ A 99233 is coded for a high-level initial hospital care visit.

9. _____ To code a preventive physical exam, the coder must first determine the level of history the provider has recorded.

10. _____ The POS for an office visit is 23.

# Fill in the Blank

**Instructions:** Using a current CPT manual, finish the statements using the correct term(s).

11. The location where care was rendered is called the _____.

12. Services provided to a patient who is presenting for a well visit are called _____ services.

13. Critical care codes are _____ -based codes.

14. When a patient is admitted and discharged on the same date of service, _____ codes are used.

15. _____ Preventative medicine counseling and risk factor reduction intervention was performed for 47 minutes for an individual patient. This would be reported with code.

16. A patient who has not received face-to-face services from a provider of the same specialty within the same group practice would be considered a(n) _____ patient.

17. A patient who has received face-to-face services from a provider of the same specialty within the same group practice would be considered a(n) _____ patient.

18. A service rendered by a provider when his or her opinion or expertise is requested by another provider or appropriate source is called a(n) _____.

19. An organized hospital-based facility that renders unscheduled episodic services to patients who require immediate attention is known as a(n) _____.

20. For services to a neonate in the intensive care unit to be coded with a 99479, the birth weight of the infant must fall between _____ and _____.

21. Transitional care management service code, _____, reports communication with a patient within two business days of discharge, high-complexity medical decision making, and a face-to-face visit within seven calendar days of discharge.

22. Seventy minutes of complex chronic care management services with one face-to-face visit would be reported with code(s) _____.

23. Add-on code 99467 would be reported for each additional 30 minutes of face-to-face services during an interfacility transport of a critically ill or injured pediatric patient, 24 months of age or younger with code _____.

24. Initial birthing center care for the evaluation and management of a normal newborn infant is reported with code _____.

25. An eight minute smoking and tobacco use cessation counseling visit is reported with code _____.

26. A preventative medicine individual counseling session of 35 minutes is reported with code _____.

27. One hour and five minutes of advance care planning would be reported with code(s) _____.

28. Joan Seap lives at home, has COPD and ASHD, and is functionally declining. Dr. Smith has revised her comprehensive care plan. Thirty minutes was spent this month completing these services. The code to report is _____.

29. Jason was seen in Dr. Jone's office as a new patient. Dr. Jone's completed a history and examination, and straightforward medical decision was completed and documented in the patient's record the findings. The time spent with the patient was 20 minutes. Code _____ should be reported for this visit.

30. Suzie, an established patient of Dr. Smith's, was seen in the office. Dr. Smith completed and documented a problem focused history, an expanded problem focused examination, and medical decision making of low complexity. The total time spent with the patient was 25 minutes. Code _____ should be reported for this service.

# Case Studies

Review each case and indicate the correct code(s).

## Case 1

Mrs. Edison was having trouble eating some of the foods the nutritionists had set up on her diabetic diet menu. Mrs. Edison talked with her doctor who, in turn, called the nutritionist overseeing Mrs. Edison's diet. The doctor and the nutritionist were on the phone, had a lengthy phone conversation, and decided to integrate a new menu that both of them felt would be more beneficial to Mrs. Edison and for the management of her diabetes. The doctor then called the patient to discuss the diet changes and decided to bill for the telephone call with the patient. The call length was 24 minutes.

CPT code(s): _____

## Case 2

Daisy, a 10-year-old girl, was very sick when she presented for an office visit at her pediatrician's office. She was running a high fever, was very lethargic, had swollen glands, and showed signs of dehydration because of the vomiting she had been doing the previous night. The doctor decided, after a comprehensive history and physical, that Daisy needed to be admitted to the hospital for lab workup, rehydration, antibiotics, and monitoring. Daisy's pediatrician stopped in to the hospital that evening to evaluate her condition and check on lab results. Medical decision making was high complexity.

CPT code(s): _____

## Case 3

Colin was having great difficulty living alone since his recent fall down the back steps of his house. His family decided that Colin should move to a skilled nursing facility (SNF), which he finally agreed to do. The physician at the SNF did a comprehensive history and physical. The medical decision making was of moderate complexity, and there was a very detailed plan of care implemented that would work on building Colin's strength and reteaching him how to get around in a safer manner.

CPT code(s): _____

## Case 4

Nick was riding his dirt bike and collided with a tree. The EMTs stabilized Nick at the scene and transported him to the nearest hospital. His doctor, Dr. Shanequa, had been contacted by the family and would meet them at the hospital emergency room. In the emergency room, Dr. Shanequa completed a history and a comprehensive physical, and ordered lab work and x-rays of the head, neck, and back, along with the right leg, because Nick was complaining of severe pain in the lower portion of the leg. Dr. Shanequa determined that although Nick was pretty banged up and should not ride the dirt bike for a while, he was fine. The x-rays showed a bad sprain in the ankle area, but nothing was broken. The total time spent treating the patient was 35 minutes.

CPT code(s): _____ (*Hint:* **Keep in mind that Dr. Shanequa is Nick's primary care physician, not the ED doctor.**)

## Case 5

Megan was admitted to the hospital on May 31 at 5:00 a.m. for chest pain with nausea and heartburn. A comprehensive history was taken, and a comprehensive exam was done. Another 12 hours later, after labs, x-rays, and monitoring had been completed, and with no repeat in symptoms, it was determined that Megan had suffered a bout of GERD, and she was released to go home. Medical decision making was of a moderate level.

CPT code(s): _____

## Case 6

*Skilled Nursing Facility Discharge Summary*

This 83-year-old has been a resident for the past 1½ years. She was admitted because she had polio with left hemiparesis with speech impediment. She was hospitalized four months ago with an exacerbation of COPD, dehydration, and low blood pressure. After physical, speech, and occupational therapy, the patient has now become more independent and is able to walk behind her wheelchair. She is able to perform all of her ADLs. Routine lab work was completed last week and was found to be within normal ranges. The patient is being discharged to her daughter's home.

*(continues)*

(*continued*)

*Final Examination of Patient*

The patient is alert. Vital signs: BP 120/66, P-64, R-12 weight –165 lb.

HEENT: Head—normocephalic EENT: clear.

NECK: No lymphadenopathy or thyromegaly.

LUNGS: Clear, good air entry.

HEART: Regular rhythm, no murmurs. Distal pulses palpable.

ABDOMEN: Soft, nondistended.

NEUROLOGICAL: Cranial nerves 2–12 grossly intact except for speech impediment. Has left hemiparesis.

Discharge records were completed, and instructions and prescriptions were given to the patient's daughter.

CPT code(s): _____

# Case 7

*Office Visit*

This patient has been a patient of mine for six years, and I saw him three months ago for his annual physical. Today he presents with a cough, which he has had for the last two days, with a fever of 101 and is short of breath.

Personal medical history is significant for appendicitis in 2003.

This well-nourished, well-developed 25-year-old patient presents with a cough and fever. BP 120/70. Height: 5 feet 9 inches. Weight: 175 lb.

Ears: Auditory canals and tympanic membranes within normal limits.

Oropharynx: No significant findings.

Lungs: Bilaterally congested.

Heart: Regular sinus rhythm.

Abdomen: Soft.

Liver and spleen: Not palpable.

Assessment: Acute bronchitis.

Plan: Patient was prescribed an antibiotic. See medication order for details. The total time for the visit was 22 minutes.

CPT code(s): _____

## Case 8

This 93-year-old was seen today in her home to reevaluate a rash that she has had for the last three weeks.

Patient appears alert and responsive. BP: 130/80.

Heart: Normal rate and rhythm.

Abdomen: Soft with no masses present.

Skin: The rash that was previously present on the patient's left arm and shoulders is resolved.

Patient was instructed to call if the rash reappears.

**CPT code(s):** _____

## Case 9

*Office Note*

This 16-year-old presents today for his annual physical. This patient has been under my care since he was 6 years old.

This patient has no known medical problems.

Please see previous family history taken in May of last year. There are no additional items to add to that history.

*Social History*

The patient is a junior in high school and denies use of drugs or alcohol. He is a swimmer and trains year round and is hoping to secure a college swimming scholarship. Denies any other social risk factors at this time. Patient was given patient educational materials on social risks that are relevant to his age.

*Physical Exam*

Vital Signs: As recorded by nurse.

HEENT: Within normal limits.

Neck: Examination and thyroid are normal.

Abdomen: There are no masses or tenderness noted. Scar from previous appendectomy at age 12.

Heart: Normal sounds, no murmurs.

Musculoskeltal: There are no significant findings. Patient has better than average muscle strength and tone.

No laboratory tests or procedures were ordered. Patient is current on all immunizations. Patient instructed to return in one year for physical, or sooner if an acute condition occurs.

**CPT code(s):** _____

## Case 10

*Smoking Cessation Program Note*

This 30-year-old male patient presents today for his fifth counseling visit as part of the Smoking Cessation Program. Reviewed self-relaxation techniques and monitoring of physical symptoms of stress that precede cravings for nicotine. Client reports reduction of three to five cigarettes per day since last visit. Patient was instructed to continue to record nicotine use and stress levels. Patient to schedule appointment in two weeks.

Time of today's session: 10:00 a.m. to 10:35 a.m.

**CPT code(s):** _____

# Anesthesia

## Chapter Outline

Introduction

Guidelines Related to the National Correct
  Coding Initiative (NCCI)

Abbreviations Relating to Anesthesia

What Is Anesthesia, and How Is
  It Administered?

Coding and Billing Anesthesia Services

Calculating Anesthesia Charges

Special Billing Consideration—Anesthetic
  Administered by Physician

Billing Concerns

Summary

Internet Links

Chapter Review

Coding Assignments

Case Studies

## Learning Objectives

### At the conclusion of this chapter, you should be able to:

1. Locate CPT codes for anesthesia services.
2. Identify the various types of anesthesia.
3. Define the abbreviations associated with anesthesia.
4. List the professionals who are certified to administer anesthesia.
5. Identify situations in which modifiers specific to anesthesia are necessary.
6. Calculate the anesthesia reimbursement amount for patient procedures.
7. Identify and code procedures for anesthesia from case studies.
8. Assign the appropriate CPT codes with modifiers for anesthesia services.

## Key Terms

anesthesia

anesthesiologist

balanced anesthesia

base unit

base unit value

basic value

Bier blocks

block

block anesthesia

bundled

certified registered
  nurse anesthetist
  (CRNA)

conduction anesthesia

conscious sedation

epidural anesthesia

epidural blocks

general anesthesia

inhalation

injection

instillation

intraspinal anesthesia

local anesthesia

moderate sedation

modifying units

peridural anesthesia

physical status
  modifiers

| postanesthesia recovery period | regional anesthesia | Relative Value Guide (RVG) | subarachnoid anesthesia |
| qualifying circumstances | relative value | spinal anesthesia | time unit |

# Introduction

This chapter introduces you to the Anesthesia section of the CPT manual, codes 00100–01999, and additional qualifying circumstance anesthesia codes 99100–99140, which are found in the Medicine section of CPT. In this chapter, we also discuss some of the nuances specific to coding anesthesia services. Anesthesia services are usually billed by a physician or certified specialist whose sole purpose is administering and monitoring anesthesia and its effect on the patient. The anesthesia provider or specialist is not typically performing the procedure in addition to the anesthesia. However, at times, a provider performing the procedure also administers the anesthetic agent.

# Guidelines Related to the National Correct Coding Initiative (NCCI)

You will need to reference the following website to obtain the most current coding guideline information related to this chapter. Follow the steps given here to access the information online:

1. Log on to *https://www.cms.gov/medicare-medicaid-coordination/national-correct-coding-initiative-ncci /ncci-medicare/medicare-ncci-policy-manual.*
2. Scroll to the section titled "View Manual by Chapter."
3. Click "Chapter 2" for guidelines specific to anesthesia coding.

# Abbreviations Relating to Anesthesia

| Abbreviations | Definitions |
| --- | --- |
| ABP | arterial blood pressure |
| anes | anesthesia |
| BaE | barium enema |
| CBF | cerebral blood flow |
| CPR | cardiopulmonary resuscitation |
| EUA | examine under anesthesia |
| IVD | intervertebral disc |
| IVPB | intravenous piggy back |
| LBBB | left bundle branch block |
| mg/dl | milligrams per deciliter |
| MVV | maximum voluntary ventilation |
| TPR | temperature, pulse, respiration |

# What Is Anesthesia, and How Is It Administered?

**Anesthesia**, which means "loss of sensation," is administered to patients to relieve pain brought on by any number of causes, including surgery. Anesthesia can be administered by a qualified professional through injection, inhalation, and agent instillation. A physician qualified to administer anesthesia and who is board certified is referred to as an **anesthesiologist**. A **certified registered nurse anesthetist (CRNA)** is a registered nurse with 36 months additional training in anesthesiology who is certified to administer anesthesia.

Various scenarios can exist for the delivery of anesthesia services, including the following:

- An anesthesiologist performing the anesthesia services alone
- A certified registered nurse anesthetist performing the anesthesia services alone
- An anesthesiologist directing one certified registered nurse anesthetist
- An anesthesiologist directing multiple CRNAs performing concurrent procedures

It is important for the coder to determine who administered the anesthesia because reimbursement will vary depending on the provider. Modifiers are used to indicate whether an anesthesiologist or a CRNA delivered the anesthetic. (The use of modifiers will be discussed later in this chapter.)

## Types of Anesthesia

Multiple techniques are used to anesthetize a patient. **General anesthesia** alters the patient's perception and affects the whole body, causing a loss of consciousness. This type of anesthesia typically is administered by injection, inhalation, instillation, or a combination of these techniques.

**Injection** of an anesthetic agent involves the anesthetic being administered directly into the bloodstream. A venous access device is used, which allows the medication to circulate through the bloodstream. **Inhalation** of anesthetic agents requires the use of the circulatory and respiratory systems to move the agent efficiently through the body. Typically, a vaporizer is used to administer this type of anesthesia. **Instillation** of an anesthetic agent is used if there are problems administering the agent by injection or inhalation. During instillation, the anesthetic agent is introduced into a cavity of the body that has a mucous membrane, such as the rectum. The mucous membrane allows the anesthetic agent to be absorbed into the circulatory system and then transported to the central nervous system, thus anesthetizing the patient. The technique is not commonly used, but it is necessary in cases where the patient is not cooperative or when other approaches have failed.

At times, general anesthesia is delivered by a combination of inhalation, injection, and instillation. This is known as **balanced anesthesia**.

**Regional anesthesia**, as the name suggests, anesthetizes a particular area or region of the body. This is accomplished through nerve or field blocking. The anesthetic is injected along a major nerve tract, thus interrupting the nerve conductivity in that region of the body. This type of anesthesia is also referred to as a **block**, **block anesthesia**, or **conduction anesthesia**. Common types of regional anesthesia include:

- **Bier blocks**—injection of an anesthetic agent into the arm below the elbow or in the leg below the knee.
- **Epidural blocks**—injection of an anesthetic agent into the epidural space above the dura mater, which contains the spinal nerves and cerebrospinal fluid. This is most commonly performed in the lumbar area. This also is commonly called **epidural anesthesia**, **intraspinal anesthesia**, **peridural anesthesia**, **spinal anesthesia**, and **subarachnoid anesthesia**.

**Local anesthesia** numbs a small area, such as a finger or toe, and occurs when an anesthetic agent is applied topically to the skin or injected subcutaneously. Local anesthesia is used for dental procedures and brief surgical procedures.

# Coding and Billing Anesthesia Services

In the hospital setting, anesthesia codes are not reported because these codes represent the professional services provided by the anesthesiologist or CRNA. Anesthesia codes are used to report the professional services of the providers who anesthetized the patient. If the hospital is billing for the professional services of the anesthesiology staff, the anesthesia codes are used.

The coding and billing of anesthesia services vary significantly depending on the payer and the state in which the service is performed. Medicare requires the use of CPT anesthesia codes, whereas some third-party payers require the use of surgery codes to bill for anesthesia services. It is of the utmost importance that coders verify the coding requirements for the area to which they are reporting the services. The codes submitted for the same anesthesia service can also differ depending on the payer.

> **EXAMPLE:** An anesthesiologist provided anesthesia services for a Medicare patient for a cranioplasty for a 2-cm skull defect. The code reported should be 00215.
>
> The same service was performed for a patient with a private payer that requires the reporting of the surgery code by the anesthesiologist. In this case, the code reported should be 62140.

Before coding from the Anesthesia section of CPT, the coder must become familiar with the guidelines that appear at the start of the section. These guidelines outline the specific features of the coding system that are unique to the Anesthesia section.

## Arrangement of the Anesthesia Section

Referencing the Anesthesia section of CPT, you will note that the subsections are organized first by anatomic site, and then by procedure. However, the following four subsections of Anesthesia, do not follow this arrangement:

| Subsection | Code Range |
|---|---|
| Anesthesia for Radiologic Procedures | 01916–01942 |
| Anesthesia for Burn Excisions or Debridement | 01951–01953 |
| Anesthesia for Obstetrics | 01958–01969 |
| Anesthesia for Other Procedures | 01990–01999 |

## Locating Anesthesia Procedure Codes

Locating the CPT codes for anesthesia procedures is not as complicated as locating other procedure codes. The main term to reference in the index is "Anesthesia." The index is divided after that term by the type of procedure performed or the body site of the procedure. For example, the start of the index for Anesthesia looks like this:

| Anesthesia | |
|---|---|
| Abbe-Estlander Procedure | 00102 |
| Abdomen | |
| Abdominal Wall | 00700, 00730, 00800–00802, 00820, 00836 |

Therefore, if the patient underwent anesthesia for a Abbe-Estlander procedure, the coder should reference the main term *Anesthesia* in the index and then the subterm *Abbe-Estlander Procedure*.

If you look through the Anesthesia section of CPT, you will notice that anesthesia codes are general or specific. An example of a general code is Code 00500—"Anesthesia for all procedures on esophagus." However, Code 00906, "Anesthesia for vulvectomy," represents a specific code.

## Exercise 4.1—Check Your Understanding

### Locating Anesthesia Codes

Using a CPT manual, locate the codes or code ranges listed in the index for the procedures that follow. This exercise will help familiarize you with the index. (To select the specific code for the procedures listed, you would need to have an operative report to identify the specific procedure completed.) The first two are completed for you.

1. Anesthesia for partial hepatectomy    00792

2. Anesthesia for procedure of the ankle    00400, 01462–01522

3. Anesthesia for cast application on leg    _____

4. Anesthesia for childbirth, vaginal delivery    _____

5. Anesthesia for inferior vena cava ligation    _____

6. Anesthesia for stomach restriction for obesity    _____

7. Anesthesia for renal procedure    _____

8. Anesthesia for cervical cerclage    _____

9. Anesthesia for procedure on the pharynx    _____

10. Anesthesia for procedure on the urinary tract    _____

11. Anesthesia for orchiectomy    _____

12. Anesthesia for reconstruction of bronchi    _____

13. Anesthesia for great vessels of chest    _____

14. Anesthesia for liver hemorrhage    _____

15. Anesthesia for hip procedure    _____

16. Anesthesia for gastrocnemius recession    _____

17. Anesthesia for biopsy of ear    _____

18. Anesthesia for humeral osteotomy    _____

19. Anesthesia for thoracotomy    _____

20. Anesthesia for procedure on the larynx    _____

## Anesthesia Modifiers

After selecting the correct CPT anesthesia code, select modifiers to describe the case further. Numerous types of modifiers are used with anesthesia codes.

### CPT Modifiers

The following CPT modifiers are used for anesthesia services:

| | | | |
|---|---|---|---|
| 22 | Unusual Procedural Services | 51 | Multiple Procedures |
| 23 | Unusual Anesthesia | 53 | Discontinued Procedure |
| 32 | Mandated Services | 59 | Distinct Procedural Service |

One common error that new coders make is assigning modifier 47, anesthesia by surgeon. This modifier is to be used only by a surgeon who administered regional or general anesthesia. Modifier 47 is added to the procedure code for the service performed. This modifier is not used for the anesthesia procedure codes 00100–01999.

 **NOTE:**

The complete definition of each of the preceding modifiers is located in Appendix A, Modifiers, of the CPT manual.

## HCPCS Level II Modifiers

As mentioned earlier in this chapter, anesthesia services are performed by anesthesiologists and CRNAs. Medicare and some other payers require the use of the two-digit alpha HCPCS modifiers. Use the following HCPCS Level II modifiers with anesthesia codes to identify the exact nature of the service provided:

**AA**—Anesthesia services performed personally by anesthesiologist. This modifier is used only by the anesthesiologist.

**AD**—Medical supervision by a physician: more than four concurrent anesthesia procedures. This modifier is used only by the anesthesiologist.

**G8**—Monitored anesthesia care (MAC) for deep complex, complicated, or markedly invasive surgical procedures.

**G9**—Monitored anesthesia care for a patient who has a history of a severe cardiopulmonary condition.

**QK**—Medical direction of two, three, or four concurrent anesthesia procedures involving qualified individuals. This modifier is used only by the anesthesiologist.

**QS**—Monitored anesthesia care services.

**QX**—CRNA service with medical direction by a physician.

**QY**—Medical direction of one certified registered nurse anesthetist (CRNA) by an anesthesiologist.

**QZ**—CRNA service without medical direction by a physician.

## Physical Status Modifiers

For each anesthesia code reported, a physical status modifier code also should be reported. (Physical status modifiers will be discussed in more detail later in this chapter.) It should be noted that Medicare does not accept physical status modifiers.

# Calculating Anesthesia Charges

To calculate the reimbursement amount for professional anesthesia services, the following formula is commonly used by third-party payers:

Basic Value + Time Units + Modifying Units = Total Units

Total Units × Conversion Factor = Total Reimbursement Amount

To understand this formula, you must understand the elements in the formula and the development of these elements.

# Basic Value

As mentioned previously, the American Medical Association (AMA) developed the CPT codes, including those for anesthesia. The American Society of Anesthesiologists (ASA) publishes supplemental codes and guidelines similar to those in CPT, as well as the **Relative Value Guide (RVG)**. The RVG contains the basic value of each of the anesthesia services and additional codes that act as supplements to the regular CPT codes, along with narratives similar to those in the CPT manual. Because anesthesiologists perform other services, the RVG contains CPT codes from the Evaluation and Management, Medicine, and Surgery sections of the CPT manual.

Each anesthesia code has a basic value attached to it. The **basic value**, **base unit**, or **base unit value** has two elements. The basic value is also referred to as the **relative value**. The first element of the basic value reflects the usual services attached to anesthesia services, which refer to services included in, or bundled into, the anesthesia procedure code. These would include the following:

- Preoperative visits—including the history and exam performed by the anesthesiology staff.

- Intraoperative care—including the administration of fluids and blood products; monitoring of noninvasive vitals, such as electrocardiography (ECG), temperature, blood pressure, pulse oximetry, capnography, and mass spectrometry; and the administration of anesthesia.

- Postoperative visits—also known as the **postanesthesia recovery period**, includes all care until the patient is released to the surgeon or to another physician.

These services are considered to be services provided at the time of the procedure and are not paid separately. If the care provided is beyond the scope of the services listed previously, those unusual services can be reported in addition to the basic anesthesia services. Unusual services that can be billed include intra-arterial, central venous, and Swan-Ganz monitoring, as well as pain management services for relief of severe postoperative pain. It should be noted that in some states, anesthesia practitioners are allowed to bill postoperative management services after the anesthesia service time ends. This would include services unrelated to the anesthesia procedure, such as postoperative pain management and ventilator management.

The second element is the value of the work associated with the anesthesia service provided. Therefore, these two elements determine the basic value for the anesthesia code.

# Time Units

The second factor in the formula to calculate the charge for anesthesia services is time. Anesthesia time is defined as the actual time spent providing the anesthesia service. This is recorded in minutes and is converted to a time unit. The **time unit** is independently determined by payers and represents a defined time increment. Commonly, the increment is 15 minutes, but some carriers use a 30-minute increment. When a 15-minute increment is used, one time unit would be reported for each 15 minutes. To determine the time to report, the time starts when the provider is in personal attendance to prepare the patient for the induction of anesthesia, and the time ends when the provider is no longer in attendance and the patient may safely be sent to the post surgery recovery area.

# Modifying Units

The last factor in the formula is the modifying units. **Modifying units** are determined by a patient's physical condition and qualifying circumstances that affect the administration of anesthesia.

All surgeries are not equal. Like people, circumstances for procedures differ. Sometimes conditions are unusual or out of the ordinary and significantly influence the administration of anesthesia. These situations are known as **qualifying circumstances** and are reported using codes 99100–99140. When these happen, an additional qualifying circumstance code is reported with the anesthesia service code. It should be noted that Medicare does not recognize the qualifying circumstances codes. The qualifying circumstance codes are never to be reported alone. Note that in the CPT manual, in front of each of the codes 99100, 99116, 99135, and 99140, is the add-on notation (+). This notation alerts the coder that these codes are used in addition to the code for the anesthesia service. The ASA assigned these codes as additional units because of the extenuating circumstances that surround their use. The qualifying circumstances codes are summarized in Table 4-1.

**TABLE 4-1** Qualifying Circumstances (99100–99140)

| Code | Description | Units Assigned by ASA |
|---|---|---|
| 99100 | Anesthesia for patient of extreme age, <1 year old and >70 years old | 1 |
| 99116 | Anesthesia complicated by utilization of total body hypothermia | 5 |
| 99135 | Anesthesia complicated by utilization of controlled hypotension | 5 |
| 99140 | Anesthesia complicated by emergency conditions (specify) | 2 |

The qualifying circumstances codes are located in the Medicine section of CPT but are explained under Qualifying Circumstances in the guidelines of the Anesthesia section. These guidelines should be read and understood fully before you assign any of these codes.

As mentioned previously, the physical status of the patient can also affect the modifying-units value. **Physical status modifiers** are used to describe the patient's health status. The explanation of physical status modifiers is found in the CPT manual in the Anesthesia Guidelines. It should be noted that Medicare does not recognize physical status modifiers. These modifiers are summarized in Table 4-2.

When a patient is given a physical status modifier of P3, P4, or P5, the modifying units are increased.

To determine the total units for the anesthesia service, add the basic value, time units, and modifying units. The total reimbursement amount can be calculated by multiplying the total units by the conversion factor used in the geographical region in which the service was performed.

**EXAMPLE:** A patient undergoes a cardiac procedure with a basic value of 20. The procedure requires 60 minutes of anesthesia time. The time units are calculated in 15-minute increments. Therefore, there are four time units for this procedure. The patient has a severe systemic disease and is 82 years old.

Therefore, modifier P3 and code 99100 are assigned.

| Calculation for Total Units | |
|---|---|
| Basic Value | 20 |
| Time Units | 4 |
| Physical Status | 1 |
| Qualifying Circumstances | 1 |
| Total Units | 26 |

**TABLE 4-2** Physical Status Modifiers

| Modifier | Description | Units Assigned by ASA |
|---|---|---|
| P1 | Normal healthy patient | 0 |
| P2 | Patient with mild systemic disease | 0 |
| P3 | Patient with severe systemic disease | 1 |
| P4 | Patient with severe systemic disease that is a constant threat to life | 2 |
| P5 | A moribund patient who is not expected to survive without the operation | 3 |
| P6 | A declared brain-dead patient whose organs are being removed for donor purposes | 0 |

Assume that the conversion factor for this geographical area is $50 per unit of anesthesia. Using the following formula, calculate the total reimbursement amount:

Total Units × Conversion Factor = Total Reimbursement Amount
26 × $50 = $1300

The total reimbursement amount for this service would be $1300.

CMS posts the anesthesiology base unit values and the conversion factors at *http://www.cms.hhs.gov/center/anesth.asp*. These units are used by Medicare to determine reimbursement amounts. The base unit values and conversion factors are also in Appendices IV and V of your textbook.

## Exercise 4.2—Calculating Anesthesia Fees

For each of the following cases, calculate the anesthesia reimbursement amount based on the information given. Assume that the anesthesia time unit is 15 minutes. Use the base unit values and conversion factors found in Appendices IV and V of your textbook. The unit values for the qualifying circumstances and physical status modifiers are located in Tables 4-1 and 4-2, respectively. Assume that the payer recognizes the physical status and qualifying circumstance units.

1. John Smith is an 86-year-old male patient who was placed under general anesthesia for 30 minutes. The code used to report the anesthesia service rendered was code 00300. John had a history of an MI and, therefore, is classified with a physical status modifier of P3. This service was performed in Birmingham, Alabama.

2. Mary Jones is a 36-year-old patient who had anesthesia for sternal debridement, reported with anesthesia code 00550. Anesthesia time was 15 minutes. She has no complicating medical diagnoses. The service was performed at a hospital in the state of Alaska.

3. Helen is a 76-year-old female placed under general anesthesia for a vulvectomy. Dr. Smith, the anesthesiologist, submitted code 00906 to his staff. The patient has anemia, and the doctor assigned modifier P2. Total anesthesia time was 30 minutes. This service was performed in Danbury, Connecticut.

4. Jackie is a 9-month-old child who had an arthroscopic procedure completed on her left hip joint while under general anesthesia for 45 minutes. The anesthesia code selected by the anesthesiologist was 01202. She has renal dysfunction; therefore, the physical status modifier for the case is P4. The procedure was performed in Madera, California.

5. Mandee is an 87-year-old patient with severe cardiovascular disease who lives in Shreveport, Louisiana. She had a needle biopsy of the thyroid, anesthesia, code 00322, and was anesthetized for 15 minutes.

# Special Billing Consideration—Anesthetic Administered by Physician

When a physician performs a surgery or procedure, anesthesia administered by the same physician performing the service is considered a bundled service. The term *bundled* means that the preoperative services, the postoperative services, and the procedure itself are included in the price that the physician receives for the procedure and should not be broken out and billed separately. This would include administering anesthesia.

**EXAMPLE:** A 10-year-old boy presented today with a 3-cm laceration on the anterior portion of the left hand, which he received while playing baseball. The wound was cleaned with Betadine, and it was determined that several stitches were needed. Xylocaine was injected, and four sutures were placed. Patient tolerated procedure well and will return in 10 days for suture removal.

In this example, the services included would be the brief evaluation, the administering of the Xylocaine anesthetic, the procedure itself, and the postoperative suture removal in 10 days. These services are considered bundled into the single procedure code and are not broken out separately for claims submission.

## Moderate or Conscious Sedation

Bundled services have been discussed; however, certain services may be billed separately if the situation warrants. Services that fall outside normal anesthesia services, for example, would be billed separately. Examples of such services would include insertion of central venous or intra-arterial catheters, prolonged preoperative or postoperative care, and moderate sedation.

Moderate sedation, or conscious sedation is a form of anesthetizing a patient, with or without analgesia, that causes a controlled state of depressed consciousness so that the patient is able to respond to stimulation. Coders are given instructions in the Anesthesia Guidelines of the CPT manual for the reporting of moderate (conscious) sedation. Codes 99151 to 99153 are reported for moderate sedation provided by a physician who is also performing the service for which the conscious sedation is being provided. Codes 99155 to 99157 are used to report moderate sedation when a second physician, other than the health care professional performing the diagnostic or therapeutic service, provides the moderate sedation in a facility setting.

## Billing Concerns

Anesthesiologists bill their services separately from the surgeon. Their charges must, however, mirror the charges submitted by the surgeon. The same diagnosis and the same procedure codes should be reported if the payer requires the anesthesiologist to submit the surgery code in place of the anesthesia code. If an anesthesia code is submitted by anesthesia staff, it should reflect the same procedure submitted by the surgeon.

## Summary

- Anesthesia services are performed by anesthesiologists and CRNAs.
- General anesthesia can be administered by injection, inhalation, and instillation.
- Regional anesthesia includes Bier blocks and epidural blocks and can be referred to as *conduction anesthesia*.
- Physical status modifiers are used to identify the physical condition of the patient.
- HCPCS modifiers are used for Medicare patients and some third-party payers.
- The RVG was developed by the American Society of Anesthesiologists.

## Internet Links

To learn more about anesthesiology and the completion of anesthesia services, visit the following sites:

**http://www.asahq.org**

**http://www.cms.gov/center/anesth.asp**

# Chapter Review

## True/False

**Instructions:** Indicate whether the following statements are true (T) or false (F).

1. _____ Documentation of time is necessary in billing anesthesia services.

2. _____ Anesthesia complicated by emergency conditions is reported with the add-on code 99140.

3. _____ Anesthesia-specific modifiers are required only if the anesthesiologist deems it necessary.

4. _____ RVG stands for *Relative Value Guide* and is published by the AMA.

5. _____ The P4 modifier is required for services rendered to a patient who has a mild systemic disease.

## Fill in the Blank

**Instructions:** Fill in the blanks in the statements that follow.

6. When an agent is administered into the peridural space of the spinal cord, _____ anesthesia is accomplished.

7. Preoperative and postoperative services are considered _____ into the procedure.

8. Each anesthesia code has a _____ or basic value attached to it.

9. A physician who is board certified to administer anesthesia is called a(n) _____.

10. Anesthesia complicated by utilization of total body hypothermia would be assigned the add-on code _____.

## Matching

**Instructions:** Match the physical status modifier with the example that best reflects it.

| Modifier | Description |
| --- | --- |
| _____ 1. P1 | A. Patient undergoes a lung transplant due to end-stage lung disease. |
| _____ 2. P2 | B. Patient with poorly controlled hypertension undergoes a colonoscopy. |
| _____ 3. P3 | C. Patient with controlled diabetes mellitus undergoes an appendectomy. |
| _____ 4. P4 | D. Patient is a healthy 80-year-old patient undergoing a bronchoscopy. |
| _____ 5. P5 | E. Patient pronounced dead following a brain aneurysm; harvesting of organs occurred. |
| _____ 6. P6 | F. Patient with advanced cardiovascular disease undergoes open reduction of fracture. |

# Coding Assignments

**Instructions:** Assign the correct anesthesia CPT code for each of the following procedures.

1. Anesthesia for procedure on the eye; corneal transplant _____

2. Anesthesia for procedure on the lumbar sympathectomy _____

3. Anesthesia for procedure on upper posterior abdominal wall _____

4. Anesthesia for interpelviabdominal amputation _____

5. Anesthesia for radical perineal procedure _____

6. Anesthesia for diagnostic arthroscopic procedures of shoulder joint _____

7. Anesthesia for femoral artery ligation _____

8. Anesthesia for total knee arthroplasty _____

9. Anesthesia for physiological support for harvesting of organ(s) from brain-dead patient _____

10. Anesthesia complicated by utilization of controlled hypotension _____

11. Anesthesia for embolectomy of femoral artery _____

12. Anesthesia for induced abortion _____

13. Anesthesia for cast application to wrist _____

14. Anesthesia for ophthalmoscopy _____

15. Anesthesia for electroconvulsive therapy _____

16. Anesthesia for heart transplant _____

17. Anesthesia for percutaneous liver biopsy _____

18. Anesthesia for amniocentesis _____

19. Anesthesia for perineal prostatectomy _____

20. Anesthesia for arthroscopy on wrist _____

21. Anesthesia for tenoplasty elbow to shoulder _____

22. Anesthesia for pancreatectomy _____

23. Anesthesia for hernia repair in upper abdomen _____

24. Anesthesia for partial rib resection _____

25. Anesthesia for subdural taps _____

26. Anesthesia for thoracoplasty _____

27. Anesthesia for CSF shunting procedure _____

28. Anesthesia for biopsy of the clavicle _____

29. Anesthesia for pneumocentesis _____

30. Anesthesia for bone marrow biopsy, iliac anterior crest _____

31. Anesthesia for iridectomy _____

32. Anesthesia for permanent transvenous pacemaker insertion _____

33. Anesthesia for procedure on seminal vesicles _____

34. Anesthesia for cervical cerclage _____

35. Anesthesia for total ankle replacement _____

# Case Studies

**Instructions:** Select the correct CPT anesthesia code for each of the following cases.

## Case 1

**Patient Name:** Matino, Greta

**MRN:** 223232

**Date:** 02/02/20XX

**Procedure:** Excision of orbital mass, left superior orbit

Anesthesiologist performed the following:

**Anesthesia:** Proparacaine was instilled in the left eye. The eye was then prepped and draped in the usual sterile manner. The superior aspect of the left orbit was injected with 2% Lidocaine with 1:200,000 epinephrine.

Procedure was performed by the eye surgeon.

CPT code assignment for the anesthesiologist would be: _____

## Case 2

**Patient Name:** Wyon, Gabbie

**MRN:**                     049586

**Date:**                    3/4/20XX

**Procedure:**               Radical hysterectomy

Anesthesiologist performed the following:

General anesthesia was administered prior to the completion of a radical hysterectomy.

CPT code assignment for the anesthesiologist would be: _____

## Case 3

**Patient Name:** Jones, Joanne

**MRN:**                     029384

**Date:**                    April 16, 20XX

**Procedure:**               Tubal ligation

Anesthesiologist performed the following:

The patient was placed under general anesthesia prior to the completion of a laparoscopic tubal ligation.

CPT code assignment for the anesthesiologist would be: _____

## Case 4

**Patient Name:** Stan Tanks

**MRN:**                     774950

**Date:**                    January 15, 20XX

**Procedure:**               Closed reduction of humerus

Dr. Jones, anesthesiologist, used general anesthesia to sedate this patient prior to a closed reduction of the humerus.

CPT code assignment for the anesthesiologist would be: _____

## Case 5

**Patient Name:** Mary Thomas

**MRN:**                  102938

**Date:**                 December 14, 20XX

**Procedure:**            Cesarean delivery of twin girls

This 29-year-old patient was placed under general anesthesia for the delivery of two infant females.

CPT code assignment for the anesthesiologist would be: _____

## Case 6

**Patient Name:** Mark Jumps

**MRN:**                  394567

**Date:**                 June 18, 20XX

**Procedure:**            Arthroscopic total knee arthroplasty

This 19-year-old soccer player sustained an injury to his left knee, and an arthroscopic total knee arthroplasty was performed with Dr. Jones administering the anesthesia.

CPT code assignment for the anesthesiologist would be: _____

## Case 7

**Patient:** Natalie Smith

**MRN:**                  893568

**Date:**                 July 7, 20XX

**Procedure:**            Liver biopsy

This 29-year-old female with a history of liver disease was placed under anesthesia for a percutaneous liver biopsy to rule out a malignant condition.

CPT code assignment for the anesthesiologist would be: _____

## Case 8

**Patient:** Jackie Edwards

**MRN:**                209385

**Date:**                September 19, 20XX

**Procedure:**        Craniotomy

This 38-year-old female has a hematoma, and a craniotomy was performed for the evacuation of the hematoma. She was placed under general anesthesia.

CPT code assignment for the anesthesiologist would be: _____

## Case 9

**Patient:** Roberto Rodriguez

**MRN:**                683940

**Date:**                October 19, 20XX

**Procedure:**        Repair of cleft palate

This 2-year-old male was placed under general anesthesia for a repair of a congenital cleft palate.

CPT code assignment for the anesthesiologist would be: _____

## Case 10

**Patient:** Jose Booth

**MRN:**                549762

**Date:**                April 19, 20XX

**Procedure:**        Needle biopsy of thyroid

This 9-month-old was placed under general anesthesia so that a needle biopsy of the thyroid could be performed.

CPT code assignment for the anesthesiologist would be: _____

# Surgery and the Integumentary System

## Chapter Outline

Introduction
Surgery Guidelines
The National Correct Coding Initiative (NCCI)
Guidelines Related to the National
   Correct Coding Initiative (NCCI)
Abbreviations Related to the
   Integumentary System
Anatomy of the Integumentary System

Procedures Performed on the Integumentary
   System
Summary
Internet Links
Chapter Review
Coding Assignments
Case Studies

## Learning Objectives

### At the conclusion of this chapter, you should be able to:

1. Define key terms related to coding procedures performed within the integumentary system.
2. Explain the organization of the Surgery section of the CPT manual.
3. Explain what is included in a surgical package.
4. Identify bundled services.
5. Explain the purpose of the National Correct Coding Initiative (NCCI).
6. Define abbreviations related to the integumentary system.
7. Define the basic anatomy and functions of the integumentary system.
8. Define common procedures performed within the integumentary system.
9. Identify and code the different types of grafts.
10. Assign the appropriate CPT code(s) and modifier(s) for surgical procedures performed within the integumentary system.
11. Identify and code procedures for surgery and the integumentary system from case studies.

## Key Terms

| | | | |
|---|---|---|---|
| acellular dermal replacement | aspiration | benign lesion | class findings |
| adjacent tissue transfer | autogenous graft | biopsy | clean-contaminated wound |
| | autograft | burn | |

clean wound

complex repair

contaminated wound

debridement

decubitus ulcer

defect site

dermal autograft

dermatome

dermis

destruction

diagnostic procedures

dirty and infected wound

donor site

epidermal autograft

epidermis

escharotomy

fine needle aspiration

first-degree burn

free graft

full thickness graft

global days

global package

graft

hematoma

heterodermic graft

homograft

homologous graft

hyperkeratotic

imaging guidance

incision and drainage (I&D)

integumentary system

intermediate repair

malignant lesion

mammary ductogram

mastectomy

mastotomy

metastasis

Mohs micrographic surgery

National Correct Coding Initiative (NCCI)

ostectomy

pedicle flap

pilonidal cyst

pinch graft

recipient site

repair

scalpel

second-degree burns

shaving

simple repair

skin tags

split-skin graft

split-thickness autograft

split-thickness graft

subcutaneous

surgical package

therapeutic procedures

third-degree burns

tissue-cultured epidermal autograft

ulcers

unbundling

wedge excision

xenografts

# Introduction

The Surgery section is the largest and most complicated section in the CPT manual. The Surgery section is organized by body system and types of procedures. Specialists may find that they code mainly from one subsection of the Surgery section, whereas general surgeons code from various subsections within the section.

Careful attention to the details of the procedure and a working knowledge of the CPT manual are essential for proper code assignment. For surgical procedures, the operative note provides the most accurate source of information for the service rendered and should be documented accordingly.

This chapter will discuss the organization of the Surgery section of the CPT manual.

The Surgery section of the CPT manual begins with general information and surgical guidelines. Prior to selecting codes, coders need to review the definitions and concepts included in the Surgery Guidelines found in the CPT manual prior to the surgery codes. The Surgery guidelines address the following:

- Services
- CPT surgical package definition
- Follow-up care for diagnostic procedures
- Follow-up care for therapeutic surgical procedures
- Supplied materials
- Reporting more than one procedure/service
- Separate procedure
- Unlisted service or procedure
- Special report
- Imaging guidance
- Surgical destruction
- Foreign Body/Implant Definition

Locate the Surgery Guidelines in the CPT manual and read the information contained in this part of the manual. Following the guidelines, the various subsections of the Surgery section appear. The Surgery section of the CPT manual is arranged by body system as follows:

- General—Codes 10004–10021
- Integumentary System—Codes 10030–19499
- Musculoskeletal System—Codes 20100–29999
- Respiratory System—Codes 30000–32999
- Cardiovascular System—Codes 33016–37799
- Hemic and Lymphatic System—Codes 38100–38999
- Mediastinum and Diaphragm—Codes 39000–39599
- Digestive System—Codes 40490–49999
- Urinary System—Codes 50010–53899
- Male Genital System—Codes 54000–55899
- Reproductive System Procedures—Code 55920
- Intersex Surgery—Codes 55970–55980
- Female Genital System—Codes 56405–58999
- Maternity Care and Delivery—Codes 59000–59899
- Endocrine System—Codes 60000–60699
- Nervous System—Codes 61000–64999
- Eye and Ocular Adnexa—Codes 65091–68899
- Auditory System—Codes 69000–69979
- Operating Microscope—Code 69990

Locate these subsections in the CPT manual. After each body system, the subsections are further divided by anatomical site, beginning with the top of the body (i.e., head or scalp) and working down to the feet and toes, and then from the trunk of the body outward. Understanding the organization of the Surgery section is valuable when a coder is attempting to determine if he or she is reviewing the correct section of the CPT manual for code selection.

Understanding whether the procedure performed is a diagnostic or therapeutic procedure can also be helpful when determining a code assignment. **Diagnostic procedures** are completed to determine a diagnosis and establish a care plan. **Therapeutic procedures** are part of the care plan and are used as treatment for a diagnosis. This chapter will discuss the Integumentary System subsection of the Surgery section in further detail.

# Surgery Guidelines

Prior to the code listings in the CPT manual, the Surgery-section-specific guidelines are presented.

## Services

The first guideline alerts the coder that codes for services that are provided in the office, home, or hospital, as a consultation or other medical service, are found in the Evaluation and Management section (codes 99202–99499) or in the Medicine section (codes 99000–99082) for Special Services and Reports.

## Surgical Package

Prior to code assignment, it is important to understand what is included in a **surgical package**, also known as a **global package**. When a code is selected, it represents specific services that are included in a

CPT surgical code. This term is defined differently by various payers, but the CPT manual defines the surgical package as follows:

- Local infiltration, metacarpal/metatarsal/digital block, or topical anesthesia
- Subsequent to the decision for surgery, one related Evaluation and Management (E/M) encounter on the date immediately prior to or on the date of procedure (including history and physical)
- Immediate postoperative care, including dictating operative notes and talking with the family and other physicians and qualified health care professionals
- Writing orders
- Evaluating the patient in the postanesthesia recovery area
- Typical postoperative follow-up care

This definition can be found in the Surgery Guidelines section of the CPT manual.

Many payers establish specific time periods for the postoperative period. This is referred to as the **global days** or global period. For example, Medicare defines surgeries as major or minor surgeries. Major surgeries have 90 postoperative days, whereas minor surgeries have 0 or 10 postoperative days.

> **EXAMPLE**: Brittney presented to her doctor's office with toe pain and swelling. After looking at her toe and discussing treatment options, Brittney and her doctor, Dr. Kilts, decided that she should have the nail plate removed to relieve the problem of an ingrown toenail, which was slightly deformed and causing problems. Dr. Kilts had a cancellation in his schedule for the next day, so Brittney's procedure was scheduled. She presented, had the procedure done, and was told to return in two days for a dressing change. Two days later, the dressing was changed, and the surgical site was healing nicely.

In the example, the decision for surgery was made one day prior to the procedure. The intent of the visit in the example was to determine a plan of care that would take care of the pain Brittney presented with. Since the intent of the visit was not to have the procedure performed, the evaluation of her problem is a separately billable service and should be coded with the appropriate E/M code. The procedure code reported in our example would be code 11750. This code has a 10-day global period attached to it by most payers. The dressing change is also included in the surgical package, so it would not be reported separately because it was a service performed as an integral part of the surgery. Keep in mind that most types of anesthesia, as well as airway access, are essential and would not be reported separately.

Payers should be consulted regarding their individual policies regarding surgical packages. Medicare's surgical package protocol is explained on the Centers for Medicare & Medicaid Services (CMS) website. For Medicare, approved payment amounts for procedures include payment for the following services related to the surgery. The payments are made according to this policy when the services are completed by the physician who performs the surgery.

Services that are included in Medicare's global surgical package include:

- Preoperative visits—All preoperative visits are included in the package after the decision is made to operate, beginning with the day before the day of surgery for major procedures and the day of surgery for minor procedures.
- Intraoperative services—Intraoperative services that are normally a usual and necessary part of a surgical procedure, including the prep for surgery, wound irrigation and closure, placement and removal of surgical drains, and dressing applications, are included here.
- Complications following surgery—These are all additional medical or surgical services required of the surgeon during the postoperative period of the surgery due to complications that do not require additional trips to the operating room.
- Postoperative visits—These are follow-up visits during the postoperative period of the surgery that are related to recovery from the surgery. Keep in mind that the postoperative period will be 0, 10, or 90 days based on the complexity of the surgery.
- Postsurgical pain management—Pain management that is managed by the surgeon is included in the package.
- Supplies—These are supplies other than those identified as exclusions in the CMS manual.

- Miscellaneous services—The following services, such as dressing changes; local incisional care; removal of an operative pack; removal of cutaneous sutures, staples, lines, wires, tubes, drains, casts, and splints; insertion, irrigation, and removal of urinary catheters; routine peripheral intravenous lines, nasogastric, and rectal tubes; and changes and removal of tracheostomy tubes.

## Follow-Up Care for Diagnostic and Therapeutic Surgical Procedures

Within the Surgery Guidelines of CPT, the guidelines state that follow-up care includes only the care related to the recovery from the procedure. Care for conditions, complications, exacerbations, recurrence, or the presence of other diseases or injuries is to be reported separately. Failure to report care for an unrelated condition, complication, exacerbation, recurrence, disease, or injury related to the recovery from the procedure performed is a loss of revenue for the provider.

## Supplied Materials

If additional supplies and materials are used over what is typically used for the procedure, the provider can bill drugs, trays, supplies, and other materials. However, caution should be used when billing these codes because the documentation has to provide evidence of the necessity for these additional materials.

## Reporting More Than One Procedure/Service

The next section in the Surgery Guidelines states that if more than one procedure/service is completed on the same date, session, or during the postoperative period, codes should be appended with CPT modifiers. This was discussed in Chapter 2 of this book.

## Separate Procedure

Following some code descriptions are the words "separate procedure." These codes report procedures that are typically part of a larger service or procedure and, therefore, are not reported if the larger procedure is performed. However, if the code description designated as a separate procedure is completed alone, then the code is reported.

## Unlisted Service or Procedure and Special Reports

Within the Surgery Guidelines is a listing of all the unlisted surgery service or procedure codes found in the CPT manual. These codes should be used only when a more specific code is not available for use. When these codes are used, it is common for payers to request a special report that outlines the description of the following:

- The nature, extent, and need for the procedure
- The time, effort, and equipment necessary to provide the service/procedure

  Use of the unlisted codes should be rare.

## Imaging Guidance

This guideline gives directions that state "when imaging guidance or imaging supervision and interpretation is included in a surgical procedure, guidelines for image documentation and report, included in the guidelines for Radiology (Including Nuclear Medicine and Diagnostic Ultrasound), will apply." Reference this guideline, located in Surgery Guideline section of the CPT manual, for additional information.

## Surgical Destruction

The next to last guideline found in the Surgery Guidelines states that surgical destruction is considered a part of a surgical procedure. Exceptions to this are listed as separate code numbers.

## Foreign Body/Implant Definition

Within the CPT coding manual in the Surgery Guidelines the term implant and foreign body are defined. An implant is defined as an object that is placed by a healthcare provider or professional for a specific purpose, such as the placement of a metal rod in a bone to treat a fracture. An object that is not placed by a healthcare provider or professional intentionally is a foreign body. Review the Surgery Guidelines in the CPT coding manual for additional information that applies to the coding of implants that have moved or have broken and have to be removed from the body.

## Exercise 5.1—Check Your Understanding

**Surgical Coding**

Indicate whether the following statements are true (T) or false (F).

1. _____ Vascular surgeons must assign codes from the Cardiovascular section of the Surgery chapter.

2. _____ CPT coders need to pay attention to detail and also have a working knowledge of the codes that their doctor usually assigns.

3. _____ Diagnostic procedures are part of the care plan and are used for treatment of a diagnosis that has already been rendered.

4. _____ Within the subsections of the Surgery section, the CPT codes are first arranged by body system, and then by anatomical site.

5. _____ Surgery and normal follow-up care are included in the surgical package.

# The National Correct Coding Initiative (NCCI)

The **National Correct Coding Initiative (NCCI)** was implemented to standardize proper coding and payment for Medicare Part B claims. The purpose of the NCCI has evolved to include outpatient hospital services and fiscal intermediaries. Payment denials are generated when a pair of codes is submitted together on one claim and the processing system rejects the claim based on coding conventions. Medicare does not allow beneficiaries to be billed if a denial occurs based on NCCI edits, which could put your practice at financial risk. The coder should study these denials in detail and avoid repeating the same mistakes. Education to avoid further denials is usually enough to stop the denials from occurring with any frequency.

The NCCI is set up in table format. Column 1/Column 2 of the Correct Coding Edits is the first table. This used to be known as the Comprehensive/Component edits. The second table is known as the Mutually Exclusive edits. The code(s) listed in column 2 of the Mutually Exclusive edits table are not payable services when billed with the code(s) in column 1.

**EXAMPLE:**

| Column 1 | Column 2 |
| --- | --- |
| 10021 | 36000, 36410, 64415, 64417, etc. |

In the example, if we billed code 10021 and code 36410 together, our claim would be rejected, or edited out due to NCCI coding guidelines. CPT code 10021 encompasses the services rendered in 36410, and, therefore, 36410 cannot be billed separately when reported with code 10021.

Mutually exclusive codes are codes that cannot physically be performed together during one encounter on the same anatomical site, or are code pairs that, by definition, would not be performed at the same encounter. Mutually exclusive code pairs, in certain instances, can be billed together if a modifier indicator is noted. Remember the following:

1. The standard of care is to accomplish the overall procedure.

2. To complete a procedure successfully, another procedure may also need to be performed, but these procedures may not be separately billable depending on NCCI.

# Guidelines Related to the National Correct Coding Initiative (NCCI)

The Centers for Medicare & Medicaid Services (CMS) maintains guidelines that relate and affect code selection. At the beginning of each surgical chapter in this textbook, the website and the link for the National Correct Coding Initiative information that relates to the chapter will be listed. The student will need to reference the following website to obtain the most current coding guideline information related to the Integumentary chapter. The student should follow these steps to access the information online:

**1.** Log on to *https://www.cms.gov/medicare-medicaid-coordination/national-correct-coding-initiative-ncci /ncci-medicare/medicare-ncci-policy-manual.*

**2.** Scroll to the section titled "View Manual by Chapter."

**3.** Click on "Chapter 3" for guidelines specific to the Integumentary System coding.

## Unbundling

Correctly coding a service means that the coder needs to be reporting the service rendered with the most comprehensive code available. Knowledge of the component parts of the procedure are important elements in coding a service correctly.

At times procedure codes are reported incorrectly by reporting additional codes. This is known as unbundling codes. **Unbundling** occurs when procedures and/or services are performed and they are separately coded and submitted to the insurance company for payment when there exists a single code to report them.

> **EXAMPLE:** Scarlet was scheduled in Dr. Johnson's office for the paring of two corns. Dr. Johnson performed the removal of the corns. (CPT code 11056 would be the correct code to report.) He filled out the encounter form as follows:
>
> 99211—For the examination
> 11055—Paring or cutting of benign hyperkeratotic lesion (e.g., corn or callus); single lesion
> 11055—Paring or cutting of benign hyperkeratotic lesion (e.g., corn or callus); single lesion

Dr. Johnson unbundled the services he rendered. The 99211 is inappropriate because the patient was scheduled for the removal of the corns due to a previous examination by Dr. Johnson. The determination had been made prior to this visit to do the procedure, so this evaluation is not separately billable. The coding of 11055 twice is also inappropriate because the description for code 11055 states only a single lesion and the description for code 11056 includes two to four lesions. Therefore code 11056—"Paring or cutting of benign hyperkeratotic lesion (e.g., corn or callus); 2 to 4 lesions"—is the appropriate code to report. Reporting code 11055 twice is considered unbundling because two codes were reported in place of one code that would accurately report the procedure performed.

The NCCI will help a coder immensely when it comes to more complex procedures that are often performed together. It is important to use all resources available when you are trying to determine whether to code a procedure with one comprehensive code or to break it out into separate codes to capture all the work done.

Medicare and other insurance carriers review claims submitted to detect billing errors. Repeated denials for unbundling of codes can be a red flag to Medicare and other insurance carriers. This red flag may trigger an audit of coding habits to determine whether the unbundling is intentional or not. If it is determined that there is intentional unbundling of services to receive additional payment, legal action may be taken by the payer.

# Abbreviations Related to the Integumentary System

Please reference the following for common abbreviations associated with the Surgery and Integumentary section of CPT.

| Abbreviations | Definitions |
|---|---|
| Bx or bx | biopsy |
| C&S | culture and sensitivity |
| derm | dermatology |
| FS | frozen section |
| HSV | herpes simplex virus |
| ID | intradermal |
| I&D | incision and drainage |
| KOH | potassium hydroxide |
| sc or sub-q | subcutaneous |
| UV | ultraviolet |

# Anatomy of the Integumentary System

The **integumentary system**, also known as the *skin*, acts as a shield for the body and is considered the largest body system. The functions of the integumentary system include the protection of deeper tissue by retaining fluid in the body and regulation of body temperature by controlling the amount of heat loss. A natural shield, the integumentary system also works as a factor in the immune system by blocking bacteria and other foreign bodies from entering the body. Receptors for touch are located on the skin. Because the skin is porous, it protects the body from ultraviolet radiation from the sun while also letting in ultraviolet light so that vitamin D can be produced by the body. The skin also temporarily stores fat, glucose, water, and salts that are absorbed by the blood and used by various organs of the body.

Coding some of the procedures listed in the Integumentary chapter of the CPT manual requires knowledge of how deep into the layers of skin the provider was when performing a surgery or procedure. The provider may use terms such as *epidermis*, *dermis*, and *subcutaneous*. The coder needs to know what these terms mean and where they are in relation to the depth of a procedure in order to assign a code properly.

The **epidermis** is the outermost layer of the skin. There are no blood vessels or connective tissue within the epidermis, so this layer of skin depends on lower layers for nourishment.

The **dermis** is the thick layer of tissue located directly below the epidermis. This is the layer of skin that enables a person to recognize touch, pain, pressure, and temperature changes. This layer of skin contains blood and lymph vessels, so it is more sensitive and self-sufficient than the epidermis.

The **subcutaneous** layer of skin connects the skin to the muscle surface. When a provider writes that he or she went "subcu" (you may see it written "sub-q"), this is the layer referred to. Figure 5-1 illustrates the three layers of the skin and the structures contained within these layers.

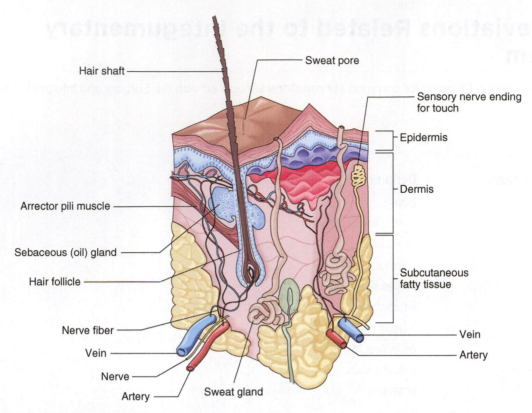

**FIGURE 5-1** Layers and Structures of the Skin

The procedures in the Integumentary subsection of the Surgery section begin with introduction and removal (codes 10030 to 10036) and then move on to incision and drainage, then debridement, paring or cutting, biopsy, removal of skin tags, shaving of epidermal or dermal lesions, and excision of benign and malignant lesions. To begin coding these procedures, the coder must have a basic understanding of the procedure being performed, the approach used, and the site of the procedure. You cannot even begin to code a procedure without knowing at least these three things.

As with every other aspect of coding a service, documentation is key. The more complicated the procedure, the more elements that become important when you select a code and the more detailed the documentation. You will see as you move through this chapter that size, or measurements, of lesions in centimeters is critical, as is the number of lesions. If measurements are given in inches or meters, the conversion to centimeters is necessary. Table 5-1 lists some of the more commonly referenced conversions for you.

A note of caution: *Never* assign a code based only on what doctors *tell* you they did. A procedure note should always be referenced when you assign a procedure code to a service. Everything goes back to "If you didn't document it, you didn't do it."

In the first subsection of the Integumentary section of Surgery, the procedures may be performed in a physician's office, an outpatient ambulatory setting, or a hospital. This is not an all-inclusive place-of-service list, but place of service makes a difference, in some instances, to insurance carriers. Be aware that just because a procedure is considered surgery does not mean that it is required to be done as an inpatient in the hospital.

**TABLE 5-1** Conversion Table

| |
|---|
| 1 inch = 2.54 centimeters (cm) |
| 1 cm = 10.0 millimeters (mm) |
| 20 grains = 1 pennyweight |
| 20 pennyweight = 1 ounce (oz) |

## Exercise 5.2—Check Your Understanding

**Integumentary System**

Indicate whether the following statements are true (T) or false (F).

1. _____ The dermis is a thick layer of tissue located below the epidermis.

2. _____ The subcutaneous layer of the skin contains sweat pores.

3. _____ The integumentary system acts as a natural shield against bacteria.

4. _____ For coding purposes, measurements need to be in centimeters for lesion size and laceration length.

5. _____ Place of service for a procedure reported from the first part of the Integumentary section of the Surgery chapter has to be the hospital.

6. _____ Sensory nerves are found in the epidermis.

7. _____ The dermal layer connects the skin to the muscle.

8. _____ A measurement given for the length of a laceration is 2 inches. The conversion to centimeters would make the length of the laceration 5.08 cm.

# Procedures Performed on the Integumentary System

As we proceed into the different systems included in the Surgery section, we will note different guidelines specific to that section as a further resource for coders.

## General (10004–10021)

The Surgery section begins with codes for Fine Needle Aspiration (FNA) Biopsy. **Aspiration** is a procedure in which fluid is surgically removed from the body. **Fine needle aspiration** is a type of aspiration in which a very fine needle is inserted into the site, and fluid is drawn. Lumps or masses that are located by touch do not typically require imaging. If a lump cannot be located by touch, imaging may need to be used. **Imaging guidance** is a radiologic procedure that assists a physician in locating the area to be addressed, usually by ultrasound or computed tomography (CT) imaging. A marker may be placed at the site so that if further surgery is necessary, the site will be easily located.

In the CPT manual, reference codes 10004 to 10021. Please note that these codes are out of numerical sequence. The coder needs to be guided by the symbols that are used in front of codes to denote that a code is out of numerical sequence. It also should be noted that the descriptions of the codes denote if imaging guidance is used or if the procedure occurs without imaging guidance. For example, code 10021 is for fine needle aspiration biopsy, without imaging guidance for the first lesion, while code 10005 reports a fine needle biopsy including ultrasound guidance for the first lesion. This range of codes denotes the following types of imaging guidance: ultrasound, fluoroscopic, CT, or MR guidance. Please review the codes in the CPT manual for the specific descriptions for each code and note the type of imaging guidance listed in the code description.

In the CPT manual, reference the instructional notation that appears after the heading of Fine Needle Aspiration (FNA) Biopsy. This is located after the guidelines for the Surgery section of the CPT manual. The instructional notation that appears after the heading for Fine Needle Aspiration (FNA) Biopsy provides guidance to coders in relation to the reporting of additional codes that relate to procedures that typically are performed at the same time as an FNA biopsy or when multiple FNA biopsies are completed at the same operative session. Read through the instructional notation noting the various guidance it provides. An example of such guidance is: "When more than one FNA biopsy is performed on separate lesions at the same session, same day, same imaging modality, use the appropriate imaging add-on code for the second and subsequent lesions." If you are coding using a CPT manual, I would suggest that you highlight the sentences in this instructional notation that give you guidance as to the reporting for this range of codes.

## Introduction and Removal (10030, 10035, 10036) and Incision and Drainage (10040–10180)

Code 10030 reports image-guided fluid collection drainage by a catheter for an abscess, hematoma, seroma, lymphocele or cyst, or the like found in soft tissue via a percutaneous approach. Code 10035 reports a placement of soft tissue localization device(s), percutaneous, including imaging guidance for the first lesion. Code 10036 is an add on code and reports the placement of the localization devices for each additional lesion. The notations that follow code 10036 need to be referenced as they provide additional instructions for the reporting of these codes. **Incision and drainage (I&D)** involves surgically cutting over the area to be drained, and then withdrawing the fluid or draining it. An I&D may be performed for any number of reasons, such as drainage of a cyst or abscess.

The codes are differentiated by the type of abscess or cyst to be incised, and whether the I&D was simple or complicated. The coder would choose a simple procedure code unless the provider indicated that surgical closure was delayed or that a Z-plasty (repair) was required. In these cases, the coder may need to select a code indicating that a more complicated procedure was performed. It should be noted that this section of codes reports incision and drainage, not excisions. Following code 10081, a note informs the coder that, if an excision of a pilondial cyst occurs, code range 11770–11772 should be referenced for proper code selection.

Codes 10120–10121 would be used for a foreign body removal no deeper than the subcutaneous level. Code 10121, for complicated removal, is used only if underlying tissue is involved and documented accordingly.

## Debridement (11000–11047)

**Debridement** is a type of cleansing. It involves removal of dirt or foreign objects along with tissue that is necrotic or damaged in a way that hinders the healing process. In the CPT manual, code range 11042–11047 is used to report debridement services for injuries, infections, wounds, and chronic ulcers. For proper code selection, the depth of the tissue removed and the surface area of the wound must be known.

The percentage of body surface debrided must be documented to use the 11000–11047 codes. Additional documentation requirements for debridement code usage would be the anatomical location and the depth of the tissue removed. Any comorbidities that would affect the patient's ability to heal should also be noted.

Diabetes or peripheral vascular disease, for example, are conditions that would directly affect healing and should be noted in the documentation and listed on claims submitted to an insurance company for payment of procedures.

Codes 11000 and 11001 are used to reflect extensive removal of infected or eczematous skin. Conditions such as aggressive streptococcal skin infections or extensive skin trauma would support use of these codes. Documentation of necrotic or damaged tissue supports the medical necessity of extensive debridement and is essential in supporting use of these codes.

The coder should note the plus sign (+), also known as the add-on symbol, in front of code 11001. This plus sign indicates that code 11001 is an add-on code and cannot be used alone. It is always coded in conjunction with code 11000.

Codes 11004–11006 are used to report the debridement of skin, subcutaneous tissue, muscle, and fascia for a necrotizing soft tissue infection. The codes are differentiated according to body site. Code 11008 is an add-on code used to report the removal of prosthetic material or mesh of the abdominal wall due to infection.

Codes 11010–11012 are used for debridement in conjunction with open fractures and dislocation(s). The use of these codes depends on the depth of the open wound.

Codes 11042–11047 are used for debridement of localized areas, such as skin ulcers and circumscribed dermal infections. This code series involves simple debridement of the dermis down to the muscle and bone level. This code series begins with code 11042 for debridement of subcutaneous tissue for the first 20 sq cm or less.

Add-on code 11045 reports each additional 20 sq cm or part thereof. It should be noted that code 11045 does not appear in numerical order in the CPT manual. Codes 11043 and 11046 report the debridement of muscle and/or fascia, with code 11046 being an add-on code used to report additional tissue debrided. The debridement of bone is reported with code 11044 and add-on code 11047. To become familiar with these codes, reference the CPT manual and note how many of the codes in the code range 11042–11047 are out of numerical sequence in the code book.

When reading documentation, the coder would look for the instrument(s) used to perform the debridement. A scalpel or dermatome is typically the instrument used. A **scalpel** is actually the handle part of a surgical knife. Variously sized knife blades are attached to the scalpel, which is then used for surgical cutting. A **dermatome** is also a cutting instrument, but the dermatome cuts slices of skin—the thickness is determined by the surgeon— and can be handheld or powered, depending on its usage. Dermatomes are used for debridement but are more often used for skin grafting.

## Paring or Cutting (11055–11057)

Codes in the 11055–11057 range are assigned based on the number of lesions that are being cut or pared. This code set is used when a provider is taking care of corns, calluses, or other **hyperkeratotic** lesions. *Hyperkeratotic* refers to an overgrowth of skin.

> **EXAMPLE:** Mrs. Mops presented with two corns on the right foot and one on the left. Dr. Smith decided to pare them down so she would have some comfort in her shoe gear. All three corns were pared.

In the example, Dr. Smith would code the procedure with code 11056—"Paring or cutting of benign hyperkeratotic lesion (e.g., corn or callus); two to four lesions." Because the code reads "two to four lesions," only one code would be reported, even though three corns were pared.

## Routine Foot Care

Codes 11055, 11056, and 11057 are sometimes referred to as part of the "routine foot care" codes. Since Medicare does not cover routine foot care, coders must understand the Medicare definition of "routine foot care" and the specific conditions for which foot care is covered by Medicare. Routine foot care can be submitted by any provider, but it is most often submitted by podiatrists.

Routine foot care, as defined by Medicare, is defined as the following:

- Cutting or removal of corns and calluses
- Clipping, trimming, or debridement of nails, including debridement of mycotic nails
- Shaving, paring, cutting, or removal of keratoma, tyloma, and heloma
- Nondefinitive simple, palliative treatments like shaving or paring of plantar warts that do not require thermal or chemical cautery and curettage

- Other hygienic and preventive maintenance care in the realm of self-care, such as cleaning and soaking the feet and the use of skin creams to maintain skin tone of both ambulatory and bedridden patients
- Any services performed in the absence of localized illness, injury, or symptoms involving the foot

Also included in the category of routine foot care are codes 11719, "Trimming of nondystrophic nails, any number;" and 11720–11721, "Debridement of nail(s) by any method." These codes require knowledge of how many toes have been treated, use of specific modifiers indicating the toes treated, and awareness of whether any comorbidities might affect the patient.

Medicare will pay for routine foot care:

- When the patient has a systemic disease, such as diabetes mellitus, peripheral vascular disease, and metabolic or neurologic diseases of sufficient severity that puts the patient at risk if the foot care is not completed by a professional.
- When the services are performed as a necessary and integral part of other covered services, such as services that are completed for the treatment of ulcers, wounds, or infections.
- When the care is for the treatment of warts on the foot, which is covered to that same extent as the treatment of warts located elsewhere on the body.
- When there is documentation of the class findings or presence of a qualifying systemic illness for the treatment of mycotic nails. **Class findings** (Class A, Class B, or Class C) reflect clinical findings of patients with severe peripheral involvement. Modifiers are assigned to the CPT code to indicate the category of class findings related to a particular patient. These modifiers are referred to as Q modifiers. Table 5-2 lists the class findings, along with the Q modifiers.

The preceding list is not exclusive for the specific conditions for which foot care is covered by Medicare. The complete listings of coverage guidelines can be found by searching online for Medicare Local Coverage Determinations (LCD). For example, to reference the LCD for routine foot care and debridement of nails found on the National Government Services (NGS) website, go to *www.NGSMedicare.com* and then search on the words "LCD for Routine Foot Care and Debridement of Nails (L33636)." This will display the full policy.

**TABLE 5-2** Class Findings and Q Modifiers

| Class | Description Including Modifier |
|---|---|
| Class A | Non-traumatic amputation of foot or integral skeletal portion thereof |
| | A Q7 modifier reflects one Class A finding. |
| Class B | Absent posterior tibial pulse |
| | Absent dorsalis pedis pulse |
| | Advanced trophic changes as evidenced by three or more of the following: |
| | 1. Increase or decrease in hair growth |
| | 2. Change in nail texture—thickening |
| | 3. Change in color—discoloring |
| | 4. Change in skin texture—thin or shiny |
| | 5. Change in skin color—redness |
| | A Q8 modifier is used if there are two Class B findings. |
| Class C | Claudication |
| | Temperature changes, such as cold feet |
| | Edema |
| | Abnormal spontaneous sensations in the feet, known as paresthesias |
| | Burning |
| | A Q9 modifier would be used if there is one Class B finding accompanied by two Class C findings. |

## Exercise 5.3—Check Your Understanding

### Codes 10021–11047

Fill in the blank with the correct term(s) or code to complete the sentence. Reference the CPT manual.

1. The handle part of the surgical knife is called the _____.

2. A complicated incision and drainage of a pilonidal cyst is reported with code _____.

3. _____ is the removal or cleansing of foreign objects or dirt to help in the healing process.

4. A puncture aspiration of a hematoma is reported with code _____.

5. A(n) _____ lesion is made up of an overgrowth of skin.

6. _____ is a procedure using a very fine needle to draw fluid out of the body.

7. The surgical cutting of an area and then the withdrawing of fluids from this area is a procedure known as a(n) _____.

8. A simple incision and removal of a foreign body from subcutaneous tissue is reported with code _____.

9. Debridement of infected skin, 8% of body surface, is reported with code _____.

10. The debridement of 12 sq cm of muscle and fascia is reported with code _____.

## Biopsy (11102–11107)

A **biopsy** is a procedure in which a sampling of tissue is removed for pathological examination to differentiate between malignant and benign tissue. A definitive diagnosis is determined by a biopsy.

In the integumentary system, the codes 11102 to 11107 are used for biopsies of skin. Codes for other anatomical sites can be located in the CPT Index under the term Biopsy.

As described in the notation that precedes code 11102, the coder should be aware that these codes are assigned when the procedure was independently performed to obtain tissue solely for diagnostic histopathologic examination or the procedure was unrelated or distinct from other procedures/services provided at that time. Read this extensive instructional notation in the CPT manual that explains how to report biopsies performed on different lesions or different sites. For example, the "instructional notation" states: "Biopsies performed on different lesions or different sites on the same date of service may be reported separately, as they are not considered components of other procedures."

For codes 11102 to 11107, one of three distinct biopsy techniques are described. The codes are differentiated as a tangential biopsy, a punch biopsy, or an incisional biopsy. For the complete definition of each type of biopsy, reference the instructional notation that appears in the CPT book prior to code 11102.

## Skin Tags (11200–11201)

**Skin tags** are skin growths that are found on many areas of the body, but usually the neck, axillae, and inguinal areas. A skin tag is a small lesion that can be brownish or flesh colored and is raised away from the body. Skin tags tend to grow with age but are almost always benign. Removal of skin tags is usually done with scissors, a scalpel, or ligature strangulation. Sometimes chemical or electrical cautery is also used.

Code 11200 is used to report the first 15 skin tags. The 11201 code is used for each additional 10 lesions or part thereof after the first 15.

**EXAMPLE:** Mr. Johnson was bothered by some small growths around his neck. His shirt collar was rubbing against some of them and irritating them. The doctor examined Mr. Johnson and said the growths were skin tags and could be removed at this visit. Mr. Johnson agreed. The doctor removed 25 skin tags.

The doctor coded the visit using 11200 (this code would be for the first 15 lesions removed) and then 11201 (this code with a quantity of 1 for the remaining 10 lesions) to report the remaining lesions.

## Shaving of Epidermal or Dermal Lesions (11300–11313)

**Shaving** a lesion involves removal of a lesion from the epidermal or dermal layer by a transverse incision or slicing to remove epidermal and dermal lesions. A full-thickness dermal excision does not occur during this type of removal. This technique is most often used when a lesion is raised from the skin; the scalpel blade is moved horizontally to remove the lesion.

The code range for this procedure is 11300–11313. To code from this range, the coder needs to know the anatomical site and the size of the lesion. When this procedure is performed, typically local anesthesia is used. To close the wound, chemical cauterization or electrocauterization is performed, and the wound is not closed via sutures. If the specimen is sent to pathology, diagnosis coding should wait until the final diagnosis determination is rendered before a code is assigned.

## Excision—Benign Lesions (11400–11471)

The code range 11400–11471 is used for removal of benign lesions. A **benign lesion** is one in which the cell growth is abnormal but not life-threatening. These types of lesions also are known as *nonmalignant tumors*.

The physician or provider may refer to the lesion as a *cyst*, a *neoplasm*, a *tumor,* or a *growth*. The coder might also see the terms *cicatricial, fibrous, inflammatory, congenital*, or *cystic*. These terms all refer to a benign lesion. The procedure note should be referenced with regard to type of lesion, anatomical site, method of lesion removal, number of lesions, and lesion size in centimeters. The lesion size, in addition to the size of the excised margins, should drive the code selection. The notation that appears before code 11400 states that the excision is defined as full-thickness removal of a lesion and the margins of tissue that surround the lesion that were also removed. To determine the size of tissue and lesion excised, the coder needs to know the clinical diameter of the lesion plus the margin required for excision.

When referencing the procedure note, attention should be drawn to whether the closure was intermediate or complex. These types of closures should be coded in addition to the excision, as explained in the paragraphs preceding code 11400 in the CPT manual. In some instances, layered closures pay more than the procedure itself. The procedure note should also indicate whether there was a skin graft or other type of closure, such as a flap. If the procedure note indicates that this is the case, review the procedural note to ensure that proper code selection was made.

## Excision—Malignant Lesion (11600–11646)

A **malignant lesion** is one in which the abnormal cell growth is found to be cancerous.

The terms that a coder might see in relation to a malignant lesion are *basal cell carcinoma, papillocystic carcinoma, squamous cell carcinoma*, and *melanoma of the skin*. It should be noted that an assumption is sometimes made that melanoma is present only in skin cancers. This is not true. Malignant melanoma can also be present in mucous membranes and the eye. This is rare, but it does occur.

Malignant tumors can grow deep and can also spread or metastasize. When a malignant growth or tumor spreads from one part of the body into another part of the body, it is called **metastasis**. This section of CPT should not be referenced if the tumor that is to be excised is part of deeper structures other than the skin. Other surgery sections within the Surgery chapter would be referenced for these types of deep excisions.

Code range 11600–11646 differentiates the codes relating to the site of the excision and the excised diameter of the lesion. Prior to code 11600, extensive notations instruct the coder to report separately each malignant lesion that is excised. The notation also states that the excision of the malignant lesion also includes a simple nonlayered closure. Intermediate or complex closures should be reported separately. Also note that, when there is a re-excision at a subsequent operative session to widen the margins, modifier 58 should be appended to the code if the procedure was performed during the postoperative period of the first excision.

Lunula

Free edge
of nail

Nail body

Cuticle

Nail bed

Bone

**FIGURE 5-2** Structures of the Fingernails
and Toenails

## Nails (11719–11765)

We briefly discussed routine nail care earlier in this chapter. For example, the trimming of nondystrophic nails falls into this category. Also in this section of CPT are codes for avulsion of nail plates, evacuation of a subungual hematoma, biopsy of the nail unit, and repair and reconstruction of the nail bed. The code set for these procedures is 11719–11765. Figure 5-2 illustrates the structure of nails.

The debridement section of the Surgery chapter goes into detail regarding the first several codes of the nails subsection of CPT, so they will not be repeated here. The codes for the Nails subsection can be assigned when the procedure performed is in relation to toenails or fingernails. Unless the code specifically makes a distinction, these codes can be used for procedures on either set of nails.

We will begin with codes 11730—avulsion of the nail plate, partial or complete, simple, single, and 11732—each additional nail plate (list these separately in addition to the code for primary procedure). In this procedure, the physician takes the nail away from the nail bed using blunt dissection. The procedure may involve the whole nail or a part of the nail. If more than one nail is done, the 11732 code is used for each additional nail.

> **EXAMPLE:** Joe presented to his podiatrist with painful great toes. The right great toe was inflamed and was painful with shoe gear on. The left great toe was not as inflamed, but there was a slight area of infection, and Joe stated that it was just as painful with shoe gear. After examination and discussion, it was decided that the doctor would perform an avulsion on each nail. On the right great toe, a complete avulsion was performed, as the nail bed was totally inflamed once the nail plate was lifted. The left great toe required only a partial avulsion, as the nail irritation occurred only on one side of the nail.

The podiatrist in our example would code 11730-T5 for the nail on the right great toe and 11732-TA for the nail on the left great toe, which required a partial avulsion.

Code 11740 reports an evacuation of a subungual hematoma. A **hematoma** is a collection of blood in a particular space or organ. A subungual hematoma is the collection of blood under the fingernail or toenail. Code 11740 reflects the draining of this blood collection. An electrocautery needle is used to pierce the nail so that the blood can drain.

Code 11750 is used when the nail and nail matrix are excised. This code represents a more permanent form of removal. Should the medical record documentation indicate that the nail plate was dissected away from the nail bed and that the entire tuft of the distal phalanx was removed, the coder should be using code 11750. The verbiage in a procedure note will help the coder in determining whether an avulsion or an excision took place. If there are any questions, the doctor needs to be asked to clarify what was actually done. In some cases, the doctor may refer to a wedge excision when trying to relieve problems with an ingrown toenail. A **wedge excision** is a procedure where the physician excises skin in the area of the ingrown portion of the nail in the hopes of freeing the nail enough to relieve pain. This is reported with code 11765—"Wedge excision of skin of nail fold."

Code 11755 reports a biopsy of a nail unit. Note that this code is a separate procedure code. When a biopsy is performed on a nail unit, any part of the nail can be sent to pathology, including the nail itself, along with samplings from the nail bed or soft tissue under the nail.

Repair and reconstruction of a nail bed are completed when the nail bed is damaged and is reported with codes 11760 and 11762.

During the repair of the nail bed, reported with code 11760, the defective nail is removed from the nail bed and the nail bed is sutured. A separate code for the suturing is not reported. Code 11762 reports a reconstruction of the nail bed by use of a skin graft, which is sutured in place. Repair may involve sutures. Reconstruction may involve grafting.

## Pilonidal Cyst (11770–11772)

Codes 11770–11772 report excisions of pilonidal cysts. A **pilonidal cyst** is a closed sac, located in the sacrococcygeal area, that contains epithelial tissue with hair nested within the sac. The hair is referred to as ingrown hair. Code 11770 reports a simple excision that involves the excision of the cyst and a sutured closure in a single layer. Codes 11771 and 11772 report more complex excisions. The coder needs to determine that the cyst has subcutaneous extensions to report codes 11771 and 11772. Code 11771 is reported for the excisions of cysts to the underlying fascia that are closed in several layers. Code 11772 reports the most complex excisions in which there are multiple subcutaneous extensions. Closure of these excisions varies depending on the size of the defect area to be closed. Because the CPT manual does not contain explicit definitions for the terms *simple*, *extensive*, and *complicated* listed in codes 11770 to 11772, it is best practice to develop specific coding guidelines for coders to follow. When assigning these codes, the coder should query the provider if the documentation contained in the record does not clearly state the extent of the excision.

## Introduction (11900–11983)

Codes 11900–11983 report various types of injections, procedures involving tissue expanders, and procedures involving drug delivery implants. Codes 11900 and 11901 report intralesional injections according to the number of lesions injected. During these procedures, the lesions are injected with a pharmacologic agent, such as a steroid or anesthetic solution, for therapeutic purposes. The instructional notation that follows code 11901 in the CPT manual states that these codes are not to be used for preoperative local anesthetic injections.

Codes 11920–11922 report procedures in which insoluble opaque pigments are injected into the skin to correct skin color defects. This is known as tattooing. The codes are differentiated according to the size of the area tattooed. Code 11920 reports an area of 6.0 sq cm or less, whereas code 11921 reports 6.1 to 20.0 sq cm. Code 11922 is used in conjunction with 11921 when greater than 20.0 sq cm is tattooed. Code 11922 is an add-on code used to report each additional 20.0 sq cm, or part thereof, tattooed above 20.0 sq cm. For example, if 25 sq cm is tattooed, code 11921 would be reported for the first 20 sq cm, and code 11922 would be reported for the additional 5 sq cm above the initial 20 sq cm reported with code 11921.

Codes 11950–11954 are used to report procedures that are completed to correct soft tissue defects or deformities by the injection of filling material into subcutaneous tissue. The injection is used to correct acne scars, facial wrinkles, or traumatic or postoperative defects. The injection fills in the dermal layer of tissue and thus decreases the depressions or defects of the skin. The codes are differentiated according to the amount of the injected substance. Code 11950 reports the injection of 1 cc or less, code 11951 reports 1.1 to 5.0 cc, code 11952 reports 5.1 to 10.0 cc, and code 11954 reports over 10.0 cc.

Codes 11960–11971 report procedures that involve the insertion, replacement, and removal of tissue expanders. Code 11960 reports the insertion of tissue expanders for sites other than the breast. Note the instructional notations that appear in the CPT manual following code 11960. Breast reconstruction with tissue expanders are reported with code 19357. At times, the tissue expanders are removed and then replaced with a permanent implant; this is reported using only one code, 11970. When a previously implanted tissue expander is removed and there is no insertion of an implant, code 11971 is reported. Reference the CPT manual and review the notations that follow code 11971. These notations provide the coder direction as it relates to the codes in which code 11971 is not reported with.

Procedures that involve the removal of implantable contraceptive capsules are reported with code 11976. This procedure involves the placement of subdermal capsules, typically in the upper arm, of a female patient. When an insertion of an implantable contraceptive capsule occurs, code 11981 is used. Removal of a capsule without the reinsertion of a capsule is reported with code 11976, whereas removal of a capsule with a reinsertion of a contraceptive capsules is reported with codes 11976 and 11981.

The remaining codes report the following:

- Code 11980 reports the implantation of a subcutaneous hormone pellet implanted below the skin.
- Code 11981 reports the insertion of a drug-delivery implant. A cylinder, containing a drug, is placed under the skin and sutured in place. The drug is then continuously released to the patient as prescribed. Reference the code 11981 in a CPT manual and review the notes that follow the code for further instruction on the coding for the manual preparation and insertion of devices and removal of implants.
- Code 11982 reports the removal of a nonbiodegradable drug delivery implant system. This code is reported when the system is not replaced. Reference code 11982 in a CPT manual and review the notes that follow the code for additional information that pertains to this code.
- Code 11983 reports the removal of a nonbiodegradable drug delivery implant with reinsertion of another. Only one code is reported for both the removal and reinsertion.

## Repair (12001–13160)

The **repair** of a wound is a surgical closure of an area that may have been injured as a result of trauma or surgery. Prior to selecting codes from the 12001–13160 repair codes, coders need to become familiar with the instructional notations that appear prior to code 12001. The instructional notation states that these codes can be used for any repair involving sutures, staples, or tissue adhesives, such as Dermabond. These codes can be used when the repair is a combination of these techniques, one of the techniques, or any of these techniques in combination with adhesive strips. For example, the lower layer of the skin may be sutured while the outermost layer is stapled.

The instructional notation also states that when chemical cauterization, electrocauterization, or wound closure utilizing adhesive strips is completed as the sole repair material that an additional code is not needed as it is included in the appropriate evaluation and management code.

Also defined in the CPT manual are three types of repair codes. The first is a **simple repair**. A simple repair is one in which there is a simple, single-layer closure of a laceration that does not go any deeper than the subcutaneous tissue. There is no involvement of muscle fascia or of deeper structures.

Simple repair codes are not billed separately when any other procedure is performed on the same wound because it is included in the other service. For example, lesion excisions include a simple closure, so the simple closure should not be billed separately.

An **intermediate repair** of a laceration or wound is defined as a repair of the epidermis, dermis, and subcutaneous tissue with a layered closure of one or more of the deeper layers of subcutaneous tissue and superficial (nonmuscle) fascia, in addition to the skin (epidermal and dermal) closure. The wound layers do not go deeper than nonmuscle fascia. If a layered closure is not performed, and there is a single-layer closure of a heavily contaminated wound, and the wound site requires extensive cleaning or removal of foreign materials, then codes 12031–12057 can be assigned. There must be documentation supporting the fact that there was extensive cleansing and/or heavy contamination of the site.

The last type of repair is a **complex repair**. A complex repair requires more than a layered closure (that is, scar revision, debridement, extensive undermining, stents, or retention sutures). Prior to the repair, it may be necessary to prepare the area by the creation of a limited defect or the debridement of complicated lacerations or avulsions. It should be noted that the following are not included as components of a complex repair and, therefore, are reported separately:

- Excision of benign lesion (codes 11400–11446)
- Excision of malignant lesion (codes 11600–11646)
- Excisional preparation of a wound bed (codes 15002–15005)
- Debridement of an open fracture or open dislocation (codes 11010–11012)

In the CPT manual following the definitions of the type of repairs, additional instructions are given for the reporting of repairs. The first instruction states that the size of a wound needs to be recorded in the medical record and reported in centimeters.

The second instruction gives coding instructions for when multiple wounds are repaired. As discussed, the code ranges are divided according to the type of repair: simple, intermediate, and complex. The codes are then further divided by anatomical site and the size of the repair. When multiple wounds are repaired, the coder needs to determine the wounds that fall into the same classification of repair: simple, intermediate, or complex. The coder then needs to review the wound in each classification of repair and determine which anatomic sites are involved. If the wounds are from the same classification and the same anatomical site, then the lengths of the repair for the specific classification are added together and reported with one code from the classification of repair.

**EXAMPLE:** Lindsay fell off her bike and was taken to the emergency department (ED) for evaluation. She was found to have a laceration on her left arm and left knee. After cleaning the area, the doctor determined that the two areas needed to be sutured. A simple 2.8-cm repair of the laceration on her left arm and a simple 4-cm repair of the laceration on her leg was completed.

To determine the correct code assignment, the coder should first note that the repairs are both simple repairs. Second, the coder needs to determine whether the anatomical sites, arm and leg, are both grouped into the same code descriptor within the CPT manual. Using the CPT index, the coder should reference the term "Integumentary system," then "repair," and then "simple" to code these repairs. The index lists codes 12001–12021. Referencing this range of codes, the coder notes that code 12001 reads, "Simple repair of superficial wounds of scalp, neck, axillae, external genitalia, trunk and/or extremities (including hands and feet); 2.5 cm or less." The coder can now conclude that the arm and leg are grouped into the same anatomic site: extremities. Now the coder should add together the lengths of the lacerations repaired. The laceration on the arm is 2.8 cm and the laceration on the knee is 4 cm. Because the procedure code is in the same category for both lacerations, the coder would add the two lengths together for a total of 6.8 cm. Code 12001 reads, "2.5 cm or less," and the laceration in the example is longer than 2.5 cm. Reviewing the codes in the CPT manual, the coder would notice that code 12002 reads the same as code 12001, except when you get to the semicolon (;). At that point, the coder would read it as 2.6 cm to 7.5 cm, which is where the sum of the two areas would fall. Therefore, the CPT code assignment for our example would be 12002.

The third coding instruction found for repair codes addresses decontamination and/or debridement. Although not discussed in the CPT manual, understanding types of wounds helps a coder assign the proper CPT code and also the correct ICD-10-CM, or diagnosis, code. Roman numerals are used to note each type of wound classification. The surgical wound classification is not assigned until after the procedure is completed. The various classes of wounds are:

- Class I—A **clean wound** has a very low infection rate (1–5%) and involves no inflammation or break in sterile technique.
- Class II—A **clean-contaminated wound** has a low infection rate (8–11%) and involves a minor break in sterile technique, but no inflammation is present. The wound may involve the genitourinary, respiratory, or digestive tracts.
- Class III—A **contaminated wound** involves a major break in sterile technique, and acute nonpurulent inflammation is present. The wound is less than four hours old, and the tracts mentioned in the Class II classifications may be involved, along with the biliary tract. There is usually spillage involved. This would be referenced as a Class III.

- Class IV—This class of wounds involves nonsterile conditions in which infection and inflammation are present. The wound is more than four hours old. The viscus would be perforated, and there may be a foreign body, fecal contamination, or necrotic tissue present. This is referred to as a **dirty and infected wound**.

Knowing the classifications will help the coder determine whether debridement of a wound should be reported. Debridement of a wound is considered bundled into the repair code. However, as outlined in the instructions in the CPT manual, a separate code for debridement should be reported in the following circumstances:

- Gross contamination of a site requires prolonged cleaning.
- Appreciable amounts of devitalized or contaminated tissue are removed.
- Debridement is carried out separately without immediate primary closure.

To report the debridement, documentation needs to reflect the extra time involved, along with details regarding any removal of necrotic or devitalized tissue. Therefore, the class of the wound will also support the reporting of the debridement.

The fourth instruction discussed in the CPT manual states that, for repairs of nerves, blood vessels, and tendons, the procedures should be reported from the appropriate body system within the CPT manual: nervous system, cardiovascular system, or musculoskeletal system. The instructional notation also states the following:

- Simple ligation of a vessel is part of any wound closure.
- Exploration of the wound also is included in the repair code, as is exploration of nerves, blood vessels, and tendons that may be exposed because of injury.

## Exercise 5.4—Check Your Understanding

### Surgical Procedures

Fill in each blank with the correct term(s) or code to complete the statement. Reference the CPT manual.

1. A 1-cc subcutaneous injection of collagen is reported with code _____.
2. To examine and differentiate between malignant and benign tissue, a(n) _____ of the lesion would be taken and sent to pathology.
3. Code _____ would be used to report partial avulsion of the nail plate for a single nail.
4. A surgical closure of an area that may have been damaged as a result of trauma or injury, or even as a result of surgery, is called a(n) _____.
5. A(n) _____ has a very low infection rate and involves no inflammation or break in sterile technique.
6. Debridement of two nails is reported with code _____.
7. An excision of a malignant lesion of the arm with an excised diameter of 2.2 cm is reported with code _____.
8. Evacuation of a subungual hematoma is reported with code _____.
9. Repair of a nail bed is reported with code _____.
10. Excision of a pilonidal cyst, complicated is reported with code _____.

## Adjacent Tissue Transfer or Rearrangement (14000–14350)

As we discussed earlier, the skin is the safeguard for the internal organs of the body against infection and other outside elements that can cause damage. When the skin is damaged in such a way that suturing or stapling cannot be performed to close a wound, a physician may perform an adjacent tissue transfer. **Adjacent tissue transfer** is exactly what its name implies: healthy tissue is manipulated or rearranged—transferred—from a site close to or next to an area that is open because of disease or injury.

Techniques indicating adjacent tissue transfer or rearrangement that may be mentioned in an operative note include rotation, Z-plasty, W-plasty, VY-plasty, advancement, Rhombic flaps, and double pedicle flaps. A **pedicle flap** is a flap of skin that hangs on a stem of skin that contains a blood vessel. This skin flap is rotated around and sutured to an adjacent site to supply blood to the new site until the injury or diseased site is healed.

When reporting codes from the 14000–14350 series, the coder would not report debridement codes or repair codes separately, because these services are included in the 14000–14350 series. Also included in this code set are the excisions of lesions. If the adjacent tissue transfer or rearrangement was performed at a different operative setting from an incision, a 58 modifier would need to be appended to indicate a staged or related procedure. If a skin graft is performed, and the type of graft performed is not noted in the 14000–14350 code set, the graft may be billed in addition to one of the 14000 codes. The coder would need to research the codes being used carefully to be sure that the proper code selection was made.

To assign a code from this series properly, the coder needs to know the site and the size of the defect in square centimeters.

## Surgical Preparation (15002–15005)

The coder will need to have an understanding of certain terms before being able to code procedures from the Surgical Preparation subsection of the Integumentary System section. Understanding terminology associated with graft procedures is essential to code from this subsection of the Surgery chapter. When surgeons refer to the **defect site** or **recipient site**, they are referring to the area that will receive a graft. This site is in need of repair because of lesion removal, a burn or other injury, or the graft itself. The **donor site** is the area that provides the tissue used to make the repair.

When coding grafts, a coder must select the code very carefully by reviewing all documentation available. Some codes include the repair of the donor site, but most codes do not, so an additional code is allowed when repair of the donor site is necessary. The coder should also keep in mind that a lesion excision is not reported separately if adjacent tissue transfer or rearrangement is performed at the site. The excision is considered an integral part of graft procedures. Other terminology that the coder may encounter and have a need to understand are *flaps*, *free skin graft*, *pedicle graft*, and *adjacent tissue transfer* or *rearrangement*. We will be explaining these terms as we progress through this chapter.

## Skin Replacement Surgery and Skin Substitutes

A **graft** is a section of tissue that is moved from one site to another in an effort to heal or repair a defect. There are different types of grafts that are performed, depending on several factors. A **homograft**, or **homologous graft**, involves tissue from an individual of the same species. An **autogenous graft** is a type of graft where tissue is taken from one part of a person's body and put on another part of the same person's body. A **heterodermic graft** is a type of graft where tissue from a different species is used for the repair. Other terms that a coder might encounter would be *free graft* and *split-skin graft*. A **free graft** is one in which the tissue is totally freed from its original site. A **split-skin graft**, or **split-thickness graft**, is one in which the tissue is about half or more of the thickness of the skin (i.e., the epidermis with a bit of the dermis layer).

To begin to code from this subsection, the coder needs to know the type of graft, the graft's location, and the size, in square centimeters, of the defect that is going to be repaired.

The 15002–15005 codes are the surgical preparation codes and are used for the preparation of a recipient site. The surgical preparation of a recipient site involves cleaning and excising tissue to a level where there is a healthy vascular bed on which to set the donor graft and promote healing. An excisional preparation of the skin is necessary to receive the graft: the surgeon excises tissue, scars, or lesions to the point where a healthy vascular tissue bed is exposed to receive the graft. In order for a graft to be successful, the site should be free of debris and infection, have a good blood supply source, and bleeding needs to be controlled.

The cleansing and excising of tissue can involve lesion removal or release of scar tissue that may be causing excessive tightening. When scar tissue is released, an open wound may result, which would require some type of closing.

Table 5-3 summarizes the code descriptions for codes 15002, 15003, 15004, and 15005.

**TABLE 5-3** Surgical Preparation (15002–15005)

| Instructions for Use of Codes |
| --- |
| Review the CPT manual and note that code 15002 reports the preparation or creation of recipient site by excision. This code is used for defects that occur on the trunk, arms or legs. To properly code the coder must identify the size or % of the defect. When assigning this code the coder needs to identify that the size of the excision is documented or that the percentage of the body area of the wound is recorded. This code can be used alone or with code 15003. |
| Review the CPT manual for the full description of code 15003. This code is an add-on code and is only reported when the documentation records the size of the area is greater than 100 sq cm. Code 15003 must be used as a second or greater listed code in conjunction with code 15002. Note that code 15003 can be used multiple times based on the size of the area treated. |
| Like code 15002 code 15004 reports the preparation or creation of recipient site by excision. This code reports the same procedure as code 15002 except that the site of the procedure for code 15004 is the face, scalp, eyelids, mouth, neck, ears, orbits, genitalia, hands, feet, and/or multiple digits. Review the CPT manual for the full code description. |
| Code 15005 is reported as an add-on code to 15004, therefore code 15005 is never reported alone. The number of times that code 15005 is reported is based on the size of the area treated. Review the CPT manual for the full description of the code. |

**EXAMPLE:** A 62-year-old woman was admitted from the Emergency Department with second- and third-degree burns received while cooking dinner for her grandchildren. Her arms were burned. A total of 10% of her body surface suffered from second- and third-degree burns. Under general anesthesia, the eschar was excised to viable subcutaneous tissue. A total of 125 sq cm was excised. The area was prepped for immediate skin grafting.

Code 15002 would be used to report the first 100 sq cm, and add on code 15003 reports the remaining 25 sq cm.

## Grafts (15040–15278)

To select a code properly from the Grafts subsection of CPT, the coder would need to know the following:

- Location of the defect
- Size in centimeters of the defect
- The type of graft (flap, free, pedicle, etc.)

The best manner in which to determine the location, size, and type of graft is for the coder to review the patient's history, the procedure note, and any additional documentation that is present in the patient's record. Keep in mind that the size of the defect must be known for the assignment of certain codes. For adults and children 10 years of age and older the measurement of 100 sq cm is used in the code descriptions. For infants and children younger than 10 years of age the percentages of body surface area is used to describe the defect area. These measurements apply to the defect area only. For example, the description for code 15100 reads: "Split-thickness autograft, trunk, arms, legs; first 100 sq cm or less, or 1% of body area of infants and children (except 15050)."

An **autograft** is a type of graft that involves only one individual; the donor and recipient sites are from the same individual. Autograft codes are described in Table 5-4.

**TABLE 5-4** Autograft (15040–15157)

| Definitions of Grafts and Use of Codes |
|---|
| Reference the CPT manual and note that code 15040 is used when skin is harvested for a tissue-cultured skin autograft. This code is only used when the area is 100 sq cm or less. This is essential that the documentation found in the patient's records support the size of the area stated in the code. Do not report this code if the area is over 100 sq cm. |
| A **pinch graft** is a smaller form of autograft. Code 15050 reports a single graft or multiple pinch grafts, except those completed on the face, that are completed for a defect of up to a defect size of a 2 cm diameter. This code is only used when the graft is completed to cover a small open area. Reference the code in the CPT manual for examples. |
| Code 15100 reports a split-thickness autograft. To use this code the autograft must be completed on the trunk, arms, and/or legs. The size of the area treated is specified as the first 100 sq cm or less, or 1% of body area of infants and children. Review the CPT manual for additional instructions for this code. **Split-thickness autograft** contains only part of the dermal layer, but the epidermis and dermis would be included. |
| Note that code 15101 is an add-on code that reports each additional 100 sq cm, or each additional 1% of body area of infants and children, or part thereof. This code cannot be reported alone and must be reported with code 15100. The number of times that code 15101 is based on the size of the area treated. |
| **Epidermal autograft** is a graft of the epidermal layer only. Code 15110 is used to report epidermal autografts that are completed on the trunk, arms and/or legs. It is important for coders to note that this code reports only the first 100 sq cm or less or 1% of the body area of infants and children. If the size of the area treated is larger the use of add-on code 15111 should occur. |
| Code 15111 is an add-on code for code 15110 and is reported for each additional 100 sq cm, or each additional 1% of body area of infants and children, or part thereof when the area treated is larger than the area stated in code 15110. Code 15111 is used as an add-on code to code 15110 and code 15111 must be reported after code 15110. |
| As with code 15110, code 15115 reports epidermal autografts. The differences is that code 15115 reports grafts of the face, scalp, eyelids, mouth, neck, ears, orbits, genitalia, hands, feet, and/or multiple digits. The size of the area treated is specified as the first 100 sq cm or less, or 1% of body area of infants and children. |
| Code 15116 is the add-on code to be used with code 15115 and is used to report each additional 100 sq cm, or each additional 1% of body area of infants and children, or part thereof. To report this code the coders must verify the size of the area treated and use code 15116 for procedures in which the size of the area treated exceeds the size stated for code 15115. |
| A split-thickness autograft of the face, scalp, eyelids, mouth, neck, ears, orbits, genitalia, hands, feet, and/or multiple digits is reported with code 15120. This code is used for the first 100 sq cm or less, or 1% of body area of infants and children. When the size of the area treated exceeds the size listed in code 15120 the add-on code of 15121 should be listed as an additional code. |
| Code 15121 is an add-on code for code 15120 and is used to report each additional 100 sq cm, or each additional 1% of body area of infants and children, or part thereof when the size of the area treated exceeds what is stated in code 15120. Code 15121 must be used in conjuction with code 15120. Note: This add-on code should be checked against codes 67961–67975 if the site of the graft is the eyelids. |
| Code 15130 reports a dermal autograft of the trunk, arms, and/or legs. Code 15130 reports the first 100 sq cm or less, or 1% of body area of infants and children. The documentation of the size of the area treated must align to the size description stated in the CPT manual for this code. Coders should note that a **dermal autograft** involves only the dermal tissue in the harvest process. |
| Code 15131 is an add-on code for code 15130 and it is used to report each additional 100 sq cm, or each additional 1% of body area of infants and children, or part thereof. Code 15131 is not be reported alone, it must be reported with code 15130. Prior to reporting these codes the coder needs to ensure that the record documentation supports the reporting of both of these codes. |
| Code 15135 reports a dermal autograft of the face, scalp, eyelids, mouth, neck, ears, orbits, genitalia, hands, feet, and/or multiple digits. This code is only used for the first 100 sq cm or less, or 1% of body area of infants and children. When the size of the area treated is larger than the area stated in code 15135, code 15135 is to be reported with code(s) 15136. |
| Review the CPT manual and note that code 15136 is an add-on code that is used with code 15135 for each additional 100 sq cm, or each additional 1% of the body area of infants and children, or part thereof. Code 15136 is reported only with 15135 and code 15136 can not be reported alone. |

*(continues)*

**TABLE 5-4** (continued)

| Definitions of Grafts and Use of Codes |
|---|
| Reference the CPT manual and note that code 15150 reports a tissue-cultured skin autograft, involving the skin of the trunk, arms or legs. Please note that code 15150 is used only for the first 25 sq cm or less. When a larger area is treated the add-on codes of 15151 and 15152 are used with code 15150. Reference the CPT manual for the full code description.<br><br>A **tissue-cultured epidermal autograft** is a type of graft where tissue is harvested in a split-tissue autograft and the cultured tissue is grafted back to the donor. |
| Code 15151 is an add-on code that is used with code 15150 when the area of the autograft treated exceeds 25 sq cm. Code 15151 is used to report an additional 1 sq cm to 75 sq cm. Documentation in the record must justify the use of this add-on code.<br><br>Note: This code can be reported only once per session. |
| Code 15152 is an add-on code that is reported with codes 15150 and 15151, when the size of the area treated exceeds the size of the descriptions found in codes 15150 and 15151. Code 15152 reports each additional 100 sq cm, or each additional 1% of body area of infants and children, or part thereof. Code 15152 is only used when codes 15150 and 15151 are reported. Review these three codes in the CPT manual. |
| Code 15155 is similar to code 15150 as both codes report tissue-cultured skin autograft. The difference is that code 15155 specifies that this code is for grafts of the face, scalp, eyelids, mouth, neck, ears, orbits, genitalia, hands, feet, and/or multiple digits. Code 15155 is for the first 25 sq cm or less. If a larger area is grafted the use of add-on codes 15156 and 15157 may be needed. |
| Code 15156 is an add-on code that is used with code 15155 when more than 25 sq cm are grafted. Code 15156 reports an additional 1 cm to 75 sq cm. Code 15156 must be used with code 15155 to be valid. Documentation must justify the area grafted when using both codes. 1 sq cm to 75 sq cm. (List separately in addition to the code for the primary procedure.)<br><br>Note: This code should be used only once per session. |
| Code 15157 is an add-on code that is used when the area grafted exceeds the area described in codes 15155 and 15156. Code 15157 documents each additional 100 sq cm, or each additional 1% of body area of infants and children, or part thereof. Code 15157 is used as the third listed code after codes 15155 and 15156 when the documentation supports the total size of the graft completed. |

## Exercise 5.5—Check Your Understanding

### Autograft Coding—Table 5-4

Fill in the blank with the correct term(s) or code to complete the sentence.

1. Epidermal autograft, back—75 sq cm
   _____

2. Split-thickness autograft, calf—200 sq cm
   _____

3. Tissue-cultured epidermal autograft, cheek—25 sq cm _____

4. Pinch graft, tip of index finger—1 cm
   _____

5. Dermal autograft, neck—85 sq cm
   _____

6. A small-type graft, or _____, is used to cover small ulcers or the tip of digits.

7. The _____ autograft involves only the dermal layer in the harvest process.

8. This type of autograft is a type of graft in which tissue is harvested in a split-tissue autograft and the cultured tissue is grafted back to the donor. This is called a(n) _____ autograft.

9. What code(s) are assigned when a 32-sq-cm epidermal autograft of the back is performed? _____

10. What code(s) are assigned when a 145-sq-cm split-thickness graft is performed on the left leg and the trunk? _____

**Acellular dermal replacement** is a skin substitute for areas that require a temporary closure. Porous lattice fibers and a synthetic substance are combined to make the replacement. A surgeon will excise a full or partial thickness until viable tissue is reached. Then the surgeon will cover the open wound with an acellular dermal replacement graft until skin autografts can be placed. Table 5-5 defines the codes used for acellular dermal replacement.

**TABLE 5-5** Full Thickness Grafts and Skin Substitute Grafts (15200–15278)

| Instructions for Use of Codes |
| --- |
| Code 15200 reports a full thickness graft, free, including direct closure of donor site, trunk. This is important for the coder to note that this code only reports a graft of 20 sq cm or less. If a graft of a larger size is completed than add-on code 15201 should be used in conjunction with this code. <br><br> A **full thickness graft** contains a portion of both the epidermis and dermis of the donor site with a section that is equal, continuous, and totally free for transfer. |
| Code 15201 is an add-on code that is used with code 15200 to report each additional 20 sq cm, or part thereof beyond what is reported using code 15200. If the graft is over 20 sq cm than code 15200 is listed first followed by code 15201. The coder needs to review the documentation to determine how many times code 15201 would be reported. Remember code 15201 reports each additional 20 sq cm. |
| Code 15220 reports a full thickness graft, free, including direct closure of donor site involving the scalp, arms, and/or legs. Prior to assigning this code the coder should verify the location of the graft and ensure that it involves the scalp, arms and or legs. The coder should also note that this code reports 20 sq cm or less. If a larger graft is completed than add-on code 15221 will need to be assigned as additional code(s). |
| Code 15221 is an add-on code that is used with code 15220 for each additional 20 sq cm, or part thereof when grafts over 20 sq cm are completed. Code 15221 is never reported alone and must be reported as a secondary code to code 15220 when the documentation supports the size of the graft described in the codes. |
| Code 15240 reports a full thickness graft, free, including direct closure of donor site. The sites for this code are the forehead, cheeks, chin, mouth, neck, axillae, genitalia, hands, and/or feet. As with code 15220 this code reports grafts of 20 sq cm or less. The coder needs to ensure that when selecting this code the site and size in the documentation are reflected in the code description. Reference the CPT manual for the description. <br><br> Note: CPT code 15050 should be referenced if a graft is performed on a fingertip. <br><br> CPT codes 26560–26562 should be referenced if repair is performed on a web finger. |
| Code 15241 is an add-on code that is used with code 15240 to report each additional 20 sq cm, or part thereof when the graft completed is larger than 20 sq cm. Code 15240 is to be listed first followed by code 15241 to accurately reflect the size of the graft as stated in the documentation for the procedure. Note that code 15241 can be reported more than once depending on the size of the graft. |
| Code 15260 is similar to codes 15200, 15220, and 15240 in that they all report a full thickness graft, free, including direct closure of donor site. The codes are differentiated by site and code 15260 reports the sites of the nose, ears, eyelids, and/or lips. Code 15260 reports a graft of 20 sq cm or less. When larger grafts are performed code 15261 is used with code 15260. |
| Code 15261 is an add-on code that is reported with code 15260 for each additional 20 sq cm, or part thereof. The procedural note needs to clearly reflect the size of the graft for this code to be assigned with code 15260. |
| Codes 15271–15278 reports the application of skin substitute grafts. Codes are differentiated by site of graft and wound surface area. Codes 15273, 15274, 15277, and 15278 designate specific criteria for body area of infants and children. Coders need to reference the CPT manual for the full description of these codes and the instructional notation that follows the heading entitled Skin Substitute Grafts. |

## Exercise 5.6—Check Your Understanding

**Full Thickness Grafts**

Code the following:

1. Full-thickness free graft, trunk—60 sq cm
_____

2. Full-thickness free graft with direct closure of donor site, trunk—10 sq cm _____

3. Full-thickness free graft, lip—10 sq cm
_____

4. Full-thickness free graft of scalp, including direct closure of donor site, scalp—17 sq cm
_____

## Exercise 5.6 (*continued*)

5. Full-thickness free graft, chin—15 sq cm
_____

6. Free, full thickness graft, right side of nose and upper lip—10 sq cm _____

7. Free, full thickness graft, forehead, cheek, neck, and hands (all on the left side)—28 sq cm _____

8. Free, full thickness graft, back—40 sq cm
_____

For each of the following statements, say whether the statement is true or false.

9. The supply of skin substitute grafts should be reported separately in conjunction with 15271 to 15278. _____

10. For a biologic implant for soft tissue reinforcement, use code 15777 in conjunction with the code for the primary procedure. _____

## Exercise 5.7—Check Your Understanding

**Code Range 15271–15278**

Complete the following statements.

1. Code 15272 is used in conjunction with code _____.

2. Code 15274 is used in conjunction with code _____.

3. Do not report codes 15275 and 15276 in conjunction with code 15277 and code _____.

4. Use code 15276 in conjunction with code _____.

5. Do not report codes 15271 and 15272 in conjunction with code 15273 and code _____.

Sometimes grafts are made up of material that is nonhuman, such as pig tissue. These grafts are known as **xenografts** and are temporary coverings used until appropriate, more compatible material is available. The location and size of the defect determine code selection and are reported with codes 15271–15278.

### Flaps (Skin and/or Deep Tissues) (15570–15738) and Other Flaps and Grafts (15740–15778)

Coding from this code range can be challenging, so attention to the detail in the code descriptions is necessary. In the CPT manual, several notations appear before code 15570. Locate these notations that appear before the code 15570 and follow the heading entitled Flaps (Skin and/or Deep Tissue). The first sentence informs the coder that the regions that are listed for this code range refer to the recipient site when a flap is being attached in a transfer or to a final site. The second sentence informs the coder that the regions listed refer to a donor site when a tube is formed for later transfer or when a delay of flap occurs prior to the transfer. Reference the CPT manual for additional notations that are found in this section of the manual.

Codes 15570–15576 report the formation of either a direct or tubed pedicle flap that is used to reconstruct the defect area. Codes 15600–15630 are reported when the direct or tubed pedicle flap is sectioned several weeks following the reconstruction of the defect. Codes 15733–15738 are described by donor site and are reported when the defect is repaired using a muscle, muscle and skin, or a fasciocutaneous flap.

The remaining graft codes, 15740–15778 in the Flaps subsection of the Integumentary section, are for other types of flaps and grafts, which include island pedicle, composite, and punch grafts (for hair transplants).

The coder should be very careful when coding flaps, grafts, and tissue transfers. As was discussed earlier, all documentation on the current procedure should be reviewed, along with any staged procedures that were performed. Review of these notes will allow for proper code assignment.

Table 5-6 summarizes flap-type repairs.

**TABLE 5-6** Flap-Type Repairs (15570–15738)

| Code(s) | Description |
|---|---|
| 15570 to 15576 | Codes 15570 to 15576 report the formation of direct or tubed pedicle. All of these code descriptions are with or without transfer. The differentiating factor for these codes is the site of the procedure. Reference the CPT manual prior to code 15570 for additional information that applies to this code range. |
| 15600 to 15630 | Codes 15600 to 15630 report delay of flap or sectioning of flap (division and inset). The codes are differentiated by site. Reference the CPT manual for the specific sites listed for each code. |
| 15650 | Code 15650 reports the intermediate transfer of any pedicle flap. This code description is not specific to any one location. |
| 15730 | In order to report this code the coder needs to ensure that the documentation states that the flap is a midface flap and there is preservation of the vascular pedicle(s). |
| 15731 | In order to report this code the documentation needs to identify a forehead flap with preservation of vascular pedicle. |
| 15733 to 15738 | Codes 15733 to 15738 report a muscle, myocutaneous, or fasciocutaneous flap. The codes are differentiated by site. Reference the CPT manual for the specific sites. |

# Other Procedures (15780–15879)

There is an array of codes in this subsection that should be reviewed. This subsection includes dermabrasion, chemical peel, rhytidectomy, blepharoplasty, and suture removal. Codes in this subsection are used by plastic surgeons and dermatologists, but they can be used by other providers as well.

Codes 15851–15854 involve suture removal and dressing change. The codes delineate if anesthesia was used or if no anesthesia was used. For example, codes 15851 and 15852 state that anesthesia was required to complete the procedure. These codes should *not* be used unless the patient received anesthesia as described in the code. If a primary procedure is being performed, or the patient is returned to the operating room for complications of a surgery that require the incision to be reopened, these codes are not to be used.

# Pressure Ulcers (Decubitus Ulcers) (15920–15999)

**Ulcers** are erosions of the skin in which the tissue becomes inflamed and is then lost. In patients who have continuous pressure in an area such as the elbows, buttocks, coccyx, hands, or wrists, the limited circulation eventually causes a breakdown, and an ulcer is formed. A **decubitus ulcer** is the result of continuous pressure in an area that eventually limits or stops the oxygen flow to the area, causing a sore. This can sometimes be referred to as a *pressure ulcer* or *bedsore*.

Codes 15920–15999 report procedures in which the physician excises the ulcer and cleanses the area until viable tissue is found. The area is then prepared for a flap or skin graft. If the underlying bone is removed before the area is repaired, the coder would select the excision code that lists the term **ostectomy**, which denotes that bone was removed. When reviewing claims, insurance companies look for the stage of the ulcer. This is reflected in documentation and the proper assignment of the ICD-10-CM diagnosis code. The coder should verify that medical documentation supports the procedural and diagnostic codes selected.

# Burns, Local Treatment (16000–16036)

A **burn** is an injury to body tissue that is a result of heat, flame, sun, chemicals, radiation, and/or electricity. The procedure codes in code range 16000–16036 encompass only local treatment of the burned surface. If the burn patient needs further related medical treatment, evaluation and management codes are used to report the management of the victim.

The degree of the burn also needs to be understood by the coder. A **first-degree burn** is the least severe burn and presents no danger to the patient. Code 16000—"Initial treatment, first-degree burn, when no more than local treatment is required," would be assigned to simple treatment of a burn. Simple treatment includes application of cream and/or a dressing. Documentation should indicate the location and size of the area treated.

**Second-degree burns** are partial-thickness burns that form blisters. A second-degree burn, if not properly treated, could result in an infection at the burn site. **Third-degree burns** also are called *full-thickness burns*. The burn goes to the subcutaneous skin layers or further. Documentation should always indicate the location, size, and depth of the burn.

Code range 16020–16030 is assigned based on body surface area treated and reports the initial or subsequent dressings and/or debridement of partial-thickness burns. The coder would need to know the percentage of body surface area affected to assign the correct code. Codes in this range address cleansing the area, as well as some debridement and dressing application. These codes can be billed each time the service is performed.

Codes 16035, "Escharotomy; initial incision," and 16036, "Each additional incision" (list separately, in addition to the code for the primary procedure) are also reported from this range of codes. Note that code 16036 is an add-on code. In the CPT manual following code 16036 a notation appears that alerts the coder that for debridement or curettement of a burn wound the coder should reference codes 16020–16030.

**Escharotomy** is the removal of necrosed tissue of severely burned skin. This procedure involves the physician releasing the underlying tissue. Repairs are made using flaps, grafts, or tissue advancement, which are separately billable.

> **EXAMPLE:** Dennis received second-degree burns to his left arm and hand, including three fingers. The burns were received while attending to a campfire on a recent camping trip. He is here for a dressing change on this area.
>
> The bandages were removed after the arm and hand were submerged in the whirlpool. The area is healing nicely. The burn area was carefully cleansed and ointment was applied to it, and impregnated gauze was laid over the same area. The 4 × 4s were placed over the gauze, and then Kerlix was fluffed and applied to the arm and hand prior to the Ace wraps. Patient will return in two days for a dressing change.

The doctor should report services rendered in the example above using code 16025.

# Destruction (17000–17286)

**Destruction** describes a procedure that totally destroys or removes a lesion. In this subsection of CPT, *destruction* refers to cryosurgery, laser, electrosurgery, surgical curettement, or chemosurgery. These procedures can take place alone or in conjunction with each other.

The coder will need to determine whether the type of lesion is benign, premalignant, or malignant. This determination will help the coder in deciding which code to select.

Locate codes 17000 to 17003 in the CPT manual. Note that code 17000 can be used with code 17003 since code 17003 is an add-on code for 17000. Following code 17003 a notation appears that states: "Use 17003 in conjunction with 17000." Now locate code 17004 in the CPT manual and review the notation following the code that states: "Do not report 17004 in conjunction with 17000–17003." When you are coding for lesions up to and including 14 lesions, codes 17000 and 17003 are used. When there is destruction of 15 or more lesions, code 17004 is used.

> **EXAMPLE:** Megan presented to Dr. Barnes with 13 plantar warts to be treated. There were six warts on the right foot and seven warts on the left. Dr. Barnes used a combination of cryosurgery and surgical curettement to treat these warts.

Dr. Barnes reported her services using 17000 × 1 (quantity is always 1 for this code) and 17003 × 12 for each additional lesion. Now, if we modify this same example, treating 15 warts instead of 13, Dr. Barnes will report her charges as follows: 17004 × 1 (the quantity is always 1 for this code). Table 5-7 summarizes codes 17000, 17003, and 17004.

The next range of codes, 17106–17108, involves destruction of cutaneous vascular proliferative lesions. These codes are reported when the destruction occurs with a laser and does not involve invasive procedures, such as cutting. The coder needs to know the size of the area in square centimeters.

**TABLE 5-7** Destruction of Lesions (17000–17004)

| Code | Description |
|------|-------------|
| 17000 | Code 17000 reports the destruction of premalignant lesions other than skin tags or cutaneous vascular proliferative lesions. The various types of destruction used are listed in the CPT code description. Reference the CPT manual for the listing. This code is used to report the destruction of the first lesion. |
| 17003 | Code 17003 is an add-on code and is used to report the second through fourteenth lesions, each. Code 17003 is not to be reported without using code 17000 as the first listed code. |
| 17004 | Code 17004 reports the destruction of 15 or more premalignant lesions. For this code to be used the documentation must report the number of lesions. |

Codes 17110 and 17111 are used to report the destruction of benign lesions other than skin tags or cutaneous vascular proliferative lesions. The procedural note needs to state specifically that the lesions destroyed were these types of lesions. These codes are never reported together. The code 17110 is for the first 14 lesions. After that, code 17111 would be reported for 15 or more lesions. Following code 17111, an instructional notation appears in the CPT manual that states: "For destruction of extensive cutaneous neurofibroma over 50–100 lesions, see 0419T, 0420T."

For code 17250—Chemical cauterization of granulation tissue (i.e., proud flesh)—the provider applies a chemical substance (e.g., silver nitrate) to destroy the granulation tissue. Referencing the instructional notations that follow code 17250, the coder is instructed that this code is not to be reported with removal or excision codes for the same lesion, when chemical cauterization is used to achieve wound hemostasis, or reported in conjunction with codes 97597, 97598, and 97602 for the same lesion.

## Destruction, Malignant Lesions, Any Method (17260–17286)

Destruction of a malignant lesion is coded from this section. A malignant lesion contains cells that are showing abnormal growth. These lesions also are referred to as *cancerous* lesions. To assign the proper code from this subsection, the coder needs to know the location of the lesions and the size of the lesions with the margins of the tissue before excision or destruction. The size of the lesion needs to be expressed in centimeters to select a code.

> **EXAMPLE:** Casey was diagnosed with a melanoma on his hand, which measured 1.2 cm. Due to the lesion's location, it was decided to remove it using laser surgery. The lesion and a small area around it were treated. In total, the area measured 1.4 cm.

Code 17272 was used to report this procedure.

## Mohs Micrographic Surgery (17311–17315)

**Mohs micrographic surgery** is a type of chemosurgery. A chemical agent, which acts as a chemical fixative, is placed onto the lesion before it is excised. This chemical fixative allows the surgeon to access the extent of the tumor and the

## Exercise 5.8—Check Your Understanding

### Coding Destruction of Lesions

Using a CPT manual, indicate the correct code(s) for the destruction of malignant lesions. If the diagnostic statement specifies the side, use the modifier RT or LT.

1. Chemosurgery on left hand—0.4 cm
   _____

2. Laser surgery, nose—2.0 cm _____
3. Cryosurgery, trunk—4.8 cm _____
4. Cryosurgery, feet—1.0 cm on left _____
   1.1 cm on right _____

5. Laser surgery, upper lip—0.5 cm _____
6. Surgical curettement, back—3.4 cm _____
7. Laser surgery, left ear—0.1 cm _____
8. Cryosurgery, right leg—2.7 cm _____
9. Chemosurgery, scalp—1.8 cm _____
10. Laser surgery, eyebrow—1.0 cm _____

margins surrounding it. Once the tumor is excised, the surgeon also acts as a pathologist as the tissue samples are divided and examination is performed. These codes are not applicable if the surgeon does not act in both capacities.

Separate procedure codes can be assigned if a repair is performed. If Mohs surgery is performed the same day as a biopsy, and no prior pathology confirmation of a malignant diagnosis was made, the Mohs surgery would be reported with the diagnostic skin biopsy code(s) and the frozen section pathology code (88331) with a modifier 59. A coder can determine the correct code by knowing the stage performed, as noted in the documentation, and the number of specimens obtained.

## Other Procedures (17340–17999)

These procedures tend to fall under the term *cosmetic*. This means that most insurance carriers do not recognize these CPT codes for payment because they are performed at the patient's request and not for medical necessity.

## Breast (19000–19499)

The coding in this subsection involves only unilateral procedures. Depending on the insurance carrier, a modifier 50, RT (right) and/or LT (left), might be needed if the procedure is performed bilaterally.

If a biopsy is done on the same lesion that is excised, the biopsy is *not* coded separately. The biopsy is considered inclusive to the lesion removal.

### Incision (19000–19030)

Code 19000—"Puncture aspiration of cyst of breast"—involves a physician inserting a needle into the breast cyst and drawing cyst fluid into a syringe. Each cyst is reported separately after the first cyst by using code 19001. The 19001 is an add-on code and must be used in conjunction with code 19000.

> **EXAMPLE:** Mrs. Page presented for a puncture aspiration of the breast. Dr. Calvin explained to her that there were three cysts that they would be aspirating fluid from. The first cyst was at the "2 o'clock" position, the second cyst was at "3 o'clock," and the third was at "6 o'clock." Mrs. Page tolerated the procedure well.

Dr. Calvin reported his services in this example using codes 19000 × 1, 19001 × 2.

A **mastotomy** is also known as a surgical incision of the breast. Code 19020 involves an incision over the tissue where a suspicious abscess, or tissue that might be suspicious, might be located. The abscess would be drained and sent for culture.

Code 19030— "Injection procedure only for mammary ductogram or galactogram"—involves injection of contrast material for radiographic study. A **mammary ductogram** is the study done on the mammary duct to the mammary gland that secretes milk from the breast. When reporting this code, remember to include the radiological piece of the procedure.

### Excision (19081–19126)

Breast biopsies, cryosurgical ablation of fibroadenoma, and nipple exploration are reported with code range 19081 to 19126. A biopsy may be taken through an open or percutaneous procedure and may be completed with or without imaging guidance. If excision of the lesion is performed on the same lesion and at the same time as the biopsy, the code for the biopsy would not be reported in addition to the code for the excision. Review the extensive notation that appears in the CPT manual prior to code 19081 for additional information that applies to this range of codes.

### Introduction (19281–19298)

These codes are for placement of devices into the breast for markers or other reasons. The markers indicate where lesions are for upcoming surgery. These markers make it easy for the surgeon to locate nonpalpable masses so the breast surgery can be done quickly and efficiently.

## Mastectomy Procedures (19300–19307)

A **mastectomy** is the excision of the breast or breast tissue. This range of codes is used to report open procedures such as a partial or complete mastectomy. Coding from this range depends on documentation. If at all possible, the coder should read the operative report before assigning a code.

Mastectomy for gynecomastia (19300) is a code that is considered gender specific. This procedure is performed on the breast tissue of a male. This procedure does not include removal of muscle or lymph nodes.

The coder needs to review documentation to see how extensive the surgery was in order to determine whether the procedure was simple, subcutaneous, or radical. Talking with your surgeon is extremely helpful in understanding what was done during the procedure. A simple mastectomy (19303) does not involve the removal of muscle or lymph nodes. The lymph nodes may be biopsied, which would be included in the surgery. As the surgeon goes deeper, the code changes. Subcutaneous mastectomies involve the removal of breast tissue, but the outer skin and nipple are left intact. An implant may or may not be performed during the same operative session.

## Repair and/or Reconstruction (19316–19499)

Justifying medical necessity is important when you are reporting these codes because some of them are considered cosmetic by insurance carriers. The reconstruction procedures include the insertion of prostheses or implants. The codes are reported for unilateral procedures, but they must be reported with a 50 modifier if done bilaterally. In the CPT manual locate code 19316. Prior to this code there is an extensive notation that provides information about the goals of breast reconstruction. This notation also contains information about different techniques that are used for breast repair and reconstruction. It is helpful for a coder to review this notation and reference the information when selecting codes from this range of the coding manual. For example this notation provides information about code 19357 and provides a definition for a tissue expander.

# Summary

- The integumentary system relates to the skin.
- There are three layers of the skin: the epidermis, dermis, and subcutaneous.
- The coder should determine whether the procedure performed is diagnostic or therapeutic.
- The surgical package includes E/M services performed the day of or one day prior to surgery, the surgery itself, and any postoperative management that falls within the norm of follow-up care.
- Understanding how to read the National Correct Coding Initiative (NCCI) is essential for any coder reporting surgical services.
- Incision and drainage (I&D) refer to surgically cutting over an area and then draining it.
- Debridement is a type of cleansing.
- Procedures performed on skin tags, benign and malignant lesions, and hyperkeratotic lesions are found in this subsection of the chapter.
- Wounds are classified into four classes: clean wound (Class I), clean-contaminated wound (Class II), contaminated wound (Class III), and dirty and infected (Class IV).
- Adjacent tissue transfer, rearrangements, and grafts are all coded to their respective subsections of the Surgery section.

# Internet Links

To learn more about issues that relate to the integumentary system visit: ***https://www.aad.org/*** and search on the word "procedure." Here you will find information about procedures, billing issues, and other information that relates to the field of dermatology.

# Chapter Review

## Fill in the Blank

**Instructions:** Fill in the blanks in the statements that follow.

1. Procedures completed to determine a diagnosis and establish a care plan are referred to as _____ procedures.

2. Procedures completed as part of the care plan and used as treatment for a diagnosis are called _____ procedures.

3. The surgical package is also referred to as the _____.

4. The _____ was implemented to standardize proper coding and payment for Medicare Part B claims.

5. Unbundling occurs when procedures are performed and services are _____ coded, and submitted to an insurance company for payment.

6. A wound that has a very low infection rate (1–5%) and involves no inflammation or break in sterile technique is called a(n) _____ wound.

7. A skin substitute for areas that require a temporary closure is called an acellular dermal _____.

8. Epidermal autograft is a graft of the _____ layer only.

9. Mohs micrographic surgery is a type of _____.

10. Incision and drainage refer to surgically cutting over an area and then _____ the area.

# Coding Assignments

**Instructions:** Using a CPT manual, select the appropriate code for each of the following procedures:

1. I&D of pilonidal cyst _____
2. Debridement of seven nails _____
3. Repair of 5.3-cm superficial wound of neck _____
4. Dermabrasion for tattoo removal _____
5. Sacral pressure ulcer excision with primary closure _____
6. Cryotherapy for acne _____
7. Simple complete mastectomy _____
8. Excision of lactiferous duct fistula _____
9. Removal of intact mammary implant _____
10. Mastotomy with exploration of deep abscess _____

11. Complex repair of nose—2.1 cm _____
12. Harvest of skin for tissue cultured skin autograft—85 sq cm _____
13. Destruction of malignant lesion of neck 2.5 cm by electrosurgery _____
14. Complete peri-implant capsulectomy, breast and removal of all intracapsular contents _____
15. Correction of inverted nipples _____
16. Shaving of dermal lesion on face, 1.3-cm lesion diameter _____
17. Paring of three benign hyperkeratotic lesions _____
18. Excision of benign lesion of foot, excised diameter—3.3 cm _____

19. Intermediate repair of laceration on face—4.5 cm _____

20. Excision of ischial pressure ulcer with primary suture _____

21. Incision and drainage of seroma _____

22. Removal of 13 skin tags from upper trunk _____

23. Excision of benign lesion and margins of skin of ear, 0.8 cm _____

24. Treatment of superficial wound dehiscence with packing _____

25. Dermal facial chemical peel _____

26. Excision of excessive skin and subcutaneous tissue from the arm _____

27. Trochanteric pressure ulcer excision with skin flap closure _____

28. Removal of 12 skin tags _____

29. Excision of malignant lesion of face with an excised diameter of 2.3 cm _____

30. Intermediate repair of wound of neck measuring 13.1 cm _____

31. Nipple reconstruction _____

32. Rhytidectomy of chin _____

33. Epidermal nonfacial chemical peel _____

34. Partial mastectomy _____

35. I&D of complex postoperative wound infection _____

# Case Studies

Review each case and indicate the correct code(s).

## Case 1

**Preoperative and postoperative diagnosis:** 4-cm laceration of the left thigh.

**Procedure:** Repair of laceration

This 4-year-old male was prepped and draped in the usual fashion. The left thigh was cleansed, and 1% lidocaine was used to anesthetize the area. The laceration was measured and found to be 4 cm in length. The wound was examined, and no foreign bodies were found in the area. Eight sutures, placed in the subcutaneous fat layer of the skin, were used to close the wound. Additional sutures were placed to close the skin. The patient tolerated the procedure with no complications and was sent to the recovery area.

**CPT code(s):** _____

## Case 2

**Preoperative diagnosis:** Warts

**Postoperative diagnosis:** One wart on third toe of right foot and two warts on fourth toe of left foot.

Due to the size of the warts, the patient was taken to the operating room for wart removal. The left foot was infiltrated with 1% lidocaine. The $CO_2$ laser was prepared, and the wart on the right third toe was vaporized. The two larger warts on the fourth toe of the left foot were then vaporized. All areas were vaporized to a depth of 1.5 cm. A 3-mm margin was vaporized around all the lesions. Noting no complications, the patient was transferred to the recovery room in stable condition.

**CPT code(s):** _____

## Case 3

**Preoperative and postoperative diagnosis:** Scar on left eyebrow/forehead

**Operation:** Left eyebrow/forehead scar revision

**Anesthesia:** General

This 14-year-old female sustained an oblique laceration to the medial aspect of the left eyebrow. The laceration extended superiorly above the eyebrow hairs to the lower aspect of the forehead. Initially, this was repaired in the emergency department over a year ago. The scar has not healed well.

The patient was placed in the supine position and prepped and draped in the normal fashion. IV Kefzol was given. The portion of the scar was marked out with a marking pen marking the 1-cm inferomedial area. After this, 1 cc of 1% Lidocaine with 1:2000,000 of epinephrine was injected. Using a #15 blade, the widened portion of the scar was incised and then excised deeply in the subcutaneous area. The superior aspect of the incision undermining was completed, and the wound was brought together without tension. The deep layers were closed with buried 4-0 PDS sutures and a running subcuticular 5-0 Moncryl was used to close the skin. There was minimal blood loss. The patient was sent to the recovery room in satisfactory condition.

**CPT code(s):** _____

# Case 4

**Preoperative and postoperative diagnosis:** Painful enlarging right vulvar cyst

**Operation performed:** Excision of right vulvar cyst

**Reason for surgery:** This 34-year-old female patient has a vulvar cyst that is causing pain and discomfort.

The patient was taken to the OR and placed in the supine position. IV analgesia was started, and then she has placed in the dorsal lithotomy position. The surgical site was prepared with Lidocaine 1%, and then epinephrine and bicarb was administered. A 20-mm cyst was seen on the medial right upper labia minora. A #15 blade was used to make a 1.2-cm incision, freeing the cyst. The cyst was removed. The area was closed with 5-0 Vicryl running interrupted sutures. The patient tolerated the procedure. She was placed back in the supine position and transferred to the recovery room in satisfactory condition.

**CPT code(s):** _____

# Case 5

**Preoperative and postoperative diagnosis:** Laxity of skin and muscle of the abdomen

**Procedure:** Abdominoplasty

The 46-year-old female patient desired to have an abdominoplasty because of the lax skin, subcutaneous tissue, and muscle of her abdomen. The risks of the procedure were explained to the patient, and she signed the consent to have the procedure.

When the patient presented to the operatory area, the midline of the abdomen was marked for the planned incisions. The abdomen was prepped, and 45 cc of a local infiltration of 1% Lidocaine with 1:1000000 dilution of epinephrine was administered along the planned incisional lines.

A skin incision was made along the marking, which was carried through the skin and subcutaneous tissue with Bovie electrocautery. Dissection of the tissue was completed down to the fascial musculature of the abdomen. A periumbical incison was made, and the umbilical stalk was freely dissected. Additional dissection occurred, and a moderate amount of redundant skin was assessed. Using a #15 blade and Bovie electrocautery, a superior incision was made. The tissue along the upper incision was thinned, and, with hemostatis achieved, the site was irrigated with aline. Above and below the umbilicus, a plication of the rectus muscle was performed. With the patient in the semiflexed position, several tacking 2-0 Vicryl sutures were placed. An incision was then made at the iliac crest bilaterally using a #15 blade. Using Bovie electrocautery, the periumbilical area was defatted. 3-0 Vicryl sutures were used to close. On both sides, drains were placed and sutured in place.

*(continues)*

*(continued)*

Closure was completed with additional 3-0 Vicryl sutures and subcuticuar 4-0 Vicryl sutures. 3-0 and 4-0 Vicryl sutures, followed by 5-0 nylon sutures, were used to close the periumbical area. The wound was dressed. There was approximately 55 cc of blood loss. After extubating the patient, she was transferred to the recovery area in stable condition.

CPT code(s): _____

# Case 6

**Preoperative and postoperative diagnosis:** Bilateral breast hypoplasia and symmetry

**Operation performed:** Bilateral augmentation mammoplasty

The patient was prepped and draped in the usual sterile fashion, and then general anesthesia was achieved. Local infiltration with 1% Lidocaine with 1:100,00 dilution of epinephrine was performed. On the right breast, using a #15 blade, an inframammary incision was made and carried through the skin and subcutaneous issue. A Bovie electrocautery dissection was completed down to the pectoralis muscle, and a submuscular pocket was created. Saline was used to irrigate the site. Hemostasis was achieved.

The same procedure then was completed on the left breast, with dissection performed in a symmetric fashion to recreate a submuscular pocket. Two implants were inspected, and they were placed in the submuscular pockets. Additional dissection was performed on the left side to achieve symmetry. 3-0 Vicryl sutures were used to close the muscle layer. The subcutaneous deep dermal layer was then closed with 3-0 Vicryl sutures and the subcuticular with 4-0 Vicryl sutures. The wounds were dressed, and a Velcro breast band was placed on the superior aspect of the breast. After extubating the patient, she was sent to recovery in stable condition.

CPT code(s): _____

# Case 7

**Preoperative diagnosis:** Cyst
**Postoperative diagnosis:** Pending review of pathology findings
**Procedure:** Fine needle aspiration cyst

This 59-year-old male patient was prepped and draped in the usual fashion for a fine needle aspiration. The cyst on his right shoulder was identified, and the area was cleansed. A 25-gauge needle was guided, by palpation, into the cyst, and the fluid was removed from the cyst. The fluid was sent to pathology. The needle was withdrawn, and a bandage was placed over the wound site. There were no complications.

CPT code(s): _____

## Case 8

**Podiatry Note**

This 67-year-old diabetic patient is seen today for debridement of all nails on his right and left feet. He states that he is having a problem walking, and his feet are painful. The nails on both feet were debrided. There were no signs of infection or open wounds. He was instructed to continue to follow up with me on a regular basis to monitor any possible podiatric conditions due to his diabetes.

CPT code(s): _____

## Case 9

**ER Note**

This 15-year-old male patient was playing and ran into a tree, and his hand was injured. His left thumb is swollen, and there is blood present beneath the nail. After the hand was cleansed, Lidocaine was used to anesthetize the area, and then an electrocautery needle was used to pierce the nail plate. The hematoma was drained successfully. For the site to drain, a loose dressing was put in place. Instructions were given on dressing changes. He was instructed to see his primary care provider if he experiences increased pain and to schedule a follow-up appointment within seven days.

CPT code(s): _____

## Case 10

**Office Procedure Note**

This 39-year-old patient returns to the office today because of a defect on the nail of his left big toe. He was seen three times in the last four months for this problem. This defect is very suspicious, and I felt it best to biopsy a portion of the nail plate and bed. The sample was sent to pathology. I told the patient that he will be called with the results, and then I will decide how to proceed.

CPT code(s): _____

# Musculoskeletal System

## Chapter Outline

Introduction

Guidelines Related to the National Correct Coding Initiative (NCCI)

Abbreviations Related to the Musculoskeletal System

Anatomy of the Musculoskeletal System

General Procedures (20100–20999)

Procedures for Musculoskeletal System by Body Site

Arthrodesis

Application of Casts and Strapping (29000–29799)

Endoscopy/Arthroscopy (29800–29999)

Summary

Internet Links

Chapter Review

Coding Assignments

Case Studies

## Learning Objectives

### At the conclusion of this chapter, you should be able to:

1. Define key terms related to coding procedures performed on the musculoskeletal system.
2. Define abbreviations related to the musculoskeletal system.
3. Describe the basic anatomy and functions of the musculoskeletal system.
4. Define common procedures performed on the musculoskeletal system.
5. Apply the specific guidelines for the musculoskeletal system to this chapter.
6. Select CPT codes for procedures completed on the musculoskeletal system.
7. Identify and code procedures for the musculoskeletal system from case studies.

## Key Terms

| | | | |
|---|---|---|---|
| arthrodesis | arthroscopy | cartilage | closed treatment |
| arthroplasty | arthrotomy | casts | curettage |
| arthroscope | augmentation | closed reduction | debridement |

diagnostic arthroscopy

diagnostic endoscopy

dislocation

dynamic splint

endoscope

excision

exostosis

external fixation

fascia

fasciectomy

fixation

genioplasty

hip arthroplasty

imaging guidance

incisions

internal fixation

knee arthroplasty

Le Fort fracture

ligaments

local autograft

manipulation

morselized allograft

morselized autograft

muscle

open reduction

open reduction internal fixation (ORIF)

open treatment

ostectomy

osteoclasis

osteoectomy

osteoplasty

osteotomy

percutaneous skeletal fixation

reconstruction

reduction

sinogram

skeletal traction

skin traction

static splint

strapping

structural allograft

structural autograft

surgical arthroscopy

surgical endoscopy

synovectomy

tendon

wound exploration

# Introduction

Procedures performed on the musculoskeletal system involve the bones, muscles, tendons, cartilage, and soft tissue. The range of codes that is used for the musculoskeletal system section of CPT includes codes 20100–29999. Coders need to become familiar with the definitions that are found throughout this section of the CPT manual. At the start of the section, under the General heading, codes 20100–20999 describe a number of general procedures. The remaining sections are then further organized from head to toe. Within each subsection, the codes are organized by the type of procedure. For example, code range 21010–21499 is used to code procedures performed on the head, and code range 21501–21899 is used to code procedures performed on the neck (soft tissue) and thorax. At the start of the chapter, an extensive note discusses coding guidance and definitions that are used for codes within the musculoskeletal system. Prior to code selection, read the note and become familiar with the coding guidance and definitions.

# Guidelines Related to the National Correct Coding Initiative (NCCI)

The student will need to reference the following website to obtain the most current NCCI guideline information related to the musculoskeletal system.

1. Log on to *https://www.cms.gov/medicare-medicaid-coordination/national-correct-coding-initiative-ncci /ncci-medicare/medicare-ncci-policy-manual.*

2. Scroll to the section titled "View Manual by Chapter."

3. Click on "Chapter 4" for guidelines specific to the Musculoskeletal System coding.

# Abbreviations Related to the Musculoskeletal System

The following is a list of abbreviations that are common to the musculoskeletal system.

| Abbreviations | Definitions |
| --- | --- |
| AE | Most often-seen in documentation when referencing above-elbow amputation |
| AK | Most often-seen in documentation when referencing above-knee amputation |
| AP | anterioposterior |
| BE | below elbow—same context as AE |
| BK | below knee—same context as AK |
| C1, C2, etc. | cervical vertebra |
| C1–C7 | cervical vertebrae, 1 through 7 |
| CR | closed reduction |
| CTS | carpal tunnel syndrome |
| DIP | distal interphalangeal joint |
| DJD | degenerative joint disease |
| DTR | deep tendon reflex |
| EMG | electromyography |
| FM | fibromyalgia |
| Fx | fracture |
| IS | intracostal space |
| L1, L2, etc. | lumbar vertebra |
| L1–L5 | lumbar vertebrae, 1 through 5 |
| MCP | metacarpophalangeal joint |
| OA | osteoarthritis |
| ORIF | open reduction internal fixation |
| PKR | partial knee replacement |
| PIP | proximal intraphalangeal joint |
| ROM | range of motion |
| S1, S2, etc. | sacral vertebra |
| T1, T2, etc. | thoracic vertebra |
| T1–T12 | thoracic vertebrae, 1 through 12 |
| TENS | transcutaneous electric nerve stimulation |
| THA | total hip arthroplasty |
| THR | total hip replacement |
| TKA | total knee arthroplasty |
| TKR | total knee replacement |

# Anatomy of the Musculoskeletal System

To code correctly for the musculoskeletal system, coders must have an understanding of the anatomy of the musculoskeletal system and medical terms that are used in describing procedures. Table 6-1 summarizes common terms that are used in relation to the musculoskeletal system. Figure 6-1 illustrates a lateral view of the adult human skeleton. Figure 6-2 shows the anterior view of the human skeleton, and Figure 6-3 shows the posterior view of the human skeleton.

**TABLE 6-1** Musculoskeletal System Terms

| Term | Definition |
|---|---|
| Arthrodesis | Surgical repair or reconstruction fixation of a joint. |
| Arthroplasty | Plastic surgery of a joint. |
| Arthroscopy | Examination of the interior of a joint by use of an arthroscope. |
| Arthrotomy | A surgical incision of a joint. |
| Cartilage | Thin sheets of fibrous connective tissue. |
| Closed treatment | Treatment of fracture sites. When closed treatment occurs, the fracture site is not surgically exposed or opened. There are three types of closed treatment: (1) treatment without manipulation, (2) treatment with manipulation, and (3) treatment with or without traction. |
| Debridement | The removal of foreign material or devitalized or contaminated tissue from an area. |
| Dislocation | The displacement of a bone from normal anatomical position. |
| Exostosis | A benign bony growth that projects from the surface of a bone. |
| Fascia | A sheet of fibrous tissue. |
| Fixation | The process of suturing or fastening a structure in place. |
| Ligaments | Bands of connective tissue that bind the joints together and connect the articular bones and cartilages to cause movement. |
| Manipulation | The reduction of a dislocation or fracture. |
| Muscle | Tissue that is composed of fibers and cells that cause movement and are able to contract. There are three types of muscle: striated, cardiac, and smooth. |
| Open treatment | Treatment of a fracture when the site is surgically exposed and visualized. The site may have been opened for placement of internal fixation, but this does not always occur. |
| Ostectomy | Removal of bone. |
| Osteoclasis | The process of creating a surgical fracture of a bone to correct a deformity. |
| Osteoplasty | Plastic surgery completed on bone tissue. |
| Osteotomy | Sawing or cutting of a bone. |
| Percutaneous skeletal fixation | Fracture treatment in which the fracture site is neither open nor closed. Fixation is placed across the fracture site, typically under the guidance of x-ray imaging. |
| Skeletal traction | The application of force to a limb by a clamp, pin, screw, or wire that is attached to bone. |
| Skin traction | The application of force to a limb using felt that is applied to the skin. |
| Tendon | A dense fibrous band of connective tissue that attaches muscles to bones. |

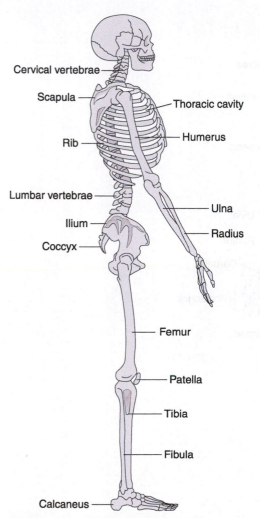

**FIGURE 6-1** Lateral View of the Adult Human Skeleton

**FIGURE 6-2** Anterior View of the Adult Human Skeleton

# General Procedures (20100–20999)

Codes 20100–20999 represent general procedures that are performed on the musculoskeletal system. These codes are used for various anatomical structures and are not limited to any one body area, such as the head or shoulder.

## Wound Exploration—Trauma (20100–20103)

Codes 20100–20103—wound exploration—trauma—are used to code wounds that occur because of a traumatic injury. **Wound exploration** is completed to determine the extent of an injury and includes surgical exploration of the wound area with enlargement of the wound. Also included is the debridement of the area, removal of any foreign material, coagulation or ligation of minor subcutaneous and/or muscular blood vessels, or the subcutaneous tissues, muscle fascia, and/or muscle. It should also be noted that this range of codes contains only separate procedure codes. Therefore, if additional procedures are reported, these codes are not reported. Coders should be familiar with the additional information that is noted in the CPT manual under the heading Wound Exploration. The codes are differentiated by site: neck, chest, abdomen/flank/back, or extremity.

> **EXAMPLE:** As a separate procedure, Dr. Wong completed an exploration of a penetrating wound of the chest. This is coded with code 20101.

**FIGURE 6-3** Posterior View of the Adult Human Skeleton

# Excisions (20150–20251)

Excisions of the epiphyseal bar and biopsies of muscles and bones are coded using the range 20150–20251. When selecting codes for the biopsies of muscle or bone, the coder needs to determine the following:

- What was the site of the biopsy?
- Was the biopsy superficial or deep?
- Was a percutaneous needle used?
- Was the procedure completed as an open procedure?

Documentation must be reviewed to answer these questions in order to select the proper code. For example, code 20206 is used to report a percutaneous needle biopsy of a muscle, while code 20251 is used to report an open biopsy of a lumbar or cervical vertebral body.

Figure 6-4 illustrates the anterior view of the major muscles of the body, and Figure 6-5 illustrates the posterior view of the major muscles of the body.

**FIGURE 6-4** Anterior View of the Major Muscles of the Body

# Introduction or Removal (20500–20705)

Code range 20500–20705 is used to report aspiration and injection procedures, as well as the application of halo devices, pins, wires, and other external fixation systems. Table 6-2 describes the codes from this subsection. Locate this code range in your CPT manual for the complete listing and definitions of the codes in this code range. For example, prior to code 20700 there is an extensive notation that governs codes for the code range 20700 to 20705. It should be noted that many of these procedures are completed with **imaging guidance**. Imaging guidance is the use of radiological techniques or procedures to visualize the placement of a needle, a catheter, or another device. When imaging guidance is used, additional codes are reported. Notations are found after the code, directing coders to use the additional imaging guidance codes.

**TABLE 6-2** Introduction or Removal (20500–20705)

| Code(s) | Description |
| --- | --- |
| 20500–20501 | This code range is used to report injections into the sinus tract. |
|  | These codes differentiate between therapeutic and diagnostic procedures. Code 20500 is used to report a therapeutic injection and is a separate procedure code. Code 20501 is a diagnostic procedure, performed on the sinus tract, also referred to as a **sinogram**. An additional code, 76080, is used to report the radiological supervision and interpretation when it occurs. |

*(continues)*

**TABLE 6-2**  (*continued*)

| Code(s) | Description |
|---|---|
| 20520–20525 | Removal of a foreign body is reported with this range of codes. |
| | Foreign bodies can become embedded in the muscle or tendon sheath. When this occurs, the foreign body is removed. These codes are used to report the removal of the foreign body and are differentiated by the term *simple, deep,* or *complicated*. Provider documentation must support the use of code 20525 by indicating the depth of the foreign body at the time of the procedure. |
| 20526 | Local anesthetics or steroids therapeutically injected into the carpal tunnel area to relieve pain are reported with this code. |
| | The code reports an injection into one extremity; however, treatment can be completed on one extremity or bilaterally. When completed bilaterally, modifier 50 is required by some payers; other payers prefer that the code be reported twice. |
| 20550–20561 | Codes 20550–20553 are used to report injections into the tendon sheath, ligament, or aponeurosis and muscles. |
| | When reporting codes 20552–20553, the coder must be able to identify the number of muscles involved, because the codes differentiate among the number of muscles involved in the procedure. Codes 20560 and 20561 report needle insertions without injections and are differentiated by the numbers of muscles. |
| 20555 | Placement of needles or catheters into muscle and/or soft tissue for subsequent interstitial radioelement application (at time of or subsequent to the procedure) is reported with this code. |
| | Prior to using this code, the CPT manual should be referenced because it provides notes that clarify proper use of this code specific to the services rendered. |
| 20600–20611 | This range of codes reports arthrocentesis, aspiration, and/or injections into joints and bursa. |
| | Code selection depends on the site of the procedure: |
| | • Small joint or bursa—such as fingers or toes, reported with code 20600 without ultrasound guidance. Code 20604 reports the procedure with ultrasound guidance, with permanent recording and reporting. |
| | • Intermediate joint or bursa—such as temporomandibular, acromioclavicular, ankle, elbow, wrist, or olecranon bursa, reported with code 20605 without ultrasound guidance. Code 20606 reports the procedure with ultrasound guidance, with permanent recording and reporting. |
| | • Major joint or bursa—such as knee joint, hip, shoulder, or subacromial bursa, reported with code 20610 without ultrasound guidance. Code 20611 reports the procedure with ultrasound guidance, with permanent recording and reporting. |
| 20612 and 20615 | Aspiration and/or injection procedures for treatment of ganglion cysts and bone cysts are reported with code 20612 for ganglion cyst(s), any location, and with code 20615 for bone cyst. |
| 20650–20694 | Insertion, application, and removal of wires, pins, and halo devices are coded to this range of codes. |
| | Coders must be able to determine the following: |
| | • Site of the procedure |
| | • Type of device used—e.g., wires, pins, halo |
| | • Type of procedure—application versus removal versus adjustment or revision |
| 20696–20705 | Applications of multiplane, unilateral, and external fixation with stereotactic computer-assisted adjustment, including imaging, are reported with codes 20696 to 20697. |
| | Code 20696 is reported for the initial and subsequent alignments, assessments, and computation(s) of adjustment schedules, while code 20697 reports the exchange of each strut or the removal and replacement. Code 20697 is not reported with codes 20692 or 20696 and is modifier 51 exempt Codes 20700 to 20705 are add-on codes. Review the CPT manual for the definitions of the codes and for a listing of the codes that these codes are used in conjunction with. |

# Replantation (20802–20838)

This range of codes, 20802–20838, is used to report the replantation of a part of the upper extremities or a foot following complete amputation. In a CPT manual locate, this range of codes and note the extensive notation that

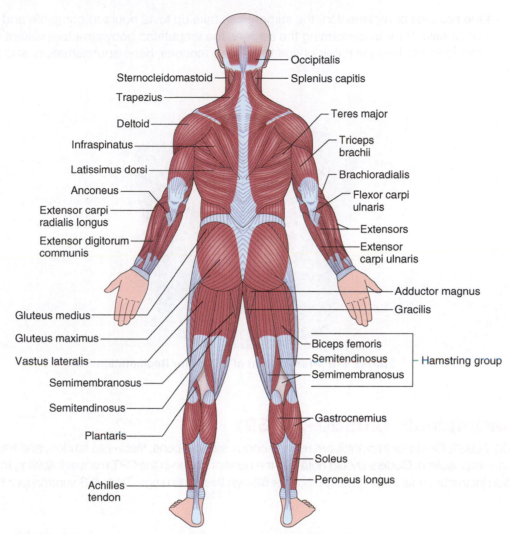

Occipitalis
Sternocleidomastoid
Splenius capitis
Trapezius
Teres major
Deltoid
Triceps brachii
Infraspinatus
Latissimus dorsi
Brachioradialis
Anconeus
Flexor carpi ulnaris
Extensor carpi radialis longus
Extensors
Extensor digitorum communis
Extensor carpi ulnaris
Adductor magnus
Gracilis
Gluteus medius
Gluteus maximus
Biceps femoris
Semitendinosus
Semimembranosus
Hamstring group
Vastus lateralis
Semimembranosus
Semitendinosus
Gastrocnemius
Plantaris
Soleus
Peroneus longus
Achilles tendon

**FIGURE 6-5**  Posterior View of the Major Muscles of the Body

appears after the heading replantation. Follow the guidance provided for selecting modifiers for this code range. Codes are differentiated by site as follows:

- Code 20802—Arm, includes surgical neck of humerus through elbow joint. The reattachment occurs between the elbow and shoulder.

- Code 20805—Forearm, includes radius and ulna to radial carpal joint. The reattachment occurs between the wrist and elbow.

- Code 20808—Hand, includes hand through metacarpophalangeal joint(s). The reattachment of the hand occurs between the wrist and fingers.

- Code 20816—Digit, excluding thumb, includes metacarpophalangeal joint to insertion of flexor sublimis tendon. The reattachment of one finger, excluding the thumb, occurs at or near the finger's articulation with its corresponding metacarpal bone.

- Code 20822—Digit, excluding thumb, includes distal tip to sublimis tendon insertion. The reattachment of one finger, excluding the thumb, between the fingertip and the attachment of the finger to the hand.

- Code 20824—Thumb, includes carpometacarpal joint to MP joint. The reattachment of the thumb to the hand.

- Code 20827—Thumb, includes distal tip to MP joint. The reattachment of the thumb distal to where the thumb attaches to the hand.

- Code 20838—Foot. The reattachment of the foot at or near the ankle.

Because of the process of replantation, the surgery can take up to 12 hours to complete and is performed under general anesthesia. Prior to performing the surgery, the amputated body structure is kept cold (see Figure 6-6).Replantation involves the repair of soft tissue and tendons, bone approximation, and blood vessel repair.

**FIGURE 6-6**  Preservation of a Digit for Replantation

# Grafts or Implants (20900–20939)

Codes 20900–20939, Grafts (or Implants), are used to code cartilage, bone, fascia lata tendon, and tissue grafts of the musculoskeletal system. Coders should note that the notation found in the CPT manual following the heading for this subsection instructs coders not to assign modifier 62 with this code range. Table 6-3 summarizes the codes in this range.

**TABLE 6-3**  Grafts or Implants (20900–20939)

| Code(s) | Description |
|---|---|
| 20900 and 20902 | These codes report bone grafts from any donor site. |
| | The codes differentiate between minor or small (code 20900) versus major or large (code 20902). Provider documentation must justify code selection. |
| 20910 and 20912 | Grafting of cartilage is reported with this code range. |
| | The site of the graft is the determining factor for code assignment. Use code 20910 for costochondral and code 20912 for the nasal septum. It should be noted that ear cartilage grafting is not coded to this subsection, but to 21235. In the CPT manual locate the notation that appears after code 20912 that gives direction for the use of code 21235. |
| 20920 and 20922 | This range reports fascia lata grafting. |
| | The codes are differentiated by the use of a stripper (code 20920) or by incision and area exposure (code 20922). |
| 20924 | This code reports tendon grafts from a distance. During this procedure, a tendon is dissected and removed. |
| +20930 | This code reports a **morselized allograft** for spine surgery or placement of osteopromotive material. |
| | During this procedure, small pieces of bone are harvested to form the graft from a source other than the patient. This is an add-on code. The CPT manual should be referenced with regard to primary codes that this code would be reported with. |

*(continues)*

**TABLE 6-3** (*continued*)

| Code(s) | Description |
|---|---|
| +20931 | A **structural allograft** for spine surgery only is reported with this add-on code.<br><br>This procedure involves a large segment of bone being harvested from a donor source, other than the patient, and placed into the interspace of the spine. This is an add-on code. The CPT manual should be referenced with regard to primary codes that this code would be reported with. |
| +20932<br>+20933<br>+20934 | These three codes are all add-on codes for allografts, which includes templating cutting, placement, and internal fixation when performed. These codes are futher differentiated as follows: code 20932 includes an osteoarticular graft including articular surface and contiguous bone, code 20933 includes a partial hemicortical intercalary graft, while code 20934 includes a complete intercalary graft. Prior to assigning these codes, the coder must reference the instructional notations that follow each code that delineate the codes that should not be reported with codes 20932, 20933, and 20934. |
| +20936 | A **local autograft** for spine surgery is reported with this code.<br><br>During this procedure, only one incision is used to harvest the graft and to complete the procedure. The graft is from the ribs, spinous process, or laminar fragments. This is an add-on code. The CPT manual should be referenced with regard to primary codes that this code is reported with. |
| +20937 | This code is used to report a **morselized autograft** for spine surgery that is completed by harvesting small pieces of the patient's own bone through a separate incision. A common harvest site is the iliac crest. This is an add-on code. The CPT manual should be referenced with regard to primary codes reported with this code. |
| +20938 | A **structural autograft** for spine surgery is reported with this code. During this procedure, a bicortical or tricortical graft is harvested through a separate incision. This is an add-on code. The CPT manual should be referenced with regard to primary codes reported with this code. |
| +20939 | This code is used for spine surgery only, to report a bone marrow aspiration for bone grafting through a separate skin or fascial incision. This code is an add-on code and is to be listed separately in addition to the code for the primary procedure completed. Coders should reference the instructional notations that appear in the CPT manual after the code description for additional instructions that impact the assignment of code 20939. |

## Other Procedures (20950–20999)

Other general procedures that are related to the musculoskeletal system are coded with code range 20950–20999, titled "Other Procedures." Procedures in this range include the following:

- Monitoring of interstitial fluid pressure
- Bone grafts with microvascular anastomosis
- Free osteocutaneous flaps with microvascular anastomosis
- Electrical stimulation and ultrasound stimulation to aid bone healing
- Ablation of bone tumors
- Computer-assisted surgical navigational procedures, with or without images

It should be noted that several guidance notes appear in this section of the CPT manual.

## Exercise 6.1—Check Your Understanding

**Other General Procedures, Code Range 20000–20999**

**Fill in the Blank**

Enter the appropriate term(s) to complete each of the following statements. Reference the CPT manual.

1. Code 20251 is used to code an open biopsy of a vertebral body in the _____ or _____ area.

(continues)

## Exercise 6.1 (*continued*)

2. Codes 20100–20103 are used to code the exploration of penetrating wounds and are differentiated by the following sites: neck, _____, abdomen/flank/back, and _____.

3. A(n) _____ autograft for spine surgery is completed by harvesting small pieces of the patient's own bone through a separate incision.

4. Electrical stimulation to aid bone healing is coded by using codes 20974 and 20975. Code 20974 is for a(n) _____ approach, whereas 20975 is for a(n) _____ approach.

5. Code 20206 is used to report a biopsy of a muscle using a(n) _____.

6. A diagnostic procedure performed on the sinus tract is known as a(n) _____.

7. When selecting codes for biopsies of muscle or bone, the coder needs to know the site of the biopsy and whether the procedure was performed as an open procedure or by using a percutaneous needle. The coder also needs to know _____.

8. The use of radiological techniques or procedures to visualize the placement of a needle, catheter, or other device is known as _____.

9. Code _____ is used to report the placement of a needle or catheter in muscle and/or soft tissue for subsequent interstitial radioelement application.

10. The determining factor for code assignment of cartilage grafting is _____.

# Procedures for Musculoskeletal System by Body Site

As mentioned at the beginning of this chapter, the codes for the musculoskeletal system are organized predominantly from head to toe. Table 6-4 lists the subsections and the codes for each.

**TABLE 6-4** Musculoskeletal Code Ranges According to Body Site

| Title of Code Range | Code Range |
| --- | --- |
| Head | 21010–21499 |
| Neck (Soft Tissues) and Thorax | 21501–21899 |
| Back and Flank | 21920–21936 |
| Spine (Vertebral Column) | 22010–22899 |
| Abdomen | 22900–22999 |
| Shoulder | 23000–23929 |
| Humerus (Upper Arm) and Elbow | 23930–24999 |
| Forearm and Wrist | 25000–25999 |
| Hand and Fingers | 26010–26989 |
| Pelvis and Hip Joint | 26990–27299 |
| Femur (Thigh Region) and Knee Joint | 27301–27599 |
| Leg (Tibia and Fibula) and Ankle Joint | 27600–27899 |
| Foot and Toes | 28001–28899 |

Within each subsection, the codes are then organized by types of procedures, mainly staying within the following outline:

1. Incision
2. Excision
3. Introduction or Removal
4. Repair, Revision, and/or Reconstruction
5. Fracture and/or Dislocation
6. Other Procedures

Additional procedural headings are added when necessary, but most of the subsection is organized as outlined here. Because the organization is repetitive, coders need to understand the main terms that relate to each procedural heading.

## Incision

**Incisions** are made into musculoskeletal structures for a variety of reasons:

- Exploration for diagnostic purposes
- Drainage of an abscess, with or without bone removal
- Drainage of a hematoma, with or without bone removal
- Removal of calcaneous deposits
- Removal of foreign bodies

These procedures are easily located in the CPT manual by referencing the terms *incision* or *incision and drainage* in the index and then locating the site into which the incision was made or the reason for the incision. These procedures also can be located in the index by referencing the procedure name. For incisions made into a joint, physicians record the medical term arthrotomy. This term also can be referenced in the index.

> **EXAMPLE:** Dr. Patel completed an incision and drainage of the hip joint area because of a hematoma. The coder should reference the terms incision and drainage in the index and then locate the reason for the incision and drainage (I&D), hematoma, and then the site hip. Code 26990 would be found in the index.

Remember to always check the main section of the code book to verify the code selection!

## Exercise 6.2—Check Your Understanding

### Incision

For each procedure listed, select the appropriate CPT code.

1. Fasciotomy of toe _____
2. Open tenotomy of hip flexor of right side _____
3. Drainage of abscess of finger _____
4. I&D of bursa of left wrist _____
5. Arthrotomy of elbow with removal of foreign body _____
6. Incision and drainage of deep abscess of the soft tissue of the thorax _____
7. Temporomandibular joint arthrotomy _____
8. Incision of bone cortex of shoulder _____
9. I&D of elbow for deep abscess _____
10. Incision of flexor tendon sheath of wrist _____

# Excision

An **excision** is the surgical removal of tissue or a structure. Excisions within the musculoskeletal system include removals of soft tissue, soft tissue tumors, bursa, bone cysts or benign tumors, bone, cartilage, synovium, tendon, and other joint structures. The musculoskeletal excision codes are differentiated by:

- Anatomical site
- Structure excised
- Partial versus complete excision
- Accompanying procedures

To locate these codes in the index, the coder should reference the term *excision* or the medical name of the procedure. For example when coding a partial fasciectomy of the plantar fascia, the coder could reference the term excision or the term fasciectomy to locate the correct code of 28060. For the index entry of excision the coder would reference the subterm of fascia and then is instructed to see fasciectomy in the index. For the entry of fasciecotmy the index lists foot and then code ranges 28060 to 28062. Coders must read the operative notes carefully to determine the extent of the excision and whether any accompanying procedures were performed. Common excisional procedures of the musculoskeletal system include:

**Fasciectomy**—Removal of fascia

**Osteoectomy**—Removal of bone

**Synovectomy**—Removal of the synovial membrane of a joint

**Curettage**—The process of removing tissue by scraping

## Exercise 6.3—Check Your Understanding

### Excision

For the following procedures, select the appropriate CPT code.

1. Interphalangeal joint excisions of the proximal end of two toes _____

2. Metatarsectomy _____

3. Radical resection for tumor of ulna _____

4. Partial acromionectomy with release of coracoacromial ligament _____

5. Excision of mandible _____

6. Radical resection of tumor of the phalanx of the toe _____

7. Arthrotomy of ankle with synovectomy _____

8. Hamstring muscle neurectomy _____

9. Ischial bursa excision _____

10. Radical resection of sarcoma of the soft tissue of the hand—3.5 cm _____

# Introduction and Removal

Codes that fall into the range titled Introduction and Removal include the following types of procedures:

- Removal of foreign bodies
- Injection procedures for radiological procedures
- Application of fixation devices
- Impression and custom preparation of prosthesis
- Implant or prosthesis removal

Codes for removals can be located in the index by referencing the term *removal* and then locating the site.

**EXAMPLE:** Dr. Jones completed the removal of a left wrist prosthesis. To locate this procedure in the index, the coder should reference the term *removal,* then *prosthesis,* and then the term *wrist.* Code range 25250–25251 is listed. Locate the codes in the body of the CPT text; the correct code to select would be 25250.

Other index entries that are applicable to this range of codes include the following:

- Injection
- Application
- Application of external fixation device
- Fixation device, application
- Implant removal
- Prosthesis

## Exercise 6.4—Check Your Understanding

**Introduction and Removal**

For each procedure listed, select the correct CPT code.

1. Impression and custom preparation of orbital prosthesis _____

2. Injection procedure for shoulder arthrography _____

3. Deep removal of a foreign body in the foot _____

4. Removal of implant of hand _____

5. Injection for temporomandibular joint arthrography _____

6. Exploration of the wrist with removal of a deep foreign body _____

7. Therapeutic injection of sinus tract _____

8. Deep removal of a foreign body in the shoulder_____

9. Removal of humeral and ulnar components of a prosthesis _____

10. Manipulation of wrist under anesthesia _____

# Repair, Revision, and Reconstruction

Repair, revision, and reconstruction procedures are completed to correct an anomaly or injury to an anatomical structure. These codes are differentiated by:

- Site
- Type of procedure; for example, reconstruction, reduction of muscle and bone, and muscle and tendon transfers and repairs
- Accompanying procedures; such as bone grafts, resection of ribs, tendon grafts, fixation, and plastic repairs

To locate these codes in the index, reference the following terms:

- Reconstruction, then the anatomical site
- Repair, then the anatomical site
- Tendon, then the anatomical site
- Muscle, then repair or revision
- The specific name of the muscle, tendon, joint, or anatomical site

**EXAMPLE:** Dr. Hand performs a repair of the carpometacarpal joint. This can be located in the index under the term *carpometacarpal joint,* then *repair.* The correct code is 25447.

Coders should also have an understanding of certain terms when coding in the various repair, revision, and reconstruction sections of the musculoskeletal system. Table 6-5 summarizes medical procedures and their definitions, and code examples for repairs, revisions, and reconstructions completed on the musculoskeletal system.

**TABLE 6-5** Repair, Revision, and Reconstruction of the Musculoskeletal System

| Term | Definition | Code Examples |
|---|---|---|
| Genioplasty | Plastic surgery of the chin<br><br>These codes are differentiated by the type of approach and the additional procedures that occur, such as augmentation, sliding osteotomy, and grafts. | 21120–21123 |
| Augmentation | Surgically increasing the size of an anatomical structure<br><br>Codes 21125–21127 are used to report mandibular body or angle augmentation. The codes are differentiated by the use of prosthetic materials or bone grafts. | 21125 and 21127 |
| Reconstruction | Surgical rebuilding of an anatomical structure<br><br>Multiple types of reconstructions are completed in the musculoskeletal system. The term *reconstruction* means that the structure was surgically rebuilt to attempt to repair the structure.<br><br>For example, reconstructions of fractures to the maxilla are relatively common. A common type of maxillar fracture is a **Le Fort fracture**, a bilateral fracture of the maxilla. Le Fort fractures are differentiated according to Le Fort I, Le Fort II, and Le Fort III, depending on the degree of injury. Figure 6-7 illustrates a reconstruction of a Le Fort I fracture. | 21141–21160<br>Le Forts |
| Arthroplasty | Plastic repair of a joint<br>Common arthroplasty procedures include<br><br>• **Hip arthroplasty**—the surgical repair or reconstruction of the hip<br>• **Knee arthroplasty**—the surgical repair or reconstruction of a knee<br><br>Figure 6-8 illustrates a total hip arthroplasty with a prosthesis in place, and a knee arthroplasty with polyethylene and metal components to replace the surfaces of the knee joint.<br><br>When coding for knee arthroplasty, the coder must reference the operative report to determine the extent of the procedure and the compartments in which the surgery was performed. The codes are differentiated by medial *or* lateral compartments versus medial *and* lateral compartments. | 27130- Arthroplasty—total hip<br>27440–27447<br>Arthroplasty—knee |

## Exercise 6.5—Check Your Understanding

**Repair, Revision, and Reconstruction**

For the following procedures, select the appropriate CPT code.

1. Arthroplasty of the patella with prosthesis _____

2. Whitman's acetabuloplasty _____

3. Fascial defect repair of the leg _____

4. Lengthening of the flexor tendon of the left hand _____

5. Release of thumb contracture _____

6. Open hamstring tenotomy of single tendon, knee to hip _____

7. Repair of dislocating peroneal tendons with fibular osteotomy _____

8. Midtarsal capsulotomy _____

9. Osteotomy of femoral neck _____

10. Anterior tibial tubercleplasty _____

**FIGURE 6-7** Reconstruction of a Le Fort I Fracture

**FIGURE 6-8** Total Hip Replacement and Total Knee Replacement with Prosthesis

# Fracture/Dislocation

Fractures and **dislocations**, a displacement of a structure, are treated in a variety of fashions. In order to select a code properly, the coder must be able to determine the following:

1. Location of the fracture
2. Whether or not manipulation occurred
3. Whether the treatment was open or closed or involved percutaneous skeletal fixation
4. Whether internal or external fixation devices were used

The fracture and dislocation codes include the application of a cast or strap and the removal of the initial cast or strap. Many of the descriptions of the treatment of fractures and dislocations include the term *each*. This means that a code is reported for each fracture or dislocation that is treated.

---

**EXAMPLE:** A surgeon completed a closed treatment of two metatarsal fractures without manipulation. The correct codes to report include the following:

For facilities, the procedure code is reported twice: listing 28470 and 28470.

For physician billing, the procedure code is listed twice, and the 51 modifier is appended to the second code: 28470, 28470-51.

---

## Manipulation

**Manipulation** or **reduction** of a bone or dislocation is performed to realign the bone or joint. This procedure is completed by open or closed reduction. **Closed reduction** occurs by manually applying force to the injured area without making an incision into the skin. **Open reduction** occurs when the site is surgically opened to realign the area. Figure 6-9 illustrates a closed reduction of a fractured left humerus.

**FIGURE 6-9**  Closed Reduction of a Fractured Left Humerus

## Fixation Devices

Fixation devices are used to immobilize fracture sites to allow for healing. There are two types of fixation used for fracture treatment. **External fixation** involves the placement of pins through soft tissue and into the bone in order to hold an external appliance in place. External fixation appliances are removed. Figure 6-10 illustrates a fracture of the epiphysis of a femur and the use of external fixation.

**Internal fixation**, also known as **open reduction internal fixation (ORIF)**, occurs when pins or a plate are internally placed into the bone to hold the fracture. The pins or plates are not typically removed after the fracture has healed. Figure 6-11 illustrates a fracture of the femoral neck and the use of internal fixation pins to correct the fracture.

**FIGURE 6-10** Fracture of the Femur (A) and External Fixation (B) to Stabilize the Bone

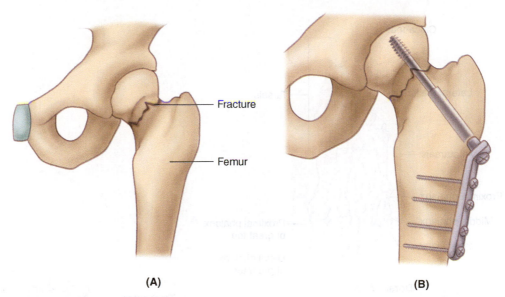

**FIGURE 6-11** Internal Fixation of Fractured Hip   (A) Fracture of the femoral neck. (B) Internal fixation pins are placed to stabilize the bone. These pins are not removed after the bone has healed.

## Detailed Skeletal Anatomy

When selecting codes for the repair of fractures and dislocations, coders must be able to identify the site of the fracture and, at times, the exact area of the bone that is treated. Codes 28470–28485 are used to code the treatment of fractures of the metatarsal bones. Codes 28490–28525 are used to code the treatment of fractures of the great toe, phalanx, or phalanges.

Coders must have a working knowledge of the skeletal system to code the treatment of fractures. Figure 6-12 illustrates the dorsal view of the bones of the lower arm, wrist, and hand. Figure 6-13 illustrates the superior and medial views of the bones of the right ankle and foot. Figure 6-14 illustrates the structures of the proximal end of the femur.

**FIGURE 6-12**  Dorsal View of the Bones of the
Lower Left Arm, Wrist, and Hand

**FIGURE 6-13**  Superior View of the Bones of the Right
Ankle and Foot

**FIGURE 6-14**  Structures of the Proximal
End of the Femur

# Arthrodesis

Earlier in the chapter, it was stated that for most anatomical sites within the musculoskeletal system, the CPT manual follows a standardized outline of the procedures within the subsections, with some subsections having additional procedures. One such additional procedure type is arthrodesis, which is reported in various subcategories with the CPT manual. Arthrodesis is defined as the surgical fusion of two bones to bind or tie them together. Arthrodesis is also referred to as surgical ankylosis. Table 6-6 summarizes the code range for various arthrodesis procedures.

**TABLE 6-6** Code Ranges for Arthrodesis

| Anatomical Site of Arthrodesis | Code Range |
|---|---|
| Spine | 22532–22819 |
| Shoulder | 23800–23802 |
| Humerus | 24800–24802 |
| Forearm and Wrist | 25800–25830 |
| Hand and Fingers | 26820–26863 |
| Pelvis and Hip Joint | 27279–27286 |
| Femur | 27580 |
| Leg and Ankle Joint | 27870–27871 |
| Foot and Toes | 28705–28760 |

To become familiar with the organization and description of these codes, locate in the CPT manual each of the code ranges that are found in Table 6-6.

In the CPT manual, locate the information that is found prior to code 22532 and follows the heading of Arthrodesis. This section of the CPT manual explains that arthrodesis may be completed alone or with other definitive procedures. When arthrodesis is performed with other definitive procedures a modifier of 51 should be appended to the code for the other definitive procedure to indicate that multiple procedures were completed when billing for professional services. It should also be noted that some arthrodesis codes are add-on codes and, therefore, modifier 51 is not to be appended to the add-on code. For example, arthrodesis codes 22585, 22614, 22632, and 22634 are add-on codes. Prior to assigning any arthrodesis codes read all of the notations that are contained in the CPT manual for additional information regarding code assignment.

# Application of Casts and Strapping (29000–29799)

Casts and strapping are used in order for fractures to heal and to immobilize an area. **Casts** are fiberglass or plaster rigid dressings. **Strapping** an area is done by using tape or bandage material to bind, protect, or immobilize an anatomical structure. At times, splints are also applied to prevent or limit mobility. There are two types of splints that are used. A **static splint** is used to prohibit mobility, whereas a **dynamic splint** is used to allow limited mobility.

As discussed earlier in this chapter, when casts or straps are used during treatment, the application and removal of the first cast or traction device is included in the code for the treatment.

**EXAMPLE:** A patient has a fracture of the femoral shaft. The procedure performed is a closed treatment of the femoral shaft fracture without manipulation and with cast application. The code to report would be 27500. Since the cast is applied during this initial treatment, a code from series 29000–29799 is not reported.

Therefore, physicians who apply the initial cast, strap, or splint and follow the patient for subsequent care of the fracture, dislocation, or other injury cannot use code series 29000–29799.

However, codes 29000–29799 are used to report the application of casts and strapping in the following situations:

- When the casting or strapping is the initial casting or strapping, and no other treatment or procedure is performed or is expected to be performed by the same physician completing the casting or strapping.
- When the casting or strapping is the initial service that is performed without any restorative treatment or procedure performed to stabilize or protect the injured area, which could include a fracture or dislocation, and/or to minimize or prevent pain.
- To report an initial cast or strapping when another physician has provided or will provide restorative treatment at a separate time.
- To report a replacement of a cast or strapping during or after the postoperative period from the original care.

**EXAMPLE:** Jim Banks injured his right arm during a construction accident. He is seen by Dr. Jones, a primary care provider. Dr. Jones immobilized the fracture by placing a long arm splint from the patient's shoulder to his hand.

This would be coded using code 29105—"Application of long arm splint (shoulder to hand)."

## Cast Removals or Repairs (29700–29750)

This range of codes is used only when the cast removal is performed by a different physician from the physician who applied the cast. These codes are differentiated by removals, repairs, and wedging of casts. Further code differentiation occurs per type of cast.

### Exercise 6.6—Check Your Understanding

**Fracture/Dislocation and Application of Casts and Strapping**

Indicate whether the following statements are true (T) or false (F).

1. _____ A static splint is used to allow for mobility.
2. _____ Code range 29000–29799 is used to report a cast replacement during the operative period.
3. _____ Dr. Smith casted the left arm of his patient. The cast was from the elbow to the finger. This service was performed after Dr. Jones performed a manipulation of the fracture site two days ago. Dr. Smith should report code 29075.
4. _____ The correct code for the strapping of a finger is 29280.
5. _____ Codes 29700–29750 are always reported for cast removals.

**Coding Assignments**

Assign the correct code(s).

6. Closed treatment of greater trochanteric fracture _____
7. Open treatment of femoral shaft fracture with placement of screws _____
8. Ankle dislocation treatment by open repair with internal fixation _____
9. Closed treatment of interphalangeal toe joint dislocation under anesthesia _____
10. Application of body cast from shoulder to hips including both thighs _____
11. Application of calf-to-foot leg splint _____
12. Open treatment of traumatic hip dislocation _____
13. Open treatment of ulnar styloid fracture _____
14. Manipulation and percutaneous skeletal fixation of medial humeral condylar fracture _____
15. Acute shoulder dislocation open treatment _____

# Endoscopy/Arthroscopy (29800–29999)

An **endoscope**, an optic illuminated instrument used for the visualization of an internal body organ or cavity, is commonly used for procedures completed on the musculoskeletal system. The common endoscopic instrument used for visualization of the interior of a joint is an **arthroscope**. The process of viewing a joint via an arthroscope is referred to as an **arthroscopy**. Figure 6-15 illustrates the use of an arthroscope to view the knee, and Figure 6-16 shows the internal view of the knee during an arthroscopy.

Endoscopic procedures completed in the musculoskeletal system are divided into diagnostic and surgical endoscopies. A **diagnostic endoscopy/arthroscopy** is completed to determine the extent of an injury or disease process and to establish a diagnosis. A **surgical endoscopy/arthroscopy** is performed to surgically treat an injury or condition or abnormality of a joint.

Diagnostic endoscopic codes are included in their surgical endoscopic code counterparts. In other words, a diagnostic arthroscope is included in a surgical arthroscope in the same area. Therefore, if a diagnostic arthroscopy is started, and then a surgical arthroscopic procedure is completed, the diagnostic arthroscope is not reported because it is included in the code for the surgical arthroscopic procedure.

The endoscopy/arthroscopy codes, 29800–29999, are differentiated by the following factors:

- Anatomical site
- Diagnostic versus surgical scope
- Additional procedure(s) performed

Coders should also note when arthroscopic procedures are performed in conjunction with an arthrotomy. When this occurs, the code for the arthrotomy should be appended with modifier 51. This instruction is given in the CPT manual following the heading Endoscopy/Arthroscopy.

To locate an endoscopic/arthroscopic procedure in the index, perform the following steps. (This process should be used for locating all endoscopic procedures, regardless of the body system. This will be referred to in subsequent chapters when additional endoscopic procedures are reviewed.)

**1.** Reference the term *endoscopy* in the index. (Please note that in the CPT manual, after the heading Endoscopy, the following notation appears: "See Arthroscopy; Thoracoscopy.")

**2.** Locate the organ/body system being viewed, examined, or treated using a scope.

**3.** If there is no endoscopy heading, reference an index entry with a descriptor that includes the suffix "-oscopy." In the case of the musculoskeletal system, this entry would be the heading "Arthroscopy."

**FIGURE 6-15** Arthroscopy of the Knee

**FIGURE 6-16** Internal View of the Knee during Arthroscopy

4. The "-oscopy" heading in the index most likely will be divided by diagnostic, surgical, and unlisted services and procedures or by body site. In the case of arthroscopy, the codes are indexed according to diagnostic, surgical, and unlisted. Select the appropriate subheading.

5. If, after you try to locate the procedure by the preceding method, you find no heading for *endoscopy*, you can be certain that the CPT manual does not have a specific code for the procedure using an endoscopic approach.

6. Query the provider who completed the procedure to determine whether the procedure was completed endoscopically.

7. After querying the provider, if it is determined that the procedure was completed endoscopically, use an unlisted procedure code in the section where the service applies. For arthroscopic procedures, for example, the appropriate code would be unlisted service code 29999—unlisted procedure, arthroscopy. The unlisted codes are always found at the end of the code section. Remember that unlisted codes should be used only after the procedure has been reviewed with the provider. When unlisted codes are used, payers review the claims carefully and usually ask for supporting documentation.

EXAMPLE: Dr. Desui performed a surgical arthroscopy of the left shoulder with lysis and resection of adhesions with manipulation. This would be coded with code 29825 and a modifier of LT since it is the left shoulder. Review the description of code 29825 in a CPT manual and note the full description of the code.

## Exercise 6.7—Check Your Understanding

**Endoscopic/Arthroscopic Procedures**

For the following procedures listed, select the appropriate CPT code.

1. Surgical arthroscopy of the shoulder with capsulorrhaphy _____

2. Arthroscopy of knee with synovial biopsy _____

3. Endoscopic release of the transverse carpal ligament of the wrist _____

4. Arthroscopy temporomandibular joint, diagnostic, with synovial biopsy _____

5. Extensive debridement of shoulder via arthroscope _____

6. Arthroscopic partial shoulder synovectomy _____

7. Lateral release via arthroscopy of knee _____

8. Endoscopic plantar fasciotomy _____

9. Surgical arthroscopy of temporomandibular joint. _____

10. Arthroscopy of wrist for internal fixation of fracture _____

# Summary

- CPT codes for the musculoskeletal system include codes 20100–29999.
- Wound exploration is completed to determine the extent of the injury and includes surgical exploration of the wound area with enlargement of the wound.
- Many procedures completed on the musculoskeletal system are completed with imaging guidance.
- Replantation involves the repair of soft tissue and tendons, bone approximation, and blood vessel repairs.
- External fixation involves the placement of pins through soft tissue and into the bone in order to hold an external appliance in place.
- Internal fixation, also known as *open reduction internal fixation (ORIF)*, occurs when pins or a plate are internally placed into the bone to hold the fracture.
- The common endoscopic instrument used for visualization of the interior of a joint is an arthroscope.

- A diagnostic endoscopy/arthroscopy is completed to determine the extent of an injury or disease process and to establish a diagnosis.
- A surgical endoscopy/arthroscopy is performed to surgically treat an injury, condition, or abnormality of a joint.

# Internet Links

To learn more about foot and ankle conditions and treatments for these conditions, visit **https://www.verywellhealth.com/foot-ankle-surgical-procedures-4012819**.

For information about knee arthroscopies, visit **https://arthroscopy.com**.

To learn more about musculoskeletal disorders overall, visit **https://bmcmusculoskeletdisord.biomedcentral.com/**.

# Chapter Review

## True/False

**Instructions:** Indicate whether the following statements are true (T) or false (F).

1. _____ Tendons are thin sheets of fibrous connective tissue.

2. _____ Debridement of the wound area is included in traumatic wound exploration codes 20100–20103.

3. _____ Local anesthetics are injected into the carpal tunnel area to relieve pain.

4. _____ An osteotomy is the completion of plastic surgery on a bone.

5. _____ Diagnostic and therapeutic arthroscopies are coded using the same code.

# Coding Assignments

**Instructions:** Using a CPT manual, select the appropriate code for each of the following procedures.

1. Single tendon tenotomy of shoulder _____

2. Correction of claw finger _____

3. Superficial biopsy of soft tissue of back _____

4. Reinsertion of spinal fixation device _____

5. Open treatment of chronic sternoclavicular dislocation _____

6. Finger sesamoidectomy _____

7. Closed treatment of coccygeal fracture _____

8. Knee arthrodesis _____

9. Diagnostic arthroscopy of wrist with synovial biopsy _____

10. Surgical arthroscopy of knee with medial meniscal transplantation _____

11. I&D in shoulder area for deep abscess _____

12. Arthrotomy of elbow with capsular excision for capsular release _____

13. Removal of humeral and ulnar prosthesis components with debridement and synovectomy _____

14. Arthrotomy with exploration of midcarpal joint _____

15. Phalangectomy of three toes _____

16. Partial excision of ulna for osteomyelitis
_____

17. Olecranon bursa excision _____

18. Injection procedure for hip arthrography
_____

19. Removal of woodlike item deep in the knee area
_____

20. Flexor tenolysis, foot, single tendon
_____

21. Manipulation of trimalleolar ankle fracture with closed treatment _____

22. Excision of two interdigital neuromas
_____

23. Arthroscopy of shoulder with synovial biopsy
_____

24. Subtalar joint arthroscopy with subtalar arthrodesis
_____

25. Application of long arm cast
_____

26. Strapping of wrist _____

27. Closed treatment of talus fracture
_____

28. Radical resection of tumor of the calcaneus
_____

29. Primary suture of infrapatellar tendon _____

30. Bilateral pelvis osteotomy _____

31. Application of shoulder to hand cast
_____

32. Wrist arthroscopy with synovial biopsy
_____

33. Shoulder arthroscopy for complete synovectomy
_____

34. Triple arthrodesis, foot joint _____

35. Superficial biopsy of soft tissue of lower leg
_____

36. Tenotomy of right shoulder involving multiple tendons via one incision _____

37. Deep incision with opening of bone cortex of left humerus for osteomyelitis _____

38. Closed treatment of right shoulder dislocation, with fracture of greater humeral tuberosity with manipulation _____

39. Decompressive fasciotomy of right hand _____

40. Replantation of left arm from complete amputation _____

# Case Studies

## Case 1

**Preoperative and postoperative diagnosis:** Left knee arthrosis

**Procedure:** Arthroscopy and debridement

The patient was prepped and brought into the operating room, where general anesthesia was administered. The knee was prepped, and a video arthroscopy was performed using the anterolateral and anteromedial portals. The scope confirmed the diagnosis. In the medial compartment, the degenerative meniscus was debrided with a shaver. The large osteophytes were removed with a bur. After removal, it was noted that there was improved extension. In the lateral compartment, a small anterior horn of the tear was debrided and shaved back to the meniscal tissue. The portals were sutured with nylon sutures. Sterile dressings were applied. The patient was in stable condition and was sent to the recovery room.

**CPT code(s):** _____

## Case 2

**Diagnosis:** Right radial shaft fracture

**Procedure:** Open reduction internal fixation of radius

The patient was placed in the supine position with an armboard extension. A nonsterile tourniquet was placed on the right arm. An incision was made proximal to the distal palmar crease and then extended to the level of the elbow crease through the subcutaneous tissue until the flexor carpi radialis tendon was identified. Further dissection of the area revealed that the fracture was at the insertion of the FPL tendon. The fracture was reduced with bone forceps and clamps. A 12-hole DC plate was fitted to the normal curvature of the volar aspect of the radius. The plate was fixed to the shaft. The screw holes were filled, and there was adequate reduction of the radial shafting. Full supination and pronation were achieved. Hemostatis was achieved, and the wound was irrigated to remove all debris. The subcutaneous tissue was closed using 2-0 Vicryl sutures, and a 3-0 nylon suture was used to close the skin. Sterile dressings were applied, and the patient's arm was placed in a sugar-tong splint. The patient was taken to the recovery room in good condition.

CPT code(s): _____

## Case 3

**Preoperative and postoperative diagnosis:** Painful bunion of the right foot

**Operation performed:** Correction of bunion—Silver bunionectomy

After being placed in the supine position, the patient was prepped and draped. IV sedation with a local consisting of 15 cc of 1:1 mixture of 0.5% Marcaine plain with 2% Xylocaine with epinephrine was administered. A 5-cm curvilinear incision was made over the first MPJ and carried deep through the subcutaneous tissue, with dissection down to the deep fascia. The prominent medial bunion was exposed, and the bunion was excised at the sagittal groove. The wound area was flushed with normal saline, and the deep structures were closed with 3-0 and 4-0 Vicryl. The skin was closed with 4-0 nylon in a horizontal mattress fashion. The wound was then dressed. The patient tolerated the procedure and was sent to the recovery area.

CPT code(s): _____

## Case 4

**Preoperative and postoperative diagnosis:** Painful left index finger due to previous crush injury

**Procedure:** Amputation of left index finger

The patient was placed under general anesthesia, and a 1% Lidocaine and 0.5% Marcaine with epinephrine was administered to perform a digital block for the left index finger. A tourniquet was inflated on the left arm. An incision was made over the mid aspect of the proximal phalanx of the left index finger with dissection of the subcutaneous tissue. The digital nerves were cut, and then sharp dissection was taken down to the bone, dividing the flexor and extensor tendons. A bone cutter was used to was taken down to the bone, dividing the flexor and extensor tendons. A bone cutter was used to divide the bone, and the finger was removed. The vessels and nerves were ligated, and the bone was smoothed off with a rongeur. The skin was closed with 5-0 nylon sutures and a dressing applied. The tourniquet was deflated. There was minimal blood loss, and the patient was taken to the recovery room in satisfactory condition.

**CPT code(s):** _____

## Case 5

**Indication for surgery**

This 49-year-old female patient sustained a proximal tibial plateau fracture three years ago, which was repaired with both internal and external fixation. Since that time, she has developed significant pain due to degenerative disease in the previous fracture area. She presents today for hardware removal.

**Postoperative diagnosis:** Retained hardware right knee

**Surgical procedure:** Removal of hardware from right knee proximal tibia

**Procedure:**

The patient was placed in the supine position. The right leg was prepped and draped after the patient was placed under general anesthesia. High on the right thigh a tourniquet was placed, and the leg was exsanguinated using an Esmarch bandage. An incision was made and carried down through the skin and subcutaneous level down to the level of the hardware. Removal of the screws and plates occurred. The fracture was united at the time of closure. The wound was closed with staples and 2-0 Dexon. The patient tolerated the procedure and was taken to the recovery area.

**CPT code(s):** _____

## Case 6

**Preoperative diagnosis:** Mass on right middle finger, middle phalanx

**Pathology:** Benign tumor from middle phalanx

**Operation:** Excision of benign tumor of middle phalanx of finger

The patient was prepped, and a digital block was achieved using 2.5 cc of 0.25% Marcaine and 1% Xylocaine. The finger was exsanguinated, and a tourniquet was placed. An incision was made over the mass and carried through the subcutaneous tissue. The mass was removed via curettes to scrape the mass from the bone. The specimen was labeled and sent to pathology. Irrigation of the wound occurred, and the skin was closed in layers. A sterile dressing was applied, and the patient was taken to the recovery area in stable condition.

**CPT code(s):** _____

## Case 7

**Operative diagnosis:** Carpal tunnel syndrome of the right hand

**Procedure:** Endoscopic carpal tunnel release

The patient was anesthetized with local anesthesia and IV sedation. After the patient was placed in the supine position, a tourniquet was placed on the right arm. A 1.5-cm horizontal incision was made at the wrist, and the subcutaneous tissue was dissected to gain entrance for the endoscope. The operative area was visualized on the monitor. The transverse carpal ligament was released. The scope was removed, and the wound was irrigated and closed with 3-0 Prolene in a running subcuticular stitch. Additionally, Steri-Strips and a sterile dressing were applied, and the tourniquet was deflated. Blood loss was minimal. Patient was stable and sent to recovery.

**CPT code(s):** _____

## Case 8

This 84-year-old patient presented today for an injection with ultrasound guidance with permanent recording and reporting due to degenerative arthritis of the left hip.

**Procedure:**

After MAC sedation, the left hip was prepped. The puncture site was injected with 1% Lidocaine with epinephrine. A 20-gauge, extra-long spinal needle was placed at the neck–head junction, and Isovue was injected. Additional injections of Lidocaine, Marcaine, and Depo-Medrol 80 mg were given. A Band-Aid was placed on the injection site. There were no complications of the procedure, and the patient was sent to recovery.

CPT code(s): _____

## Case 9

**Procedural Note**

This patient presents with a subfascial soft tissue abscess for incision and drainage of the right upper arm.

After local anesthesia was administered, an incision was made over the abscess on the right arm and continued down to the fascia until the abscessed area was visualized below the deep fascia. The deep abscess was viewed, debrided, and then drained. The area was irrigated, and packing was placed. The patient tolerated the procedure and was instructed to follow up with me in one week.

CPT code(s): _____

## Case 10

**Procedural Note**

**Preoperative diagnosis:** Possible malignancy on muscle of left thigh

After local anesthesia, a percutaneous bore needle was used to pierce the skin and fascia into the muscle to obtain a biopsy of the muscle tissue. The needle was removed with minimal blood. A bandage was placed on the site. The tissue sample was sent to pathology. The patient was in satisfactory condition after the procedure.

CPT code(s): _____

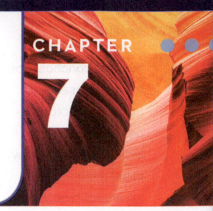

# Respiratory System

## Chapter Outline

Introduction

Guidelines Related to the National Correct
Coding Initiative (NCCI)

Abbreviations Related to the Respiratory
System

Anatomy of the Respiratory System

Procedures Completed on the Nose
(30000–30999)

Procedures Completed on the Accessory
Sinuses (31000–31299)

Procedures Completed on the Larynx
(31300–31599)

Procedures Completed on the Trachea
and Bronchi (31600–31899)

Procedures Completed on the Lungs
and Pleura (32035–32999)

Summary

Internet Links

Chapter Review

Coding Assignments

Case Studies

## Learning Objectives

### At the conclusion of this chapter, you should be able to:

1. Define key terms related to coding procedures performed on the respiratory system.
2. Define abbreviations related to the respiratory system.
3. Describe the basic anatomy and functions of the respiratory system.
4. Define common procedures performed on the respiratory system.
5. Apply specific guidelines for the respiratory system to this chapter.
6. Select CPT codes for procedures completed on the respiratory system.
7. Identify and code procedures for the respiratory system from case studies.

## Key Terms

arytenoidectomy

backbench work

bronchi

bronchoscopy

chemical pleurodesis

choanal atresia

diagnostic nasal
endoscopy

direct laryngoscopy

drainage procedures

endotracheal intubation

epiglottidectomy

ethmoidectomy

ethmoid sinuses

extensive nasal polyp
excision

extraperiosteal
  pneumonolysis

flexible bronchoscope

frontal sinuses

frontal sinusotomy

hemilaryngectomy

indirect laryngoscopy

initial rhinoplasty

intranasal biopsy

laryngectomy

larynx

lateral nasal wall
  reconstruction

lungs

maxillary sinuses

maxillary sinusotomy

maxillectomy

microlaryngoscopy

nasal polyps

nasal vestibular stenosis

open-tube
  bronchoscope

partial laryngectomy

pharyngolaryngectomy

pharynx

pleurectomy

pneumonectomy

pneumothorax

primary rhinoplasty

revision rhinoplasty

rhinectomy

rhinophyma

rhinoplasty

rhinotomy

rigid bronchoscope

secondary rhinoplasty

septoplasty

simple nasal polyp
  excision

sinus

sphenoid sinuses

sphenoid sinusotomy

spreader grafting

surgical nasal
  endoscopy

synechia

thoracoscopy

thoracostomy

thoracotomy

trachea

tracheostomy

# Introduction

Procedures performed on the respiratory system include procedures that involve the nose, sinuses, pharynx, larynx, trachea, bronchi, and lungs. The range used for the respiratory system includes codes 30000–32999. The respiratory system consists of a number of organs that allow air to enter the body and waste gases to leave the body.

# Guidelines Related to the National Correct Coding Initiative (NCCI)

Reference the following website to obtain the most current NCCI guideline information related to the Respiratory System.

1. Log on to *https://www.cms.gov/medicare-medicaid-coordination/national-correct-coding-initiative-ncci /ncci-medicare/medicare-ncci-policy-manual*.
2. Scroll to the section titled "View Manual by Chapter."
3. Click on "Chapter 5" for guidelines specific to the Respiratory System coding.

# Abbreviations Related to the Respiratory System

| Abbreviations | Definitions |
|---|---|
| ARD | acute respiratory distress |
| ARF | acute respiratory failure |
| BAL | bronchial alveolar lavage |
| COLD | chronic obstructive lung disease |
| COPD | chronic obstructive pulmonary disease |
| CPAP | continuous positive airway pressure |
| CXR | chest x-ray |

*(continues)*

(continued)

| Abbreviations | Definitions |
|---|---|
| DOE | dyspnea on exertion |
| LLL | left lower lobe (of lung) |
| LUL | left upper lobe (of lung) |
| PFT | pulmonary function testing |
| RF | respiratory failure |
| RLL | right lower lobe (of lung) |
| RUL | right upper lobe (of lung) |
| SOB | shortness of breath |
| TLC | total lung capacity |
| V/Qscan | ventilation-perfusion scan |

# Anatomy of the Respiratory System

Coders must understand the anatomy of the respiratory system to assign codes accurately. Figure 7-1 illustrates the anatomy of the upper respiratory system, and Figure 7-2 illustrates the lower respiratory system. Table 7-1 is a summary of common terms related to the respiratory system.

**FIGURE 7-1** View of the Nasal Cavity and Structures of the Upper Respiratory System

**FIGURE 7-2** Structures of the Lower Respiratory System

**TABLE 7-1** Respiratory System Terms

| Term | Description |
| --- | --- |
| Bronchi | Large air passages in the lung through which air is inhaled and exhaled |
| Laryngectomy | Surgical removal of the larynx |
| Larynx | The voice organ that connects the pharynx with the trachea |

*(continues)*

**TABLE 7-1** *(continued)*

| Term | Description |
|------|-------------|
| Lungs | Pair of organs that are located in the thorax that constitute the main organ of the respiratory system |
| Pharynx | Tubular structure that extends from the base of the skull to the esophagus |
| Sinus | Cavity that is located in the skull close to the paranasal area |
| Trachea | Tube-shaped structure in the neck that extends from the larynx to the bronchi |

# Procedures Completed on the Nose (30000–30999)

Procedures completed on the nose are divided into the following subcategories:

- Incision
- Excision
- Introduction
- Removal of foreign body
- Repair
- Destruction
- Other procedures

When coding procedures that are completed on the nose, the coder must determine whether the procedure was completed unilaterally or bilaterally. Code descriptions must be reviewed because notations will specify the correct manner in which to report the codes.

> **EXAMPLE:** Code 30110 is used to report an excision of a nasal polyp, simple. This code is considered a unilateral procedure. To report a bilateral excision of nasal polyps, the 30110 code would be reported with modifier 50.

There is a notation in parentheses following the code listing in the CPT manual that instructs the coder to use the modifier. Within this subcategory of procedures completed on the nose, the coder should review carefully all the notations that are present because specific instructions are given for the various codes found in this section.

## Incision (30000, 30020)

Two codes are found in CPT for incisional procedures completed on the nose. Code 30000 is used to code the drainage of an abscess or hematoma of the nose using an internal approach. Code 30020 is used to code the drainage of an abscess or hematoma of the nasal septum. **Drainage procedures** are completed to remove the fluid from an area—in the case of these codes, abscess material or blood.

## Excisions (30100–30160)

This subcategory includes biopsies, excisions, and destructions. Table 7-2 summarizes this range of codes.

**TABLE 7-2** Excisions (30100–30160)

| Code | Description |
|------|-------------|
| 30100 | This code is used to report an **intranasal biopsy**, which is a biopsy that is completed within the nasal cavity. If the biopsy is completed on the skin of the nose, the CPT manual instructs the coder to reference codes 11102–11107. |
| 30110 and 30115 | **Nasal polyps** are growths in the nasal cavity that are commonly associated with rhinitis. Excisions of nasal polyps are differentiated by simple and extensive excisions. During a **simple nasal polyp excision**, the polyp's shape allows it to be removed easily because it is usually hanging from a stalk. During an **extensive nasal polyp excision**, the polyp's shape or thickness, or the number of polyps present, may require more skill and effort for removal. The physician should document that the removal was more than simple, to justify the selection of the code. To report bilateral excisions, use modifier 50. |
| 30117 and 30118 | These codes are used to report the excision or destruction of an intranasal lesion. The codes are differentiated by internal or external approaches. Code 30117 reports the internal approach and code 30118 reports the external approach or a lateral rhinotomy. |
| 30120 | This code is used to report an excision or surgical planing of the skin of the nose for rhinophyma. **Rhinophyma** is a rosacea condition of the skin of the nose. The skin appears red, swollen, and distorted with sebaceous hyperplasia. |
| 30124 and 20125 | This code range is used to report the simple or complex excision of dermoid cysts of the nose. Code 30124 reports a simple excision, whereas code 30125 reports a complex excision that extends under the bone or cartilage. |
| 30130 and 30140 | Excision or submucous resection of the inferior turbinate is reported using these codes. These codes report the removal of part or all of the inferior turbinates. Code 30140 is used when the resection of the inferior turbinate extends into the submucosal layer of tissue. It should be noted that, for the excision or submucous resection of the superior or middle turbinate, code 30999 is assigned. |
| 30150 and 30160 | A **rhinectomy** is the removal of the nose and is differentiated in CPT by partial or total removal by reporting code 30150 for a partial rhinectomy and code 30160 for a total rhinectomy. |

# Introduction (30200–30220)

There are only three codes in this subcategory of the CPT manual:

- Code 30200—Used for the therapeutic injection of a substance into the turbinates
- Code 30210—Displacement therapy, which would include Proetz type
- Code 30220—Nasal septal prosthesis insertion

# Removal of Foreign Body (30300–30320)

Codes 30300–30320 are used to report the removal of a foreign body from the intranasal area. Codes are differentiated by the complexity of the procedure:

- Code 30300—This code is reported for the removal of a foreign body from the intranasal area when the procedure is an office-type procedure.
- Code 30310—When general anesthesia is used during the removal of a foreign body from the intranasal area, code 30310 is reported.
- Code 30320—Report code 30320 when the removal of a foreign body requires the completion of a lateral rhinotomy. A **rhinotomy** is a surgical procedure in which an incision is made along one side of the nose.

## Exercise 7.1—Check Your Understanding

**Incisions, Excisions, Introduction, and Removal of Foreign Bodies of the Nose**

Using the CPT manual, select the appropriate code for each of the following procedures.

1. Total rhinectomy _____

2. Drainage of hematoma of the nasal septum _____

3. Laser destruction of intranasal lesion via internal approach _____

4. Removal of foreign body from nasal cavity, under general anesthesia _____

5. Excision of nasal polyp _____

6. Nasal septal prosthesis insertion _____

7. Bilateral extensive excision of multiple nasal polyps _____

8. Removal of a foreign body in the nose by lateral rhinotomy _____

9. Surgical planing of the skin of the nose for rhinophyma _____

10. Simple excision of a dermoid cyst of the nose involving the skin and subcutaneous layers _____

## Repair (30400–30630)

Surgical repair of the nose is known as **rhinoplasty** and is reported in CPT by using codes 30400–30630. Most rhinoplasty procedures are considered cosmetic in nature, and third-party payers may not reimburse physicians for the completion of these procedures. However, there are times when rhinoplasty procedures are completed because of a congenital anomaly or an injury to the nose. When noncosmetic procedures are completed, it is important for the provider to document this clearly in the operative report because the report can be used to justify the need for the procedure.

During rhinoplasty, incisions are usually created within the nose; however, some surgeons perform the procedure by making external incisions at the base of the nostrils or along the columella. Figure 7-3 illustrates this approach.

To select codes from this subcategory, coders should reference the following entries in the index:

- Rhinoplasty
- Repair, then nose, then vestibular stenosis
- Repair, then nasal septum

Table 7-3 summarizes the codes in the range 30400–30630.

**FIGURE 7-3**  Rhinoplasty   (A) Preoperative; (B) Postoperative

**TABLE 7-3**  Repair (30400–30630)

| Code | Description |
|---|---|
| 30400–30420 | This range of codes is used to report **primary rhinoplasty**, also known as **initial rhinoplasty**, which is the surgical repair of the nose. These codes are differentiated according to the extent of the repair. Code 30400 is used to report a rhinoplasty that involves the lateral and alar cartilages and/or elevation of the nasal tip, whereas code 30410 reports a complete rhinoplasty. Code 30420 is used to report a rhinoplasty that includes a major septal repair, also known as a **septoplasty**. Code 30420 includes rhinoplasty and septoplasty, so it is not necessary to report the septoplasty separately. |
| 30430–30450 | **Secondary rhinoplasty**, also known as **revision rhinoplasty**, is differentiated in CPT according to the following:<br>• Minor revisions—including only a small amount of nasal tip work<br>• Intermediate revisions—including bony work with osteotomies<br>• Major revisions—including nasal tip work and osteotomies<br>Coders must read the operative report carefully to select the appropriate code based on provider documentation of the procedure. |
| 30460 and 30462 | Codes 30460–30462 are used to code rhinoplasty procedures completed due to a nasal deformity that is secondary to a congenital cleft lip and/or palate. Code selection is based on repair of the tip only, versus repair of the tip, septum, and osteotomies. |
| 30465, 30468, and 30469 | Code 30468 reports the bilateral repair of **nasal vestibular stenosis**, which is the narrowing of the nasal vestibule. This procedure also is referred to as **spreader grafting** or **lateral nasal wall reconstruction**. During this procedure, an incision is made in the upper lateral cartilage of the nose and continued into the medial aspect of the nasal bones. A graft is inserted to widen the nasal vestibule area. Code 30465 is a bilateral procedure; therefore, when this procedure is performed unilaterally, modifier 52 should be used. This is also true for code 30468. Code 30468 is reported when there is a repair of a nasal valve collapse. When the repair is completed there also needs to be the implantation of subcutaneous/submucosal lateral wall implant(s) for the reporting of code 30468. Reference the CPT manual and review the notations that follow the code for additional information that relates to the code. Also reference the CPT manual for the full description of code 30469. |
| 30520 | Code 30520 is used to report a septoplasty or submucous resection with or without cartilage scoring, contouring, or replacement with graft. During a septoplasty, cartilage may be removed as grafting material. When this occurs, do not assign an additional code for the harvesting of the graft because it occurred through the same incision. However, when the graft is secured through a separate incision, an additional code from code range 20900–20926 should be assigned to report the harvesting of the graft. |
| 30540–30630 | The remaining codes in the Repair subcategory are used to report the following procedures:<br>• Repair of choanal atresia with codes 30540 and 30545—**Choanal atresia** occurs when there is an occlusion of the openings between the nasal cavity and the pharynx. Typically, this is a congenital defect, but it also can be acquired. Code 30540 reports an intranasal choanal atresia repair while code 30545 reports a transpalatine choanal atresia repair.<br>• Lysis intranasal synechia with code 30560. **Synechia** is an adhesion.<br>• Repair of fistula with code 30580—During this procedure, an opening between the mouth and the maxillary sinus is closed.<br>• Septal or other intranasal dermatoplasty with code 30620—It should be noted that this code does not include obtaining the graft.<br>• Repair of nasal septal perforations with code 30630—If a large defect exists, the physician has to complete a separately reportable autogenous graft, in addition to the local flaps that are routinely completed during this procedure. |

## Destruction and Other Procedures (30801–30999)

The final range of codes that are used to report procedures on the nose include the following:

- Codes 30801 and 30802—These codes are used to report the cautery or ablation of the mucosa of the inferior turbinates, and are differentiated by whether the extent of the procedure was superficial or intramural. Instructional notations are given that direct the coder to use code 30999 for the ablation of the superior or middle turbinates. The additional instructional notations that appear after code 30802 need to be reviewed by the coder prior to code assignment as these notations give instruction as to codes that should not be used with code 30802.

- Codes 30901–30906—These codes are used to report procedures that are completed to control nasal hemorrhages. Codes are differentiated by:
  - Simple or complex cautery.
  - Simple or complex packing.
  - Anterior versus posterior packing.

It should be noted that these codes are not used when the control of bleeding is performed during a procedure. In these cases, the control of the bleeding is considered part of the procedure.

- Codes 30915 and 30920—These codes are used to report ligation of arteries and are differentiated by the artery ligated.
- Code 30930—This code is used to report the therapeutic fracture of the nasal inferior turbinates.
- Code 30999—This is the unlisted procedure code for procedures completed on the nose. It should be noted that there are multiple notations within the subcategory for the nose that instruct coders to assign this code. Coders should be sure to read the notations that appear after the code description entries. Some procedures that are reported with this code include:
  - Therapeutic fracture of superior or middle turbinate.
  - Ablation of superior or middle turbinate.
  - Excision of superior or middle turbinate.
  - Submucous resection of superior or middle turbinate.

## Exercise 7.2—Check Your Understanding

**Repair (30400–30630) and Destruction and Other Procedures (30801–30999)**

Using the CPT manual, select the appropriate code for each of the following procedures.

1. Septal dermatoplasty _____
2. Superficial bilateral cautery of mucosa of inferior turbinates _____
3. Primary rhinoplasty with elevation of nasal tip _____
4. Ethmoidal artery ligation _____
5. Lysis intranasal synechia _____
6. Septoplasty with cartilage scoring _____
7. Anterior, simple control of nasal hemorrhage _____
8. Therapeutic fracture of nasal inferior turbinate _____
9. Intranasal repair of choanal atresia _____
10. Repair of nasal septal perforation _____

# Procedures Completed on the Accessory Sinuses (31000–31299)

There are four pairs of sinuses that are named according to the bone that encloses the particular sinus area. Figure 7-4 illustrates these sinuses:

- **Frontal sinuses**—These sinuses are located within the frontal bone behind the eyebrows.
- **Ethmoid sinuses**—These are located between the eyes.
- **Sphenoid sinuses**—These are located directly behind the nose at the center of the skull.
- **Maxillary sinuses**—These are located below the eye and lateral to the nasal cavity.

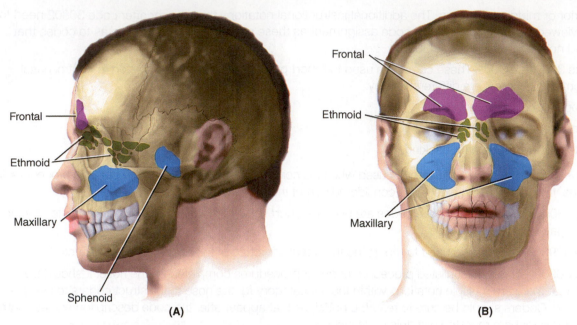

Frontal

Ethmoid

Maxillary

Sphenoid

(A)

Frontal

Ethmoid

Maxillary

(B)

**FIGURE 7-4**  Sinuses    (A) Lateral view; (B) Anterior view

Code range 31000–31299, titled Accessory Sinuses, is used to report procedures that are completed on the sinuses. There are four types of procedures found in this subcategory of CPT:

- Incision
- Excision
- Endoscopy
- Other procedures

## Incisions (31000–31090)

Incisions are made into the sinuses for a variety of reasons, including drainage, biopsy, and other reasons. To code in this section, coders need to identify the sinus in which the procedure was completed. The codes are differentiated by the specific sinus and the procedure completed. Table 7-4 summarizes the procedures that are coded by using this section.

**TABLE 7-4**  Incisions (31000–31090)

| Code | Description |
|------|-------------|
| 31000 and 31002 | These codes are used to report lavage by cannulation of the maxillary or sphenoid sinus. Code 31000 reports a lavage by cannulation of the maxillary sinus (antrum puncture or natural ostium) and code 31002 reports the same procedure completed on the sphenoid sinus. |
| 31020–31032 | **Maxillary sinusotomy**, an incision made into the maxillary sinus, is reported with this range of codes. These codes are for unilateral procedures; therefore, if a bilateral procedure is completed, the code is reported with modifier 50. The codes are differentiated by intranasal or radical procedures. |
| 31040 | Pterygomaxillary fossa surgery, any approach, would be reported using this CPT code. |
| 31050 and 31051 | **Sphenoid sinusotomy** codes, which code incisions made into the sphenoid sinus, are differentiated according to the following:<br>• With or without biopsy<br>or<br>• With mucosal stripping or removal of polyps |

*(continues)*

**TABLE 7-4** (*continued*)

| Code | Description |
|------|-------------|
| 31070–31087 | **Frontal sinusotomy** codes are used to report incisions made into the frontal sinuses to drain the frontal sinus, to remove osteomas, and for other reasons. Proper code selection also is based on the location of the incision: brow versus coronal. |
| 31090 | This code is used to report a unilateral sinusotomy of three or more paranasal sinuses. |

## Excisions (31200–31230)

Sinus excision codes are divided in CPT into two areas:

- **Ethmoidectomy**, codes 31200–31205—These codes are used to report the removal of the ethmoid sinus. The approach must be identified for code selection: intranasal versus extranasal.
- **Maxillectomy**, codes 31225 and 31230—These codes are used to report the removal of the maxillary sinus and are differentiated by the completion of the maxillectomy without or with an orbital exenteration.

## Endoscopy (31231–31298)

Codes 31231–31298 are used to report endoscopic procedures completed on the sinuses. Codes 31233–31298, unless otherwise specified, are used to report unilateral procedures, therefore, when the procedure is completed bilaterally, modifier 50 is added to the code. To complete these procedures, a physician uses an endoscope to visualize, examine, and magnify the internal structure of the sinus. A diagnostic sinus endoscopy is included with the surgical endoscopy. A surgical endoscopy also includes a sinusotomy if it is performed.

**Diagnostic nasal endoscopy** codes use code range 31231–31235 and include the inspection of the entire nasal cavity, the meatus, the turbinates, and the sphenoethmoid recess. Therefore, only one code is needed to report the inspection of all of these areas.

**Surgical nasal endoscopy** procedures are reported using codes 31237–31298 and are used when a nasal endoscope is used to complete a surgical procedure. When coding surgical nasal endoscopy procedures, the coder must read the operative report to ensure that the procedure was completed endoscopically, and then the report must be reviewed to determine the procedure that was completed. Prior to code assignment the coder should review the numerous instructional notations that follow codes in the code range 31241–31297. Locate and review these instructional notations in the CPT manual.

### Exercise 7.3—Check Your Understanding

**Accessory Sinuses (31000–31299)**

Using the CPT manual, select the appropriate code for each of following procedures.

1. Sinus endoscopy with maxillary antrostomy _____
2. Sphenoid sinusotomy with biopsy _____
3. Maxillectomy with orbital exenteration _____
4. Repair of cerebrospinal fluid leak of the sphenoid region via endoscope _____
5. Nasal endoscopy with sphenoidotomy _____
6. Endoscopic balloon dilation of sphenoid sinus ostium _____
7. Unilateral sinusotomy of four paranasal sinuses _____
8. Maxillary sinus lavage by cannulation _____
9. Radical maxillary sinusotomy _____
10. Total extranasal ethmoidectomy _____

# Procedures Completed on the Larynx (31300–31599)

Procedures completed on the larynx are divided into the following subcategories:

- Excision
- Introduction
- Endoscopy
- Repair
- Other procedures

Figure 7-5 illustrates the larynx and related structures.

**FIGURE 7-5**  Larynx and Related Structures   (A) Anterior view; (B) Lateral view

## Excision and Introduction (31300–31502)

Excisions and introduction, or insertion, of tubes completed on the larynx are coded by using this range of codes. Table 7-5 summarizes codes found in this range.

**TABLE 7-5** Excision and Introduction (31300–31502)

| Code | Description |
|------|-------------|
| 31300 | This code is reported when the physician performs a laryngotomy (thyrotomy, laryngofissure), with removal of tumor or laryngocele, cordectomy. |
| 31360–31368 | Codes 31360–31368 report a laryngectomy. Code selection is determined by whether the procedure was total or subtotal and whether radical neck dissection occurred. |
| 31370–31382 | A **partial laryngectomy**, also known as a **hemilaryngectomy**, is the partial removal of the larynx. Code selection is based on the approach. |
| 31390–31420 | This range of codes includes: <br>• **Pharyngolaryngectomy**—Surgical excision of the hypopharynx and larynx, reported with codes 31390 or 31395. These codes are differentiated by without reconstruction (Code 31390) or with reconstruction (Code 31395). <br>• **Arytenoidectomy**—Surgical excision of the arytenoid cartilage, which is the cartilage to which the vocal cords are attached, reported with code 31400. <br>• **Epiglottidectomy**—Surgical excision of the epiglottis, reported with code 31420. |
| 31500 | This code is used to code an emergency procedure called an **endotracheal intubation**. In this procedure, an endotracheal tube is placed into the trachea to keep it open. |
| 31502 | This code is used to report the changing of a tracheotomy tube prior to the establishment of a fistula tract. |

# Endoscopy of the Larynx (31505–31579)

There are two types of laryngoscopy procedures that can be performed:

- **Direct laryngoscopy**—The direct viewing of the larynx and adjacent structures by use of a laryngoscope.
- **Indirect laryngoscopy**—The viewing of the larynx by use of two mirrors: a laryngeal mirror that is placed in the back of the throat, and a second mirror held outside the mouth. Through manipulation of the mirrors and using a light source, the larynx is viewed indirectly.

In the CPT manual, locate the guidelines for endoscopies of the larynx that appear prior to code 31505. These guidelines state that a laryngoscopy includes an examination of the tongue base, larynx, and hypopharynx. Read the remaining guidelines in the CPT manual for additional information that pertains to coding laryngoscopy procedures. CPT codes 31505–31513 are used to code indirect laryngoscopic procedures. Codes 31515–31571 are used to code direct laryngoscopic procedures. Codes 31575–31579 are used to code laryngoscopic procedures that are performed using flexible fiber-optic equipment. These code ranges are further differentiated according to the reason the laryngoscopic procedure was completed, such as:

- Biopsy
- Removal of foreign bodies
- Removal of lesions
- Injections
- Insertion of obturator
- Diagnostic examinations
- Arytenoidectomy
- Reconstruction

Therefore, when reading through an operative report, the coder should identify the type of laryngoscope used, as well as the reason for the laryngoscopy.

Some codes (for example, code 31536) identify the use of an operating microscope or telescope. If documentation states that the procedure was completed using an operating microscope or telescope, these specialized codes should be used. If both an operating microscope and a telescope was used during the same operative session, the code should be reported only once. Use of an operating microscope is also identified by the physician stating the performance of a **microlaryngoscopy**.

## Repair and Other Procedures Completed on the Larynx (31580–31599)

The remaining codes, 31580–31599, are used to report repairs and other procedures completed on the larynx. The repair codes are located in the index by referencing the terms *repair* and then *larynx,* or by referencing the term *laryngoplasty.* Codes 31580–31592 contain numerous instructional notations that follow the codes that must be reviewed by the coder prior to code assignment. Review this range of codes to become familiar with the instructional notations that appear for these codes.

Code 31599 is used to report unlisted procedures that are completed on the larynx.

### Exercise 7.4—Check Your Understanding

**Procedures Completed on the Larynx (31300–31599)**

Using the CPT manual, select the appropriate code for each of the procedures listed.

1. Partial horizontal laryngectomy
_____

2. Direct operative laryngoscopy with biopsy
_____

3. Indirect laryngoscopy with foreign body removal _____

4. Flexible laryngoscopy with removal of lesion
_____

5. Direct laryngoscopy with stripping of vocal cords _____

6. Laryngoplasty for laryngeal web with indwelling keel _____

7. Laryngeal reinnervation by neuromuscular pedicle _____

8. Epiglottidectomy _____

9. Indirect laryngoscopy for diagnosis
_____

10. Flexible laryngoscopy with removal of foreign body _____

# Procedures Completed on the Trachea and Bronchi (31600–31899)

Procedures completed on the trachea and bronchi are found in code range 31600–31899. Figure 7-6 illustrates the trachea and the bronchi. The code ranges in this subsection include:

- Incision
- Endoscopy
- Bronchial Thermoplasty
- Introduction
- Excision, Repair
- Other procedures

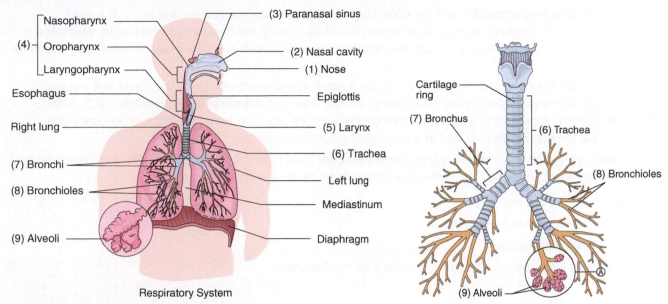

**FIGURE 7-6**  Trachea and Bronchi

# Incision (31600–31614)

An incision made into the trachea is referred to as a **tracheostomy**. Codes 31600–31610 are used to report tracheostomies. These codes are differentiated according to whether the procedure was:

- Planned
- An emergency procedure
- A fenestration procedure

**EXAMPLE:** Dr. O'Hara has just performed a **tracheostomy** on a 1-year-old.

When submitting this charge, the coder in his office reports code 31601.

# Endoscopy of Trachea and Bronchi (31615–31654)

A commonly completed procedure of the respiratory system is a **bronchoscopy**, an examination of the bronchi using an endoscope. Figure 7-7 illustrates a bronchoscopy. During a bronchoscopy, the scope is inserted

**FIGURE 7-7**  Fiber-Optic Bronchoscopy

through the oropharynx, or mouth, past the vocal cords, and beyond the trachea into the bronchi. A **rigid bronchoscope**, often referred to as an **open-tube bronchoscope**, is inserted through the mouth, whereas a **flexible bronchoscope** is inserted through the mouth or nose. CPT does not differentiate between the scopes for code selection.

At the start of this subsection in the CPT manual, a notation appears that informs the coder that a surgical bronchoscopy always includes a diagnostic bronchoscopy. The note elaborates that for codes 31622–31651, 31660, and 31661, fluoroscopic guidance is included in the code when performed with the procedure listed. Therefore, it is not necessary to code the fluoroscopic guidance separately.

To select a code for a bronchoscopy properly, the coder must read the operative report to determine why the bronchoscopy was performed. The codes are differentiated by the following:

- With or without cell washing
- Brushing or protected brushings
- Bronchial alveolar lavage
- With biopsy (or biopsies), according to various types of biopsies
- Dilation
- Placement of stents
- Removal of foreign bodies
- Excisions or destruction of tumors
- Placement of catheters
- Therapeutic aspiration
- Injection of contrast material

To locate these codes in the index, the coder should reference the term *bronchoscopy* and then reference the subterm that describes the procedure that was completed. Complete services that include sampling of lymph node(s) or adjacent structure(s) using endobronchial ultrasound (EBUS) are reported separately using codes 31652 and 31653. Code 31654 is an add-on code that reports the identification of one or more peripheral lesion(s) using transendoscopic ultrasound. Review the instructional notation found in the CPT manual following code 31654 for additional information about the use of this code. Codes 31652, 31653, and 31654 are reported only once per session.

## Bronchial Thermoplasty (31660–31661)

Codes 31660 and 31661 report a rigid or flexible bronchoscopy with bronchial thermoplasty, including fluoroscopic guidance when performed. The codes are differentiated by the number of lobes viewed. Bronchial thermoplasty is a therapeutic procedure generally used to treat patients with severe asthma that is not controlled by medications. A bronchoscope is used with a radiofrequency ablation device to reduce smooth muscle tissue in all central airways.

## Introduction, Excision Repair, and Other Procedures Completed on the Trachea and Bronchi (31717–31899)

The introduction codes in this subsection include codes for the catheterization of the area and the instillation of contrast material. Codes are differentiated by site, such as trachea versus bronchi, and by any additional procedures that may be performed.

The repair codes, 31750–31830, also are differentiated by site (trachea versus bronchi) and are further defined according to the type of repair completed. Operative reports must be read to determine:

- The site of the repair
- The type of repair—graft versus fistulization

- The reason for the repair, such as the excision of a tumor or carcinoma
- Whether there was a revision of a tracheostomy scar

---

## Exercise 7.5—Check Your Understanding

**Procedures Completed on the Trachea and Bronchi (31600–31899)**

Using the CPT manual, select the appropriate code for each of the following procedures.

1. Tracheostoma complex revision with flap rotation _____

2. Flexible bronchoscopy with brushing _____

3. Tracheobronchial catheter aspiration done with a fiberscope at the bedside _____

4. Suture of cervical tracheal wound _____

5. Excision of thoracic tracheal carcinoma _____

6. Intrathoracic tracheoplasty _____

7. Bronchoplasty graft repair _____

8. Tracheobronchoscopy through established tracheostomy incision _____

9. Nasotracheal catheter aspiration _____

10. Surgical closure tracheostomy with plastic repair _____

---

# Procedures Completed on the Lungs and Pleura (32035–32999)

Code range 32035–32999—Lungs and Pleura—is used to code procedures completed on the lungs and pleura. Figure 7-2, shown earlier in this chapter, illustrated the location of the lungs and pleura in relation to other structures of the respiratory system. This subsection is divided into the following areas:

- Incision
- Excision/Resection
- Removal
- Introduction and removal
- Destruction
- Thoracoscopy (Video-assisted thoracic surgery [VATS])
- Stereotactic radiation therapy
- Repair
- Lung transplantation
- Surgical collapse therapy: thoracoplasty
- Other procedures

## Incision (32035–32225)

Incisions are made into the lungs and pleura space for a variety of reasons, including to remove air or fluid from the area, control hemorrhaging, repair a tear, or remove a foreign body. The codes found in this area of CPT are summarized in Table 7-6.

**TABLE 7-6**  Incisions (32035–32225)

| Code | Description |
|------|-------------|
| 32035 and 32036 | A **thoracostomy**, an incision made into the chest wall, is differentiated in CPT with two codes. Code 32035 is used when rib resection for empyema occurs, and code 32036 is used when an open flap drainage for empyema is completed. |
| 32096–32160 | This range of codes is used to report **thoracotomy**, a surgical opening into the thoracic cavity. The codes are differentiated by accompanying procedures or the reason for the thoracotomy. |
| 32200–32225 | This range of codes is used to report pneumonostomy, pleural scarification, and decortication. |

# Excision/Resection, Removal, Introduction and Removal, and Destruction (32310–32562)

Excisions, removals, introductions and removals, and destructions that are performed on the lungs and pleura are coded in CPT by using code range 32310–32562. Codes for this range are summarized in Table 7-7.

**TABLE 7-7**  Excision/Resection, Removal, Introduction and Removal, and Destruction (32310–32562)

| Code | Description |
|------|-------------|
| 32310–32320 | **Pleurectomy**, the surgical removal of the pleura, is coded in CPT by use of one of two codes. Code 32310 reports a parietal pleurectomy, which is considered a separate procedure in CPT, and decortication and parietal pleurectomy are reported with code 32320. |
| 32400 and 32408 | Percutaneous needle biopsies of the pleura, lungs, or mediastinum is report with code 32400 for the pleura and code 32408 for a core needle biopsy of the lung or mediastinum. The CPT manual instructs the coder to see codes 76942, 77002, 77012, and 77021 if imaging guidance is used with code 32400. Additional instructions are also present that coders must adhere to for these codes. Reference the CPT manual and note that for code 32408 the imaging guidance is included in the code when it is performed. The note that follows the code indicates that code 32408 is not used in conjunction with the imaging codes listed in the note. |
| 32440–32491 | This range of codes is used to report the removal of a lung, known as a **pneumonectomy**. Coders must determine whether the procedure was a total pneumonectomy or other than a total pneumonectomy, because this affects code selection. If the procedure was not a total pneumonectomy, code selection is based on the removal of a single lobe, of two lobes, or of a single segment. Codes in this range are divided further according to accompanying procedures. |
| +32501 | This is considered an add-on code. This code is used only in conjunction with code 32480, 32482, or 32484. These codes are the primary codes, and code 32501 is added when a resection and repair of a portion of the bronchus is performed at the time of a lobectomy or segmentectomy. |
| 32503 and 32504 | A resection of an apical lung tumor is reported by these codes. The codes are differentiated between the procedure being performed, with or without chest wall reconstruction. |
| 32505 +32506 +32507 | Code 32505 reports an initial thoracotomy with therapeutic wedge resection. Codes 32506 and 32507 are add-on codes. Code 32506 reports each additional ipsilateral therapeutic wedge resection after the initial resection for a thoracotomy. Code 32507 reports a thoracotomy with diagnostic wedge resection followed by anatomic lung resection. In the CPT manual, review the instructional notations that follow codes 32506 and 32507 identify the primary procedures for which these codes are used. |
| 32540 | This code reports an empyemectomy, which is also known as an extrapleural enucleation of empyema. |
| 32550 | This code is used to report the insertion of an indwelling tunneled pleural catheter with cuff. Coders should note the notation found in the CPT manual that instructs the coder that code 32550 should not be reported with codes 32554, 32555, 32556, and 32557 when performed on the same side of the chest. |
| 32551 | This is a separate procedure code for tube thoracostomy, with or without water seal. This procedure is commonly completed for abscess removal, hemothorax, or empyema. |
| 32552 and 32553 | Code 32552 is used to report the removal of an indwelling tunneled pleural catheter with cuff. Code 32553 reports the placement of interstitial devices for radiation therapy guidance. Coders should look at the notations that follow this code, which direct them to report the supply of the device separately and to report the imaging guidance. |

*(continues)*

**TABLE 7-7** *(continued)*

| Code | Description |
|---|---|
| 32554 and 32555 | These codes report a needle or catheter thoracentesis aspiration of the pleural space. The codes are differentiated as to whether imaging guidance is used or not. |
| 32556 and 32557 | Percutaneous pleural drainage with the insertion of an indwelling catheter is reported with these codes. These codes are also differentiated as to whether imaging guidance is used or not. Coders should look at the notation that follows code 32557, which provides guidance on the use of codes 32554–32557. |
| 32560–32562 | These codes are used to report destructions. **Chemical pleurodesis** is coded with code 32560. In this procedure, a chemical is placed into the pleural space to cause inflammation and thereby reduce the effusion of the area. This procedure is commonly completed for persistent or recurrent **pneumothorax**, an accumulation of air or gas in the pleural cavity. Code 32561 is used to report the instillation of an agent for fibrinolysis on the initial day of treatment. Code 32562 is used to report the instillation on a subsequent day. Although the instillation of a fibrinolytic agent can be performed multiple times on the same day, code 32561 or 32562 is reported only once per day, depending on whether it is the initial or a subsequent day of treatment. |

**EXAMPLE:** Tom Jones had a chest x-ray that revealed a tumor-like spot on his right lung. Dr. Smith performed a percutaneous core needle biopsy of the lung.

This procedure would be coded using code 32408-RT.

# Thoracoscopy (Video-Assisted Thoracic Surgery [VATS]) (32601–32674)

Code range 32601–32674 is used to report **thoracoscopy**, the examination of the pleura, lungs, and mediastinum using an endoscope to visualize the area. As noted in the CPT manual, a surgical thoracoscopy always includes a diagnostic thoracoscopy. Codes 32601–32609 report diagnostic thoracoscopy, whereas codes 32650–32674 are used to report surgical thoracoscopy.

Diagnostic thoracoscopy codes are differentiated by site, and then by biopsy or without biopsy. Coders must read the operative report carefully to locate the site and determine whether a biopsy was performed.

**EXAMPLE:** Steven Ashton underwent a diagnostic thoracoscopy of the pericardial sac without biopsy. This would be given the code 32601.

Susan Paign underwent a diagnostic thoracoscopy of the pericardial sac with biopsy. This would be given the code 32604.

Surgical thoracoscopy codes are differentiated according to the type of procedure performed via the scope. To locate these codes in the index, the coder would reference the terms *thoracoscopy,* then *surgical,* and then the type of procedure.

**EXAMPLE:** Dr. Carl performed a therapeutic wedge resection, initial unilateral, via a thoracoscope.

To code Dr. Carl's procedure, a coder should reference *thoracoscopy* in the index, then *surgical,* then search code range 32650–32674. This would be coded using code 32666.

# Stereotactic Radiation Therapy (32701)

Code 32701 reports thoracic target delineation for stereotactic body radiation therapy. During this procedure a surgeon and radiation oncologist may work together. The surgeon will determine the targeted treatment area for therapy reported with code 32701, while the radiation oncologist will perform services that relate to radiation oncology. Code 32701 should be reported only once per the entire course of treatment regardless of the number of treatment sessions. Coders should become familiar with the extensive notes for code 32701 that appear before the code in the CPT manual.

## Repair (32800–32820)

There are only four codes that are used to code repairs completed on the lungs. The four codes are as follows:

- Code 32800—used to report a repair of a lung hernia through the chest wall.
- Code 32810—used to report a Clagett-type procedure, which is the closure of the chest wall following open flap drainage for empyema.
- Code 32815—used to report the open closure of a major bronchial fistula. When using this code, make sure that the operative reports describe an open procedure.
- Code 32820—used to report major reconstruction of the chest wall.

## Lung Transplantation (32850–32856)

During a transplantation of a lung or lungs, three distinct components are performed. Codes 32850–32856 are used to report these components. Coders should reference and read the notations that appear under the heading "Lung Transplantation" and before the codes.

Code 32850 is used to report the first component of the transplantation. This is the donor pneumonectomy, or the removal of the lung or lungs from the cadaver. The physician removes the lung and places the organ in cold preservation.

Codes 32855–32856 are used to report the **backbench work,** in which the physician prepares the donor organ prior to transplantation. Remember, the organ has been preserved for a period of time, especially if the organ has had to be transported to another site. Backbench work includes the preparation of the donor lung, including the dissection of the tissue to prepare the pulmonary venous/atrial cuff, pulmonary artery, and bronchus. If the procedure to be performed is a unilateral transplant, code 32855 is used to report the backbench work. If the procedure to be performed is a bilateral transplantation, code 32856 is used to report the backbench work.

The transplantation of the lung or lungs into the recipient is reported using codes 32851–32854. Codes 32851–32852 are used to report the transplant of a single lung and are differentiated by the procedure being performed without or with a cardiopulmonary bypass. Codes 32853–32854 are used to report the transplantation of two lungs and are also differentiated by the procedure being performed, without or with a cardiopulmonary bypass.

## Surgical Collapse Therapy, Thoracoplasty, and Other Procedures (32900–32999)

Code range 32900–32960 reports various procedures that are completed for therapeutic purposes to treat pulmonary conditions. Table 7-8 summarizes these codes, as well as codes that fall within code range 32997–32999.

**TABLE 7-8** Surgical Collapse Therapy, Thoracoplasty, and Other Procedures (32900–32999)

| Code | Description |
|---|---|
| 32900 | This code is used to report the extrapleural resection of the ribs. During this procedure, the rib is resected via an incision in the skin without entering the chest cavity. To prevent air from entering the chest cavity, the pleural membrane on the inside surface of the rib is not punctured. The portion of the rib is then removed. |
| 32905 and 32906 | These codes are used to report the performance of an extrapleural thoracoplasty or Schede-type thoracoplasty. This procedure is performed to treat thoracic empyema. During this procedure, the chest wall skeletal support is removed to create an area, previously filled with the accumulation of pus in the chest cavity which will fill in with granulation tissue during the healing process. If closure of a bronchopleural fistula occurs, code 32906 is reported. |
| 32940 | This code reports **extraperiosteal pneumonolysis,** which is the separation of the surface of the lung from the inside surface of the chest cavity. |

*(continues)*

**TABLE 7-8** *(continued)*

| Code | Description |
|---|---|
| 32960 | Therapeutic pneumothorax, the partial collapsing of the lung by the intrapleural injection of air, is reported with this code. Note that the physician is intentionally collapsing the lung for therapeutic reasons. |
| 32997 | This code reports a unilateral total lung lavage to treat specific lung diseases or injuries. |
| 32998 and 32994 | The 32998 code is used to report the unilateral ablation therapy of one or more pulmonary tumor(s) including pleura or chest wall when involved by tumor extension, percutaneous, including imaging guidance when performed, via radiofrequency. High-frequency radio waves create heat that destroys the tumors in the lung, pleura, or chest wall. Code 32994, an out of sequence code, reports the procedure via cryoablation. |
| 32999 | This code is used to report unlisted procedures completed on the lungs and pleura. |

## Exercise 7.6—Check Your Understanding

**Procedures Completed on the Lungs and Pleura (32035–32999)**

Using the CPT manual, select the appropriate code for each of the following procedures.

1. Percutaneous core needle biopsy of lung _____

2. Pneumonostomy with open drainage of cyst _____

3. Thoracotomy for postoperative complications _____

4. Repair of a lung hernia via the chest wall _____

5. Thoracoscopy with removal of a clot from the pericardial sac _____

6. Parietal pleurectomy _____

7. Thoracostomy with rib resection for empyema _____

8. Open biopsy of pleura _____

9. Removal of indwelling tunneled pleural catheter with cuff _____

10. Thoracotomy for exploration _____

# Summary

- Procedures completed on the nose are divided into the following subcategories: incision, excision, introduction, removal of a foreign body, repair, destruction, and other procedures.
- Drainage procedures are completed to remove a fluid from an area.
- Nasal polyps are growths in the nasal cavity that are commonly associated with rhinitis.
- A rhinotomy is a surgical procedure in which an incision is made along one side of the nose.
- Surgical repairs of the nose are known as *rhinoplasty* and are reported in CPT by using codes 30400–30630.
- A primary rhinoplasty, also known as an *initial rhinoplasty*, is the surgical repair of the nose.
- Secondary rhinoplasty is differentiated in the CPT manual according to minor revisions, intermediate revisions, and major revisions.

- There are four groups of sinuses: frontal, ethmoid, sphenoid, and maxillary.
- A partial laryngectomy, also known as a *hemilaryngectomy*, is the partial removal of the larynx.
- The *direct* viewing of the larynx and adjacent structures by use of a laryngoscope is known as a *direct laryngoscopy*.
- The viewing of the larynx by use of a laryngeal mirror that is placed in the back of the throat with a second mirror held outside of the mouth is known as an *indirect laryngoscopy*.
- A bronchoscopy is an examination of the bronchi using a flexible endoscope.
- To perform a thoracentesis, a physician inserts a needle through a patient's skin and chest wall into the pleural space.
- Pneumocentesis is the surgical puncturing of a lung.
- A thoracoscopy is the examination of the pleura, lungs, and mediastinum using an endoscope to visualize the area.
- Lung transplantation involves three components: cadaver donor pneumonectomy, backbench work, and recipient lung allotransplantation.

# Internet Links

To research diseases of sinuses and nose and their treatments, visit ***https://ent.weill.cornell.edu/patients/clinical-specialties/nose-sinus-disease***

To view information about thoracentesis, visit ***http://www.fpnotebook.com***, and search for thoracentesis.

# Chapter Review

## Fill in the Blank

**Instructions:** Fill in the blanks in the statements that follow.

1. A primary rhinoplasty is also known as a(n) _____ rhinoplasty.

2. A(n) _____ is a surgical procedure in which an incision is made along one side of the nose.

3. Secondary rhinoplasty is also known as _____ rhinoplasty.

4. The narrowing of the nasal vestibule is called _____.

5. The sinuses that are located within the frontal bone behind the eyebrows are the _____ sinuses.

6. The sinuses that are located directly behind the nose at the center of the skull are the _____ sinuses.

7. There are two types of nasal endoscopies: _____ and _____.

8. The removal of a lung is known as a(n) _____.

9. Surgical repairs of the _____ are known as rhinoplasty.

10. The surgical puncturing of a lung for aspiration is a(n) _____.

# Coding Assignments

**Instructions:** Using a CPT manual, select the appropriate code for each of the following procedures.

1. Transpalatine repair of choanal atresia _____

2. Initial posterior control of nasal hemorrhage with posterior cautery _____

3. Intranasal biopsy _____

4. Complete excision of inferior turbinate _____

5. Medial orbital wall decompression via nasal endoscopy _____

6. Diagnostic nasal endoscopy with maxillary sinusoscopy _____

7. Maxillary antrostomy using a sinus endoscope _____

8. Cervical tracheoplasty _____

9. Transtracheal tracheostomy, emergency procedure _____

10. Rigid bronchoscopy with fluoroscopic guidance with bronchial alveolar lavage _____

11. Cricoid split laryngoplasty _____

12. Single segment removal of lung _____

13. Removal of lung, pneumonectomy _____

14. Diagnostic thoracoscopy with biopsy of the mediastinal space _____

15. Thoracic sympathectomy via thoracoscope _____

16. Unilateral diagnostic nasal endoscopy _____

17. Maxillectomy _____

18. Excision of an intranasal lesion via internal approach _____

19. Intranasal maxillary sinusotomy _____

20. Pneumonostomy with open drainage of abscess _____

21. Revision of tracheostomy scar _____

22. Extrapleural pneumonectomy _____

23. Unilateral total lung lavage _____

24. Total intranasal ethmoidectomy _____

25. Rigid bronchoscopy, one lobe, with bronchial thermoplasty _____

26. Catheterization with bronchial brush biopsy _____

27. Suture of intrathoracic tracheal wound _____

28. Thoracentesis, needle, for aspiration of the pleural space _____

29. Planned tracheostomy _____

30. Laryngoscopy, flexible fiberoptic with removal of lesion _____

31. Submucous resection of superior turbinate _____

32. Total rhinectomy _____

33. Secondary rhinoplasty, minor revision _____

34. Indirect diagnostic laryngoscopy _____

35. Direct operative laryngoscopy with biopsy using operating microscope _____

36. Secondary rhinoplasty with intermediate revision _____

37. Repair of oronasal fistula _____

38. Radical maxillary sinusotomy with removal of antrochoanal polyps _____

39. Indirect laryngoscopy with vocal cord injection _____

40. Percutaneous transtracheal introduction of indwelling tube for oxygen therapy _____

# Case Studies

**Instructions:** Review each case and indicate the correct code(s).

## Case 1

**Preoperative diagnosis:** Mass on larynx

**Postoperative diagnosis:** Pending pathology report

**Procedure:** Laryngoscopy

The patient was prepped and draped in the usual fashion and placed in the supine position. The operating table was turned to 90 degrees, and a donut headrest was used for stabilization. Mirrors were placed for indirect visualization. A laryngoscope was inserted and suspended for visualization. The larynx and the surrounding area were inspected, and a biopsy of the larynx was taken. Hemostasis was verified, and the scope was extracted. The patient tolerated the procedure and was sent to the recovery room.

**CPT codes:** _____

## Case 2

**Preoperative diagnosis:** Foreign body in bronchus

**Postoperative diagnosis:** Foreign body in bronchus

**Procedure:** Removal of a foreign body in the bronchus of the left lung via scope

The patient was consciously sedated, and a bronchoscope was introduced into the left nasal passage. There were no abnormal structures noted as the scope was placed into the left bronchial tree. In the left bronchial tree, there was a foreign body, and the bronchial tree appeared slightly inflamed. The foreign body was removed and sent to pathology for inspection. The scope was removed, and the patient tolerated the procedure and was sent to recovery in stable condition.

**CPT codes:** _____

## Case 3

**Procedure Note**

This 32-year-old female was brought to the emergency department by her sister with right-side chest pain. Patient states that pain is between 9 and 10 on the pain scale. She has been having shortness of breath for the last four hours. She was fine yesterday except for a little fatigue. The pain started when she woke up this morning. A chest x-ray showed some suspicious area at the left base. At this time it was determined that a percutaneous core needle biopsy of the left lung should be completed. This procedure was performed, and the patient is resting.

**CPT codes:** _____

## Case 4

This 24-year-old patient was brought to the emergency room with difficulty breathing after being stung by a bee. The patient is experiencing a severe reaction to the bee sting. She was able to administer the EpiPen but she is still in need of breathing assistance. An emergency transtracheal tracheostomy was performed, after which the patient was resting comfortably.

CPT codes: _____

## Case 5

**Preoperative diagnosis:** Small unidentified mass in the right lung

**Postoperative diagnosis:** Same

**Procedure:** Bronchoscopy with biopsy with washings

Conscious sedation of Fentanyl, 20 mcg, and 2 mg of Versed was administered to this patient. A bronchoscope was introduced through the left nostril and moved down past normal vocal cord structure and into the bronchial tree on the right side. There were no ulcerations of the mucosa. Fluoroscopic guidance allowed for the bronchoscope to move into the upper lobe of the right lung. Endobronchial biopsy of a small mass was noted, and washings and brushings were taken. The sample was sent for histology. The patient tolerated the procedure well.

CPT codes: _____

## Case 6

**Physician Office Procedure Note**

This 76-year-old patient is being seen today because of spontaneous nasal hemorrhages. This patient has leukemia and is experiencing frequent bleeding from his nose. He was seen on Monday of this week, and I packed his nose with posterior nasal packing. He returned today and is still bleeding, and I again posteriorly packed his nose to control the nasal hemorrhage. He was instructed to go directly to the emergency department if the bleeding increases at any point.

CPT codes: _____

## Case 7

**Endoscopy Report**

**Preprocedure diagnosis:** Rule out malignant lesion of right upper lobe of bronchus

**Postprocedure diagnosis:** Pending pathology report

**Procedure:** Under conscious sedation, this 82-year-old female was sedated. The airway was anesthetized, and a flexible bronchoscope has advanced through the oral cavity through the larynx using fluoroscopic guidance. The bronchus was viewed, and a lesion was identified. A biopsy of the tissue was taken from the right upper lobe of the bronchus. No other lesions were visualized. Bleeding was found to be minimal, and the scope was removed. The tissue sample was sent to pathology. The patient was sent to the recovery area in stable condition.

**CPT codes:** _____

## Case 8

**Preoperative and postoperative diagnosis:** External and internal nasal deformity

**Procedure:** Septorhinoplasty with major septal repair

The patient was placed in the supine position under general anesthesia. This is the first time that this patient has undergone rhinoplasty. A cocaine-soaked pledget was placed in the nasal cavity, and the nasal septum and cartilaginous regions were exposed. After the blood vessels shrank, 1% Lidocaine with 1:100,000 epinephrine was injected into the nasal mucosa. The deformity was visualized via incisions noting the concave of the nasal septum. The cartilage was trimmed, and fat was removed from the subcutaneous regions. The dorsum was reshaped with files, and the periosteum was incised at the caudal aspect of the nasal bones, with a small portion of the bone resected. A vertical incision was made in the septal mucosa, and the cartilage was removed. All incisions were closed in single layers. The nose was dressed with the standard rhinoplasty dressing, and a Denver splint was placed to support the changes in the bone. Estimated blood loss was minimal. The patient was taken to the recovery area in stable condition.

**CPT codes:** _____

## Case 9

**Ambulatory Surgery Center Report**

**Patient history:** This 34-year-old male patient was in an accident five years ago, and at that time had a permanent tracheostomy due to the extent of the injury. He now presents with scar tissue in the area of the tracheostomy.

**Preoperative and postoperative diagnosis:** Redundant scar tissue surrounding a tracheal stoma

**Procedure:** Repair of the tracheal stoma

The patient was placed under general anesthesia, and the airway was established for proper ventilation during the procedure. An incision was made to resect the redundant scar tissue that had formed around the tracheal stoma. The skin was reanastomosed and closed in sutured layers. Blood loss was minimal. The patient was sent to the recovery area in satisfactory condition.

**CPT codes:** _____

## Case 10

**Endoscopy Report**

**Preoperative diagnosis:** Foreign body in larynx

**Postoperative diagnosis:** Same as above; material sent to pathology

**Procedure:** This 69-year-old female was brought to the endoscopy suite and topical anesthesia was applied to the oral cavity and pharynx. The laryngoscope was then placed through the oral cavity into the laryngeal area. An aspirator device was fed through the scope and cleared of all saliva to better visualize the foreign body that was present. The foreign body was then removed and sent to pathology. The patient was stable and sent to the postprocedure area. There were no noted complications.

**CPT codes:** _____

## Chapter Outline

Introduction

Guidelines Related to the National
    Correct Coding Initiative (NCCI)

Abbreviations Relating to the
    Cardiovascular System

Anatomy of the Cardiovascular System

Coding Cardiovascular Procedures

Coronary Artery Bypass Grafts Procedures

Arteries and Veins

Vascular Injection Procedures (36000–36598)

Arterial and Arteriovenous Procedures
    (36600–37799)

Summary

Internet Links

Chapter Review

Coding Assignments

Case Studies

## Learning Objectives

### At the conclusion of this chapter, you should be able to:

1. Define key terms related to coding procedures on the cardiovascular system.
2. Define abbreviations related to the cardiovascular system.
3. Describe the basic anatomy and functions of the cardiovasular system.
4. Define common procedures performed on the cardiovascular system.
5. Apply specific coding guidelines for the cardiovascular system.
6. Select CPT codes for procedures completed on the cardiovascular system.
7. Identify and code procedures for the cardiovascular system from case studies.

## Key Terms

| | | | |
|---|---|---|---|
| aneurysm | atrioventricular node (AV node) | complete replacement | epicardium |
| angioplasty | bundle of His | coronary artery bypass grafts (CABG) | heart |
| angioscopy | cardiac pacemaker | dual-chamber system | insertion |
| anomaly | cardiovascular system | electrode | ligation |
| aortic valve | central venous access device (CVA device) | endarterectomy | mitral valve |
| arteries | | endocardium | myocardium |
| atria | | | nonselective placement |

pacing cardioverter-
    defibrillator

parietal pericardium

partial replacement

percutaneous ventricular
    assist device (pVAD)

pericardial fluid

pericardial sac

pericardiocentesis

pericardium

pulmonary valve

pulse generator

removal

repair

selective placement

serous pericardium

single-chamber system

sinoatrial node (SA node)

thromboendarterectomy

tricuspid valve

veins

venous access device

ventricles

vessels

visceral pericardium

# Introduction

The **cardiovascular system** is the system that pumps blood through the body via the heart and blood vessels. Oxygen and nutrients are carried through the body by the blood, and waste products are transported for disposal from the body. The code range for the coding procedures performed within the cardiovascular system is 33016–37799. Within the CPT manual are two subsections with the following headings: Heart and Pericardium and Arteries and Veins.

# Guidelines Related to the National Correct Coding Initiative (NCCI)

Reference the following website to obtain the most current NCCI guideline information related to the Cardiovascular System.

1. Log on to *https://www.cms.gov/medicare-medicaid-coordination/national-correct-coding-initiative-ncci /ncci-medicare/medicare-ncci-policy-manual*.
2. Scroll to the section titled "View Manual by Chapter."
3. Click on "Chapter 5" for guidelines specific to the Cardiovascular System coding.

# Abbreviations Relating to the Cardiovascular System

The following is a list of the most common abbreviations related to the cardiovascular system.

| Abbreviations | Definitions |
|---|---|
| AED | automated external defibrillator |
| A-fib | atrial fibrillation |
| AICD | automated implantable cardioverter-defibrillator |
| AS | aortic stenosis |
| ASD | atrial septal defect |
| ASHD | arteriosclerotic heart disease |
| BBB | bundle-branch block |

*(continues)*

| (continued) | |
|---|---|
| CABG | coronary artery bypass graft |
| CAD | coronary artery disease |
| CC | cardiac catheterization |
| CCU | coronary care unit |
| CHD | coronary heart disease |
| CHF | congestive heart failure |
| DVT | deep vein thrombosis |
| EKG | electrocardiogram |
| HTN | hypertension |
| MI | myocardial infarction |
| MVP | mitral valve prolapse |
| PAD | peripheral artery disease |
| pVAD | percutaneous ventricular assist device |
| PVD | peripheral vascular disease |

# Anatomy of the Cardiovascular System

The **heart** is a large muscle that acts like a pump, moving blood through the arteries and veins. It is the major organ of the cardiovascular system. It is located between the lungs in the thoracic cavity. Figure 8-1 illustrates the location of the heart and associated structures that are found within the thoracic cavity.

The heart is enclosed in the **pericardium**, or **pericardial sac**, a double-walled sac composed of membranous tissue that surrounds the heart. The **parietal pericardium**, also known as the fibrous pericardium, is the outermost layer. The **visceral pericardium**, also known as the **serous pericardium**, is the inner layer of this double-walled sac. Between the two pericardial layers is a space that is filled with **pericardial fluid**, which prevents the two layers from rubbing against each other. There are three layers of the heart. The outermost layer of the heart is the **epicardium**. The middle layer is the **myocardium**, which is the thickest layer and is the cardiac muscle. The innermost layer is the **endocardium**, which is sometimes referred to as the *lining of the heart*. Figure 8-2 illustrates the linings and layers of the heart.

The heart is divided into four chambers. The upper chambers, called the **atria**, receive blood from the veins. The lower chambers, called **ventricles**, send blood to the arteries. Blood enters the right atrium through the superior vena cava from the upper part of the body and through the inferior vena cava from the lower part of the body. Blood leaves the heart through the aorta and the pulmonary artery. Figure 8-3 illustrates the blood flow through the heart.

The heart pumps blood rhythmically through the body. The rhythm of the pumping is the job of cells that generate and conduct electrical impulses. The **sinoatrial node (SA node)** is found where the superior vena cava and the right atrium meet. Impulses from the SA node move across the atria, causing contractions, pushing the blood into the ventricles of the heart.

When the impulse reaches the junction of the atria and the ventricles, the **atrioventricular node (AV node)**, directs the impulses to the ventricles, causing them to contract. The conduction fibers that cause contraction are called the **bundle of His**.

A coder who is trying to code procedures performed on the cardiovascular system needs to have at least a basic understanding of the anatomy of the heart and how the blood flows through it.

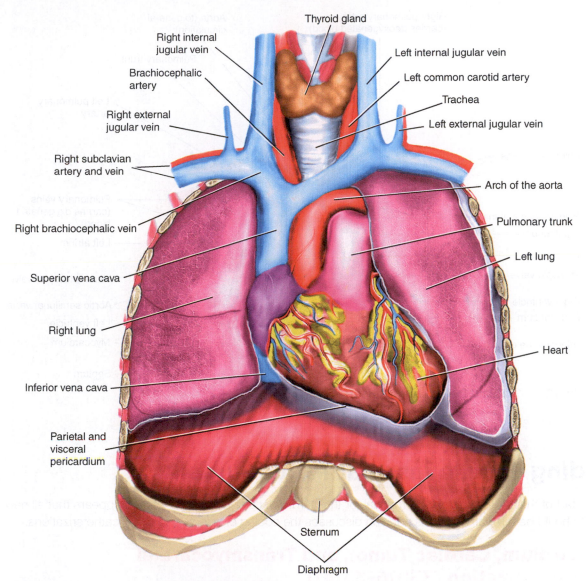

**FIGURE 8-1** Heart and Associated Structures

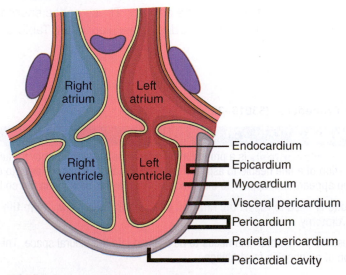

**FIGURE 8-2** Linings and Layers of the Heart

**FIGURE 8-3** Blood Flow of Normal Heart

# Coding Cardiovascular Procedures

At the start of the section in the CPT manual for the Cardiovascular System, a notation appears that all new coders should be familiar with. This notation discusses the coding of selective vascular catheterizations.

## Pericardium, Cardiac Tumor, and Transmyocardial Revascularization (33016–33141)

The first major section of codes discussed in the cardiovascular section is related to the heart and pericardium. The code range 33016–33141 begins the chapter. These codes encompass procedures on the pericardium, cardiac tumor excision, and transmyocardial revascularization. Table 8-1 summarizes the codes in this range.

**TABLE 8-1** Cardiovascular Procedures (33016–33141)

| Code(s) | Description |
| --- | --- |
| 33016–33019 | A **pericardiocentesis** is a procedure in which the physician removes fluid from the pericardial space by insertion of a fine needle to aspirate the fluid. In the CPT manual prior to code 33016 an extensive notation appears that applies to these codes. Review this notation in the coding manual. |
| 33020 | This code is used to report the removal of a clot or foreign body from the pericardium via a pericardiotomy. |
| 33025 | At times, the pericardial fluid needs to be drained into the pleural space. This code is used to report the creation of an opening for drainage. |

*(continues)*

**TABLE 8-1** (continued)

| Code(s) | Description |
|---------|-------------|
| 33030–33031 | These codes are used to report a pericardiectomy without or with cardiopulmonary bypass. |
| 33050 | Code 33050 reports resection of a pericardial cyst or tumor via an incision through the sternum. During this procedure, the patient is placed on cardiopulmonary bypass. |
| 33120 and 33130 | These codes are used to report procedures completed to remove cardiac tumors. The codes are differentiated according to whether the tumor is intracardiac or an external tumor. Code 33120 reports the excision of an intracardiac tumor. During the procedure, cardiopulmonary bypass is employed, and any defects due to the removal of the tumor are repaired. Code 33130 reports the resection of an external cardiac tumor. Cardiopulmonary bypass may or may not be employed and depends on the margins of heart or vessel tissue that is removed with the tumor. |
| 33140 and 33141 | Code 33140 is a separate procedure code that is used to report transmyocardial laser revascularization by thoracotomy. Code 33141 reports the same procedure when it is completed at the time of another open cardiac procedure. Code 33141 is secondary to the primary procedure code. Code 33141 is used in conjunction with 33390, 33391, 33404–33496, 33510–33536, and 33542. |

## Exercise 8.1—Check Your Understanding

**Cardiac Anatomy and Cardiovascular Codes (33010–33141)**

Fill in the blanks in the statements that follow.

1. When the impulse reaches the junction of the atria and the ventricles, the _____ directs the impulse to the ventricles, causing them to contract.

2. The heart is divided into _____ chambers.

3. The middle layer of the heart is the _____.

4. Blood enters the right atrium through the superior vena cava from the upper part of the body and through the _____ from the lower part of the body.

5. The heart is enclosed in the _____, a double-walled sac.

6. The "AV" in the term "AV node" means _____ node.

7. Fluid is drained from the pericardial space by a long needle. This procedure is called _____.

8. The _____ is found where the superior vena cava and the right atrium meet.

**Coding Assignment**

**Select the correct CPT code.**

9. Resection of pericardial tumor _____

10. Resection of external cardiac tumor _____

11. Pericardiocentesis with imaging guidance _____

12. Complete pericardiectomy _____

## Pacemaker or Pacing Cardioverter-Defibrillator (33202–33275)

A **cardiac pacemaker** is used to correct and manage heart dysrhythmias. The pacemaker is made up of a **pulse generator** that contains a lithium battery as its source of power. In most cases, it lasts six to ten years before it needs to be surgically replaced. The generator controls the heart's rate, the energy output, and the pacing modes. The other part of the pacemaker is the electrodes. An **electrode** is inserted into the heart through the subclavian vein and advanced to the right ventricular apex. If a second electrode, or lead, is needed, it is fixed in the right atrial appendage. The electrodes are then attached to the pulse generator. The pulse generator is implanted internally under the skin (considered permanent) or temporarily attached externally. To place the generator below the skin, an incision is made to create a pocket into which it is placed. The pacemaker system is referred to as either a *single-chamber* or a *dual-chamber* system. The **single-chamber system** has one electrode in either the right atrium or the right ventricle. The **dual-chamber system** has two electrodes: one in the right atrium and one in the right ventricle.

Also coded in this section of the CPT manual are procedures completed for pacing cardioverter-defibrillators. A **pacing cardioverter-defibrillator** differs from a pacemaker in that it emits defibrillating shocks that stimulate the heart and treat ventricular fibrillation or ventricular tachycardia. See Table 8-2.

**TABLE 8-2** Pacemaker or Pacing Cardioverter-Defibrillator (33202–33249)

| Code(s) | Description |
|---|---|
| 33202–33213 | This range of codes is used to report insertion or replacement of pacemaker, single or dual chamber. When coding the insertion or replacement of pacemakers, coders must determine the following:<br>• Is the pacemaker temporary or permanent?<br>• Was the pacemaker inserted with transvenous leads?<br>• What approach was used, thoracotomy, median sternotomy, subxiphoid approach versus endoscopic approach?<br>• Was the device single or dual chamber?<br>Figure 8-4 illustrates the placement of a pacemaker that is implanted under the skin. It should be stated that this section of codes contains instructional notations after the codes. For example, after code 33203, a notation instructs the coder of the following: When epicardial lead placement is performed with insertion of the generator, report 33202, 33203 in conjunction with 33212, 33213, 33221, 33230, 33231, and 33240.<br>Notations also appear after codes 33208 and 33221. |
| 33214 | Code 33214 reports the upgrade of implanted pacemaker system, conversion of single-chamber system to dual-chamber system (includes removal of previously placed pulse generator, testing of existing lead, insertion of new lead, insertion of new pulse generator). |
| 33215 | Repositioning of previously implanted transvenous pacemaker or implantable defibrillator (right atrial or right ventricular) electrode is reported using this code. The electrode is repositioned because the system is not functioning correctly due to improper placement of the electrode wire. |
| 33216 | Code 33216 codes the insertion of a single transvenous electrode, permanent pacemaker, or implantable defibrillator. |
| 33217 | Code 33217 codes the insertion of 2 transvenous electrodes, permanent pacemaker, or implantable defibrillator. It should be noted that codes 33216 and 33217 are not reported with numerous codes that are listed in the CPT manual after the description of codes 33216 and 33217. Reference these instructional notations for clarification. |
| 33218–33220 | Repair of transvenous electrode(s) for pacemakers is reported with these codes. Code 33218 reports the repair of a single transvenous electrode for a permanent pacemaker or implantable defibrillator, whereas code 33220 reports the repair of two electrodes for a permanent pacemaker or implantable defibrillator. |
| 33222–33223 | Procedures completed on skin pockets for pacemakers are reported using these codes. Code 33222 is for the relocation of a skin pocket for a pacemaker, while code 33223 reports the relocation of a skin pocket for an implantable defibrillator. |
| 33224 | This code reports the insertion of pacing electrode, cardiac venous system, for left ventricular pacing, with attachment to a previously placed pacemaker or implantable defibrillator pulse generator (including revision of pocket, removal, insertion, and/or replacement of the existing generator). This code is used to report the placement of an additional left ventricular electrode to a previously placed pacemaker or implantable defibrillator. |

*(continues)*

**TABLE 8-2** *(continued)*

| Code(s) | Description |
| --- | --- |
| 33225 <br><br> (must be used in conjunction with codes listed in the CPT manual) | This code is considered an add-on code that is used to report the insertion of a pacing electrode, cardiac venous system, for left ventricular pacing, at time of insertion of implantable defibrillator or pacemaker pulse generator. This code can include an upgrade to a dual-chamber system. This code is listed as secondary to the primary procedure code. The CPT manual lists the primary codes that are used with this code. |
| 33226 | At times, it is necessary to reposition a previously implanted cardiac venous system. This code is used to report this procedure for a left ventricular electrode (including removal, insertion, and/or replacement of existing generator). |
| 33233–33238 | Code range 33233–33238 is used to report the removal of a permanent pacemaker pulse generator and electrode(s). The codes are differentiated according to the items that are removed. The coder needs to read the operative report to determine which items were removed. |
| 33240 | This code is used to report the insertion of an implantable defibrillator pulse generator only with an existing single lead. |
| 33241 | During this procedure, the removal of an implantable defibrillator pulse generator occurs. It should be noted that only the pulse generator is removed. |
| 33243–33244 | Codes 33243–33244 are used to report the removal of a single- or dual-chamber implantable defibrillator electrode(s). The codes are differentiated by thoracotomy or transvenous extraction of the electrodes. It is common for the physician to attempt to remove the electrodes by transvenous extraction. During this procedure, the electrode wire is disconnected from the generator and then is withdrawn from the site. This is reported with code 33244. If the wire cannot be removed by the transvenous extraction technique, then a thoracotomy is required to gain access to the electrode for removal. Code 33243 reports removal by thoracotomy. |
| 33249 | The final code in this section reports the insertion or replacement of permanent implantable defibrillator system with transvenous lead(s) for single- or dual-chamber systems. This procedure is commonly completed using conscious sedation. |

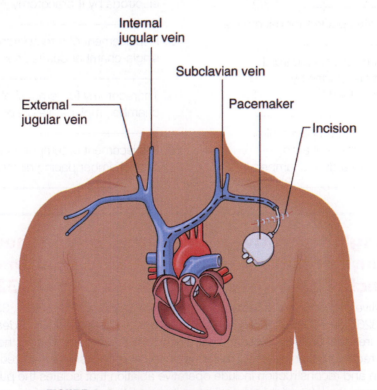

**FIGURE 8-4** Implanted Pacemaker

Additional coding guidance for the reporting of this code range includes the following:

- Radiological supervision and interpretation related to pacemaker or implantable defibrillator procedure is included in codes 33206–33249, 33262, 33263, 33264, 33270, 33271, 33272, 33273, 33274, and 33275. It should also be noted, as stated in the instructional notation for pacemaker or implantable defibrillator procedures that fluoroscopy (76000, 77002), ultrasound guidance for vascular access (76937), right ventriculography (93566), and femoral venography (75820) are included in 33274, 33275, when performed. To report fluoroscopic guidance for diagnostic lead evaluation without lead insertion, replacement or revision procedures use code 76000.

- In the CPT manual locate instructional notations that follow the heading Pacemaker or Implantable Defibrillator, which precedes code 33202. In this section of the CPT manual, the coding for the replacement of a pulse generator is discussed. The replacement of a pulse generator is also known as the changing of the battery of a pacemaker or implantable defibrillator. When selecting codes, the coder needs to determine which devices (pacemaker, lead pulse generator, etc.) are removed and/or replaced. Various codes exist for different scenarios. For example, if the pulse generator for a pacemaker is removed without replacement, code 33233 is reported. However, if the pulse generator for a pacemaker is removed with replacement of a pulse generator for only a single-lead system, then code 33227 is reported. If there is a removal of a pacemaker pulse generator with replacement of a pacemaker pulse generator for a dual-lead system, then code 33228 is reported.

## Exercise 8.2—Check Your Understanding

**Pacemaker or Pacing Cardioverter-Defibrillator (33202–33249)**

Using the CPT manual, select the appropriate code for each of the following procedures.

1. Insertion of epicardial electrodes by thoracotomy _____

2. Insertion of a permanent pacemaker with transvenous electrode; atrial _____

3. Relocation of a skin pocket for pacemaker _____

4. Removal of a permanent epicardial pacemaker and electrodes by thoracotomy; dual-lead system _____

5. Upgrade of an implanted pacemaker system with conversion of a single-chamber system to a dual-chamber system _____

6. Repositioning of a previously implanted transvenous pacemaker electrode _____

7. Removal of a permanent transvenous electrode by thoracotomy _____

8. Replacement of a temporary transvenous single-chamber cardiac electrode _____

9. Thoracotomy for removal of a dual-chamber implantable defibrillator _____

10. Replacement of temporary transvenous dual-chamber pacing electrodes _____

# Electrophysiologic Operative Procedures, Subcutaneous Cardiac Rhythm Monitor, Implantable Hemodynamic Monitors, and Wounds of the Heart (Including Valves) and Great Vessels (33250–33340)

Electrophysiologic operative procedures are reported using codes 33250, 33251, 33254, 33255, 33256, 33257, 33258, 33259, 33261, 33267, and 33268. This group of codes contain  resequenced codes. This range of codes is used to report procedures that are completed to treat dysrhythmias surgically. During these procedures, tissue ablation, disruption, and reconstruction occurs. The terms *limited* and *extensive* are utilized in this code range. Limited operative ablation and reconstruction include operative ablation that isolates the pulmonary veins or other anatomically defined areas in the left or right atrium. Extensive operative ablation and reconstruction include the services that are included in the limited procedure and additional ablation of atrial tissue, such as the right atrium, atrial septum, or left atrium with the atrioventricular annulus. The notations that appear in the CPT manual prior to code 33250 should be referenced. Codes 33265 and 33266 report surgical endoscopies consisting of operative tissue ablation and reconstruction of atria without cardiopulmonary bypass. Code 33265 reports the limited procedure, while code 33266 reports the extensive procedure based on the definitions in the CPT manual.

Codes 33269, 33265, and 33266 report endoscopic procedures. Locate code 33269 and review the instructional notation that follows the code for additional information.

Codes 33285 and 33286 report the insertion and removal of subcutaneous cardiac rhythm monitors. These monitors are also known as a cardiac event recorder or an implantable or insertable loop recorder (ILR). These procedures involve the physician inserting an event recorder at the subcutaneous level. The recorder keeps a continuous record of the heart's electrical activity. In the CPT manual, locate code 33285 and read the instructional notation that precedes it. This notation provides additional detail about codes 33285 and 33286. Also note the instructional notation that follows code 33286, which states that the initial insertion of the monitoring device includes the programming of the device. If subsequent electronic analysis and/or programming is needed, the coder is instructed to see codes 93285, 93291, or 93298.

The transcatheter implantation of an implantable hemodynamic monitor is reported with code 33289. As stated in the code description, the monitor is a wireless pulmonary artery pressure sensor implanted for long-term hemodynamic monitoring. This code also includes the deployment and calibration of the sensor, a right catherization, radiological supervision and interpretation, and pulmonary artery angiography, when performed. In the CPT manual following code 33289, an instructional notation appears that states code 93264 is used to report the remote monitoring of an implantable wireless pulmonary artery pressure sensor. An additional instructional notation also lists the codes that should not be reported in conjunction with code 33289. Reference the CPT manual for the complete listing of these non-reportable codes.

The repair of wounds of the heart and great vessels is reported using codes 33300–33340. This code range contains codes used to report the repair of cardiac wounds, cardiotomy, and the insertion of a graft, aorta, or great vessel. When coding from this range of codes, it is important for the coder to identify whether the procedures were completed with or without bypass. Many of the codes are differentiated by various types of bypass, such as cardiopulmonary bypass or shunt bypass.

## Cardiac Valve Procedures (33361–33496)

Procedures on the cardiac valves and other valvular procedures are reported using codes 33361–33496. These codes are summarized in Table 8-3.

**TABLE 8-3** Cardiac Valve Procedures (33361–33496)

| Code(s) | Description |
| --- | --- |
| 33361–33366 | These codes are used to report transcatheter aortic valve replacement with a prosthetic valve. Since these procedures require two physicians, all components of the procedures are reported by adding modifier 62, which denotes that two surgeons are working together as primary surgeons performing distinct parts of the procedure. In the CPT manual, preceding code 33361, an extensive notation appears that lists the work components of these codes. When performed, the following are included: percutaneous access, placing the access sheath, balloon aortic valvuloplasty, advancing the valve delivery system into position, repositioning the valve if needed, deploying the valve, insertion of a temporary pacemaker, and closure of the arteriotomy. Prior to assigning these codes, the coder should read the notations. Note that the codes in this code range are differentiated according to the approach. |
| 33367–33369 | These codes are all add-on codes that are added to codes 33361 to 33366, codes 33418, 33477, 0483T, 0484T, 0544T, 0545T, 0569T, 0570T, 0643T, and 0644T. Only one of these add-on codes can be reported per primary code assignment. This is noted following each add-on code. For example, following code 33367, a notation appears that states, "Do not report 33367 in conjunction with 33368, 33369." Reference the CPT manual to identify these codes and notations. |
| 33370 | Code 33370 is an add-on code that reports the placement and subsequent removal of cerebral embolic protection device(s) via a transcatheter approach. Locate this code in the CPT manual and review the entire description of the code and note the instructional notation that follows the code that states the codes that 33370 can be used in conjunction with. |

*(continues)*

**TABLE 8-3** *(continued)*

| Code(s) | Description |
|---|---|
| 33390 and 33391 | Codes 33390 and 33391 report an open valvuloplasty of the aortic valve with cardiopulmonary bypass. These codes are differentiated as simple or complex. It is essential that the documentation clearly records simple or complex. Review the CPT coding manual and note the examples of a simple or complex procedure. |
| 33404–33417 | This code range is used to report services performed on the **aortic valve**. The aortic valve sits between the aorta and the left ventricle and is one of the main valves of the heart. The procedures in this section include valvuloplasty, valve replacement, valve repair, resection, incision, and ventriculomyotomy. It should be noted that in this range of codes an out of sequence code (code 33440) appears. Code 33440 reports an aortic valve replacement by translocation of autologous pulmonary valve and transventricular aortic annulus enlargement of the the left ventricular outflow tract with valved conduit replacement of the pulmonary valve. This is known as a Ross-Konno procedure. In the CPT manual following code 33440 an instructional notation appears that lists the codes that are not be be used in conjunction with code 33440. Reference the CPT manual for the complete listing of these codes. |
| 33418–33430 | These procedures report services performed on the **mitral valve**. The mitral valve is the valve between the left atrium and left ventricle. It is also called the *bicuspid valve*. Valvotomy, valvuloplasty, transcatheter mitral valve repair (TMVR), and mitral valve replacement are reported using these codes. |
| 33460–33468 | The **tricuspid valve** is the valve that lies between the right atrium and right ventricle. The procedures on the tricuspid valve, such as a valvotomy, valvuloplasty, or valve replacement, are reported using these codes. |
| 33471–33478 | This code set involves procedures regarding the **pulmonary valve**. The pulmonary valve is one of the main valves of the heart and sits between the pulmonary artery and the right ventricle. The procedures on the pulmonary valve, such as a valvotomy, valvuloplasty, or valve replacement, are reported using these codes. |
| 33496 | This code reports a repair of nonstructural prosthetic valve dysfunction with cardiopulmonary bypass (separate procedure). This code would be used to report the repair of a malfunctioning prosthetic valve that may be leaking around the valve or malfunctioning because of a clot or growth. |

# Coronary Artery Anomalies and Endoscopy (33500–33509)

Procedures completed on coronary artery anomalies are reported using code range 33500–33507. Codes in this series include endarterectomy or angioplasty. An **endarterectomy** is a procedure used to remove the plaque deposits from blood vessels. An **angioplasty** is a procedure in which a balloon is inflated in the vessel to push and flatten plaque against the vessel wall. Figure 8-5 illustrates an angioplasty. Code 33508 is used

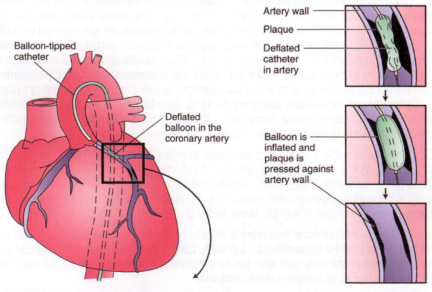

**FIGURE 8-5** Angioplasty

to report a surgical endoscopy including a video-assisted harvest of a vein(s) for a coronary artery bypass procedure. This code is used in conjunction with codes 33510–33523 as an add-on code in addition to the code for the primary procedure. Code 33509 reports the endoscopic harvesting of one segment of an upper extremity artery to be used for a coronary bypass procedure. If this is performed bilaterally add modifier 51. Review the instructional notations that follow this code for additional information.

## Exercise 8.3—Check Your Understanding

**Coronary Artery Anomalies (33250–33507)**

Using the CPT manual, assign the correct code to each of the following.

1. Replacement, pulmonary valve
   _____

2. Valvuloplasty, aortic valve; open, with cardiopulmonary bypass
   _____

3. Repair of anomalous coronary artery from pulmonary artery origin; by graft, without cardiopulmonary bypass
   _____

4. Valvotomy, pulmonary valve, closed heart; via pulmonary artery _____

5. Replacement, mitral valve, with cardiopulmonary bypass
   _____

6. Modified maze procedure for operative tissue ablation and reconstruction of atria
   _____

7. Aortoplasty completed for supravalvular stenosis _____

8. Tricuspid valve valvectomy with cardiopulmonary bypass
   _____

9. Incision of subvalvular tissue for discrete subvalvular aortic stenosis
   _____

10. Infundibular stenosis corrected by right ventricular resection _____

# Coronary Artery Bypass Grafts Procedures

**Coronary artery bypass grafts (CABG)**, are types of grafts performed on the heart that are completed using a vein, an artery, or a combination of a vein and an artery.

As discussed previously, code 33508 is an add-on code and is used in conjunction with code range 33510–33523. This code reflects the harvesting of a vein for bypass surgery. The procedure is performed using an endoscope to visualize the area on a monitor. A harvesting cannula is used to remove the portion of the vein to be used for bypass.

## Venous Grafting Only for Coronary Artery Bypass (33510–33516)

The 33510–33516 codes are used for reporting coronary artery bypass surgery when *only* veins are used for the bypass. This code range is *not* used to report bypass procedures that use arterial grafts *and* venous grafts during the same procedure. A saphenous vein is typically used, but a vein from the arm, the back of the leg, or a cadaver may also be used. Harvesting of any vein other than the saphenous is separately reportable. To report the harvesting of an upper extremity vein, use code 35500. To report the harvesting of a femoropopliteal vein segment, use code 35572. Harvesting the saphenous vein in the bypass procedure is included in the code reported for the bypass. After the vein is harvested, the heart is stopped and the bypass is performed. The code selection is based on the number of coronary venous grafts. For example, code 33510 reports a coronary artery bypass using a single coronary venous graft, whereas code 33511 is used when two coronary venous grafts are used.

## Combined Arterial-Venous Grafting for Coronary Bypass (33517–33530)

Codes 33517–33530 are used to report bypass procedures using both venous and arterial grafts that are done during the same operative session. Because codes from this range are add-on codes, they need to be reported with a primary code that is listed in the instructional notations that follow each code in code range 33517 to 33530. The codes read as combination codes and guide the coder to locate the additional code. An example can be found by referencing CPT code 33522—"Coronary artery bypass, using venous graft(s) and arterial graft(s); five venous grafts (list separately in addition to code for primary procedure)."

The coder needs to pay close attention to the operative report when assigning these codes, not only to be sure the correct number of grafts are captured, but also when there are grafts involving veins and arteries. The coder should also pay attention to who is harvesting the graft: in some cases, one surgeon will harvest the graft, and another surgeon will perform the bypass. In these instances, the surgeon performing the harvest should report his or her service as an assistant surgeon by appending the 80 modifier to the bypass procedure code.

## Arterial Grafting and Code for Coronary Artery Bypass (33533–33548)

The 33533–33548 codes would be used to report coronary artery bypass surgeries with the use of arteries or a combination of arterial-venous grafts. The arterial-venous grafts require the reporting of codes from this code range and the 33517–33523 code range, for a total of two codes for this service. Like venous grafting, harvesting the artery is included and is not reported separately except when the artery is taken from the upper extremities; when this occurs, codes 33509 or 35600 are reported in addition to the code for the bypass procedure. When an upper-extremity vein is harvested, code 35500 is additionally reported. When a femoropopliteal vein segment is harvested, code 35572 is also reported.

When a coronary artery bypass graft procedure is performed with a coronary endarterectomy, add-on code 33572 should be reported with the primary procedure code from the 33510–33516 and 33533–33536 code sets.

## Anomaly Repair and Other Procedures (33600–33926)

Code range 33600–33926 is used to report procedures completed on various cardiovascular structures and to report procedures to correct a heart anomaly. An **anomaly** is an abnormality or a deviation from the norm in a structure.

The coding in this subsection includes repairs, closures, shunting procedures, transections, and other complex procedures on the heart. The codes involve procedures performed on the aorta, on the pulmonary artery, and on septal and ventricular defects. Because of the complexity of this coding, it is essential that a coder have all appropriate documentation, along with input from the surgeon if needed, to assign the proper code(s) for the services rendered.

Review code 33741. The code reports a transcatheter atrial septostomy (TAS). Note that the code states that this procedure is completed for congenital cardiac anomalies. Documentation in the record needs to reflect the congenital anomaly. The description of the code also states that the code includes all imaging guidance that is performed by the person completing the procedure. Code 33741 is used to report any method of a TAS.

Codes 33745 and 33746 (an add-on code) report transcatheter intracardiac shunt (TIS) creation by stent placement. In reviewing these code note the additional information present in the code descriptions. These codes are for procedures that are completed for congenital cardiac anomalies. Code 33745 reports the initial intracardiac shunt while code 33746 reports each additional location. Therefore code 33745 is reported first and then code 33746 is added. If two additional shunt locations are involved as well as the primary location, the codes reported would be 33745, 33746, and 33746. Reference the CPT coding manual and note the instructional notations that follow code 33746.

Endovascular repairs of congenital heart and vascular defects are reported with codes 33894, 33895, and 33897. Locate the codes in the CPT manual for the full descriptions of the codes and review the instructional notes that appear before code 33894 and the additional notations that appear after codes 33895 and 33897. These notations provide guidance for coding and state how to use these codes in conjunction with other codes.

Many of the procedures that code to this range can be located in the CPT manual index by referencing the name of the procedure and the anomaly that is being corrected.

> **EXAMPLE:** To code a complete repair of Tetralogy of Fallot without pulmonary atresia, the following could be referenced in the index:
>
> The term *repair*, then *heart*, then *Tetralogy of Fallot*. The index instructs the coder to use code range 33692–33697.
>
> Alternatively, the coder could reference the following:
>
> The term *Tetralogy of Fallot*. When referencing this term, the coder is instructed to reference codes 33692, 33694, and 33697.
>
> Using either of these approaches, the coder will find the correct code.

## Exercise 8.4—Check Your Understanding

### Venous and Arterial Grafting, Anomaly Repair, and Other Procedures (33508–33926)

Using the CPT manual, assign the proper code(s) to each of the following:

1. Repair of pulmonary artery stenosis by reconstruction with patch _____

2. Blalock-Hanlon procedure _____

3. Repair, by ligation, of patent ductus arteriosus _____

4. Descending thoracic aorta graft, with bypass _____

5. Repair of atrial septal defect and ventricular septal defect with patch closure _____

6. Repair of pulmonary venous stenosis _____

7. Pulmonary artery embolectomy _____

8. Sinus of valsalva fistula repair with repair of ventricular septal defect via cardiopulmonary bypass _____

9. Division of aberrant vessel _____

10. Reimplantation of an anomalous pulmonary artery _____

## Heart/Lung Transplantation (33927–33945)

Only corneal and kidney transplants are more common than heart transplants. The patient who presents for heart transplant surgery has had heart damage caused by coronary artery disease, cardiomyopathy, congestive heart failure, or severe congenital heart disease.

Heart/lung transplants are usually performed on patients who will not survive unless both organs are replaced. End-stage lung disease that involves the heart is typically what leads to a heart/lung transplant. The documentation will guide the coder as to what organs were transplanted.

The coder will need to take into consideration whether the organs were harvested from a cadaver donor or if the transplanted heart was an artificial heart. As noted in Chapter 7, Respiratory System, donor transplants involve three distinct components of physician work. The components for a cadaver donor heart/lung transplantation include:

- Cadaver donor cardiectomy with or without pneumonectomy

- Backbench work, including the preparation of the donor organ(s) prior to transplantation

- Transplantation of heart, with or without lung allotransplantation

During the transplant procedure, the heart is inspected while being packed in ice-cold saline. Code 33930 is used to report the removal of the heart and lung(s) from a donor cadaver, and code 33940 is used to report the removal of only the heart. Both codes include the cold preservation of the organ(s).

Backbench work is reported by using code 33933 or 33944. Code 33933 reports the backbench work for a heart and lung transplant, while code 33944 is used to report the backbench work for a heart transplant.

The transplant is coded by use of code 33935 for a heart/lung transplant with recipient cardiectomy-pneumonectomy or by code 33945 for a heart transplant with or without recipient cardiectomy. Figure 8-6 illustrates the procurement of a donor heart, and Figure 8-7 illustrates a transplanted heart.

**FIGURE 8-6**  Donor Heart

(A)

(B)

(C)

**FIGURE 8-7**  Transplanted Heart   (A) The heart and valves are brought into place. (B) The valves are attached. (C) The heart is secured.

Codes 33927 to 33929 are used to report procedures in which an artificial heart is implanted, removed or replaced. Code 33927 reports the implantation of a total replacement heart system, (artificial heart), with a recipient cardiectomy. The removal and replacement of a total replacement heart system is reported with code 33928. Code 33929 is an add on code and is reported for the removal of a total replacement heart system for heart transplantation. Code 33929 is to be used in conjunction with primary code 33945.

## Extracorporeal Membrane Oxygenation or Extracorporeal Life Support Services (33946–33989)

At times when a patient's heart and/or lungs are not functioning correctly due to sickness or injury, the patient has to be placed on extracorporeal membrane oxygenation or extracorporeal life support services, which allow the heart or lungs to rest and recover. These services are commonly abbreviated as ECMO for extracorporeal membrane oxygenation or ECLS for extracorporeal life support. Codes 33946 to 33989 reports these services. The code range is differentiated according to the initiation of the services, daily management, and other services that are component parts of the services. Some of the codes are also differentiated by the patient's age. Locate the instructional notes for code range 33946 to 33989 that appear prior to code 33946. Read these extensive notes to become familiar with this range of codes.

## Cardiac Assist (33967–33997) and Other Procedures (33999)

This subsection of the chapter includes the insertions and removals of ventricular assist devices, extracorporeal circulation, and intra-aortic balloon assist devices. These cardiac assist device procedures are performed to help the heart function properly. The coder will need to read the operative note carefully to assign the code that most accurately reflects the service rendered. Table 8-4 summarizes the codes found in this section.

**TABLE 8-4** Cardiac Assist (33967–33999)

| Code(s) | Description |
|---|---|
| 33967–33974 | This group of codes is used to report the insertion and removal of intra-aortic balloon assist devices. The codes are grouped in pairs, with the first code used to report the insertion and the second code used to report the removal of the device. For example, code 33967 reports the insertion of an intra-aortic balloon, and the following code, 33968, reports the removal. There are three groups of codes in this range, and they are differentiated as follows:<br>• Codes 33967 and 33968—percutaneous approach<br>• Codes 33970 and 33971—insertion and removal of device involving the femoral artery<br>• Codes 33973 and 33974—insertion and removal of device involving the ascending aorta |
| 33975–33978 | These codes are used to report the insertion and removal of a ventricular assist device. The codes are differentiated by the number of ventricles involved in the procedure. |
| 33979–33980 | Codes 33979 and 33980 are used to report the insertion and removal of an implantable intracorporeal ventricular assist that involves a single ventricle. |
| 33981–33983 | Code 33981 reports replacement of extracorporeal ventricular assist device for single or biventricular, pump(s), single or each pump. Codes 33982 and 33983 report the replacement of ventricular assist device pump(s); implantable intracorporeal, single ventricle. Code 33982 reports this procedure without cardiopulmonary bypass, while code 33983 reports the procedure with a cardiopulmonary bypass. |
| 33995, 33990–33991 | Code 33995 is a code that is out of numerical order in the CPT manual. Code 33995 appears directly before code 33990. These codes report the insertion of a percutaneous ventricular assist device. A **percutaneous ventricular assist device (pVAD)** is inserted to assist a weakened heart in ejecting blood to the body via a mechanical pump. These codes include the radiological supervision and interpretation and are differentiated according to the access. Code 33995 reports insertion into the right heart with venous access only. Code 33990 reports insertion into the left heart with arterial access only while code 33991 reports both arterial and venous access of the left heart with transseptal puncture. Therefore documentation needs to clearly state the specific detail that is found in these codes. |

*(continues)*

**TABLE 8-4** (*continued*)

| Code(s) | Description |
|---|---|
| 33992 and 33997 | Code 33992 is used to report the removal of a percutaneous left heart ventricular access device when it occurs separate and distinct from the session in which the device was inserted. Reference the CPT coding manual and note the instructional notation that follows this code to provide direction in coding removal of an implantable aortic counterpulsation ventricular assist system. Code 33997 is an out of sequence code that reports a removal of a percutaneous right heart ventricular assist device. The description of this code also notes that the procedure must be performed at a separate session from the insertion of the device. When codes 33992 and 33997 are reported the documentation must clearly state that the procedure was performed using a percutaneous approach. |
| 33993 | This code reports the repositioning of a percutaneous ventricular access device that occurs at a separate and distinct session from the insertion of the device. The imaging guidance is included in the code. |
| 33999 | Code 33999 is used to report cardiac surgery procedures that are not listed in the CPT manual. Prior to reporting this code, the coder should query the provider to ensure that codes within the CPT manual do not represent the procedure completed because reporting this code most likely will trigger a review by the third-party payer. |

# Arteries and Veins

It is just as important to understand the anatomy of the vessels as it is to understand the anatomy of the heart when you are selecting codes in the cardiovascular system. **Vessels** are structures that move fluid through the body. Arteries and veins are considered vessels. **Arteries** move oxygen-rich blood from the heart to the rest of the body (with the exception of the pulmonary artery). **Veins** move the deoxygenated blood back to the heart (with the exception of the pulmonary vein). Arteries usually have one vein accompanying them throughout the vascular system. Figure 8-8 illustrates arteries and Figure 8-9 illustrates veins of the body.

## Embolectomy/Thrombectomy (34001–34490)

Codes from the 34001–34490 series are used to report embolectomy/thrombectomy procedures completed on arteries or veins, with or without catheter placement. The object of these procedures is to remove a clot in the vessel. The code selection is made by vessel, as well as by approach or method of entry.

### Exercise 8.5—Check Your Understanding

**Embolectomy/Thrombectomy (34001–34490)**

Using the CPT manual, note whether each procedure is being performed in a vein or artery, and then note the approach for each of the codes given. The student can assume that in each example, the surgeon is performing either an embolectomy or a thrombectomy.

| Code | Vein/Artery | Approach |
|---|---|---|
| 1. 34451 | _____ | _____ |
| 2. 34471 | _____ | _____ |
| 3. 34201 | _____ | _____ |
| 4. 34051 | _____ | _____ |
| 5. 34203 | _____ | _____ |

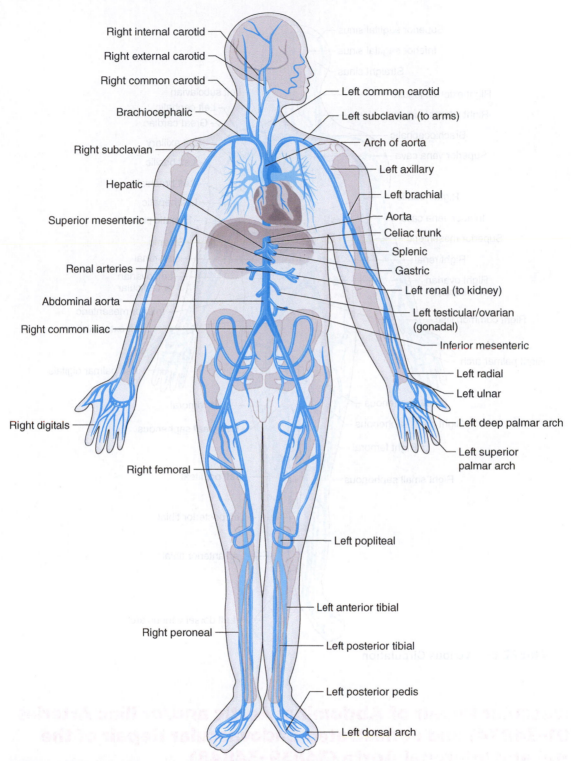

**FIGURE 8-8** Arterial Circulation

# Venous Reconstruction (34501–34530)

Codes 34501–34530 are the codes used to report reconstruction of a vein. The type of reconstruction dictates code assignment. Transposition, grafts, anastomosis, and sutures are used for reconstruction.

Superior sagittal sinus
Inferior sagittal sinus
Straight sinus
Right external jugular
Right internal jugular
Brachiocephalic
Superior vena cava
Right hepatic
Inferior vena cava
Superior mesenteric
Right renal
Right ovarian or testicular
Right common iliac
Right palmar arch
Small saphenous
Right great saphenous
Right femoral
Right small saphenous

Left subclavian
Left cephalic
Great cardiac
Left axillary
Left basilic
Left brachial
Left hepatic
Hepatic portal
Splenic
Left renal
Left ovarian or testicular
Inferior mesenteric
Left external iliac
Left palmar digitals
Left femoral
Left great saphenous
Left popliteal
Left posterior tibial
Left anterior tibial
Left dorsal venous arch

**FIGURE 8-9** Venous Circulation

# Endovascular Repair of Abdominal Aortic and/or Iliac Arteries (34701–34834) and Fenestrated Endovascular Repair of the Visceral and Inferenal Aorta (34839–34848)

Codes 34701–34834 are the codes used to report endovascular repair of an abdominal aortic aneurysm. An **aneurysm** is an area in an artery that becomes weakened. With each pulse of blood through the artery, the weakened area balloons out, or expands, causing more weakness of the vessel. Figure 8-10 illustrates the placement of iliac and aortic clamps prior to procedures to address an abdominal aortic aneurysm.

This type of coding has several components. Coders must read the notations that appear before code 34701 in the CPT manual to understand fully the coding for this section. Review the instructional notation that states that

**FIGURE 8-10** Abdominal Aortic Aneurysm

Labels: Vena cava, Aortic clamp, Kidney, Renal artery, Intended incision sites, Ureter, Common iliac artery, Iliac clamp

fluoroscopic guidance and radiological supervision and interpretation in conjunction with endograft repair is not separately reported. Guidance on the coding of wireless physiologic and pressure sensors is also given.

Table 8-5 summarizes the codes in range 34701–34834. The organization of codes found in this range of the coding manual can be difficult to understand as a number of the codes are out of sequence codes. To get the best understanding of the organization of the codes in range 34701 to 34834, locate code 34701 and review the codes throughout the manual until you locate code 34834. As you are reviewing the codes note the # symbol that identifies resequenced codes. These are the codes that are out of numerical order. Codes 34841 to 34848 report the placement of a fenestrated endovascular graft in the visceral aorta, either separately or in combination with the infrarenal aorta. The graft is placed to repair an aneurysm, pseudoaneurysm, dissection, penetrating ulcer, intramural hematoma, or a traumatic disruption.

**TABLE 8-5** Endovascular Repair of Abdominal Aortic Aneurysm (34701–34834)

| Code(s) | Description |
|---|---|
| 34701–34718 | These codes are used to report the endovascular repair of an aortic and/or iliac artery(ies). The code descriptions are very detailed and must be read carefully prior to code assignment. |
| 34808 | This code is an add-on code. Code 34808 is used with code 34701, 34702, 34703, 34704, 34707, 34708, 34709, 34710, 34813, 34841, 34842, 34843, or 34844 to report the endovascular placement of an iliac artery occlusion device. |
| 34812–34813 | These add-on codes are used for procedures completed on the femoral artery. Code 34812 is used to report an open femoral artery exposure for delivery of endovascular prosthesis by groin incision. If this procedure is completed bilaterally, modifier 50 should not be added to 34812. In the CPT coding manual locate code 34812 and review the instructional notation that instructs the coder to report code 34812 twice. Also note the codes that code 34812 would not be reported with. Code 34813 is an add-on to code 34812 and codes the placement of a femoral-femoral graft during endovascular aortic aneurysm repair. |
| 34820 | This add-on code is used for unilateral open iliac artery exposure for delivery of endovascular prosthesis or iliac occlusion during endovascular therapy, by abdominal or retroperitoneal incision. If the procedure is performed bilaterally, modifier 50 should not be added. Locate code 34820 in the CPT coding manual. Note the three instructional notations that follow the code description. The second notation states not to use the 50 modifier and to report code 34820 once per side if necessary. Documentation must clearly justify the assignment of the code twice. |
| 34830–34832 | Open repair of an infrarenal aortic aneurysm or dissection, plus the repair of an associated arterial trauma following the unsuccessful endovascular repair, are coded using this range of codes. The codes are differentiated by the type of prosthesis used: tube, aorto-bi-iliac, or aorto-bifemoral. |
| 34833 | A unilateral open iliac artery exposure with creation of a conduit for the delivery of an endovascular prosthesis or for establishment of cardiopulmonary bypass, by either an abdominal or retroperitoneal incision is reported using this code. To report a bilateral procedure, report code 34833 twice. This is so noted in the second instructional notation that appears after the code. Review the instructional notations that follow code 34833 in the CPT manual to reference the codes that code 34833 are used in conjunction with and codes that 34833 are not to be used in conjunction with. Please note that code 34833 is an add-on code. |
| 34834 | Code 34834 is used to report a unilateral open brachial artery exposure for delivery of endovascular prosthesis. The bilateral procedure is reported by reporting code 34834 twice. Please note that code 34834 is an add-on code. |

## Exercise 8.6—Check Your Understanding

**Endovascular Repair of Abdominal Aortic Aneurysm (34701–34834)**

Using the CPT manual, assign the proper code(s) or add-on codes to each of the following:

1. List the add-on code for an open iliac artery exposure for delivery of endovascular prosthesis by abdominal incision, unilateral _____

2. Endovascular repair of infrarenal abdominal aortic aneurysm using aorto-uni-iliac prosthesis _____

3. List the add-on code for an unilateral open brachial artery exposure for delivery of endovascular prosthesis _____.

4. Open repair of infrarenal aortic aneurysm in addition to repair of associated arterial trauma following unsuccessful endovascular repair with aorto-bi-iliac prosthesis _____

5. List the add-on code for an open femoral artery exposure for delivery of endovascular prosthesis by groin incision, bilateral _____

6. List the add-on code for an open brachial artery exposure to assist in the deployment of aortic endovascular prosthesis by incision into the right arm _____

7. List the add-on code for an open femoral artery exposure for delivery of endovascular prosthesis, by groin incision, unilateral _____

8. Open repair of infrarenal aortic aneurysm plus repair of associated arterial trauma, following unsuccessful endovascular repair, aorto-bifemoral prosthesis _____

# Direct Repair of Aneurysm or Excision (Partial or Total) and Graft Insertion for Aneurysm, Pseudoaneurysm, Ruptured Aneurysm, and Associated Occlusive Disease (35001–35152)

Code range 35001–35152 includes the artery preparation when an anastomosis is to be completed and includes the endarterectomy. This range reports direct repair of an aneurysm, a pseudoaneurysm, or excision and graft insertion in the various arteries of the body. Knowledge of the site of surgery is essential to select a code properly from this range because the codes identify the artery repaired. For example, code 35002 is for the carotid subclavian artery, and code 35005 is for a vertebral artery. The codes are also differentiated by whether the repair was for:

- An aneurysm and associated occlusive disease

- A ruptured aneurysm

- An aneurysm, pseudoaneurysm, and associated occlusive disease

Careful reading of the operative report must occur to identify the necessary elements for code selection.

# Repair of Arteriovenous Fistula (35180–35190)

Code range 35180–35190 is used to report the repair of an arteriovenous fistula. Codes 35180–35184 are used to report the repair of a congenital arteriovenous fistula. These codes are differentiated by the site of the procedure. Codes 35188–35190 are used to code the repair of an acquired or traumatic arteriovenous fistula. These codes are also differentiated by site.

# Repair of a Blood Vessel for Reasons Other Than Fistula (35201–35286)

Code range 35201–35286 is used to report the repair of a blood vessel for reasons other than a fistula, with or without patch angioplasty. There are three groupings of codes in this code range:

- Direct repair of a blood vessel—Differentiated by site; codes 35201–35226

- Repair of a blood vessel with a vein graft—Differentiated by site; codes 35231–35256

- Repair of blood vessel with a graft other than a vein—Differentiated by site; codes 35261–35286

# Thromboendarterectomy (35301–35390)

Code range 35301–35390 is used to code a **thromboendarterectomy**, a surgical incision that is made into an artery to remove a thrombus or plaque and the arterial lining. This procedure can occur with or without a patch graft. The codes in this range are differentiated according to the artery on which the procedure was completed. Code 35306 is an add-on code that is additionally reported for each additional tibial or peroneal artery. This code is to be listed as an additional code to the primary procedure code 35305. In the CPT manual following code 35306, a notation instructs the coder that codes 35304, 35305, and 35306 are not to be reported with codes 37229, 37231, 37233, and 37235.

# Angioscopy (35400)

The angioscopy code, 35400, is an add-on code and is used in conjunction with a code for the therapeutic intervention. **Angioscopy** is a procedure in which a fiber-optic scope is used to visualize the interior of a noncoronary vessel.

## Exercise 8.7—Check Your Understanding

### Code Range 35001–35400

Using the CPT manual, identify and assign the correct code to each of the following procedures:

1. Direct repair of blood vessel of the neck

   _____

2. Repair of congenital arteriovenous fistula of head and neck

   _____

3. Repair of blood vessel with vein graft, intra-abdominal

   _____

4. Repair, acquired arteriovenous fistula, thorax and abdomen

   _____

5. Direct repair of aneurysm with patch graft by arm incision for ruptured aneurysm of the axillary-brachial artery

   _____

## Bypass Graft—Vein (35500–35572) and In-Situ Vein (35583–35587)

This code range reports bypass grafts that are completed using veins. The codes are differentiated according to the location of the vein graft anastomosis. For example, code 35571 reports a procedure whereby the surgeon creates a bypass around the popliteal artery using a vein that is then sutured to the tibial artery. It should be noted that in the CPT manual, prior to code 35500, notations give directions for code assignment. For code range 35501–35587, procurement of the saphensous vein graft is included in the codes and, therefore, is not reported as a separate service. Codes 35583 to 35587 report in-situ vein bypass. The codes are differentiated according to the veins sutured.

## Bypass Graft—Other Than Vein (35600–35671)

Sometimes veins are not used for bypass. An artery or other material might be used. If this is the case, the coder would reference the Bypass Graft—Other Than Vein subsection of the cardiovascular chapter of the CPT manual. Codes 35600–35671 offer other reporting options for bypass grafts done with materials other than a vein.

## Composite Grafts, Adjuvant Techniques, and Arterial Transposition (35681–35697)

Composite grafts are made from donor and synthetic materials. Codes 35681–35683 are add-on codes and need to be used in conjunction with the codes that are listed in the CPT manual after each code. The harvesting and anastomosis of multiple vein segments from distant sites for use as an arterial bypass graft conduit is reported with codes 35682 and 35683. It should also be noted that, following codes 35681, 35682, and 35683, notations state the codes that are not to be reported together and the codes that these codes should be reported in conjunction with.

Adjuvant technique codes, codes 35685 and 35686, are add-on codes that are used with various codes as listed in the CPT manual. The adjuvant technique involves the surgeon placing a vein patch, placing a cuff at a distal arterial anastomosis site, or creating a fistula between artery and vein during bypass surgery. These adjuvant techniques are used to improve the patency of the lower extremity autogenous or synthetic bypass graft.

Codes 35691–35697 report arterial transposition procedures that are completed to improve blood flow within the arteries. The codes are differentiated according to whether the arteries were anastomosed. Code 35697 is an add-on code.

## Excision, Exploration, Repair, and Revision (35700–35907)

Codes 35700–35907 report excision, exploration, repair, and revision of bypass surgery. Code 35700 is an add-on code that reports the return of the patient to the operating room more than one month after an original operation was completed on the femoral-popliteal or femoral anterior tibial, posterior tibial, peroneal artery, or other distal vessel.

Codes 35701–35703 report the exploration of an artery not followed by surgical repair. Exploration for postoperative hemorrhage, thrombosis, or infection is reported with codes 35800–35860. Codes 35870–35884 report repairs, excisions, and revisions. Excisions of infected grafts are reported with codes 35901–35907 and are differentiated according to anatomical site.

# Vascular Injection Procedures (36000–36598)

The coding for this subsection of the cardiovascular chapter is difficult for new coders. Two terms that a coder needs to understand in this type of coding are *selective* and *nonselective*. The terms refer to catheter placement. **Nonselective placement** of a catheter means the catheter is functioning in the vessel punctured and does not go into any other vessel or vascular family. **Selective placement** means that the catheter moves into one of the great vessels off the aorta, not including the vessel punctured for access. This is a simplified version, but it is the basic concept for this coding.

Movement of the catheter from one vascular family to another should be reported separately. Radiological services performed in conjunction with catheter movement should also be reported separately. CPT identifies services that are included and those that are not included. Careful attention to these details can make a significant difference in the reimbursement that your surgeon does or does not receive for these services.

Code sets begin with intravenous procedures (36000–36015). The intra-arterial/intra-aortic procedures follow and are reported using codes 36100–36299.

Venous procedures, including venipuncture or intravenous therapy, are reported using codes 36400–36598. Included in the venous procedures are the central venous access (CVA) procedures. A **venous access device** is a device or catheter that allows access to the venous system. It can be used for intravenous medications or fluid delivery and is typically used for patients who require these services for more than 24 hours. A **central venous access device (CVA device)**, is a catheter classified as such if the tip ends in the subclavian, brachiocephalic, superior or inferior vena cava, or right atrium. The device can be inserted into the jugular, subclavian, femoral vein, or inferior vena cava to be considered centrally inserted. If the device is inserted peripherally, it is inserted in the basilica or cephalic vein.

There are five categories for procedures involving these devices. When a catheter is placed in a newly established venous access, it is considered an **insertion**. The **repair** procedures involve fixing, not replacing, either the catheter or port/pump. The repair is one that is other than a pharmacologic or mechanical repair of a intracatheter or pericatheter occlusion. **Partial replacement** involves replacement of only a catheter component, not the whole device. Replacement of the whole device at the same access site is considered a **complete replacement**. The final category, **removal**, involves the removal of the entire device.

When coding the replacement of an existing CVA device, the coder should code for the removal of the old device and assign a code for the new device if it is placed in a separate venous access site.

# Arterial and Arteriovenous Procedures (36600–37799)

The next group of codes in the CPT manual is used for procedures that involve arteries and veins. Many involve accessing an artery or a vein for a variety of purposes.

## Arterial and Intraosseous Codes (36600–36680)

Codes 36600–36680 are used to report services that involve arterial and intraosseous procedures such as:

- Arterial puncture, code 36600, for withdrawal of blood for diagnosis
- Arterial catheterization, codes 36620–36640, for sampling or for prolonged infusion therapy
- Catheterization of an umbilical artery, code 36660, for diagnosis or therapy on a newborn
- Placement of needle, code 36680, for intraosseous infusion

## Hemodialysis Access, Intervascular Cannulation for Extracorporeal Circulation or Shunt Insertion (36800–36861)

Code range 36800–36861 is used to report procedures completed for:

- Hemodialysis access
- Intervascular cannulation for extracorporeal circulation
- Shunt insertion

Numerous notations are present in this range of codes that must be referenced for proper code selection. For example, a notation appears under code 36818 that instructs the coder that this code is not to be reported with codes 36819, 36820, 36821, or 36830 during a unilateral upper-extremity procedure. It should also be noted that many of the procedures in this range are separate procedure codes and are reported only if no other procedure is completed. It should be noted that some of the procedures are completed via a percutaneous approach. Review codes 36836 and 36837 and note the descriptions for these two percutaneous procedures.

## Dialysis Circuit (36901–36909)

Code ranges 36901–36909 reports angioplasty, stent placement, thrombectomy, and embolization within dialysis circuit procedures. In the CPT manual prior to these codes, extensive guidelines and definitions are listed that impact the selection of codes in this range. In the CPT manual, review the definitions including dialysis circuit, peripheral dialysis segment, central dialysis segment, and so on.

Codes 36901 to 36906 are built as progressive hierarchies that include less intensive services, and only one code from 36901 to 36906 is to be reported for the service provided in a dialysis circuit. This is highlighted in the guidelines that are found in the CPT manual prior to the codes.

Codes 36907 to 36909 are add-on codes. Following each code there are extensive instructional notations in the CPT manual that outline the codes used in conjunction with these add-on codes. It is essential that coders read all of the guidelines, definitions, and instructional notations that are present in the CPT manual for this range of codes. Locate all of these items and read them prior to code selection.

## Portal Decompression Procedures (37140–37183)

Code range 37140–37183 is used to report portal decompression procedures. These procedures, which include venous anastomosis, insertion of shunts, and revision of shunts, are completed to manage venous pressures. Like other sections of this chapter, all notes need to be referenced before codes are assigned.

## Transcatheter Procedures (37184–37218)

Transcatheter procedures are completed by using a catheter to complete the following:

- Perform arterial mechanical thrombectomy—codes 37184–37186.
- Perform venous mechanical thrombectomy—codes 37187–37188.
- Inject a drug into the vessel—codes 37195 and 37211–37214.
- Obtain a biopsy sampling—code 37200.
- Retrieve a foreign body—code 37197.
- Transcatheter therapy procedures for thrombosis—codes 37211–37214.
- Placement of intravascular stents—codes 37215–37218.

Coders need to read the notations that are present at the start and end of this code range in the CPT manual for additional instructions on selecting codes from this range.

# Endovascular Revascularization (Open or Percutaneous, Transcatheter) (37220–37239)

Code range 37220–37235 reports endovascular revascularization procedures performed on the lower extremities for occlusive disease. When reporting these codes, the coder should report only one primary code from 37220 to 37235 for each extremity vessel treated because the codes are inclusive of all the services provided for that vessel. Therefore, the code for the most intensive service provided should be reported.

As discussed in the CPT manual, in the paragraphs preceding these codes, the codes include the following:

- Accessing and selectively catheterizing the vessel
- Traversing the lesion
- Radiological supervision and interpretation directly related to the intervention
- Embolic protection
- Closure of the arteriotomy
- Imaging completed
- Balloon angioplasty, if performed
- Atherectomy
- Stenting

The organization of the codes is divided into three arterial vascular territories: iliac, femoral/popliteal, and tibial/peroneal. There are specific guidelines for each of the three territories. Prior to code selection, coders must read the notations in the numerous paragraphs before the code descriptions. The guidelines give instructions for coding when multiple territories are treated, coding for lesions that extend across margins of one vessel into another, and for the use of modifier 59, to name a few. It should also be noted that, following individual codes in this section, notations are present in relation to codes used in conjunction with other codes. Codes 37246 to 37249 are out of sequence codes. These codes report transluminal balloon angioplasty, open or percutaneous, and related radiological imaging. These codes are, therefore, considered bundled codes, and the instructional notations that precede and follow the codes must be read and understood prior to assigning these codes. Locate and read the instructional notations that precede and follow these codes. Codes 37236–37239 report transcatheter placement of an intravascular stent(s) for vessels other than in the lower extremities, cervical carotid, extracranial vertebral or intrathoracic, carotid, intracranial, or coronary. These procedures can be performed as an open or percutaneous approach.

# Vascular Embolization and Occlusion (37241–37244) and Intravascular Ultrasound Services (37252–37253)

Codes 37241–37244 are used to report vascular embolization and occlusion procedures, excluding the CNS and the head and neck, as well as ablation and sclerotherapy procedures for venous insufficiency/telangiectasia of the extremities/skin. Codes 37252 and 37253 are add-on codes and report intravascular ultrasound of a noncoronary vessel during diagnostic evaluation and/or therapeutic intervention. These codes include radiological supervision and interpretation. Code 37252 reports the initial noncoronary vessel while code 37253 reports each additional noncoronary vessel. Review the instructional notations following code 37253 for additional guidance for reporting these codes.

# Endoscopy (37500–37501)

Two endoscopy codes are used for coding in the cardiovascular system. They are code 37500, surgical vascular endoscopy with ligation of perforator veins, subfascial (also known as SEPS); and code 37501, unlisted vascular endoscopy procedures.

## Ligation and Other Procedures (37565–37799)

**Ligation**, the act of tying off blood vessels and dividing and stripping vessels, is reported using code range 37565–37785. These codes are differentiated by the type of procedure and the site of the procedure—in other words, the vein or artery on which the procedure was performed. Codes 37788–37799 are referenced for other procedures that would fall into this subsection of the surgery section, and they include code 37788, penile revascularization; and code 37790, penile venous occlusive procedure.

# Summary

- The cardiovascular system is the system that pumps blood through the body via the heart and blood vessels.
- The sinoatrial node, or SA node, is found where the superior vena cava and the right atrium meet.
- At the junction of the atria and the ventricles, the atrioventricular node, or AV node, directs the cardiac impulses to the ventricles, causing them to contract.
- Pericardiocentesis is a procedure in which the physician removes fluid from the pericardial space by insertion of a fine needle.
- A cardiac pacemaker is used to correct and manage heart dysrhythmias.
- A pacemaker is made up of a pulse generator and electrodes.
- Pacemaker systems are referred to as either a *single-chamber* or a *dual-chamber system.*
- An endarterectomy is performed to remove plaque deposits from blood vessels.
- An angioplasty is a procedure in which a balloon is inflated in a vessel to push and flatten plaque against the vessel wall.
- A surgical incision that is made into an artery to remove a thrombus or plaque and the arterial lining is known as a *thromboendarterectomy.*
- A venous access device is a device or catheter that allows for access to the venous system.
- A central venous access device, or CVA device, is a catheter classified as such if the tip ends in the subclavian, brachiocephalic, superior or inferior vena cava, or right atrium.

# Internet Links

To learn more about coronary angioplasty, visit **http://www.nhlbi.nih.gov** and search on coronary angioplasty.

To learn about various vascular procedures, such as thrombectomy, placement of vascular stents, endarterectomy, and other vascular stenting, visit **http://vasculardiseasemanagement.com**.

For information on the history of and reasons for heart transplantation, visit **http://www.texasheart.org**.

# Chapter Review

## Fill in the Blank

**Instructions:** Fill in the blanks in the statements that follow.

1. Codes 35180–35184 are for the repair of congenital arteriovenous fistula, whereas codes 35188–35190 are the codes for the repair of a(n) _____ or traumatic arteriovenous fistula.
2. The act of tying off blood vessels is known as _____.
3. The node found where the superior vena cava and the right atrium meet is called the _____ or _____ node.

4. The part of the pacemaker that controls the heart rate, the energy output, and the pacing modes is known as the _____.

5. A pacemaker system that has one electrode in either the atrium or ventricle is called a _____ system.

6. A procedure in which a physician removes fluid from the pericardial space by inserting a fine needle is known as _____.

7. The lower chambers of the heart are the _____.

8. Plaque deposits are removed from blood vessels by the completion of a(n) _____.

9. When an angioplasty is completed, a(n) _____ is inflated in a vessel to push and flatten plaque against the vessel wall.

10. A device or catheter that allows access to the venous system is known as a(n) _____.

11. A central venous access device, or CVA device, is a catheter classified as such if the tip ends in the subclavian or brachiocephalic vein, superior or inferior vena cava, or _____.

12. Intravascular ultrasound services are performed for _____ or therapeutic purposes on a noncoronary artery or vein.

13. The heart is enclosed in a double-walled sac called the _____.

14. Vessels that move oxygen-rich blood from the heart to the rest of the body are _____.

15. Deoxygenated blood is moved back to the heart by _____, with the exception of the pulmonary _____.

# Coding Assignments

**Instructions:** Using the CPT manual, select the appropriate CPT code for each of the following procedures.

1. Thrombectomy of the radial artery by arm incision _____

2. Excision of pericardial cyst _____

3. Suture repair of aorta with shunt bypass _____

4. Coronary artery bypass using three coronary venous grafts, saphenous vein graft _____

5. Banding of pulmonary artery _____

6. Closure of pulmonary semilunar valve by patch _____

7. Repair of patent ductus arteriosus by division of a 14-year-old patient _____

8. Division of vascular ring with reanastomosis _____

9. Femoral vein valvuloplasty _____

10. Repair of blood vessel of upper extremity with vein graft _____

11. Stab phlebectomy of varicose veins in left leg; 12 stab incisions completed _____

12. Ligation of common iliac vein _____

13. Catheterization of umbilical artery of newborn _____

14. Extracorporeal photopheresis _____

15. Saphenopopliteal vein anastomosis _____

16. Ligation, major artery of the abdomen _____

17. Ligation of angioaccess arteriovenous fistula _____

18. Ligation of inferior vena cava _____

19. Direct thrombectomy, vena cava, iliac vein by abdominal incision _____

20. Coronary artery bypass, vein, two coronary venous grafts _____

21. Repositioning of pVAD with imaging guidance, separate session _____

22. Ligation of common carotid artery _____

23. Penile revascularization, artery with vein graft _____

24. Repair of supravalvular mitral ring by resection of left atrial membrane _____

25. Complete repair of tetralogy of Fallot with transannular patch _____

26. Percutaneous insertion of ventricular assist device via venous access of right heart with radiological supervision and interpretation _____

27. Insertion of implantable intracorporeal ventricular assist device of single ventricle _____

28. Insertion of intra-aortic balloon assist device via ascending aorta _____

29. Repair of Valsalva aneurysm with cardiopulmonary bypass _____

30. Repair of postinfarction ventricular septal defect with myocardial resection _____

# Case Studies

**Instructions:** Review each case and indicate the correct code(s).

## Case 1

**Procedure:** Replacement of pacemaker generator

The patient was brought to the operating room and was prepped and draped in the usual fashion. The patient was consciously sedated. The previous subcutaneous right infraclavicular skin pocket was identified, and an incision was made in this area to remove the previously inserted generator. The atrial and ventricular leads were checked. Since the pocket was clean, it was determined that the same pocket could be used for the reinsertion of a new generator. A pulse generator was placed and tested. Noting no complications, the physician sutured the site. The patient was found to be in stable condition and was returned to the recovery room in satisfactory condition.

**CPT code(s):** _____

## Case 2

**Preoperative diagnosis:** Leukemia, in remission

**Postoperative diagnosis:** Same

**Procedure:** Tunneled venous access port removal

**Reason for procedure:** This 8-year-old male completed chemotherapy.

The patient was prepped and draped in the normal sterile fashion. His right side was anesthetized, and an incision was made above the port area. The port was a tunneled device with a subcutaneous port that was peripherally inserted. The incision was taken down to the device, which was freed. The retention sutures were identified and cut. After confirmation that the device was free, it was removed. Hemostasis was obtained, and the wound was closed in

*(continues)*

(*continued*)

layers using 3-0 nylon. A sterile dressing was applied to the area. Patient vitals were taken, and the patient was noted to be stable. He was sent to the recovery room in stable condition.

CPT code(s): _____

# Case 3

**Preoperative and postperative diagnosis:** Excessive fluid in pericardial sac

**Procedure:** Initial removal of fluid from pericardial sac

After the patient was prepped and draped in the usual fashion, general anesthesia was administered. Using the sternum as an anatomical landmark, a long needle was placed below the sternum. The needle was advanced into the pericardial sac, and 5 cc of fluid were aspirated and sent to pathology for review. The patient was stable, and the wound was dressed. The patient was sent to the recovery area in satisfactory condition.

CPT code(s): _____

# Case 4

**Preoperative diagnosis:** Malignant carcinoma of breast

**Postoperative diagnosis:** Same

This 39-year-old female presents today for insertion of catheter for central venous access for chemotherapy.

The patient was placed in the supine position and sterile prep occurred. Lidocaine was injected into the right clavicular area. A needle was inserted into the right subclavain vein, and a J-wire was then passed into place. A tunnel was created from the area over the clavicle to the venotomy site, and a dilator was placed over the wire and then dilated. The catheter was then placed into the subclavian vein and secured. The area was flushed, and incisions were sutured. There was minimal blood loss, and the patient was stable and sent to the recovery area.

CPT code(s): _____

# Case 5

**Preoperative diagnosis:** Possible hemorrhage

**Postoperative diagnosis:** Abdominal hemorrhage of previous operative area

This patient underwent abdominal surgery 36 hours ago. An exploration of the abdominal incision site is planned.

(*continues*)

*(continued)*

After being placed under general anesthesia, the original abdominal incision site was reopened. A small bleeding site was noted, and electrocautery was used. The wound was closed. The patient tolerated the procedure and was sent to the recovery area.

**CPT code(s):** _____

# Case 6

**Preoperative diagnosis:** Chest wound

**Postoperative diagnosis:** Foreign body on the surface of the heart

**Anesthesia:** General

**Procedure:** Exploratory cardiotomy

This 59-year-old patient sustained an injury to his chest while loading logs onto a truck at work. He was brought to the ER, and imaging showed a chest wound with a possible foreign body on the surface of the heart. He was then taken to the operating room for exploration of the area. An incision was made in the sternum, and the heart was exposed. A foreign body was visualized on the heart and was removed. There were no penetrating cardiac wounds to be sutured. The operative wound was closed, and the patient was sent to the recovery area in stable condition.

**CPT code(s):** _____

# Case 7

**Preoperative and postoperative diagnosis:** Cardiac ischemia

**Procedure:** Thoracotomy for transmyocardial laser revascularization

**Anesthesia:** General

The patient was prepped and draped in the usual sterile fashion and placed under general anesthesia. A 12-cm incision was made on the left side of the chest. The incision was made between the ribs and was carried down to expose the heart's surface. An ischemia was visualized on the right side of the heart. The laser was inserted into the cardiac area, and between heartbeats, 15 channels were made and pressure was applied to close the opened areas. Prior to closure of the incision, there was no significant bleeding from the cardiac tissue. The laser was removed, the incision was closed, and dressings were placed on the wound. The patient tolerated the procedure with no complications and was sent to the recovery area in stable condition.

**CPT code(s):** _____

## Case 8

**Preoperative and postperative diagnosis:** Bleeding from pacemaker site

**Procedure:** Relocation of skin pocket for pacemaker

With the patient under general anesthesia, the previous skin pocket was opened, and the generator was removed. The skin pocket was explored and bleeding stopped in the area. The generator was then relocated, and the pocket was closed with sutures. A sterile dressing was applied. The patient was in stable condition.

**CPT code(s):** _____

## Case 9

**Preoperative and postoperative diagnosis:** Thrombus and atherosclerosis of iliac artery

**Procedure:** Iliac thromboendarterectomy

The patient was prepped and draped in the usual sterile fashion and placed under general anesthesia. An abdominal incision was made, and dissection past the large and small bowel occurred to expose the iliac artery. Clamps were placed to isolate the iliac area. A longitudinal incision was made in the artery, and the thrombus and plaque were removed. Then the area was sutured. The diameter of the artery was significantly improved after the procedure. Blood loss was minimal, and the wounds were closed and dressed. No complications were noted. The patient was sent to recovery.

**CPT code(s):** _____

## Case 10

**Neonatal Intensive Care Unit Note**

This 4-day-old neonate is suspected to be anemic. A blood sample was ordered by the attending, who completed the collection due to the size of the neonate.

**Procedure:** Venipuncture for collection of venous blood, nonroutine, upper-extremity vein

**CPT code(s):** _____

# Hemic and Lymphatic Systems

## Chapter Outline

Introduction

Guidelines Related to the National Correct
   Coding Initiative (NCCI)

Structures of the Hemic and Lymphatic
   Systems

Procedures Completed on the Spleen
   (38100–38200)

General Procedures (38204–38232) and
   Transplantation and Post-Transplantation
   Cellular Infusions (38240–38243)

Procedures Performed on the Lymph Nodes
   and Lymphatic Channels (38300–38999)

Summary

Internet Links

Chapter Review

Coding Assignments

Case Studies

## Learning Objectives

### At the conclusion of this chapter, you should be able to:

1. Define key terms related to coding procedures on the hemic and lymphatic systems.
2. Describe the basic anatomy and functions of the hemic and lymphatic systems.
3. Define common procedures performed on the hemic and lymphatic systems.
4. Apply specific coding guidelines to the hemic and lymphatic systems.
5. Select CPT codes for procedures completed on the hemic and lymphatic systems.
6. Identify and code procedures for the hemic and lymphatic systems from case studies.

## Key Terms

allogenic bone
   marrow transplants

autologous bone marrow
   transplants

axillary lymph nodes

cervical lymph nodes

deep biopsy

deep removal

hematopoietic
   progenitor cell (HPC)
   boost

inguinal lymph nodes

lymphadenitis

lymphangiotomy

lymphatic channels

lymphatic vessels

lymph glands

lymph nodes

radical
   lymphadenectomy

spleen

splenectomy

splenorrhaphy

submandibular lymph
   nodes

superficial biopsy

superficial removal

# Introduction

The hemic and lymphatic systems often are viewed as subsystems of the circulatory system. The unique functions of the hemic and lymphatic systems connect them to the circulatory system. CPT code range 38100–38999 is used to report procedures completed on the hemic and lymphatic systems.

# Guidelines Related to the National Correct Coding Initiative (NCCI)

Reference the following website to obtain the most current NCCI guideline information related to the Hemic and Lymphatic System.

1. Log on to *https://www.cms.gov/medicare-medicaid-coordination/national-correct-coding-initiative-ncci /ncci-medicare/medicare-ncci-policy-manual.*
2. Scroll to the section titled "View Manual by Chapter."
3. Click on "Chapter 5" for guidelines specific to the Hemic and Lymphatic System coding.

# Structures of the Hemic and Lymphatic Systems

Structures included in CPT for the hemic and lymphatic systems are the spleen, bone marrow, lymph nodes, and lymphatic channels. The **spleen**, the largest organ of the lymphatic system, is located in the left upper quadrant of the abdomen, behind the stomach and just below the diaphragm. The main role of the spleen is to filter blood. Figure 9-1 illustrates the location of the spleen in the abdominal cavity.

The **lymphatic channels** or **lymphatic vessels**, also illustrated in Figure 9-1, transport fluid away from the tissues of the body and toward the thoracic cavity. Lymphatic vessels transport fluid in only one direction.

**Lymph nodes**, also known as **lymph glands**, are located at various areas along the lymphatic vessels. The nodes are a collection of lymphatic tissue.

# Procedures Completed on the Spleen (38100–38200)

Codes 38100–38200 are used to report procedures completed on the spleen. There are four subsections:

- Excision
- Repair
- Laparoscopy
- Introduction

## Excisions (38100–38102)

This subsection is used to report a **splenectomy**, the surgical removal of the spleen. Codes 38100 and 38101 are considered separate procedure codes and, therefore, would not be reported if another procedure was completed. Code 38100 is used to report a total splenectomy, and code 38101 is used to report a partial splenectomy. Code 38102 is considered an add-on procedure and is reported when a total splenectomy is completed in conjunction with another procedure. Code 38102 is listed as the secondary code, with the code for the primary procedure listed first. Figure 9-2 illustrates a splenectomy.

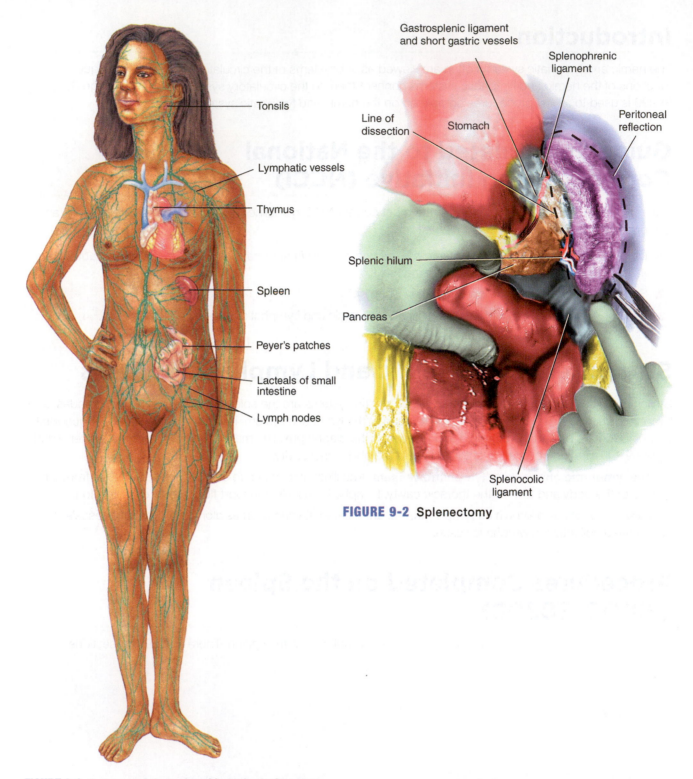

**FIGURE 9-1** Spleen and Associated Lymphatic Structures

**FIGURE 9-2** Splenectomy

# Repair (38115)

There is only one code in this subsection: code 38115. This code is used to report the repair of a ruptured spleen, which also is known as a **splenorrhaphy**. This code does not differentiate between a splenorrhaphy that is completed with a partial splenectomy and one that is completed without it. Therefore, if a repair of a ruptured spleen occurs with a partial splenectomy, it is necessary to report only code 38115 because it includes the partial splenectomy.

## Laparoscopy of the Spleen (38120 and 38129)

Coders should read the notation that appears under the heading Laparoscopy and before code 38120. It informs the reader that a surgical laparoscopic procedure includes a diagnostic procedure. Code 49320 is used to report a diagnostic laparoscopy. There are two codes for surgical laparoscopic procedures completed on the spleen:

- Code 38120—This code is used when a surgical laparoscopic splenectomy is completed.
- Code 38129—This code is for an unlisted laparoscopic procedure completed on the spleen.

## Introduction (38200)

The next code in this subsection is 38200, which is used for the injection procedure for a splenoportography. If radiological supervision and interpretation occurs for this procedure, code 75810 should also be used.

# General Procedures (38204–38232) and Transplantation and Post-Transplantation Cellular Infusions (38240–38243)

The section titled General includes codes 38204–38232 and is used to report bone marrow or stem cell services and procedures. Codes 38240–38243 report transplantation and post-transplantaion cellular infusions. There are a number of notations found in this subsection that instruct the coder on the use of codes for this section. For example, a notation appears that instructs the coder that each of the codes in the range 38207–38215 can be reported only once per day.

Code 38220 reports diagnostic bone marrow aspiration(s) and code 38221 reports a diagnostic bone marrow biopsy(ies). Code 38222 reports diagnostic bone marrow biopsy(ies) and aspiration(s). Refer to the instructional notations that follow codes 38220, 38221, and 38222 for additional instructions that impact the assignment of these codes. Code 38230 is used for bone marrow harvesting for transplantation; allogenic.

Bone marrow or blood-derived peripheral stem cell transplantation is coded using codes 38240–38243. These codes are differentiated by allogenic transplantation, autologous transplantation, and allogenic donor lymphocyte infusions. In **autologous bone marrow transplants**, cells are cultivated from the patient's own marrow, whereas in **allogenic bone marrow transplants**, cells are taken from a donor and then transplanted into the patient needing the cells. It should be noted that following code 38242, numerous notations direct the coder to additional codes for various types of procedures that involve bone marrow. Code 38243 reports a **hematopoietic progenitor cell (HPC) boost**. During this procedure the patient receives an infusion of hematopoietic progenitor cells from the original donor. This can be completed to treat a relapse or post-transplant cytopenias.

## Exercise 9.1—Check Your Understanding

### Codes for the Hemic and Lymphatic System

Using the CPT manual, select the appropriate response to each of the following questions.

1. The four subcategories for procedures completed on the spleen are

   _____, _____, _____, and _____.

2. A surgical laparoscopy of the spleen always includes a(n) _____ laparoscopy.

3. Bone marrow aspiration is coded using code _____.

4. True or false: Interpretation of a bone marrow biopsy is included in code 38221 _____.

5. Code 38100 is considered a(n) _____ procedure code; therefore, it is not reported with another code but is reported when the splenectomy is the only procedure completed.

# Procedures Performed on the Lymph Nodes and Lymphatic Channels (38300–38999)

Procedures completed on the lymph nodes and lymphatic channels, codes 38300–38999, are divided into the following subsections:

- Incision
- Excision
- Limited Lymphadenectomy for Staging
- Laparoscopy
- Radical Lymphadenectomy (Radial Resection of Lymph Nodes)
- Introduction
- Other Procedures

At times, the coder must identify the site of the lymphatic duct or node to select a code properly. Figure 9-3 illustrates the location of lymphatic ducts and nodes. There are two lymphatic ducts: the right lymphatic duct and

**FIGURE 9-3** Lymphatic Ducts and Nodes

the thoracic duct. Although lymph nodes are located throughout the body, there are four major concentrations of lymph nodes:

- **Cervical lymph nodes**—Located in the neck area
- **Submandibular lymph nodes**—Located under the mandible or lower jaw
- **Axillary lymph nodes**—Located in the armpit
- **Inguinal lymph nodes**—Located in the upper femoral triangle of the thigh

## Incision (38300–38382)

Incisions completed on the lymph nodes and lymphatic channels are reported using codes 38300–38382. Codes 38300 and 38305 are used to report the drainage of a lymph node abscess or drainage of an enlarged or inflamed lymph node, known as **lymphadenitis**. These codes are differentiated by the terms *simple* and *extensive*. When code 38305—"Drainage of lymph node abscess or lymphadenitis, extensive"—is reported, the patient's record must document the reason for and the description of the extensive treatment.

**Lymphangiotomy**, an incision made into a lymph node, or other operations on the lymphatic channels are coded using code 38308.

Suturing and/or ligation of thoracic ducts are reported using codes 38380–38382. For the proper selection of a code, the operative report must identify the approach of the procedure. The codes are differentiated by the cervical, thoracic, or abdominal approach.

## Excisions (38500–38555)

The biopsy, excision, or dissection of lymph nodes is coded by using codes 38500–38555. When reading an operative report, coders must be able to identify how the procedure was completed. Was it completed as an open procedure, or was it completed by using a needle? Also, the coder needs to determine whether the biopsy or removal was superficial or deep. A **superficial biopsy** or **superficial removal** is performed on a lymph node that is close to the surface of the skin and subcutaneous tissue. Providers may document these procedures as a biopsy or removal of a superficial lymph node. A **deep biopsy** or **deep removal** refers to nodes that are located by or below the muscle tissue. Sometimes providers will document a biopsy or removal of a deep lymph node. Codes are differentiated by using the term *deep biopsy* or *deep removal*.

**EXAMPLE:** The patient had an open superficial biopsy of an axillary lymph node.

This would be coded by using code 38500.

**EXAMPLE:** The patient had an open biopsy of a deep axillary node.

This would be coded by using code 38525.

Therefore, before selecting a code for this range, the coder must determine the site of the biopsy and how deep the node is: superficial or deep.

The Excisions subsection of CPT also contains numerous notes that instruct the coder that some of these codes are not to be assigned with other codes listed in the notation. For example, code 38500 is not to be used with codes 38700–38780, and code 38530 is not to be used with codes 38720–38746. When selecting codes from this subsection, be sure to read these notations.

To locate the codes for excisions of lymph nodes in the CPT Index, the coder would reference the main entry, "Excision," and then the subterm, "Lymphatic System" and then "Nodes." Here, additional codes are listed by anatomical site or type of excision. To locate codes for biopsy of lymph nodes in the CPT Index, the coder would reference the main entry, "Biopsy," and then the subterm, "Lymph Nodes." The type of biopsy then divides the listing.

## Limited Lymphadenectomy for Staging (38562, 38564)

There are two codes for limited lymphadenectomy for staging: 38562 and 38564. Both of these codes are separate procedure codes. The codes are differentiated by location. Code 38562 is for the pelvic and para-aortic area, whereas code 38564 is for the retroperitoneal area. Following code 38562, coders should read the notations that state, "When combined with prostatectomy, use 55812 or 55842" and "When combined with insertion of radioactive substance into prostate, use 55862." This notation directs the coder to another section in the CPT manual.

## Laparoscopy (38570–38589)

Laparoscopic procedures completed on the lymph nodes are coded to range 38570–38589. As seen in previous sections of the CPT manual, a completed surgical laparoscopic procedure always includes a diagnostic laparoscopic procedure. It should be noted that in the CPT manual, a notation appears that instructs the coder that if a diagnostic laparoscopic procedure is completed as a separate procedure, code 49320 should be reported. The codes found in this subsection are summarized in Table 9-1.

**TABLE 9-1**  Laparoscopy of Lymph Nodes (38570–38589)

| Code | Description |
|------|-------------|
| 38570 | This code is used to report a surgical laparoscopy with a biopsy of the retroperitoneal lymph nodes. This is for a single biopsy or multiple biopsies. Therefore, if two or more samples of tissue are biopsied, report the code only once. |
| 38571 | When a bilateral total pelvic lymphadenectomy is completed using a laparoscope, this code should be reported. |
| 38572 | This code is used to report a bilateral total pelvic lymphadenectomy that is completed with a periaortic lymph node biopsy. This is for a single biopsy or multiple biopsies. |
| 38573 | This code is used to report a surgical laparoscopy with a bilateral total pelvic lymphadenectomy and periaortic lymph node sampling, peritoneal washings, peritoneal biopsy(ies), omentectomy and diaphragmatic washings, including diaphragmatic and other serosal biopsy(ies), when performed. |
| 38589 | Unlisted laparoscopy of the lymphatic system is reported using this code. |

## Radical Lymphadenectomy (Radical Resection of Lymph Nodes) (38700–38780)

Codes 38700–38780 are used to report the radical resection of lymph nodes, which is commonly referred to as a **radical lymphadenectomy**. To code from this range, the lymphadenectomy must be a radical procedure, not a limited one. When these radical procedures are completed, all the lymph nodes are dissected and removed, in addition to the tissue under the skin. To select a code from this section, coders must be able to identify the site of the lymph nodes and the extent of the removal. It should also be noted that in the CPT manual, notations appear that instruct coders to add modifier 50 for bilateral procedures. So, when reading through the operative note, the coder should determine whether the procedure was completed unilaterally or bilaterally. Codes for this range are summarized in Table 9-2.

**TABLE 9-2**  Radical Lymphadenectomy (38700–38780)

| Code(s) | Description |
|---------|-------------|
| 38700 | Removal of lymph nodes in the suprahyoid area is reported with this code. If this is a bilateral procedure, modifier 50 is added for some payers. |
| 38720 | A complete cervical lymphadenectomy done unilaterally is reported with code 38720. It is reported as a bilateral procedure with the addition of modifier 50. |
| 38724 | A modified radical neck dissection of the cervical lymph nodes, also known as a cervical lymphadenectomy, is coded by using code 38724. |

*(continues)*

**TABLE 9-2** (*continued*)

| Code(s) | Description |
|---------|-------------|
| 38740 and 38745 | These codes are used to report axillary lymphadenectomy. The codes are differentiated by a superficial or a complete procedure. The term *complete* refers to the removal of all the nodes. |
| 38746 and 38747 | These are considered add-on codes and are listed separately in addition to the code for the primary procedure. Code 38746 reports a thoracic lymphadenectomy by thoracotomy, mediastinal, and regional lymphadenectomy; and code 38747 reports an abdominal lymphadenectomy, regional. |
| 38760 | When lymph nodes are removed in the inguinofemoral area, including Cloquet's node, code 38760 is listed for the unilateral procedure. Modifier 50 is added for a bilateral procedure. It should be noted that this is also a separate procedure code. |
| 38765 | A superficial inguinofemoral lymphadenectomy that is performed in continuity with a pelvic lymphadenectomy is reported as a unilateral procedure with code 38765 and as a bilateral procedure with code 38675-50. This procedure also includes the removal of the external iliac, hypogastric, and obturator nodes. This is also a separate procedure code. |
| 38770 | This separate procedure code is used to report a pelvic lymphadenectomy that can include the removal of the external iliac, hypogastric, and obturator nodes. Modifier 50 is added for a bilateral procedure. |
| 38780 | Extensive retroperitoneal transabdominal lymphadenectomy is coded with this code. Reporting this code also includes the removal of the pelvic, aortic, and renal nodes. Note that this is a separate procedure code. |

## Exercise 9.2—Check Your Understanding

### Codes from Code Range 38300–38780

Using the CPT manual, select the appropriate CPT code for each of the following.

1. Suture and ligation of the thoracic duct via the abdominal approach _____

2. Limited lymphadenectomy for staging in the pelvic and para-aortic region _____

3. Laparoscopic bilateral total pelvic lymphadenectomy _____

4. Complete axillary lymphadenectomy _____

5. Superficial inguinofemoral lymphadenectomy including Cloquet's node _____

## Introduction and Other Procedures (38790–38999)

The last two subsections include the following codes:

- Code 38790—An injection procedure for a lymphangiography
- Code 38792—An injection procedure of a radioactive tracer for the identification of sentinel nodes
- Code 38794—The cannulation of the thoracic duct
- Code 38900—Intraoperative identification of sentinel lymph nodes. Code 38900 includes the injection of a non-radioactive dye when it is performed. This is an add-on code used with numerous codes. Reference the CPT manual for the primary codes in which code 38900 is used as an add-on code. The primary codes are listed after the description of code 38900.
- Code 38999—Unlisted procedures on the hemic or lymphatic system

# Summary

- The hemic and lymphatic systems are often viewed as subsystems of the circulatory system.
- The repair of a ruptured spleen is also known as a *splenorrhaphy*.
- The spleen is located in the left upper quadrant of the abdomen, behind the stomach and just below the diaphragm.
- The lymphatic channels, or vessels, transport fluid away from the tissues of the body and toward the thoracic cavity.
- Lymph nodes, also known as *lymph glands*, are located at various areas along the lymphatic vessels.
- In an autologous bone marrow transplant, cells are cultivated from the patient's own marrow.
- In an allogenic bone marrow transplant, cells are taken from a donor and then transplanted.
- There are four major concentrations of lymph nodes: cervical lymph nodes, submandibular lymph nodes, axillary lymph nodes, and inguinal lymph nodes.

# Internet Links

To learn more about a splenectomy, visit **http://www.mayoclinic.org/tests-procedures/splenectomy/basics/definition/PRC-20014837**.

To learn more about lymph and lymph nodes, visit **http://www.breastcancer.org**.

To learn more about bone marrow transplantations, visit **http://www.stjude.org** and search for "bone marrow transplant."

To learn more about bone marrow transplantations from the National Institutes of Health (NIH), visit **http://www.nlm.nih.gov** and search for "bone marrow transplant."

# Chapter Review

## Fill in the Blank

Instructions: Fill in the blanks in the statements that follow.

1. The largest organ of the hemic and lymphatic systems is the _____.

2. A patient's own cells are cultivated to perform the transplant in a(n) _____ bone marrow transplant.

3. A biopsy of a superficial lymph node is completed close to the skin and _____.

4. Code 38505 is used to report a biopsy or excision of a superficial lymph node performed by use of a(n) _____.

5. Cells are taken from a donor and then transplanted into the patient who needs the cells in a(n) _____ bone marrow transplant.

6. An enlarged or inflamed lymph node is known as _____.

7. The repair of a ruptured spleen is also known as a(n) _____.

8. Lymph nodes that are located by or below the muscle tissue are referred to as _____ nodes.

9. Cervical lymph nodes are located in the _____.

10. Inguinal lymph nodes are located in the _____ triangle of the thigh.

# Coding Assignments

**Instructions:** Using the CPT manual, select the appropriate code for each of the following procedures.

1. Open excision of deep cervical node _____

2. Splenorrhaphy _____

3. Partial splenectomy _____

4. Laparoscopic splenectomy _____

5. Thoracic approach for ligation of the thoracic duct _____

6. Deep jugular lymph node dissection _____

7. Suprahyoid lymphadenectomy _____

8. Lymphangiography injection procedure _____

9. Cannulation of thoracic duct _____

10. Complete cervical lymphadenectomy _____

11. Axillary excision of cystic hygroma with deep neurovascular dissection _____

12. Thawing of previously frozen cells harvested for transplant without washing _____

13. Bone marrow transplantation from autologous marrow _____

14. Harvesting of bone marrow for transplantation; allogenic _____

15. Drainage of abscess of cervical lymph node _____

# Case Studies

**Instructions:** Review each case and indicate the correct code(s).

## Case 1

**Preoperative diagnosis:** Enlarged lymph node in left axillary area

**Postoperative diagnosis:** Left axillary lymphadenitis

**Procedure:** Excision of one axillary lymph node

The patient was prepped and draped in the usual fashion and sedated via IV. The left axillary area was cleansed with Betadine, and 1% Xylocaine was injected. An incision was made through the skin, and the enlarged node was identified deep in the fascia. The surrounding vessels in the area were clamped, and the deep node was excised. The node, measuring 2.3 by 2.5 cm, was sent to pathology for further analysis. The subcutaneous tissue and skin were closed. There was minimal blood loss, and the patient tolerated the procedure in good condition and was sent to the recovery room.

**CPT code(s):** _____

## Case 2

**Preoperative diagnosis:** Pain over spleen after falling down stairs

**Postoperative diagnosis:** Ruptured spleen

**Indications for surgery:** This 78-year-old male fell while completing yard work. It is believed that his spleen was ruptured due to this injury.

**Procedure:** This 78-year-old male was prepped and draped in the usual fashion. General anesthesia was administered, and he was placed in the supine position. An incision was made in the upper midline area. Retractors were then placed. The splenic ligaments and the gastric veins were located and divided so that the left upper quadrant of the abdomen could be viewed. The spleen was ruptured. The splenic hilum was dissected, and the splenic artery and vein were identified and double-ligated. They were then suture-ligated and divided. Removal of the spleen occurred, and hemostasis was achieved. A drain was placed, and the area was closed in layers. There was minimal blood loss. The patient's vitals were taken, and then he was sent to the postop recovery room in stable condition.

**CPT code(s):** _____

## Case 3

**Preoperative diagnosis:** Non-Hodgkin's lymphoma

**Postoperative diagnosis:** Non-Hodgkin's lymphoma

**Procedure:** Bone marrow biopsy and bone marrow aspiration

**Indications for surgery:** Non-Hodgkin's lymphoma

**Procedure:** This 25-year-old male was placed in the prone position on the operating table. Posterior superior iliac spines were prepped and draped in the usual sterile fashion. 1% Lidocaine was administered to anesthetize the area. The needle was inserted into the left iliac spinal region, rotated to the right, then left, and removed. The needle was then inserted into the left iliac spinal region at a 45-degree angle, and the procedure was repeated. Bone marrow aspiration and biopsy were performed and sent for contingent flow and contingent cytogenetics. The patient tolerated the procedure well and will return for follow-up and results.

**CPT code(s):** _____

## Case 4

This 42-year-old female presents today with an abscess in the right inguinal area. The patient is not suffering from fever or chills but is in pain in this area from the abscess. The options were explained to the patient, and she decided to proceed with an incision and drainage of the lymph node. All risks and benefits were explained, after which the patient signed the consent form for the procedure.

**Procedure:** After the patient was made comfortable on the procedure table, the right inguinal area was prepped and draped in the usual sterile fashion. An incision was made over the abscess and carried down until the lymph node was visualized. The lymph node was identified, and the syringe was inserted. At this time, 6 cc of fluid was removed from the node and sent to pathology. Pressure was applied to the area until the bleeding stopped, and the area was closed with Steri-Strips. The patient tolerated the procedure well and will return in 10 days for follow-up.

CPT code(s): _____

## Case 5

This 54-year-old male presents with an enlarged cervical lymph node that is deep within the fat pad. The node has been enlarged for the last six months and has been painful. Various treatments occurred with no success.

**Procedure:** The cervical area was anesthetized, and an incision was made to identify the node. The node was deep within the fat layer and enlarged. The node was excised with additional excision of the scalene fat pad. After bleeding was controlled, the area was sutured. The patient was sent to the recovery area in stable condition.

CPT code(s): _____

## Chapter Outline

Introduction

Guidelines Related to the National Correct
Coding Initiative (NCCI)

Procedures Completed in the Mediastinum
(39000–39499)

Procedures Completed on the Diaphragm
(39501–39599)

Summary

Internet Links

Chapter Review

Coding Assignments

Case Studies

## Learning Objectives

### At the conclusion of this chapter, you should be able to:

1. Define key terms related to coding procedures on the mediastinum and diaphragm.
2. Explain the location of the mediastinum and diaphragm.
3. Define common procedures performed on the mediastinum and diaphragm.
4. Select CPT codes for procedures completed on the mediastinum and diaphragm.
5. Identify and code procedures for the mediastinum and diaphragm from case studies.

## Key Terms

| | | | |
|---|---|---|---|
| anterior mediastinotomy | diaphragm | mediastinoscope | mediastinum |
| cervical mediastinotomy | imbrication of the diaphragm | mediastinotomy | transthoracic mediastinotomy |

## Introduction

The Mediastinum and Diaphragm subsection of the CPT surgery section is used to code procedures completed in the mediastinum and on the diaphragm. The **mediastinum** is the space in the thoracic cavity behind the sternum and in between the two pleural sacs that contain the lungs and pleurae. The **diaphragm** is a dome-shaped muscle that separates the thoracic cavity from the abdominal cavity. Figure 10-1 illustrates the location of the mediastinum and diaphragm.

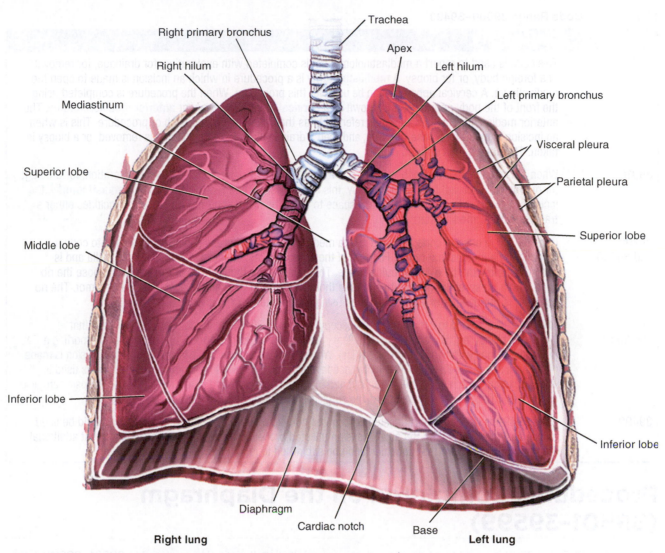

Right primary bronchus

Trachea

Apex

Right hilum

Left hilum

Mediastinum

Left primary bronchus

Superior lobe

Visceral pleura

Parietal pleura

Middle lobe

Superior lobe

Inferior lobe

Inferior lobe

Diaphragm

Cardiac notch

Base

**Right lung**

**Left lung**

**FIGURE 10-1** Location of Mediastinum and Diaphragm

# Guidelines Related to the National Correct Coding Initiative (NCCI)

There is no coding guideline information related to this chapter at this time.

# Procedures Completed in the Mediastinum (39000–39499)

The Mediastinum section, code range 39000–39499, is used to code procedures completed in the mediastinum. Codes are located in one of four groups, depending on the procedure performed:

- Incision
- Excision/Resection
- Endoscopy
- Other Procedures

Table 10-1 summarizes this code range.

**TABLE 10-1**  Code Range 39000–39499

| Code(s) | Description |
|---|---|
| 39000 | This code is used to report a mediastinotomy that is completed with exploration, for drainage, for removal of a foreign body, or for biopsy. A **mediastinotomy** is a procedure in which an incision is made to open the mediastinum. A cervical approach can be used for this procedure. When the procedure is completed using the front of the body approach, it is known as a **cervical mediastinotomy** or **anterior mediastinotomy**. The anterior mediastinotomy is sometimes referred to as the Chamberlain approach or procedure. This is when an incision is made to expose the area, and then a drain is placed, a foreign body is removed, or a biopsy is taken. The area is then sutured closed. |
| 39010 | When a transthoracic approach is used for a mediastinotomy that is completed with exploration, for drainage, for removal of a foreign body, or for biopsy, this code is used. During a **transthoracic mediastinotomy**, the incision is made in the fourth intercostal space to enter the mediastinum. This code also includes either a transthoracic or median sternotomy. |
| 39200 and 39220 | Code 39200 is used to code a resection of a mediastinal cyst, whereas code 39220 is used to code a resection of a mediastinal tumor. For both of these procedures, an incision is made in the axilla and is extended below the tip of the shoulder blade. The muscles are then moved or retracted to expose the rib cage, and a rib spreader is used to enter the thoracic cavity to view and remove the cyst or tumor. The rib spreader is removed, and the site is closed using either sutures or staples. |
| 39401 and 39402 | These codes are used to code a mediastinoscopy, with code 39401 reporting a mediastinoscopy that includes a biopsy(ies) of mediastinal mass (e.g., lymphoma), when performed, and code 39402 reporting a mediastinoscopy with lymph node biopsy(ies). When these procedures are performed, a small incision is made in the area above the sternum. The lighted scope, known as a **mediastinoscope**, is inserted and is used to visually examine the mediastinum, trachea, and the major vessels found in this area. At times, biopsies are also completed. After the scope is removed, the surgical wound is closed with Steri-Strips or sutures. |
| 39499 | Code 39499 is used to report unlisted procedures completed in the mediastinum. Caution should be used before assigning this code. Because this is an unlisted procedure code, most payers will request additional information and require that documentation be submitted to justify the selection of this code. |

# Procedures Completed on the Diaphragm (39501–39599)

Code range 39501–39599 is used to code procedures completed on the diaphragm. Codes 39501–39561 are used to report repairs, imbrications, and resections of this area, and code 39599 is used to report unlisted procedures completed on the diaphragm. Table 10-2 summarizes the codes found in this section.

It should be noted that the only hernia repair codes that are not located in the digestive-system range of codes are the diaphragmatic hernia repair procedures.

**TABLE 10-2**  Procedures Completed on the Diaphragm

| Code(s) | Description |
|---|---|
| 39501 | This code is used to code a repair of a laceration of the diaphragm using any approach that could include an abdominal or chest incision. The incision is completed to expose the tear in the diaphragm, which is repaired using sutures and at times is reinforced by an artificial patch. |
| 39503 | This code is used to report a repair of a diaphragmatic hernia that is completed on a neonate. This code includes the repair with or without chest tube insertion and with or without the creation of a ventral hernia. Following the code description, a notation appears stating that modifier 63 should not be used with code 39503. |
| 39540 and 39541 | These codes are used to report a diaphragmatic hernia repair that has occurred because of trauma. These codes are not used for neonates. The codes are differentiated by acute hernia (code 39540) and chronic hernia (code 39541). Because the abdominal organs are protruding into the chest cavity, the physician makes an incision into the chest or abdomen to draw the organs back into the abdominal cavity. The opening in the diaphragm is repaired by suturing or by inserting a patch. |

*(continues)*

**TABLE 10-2** *(continued)*

| Code(s) | Description |
|---------|-------------|
| 39545 | This code is used to report the **imbrication of the diaphragm**. During this procedure, the physician makes a transthoracic or transabdominal incision to draw back the abdominal organs. Folds or tucks are then made in the connective tissue, suturing the tissue to the diaphragm to restore the diaphragm to its correct anatomical position. |
| 39560 and 39561 | These two codes are used to report the resection of the diaphragm. Code 39560 is used to report the procedure when a simple repair closes the site. Code 39561 is used to report the procedure when a complex repair closes the site. A complex repair involves repairing the site with a local muscle flap or synthetic material to patch the area. |
| 39599 | This code is used to report unlisted procedures completed on the diaphragm. Additional information is provided following code 39599. Reference a CPT manual and review the information that follows code 39599. |

# Summary

- The mediastinum is the space in the thoracic cavity behind the sternum and between the two pleural sacs that contains all the viscera of the chest except the lungs and pleurae.
- The diaphragm is a dome-shaped muscle that separates the thoracic cavity from the abdominal cavity.
- A mediastinotomy is a procedure in which an incision is made to open the mediastinum.
- A cervical or anterior mediastinotomy is completed from the front of the body.
- During a transthoracic mediastinotomy, the incision is made in the fourth intercostal space to enter the mediastinum.
- A mediastinoscope is a lighted instrument that is used to visually examine the mediastinum.
- A transabdominal approach occurs when an incision is made across the abdomen.

# Internet Links

For information on symptoms and treatment of diaphragmatic hernias, visit *http://www.umm.edu*.

# Chapter Review

## Fill in the Blank

**Instructions:** Fill in the blanks in the statements that follow.

1. During a(n) _____ of the diaphragm, the physician makes a transthoracic or transabdominal incision to draw back the abdominal organs, and then makes folds in the connective tissue, suturing the tissue to the diaphragm to restore it to its correct anatomical position.

2. Code _____ is used to report the repair of a traumatic (acute) diaphragmatic hernia.

3. A lighted scope, known as a(n) _____, is used to examine the mediastinum visually.

4. When performing a transthoracic mediastinotomy, the surgeon makes an incision in the _____ to enter the mediastinum.

5. Code 39503 is used to report a repair of a diaphragmatic hernia that is completed on a(n) _____.

## True/False

**Instructions:** Indicate whether the following statements are true (T) or false (F).

6. _____ When a biopsy is performed in the mediastinum using a cervical approach, CPT code 39200 is reported.

7. _____ A laparoscopic repair of a diaphragmatic hernia and fundoplication are reported using CPT code 39540.

8. _____ CPT code 39560 is used to report a simple resection of the diaphragm.

9. _____ The diaphragm is a dome-shaped ligament that separates the thoracic and abdominal cavities.

10. _____ A cervical mediastinotomy is completed by an approach from the front of the body.

# Coding Assignments

**Instructions:** For each of the following procedures, select the appropriate CPT code.

1. Mediastinoscopy with biopsy of mediastinal mass
   _____

2. Excision of a cyst of the mediastinum
   _____

3. Exploration of the mediastinum with mediastinotomy for drainage via the cervical area
   _____

4. Diaphragmatic hernia repair due to acute trauma
   _____

5. Endoscopy of mediastinum _____

6. Imbrication of the diaphragm for eventration
   _____

7. Resection of the diaphragm with complex repair
   _____

8. Repair of chronic diaphragmatic hernia
   _____

9. Repair of diaphragmatic hernia with chest tube insertion, 23-hour-old newborn
   _____

10. Mediastinal cyst resection _____

# Case Studies

**Instructions:** Review each case and indicate the correct code(s).

## Case 1

**Preoperative diagnosis:** Carcinoma of the mediastinum

**Postoperative diagnosis:** Tumor of mediastinum, carcinoma

**Reason for procedure:** Two weeks ago, the patient had a biopsy of a mass found in the mediastinum. Pathology confirmed that the mass was a carcinoma of the mediastinum.

**Procedure:** The patient was prepped and draped in the usual sterile fashion. General anesthesia was administered. An incision was made in front of the left axilla area just below the nipple. The incision was then extended to below the tip of the left shoulder blade. The muscles were resected to expose the rib cage, and all bleeding points were controlled.

*(continues)*

(continued)

The rib cage was entered by using a rib spreader that revealed a 2.2 by 1.4 cm mass. The mass and surrounding tissue were resected. The wound was closed in a layered fashion with sterile dressings applied. The mass was sent to pathology. The patient tolerated the procedure well and was taken to the recovery room in stable condition.

**CPT code(s):** _____

# Case 2

**Preoperative and postoperative diagnosis:** Diaphragmatic hernia

**Procedure:** Repair of a neonatal diaphragmatic hernia

The patient was prepped and draped in the usual sterile fashion, and general anesthesia was administered. An abdominal incision was made under the upper ribs to view the abdominal cavity. The herniated stomach tissue was pulled through the opening in the diaphragm and returned to the correct anatomical position. The diaphragmatic opening was sutured to reduce the size of the opening. A chest tube was inserted. The patient tolerated the procedure and was sent to the recovery room in satisfactory condition.

**CPT code(s):** _____

# Case 3

**Procedure:** Mediastinoscopy

**Reason for procedure:** Lymph node biopsy-staging procedure

**Diagnosis:** Lung cancer

Patient was brought into the operating suite after all consents had been discussed and signed. Patient is aware that this is a lymph node biopsy being performed for staging of his recently diagnosed lung cancer.

Patient was prepped and draped in the usual sterile fashion. General anesthesia was administered. An incision was made approximately 1 cm above the suprasternal notch of the breast bone. Dissection was then carried down to the cartilaginous ridge within the trachea at the tracheal bifurcation. A mediastinoscope was then introduced, which provided good visualization of the mediastinum and its structures.

Lymph nodes 2, 4, 5, and 7 were removed and sent to pathology. The scope was removed, and the incision was closed. The patient was removed from the operating suite with minimal blood loss and in good condition.

**CPT code(s):** _____

# Digestive System

## Chapter Outline

Introduction

Guidelines Related to the National Correct
   Coding Initiative (NCCI)

Abbreviations Related to the Digestive System

Procedures Completed on the Lips, Mouth,
   Tongue, Teeth, Palate, Uvula, and Salivary
   Glands and Ducts (40490–42699)

Procedures Completed on the Pharynx,
   Adenoids, and Tonsils (42700–42999)

Procedures Completed on the Esophagus
   (43020–43499)

Stomach (43500–43999)

Intestines, Except Rectum (44005–44799)

Meckel's Diverticulum and the Mesentery
   (44800–44899)

Appendix (44900–44979)

Colon and Rectum (45000–45999)

Anus (46020–46999)

Liver (47000–47399)

Biliary Tract (47400–47999)

Pancreas (48000–48999)

Abdomen, Peritoneum, and Omentum
   (49000–49999)

Summary

Internet Links

Chapter Review

Coding Assignments

Case Studies

## Learning Objectives

### At the conclusion of this chapter, you should be able to:

1. Define key terms related to coding procedures on the digestive system.
2. Define abbreviations related to the digestive system.
3. Describe the basic anatomy and functions of the digestive system.
4. Define common procedures performed on the digestive system.
5. Select CPT codes for procedures completed on the digestive system.
6. Identify and code procedures for the digestive system from case studies.

# Key Terms

abdomen
adenoids
alimentary canal
allotransplantation
alveolus
anastomosis
anoscopy
anus
appendix
ascending colon
bariatric surgery
biliary tract
cheiloplasty
colonoscopy
combined hemorrhoids
descending colon
digestive system
dilation
direct inguinal hernia
duodenotomy
endoscopic procedure
endoscopic retrograde
cholangiopancreatog-
raphy (ERCP)

enteroenterostomy
enterolysis
enterotomy
esophagogastroduode-
noscopy (EGD)
procedures
esophagus
external hemorrhoids
frenum
gastric bypass surgery
gastrotomy
glossectomy
hemorrhoid
hernia
hiatal hernia
incisional hernia
indirect inguinal hernia
inguinal hernia
internal hemorrhoids
intestine
island flap
laparoscopy
large intestine
ligation

lingual
lingual tonsils
liver
manipulation
Meckel's diverticulum
mesentery
mixed hemorrhoids
nasopharyngeal tonsils
nasopharynx
omentum
open colectomy
palate
palatine tonsils
palatoplasty
pancreas
parotid glands
peritoneum
pharyngeal flap
pharyngoplasty
pharyngostomy
pharynx
proctosigmoidoscopy
prolapsed hemorrhoid
pyloromyotomy

rectum
salivary glands
sigmoid colon
sigmoidoscopy
small intestine
stoma
stomach
strangulated hemorrhoid
strangulated hernia
sublingual
sublingual glands
submandibular glands
thrombosed hemorrhoid
tonsils
tracheostomy
transverse colon
ulcerated hemorrhoid
uvula
vagotomy
ventral hernia
vermilion
vestibule of the mouth
V-excision

# Introduction

This subsection of the surgical section of the CPT manual codes procedures performed on the digestive system. The **digestive system** performs numerous functions that include the intake of nourishment, breakdown of food during digestion, absorption of nutrients, and elimination of waste products.

The digestive system begins at the lips when food is taken in and chewing starts. The food then moves to the oral cavity (mouth), the pharynx (throat), and the esophagus, and then on to the stomach, small intestine, large intestine, rectum, and anus. The procedures in this subsection of the CPT manual follow the same order. The procedures of the lips and mouth begin the subsection and move on to the pharynx, esophagus, stomach, intestines, rectum, and anus. The coder should be able to locate a code easily by knowing the area or structure the particular procedure was performed on. It is also helpful if the coder recognizes that the digestive system is sometimes referred to as the **alimentary canal**. Figure 11-1 illustrates the structures of the digestive system.

The digestive system section also includes procedure codes for services pertaining to the liver, biliary tract, pancreas, abdomen, peritoneum, and omentum.

# Guidelines Related to the National Correct Coding Initiative (NCCI)

The student will need to perform the following steps to obtain the most current coding guideline information related to this chapter online:

1. Log on to *https://www.cms.gov/medicare-medicaid-coordination/national-correct-coding-initiative -ncci/ncci-medicare/medicare-ncci-policy-manual*.
2. Scroll to the section titled "View Manual by Chapter."
3. Click "Chapter 6" for guidelines specific to the digestive system.

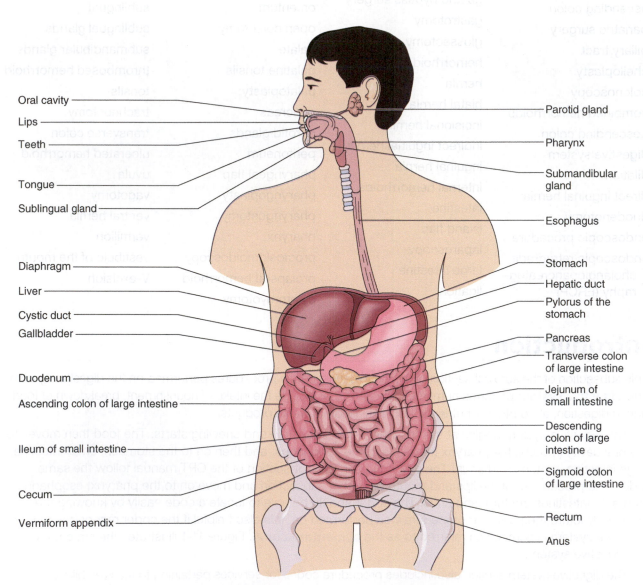

**FIGURE 11-1** Organs of the Digestive System

# Abbreviations Related to the Digestive System

The following are some of the most common abbreviations related to the digestive system:

| Abbreviations | Definitions |
|---|---|
| BE | barium enema |
| COL | colonoscopy |
| EGD | esophagogastroduodenoscopy |
| GERD | gastroesophageal reflux disease |
| GI | gastrointestinal |
| IBD | inflammatory bowel disease |
| IBS | irritable bowel syndrome |
| NG tube | nasogastric tube |
| NPO | nothing by mouth |
| PEG tube | percutaneous endoscopic gastrostomy tube |
| SBF | small bowel follow-through |
| TPN | total parenteral nutrition |
| UC | ulcerative colitis |

# Procedures Completed on the Lips, Mouth, Tongue, Teeth, Palate, Uvula, and Salivary Glands and Ducts (40490–42699)

Figure 11-2 illustrates the oral cavity and many of the structures discussed in this subsection of the chapter. As in other subsections of the Surgery section, the organization of this subsection includes incisions, excisions, repairs, and other procedures.

## Lips (40490–40799)

This section begins with codes for excision procedures. A term that coders should be familiar with is **vermilion**, the pinkish border of the lips. Codes 40490–40530 reflect the procedures performed on and around the lips. Table 11-1 summarizes codes from this range.

**TABLE 11-1** Lips (40490–40530)

| Code(s) | Description |
|---|---|
| 40490 | This code is used to report a biopsy of the lip. |
| 40500 | Vermilionectomy, also known as lip shave, is reported with this code, which also includes the mucosal advancement during the procedure. |
| 40510–40527 | This range of codes is used to report excisions of the lip. The codes are differentiated by the type of excision and type of closure or reconstruction. Coders must read the operative report to determine the type of closure or reconstruction completed. A term that coders should be familiar with is **V-excision**, a V-shaped cut made by the doctor. |
| 40530 | Code 40530 reports a resection of the lip. This code specifies that "more than one-fourth" of the lip is involved. There is usually layered closure involved in this procedure. Be sure to reference the documentation for support of the use of this code. It should also be noted that an instructional notation follows code 40530 that instructs the coder that for reconstruction the coder should see code range 13131 et seq. |

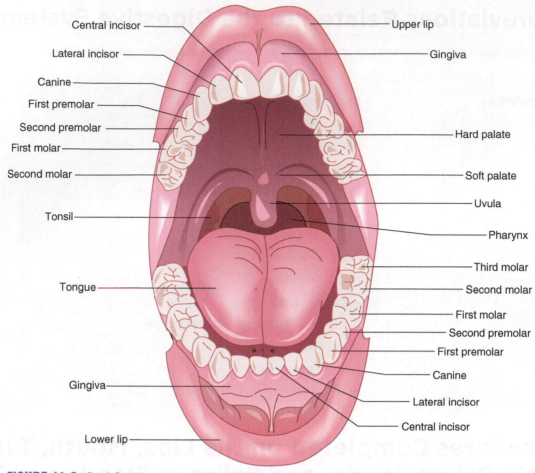

Central incisor — — Upper lip

Lateral incisor — — Gingiva

Canine —

First premolar —

Second premolar — — Hard palate

First molar —

Second molar — — Soft palate

— Uvula

Tonsil — — Pharynx

— Third molar

— Second molar

Tongue — — First molar

— Second premolar

— First premolar

— Canine

Gingiva — — Lateral incisor

— Central incisor

Lower lip —

**FIGURE 11-2** Oral Cavity

Codes 40650 to 40761 reports repairs that are completed on the lips. The term **cheiloplasty** refers to the repair of the lips. This section of codes should be reviewed carefully before codes are assigned. The coder needs to be aware of the type of deformity being corrected. Partial, complete, unilateral, and bilateral repairs are reported using the codes from this range of codes. There are several notes that are present for codes in this code range. Review the notes that are found in the CPT manual to become familiar with the instructional notations. The coder also needs to know whether a rhinoplasty was performed in addition to or separate from the repair of the lip. Attention to documentation is imperative. Table 11-2 summarizes codes in this section.

Code 40799 is used to report other unlisted procedures that are completed on the lips.

**TABLE 11-2** Lips (40650–40761)

| Code(s) | Description |
| --- | --- |
| 40650–40654 | Repair of the lip is reported with this range of codes. The codes are differentiated by the amount of the lip repaired:<br><br>   Code 40650—vermilion only<br><br>   Code 40652—up to half vertical height<br><br>   Code 40654—over one-half vertical height, or complex |
| 40700–40761 | This range of codes is used to report the plastic repair of a cleft lip or nasal deformity. The codes are differentiated by whether the repair is the primary or secondary repair and also if the procedures are unilateral or bilateral. The codes are also defined by the number of stages for the procedure: code 40701 is for a one-stage procedure, whereas codes 40702 and 40720 represent a two-stage procedure. It should be noted that code 40720 is a unilateral procedure and, if it is performed bilaterally, modifier 50 should be added to the code. |

# Vestibule of the Mouth (40800–40899)

The mucosal tissue and submucosal tissue of the lips and cheeks comprise the **vestibule of the mouth**. Keep in mind that the teeth and the alveolar process are not part of the vestibule.

This code range begins with codes used to report incision procedures, codes 40800–40806. Codes 40800 and 40801 report the drainage of an abscess, cyst, or hematoma and are differentiated by whether the case is simple or complicated. Here, the term *complicated* is interpreted as treatment of larger lesions or the completion of multiple incisions. Codes 40804–40805 are used to report the removal of an embedded foreign body from the vestibule of the mouth.

Excision and destruction of lesions found in the vestibule of the mouth are coded using code range 40808–40820. Code 40808 reports a biopsy of the mouth. Excisions in this range are differentiated by the type of repair completed.

> **EXAMPLE:** Dr. Maki completes an excision of a 1-cm lesion of the mucosa and submucosa on the vestibule of the mouth with a simple repair.

This should be coded using code 40812. If this same procedure was completed but the repair was complex, code 40814 should be reported.

Repair codes are reported using codes from the 40830–40845 code range. Knowing whether the procedure was complex and whether the procedure was done bilaterally or unilaterally is necessary when you are coding from this code range. Knowledge of whether the procedure was done in the posterior or anterior portion is also necessary.

The last code in this subsection is code 40899, used for unlisted procedures completed on the vestibule of the mouth. This code should be used only if no other procedure code is appropriate.

# Tongue and Floor of Mouth (41000–41599)

Understanding terminology is very important in selecting the correct code from this subcategory. **Lingual** refers to the tongue, and at times, the physician will refer to a procedure being done in the sublingual area. The **sublingual** area refers to the area under the tongue.

Code range 41000–41599 is organized into the following groups of codes:

- Incision—code range 41000–41019
- Excision—code range 41100–41155
- Repair—code range 41250–41252
- Other Procedures—code range 41510–41599

## Incision (41000–41019)

Codes 41000–41009 are used to report intraoral incision and drainage of an abscess, cyst, or hematoma of the tongue or the floor of the mouth. The codes are differentiated by the area of the tongue or the floor of the mouth treated. Code 41010 reports an incision of the lingual frenum, or tongue. The **frenum** is a connection. In this case, the connection is between the tongue and the floor of the mouth. The coder should always use as many references as necessary to be sure that a proper code assignment is made and that the documentation supports that code assignment.

Codes 41015–41018 report extraoral incision and drainage of an abscess, cyst, or hematoma of the floor of the mouth. These codes are also differentiated by the site of the procedure.

Code 41019 reports the placement of needles, catheters, or other devices that are used for subsequent interstitial radioelement application. If imaging guidance, stereotactic insertion of intracranial brachytherapy radiation sources, or interstitial radioelement application occurred, the notations that follow code 41019 in the CPT manual should be referenced prior to code assignment.

## Excision (41100–41155)

This range is used to report excision codes and biopsies of the tongue and floor of the mouth. Codes 41100 and 41105 are used to report a biopsy of the tongue. When selecting a code from this range, the coder must be able to identify the area of the tongue from which the biopsy was taken. Code 41108 reports a biopsy taken from the floor of the mouth. Codes 41110–41114 report the excision of lesions of the tongue. The coder must determine the extent of the excision when reading the operative note for the procedures. A biopsy that is performed during the same operative session as an excision will affect code selection. Code 41115 reports a frenectomy, which is an excision of the lingual frenum, while code 41116 is used to report an excision of a lesion from the floor of the mouth.

A **glossectomy** is a procedure in which there is a partial or complete removal of the tongue. It is reported using code range 41120–41155. The glossectomy procedures are based on how much of the tongue is removed and whether a tracheostomy is performed. A **tracheostomy** is a surgical opening into the trachea through the neck. This code range also identifies whether there is any radical neck dissection.

## Repair and Other Procedures (41250–41599)

After incision and excision codes, the repair codes and other procedures are listed in the CPT manual. Repair of lacerations (code range 41250–41252) is differentiated by the size of the laceration repaired and the site of the repair.

Other procedures that are completed on the tongue are reported with codes 41510–41599. These codes include the following procedures:

- Suture of the tongue to lip for micrognathia—code 41510
- Tongue base suspension—code 41512. Review the instructional notations that follow this code in the CPT manual.
- Frenoplasty—code 41520. Review the instructional notation that follows this code in the CPT manual.
- Submucosal ablation of tongue base—code 41530
- Unlisted procedure—code 41599

## Dentoalveolar Structures (41800–41899)

This code range contains procedures performed on the gums and alveolus. The **alveolus** is the socket where the tooth sits. Like the other code ranges, this code set begins with incisions. Code 41800 reports the drainage of an abscess, cyst, or hematoma from dentoalveolar structures. Codes 41805 and 41806 code the removal of an embedded foreign body from dentoalveolar structures and are differentiated by the removal from the soft-tissue area or bone.

Excisions and destructions are coded with code range 41820–41850. Terms that are referenced in the index to select codes from this range include:

- Gingivectomy
- Operculectomy
- Excision, then lesion, then gum
- Alveolectomy
- Destruction, then lesion, then gum

The remaining codes, 41870–41899, report other procedures completed on the dentoalveolar structures. Code 41870 is used for grafting around the teeth. Code 41872, gingivoplasty, and code 41874, alveoloplasty, are reported for each quadrant in which the procedure is completed. Prior to assigning code 41874 coders need to review the instructional notations that follow the code for additional guidelines. Code 41899 reports an unlisted procedure of dentoalveolar structures.

# Palate and Uvula (42000–42299)

The **palate** is more commonly called the *roof of the mouth*. The **uvula** is located in the posterior border of the soft palate. It is a small, cone-shaped mass of flesh that hangs from the soft palate. Code range 42000–42299 is divided into the following:

- Incision
- Excision, Destruction
- Repair
- Other Procedures

There is only one incision code in this code range: 42000, drainage of abscess of palate, uvula. Code 42100 is used to report a biopsy of the palate or uvula. The next code range, 42104–42107, reports the excision of a lesion of the palate or uvula. The codes are differentiated by whether a closure was completed. If a closure was completed, the coder must determine whether the closure was a simple primary closure or a local flap closure. Code 42120 reports a resection of the palate or extensive resection of a lesion. Following this code an instructional notation appears providing guidance in the reporting of reconstructions of the palate with extraoral tissue. Review this notation in the CPT manual. Code 42140 reports an excision of the uvula and code 42145 reports a palatopharyngoplasty. In the CPT manual review the instructional notation that follows code 42145. Code 42160 reports the destruction of a lesion on the palate or uvula by thermal, cryo, or chemical means.

Repair codes are found in the 42180–42281 code range. Repairs of lacerations of the palate, codes 42180 and 42182, are differentiated by the length of the repair and whether the repair is complex. Palatoplasty for a cleft palate is reported with codes 42200–42225. A **palatoplasty** is a repair of the roof of the mouth. Also found in the repair section of this code range, codes 42226–42235, are pharyngeal and island flap codes. A **pharyngeal flap** is formed by making an incision through the soft palate to the posterior pharyngeal wall. The incision is advanced to the muscle, and the flap is formed. The **island flap** is made using subcutaneous tissue with nutrient vessels. A maxillary impression for palatal prosthesis is reported with code 42280 while code 42281 reports an insertion of a pin-retained palatal prosthesis. Code 42299 reports unlisted procedures completed on the palate and uvula.

# Salivary Glands and Ducts (42300–42699)

The **salivary glands** secrete saliva, which contains an enzyme that aids in digestion. There are actually three pairs of salivary glands. The first are called the **parotid glands** and are located in front of each ear. The **sublingual glands** are located under the tongue. The third set is the **submandibular glands**, which are found on the floor of the mouth.

This code range begins with incision codes that report the following:

- Drainage of abscess—differentiated by site: parotid versus submaxillary or sublingual (codes 42300–42320)
- Sialolithotomy—differentiated by site and whether the case was complicated or uncomplicated (codes 42330–42340)

Code range 42400–42450 then follows, which reports the excisional procedures completed on the salivary glands and ducts. Table 11-3 summarizes the codes in this range.

**TABLE 11-3** Salivary Glands, Excision 42400–42450

| Code(s) | Description |
| --- | --- |
| 42400 and 42405 | Biopsies of the salivary gland are reported by using these codes, which are differentiated by needle biopsy in code 42400 and incisional biopsy in code 42405. |
| 42408 | Excision of sublingual salivary cyst is reported with this code. |
| 42409 | Marsupialization of sublingual salivary cyst is reported with this code. |
| 42410–42450 | This group of codes reports the excisions of various tumors or glands. To select a code, the coder must determine the location of the procedure: parotid, submandibular, or sublingual gland area. For codes 42410–42426, the coder must also determine the lobes involved and any accompanying procedures, such as en bloc, unilateral radical neck dissection, and others. |

This code range finishes with repair codes, which include plastic repair and diversion codes of the salivary glands. The other procedure codes in this code set include injection procedures, dilation, and ligation of the salivary duct, along with the unlisted procedure code for salivary glands or ducts.

## Exercise 11.1—Check Your Understanding

**Understanding Code Range 40490–42699**

Using a CPT manual, locate the correct code for each procedure given, and make note of the subcategory in which the code was found (i.e., Lips, Vestibule of Mouth, Tongue and Floor of Mouth, Dentoalveolar Structures, Palate and Uvula, or Salivary Gland and Ducts). The first one is done for you.

1. Drainage of abscess; parotid, simple
   42300; Salivary Gland and Ducts

2. Palatoplasty for cleft palate, with closure of alveolar ridge; soft tissue only _____

3. Unilateral posterior vestibuloplasty _____

4. Excision of lingual frenum _____

5. Resection of lip, more than one-fourth, without reconstruction _____

6. Excision of sublingual salivary cyst _____

7. Biopsy of lip _____

8. Biopsy of floor of mouth _____

9. Periodontal mucosal grafting _____

10. Closure of salivary fistula _____

# Procedures Completed on the Pharynx, Adenoids, and Tonsils (42700–42999)

The **pharynx** is the passageway that connects the oral cavity to the esophagus for the digestive system but also connects to the larynx as part of the respiratory system. This structure is part of both the digestive and respiratory systems. The pharynx is also called the *throat*.

The **tonsils** are located in the posterior wall of the **nasopharynx**. The nasopharynx is the part of the pharynx that is located posterior to the nasal cavity. The tonsils are made up of lymphatic tissue and are considered the first line of defense for the respiratory system.

There are actually three pairs of tonsils in the body: the **nasopharyngeal tonsils**, which are also referred to as the **adenoids**; the **lingual tonsils**, which are located at the base of the tongue on the posterior surface; and the **palatine tonsils**, which are the pair that are most commonly referred to as the *tonsils*. This pair of tonsils comes off the soft palate to the base of the tongue. Figure 11-3 illustrates the location of the tonsils.

Code range 42700–42999 is divided as follows:

- Incision
- Excision, Destruction
- Repair
- Other Procedures

The incision codes are listed first, and report the incision and drainage of abscesses, which are differentiated by location: peritonsillar, retropharyngeal or parapharyngeal (intraoral approach), or retropharyngeal or parapharyngeal (external approach).

Codes 42800–42894 follow and are used to report excisions and destructions of the pharynx, adenoids, and tonsils. The codes for tonsillectomy and adenoidectomy, codes 42820–42836, are found in this code range and are assigned according to the age of the patient. It should be noted here that these procedures are implied to be bilateral, so the addition of the 50 modifier is not appropriate for these codes.

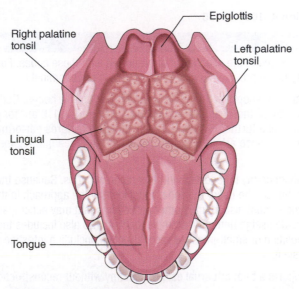

**FIGURE 11-3** Types of Tonsils

Repair codes and other procedures on the pharynx are listed next in the CPT manual. Codes that fall into this range include the following:

- Suture of pharynx for wound or injury—code 42900. Medical documentation must support that the suture occurred because there was a wound or injury to the pharynx.
- **Pharyngoplasty**—code 42950. This is for plastic surgery or a reconstructive operation on the pharynx.
- Pharyngoesophageal repair—code 42953.
- **Pharyngostomy**—code 42955. This term is used to identify a procedure in which an artificial opening is made into the pharynx.
- Control of oropharyngeal or nasopharyngeal hemorrhage—codes 42960–42972. These codes are differentiated by whether the procedure was simple, complicated, or involved secondary surgical intervention.
- Drug-induced sleep endoscopy—code 42975. This code reports the endoscopy and includes a dynamic evaluation for evaluation of sleep-disordered breathing. Locate code 42975 in the CPT manual for the full description of the code. Also note the instructional notations that appear after the code that provides guidance for code assignment.
- Unlisted procedures completed on the pharynx, adenoids, or tonsils—code 42999. Remember that this code should be used only when a more specific code is not found.

# Procedures Completed on the Esophagus (43020–43499)

The **esophagus** is a muscular structure that moves food from the pharynx to the stomach. The procedures in this code range follow the same format as previous code ranges beginning with incision codes. Codes here report the esophagotomy cervical approach with removal of a foreign body (Code 43020), cricopharyngeal myotomy (Code 43030), and the esophagotomy thoracic approach with removal of a foreign body (Code 43045).

Codes 43100–43135 report excisions completed on the esophagus. Table 11-4 summarizes the codes found in this range.

Please remember that excision codes are determined by how much of the esophagus is removed, so attention to detail in the operative report is necessary.

**TABLE 11-4** Esophagus, Excision 43100–43135

| Code(s) | Description |
| --- | --- |
| 43100 and 43101 | Excisions of lesions of the esophagus are reported with these codes. For proper code selection, the coder must identify the approach: cervical versus thoracic or abdominal. |
| 43107–43113 | Total or near-total esophagectomy are reported with these codes. Codes 43107 and 43108 are for procedures without thoracotomy, and codes 43112 and 43113 are for procedures with thoracotomy. The codes are also further differentiated by other procedures performed at the time of the surgery. Coders must pay close attention to the details of the procedures noted in the operative report for code selection. |
| 43116–43123 | Partial esophagectomy is reported with this range of codes. Because there are various types of approaches that can be used, the coder must identify the approach in the operative report to select a code. The coder must also identify other procedures that may accompany the partial esophagectomy that may affect code assignment. For example, code 43123 also includes the accompanying procedure of a colon interposition or small-intestine reconstruction, including intestine mobilization, preparation, and anastomosis(es). |
| 43124 | This code reports a total or partial esophagectomy without reconstruction, with cervical esophagostomy. |
| 43130 and 43135 | This range of codes reports a diverticulectomy of hypopharynx or esophagus with or without myotomy. Code 43130 reports a cervical approach, while code 43135 reports a thoracic approach. |

# Endoscopy Procedures (43180–43278)

Code range 43180–43278 reports endoscopic procedures completed via the esophagus. An **endoscopic procedure** involves insertion of a flexible or rigid instrument called an *endoscope*, which is used to view the internal structures.

These procedures may be diagnostic, which determines whether an abnormality is present. If an abnormality is found, a determination should be made as to the extent of the abnormality. If the surgeon is doing anything more than a visual examination, the procedure then becomes a surgical procedure. A diagnostic endoscopy should not be reported in addition to a surgical endoscopy because the diagnostic endoscopy is bundled into the surgical endoscopy. When an endoscopic procedure turns into an open procedure, the endoscopic procedure can be reported separately with modifier 58 to indicate a staged or related procedure.

## Codes 43180–43232

The endoscope can be moved down the esophagus for visualization or obtaining biopsies of the esophagus. Code 43180 reports a rigid esophagoscopy, transoral with diverticulectomy of hypopharynx or cervical esophagus with a cricopharyngeal myotomy with or without the use of a telescope or operating microscope. Code 43191 reports a diagnostic esophagoscopy using a rigid scope. Codes 43192 to 43196 report the use of a rigid esophagoscope for therapeutic procedures, such as removal of a foreign body or other procedures.

Code 43197 reports the use of a flexible esophagoscope for diagnostic purposes. Codes 43198 to 43232 reports the use of a flexible esophagoscope for diagnostic and therapeutic procedures. Please note, in the CPT manual, the numerous instructional notations that appear following the codes in this range of codes.

**EXAMPLES:**
1. Mr. George presented for a biopsy of a lesion on the esophagus. Dr. Dennis moved the flexible esophagoscope to the area of the lesion, and a biopsy was taken of the lesion in question, along with a biopsy of another lesion viewed during the procedure.
2. Mr. George presented for a biopsy of a lesion on the esophagus. Dr. Dennis moved the flexible esophagoscope to the area of the lesion and decided to remove the whole lesion by bipolar cautery, along with removing another lesion viewed during the procedure using the same bipolar cautery technique.

In the first example, a simple biopsy was performed on each lesion. This procedure would be reported using code 43202. The second procedure would be reported using code 43216 because a more extensive procedure was performed.

For some codes, such as codes 43216–43217, the documentation should note what specific method or technique was used to remove a lesion. The different techniques are noted in the code descriptions and should be reviewed carefully. If necessary, the surgeon should be consulted to ensure that the proper code is selected.

Codes 43200–43232 report the use of an endoscope to view the esophagus or to perform a surgical procedure via the scope. Codes that report surgical endoscopy procedures completed on the esophagus include the following:

- Code 43215—esophagoscopy, flexible, with removal of foreign body
- Code 43211—esophagoscopy, flexible, with endoscopic mucosal resection
- Code 43226—esophagoscopy, flexible, with insertion of guidewire followed by passage of dilator(s) over guide wire
- Code 43231—esophagoscopy, flexible, with endoscopic ultrasound examination

The preceding list is not all-inclusive of the codes in this range. It is used to demonstrate the types of procedures that are completed via the endoscope. To become familiar with all the codes in this section, a new coder should read the codes found in code range 43180–43232. It should also be noted that there are codes within this code range that are out of numerical sequence. Review the notes that are found in the CPT manual following code 43206 for the listing of codes that are out of numerical sequence within this code range of CPT.

## Codes 43233–43259 and Codes 43210, 43270, and 43266

Codes 43233 through 43259 and codes 43210, 43270, and 43266 are used for endoscopic procedures in which the scope is moved down the esophagus into the stomach, and then into the duodenum with the possibility of the scope entering into the upper part of the jejunum. Once the endoscope passes through the diaphragm, the procedure becomes an esophagogastroscopic procedure.

Codes 43233–43259 and codes 43210, 43270, and 43266 are used to report **esophagogastroduodenoscopy (EGD) procedures**. During this procedure, the scope is passed to view the esophagus and upper portion of the gastrointestinal tract, including the stomach, upper duodenum, and/or jejunum. This procedure is also known as an *upper gastrointestinal endoscopy*. To locate these codes in the index, the coder would reference the term *endoscopy* and then *gastrointestinal, upper*. It should be noted that there are codes that are out of numerical sequence in this range of codes. For example code 43233 is out of numerical sequence. Be guided by the notes that appear in the CPT manual for the location of codes that are out of numerical order.

Reviewing the CPT manual in this section, the coder should note that there are instructional notes that need to be reviewed before codes are selected from this range. These notations instruct coders about accompanying codes or combinations of codes that are not reported together.

> **EXAMPLE:** By referencing CPT code 43238, the coder will find a notation that says not to report code 43238 in conjunction with numerous codes that are listed, including codes 76942 or 76975. Locate the listing of codes in the CPT manual following code 43238. Ultrasound procedure codes 76942 and 76975 cannot be reported separately, as these services are bundled into code 43238.

As can be noted from reviewing codes 43233–43259 and codes 43210 and 43270 and 43266, there are numerous endoscopic procedures performed on the upper gastrointestinal area. New coders must read operative notes carefully to identify the procedure completed and match it with the correct code from this range, reporting only the procedures completed via the scope. Coders should review documentation to determine the following before assigning codes for endoscopies:

1. Was the procedure diagnostic or surgical?
2. How was the scope inserted? In other words, what was the approach?
3. What was the reason for the endoscopy?
4. To what location was the scope advanced?

It is essential that coders review the documentation found in the patient's record and compare the documentation to the description of the CPT code. Review code 43290 and note that this code reports a flexible esophagogastroduodenoscopy (denoting how far the scope is placed). The description of the code also notes that the approach is transoral. The code description also states that there is a deployment of intragastric bariatric ballon, thus denoting the scope is surgical in nature.

### Codes 43260–43289

The next range of codes is for **endoscopic retrograde cholangiopancreatography (ERCP)**, codes 43260–43278. ERCP is an endoscopic procedure that combines a retrograde cholangiography and a transhepatic cholangiography. Other procedures performed at the same time as the ERCP determine code assignment. Other procedures include the insertion of a tube or stent into the pancreas, pressure measurement, biopsies, and ablation of polyps or tumors. If separate approaches are used, modifier 51 can be used to indicate multiple procedures at the same operative session for the professional services. When assigning codes from code range 43260–43278, make sure all notations are read, as instructions for code assignment are given there.

Take your time when assigning codes to make sure that all notes are read and all additional codes are assigned as necessary. Code 43273 is an add-on code that can be used in conjunction with codes 43260–43265 and 43274–43278 when there is also endoscopic cannulation of papilla with direct visualization of the common bile duct(s) and/or pancreatic duct(s) occurring in the same operative session.

Code range 43279–43289 is used to report **laparoscopy**, a procedure using a scope much like an endoscope, which views the interior structures of the abdomen. Laparoscopic surgical procedures always include diagnostic procedures.

## Repairs (43300–43425)

The various types of repairs of the esophagus are reported by the 43300–43425 code range. The approach will guide the coder as to the proper code selection. Types of approaches for esophagoplasty help differentiate the codes by noting whether the approach is abdominal, cervical, or thoracic. These codes are also differentiated by any procedures that are performed in addition to the esophagoplasty. These additional procedures include repairs of tracheoesophageal fistulas, both acquired and congenital, and the repair of a paraesophageal hiatal hernia.

Codes 43320–43328 are used to report esophagogastrostomy and esophagogastric fundoplasty. When reporting codes 43330–43352, for esophagomyotomy, esophagojejunostomy, and esophagostomy, the coder must be able to identify the approach, which could be abdominal, thoracic, or cervical. Codes 43360 and 43361 report a gastrointestinal reconstruction for a previous esophagectomy, for an obstructing esophageal lesion or fistula, or for a previous exclusion. Code 43360 reports the reconstruction of a stomach with or without pyloroplasty, while code 43361 is for the reconstruction of a colon interposition or small intestine reconstruction, including intestine mobilization, preparation, and anastomosis(es).

The remaining codes report the following types of procedures:

- **Ligation**—codes 43400 and 43405. This is a procedure that ties or binds something together with catgut, cotton, wire, or silk.
- Suture of esophageal wound or injury—codes 43410 and 43415. The suturing of this type of wound is differentiated by the type of approach used.
- Closure of esophagostomy or fistula—codes 43420–43425. These closure codes are differentiated by the type of approach used.

## Manipulation Codes and Other Procedures (43450–43499)

Manipulation codes (43450–43460) and Other Procedures (codes 43496–43499) finish the range of codes for procedures completed on the esophagus. **Manipulation** is a maneuver by hand to treat or perform therapy.

Dilation procedures are also coded by using this range of codes. **Dilation** is performed when an expansion or stretching is necessary. When a dilation of the esophagus occurs, the provider dilates the esophagus using a balloon or dilator. A peroral endoscopic myotomy (POEM) is reported with code 43497 as is a transoral lower esophageal myotomy. Reference code 43497 in a CPT manual and note the instructional notation that follows the code for codes that should not be reported with 43497.

## Exercise 11.2—Check Your Understanding

**Vocabulary**

Fill in the blanks in the statements that follow.

1. _____ is performed when an expansion or stretching is necessary.
2. A(n) _____ endoscopy would not be reported in addition to a surgical endoscopy.
3. The _____ is a muscular structure that moves food from the pharynx to the stomach.
4. A(n) _____ can be rigid or flexible and is used to view internal structures.
5. _____ is a procedure that ties or binds something together with catgut, cotton, wire, or silk.
6. The _____ are located in the posterior wall of the nasopharynx.
7. An endoscopic procedure that combines a retrograde cholangiography and transhepatic cholangiography is known as a(n) _____.
8. A(n) _____, or maneuver by hand, is used to treat or perform therapy.

# Stomach (43500–43999)

The **stomach** is a pouchlike structure that aids in the breakdown and digestion of food. The stomach is positioned at the base of the esophagus on one end and connects to the duodenum on the other end. It is found in the upper left quadrant of the abdomen. Figure 11-4 illustrates the positioning of the stomach in relation to the liver and intestines.

Procedures completed on the stomach are grouped in CPT according to the following:

- Incision
- Excision
- Laparoscopy
- Introduction
- Bariatric Surgery
- Other Procedures

## Incision (43500–43520)

Codes 43500–43510 would be used to report **gastrotomy** procedures, surgical incisions made into the stomach. The reasons for the completion of a gastrotomy differentiate the codes as follows:

- Exploration or foreign body removal
- Suture repair of bleeding ulcer
- Suture repair of preexisting esophagogastric laceration
- Esophageal dilation and insertion for permanent intraluminal tube

The final code in this range is code 43520, which reports a **pyloromyotomy**, the cutting of the pyloric muscle.

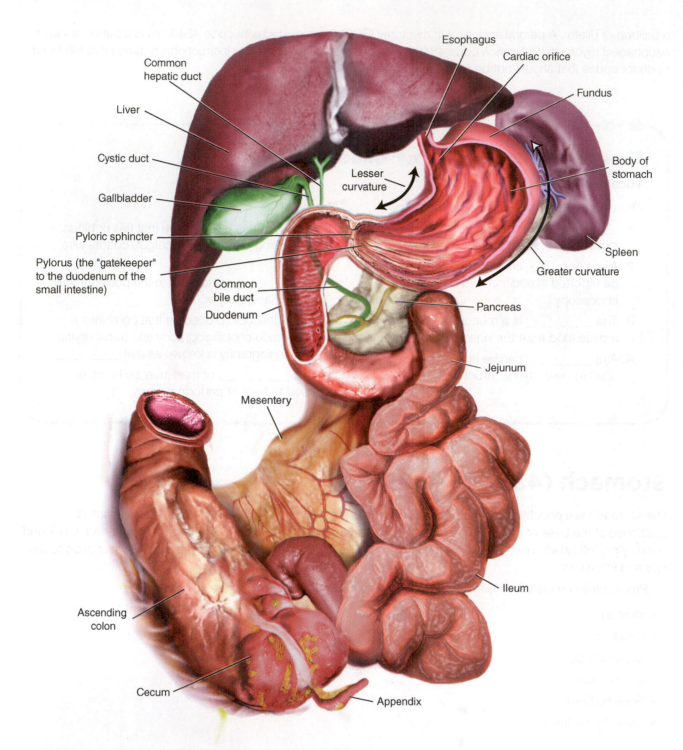

**FIGURE 11-4**  Position of the Stomach, Liver, and Intestines

# Excision (43605–43641)

Biopsies and excisions completed on the stomach are reported using code range 43605–43641. Terms that would be referenced in the CPT index to select codes from this section include:

- Biopsy, then stomach—code 43605
- Excision, then tumor, then stomach—codes 43610–43611
- Gastrectomy—codes 43620–43634. These codes are differentiated between total and partial gastrectomy and accompanying procedures.

- Vagotomy—codes 43635–43641. A **vagotomy** is the surgical cutting of the vagus nerve with the intent of reducing acid secretions in the stomach. These codes are assigned by identifying the additional procedures completed with the vagotomy. Code 43635 is an add-on code, so all notes in this section need to be referenced before a code is assigned.

## Laparoscopy (43644–43659)

The laparoscopic procedures completed on the stomach begin with code range 43644–43645, which is used to report gastric bypass surgery. **Gastric bypass surgery** is performed by dividing the small bowel with anastomosis to the proximal stomach to bypass the major portion of the stomach. Some morbidly obese patients have health issues that can be indications for this type of surgery.

The remaining codes in the range, codes 43647–43659, are used to report other surgical laparoscopic procedures. These codes are assigned according to the completion of the following: implantation or replacement of gastric neurostimulator electrodes, transection of vagus nerves (selective or highly selective), or gastrostomy without construction of a gastric tube. Code 43659 is used to report an unlisted laparoscopy procedure completed on the stomach.

## Introduction (43752–43763)

The next code set, 43752–43763, is used to report the introduction or change of gastric or nasogastric tubes. When assigning code 43752, closely review the patient's medical documentation. The notation that appears after code 43752 needs to be understood by the coders. This notation instructs the coder that if critical care codes are reported, code 43752 should not be reported. Codes in this range would be used to report gastric or duodenal intubation and aspiration. The change or repositioning of these tubes is also found in this code range.

## Bariatric Surgery (43770–43775)

**Bariatric surgery** is a type of operative procedure using bands and port insertion, and is performed as a treatment of morbid obesity. The bariatric procedures are reported using code set 43770–43775. These codes are differentiated by the components of the procedure completed in relation to the gastric restrictive device. These components include placement of adjustable gastric band, revision of adjustable gastric band, and removal of adjustable gastric band and subcutaneous port components.

## Other Procedures Completed on the Stomach (43800–43999)

Other procedure codes used to report gastric procedures are reported using the 43800–43999 code set. Some of the gastric restrictive procedures that cannot be reported with the bariatric or gastric bypass codes are found in this code range. Revision codes and repair codes that are not found elsewhere are coded from this code range as well.

### Exercise 11.3—Check Your Understanding

**Code Range 43500–43999**

Using the CPT manual, assign the correct code for each statement given.

1. Pyloroplasty _____
2. Open gastrotomy with suture repair of bleeding ulcer _____
3. Gastrectomy, partial, distal, with Roux-en-Y reconstruction _____
4. Selective transection of vagus nerves done laparoscopically _____
5. Local excision of malignant tumor of stomach _____
6. Therapeutic gastric intubation and aspiration(s), including lavage (physician skill needed) _____
7. Open gastric restrictive procedure with removal of subcutaneous port component only _____
8. Vagotomy including pyloroplasty, with gastrostomy, truncal _____
9. Gastroduodenostomy _____
10. Surgical closure of gastrostomy _____

# Intestines, Except Rectum (44005–44799)

The **intestine** is a membranous tube that begins at the pyloric opening of the stomach and ends at the anus. It is divided into the small and large intestine. The **small intestine** begins at the pyloric sphincter and moves through the duodenum, jejunum, ileum, and the ileocecal sphincter. It is approximately 20 feet long and encompasses most of the abdominal cavity. Most of the nutrient absorption and digestive process is completed in the small intestine before waste is moved into the large intestine.

The **large intestine** begins with the cecum and then moves to the colon, rectum, and anus. The large intestine further breaks down food and holds it until it can be further broken down and expelled from the body. Liquid is absorbed in both the large and small intestine. The longest part of the large intestine is the colon.

The colon is made up of four specific sections. The first is the **ascending colon**, which begins at the ileocecal junction; at the undersurface of the liver, it becomes the transverse colon. The **transverse colon** moves in a horizontal direction, and at the splenic flexure, it makes a downward turn to the **descending colon**. The descending colon moves down the left side of the abdomen to the **sigmoid colon**, which connects to the rectum. The coder will need to be familiar with the parts of the colon, as well as the intestines, in order to assign the correct code described in an operative note.

Figure 11-5 illustrates the structures of the small intestine, and Figure 11-6 illustrates the anatomy of the large intestine.

**FIGURE 11-5**  Small Intestine

**FIGURE 11-6** Large Intestine

## Exercise 11.4—Check Your Understanding

### Understanding the Division of the Small and Large Intestine

Indicate whether the site noted is in the large (L) or small (S) intestine.

**1.** Transverse colon _____        **4.** Cecum _____

**2.** Jejunum _____        **5.** Ascending colon _____

**3.** Ileum _____

Coding for the procedures performed in the intestines is organized into the following groups of codes:

- Incision
- Excision
- Laparoscopy
- Enterostomy—External Fistulization of Intestines
- Endoscopy, Small Intestine and Stomal
- Introduction
- Repair
- Other Procedures

# Incision (44005–44055)

Procedures that are reported using code range 44005–44055 include the following:

- **Enterolysis**, code 44005, is the freeing of intestinal adhesions. This is a separate procedure code and is reported only when no other procedure is performed. It should also be noted that code 44005 is not to be reported with code 45136.
- **Duodenotomy**, code 44010, is the process of making an incision into the duodenum. This procedure is completed to explore the area, to obtain biopsies, or to remove a foreign body.
- Tube or needle catheter jejunostomy for enteral alimentation, code 44015, is an add-on procedure. This is an intraoperative procedure, and this code can be added to any primary procedure. Code 44015 is always reported as a secondary code to a primary procedure.
- **Enterotomy**, codes 44020–44021, is the process of making an incision into the intestines. These codes are differentiated by the reason for the procedure.

# Excision (44100–44160)

Code range 44100–44160 is used to report excisions completed on the intestines. A term that coders will see associated with these procedures is **anastomosis**, which is the process of surgically connecting two structures that are usually hollow tubular parts, such as the intestines. Codes 44100–44130 report the following procedures:

- Biopsy of intestine—code 44100.
- Excisions of one or more lesions of small or large intestines—codes 44110–44111.
- Enterectomy, resection of small intestine—codes 44120–44128. These codes are differentiated according to the accompanying procedures and the reason for the enterectomy.
- **Enteroenterostomy**—code 44130. This is a separate procedure code that is used to report the surgical anastomosis of two parts of the intestine with the creation of an opening between the two areas.

Also included in this range are codes for excision procedures that are completed for intestinal transplant surgery. As in other sections of CPT, these codes involve three distinct components of work associated with the transplantation:

- Donor enterectomy—either from a cadaver (code 44132) or from a living donor (code 44133)
- Backbench work—codes 44715 and 44720–44721
- Recipient intestinal allotransplantation with or without recipient enterectomy—codes 44135 and 44136

Codes 44140 to 44160 are used to report an **open colectomy**, an excision of all or part of the colon by making an incision into the area. These codes are differentiated according to whether the colectomy was partial, codes 44140–44147 and 44160, or whether the procedure was a total colectomy, codes 44150 to 44158. The codes are further differentiated by accompanying procedures. Therefore, when selecting codes from this area, the coder needs to determine the following:

- Was the colectomy partial or total?
- What were the accompanying procedures (such as coloproctostomy, ileostomy, or mucosectomy)?

Figure 11-7 illustrates various colectomy options.

# Laparoscopy (44180–44238)

Laparoscopic enterolysis of adhesions, code 44180, allows surgeons the ability to report extensive removal of adhesions that have to be passed through to get to the operative site. Most insurance carriers will not reimburse separately for this procedure because they consider it bundled into the other, more complex operative services provided. However, in some instances, there are such extensive adhesions that the destruction of these

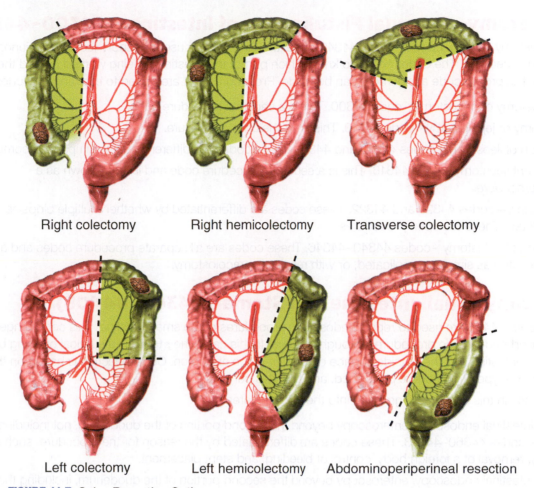

Right colectomy          Right hemicolectomy          Transverse colectomy

Left colectomy          Left hemicolectomy          Abdominoperineal resection

**FIGURE 11-7** Colon Resection Options

adhesions adds more time to the other surgery being performed. If the surgeon documents this additional time and why this is above and beyond the norm for the service being provided, an appeal may be successful if the claim is rejected by the insurance company.

As with other laparoscopic procedures, a diagnostic laparoscopy is always included in the surgical laparoscopy. However, in this section of CPT, the diagnostic laparoscopy is reported using code 49320, which does not fall within this range of codes. Codes 44180 to 44238 include only surgical laparoscopic procedures and are divided into the following groups of codes:

- Incision—code 44180
- Enterostomy—External Fistulization of Intestines—codes 44186–44188
- Excision—codes 44202–44213
- Repair—code 44227
- Other Procedures—code 44238

In reviewing these codes further, note that all of these laparoscopic procedures are also completed as open procedures. After each of the codes in this section, a notation appears that references the open procedure.

**EXAMPLES:** Code 44204 is used to report a surgical laparoscopy with a partial colectomy with anastomosis. Code 44140 is used to report a partial colectomy with anastomosis that was completed as an open procedure.

Therefore, it is of utmost importance that, when reading the operative report, the coder identify whether the procedure was completed via a laparoscope or as an open procedure.

# Enterostomy—External Fistulization of Intestines (44300–44346)

The Enterostomy section, codes 44300–44346, is next. This section is used to report ileostomy, jejunostomy, or colostomy procedures. The coder needs to know which part of the intestine is being worked on and the division of each so that proper code assignment can be made. Procedures that are coded to this range include:

- Enterostomy or cecostomy—code 44300. This is a separate procedure code.
- Ileostomy or jejunostomy—code 44310. This is for the open procedure.
- Revision of ileostomy—codes 44312 and 44314. These codes are differentiated by simple and complicated.
- Continent ileostomy—code 44316. This is a separate procedure code and is also known as a *Kock procedure*.
- Colostomy—codes 44320 and 44322. These codes are differentiated by whether multiple biopsies were completed. These are open procedures.
- Revision of colostomy—codes 44340–44346. These codes are all separate procedure codes and are differentiated as simple, complicated, or with repair of paracolostomy.

# Endoscopy, Small Intestine and Stomal (44360–44408)

Codes 44360–44408 are used to report endoscopic procedures of the small intestine. This code range is also used to report endoscopic procedures through a stoma. In this case, the **stoma** is a surgical opening between a part of the intestine and the outside surface of the skin of the abdomen. Code selection is based on the scope placement, the type of procedure performed, and how it is performed.

The codes in this section are grouped into the following areas:

- Small intestinal endoscopy, enteroscopy beyond the second portion of the duodenum, not including the ileum—codes 44360–44373. These codes are differentiated by the reason for the procedure, such as biopsy, removal of a foreign body, control of bleeding, and stent placement.
- Small intestinal endoscopy, enteroscopy beyond the second portion of the duodenum, including the ileum—codes 44376–44379. These codes are also differentiated by the reason for the procedure.
- Ileoscopy—codes 44380–44384. Code selection is based on whether the procedure was diagnostic, completed with a biopsy, or for placement of a transendoscopic stent.
- Endoscopic evaluation of a small intestinal pouch—codes 44385–44386. Codes are differentiated by a diagnostic procedure or by a biopsy.
- Colonoscopy—codes 44388–44408. These codes are selected based on whether the colonoscopy was diagnostic (code 44388) or whether the colonoscopy was completed to perform a procedure (codes 44389 to 44408) such as a biopsy, removal of a foreign body, or stent placement.

# Codes 44500 to 44799

Introduction of a long gastrointestinal (GI) tube is reported with code 44500. This GI tube placement is not the same as the nasogastric tube placement (43752). This procedure is typically referred to as a Miller-Abbott, in which a mercury-filled balloon is swallowed that carries it to the small intestine. The patient is seated lower than the person performing the service. The balloon is then inflated slightly and pulled outward until the obstruction is encountered. The procedure may be done with or without fluoroscopy.

Repair codes and other procedures complete this subsection. The services reported with codes 44602 to 44680 include closure procedures of the large or small intestine. Procedures reported from this range include:

- Suturing of small intestine
- Closure of enterostomy
- Closure of intestinal fistula
- Intestinal plication

Other procedures are reported with codes 44700 to 44799 and include codes for backbench work. Remember that backbench work is the work completed to prepare for a transplant.

## Exercise 11.5—Check Your Understanding

**Code Range 44005–44799**

Using the CPT manual, assign the proper code to each of the following statements.

1. Enterorrhaphy for perforated ulcer small intestine, single perforation _____
2. Revision of colostomy, simple _____
3. Ileoscopy, through stoma, with biopsy _____
4. Laparoscopic lysis of adhesions of the abdomen _____
5. Simple revision of ileostomy _____
6. Duodenotomy for biopsy _____
7. Laparoscopic nontube ileostomy _____
8. Complete removal of transplanted intestinal allograft _____
9. Kock procedure _____
10. Closure of intestinal cutaneous fistula _____

# Meckel's Diverticulum and the Mesentery (44800–44899)

**Meckel's diverticulum** is a form of diverticulum of the ileum. The **mesentery** is the membranous attachment of an organ to the body wall. The codes found in this subcategory include excision codes 44800 and 44820, and a code for the suturing of the mesentery, code 44850. Code 44899 is used to report unlisted procedures completed on Meckel's diverticulum and the mesentery.

# Appendix (44900–44979)

The **appendix** is a small, twisted, tubelike structure located at the blind end of the cecum. The location of the appendix in relation to the cecum is previously illustrated in Figure 11-6.

The appendix does not serve any known purpose in the digestive system. The coding begins with incision and excision codes and moves on to laparoscopic codes. An open appendectomy is code 44950 if performed on its own and *not* in conjunction with any other abdominal procedure. If the removal is performed in addition to another major procedure for a clinically indicated reason, add-on code 44955 should be used to report the removal of the appendix. Code 44970 is used to report an appendectomy performed laparoscopically. If this is done at the time of a diagnostic procedure, the diagnostic procedure is considered inclusive to the surgical procedure and is not reported separately.

# Colon and Rectum (45000–45999)

At the distal end of the large intestine is the **rectum**, which aids the removal of waste from the body.

The 45000–45020 code range is used to report incision procedures. Procedures reported with this range of codes include incision and drainage of abscesses that are located in the rectum.

Excision procedures are reported using code range 45100–45172. The terms to reference in the index to locate codes from this section include:

- Biopsy, then rectum—code 45100
- Myomectomy, then anorectal—code 45108

- Proctectomy, then partial (open) or total (open)—codes 45110–45123
- Rectum, then prolapse, then excision—codes 45130–45135
- Rectum, then stricture, then excision—code 45150

Destruction of a rectal tumor by electrodesiccation, electrosurgery, laser ablation, laser resection, or cryosurgery via a transanal approach is recorded using code 45190.

Endoscopic procedures can be either surgical or diagnostic in nature and are reported using codes 45300–45398.

Endoscopic procedures are determined by how far into the large intestine the scope is moved. Codes for this subcategory are set up in the order of examinations, which go from least invasive to most invasive.

Examination of the rectum with scope advancement into the sigmoid colon is called a **proctosigmoidoscopy**. The code range for proctosigmoidoscopy is 45300–45327.

A **sigmoidoscopy** is a procedure in which the endoscope is moved all the way through the rectum and sigmoid colon and may even advance slightly into the descending colon. The code range for sigmoidoscopy procedures is 45330–45350.

An examination in which the entire colon, from the rectum to the cecum, is visualized is known as a **colonoscopy**. A colonoscopy may include examination of the terminal ileum as well. The endoscope may be flexible or rigid. The procedure codes used to report a colonoscopy are 45378–45398. Coding guidelines for endoscopic procedures dictate that only the most extensive procedure performed should be reported.

> **EXAMPLE:** Dr. Dodd performed a sigmoidoscopy for lesion removal on his patient, but because of his findings, it was determined that he needed to perform a colonoscopy for polyp removal by snare technique farther up in the large intestine and proximal to the splenic flexure.

Dr. Dodd should be using code 45385—colonoscopy, flexible, proximal to splenic flexure; with removal of polyps, by snare technique. The sigmoidoscopy should not be reported, since the colonoscopy is more extensive and includes the sigmoidoscopy.

Laparoscopy, repairs, manipulation, and other procedures complete this subcategory of the digestive system. A coder uses code range 45395–45999 for surgical laparoscopic procedures, proctoplasty, protopexy, and unlisted procedures completed on the rectum. The coder needs to review the operative notes carefully to be sure that the service was captured correctly.

Repair codes are reported using codes 45500 to 45825. When coding from this range, the coder needs to note the approach that was used in order to select codes from 45540 to 45550. It should also be noted that codes in range 45562–45825 are differentiated by whether a colostomy was performed.

Manipulation procedures of the rectum are reported with codes 45900–45915. These codes are used to report the following procedures:

- Reduction of procidentia
- Dilation of anal sphincter or rectal stricture
- Removal of fecal impaction or a foreign body

Dilation in the rectum is reported using codes 45905 and 45910. Dilation procedures are performed digitally or by using a dilating instrument and are typically done under some type of anesthesia.

# Anus (46020–46999)

The **anus** is the most distal structure of the digestive system. The anus is typically where hemorrhoids appear. A **hemorrhoid** is an enlarged varicose vein in or near the anus.

Understanding terminology related to types and complications of hemorrhoids is important in assigning the correct CPT code. Hemorrhoid types can be internal, external, combined, or mixed. **Internal hemorrhoids** are located in the superior vein. **External hemorrhoids** are found outside of the external sphincter. **Combined hemorrhoids** or **mixed hemorrhoids** are found in both places and are usually dilated.

Some of the complications that a coder might need to take into consideration when choosing the correct code are notations from the provider that the hemorrhoid might have been diagnosed as a **prolapsed**, **thrombosed**, **strangulated**, or **ulcerated hemorrhoid**.

When a hemorrhoid becomes prolapsed, it has descended past the anal sphincter. A thrombosed hemorrhoid is one that contains a blood clot and is extremely painful. When the anal sphincter causes the blood supply to be occluded in a hemorrhoid, it is referred to as a *strangulated hemorrhoid*. A hemorrhoid that is inflamed and may have necrotic changes in surrounding tissue is referred to as an *ulcerated hemorrhoid*.

Because of the complications and types of hemorrhoids, code assignment can be tricky, and coders should take these things into account, as well as the type of treatment used and any other modifying factors, such as a fissure or fistula. The guidelines that start this code range have additional information that is extremely helpful and should be referenced prior to code assignment.

Codes in this subcategory include incision (codes 46020 to 46083) and excision (codes 46200 to 46320). Codes 46221, 46945, 46946, 46948, and 46250–46262 report hemorrhoidectomy. The codes are differentiated by whether the hemorrhoids are internal versus external, and by accompanying procedures. The coder should note that there is resequencing in the Excision code range. Attention to detail is essential prior to assigning a code.

Endoscopy procedures completed on the anus, known as **anoscopy**, are reported using codes 46600–46615. Code 46600 reports a diagnostic anoscopy, and the remaining codes report anoscopy procedures that are completed for the following reasons: dilation, biopsy, removal of a foreign body, removal of tumors and polyps, control of bleeding, and ablation of lesions.

Codes 46700–46761 and 46947 are used to report repairs completed on the anus. Terms to reference in the index for code selection in this range include:

- Anoplasty
- Anus, then repair
- Repair, then anal
- Sphincteroplasty, then anal

## Exercise 11.6—Check Your Understanding

### Vocabulary

Fill in the blanks in the statements that follow.

1. The examination in which the entire colon, from the rectum to the cecum, is visualized is known as a(n) _____.

2. A(n) _____ hemorrhoid is one that contains a blood clot and is extremely painful.

3. The _____ is the most distal structure of the digestive system.

4. The _____ is a small, twisted, tubelike structure located at the blind end of the cecum.

5. _____ is a form of diverticulum of the ileum.

6. A _____ is an enlarged varicose vein near the anus.

7. A _____ is a procedure in which the endoscope is moved all the way through the rectum and sigmoid colon.

8. The _____ is located at the distal end of the large intestine.

Destruction codes are reported by using code range 46900–46942. These codes include the destruction of lesions of the anus by various methods. The coder must be able to identify the method of destruction for code selection: chemical, electrodesiccation, cryosurgery, laser, or surgical excision.

# Liver (47000-47399)

The **liver** filters red blood cells, stores essential vitamins, contains enzymes that break down poisons in the body, and produces bile that helps break down fats.

The code selection depends on the service provided and whether the procedure was performed as an open procedure or a laparoscopic procedure. Incision and excision codes start the subcategory and then move into the codes for liver transplantation procedures. The coder should refer to operative notes to see whether imaging guidance was used because additional codes may be necessary for some of the procedures listed.

Liver transplantation codes begin with code 47133 and go through code 47147. These transplant codes have three components encompassing the physician work involved. The harvesting of the graft, including preservation, is the first component. The codes used to report the harvesting are 47133–47142. The next component reflects the physician's part in the benchwork. The codes used for this component are 47143–47147. Code 47135 reports the final component, which is recipient liver allotransplantation. **Allotransplantation** is a transplant that occurs between like species. Allotransplantation includes the recipient hepatectomy (partial or whole) and the transplantation of the allograft (partial or whole), along with care of the recipient patient.

The subcategory continues with repair codes, laparoscopic procedures, and other procedures, including ablation of liver tumors with radiofrequency. Repair codes 47300–47362 include repair of liver hemorrhage. Code 47361 includes wound exploration with extensive debridement, coagulation, and sutures with or without packing. If packing is used, code 47361 should be used. Some types of packing are removed within three days of placement. When the patient returns for removal of the packing, code 47362 should be used to report this service.

# Biliary Tract (47400-47999)

The **biliary tract** is composed of organs and ducts that are involved in the processing and movement of bile into the duodenum. The organs and ducts include the liver, gallbladder, and bile ducts. Knowing the approach that the surgeon used is very important to determine the correct code selection.

The codes for incision of these structures are 47400–47480. This range includes such procedures as:

- Hepaticotomy
- Hepaticostomy
- Choledochotomy
- Choledochostomy
- Transduodenal sphincterotomy or sphincteroplasty

Introduction codes begin with code 47490, percutaneous cholecystostomy complete procedure (including imaging guidance, catheter placement, cholecystogram when performed and radiological supervision and interpretation), and include codes 47531–47544 for various biliary procedures that include stent or catheter placement, exchange and/or removal. Codes 47542–47544 are add-on codes. The entire range of codes 47490–47544 include numerous notations prior to the listing of codes and within the code description listings. Read all of the notations that are listed in the CPT manual for these codes.

Endoscopic and laparoscopic procedures are covered by the next set of codes. These codes can be reported as surgical or diagnostic, but as coding guidelines note, surgical procedures include diagnostic ones, so the diagnostic procedures should not be reported separately if a more extensive surgical procedure is being performed at the same operative session on the same problem. These codes are differentiated according to accompanying procedures, such as biopsy, removal of calculus, dilation, cholangiography, cholecystectomy, and types of exploration. A very common procedure is a laparoscopic cholecystectomy. Figure 11-8 illustrates a lateral view of a laparoscopic cholecystectomy, whereas Figure 11-9 illustrates the cross-sectional view.

Excision codes are reported using code range 47600–47715. This code range includes codes for various types of cholecystectomies, excision of a bile duct tumor, and portoenterostomy and other excision procedures.

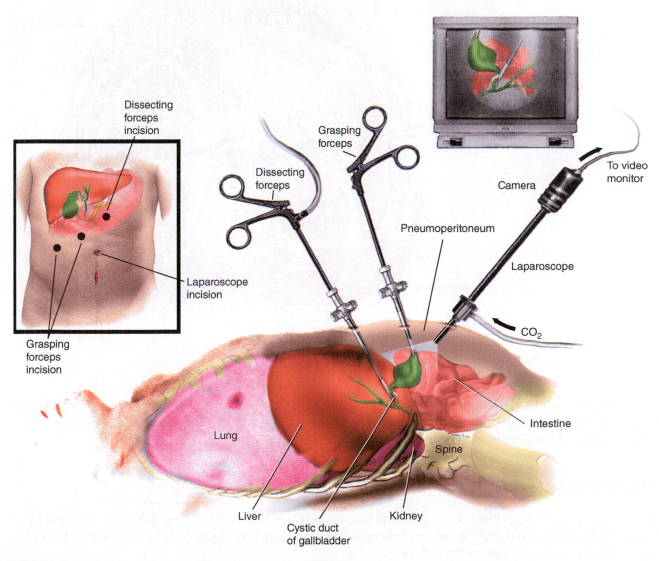

**FIGURE 11-8** Laparoscopic Cholecystectomy—Lateral View

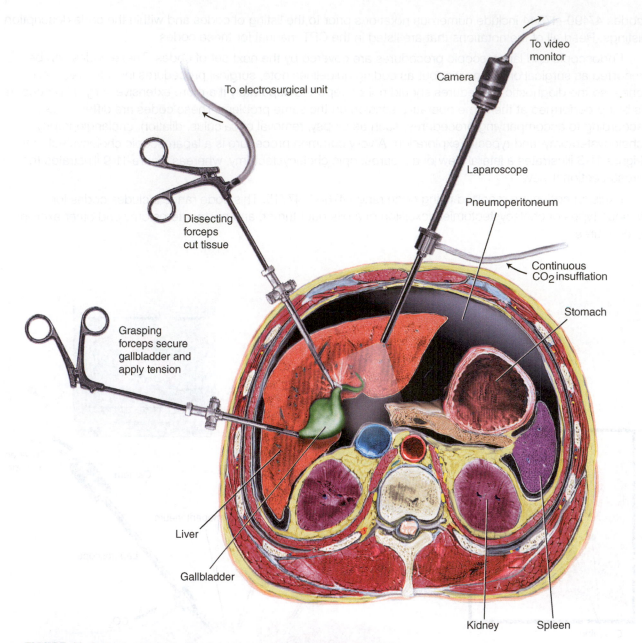

To video monitor

Camera

To electrosurgical unit

Laparoscope

Pneumoperitoneum

Dissecting forceps cut tissue

Continuous $CO_2$ insufflation

Stomach

Grasping forceps secure gallbladder and apply tension

Liver

Gallbladder

Kidney    Spleen

**FIGURE 11-9** Laparoscopic Cholecystectomy—Cross-Section View

Attention to detail is necessary because anastomosis procedures are also found in the Repair section. Repair codes as they relate to the biliary tract are reported with codes 47720–47900. The code 47999 would be used to report unlisted procedures in relation to the biliary tract.

# Pancreas (48000–48999)

The **pancreas** is an organ that is located behind the stomach and is connected to the gallbladder and liver by way of the common bile duct. The pancreas secretes juices necessary for digestion but also regulates blood sugar levels with the secretion of the hormone insulin.

Incisions are reported using code set 48000–48020, and excisions are reported using code set 48100–48160.

There is one introduction code, which is code 48400. This is an add-on code and should not be used alone. This code should be used in conjunction with a primary procedure code, as well as a radiological code if appropriate. Codes 48500–48548 report repairs completed on the pancreas and include:

- Marsupialization of pancreatic cyst
- Open external drainage of pseudocyst of pancreas
- Direct internal anastomosis of pancreatic cyst to gastrointestinal tract
- Pancreatorrhaphy for injury
- Duodenal exclusion with gastrojejunostomy for pancreatic injury
- Pancreaticojejunostomy, side-to-side anastomosis

Codes 48550–48556 are used to report pancreas transplant procedures. Like the liver transplant services, pancreatic transplants also have three components: harvesting, backbench work, and transplant. It is essential that the coder review operative notes to be sure all services are captured.

# Abdomen, Peritoneum, and Omentum (49000–49999)

The **abdomen** is the area of the body that lies between the thorax and the pelvis. The **peritoneum** is the membranous lining of the abdomen. The **omentum** is the part of the peritoneum that connects the stomach to other structures of the abdomen.

This subcategory of codes begins with incision, excision, and destruction codes. The code range is 49000–49255. The services reported from this code range include drainage, peritoneocentesis, excision, and biopsies.

Laparoscopic procedures are reported with codes 49320–49329. As with any laparoscopic procedure, diagnostic laparoscopic procedures are included in the surgical procedures.

Introduction, revision, and/or removal codes are reported using code set 49400–49465. Insertion of a cannula and peritoneal-venous shunt are reported from this code set.

## Repair—Hernioplasty, Herniorrhaphy, Herniotomy, Suture, and Other Procedures (49491–49999)

A **hernia** is a protrusion or bulge through the tissue that normally contains a structure. Hernioplasty, herniorrhaphy, and herniotomy are all terms used when referring to hernia repair. Repairs are usually made with sutures, mesh, or wire. Unless the code states otherwise, the code is for unilateral repair. If a bilateral repair is performed, the coder needs to append modifier 50 to the CPT code.

Hernia repairs are coded according to the type of hernia. There are several types of hernias, and a coder needs to be able to distinguish the differences to be able to assign the correct code. An **inguinal hernia** (codes 49491–49525) is a bulging at the inguinal opening. An **indirect inguinal hernia** is a sac that extends through the inguinal ring and into the inguinal canal, sometimes descending into the scrotum. A **direct inguinal hernia** is a type of inguinal hernia that protrudes into the abdominal wall by the Hesselbach triangle. A **hiatal hernia** is a type of hernia that pushes the stomach upward into the mediastinal cavity through the diaphragm. An **incisional hernia** is a hernia that develops through a surgical scar or scar tissue. A **strangulated hernia** is a hernia that develops gangrene because the sac is tightly constricted. A **ventral hernia** is a hernia that protrudes through an abdominal scar where the abdominal wall is protected only by scar tissue.

Some of the hernia repair codes are further distinguished as initial or recurrent based on whether the hernia has previously been repaired. For some of the codes, the patient age and clinical presentation is a factor in code selection. The clinical presentation of the hernia can be reducible, incarcerated, or strangulated.

Surgical hernia repair completed laparoscopically is reported using codes 49650, 49651, and 49659. Secondary repair of abdominal wall evisceration or dehiscence is reported with code 49900. Other procedures not located elsewhere for this subcategory are reported using codes in the 49904–49999 code range.

# Summary

- The digestive system is sometimes referred to as the *alimentary canal.*
- The procedure codes begin with procedures on the mouth and oral cavity and move through the entire digestive system.
- The vestibule of the mouth is the mucosal tissue and submucosal tissue of the lips and cheeks.
- *Lingual* refers to the tongue, and the *sublingual area* refers to the area under the tongue.
- A tracheostomy is a surgical opening in the trachea through the neck.
- An endoscopic procedure involves insertion of a flexible or rigid instrument called an *endoscope*, which is used to view internal structures.
- Endoscopic and laparoscopic procedures are frequently completed on the digestive system.
- Manipulation is a maneuver by hand to treat or perform therapy.
- Dilation is performed when expansion or stretching is necessary.
- Enterolysis is the freeing of intestinal adhesions.
- Duodenotomy is the process of making an incision into the duodenum.
- A hemorrhoid is an enlarged varicose vein in or near the anus and includes the following types: internal, external, combined, and mixed.
- Meckel's diverticulum is a form of diverticulum in the ileum.
- A proctosigmoidoscopy is the examination of the rectum with scope advancement into the sigmoid colon.
- A sigmoidoscopy is a procedure in which the endoscope is moved all the way through the rectum and sigmoid colon and may even advance slightly into the descending colon.
- The examination in which the entire colon, from the rectum to the cecum, is visualized is known as a *colonoscopy.*

# Internet Links

To learn more about the digestive system and surgical procedures associated with this system, visit
**https://www.merckmanuals.com/home**

Type the name of a procedure, such as biopsy of the intestine, into a search engine, extensive  information will be available.

# Chapter Review

## True/False

**Instructions:** Indicate whether each of the following statements is true (T) or false (F).

1. _____ The nasopharynx is part of the pharynx and contains the tonsils.

2. _____ Cheiloplasty refers to repair of the lips.

3. _____ The digestive system aids the body in eliminating waste.

4. _____ The mouth, throat, intestines, and anus are all structures of the digestive system.

5. _____ For surgical endoscopy, the diagnostic endoscopy should be reported separately because it indicates where the surgery needed to take place.

## Fill in the Blank

**Instructions:** Fill in the blanks in the following sentences.

6. The abdomen is the area of the body that lies between the thorax and the _____.

7. A procedure that is performed by dividing the small intestine with anastomosis to the proximal stomach in the treatment of obesity is known as _____.

8. A type of hernia that pushes the stomach upward into the mediastinal cavity through the diaphragm is called a(n) _____ hernia.

9. The anatomical structure that is positioned at the base of the esophagus on one end and connects to the duodenum on the other end is the _____.

10. An examination of the entire colon, from the rectum to the cecum, is known as a(n) _____.

# Coding Assignments

**Instructions:** For each of the following procedures, select the appropriate CPT code.

1. Free omental flap with microvascular anastomosis _____

2. Ligation of internal hemorrhoids

   _____

3. Incision and drainage of perirectal abscess

   _____

4. Single resection of small intestine with anastomosis _____

5. A 1.3-cm laceration repair, vestibule of mouth

   _____

6. Biopsy of the lip _____

7. Periodontal mucosal grafting

   _____

8. Lengthening of palate, and pharyngeal flap

   _____

9. Frenoplasty _____

10. Cricopharyngeal myotomy

    _____

11. Total esophagectomy with thoracotomy with cervical esophagogastrostomy, without pyloroplasty _____

12. Diagnostic esophagoscopy, flexible, no collection of specimen, transoral _____

13. Upper gastrointestinal flexible endoscopy, from esophagus to stomach through jejunum, with collection of specimen by brushing

    _____

14. Retrograde cholangiopancreatography, diagnostic endoscopic with collection of specimen using brushing technique _____

15. Transrectal drainage of pelvic abscess

    _____

16. Appendectomy _____

17. Proctosigmoidoscopy with removal of three polyps by snare technique

    _____

18. Flexible colonoscopy proximal to splenic flexure; diagnostic, no specimen, no colon decompression

    _____

19. Umbilical hernia repair of 17 year old, incarcerated 2 cm _____

20. Repair lumbar hernia _____

21. Secondary suture of abdominal wall for dehiscence _____

22. Open drainage of retroperitoneal abscess

    _____

23. Laparoscopic cholecystectomy with cholangiography _____

24. Cryosurgery of malignant rectal tumor

_____

25. Biopsy of intestine by capsule, three specimens _____

26. Removal of esophageal sphincter augmentation device _____

27. Removal of transplanted pancreatic allograft

_____

28. Resection of omentum

_____

29. Open drainage of subphrenic abscess

_____

30. Marsupialization of abscess of liver

31. Vermilionectomy with mucosal advancement

_____

32. Vestibuloplasty posterior, bilateral

_____

33. Excision of lesion of tongue without closure

_____

34. Gingivoplasty quadrant 1

_____

35. Lengthening of palate with island flap

_____

# Case Studies

**Instructions:** Review each case and indicate the correct code(s).

## Case 1

**Preoperative and postoperative diagnosis:** Chronic calculus cholecystitis

**Anesthesia:** General

**Procedure:** Cholecystectomy via scope

This 12-year-old patient was brought to the operating room and placed on the operating table, and general anesthetic was induced. The abdomen was prepped and draped. An infraumbilical incision was made, and dissection was made down to the fascia, which was lifted and cut. The blunt port trocar was placed, and the abdomen was insufflated with carbon dioxide. Additional 5-mm trocars were placed in the upper abdomen. The gallbladder was identified and retracted. At the level of the Calot triangle, dissection was started, dissecting the peritoneum and adipose tissues from the underlying cystic duct. The cystic artery was taken down with shears. The gallbladder was dissected to free it from the liver bed. The cystic duct was ligated on its proximal and distal aspects with a 0 Vicryl endoloop. The cystic duct was transected and brought through the umbilical site. The area was inspected, with no complications noted. The trocars were removed, and no hemorrhage was noted. Deflation of the abdomen occurred. The umbilical site at the fascia was closed with interrupted 0 Vicryl sutures, and the skin was closed with 4-0 Vicryl sutures. The patient tolerated the procedure well and was sent to the recovery room in stable condition.

**CPT code(s):** _____

# Case 2

**Preoperative diagnosis:** Bilateral hernias

**Postoperative diagnosis:** Bilateral inguinal hernias

**Anesthesia:** MAC

**Procedure:** Bilateral inguinal hernia repair

This 54-year-old patient was prepped and draped in the usual fashion, and sedation was introduced. The left inguinal region was anesthetized, and an incision was made with a scalpel. Dissection was carried through to the subcutaneous tissue with Bovie electrocautery. The ilioinguinal nerve was identified and was separated from the operative field. The spermatic cord was surrounded with a Penrose drain, and the cord was dissected. A small hernia sac was seen and ligated near its base, and a large Bard PerFix plug was placed into the defect and sutured to the edges. At the floor of the canal, a patch was placed and sutured to the shelving edge of the inguinal ligament midway through the canal and transversalis fascia. The spermatic cord structures were returned to the canal. The underlying tissue was closed with 3-0 Vicryl sutures. The skin was closed with 4-0 Vicryl sutures in a running subcuticular fashion. Next, the same procedure was completed on the right side after seeing a small indirect hernia. A Bard PerFix plug and a large patch were used. Closure was completed in the same fashion. The patient tolerated the procedure well and was sent to the recovery room in satisfactory condition.

**CPT code(s):** _____

# Case 3

This 58-year-old female presented with a history of bleeding hemorrhoids. Today, her chief complaint was some rectal bleeding. We discussed the risks and benefits of an anoscopy to see what was going on. The patient agreed and was prepped for the procedure. She was accompanied by her husband. She had high anxiety about the procedure but was more nervous about the bleeding, so we administered 10 mg of Versed to help her get through this.

**Procedure:** The anascope was introduced to the rectum, and visualization was performed for the entire rectum. A small polyp appeared to have ruptured. This was not a hemorrhoid and did not look threatening. Another polyp was visualized and appeared to be inflamed. Using snare technique, this one polyp was removed. Samplings were taken and sent for pathology. Patient tolerated the procedure well and was scheduled to return in one week for pathology report results.

**CPT code(s):** _____

## Case 4

**Preoperative diagnosis:** Gastrointestinal bleeding, chronic calculus cholecystitis

**Postoperative diagnosis:** Same

**Procedure:** Gastroscopy with biopsy

**Indications:** This 32-year-old female had some GI bleeding. A colonoscopy was performed last week that showed no abnormalities, so it was decided that the upper GI tract should be viewed as well.

**Procedure:** The patient was brought to the procedure suite, at which time she received 10 mg of intravenous Versed and 50 mg of intravenous Demerol for sedation. We used Cetacaine spray to anesthetize the oropharynx. An Olympus video gastroscope was then passed through the oropharynx and into the esophagus, which was unremarkable. The stomach was next visualized. There, multiple gastric ulcers were seen in the antrum and pyloric area. There was some evidence of bleeding, but nothing active at this time. Biopsies of these lesions were taken for histology. The scope was moved to the duodenum, which was clear. The patient tolerated the procedure well.

CPT code(s): _____

## Case 5

This 10-year-old male suffered from recurrent strep throat. It was decided by his parents that a tonsillectomy would be the best course to take for this young man.

**Procedure:** The child was placed supine on the operating table. General endotracheal anesthesia was administered. The patient was prepped and draped in the usual sterile fashion. The right tonsil was grabbed near the superior pole and was retracted medially and inferiorly. The anterior pillar was incised with Bovie cautery, and dissection was carried from the superior to inferior direction and anterior to posterior with care to preserve the posterior pillar. The left tonsil was removed in a similar fashion. The adenoids were left intact.

CPT code(s): _____

## Case 6

**Preoperative and postoperative diagnosis:** Acute abdominal sepsis

**Procedure:** Exploratory laparotomy with partial excision of colon with end-to-end anastomosis

**Description of procedure:** The patient was brought to the operating room, and general endotracheal anesthesia was administered. The abdomen was prepped and draped in the usual sterile fashion. A midline abdominal incision was placed. Reaching the fascial area, the omentum was pulled up from over the top of the small intestine. The bowel was greatly distended, and exploration was difficult. The small bowel was then removed from the peritoneal cavity. A Bookwalter retractor was placed to expose the pelvis. A segment of the colon was resected, and the remaining ends of the colon were reapproximated with sutures, thus creating an end-to-end anastomosis. The retention sutures were tied in place, and the wound was packed with saline moistened gauze.

The patient tolerated the procedure well and was sent to the recovery room in good condition.

CPT code(s): _____

## Case 7

**Preoperative diagnosis:** Small bowel obstruction due to extensive bowel adhesions

**Postoperative diagnosis:** Same

**Procedure:** Lysis of adhesions with side-to-side ileocolostomy

**Description of procedure:** The 68-year-old female patient was taken to the operating room and, after induction of general anesthesia, was placed in a supine position. The abdomen was prepped with Betadine solution and draped in the usual sterile fashion. A midline incision was made over the old incision from a previous surgery. The incision extended from the umbilicus down to the pubis. Upon entering the abdominal cavity, adhesions were found anterior to the abdominal wall. These adhesions were removed, and the area was cleaned up, allowing for the small bowel to be better visualized. The obstruction appeared secondary to the distal ileum, being slightly twisted and wedged into the pelvis. In total, there was about 3 feet of small bowel involved. It was possible to bring some of the bowel proximal to the obstruction, and it would easily reach the cecum, which was mobilized. Approximately 2 feet from the ileocecal valve, the small bowel was anastomosed side to side to the cecum by firing a TX 60 stapler distal to the anastomosis and transecting its attachment. Once this was completed, the bowel was able to be brought up through the opening in the abdominal wall.

*(continues)*

*(continued)*

The midline incision was closed with #1PDS sutures first; then retention sutures were tied in place. The stoma was matured to the skin, and an appliance was placed.

The patient tolerated the procedure well and was sent to the recovery room in stable but serious condition.

CPT code(s): _____

# Case 8

**Preoperative diagnosis:** Retroperitoneal abscess

**Postoperative diagnosis:** Same

**Description of procedure:** This 47-year-old female was taken to the operating room and placed in a supine position. The right flank was prepped with Betadine and draped in a sterile fashion. The previous incision was taken down to the retroperitoneum, which allowed immediate visualization of the abscess. The abscess was opened and drained, yielding about 15 cc of exudate, which was sent to pathology for culture. A Jackson-Pratt was placed within the abscess, and another was placed along the retroperitoneum. They were brought out through two separate puncture sites and sutured in place. The wounds were closed in layers of running #1 PDS, and the skin was closed using staples. All sites were dressed, and the patient was sent to recovery in good condition.

CPT code(s): _____

# Case 9

**Procedural Notes**

This 75-year-old patient was placed in the upright position for placement of a nasogastric tube. The left nostril was examined, and there was no obstruction or foreign body present. The nostril was sprayed to numb the area. The tube was inserted into the nostril and advanced and viewed via fluoroscopic guidance. The tube was advanced into the stomach, and air was injected; using a stethoscope, the air sounds were then heard in the stomach. Tape was placed on the nostril to hold the tube in place.

CPT code(s): _____

## Case 10

This 67-year-old male patient has been experiencing chronic anal pain for the last six months. Previous colonoscopy, performed three months ago, was negative. The patient has been treated medically with no pain relief. Today, an examination of the anus and rectum under anesthesia is scheduled.

After obtaining sedation with anesthesia, the patient was prepped and draped in the usual fashion and placed in the lithotomy position. A digital rectal examination was found to be negative. Following the manual rectal examination, a rigid proctoscope was introduced into the anus and the scope was advanced. The anal canal and distal rectal mucosa were visualized and carefully examined. No hemorrhoids, polyps, fistula, or fissures were visualized, and no other pathology was identified. The proctoscope was removed. The patient tolerated the procedure and was taken to the recovery area in satisfactory condition.

CPT code(s): _____

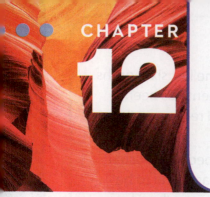

# Urinary System

## Chapter Outline

Introduction

Guidelines Related to the National Correct
Coding Initiative (NCCI)

Abbreviations Related to the Urinary
System

Anatomy of the Urinary System

Procedures Completed on the Kidneys
(50010–50593)

Procedures Completed on the Ureter
(50600–50980)

Procedures Completed on the Bladder
(51020–52700)

Procedures Completed on the Urethra
(53000–53899)

Summary

Internet Links

Chapter Review

Coding Assignments

Case Studies

## Learning Objectives

**At the conclusion of this chapter, you should be able to:**

1. Define key terms related to coding procedures on the urinary system.
2. Define abbreviations associated with the urinary system.
3. Describe the basic anatomy of the urinary system.
4. Define common procedures completed on the urinary system.
5. Apply specific coding guidelines for the urinary system.
6. Select CPT codes for procedures completed on the urinary system.
7. Identify and code procedures for the urinary system from case studies.

## Key Terms

cystostomy

cystotomy

cystourethroscopy

external sphincter

kidneys

nephrectomy

nephrolithotomy

nephrorrhaphy

nephrotomy

open drainage of a
perirenal abscess

open drainage of a renal
abscess

partial nephrectomy

pyeloplasty

pyelotomy
renal endoscopic
  procedures

symphysiotomy for
  horseshoe kidney
ureterectomy

ureters
urethra

urinary bladder
urodynamics

# Introduction

CPT code range 50010–53899 is used to code procedures completed on the urinary system. The codes are divided into four sections based on the structures that comprise the urinary system. The urinary system removes waste from the body.

# Guidelines Related to the National Correct Coding Initiative (NCCI)

The student should follow these steps to obtain the most current coding guideline information related to this chapter.

1. Log on to *https://www.cms.gov/medicare-medicaid-coordination/national-correct-coding-initiative-ncci/ncci-medicare/medicare-ncci-policy-manual*.
2. Scroll to the section titled "View Manual by Chapter."
3. Click "Chapter 7" for guidelines specific to the urinary system.

# Abbreviations Related to the Urinary System

| Abbreviations | Descriptions |
| --- | --- |
| ARF | acute renal failure |
| BPH | benign prostatic hypertrophy |
| BUN | blood, urea, nitrogen |
| CRF | chronic renal failure |
| C&S | culture and sensitivity |
| cysto | cystoscopy |
| ESRD | end stage renal disease |
| ESWL | extracorporeal shock-wave lithotripsy |
| IVP | intravenous pyelogram |
| IVU | intravenous urography |
| KUB | kidneys, ureters, bladder |
| PD | peritoneal dialysis |
| RP | retrograde pyelogram |
| TURP | transurethral resection of the prostate |
| U/A | urinalysis |
| UTI | urinary tract infection |
| VCUG | voiding cystourethrogram |

# Anatomy of the Urinary System

The structures found in the urinary system include bilateral kidneys, bilateral ureters, the urinary bladder, and the urethra. Figure 12-1 illustrates these structures.

The **kidneys** are located in the back of the abdominal region of the body on either side of the vertebral column. The main functions of the kidneys are to remove waste products from the blood and to regulate the volume and composition of the blood by allowing the reabsorption of water and other substances into the bloodstream. An adult kidney weighs about 5.5 ounces and is 10 cm long by 5.5 cm wide and 3 cm thick.

Leading from the kidneys are muscular tubes known as **ureters** that are lined with a mucous membrane. The ureters, which measure approximately 30 cm, move urine from the kidneys into the urinary bladder by means of peristalsis.

The **urinary bladder** is located in the pelvic cavity and serves as a temporary reservoir for the urine. An average-sized bladder can hold about one quart of urine.

A single structure known as the **urethra** is a mucous membrane–lined tube that transports the urine from the bladder to be excreted from the body. The length of the urethra is different for males and females. In the female, the urethra is approximately 3 to 5 cm long, whereas in the male, the urethra is approximately 18 to 20 cm long.

Below the neck of the bladder is an **external sphincter** that controls the release of the urine from the bladder. The sphincter contracts around the urethra, sending a message to the bladder to relax and not release urine. When the sphincter relaxes, the bladder neck contracts and releases urine from the body. Figure 12-2 illustrates this process.

**FIGURE 12-1**  Organs of the Urinary System

In males and females, the placement of the ureters and bladder is also different because of the reproductive organs. Figure 12-3 illustrates the location of the urinary bladder in females.

**(A) Full bladder**

Bladder

External sphincter

Bladder neck

Urethra

**(B) Release of urine from the bladder**

Bladder

External sphincter

Bladder neck

Urethra

**FIGURE 12-2**  Release of Urine Process

Ureter

Ovary

Cervix of uterus

Anus

Fallopian tube

Body of uterus

Urinary bladder

Clitoris

Urethra

Vagina

**FIGURE 12-3**  Position of the Urinary Bladder in the Female

# Procedures Completed on the Kidneys (50010–50593)

Codes 50010–50593 are used to report procedures completed on the kidneys. There are eight subsections:

- Incision
- Excision
- Renal Transplantation
- Introduction
- Repair
- Laparoscopy
- Endoscopy
- Other Procedures

## Incision (50010–50135)

Codes 50010–50135 are used to report procedures in which an incision is made into the kidney. Table 12-1 summarizes codes from this subsection.

**TABLE 12-1**  Incision (50010–50135)

| Code(s) | Description |
|---------|-------------|
| 50010 | This code is used when no other specific procedure is completed on the urinary system and there is renal exploration. |
| 50020 | At times, it is necessary to drain an abscess that is located in the renal or perirenal area. Code 50020 reports the open drainage of a perirenal or renal abscess. When an **open drainage of a perirenal abscess** or **open drainage of a renal abscess** is completed, an incision is made into the area, the site is irrigated, and drain tubes are placed. |
| 50040 | This code is used to report a nephrostomy, nephrotomy with drainage. During this procedure, an incision is made through the skin and then through the muscles, fat, and other tissue structures to the kidney. An incision is made into the kidney, and a catheter tip is placed. The physician then inserts a drain tube, and the area is closed. |
| 50045 | A **nephrotomy** with exploration is reported by using this code. During this procedure, an incision is made into the kidney, and the physician explores the interior area. |
| 50060–50075 | These codes are used to code **nephrolithotomy**, the removal of a kidney stone by making an incision into the kidney. The codes are differentiated by whether the procedure is a primary or secondary operation for calculus, complicated by kidney abnormality, or for removal of a large staghorn calculus. |
| 50080 and 50081 | These codes are differentiated by the size of the calculus removed by percutaneous nephrostolithotomy or pyelostolithotomy. The procedures can include a lithotripsy, stenting, or stone extraction. It is imperative that the size of the calculus be recorded in the medical documentation to allow you to select a code accurately. It should also be noted that if imaging guidance is performed an additional code is not to be reported as codes 50080 and 50081 include the imagining guidance. Review the codes and note the size of the stone(s) noted in the codes. |
| 50100 | This is a separate procedure code that is used to report the transection or repositioning of renal vessels. |
| 50120–50135 | **Pyelotomy**, an incision made into the renal pelvis, is reported by this range of codes. The codes are differentiated by the reason for the incision: exploration, drainage, removal of calculus, secondary operation, and complications such as a secondary operation or a congenital kidney abnormality. |

## Excision (50200–50290)

An excision completed on a kidney is known as **nephrectomy**. There are various techniques and reasons why a nephrectomy is completed. Table 12-2 summarizes the codes found in code range 50200–50290.

**TABLE 12-2** Excision Procedures (50200–50290)

| Code(s) | Description |
| --- | --- |
| 50200 and 50205 | There are two codes that report a renal biopsy. Code 50200 reports a percutaneous renal biopsy completed by a trocar or needle. Code 50205 codes a renal biopsy by surgical exposure of the kidney. |
| 50220–50230 | This range of codes is used to report a nephrectomy, a removal of a kidney, that includes a partial **ureterectomy**, the removal of a ureter. The codes are differentiated by other issues that influence the case: rib resection, previous surgery on the same kidney, regional lymphadenectomy, and so on. |
| 50234 and 50236 | When a nephrectomy is completed through the same incision, with a total ureterectomy and bladder cuff, code 50234 is used to report the case. When different incisions are made, code 50236 is reported. |
| 50240 | A partial removal of the kidney, known as a **partial nephrectomy**, is coded using this code. During this procedure (illustrated in Figure 12-4), part of the kidney is removed, and the area is then closed. It should be noted that if this procedure is performed via a laparoscope, code 50543 should be used. |
| 50250 | An open ablation of one or more renal mass lesions by cryosurgery is reported with this code. This code also includes intraoperative ultrasound if the ultrasound was performed. |
| 50280 and 50290 | These codes are used for excisions of cysts. The codes are differentiated by the location of the cyst. Code 50280 is used for excision or unroofing of a kidney cyst, and code 50290 is used for excision of a perinephric cyst. |

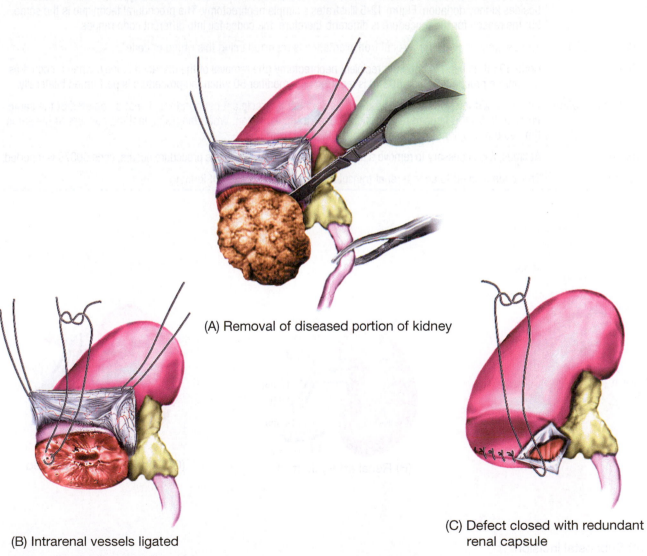

(A) Removal of diseased portion of kidney

(B) Intrarenal vessels ligated

(C) Defect closed with redundant renal capsule

**FIGURE 12-4** Partial Nephrectomy

# Renal Transplantation (50300–50380)

Code range 50300–50380 is used to report renal transplantation that involves three components of physician work. The three components are as follows:

- Harvesting of kidney—this can include a cadaver donor nephrectomy, unilateral or bilateral, or the harvesting of a graft from a living donor. This phase includes the harvesting of the graft and the preservation of the kidney.
- Backbench work—this includes the preparation of the harvested graft prior to transplantation.
- Recipient renal allotransplantation—during this component of the surgery, the transplant occurs and the recipient is cared for.

Codes from this range are summarized in Table 12-3.

**TABLE 12-3** Codes for Renal Transplantation (50300–50380)

| Code(s) | Description |
|---|---|
| 50300 and 50320 | These codes are to report a donor nephrectomy and are differentiated by whether the kidney is from a cadaver or from a living donor. Code 50300, used for a cadaver donor, is for a unilateral or bilateral kidney removal. It is important that code 50320 is assigned only when the nephrectomy is for a kidney donation. Do not confuse code 50320 with codes 50220 to 50236, which are used for nephrectomies that are performed for reasons besides kidney donation. Figure 12-5 illustrates a simple nephrectomy. The procedural technique is the same, but the reason for the procedure is different; therefore, the codes fall into different code ranges. |
| 50323–50329 | The backbench work for a renal transplantation is reported using this range of codes. |
| 50340 | Code 50340 is used to code the recipient nephrectomy (the removal of the diseased kidney) when it occurs as a separate procedure. Code 50340 is reported with modifier 50 when the procedure is performed bilaterally. |
| 50360 and 50365 | When the kidney graft is implanted and performing the recipient nephrectomy is not completed at the same time, code 50360 is used to report the kidney transplantation. When the transplantation occurs at the same time as the recipient nephrectomy, code 50365 is used. |
| 50370 | At times, it is necessary to remove a transplanted renal graft. When this procedure occurs, code 50370 is reported. |
| 50380 | This code is used to code a renal transplantation, reimplantation of kidney. |

(A) Subcostal incision

(B) Renal artery ligated

(C) Renal artery transected

**FIGURE 12-5** Simple Nephrectomy

# Introduction (50382–50396 and 50430–50437)

Code range 50382–50396 and codes 50430–50437 are used to code the introduction of catheters into the renal area and other introduction, injection, change, and removal procedures of the renal pelvis. Codes 50382–50386 report the removal or the removal and replacement of an internally dwelling stent, whereas codes 50387 and 50389 report the removal of an externally accessible stent. When assigning codes, coders should read the notations that appear throughout this section. Many of these codes can be reported bilaterally, and a modifier would be added.

Other introduction procedures are coded by using code range 50390–50396 and codes 50430–50437. Codes 50430 and 50431 are diagnostic procedures that report the injection procedure for an antegrade nephrostogram and/or ureterogram. Codes 50432 to 50435 report therapeutic procedures. Review these codes and note that these codes are out of sequence codes and they also include imaging guidance. Also review the numerous notations that appear prior to code 50390 and throughout the code descriptions. Codes 50436 and 50437 are out of sequence codes. Code 50436 reports a percutaneous dilation of existing tract for an endourolgic procedure including the imaging guidance and all associated radiological supervision and interpretation with postprocedure tube placement, when it is performed. Code 50437 reports the same procedural components for code 50436 with the addition of a new access into the renal collecting system. For additional information regarding the reporting of these codes, reference the notations following code 50437.

# Repair (50400–50540)

This range of codes is used to report repairs that are completed on the kidneys. To select these codes from the index, the coder should reference the following terms:

- **Pyeloplasty**—codes 50400 and 50405. This is plastic surgery that is completed on the renal pelvis of the kidney.
- **Nephrorrhaphy**—the suturing of a kidney wound or injury. Use code 50500.
- Fistula, then the subterm kidney—code range 50520–50526.
- Symphysiotomy, then horseshoe kidney—a **symphysiotomy for horseshoe kidney** is completed to correct a horseshoe kidney, a condition in which there is an abnormal union of the kidneys. Code 50540 should be reported.

# Laparoscopy (50541–50549)

As in the other sections of Surgery, a diagnostic laparoscopy is always included in a surgical laparoscopy. This also holds true for code range 50541–50549, laparoscopic procedures involving the renal area. It is important for the coder to read the operative reports carefully before assigning codes from this section. Many procedures can be completed as open or laparoscopic procedures. Therefore, before assigning codes from this range, the coder needs to verify that the procedure was completed via a laparoscope.

**EXAMPLE:** Dr. Jones completes a partial nephrectomy as an open procedure.

This should be coded using code 50240.

**EXAMPLE:** Later in the day, he completes surgery on another patient in which he completes a laparoscopic partial nephrectomy.

This should be assigned a different code because of the use of a laparoscope. The correct code assignment is 50543.

The coder is reminded of the different code assignments by the presence of notations in the CPT manual. Following the code descriptions for codes 50240 and 50543, notations are present that reference the other codes. Make sure that all notations are read for accurate code assignment.

## Endoscopy (50551–50580)

Code range 50551–50580 is used to report endoscopic procedures completed on the kidney. These procedures are known as **renal endoscopic procedures**. Codes in this range are differentiated according to the reason for the endoscopy, such as a biopsy, removal of a foreign body, or other accompanying procedures that can include catheterization, fulguration, or endopyelotomy.

## Other Procedures (50590–50593)

A common procedure completed to break up urinary calculi is extracorporeal shock wave lithotripsy. This procedure is noninvasive and uses two x-ray beams to shock the calculi repeatedly, causing the calculi to fracture. This is done through a liquid medium. One technique used is to submerge the patient into degassed, deionized water and direct shock waves through the liquid to the stone. A second, more common technique directs the shock waves through a water cushion to the stone. Code 50590 is used to report this procedure (illustrated in Figure 12-6).

X-ray beams crossing at focal point for positioning on the stone

Focal point

Reflection of shock waves on stone and surrounding fluid with fracture of the stone

**FIGURE 12-6** Extracorporeal Shock Wave Lithotripsy

---

### Exercise 12.1—Check Your Understanding

Laparoscopic Procedures Completed on the Kidneys

Using the CPT manual, provide the appropriate responses to the following questions.

1. Code 50230 is used to code a radical nephrectomy with regional lymphadenectomy. The correct code to use if this procedure is performed via a laparoscope is

   _____.

2. True or false: A laparoscopic ablation of a renal cyst includes the diagnostic laparoscopic procedure, if performed. The coder should use code 50541 to report this service.

   _____

*(continues)*

## Exercise 12.1 (*continued*)

3. An unlisted laparoscopy procedure completed on the kidneys should be reported with code _____.

4. True or false: Code 50547 is used to report a nephrectomy from a cadaver and includes cold preservation. _____

5. True or false: Dr. Smith performed a laparoscopy and a radical nephrectomy. In addition to this, he completed an adrenalectomy. Code 50545 should be reported with an additional code for the adrenalectomy. _____

6. A nephrotomy with exploration for calculus is reported using CPT code _____.

7. A removal of a transplanted renal allograft is reported with CPT code _____

8. An excision of a cyst of the kidney is reported using CPT code _____.

9. True or false: A laparoscopic nephrectomy is reported using CPT code 50240. _____

10. True or false: An excision of a perinephric cyst is reported using CPT code 50290. _____

# Procedures Completed on the Ureter (50600–50980)

Code range 50600–50980 is used to report procedures completed on the ureter. Remember that there are two ureters in the body. Therefore, modifier 50 may have to be added for bilateral procedures. Notations are found throughout this section of CPT to guide coders in the assignment of modifier 50. For example, code 50715 has a notation that instructs the coder to add modifier 50 for a bilateral procedure.

The codes are organized into the following subsections:

- Incision/Biopsy
- Excision
- Introduction
- Repair
- Laparoscopy
- Endoscopy

## Incision, Excision, and Introduction (50600–50695)

Terms that are used to locate these codes in the index include the following:

- Ureterotomy—codes 50600 and 50605. Separate codes are present for exploration or drainage and for insertion of an indwelling stent.
- Ureterolithotomy—codes 50610–50630. When selecting a code from this range, the coder must identify the section of the ureter on which the procedure was completed: upper one-third, middle one-third, or lower one-third.

Locate code 50606 in the CPT manual. Code 50606 is an add-on code that reports an endoluminal biopsy of the ureter and/or renal pelvis, nonendoscopic. In the CPT manual review code 50606 for the full code description and for the primary codes that this add-on code is used with. Also note the codes that should not be reported in conjunction with code 50606. There are two excision codes (codes 50650 and 50660), and these codes are located in the index by referencing the term *ureterectomy*. Injection procedures, manometric studies, and the changing of ureterostomy tubes are coded by using codes 50684 to 50690, titled Introduction.

Codes 50693 to 50695 report the percutaneous placement of a ureteral stent. Code differentiation is based on whether there was a pre-existing nephrostomy tract or whether new access was established, as well as whether or not a separate nephrostomy catheter was used. Review these codes in the CPT manual and note the instructional notation that follows code 50695.

## Repair (50700–50940)

Code range 50700–50940 is used to report repairs that are completed on the ureter. Codes 50705 and 50706 are add-on codes. Review their full descriptions in the CPT manual and note the instructional notations that follow each of the codes to determine which primary codes can be used with these add-on codes. Terms to reference in the index to locate codes from this code range include:

- Ureteroplasty
- Ureterolysis
- Ureteropyelostomy
- Ureteroneocystostomy
- Ureteroenterostomy
- Ureterosigmoidostomy
- Ureterostomy

Many of these procedures are performed as unilateral procedures; however, they also may be performed as bilateral procedures. Therefore, coders must read the operative report to determine the extent of the procedure and make the determination regarding the need for modifier assignment.

## Laparoscopy and Endoscopy Procedures (50945–50980)

Surgical laparoscopic procedure codes for procedures completed on the ureters include a diagnostic laparoscopy. These codes, 50945–50949, are differentiated according to the type of procedure performed, such as ureterolithotomy, ureteroneocystostomy with or without cystoscopy, and ureteral stent placement.

Endoscopy codes for ureteral procedures completed through an established ureterostomy are found in code range 50951 to 50961. It is important that the coder identify that the endoscopy was performed through an established ureterostomy and also identify the reason for the endoscopy, such as biopsy, ureteral catheterization, fulguration, or removal of a foreign body or calculus.

Code range 50970 to 50980 is used to report ureteral endoscopy through a ureterotomy. The codes are differentiated by the reason for the procedure: ureteral catheterization, biopsy, fulguration, or removal of a foreign body or calculus.

# Procedures Completed on the Bladder (51020–52700)

The next section reports procedures completed on the bladder: codes 51020–52700. This range contains numerous subsections of codes:

- Incision
- Removal
- Excision
- Introduction

- Urodynamics
- Repair
- Laparoscopy
- Endoscopy—Cystoscopy, Urethroscopy, Cystourethroscopy
- Transurethral Surgery
- Vesical Neck and Prostate

## Incision, Removal, Excision, and Introduction (51020–51720)

Codes 51020–51102 are used to code incisional and removal procedures completed on the bladder that include bladder aspiration, cystotomy or cystostomy, transvesical ureterolithotomy, and drainage of an abscess. Many of these procedures include the insertion of ureteral catheters. An alternate method of catheterizing the bladder for drainage is completed by performing a **cystostomy**. During a cystostomy, an incision is made in the midline and carried through until the bladder is incised. A tube is then inserted and sutured in place. Figure 12-7 illustrates an open cystostomy.

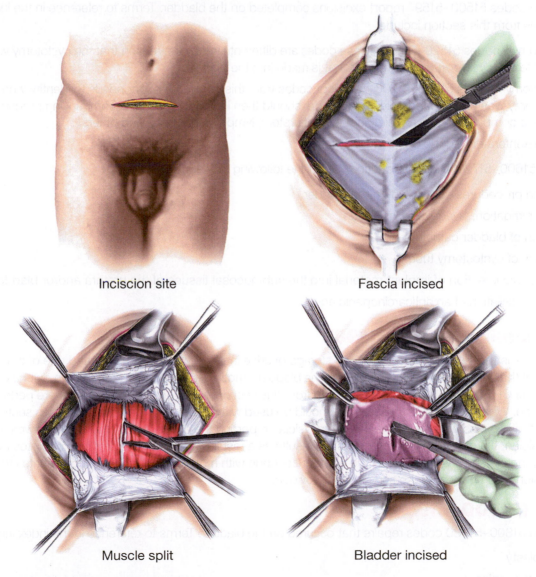

Inciscion site

Fascia incised

Muscle split

Bladder incised

**FIGURE 12-7** Open Cystostomy

Cystostomy tube inserted        Cystostomy tube secured with sutures

**FIGURE 12-7**  *(continued)*

Excision codes 51500–51597 report excisions completed on the bladder. Terms to reference in the index to locate codes from this section include:

- Cystotomy—codes 51520–51535. These codes are differentiated by the reason that the cystotomy was completed. A **cystotomy** is an incision that is made into the bladder.
- Cystectomy—codes 51550–51596. To select codes from this range, the coder needs to identify whether the cystectomy was partial or complete. The coder should then identify any other accompanying procedures that were completed, such as reimplantation of ureters, lymphadenectomy, and others.
- Pelvic exenteration—code 51597

Codes 51600–51720, titled Introduction, report the following procedures:

- Injection procedures completed on the bladder
- Bladder irrigation, lavage, and instillation
- Insertion of bladder catheters
- Changes of cystostomy tubes
- Endoscopic injection of implant material into the submucosal tissues of the urethra and/or bladder neck
- Bladder instillation of an anticarcinogenic agent

## Urodynamics (51725–51798)

**Urodynamics** is the study of the holding and storage of urine in the bladder, the motion and rate of the movement of the urine, and the analysis of how the bladder empties. It should be noted that an extensive notation appears in the CPT manual with regard to coding from this section. Many of these procedures are performed at the same time. When this occurs, modifier 51 should be used with the codes. The codes from this section also reflect that the services were performed by the physician reporting the codes and that all supplies were provided by the physician. If a physician only interprets the results as a result of the testing and/or only operates the equipment, the physician should report the appropriate code with modifier 26. Modifier 26 designates that only the professional component of the service was provided.

## Repair (51800–51980)

Code range 51800–51980 codes repairs that occured on the bladder. Terms to reference in the index include:

- Cystoplasty
- Cystourethroplasty

- Urethropexy
- Cystorrhaphy
- Closure, then cystostomy
- Enterocystoplasty

These codes are differentiated by accompanying procedures and by the reason for the procedure.

## Laparoscopy and Endoscopy (51990–52010)

Laparoscopic procedure codes 51990 and 51992 are surgical laparoscopy codes and are differentiated by whether the procedure was performed for a urethral suspension for stress incontinence or for a sling operation for stress incontinence. Code 51999 reports an unlisted laparoscopic procedure of the bladder.

Codes 52000 to 52010 are used to report endoscopic procedures completed on the bladder. Code 52000 is a separate procedure code and is used to report a cystourethroscopy. Codes 52001–52010, cystourethroscopy, are differentiated according to the procedure performed through the scope. Procedures include:

- Irrigation and evacuation of multiple obstructing clots
- Ureteral catheterization
- Biopsy
- Ejaculatory duct catheterization

Figure 12-8 illustrates the completion of a cystourethroscopy on a male patient.

**FIGURE 12-8** Cystourethroscopy of Male Patient

# Transurethral Surgery (52204–52356)

Code range 52204–52356 is used to report transurethral surgery that is completed by the use of a cystourethroscope. This code range is divided into two subsections:

- Codes 52204 to 52318 for procedures that are completed on the urethra and bladder
- Codes 52320 to 52356 for procedures that are completed on the ureter and pelvis

These codes are further differentiated by the type of accompanying procedures. Coders also need to note the sex of the patient, as some codes specify the sex of the patient.

> **EXAMPLE:** Code 52270 is used to report a cystourethroscopy with internal urethrotomy for a female patient.

To report this procedure for a male patient, code 52275 should be used.

An extensive notation appears prior to code 52320 that affects the coding of a cystourethroscopy of the ureter and pelvis. Coders are given guidance as to codes that cannot be reported together, and the use of modifier 50 when the insertion of bilateral indwelling ureteral stents occurs. New coders need to read and understand the instructions given.

# Vesical Neck and Prostate (52400–52700)

This range of codes is used for male patients to report procedures completed on the vesical neck and prostate. Procedures included in this range of codes include:

- Cystourethroscopy for the resection or incision of ejaculatory ducts
- Transurethral procedures performed on the prostate
- Laser coagulation, laser vaporization, and laser enucleation of prostate
- Drainage of prostatic abscess

## Exercise 12.2—Check Your Understanding

**Procedures Completed on the Ureters and Bladder**

Using the CPT manual, select the appropriate responses to the following questions.

1. True or false: Ureteroplasty is a type of repair _____.
2. The correct code for a ureterolithotomy completed on the middle one-third of the ureter is _____.
3. True or false: All procedures performed on the ureters are bilateral procedures _____.
4. Code 51580 is found in the _____ section of codes for procedures completed on the bladder.
5. True or false: Code 52000 can be reported when other procedures are completed _____.
6. A procedure in which an incision is made into the bladder is called a(n) _____.
7. An injection procedure and placement of a chain for contrast and chain urethrocystography are reported using CPT code _____.
8. A cystourethroscopy with a direct vision internal urethrotomy is reported using CPT code _____.
9. An ureterotomy for the insertion of an indwelling stent is reported with code _____.
10. Aspiration of bladder by trocar is reported with code _____.

# Procedures Completed on the Urethra (53000–53899)

The final range of codes for procedures completed on the urinary system is code range 53000–53899. This range is divided into the following:

- Incision
- Excision
- Repair
- Manipulation
- Other Procedures

## Incision, Excision, and Repair (53000–53520)

Incision codes can be located in the index by referencing terms such as *urethrotomy, urethrostomy, meatotomy,* and *incision* then *urethra*. Excision codes are located in the index by referencing *urethrectomy, excision* then *urethra,* or *excision* then *polyps* then *urethra*.

Repair codes are located in the index by referencing the terms *urethroplasty, sling operation, urethromeatoplasty, urethrolysis,* and *urethrorrhaphy*.

## Manipulation and Other Procedures (53600–53899)

Code range 53600–53665 includes codes to report the dilation of the urethra. These codes are differentiated by procedures completed on males and procedures completed on females.

Code range 53850–53854 reports transurethral destruction of prostate tissue. These codes are differentiated by one of three methods: microwave thermotherapy, radiofrequency thermotherapy, or radiofrequency generated water vapor thermotherapy. Code 53855 is used to report the insertion of a temporary prostatic urethral stent. Transurethral radiofrequency microremodeling of the female bladder neck and proximal urethra for stress urinary incontinence is reported with code 53860. To report this code, the diagnosis of stress urinary incontinence must be recorded in the patient's record.

# Summary

- The structures that are found in the urinary system include bilateral kidneys, bilateral ureters, the urinary bladder, and the urethra.
- The external sphincter controls the release of the urine from the bladder.
- The kidneys are located in the back of the abdominal region of the body on either side of the vertebral column.
- The ureters are muscular tubes that transport urine from the kidneys to the bladder.
- The urinary bladder is located in the pelvic cavity and serves as a temporary reservoir for the urine.
- The urethra is a mucous membrane–lined tube that transports urine from the bladder to be excreted from the body.
- A pyelotomy is an incision made into the renal pelvis.
- Endoscopy codes for ureteral procedures completed through an established ureterostomy are reported with codes 50951 to 50961.
- Code range 50970 to 50980 is used to report ureteral endoscopy through a ureterotomy.
- An alternate method of catheterizing the bladder for drainage is completed by performing a cystostomy.
- Code range 52400–52700 is used for male patients to report procedures completed on the vesical neck and prostate.

# Internet Links

To learn more about kidney stones and their treatment and about the completion of a cystoscopy and ureteroscopy, visit **https://www.niddk.nih.gov** and search on the item you want to learn about (ie. kidney stones, urinary system, etc.)

To research various kidney diseases and the treatment of the diseases, visit **http://www.kidney.org**.

# Chapter Review

## Fill in the Blank

**Instructions:** Fill in the blanks in the statements that follow.

1. The removal of a kidney stone by making an incision in the kidney is known as a(n) _____.

2. During a percutaneous drainage of a renal abscess, a CAT scan or _____ is used to guide the placement of a drainage needle.

3. A single structure known as the _____ is a mucous membrane–lined tube that transports urine from the bladder to be excreted from the body.

4. A partial removal of the kidney is known as a(n) _____.

5. Plastic surgery that is completed on the renal pelvis of the kidney is known as _____.

6. Nephrorrhaphy is _____ of the kidney.

7. Surgical laparoscopic procedure codes for procedures completed on the ureters always include a(n) _____.

8. Codes 50951 to 50961 are used to report endoscopy ureteral procedures completed through an established _____.

9. The study of the holding and storage of urine in the bladder, the motion and rate of the movement of the urine, and the analysis of how the bladder empties is called _____.

10. Code 52000 is a separate procedure code and is used to report a(n) _____.

# Coding Assignments

**Instructions:** Using the CPT manual, identify the appropriate code for each of the following procedures.

1. Ureterolithotomy involving the upper one-third of the ureter _____

2. Ureterectomy with bladder cuff _____

3. Percutaneous needle biopsy of the kidney _____

4. Excision of perinephric cyst _____

5. Open drainage of renal abscess _____

6. Partial nephrectomy _____

7. Unroofing of cyst of kidney _____

8. Partial cystectomy _____

9. Ureteral endoscopy by means of ureterotomy with removal of calculus _____

10. Cystourethroplasty with bilateral ureteroneocystostomy _____

11. Cystourethroscopy _____

12. Drainage of deep periurethral abscess _____

13. Insertion of tandem cuff of urethra _____

14. Urethromeatoplasty with partial excision of distal urethral segment _____

15. Bladder lavage _____

16. Complex uroflowmetry _____

17. Ureterotomy with drainage _____

18. Extracorporeal shock wave lithotripsy

_____

19. Ureterolysis for ovarian vein syndrome

_____

20. Closure of pyelocutaneous fistula

_____

21. Cystourethroscopy with transurethral resection of ejaculatory ducts _____

22. Initial dilation of female urethra, including suppository and installation _____

23. Excision of Skene's gland _____

24. Closure of vesicovaginal fistula; abdominal approach _____

25. Cystotomy with insertion of ureteral catheter

_____

26. Percutaneous unilateral radiofrequency ablation for two renal tumors _____

27. Insertion of non-indwelling bladder catheter

_____

28. Cystourethroscopic vasotomy with transurethral resection _____

29. Biopsy of urethra _____

30. Fulguration of carcinoma of urethra

31. Nephrolithotomy, removal of calculus

_____

32. Transection of aberrant renal vessels

_____

33. Nephrectomy with total ureterectomy and bladder cuff using same incision _____

34. Nephrorrhaphy suture of kidney injury

35. Closure of nephrovisceral fistula including visceral repair via abdominal approach _____

# Case Studies

**Instructions:** Review each case and indicate the correct code(s).

## Case 1

**Preoperative and postoperative diagnosis:** Ureteral calculus

**Anesthesia:** General

**Procedure:** Ureteroscopy of left ureter for removal of calculus; stent placement

The patient was taken from the presurgery area to the operating room and prepped and draped in the usual fashion. General anesthesia was administered. The endoscope was placed into the urethra, which appeared to be inflamed. The scope was then carefully passed through the bladder, which appeared normal. The guidewire was introduced, and a balloon was used to dilate the left ureter. The scope was advanced to view the ureter, where a small stone was extracted and a stent was placed. The area was checked for bleeding, and the scope was then removed. The stent was attached to a string, which was in the correct position. Blood loss was minimal and the patient was sent to the recovery room in good condition.

**CPT code(s):** _____

## Case 2

**Preoperative and postoperative diagnosis:** Urethral stricture

**Procedure:** Dilation of urethra, first attempt

This 45-year-old male patient was brought to the operating room and prepped and draped in the usual fashion. After the patient was anesthetized, a urethral dilator was inserted into the urethra. The urethra was then dilated to normal range. The dilator was removed, and no bleeding was noted. The patient tolerated the procedure well and was taken to the recovery room.

**CPT code(s):** _____

## Case 3

The patient is a 70-year-old female with a history of bladder cancer. She presents today for a cystoscopy, biopsy, and fulguration of an erythematous area that appeared suspicious in previous testing. The area is the right trigone.

The patient was placed in the supine position, where spinal anesthesia was administered. She was then turned to the dorsal lithotomy position, where she was prepped and draped in the usual sterile manner. A #22 French cystoscopy sheath was passed in atraumatic fashion per the urethra. The bladder was resected with the 70-degree lens, and the right trigone area was found slightly erythematous and hypervascular and was fulgurated. No tumors were found, and no mucosal abnormalities were noted. A biopsy of the area was taken and sent for pathology.

**Pathology findings:** Chronic cystitis with squamous cell metaplasia

**CPT code(s):** _____

## Case 4

A 68-year-old male presents today for laser coagulation of the prostate due to urinary retention with urgency and difficulty urinating.

**Procedure:** The patient was placed on the operating table in the lithotomy position. Spinal anesthesia was administered, and external genitalia was prepped and draped. A 21-French cystoscope was introduced into the bladder. Upon inspection, there was no evidence of a tumor. Mild trabeculations were observed on both ureteral orifices. The retroscope was introduced with a resection of the lateral lobes of the prostate being done; complete opening of the prostatic urethra was allowed. The bladder was examined, and all prostatic chips were removed. The bladder was coagulated and smoothed out with the VaporTrode. An indwelling Foley catheter was inserted into the bladder.

**CPT code(s):** _____

# Case 5

**Preoperative diagnosis:** Sigmoid diverticulitis

**Postoperative diagnosis:** Same

**Procedure:** Ureteral catheterization via scope

Patient was placed in the lithotomy position after administration of general anesthesia. A size 22 cystoscope with a 30-degree lens was placed with care under direct visualization. A lighted catheter was placed to the side for the scope, and then the left ureteral orifice was visualized. The lighted catheter was moved to the ureteral orifice and then advanced into the left renal pelvis without any problems or difficulty. After this, the cystoscope was removed. The lighted catheter was then connected to the light source. A size 18 Foley catheter was inserted into the bladder without any difficulty, and in balloon, the fluid was 10 cc. There was no blood loss during surgery, and the patient was taken to the recovery area in good condition.

CPT code(s): _____

# Case 6

**Preoperative diagnosis:** Neurogenic bladder with urinary retention

**Postoperative diagnosis:** Same

**Procedure:** Bladder aspiration with suprapubic tube placement

**Blood Loss:** < 10 mL

**Indications for procedure:** This is a mentally challenged 49-year-old white male who is currently a resident in a long-term care facility who presents today for placement of a suprapubic tube due to erosion of the Foley catheter drain his neurogenic bladder.

**Procedure:** The patient was brought to the operating room and placed in the supine position. Anesthesia was administered, and the patient was then moved to the dorsal lithotomy position. He was prepped and draped in normal sterile fashion after the Foley catheter was removed. A cystoscopy was used to explore the bladder for tumor or other foreign bodies. None were identified. The bladder was then filled with about 500 cc of sterile water, which allowed for identification of the tract needed to insert the Rauch suprapubic trocar. The skin was anesthetized with Marcaine and Lidocaine. A needle was then inserted through the lower abdominal wall into the bladder, and the trocar was advanced until the sheath of the trocar was in the bladder. A 16 French catheter was placed through the sheath into the bladder, and the balloon was inflated with 10 cc of sterile water. The sheath was then removed, and we noted good placement of the suprapubic tube in the bladder. The tube was then secured with a 0 Prolene suture, and the skin incision was cauterized and hemostasis was achieved. The patient was transferred to the recovery room in good condition.

CPT code(s): _____

# Case 7

**History:** This is a 67-year-old female who has a history of bladder cancer. She has been in remission from grade II superficial transitional cell carcinoma for 18 months now. During her follow-up visit, a cystoscopy was performed, which identified a suspicious area on the right lower portion of the trigone.

Today, she presents for a cystoscopy, biopsy, and fulguration of this area.

**Procedure:** The patient was placed on the procedure table in supine position with conscious sedation of Versed given. The patient was then placed in the lithotomy position. She was prepped and draped in normal sterile fashion. A #22 French cystoscopy sheath was passed through the urethra in atraumatic fashion. The bladder was resected with the 70-degree lens. The urethra was normal, the bladder was 1+ trabeculated, the lower-right portion of the trigone were erythematous and hypervascular. No papillary tumors or masses were found. No mucosal abnormalities were noted. A total of three cup biopsies were taken using forceps from the erythematous area of the trigone and sent to pathology. This area was fulgurated with the Bugby electrode, no active bleeding was encountered. The pathology came back as chronic cystitis.

**CPT code(s):** _____

# Case 8

**Preoperative and postoperative diagnosis:** Right renal calculus, 5 mm

**Anesthesia:** Conscious sedation under supervision of urologist for 45 minutes

**Procedure:** Extracorporeal shock wave lithotripsy

This twenty-five-year-old patient was placed on the treatment table, and a water cushion was placed over the location of the kidney stone. X-rays were then taken to determine the exact location of the stone, which was then treated with a total of 3,200 shocks. Films confirmed that the stone was pulverized into small fragments. There were no complications and the patient was sent to the recovery area.

**CPT code(s):** _____

## Case 9

**Preoperative and postoperative diagnosis:** Transitional cell carcinoma of the bladder

**Anesthesia:** General

**Procedural Notes:**

After the patient was prepped, draped, and anesthetized, he was placed in the lithotomy position. A cystourethroscope was inserted through the urethra into the bladder. In the bladder, there was a large amount of tumor that was then fulgurated via electric current. The tumor was noted to be 3 cm in size. There was minimal blood loss. The patient tolerated the procedure well and was sent to recovery in stable condition.

CPT code(s): _____

## Case 10

**Preoperative diagnosis:** Possible recurrence of bladder cancer

**Postoperative diagnosis:** No findings

**Indications for procedure:** This 56-year-old female patient had bladder cancer three years ago that was treated. She is undergoing this procedure to determine if the cancer has returned.

**Procedural Notes:**

A cystourethroscope was passed through the urethra into the bladder. The urethra, bladder, and ureteric openings were carefully visualized for any evidence of cancer recurrence. The examination showed all structures to be normal with no evidence of cancer at this time. The scope was withdrawn and the patient was sent to the recovery area in satisfactory condition.

CPT code(s): _____

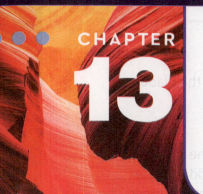

# Male Genital System

## Chapter Outline

Introduction

Guidelines Related to the National Correct Coding Initiative (NCCI)

Abbreviations Related to the Male Genital System

Procedures Completed on the Penis (54000–54450)

Procedures Completed on the Testis (54500–54699)

Procedures Completed on the Epididymis and Tunica Vaginalis (54700–55060)

Procedures Completed on the Scrotum, Vas Deferens, Spermatic Cord, and Seminal Vesicles (55100–55680)

Procedures Completed on the Prostate (55700–55899)

Reproductive System Procedures (55920) and Intersex Surgery (55970–55980)

Summary

Internet Links

Chapter Review

Coding Assignments

Case Studies

## Learning Objectives

### At the conclusion of this chapter, you should be able to:

1. Define key terms related to coding procedures on the male genital system.
2. Define abbreviations associated with the male genital system.
3. Describe the basic anatomy and functions of the male genital tract.
4. Define common procedures completed on the male genital organs.
5. Apply specific coding guidelines for the male genital system.
6. Select CPT codes for procedures completed on the male genital organs.
7. Identify and code procedures for the male genital organs from case studies.

## Key Terms

circumcision

corpora cavernosa

cryosurgical ablation of prostate

epididymis

foreskin

glans penis

hypospadias

| orchiopexy | prostate gland | sperm | tunica vaginalis |
| penis | scrotum | spermatic cord | vas deferens |
| Peyronie's disease | seminal vesicle | spermatozoa | vasectomy |
| prepuce | shaft | testes | |

# Introduction

The procedures performed on the male genital organs are reported using CPT codes 54000–55899. The organs and structures of the male genital system include the penis, testes, epididymis, tunica vaginalis, scrotum, vas deferens, spermatic cord, seminal vesicles, and prostate. These structures are illustrated in Figure 13-1.

The male genital system is primarily for reproduction, but it also functions as part of the urinary system. When a coder is making a selection that reports a service performed as part of urinary system surgery, the codes in this subsection should be reviewed, as well as those found in the urinary system, to be sure that the proper code is selected. Code descriptions may indicate unilateral or bilateral procedures. If the description does not specify unilateral or bilateral, the coder should assume that the code is for a unilateral procedure; if performed bilaterally, it may need modifier 50 appended to it. Also discussed in this chapter is Reproductive System Procedures (55920) and Intersex Surgery, codes 55970 and 55980.

# Guidelines Related to the National Correct Coding Initiative (NCCI)

Perform the following steps to obtain the most current coding guideline information related to this chapter.

1. Log on to *https://www.cms.gov/medicare-medicaid-coordination/national-correct-coding-initiative-ncci /ncci-medicare/medicare-ncci-policy-manual*.
2. Scroll to the section titled "View Manual by Chapter."
3. Click "Chapter 7" for guidelines specific to the male genital system.

# Abbreviations Related to the Male Genital System

The following is a list of the most common abbreviations related to the male genital system.

| Abbreviations | Definitions |
| --- | --- |
| BPH | benign prostatic hyperplasia |
| DRE | digital rectal examination |
| TRUS | transrectal ultrasound |
| TUIP | transurethral incision of the prostate |
| TUMT | transurethral microwave thermotherapy |
| TUNA | transurethral needle ablation |
| TURP | transurethral resection of the prostate |

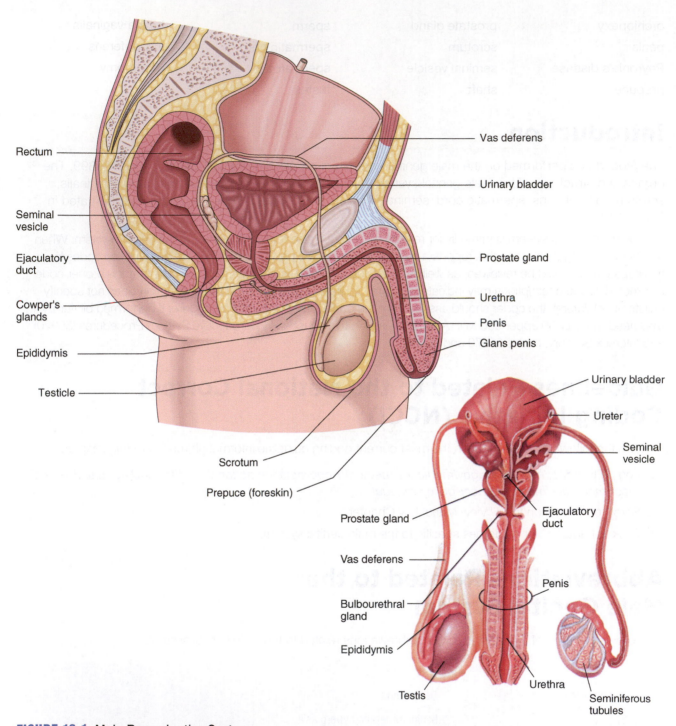

Rectum

Seminal vesicle

Ejaculatory duct

Cowper's glands

Epididymis

Testicle

Vas deferens

Urinary bladder

Prostate gland

Urethra

Penis

Glans penis

Scrotum

Prepuce (foreskin)

Urinary bladder

Ureter

Seminal vesicle

Ejaculatory duct

Prostate gland

Vas deferens

Penis

Bulbourethral gland

Epididymis

Testis

Urethra

Seminiferous tubules

**FIGURE 13-1**  Male Reproductive System

# Procedures Completed on the Penis (54000–54450)

The **penis** is the organ through which the urethra passes to allow urine to be expelled from the body as part of the urinary system. As part of the reproductive system, the penis delivers spermatozoa to the female reproductive tract. The distal end of the penis is known as the **glans penis**. The loose skin covering the glans penis is referred to as **foreskin** or **prepuce**. The glans penis connects to the **shaft**, which is the proximal end of the penis.

The procedures performed on the penis should be reported using codes 54000–54450. Incision, destruction, and excision codes begin this subsection of the male genital system codes.

Codes for reporting a circumcision are found in the Excision subsection. A **circumcision** is an elective procedure used to remove the foreskin completely from the glans penis. The surgical method should be documented, which will affect the code selection.

The coder should be aware that even though these procedures are typically performed on infants (newborn to 28 days), there is a code that allows reporting of the procedure for patients more than 28 days old. The medical necessity should be documented in the patient's medical record when the procedure is done later in life.

The introduction codes (54200–54250) refer to a structure called the **corpora cavernosa**. The corpora cavernosa refers to the erectile tissue of the penis. **Peyronie's disease** is a condition in which the corpora cavernosa becomes hardened. It can be painful and cause deformity if not treated. This code range also contains codes for injection and irrigation procedures performed on the corpora cavernosa.

The next range of codes consists of repair codes (54300–54440). If plastic surgery is performed on the penis, the codes to be referenced are found in this subcategory. Also found in this subcategory are urethroplasty codes. These are codes used to report repair of the penis when it is abnormally curved, or when the ureter opening is not properly located, affecting the flow of urine out of the body. The medical term (and the term the coder will find in CPT for this condition) is **hypospadias**.

Manipulation code 54450 is the last code in this subcategory. This code is used to report the lysis of adhesions that form between the foreskin and the head of the penis in an uncircumcised male.

## Procedures Completed on the Testis (54500–54699)

The **testes** are glands located in the scrotal sac that produce sperm and are referred to as the *testicles*. Figure 13-2 illustrates the anatomy of the testis.

Excision codes begin this subcategory. Codes for biopsy, excision of lesions, and exploration for undescended testes are found here. The code for biopsy of the testes contains notes that guide the coder to additional codes if a vasogram, seminal vesiculogram, or epididymogram is performed at the same time.

Sometimes a testicle fails to drop to the scrotum during development. As a male child grows, the testicle will usually drop on its own; however, in some cases this does not happen, and surgical intervention is required. Open exploration for an undescended testis is reported with CPT codes 54550–54560.

Repair codes are next, in which orchiopexy procedures are reported. An **orchiopexy** is a surgical fixation of the testis in the scrotal sac. Laparoscopic repair of a hernia performed at the same time as the orchiopexy would be reported with two repair codes, one indicating the hernia repair and one for the orchiopexy.

## Procedures Completed on the Epididymis and Tunica Vaginalis (54700–55060)

The **epididymis** is a tubular structure that is found at the posterior border of a testis and carries sperm to the ductus deferentia (vas deferens). The **tunica vaginalis** is the membranous sac within the scrotum that covers the sides and front of the testis and epididymis.

The coding for these subsections begins with incision and excision codes. Note that there is a notation that follows code 54800 that states for fine needle aspiration biopsy see codes 10004, 10005, 10006, 10007, 10008, 10009, 10010, 10011, 10012, and 10021.

Code 54865 is used to report exploration of epididymis with or without biopsy. The subsection for epididymis concludes with code 54900 for a unilateral epididymovasostomy, anastomosis of epididymis to vas deferens and code 54901 for a bilateral epididymovasostomy, anastomosis of epididymis to vas deferens.

Codes 55000 to 55060 report codes for procedures on the tunica vaginalis. There are three subsections: incision, excision, and repair procedures.

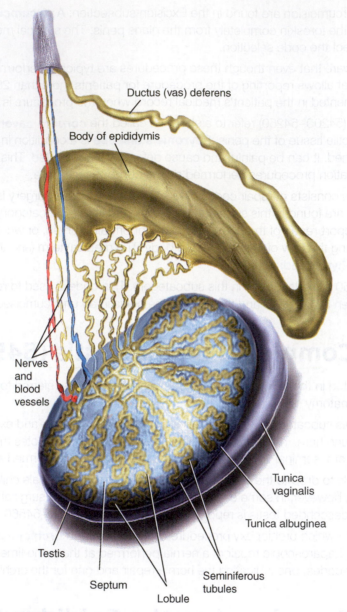

Ductus (vas) deferens

Body of epididymis

Nerves and blood vessels

Tunica vaginalis

Tunica albuginea

Testis

Septum

Lobule

Seminiferous tubules

**FIGURE 13-2** Anatomy of the Testis

# Procedures Completed on the Scrotum, Vas Deferens, Spermatic Cord, and Seminal Vesicles (55100–55680)

The subsection for procedures completed on the scrotum contains codes for incisions, excisions, and repairs. The vas deferens subsection includes codes for incisions, excisions, introduction, and repairs.

The spermatic cord subsection has codes for excisions, using codes 55500 to 55540, and codes for laparoscopic procedures using codes 55550 and 55559 to report these procedures. Codes for procedures completed on the seminal vesicles include codes 55600 and 55605 for incisions and codes 55650 and 55680 for excisions.

## Scrotum (55100–55180)

Understanding the terminology is essential to being able to code these procedures. The **scrotum** encloses, protects, and supports the testicles. The code range for procedures performed on the scrotum consists of codes 55100–55180, which include drainage, exploration, resection, and scrotoplasty.

## Vas Deferens (55200–55400)

The **vas deferens** is also referred to as the *ductus deferens* or the *seminal duct*. Procedures completed on the vas deferens are coded from the 55200–55400 code range. The vas deferens is a tube that starts as the epididymis. The epididymis moves upward and takes a turn over the top of the urinary bladder. At the turn, the epididymis becomes the vas deferens. The vasectomy procedures are coded from this code range. A **vasectomy** is the excision of the vas deferens that prevents sperm from moving outside the system, which renders a man sterile. **Sperm** is a germ cell secretion of the testicles. Vasotomy, vasovasostomy, and vasovasorrhaphy procedures are also found in this code range.

## Spermatic Cord and Seminal Vesicles (55500–55680)

The **spermatic cord** is a covering around the nerves and vessels that encloses the seminal duct. The **seminal vesicle** is part of the ejaculatory duct. The seminal vesicle and the vas deferens come together to form the ejaculatory duct posterior to the urinary bladder. The surgeon may report that at the time of an inguinal hernia repair, a lipoma of the spermatic cord was also excised. This is typically done and is considered bundled into the hernia repair, so code 55520 would not be reported separately.

---

### Exercise 13.1—Check Your Understanding

Fill in the blanks in the statements that follow.

1. The _____ is a tubular structure that is found at the posterior border of a testis and carries sperm to the ductus deferentia (vas deferens).
2. Code 54512 is found in the _____ subcategory of the male genital system code set.
3. The _____ is a covering around the nerves and vessels that encloses the seminal duct.
4. Laparoscopic orchiopexy for intra-abdominal testis is reported using CPT code _____.
5. A repair of an incomplete circumcision is reported with CPT code _____.
6. Irrigation of corpora cavernosa for priapism is coded using CPT code _____.
7. A surgical fixation of the testis in the scrotal sac is known as a(n) _____.
8. A condition in which the corpora cavernosa becomes hardened is known as _____.
9. The seminal vesicle and the vas deferens form the _____.
10. When performing a circumcision without a dorsal penile or ring block, modifier _____ should be used.

---

# Procedures Completed on the Prostate (55700–55899)

The **prostate gland** secretes fluid that is part of the semen and aids in the motility of sperm. It is located below the urinary bladder and on the upper end of the urethra.

The Prostate subcategory contains notes that the coder will need to pay close attention to when selecting a proper code for the service rendered. Incision codes (55700–55705) instruct the coder to report imaging guidance if appropriate. Needle aspiration and transurethral drainage are also noted for the most specific code assignment possible.

Excision codes (55801–55865) follow the incision subsection. Prostatectomy, transperineal placement of catheters, and exposure of the prostate for insertion of a radioactive substance are found in this code range. The excision codes also contain instructional notes regarding the frequency of the procedure being done. Careful attention to detail must be paid here to be sure that the proper codes and any necessary modifiers are assigned to convey the service properly.

Laparoscopic and other procedures finish this group of codes. Diagnostic procedures are always included in surgical procedures, so the coder must read the operative note to be sure that the code assignment is correct. Coders should also read the instructional notations that appear in the CPT manual. For example, review codes 55866 and 55867 and read the notations that appear before and after these codes for additional information that applies to each codes.

Code 55870—electroejaculation is assigned when the physician uses an electrovibratory device that stimulates ejaculation for semen collection, usually for artificial insemination. The actual artificial insemination is not reported with this code.

Code 55873, **cryosurgical ablation of the prostate**, is a surgical procedure used for the ablation of the prostate. Ultrasonic guidance and monitoring is included in the code. Care is taken that the scrotum and ureter are not affected.

Malignant prostate tissue can be treated with ablation. At times ultrasound is used during the ablation. If a transrectal approach is used to complete the ablation of malignant prostate tissue code 55880 should be used. Reference code 55880 in the CPT manual.

# Reproductive System Procedures (55920) and Intersex Surgery (55970–55980)

At this time there is only one code listed for Reproductive System Procedures. Code 55920 reports the placement of needles or catheters into pelvic organs and/or genitalia (except the prostate) for subsequent interstitial radioelement  application. Following code 55920 the coder should note the instructional notations that provide the coder guidance in reporting the placement of needles or catheters into the prostate (code 55875), the insertion of uterine tandems and/or vaginal ovoids for clinical brachytherapy (code 57155), and the insertion of Heyman capsules for clinical brachytherapy (code 58346). Codes 55970–55980 reflect a series of staged procedures when a patient is undergoing a sex-change operation. These surgical codes are used to report the removal and creation of genital organs.

# Summary

- The procedures performed on the male genital organs are reported using CPT codes 54000–55899.
- The organs and structures of the male genital system include the penis, testes, epididymis, tunica vaginalis, scrotum, vas deferens, spermatic cord, seminal vesicles, and prostate.
- Some structures of the male genital system are also part of the urinary system.
- The coder needs to understand whether a procedure was performed unilaterally or bilaterally.

# Internet Links

Using the search field on the following website, search by name of the procedure that you wish to research: **http://www.aafp.org**.

# Chapter Review

## True/False

**Instructions:** Indicate whether the following statements are true (T) or false (F).

1. _____ The male genital system is primarily for reproduction, but it also functions as part of the urinary system.

2. _____ Diagnostic procedures are always included in surgical procedures in the laparoscopic section of prostate procedures.

3. _____ The vas deferens is also referred to as the *seminal deferens* and is coded from the 55200–55550 code range.

4. _____ If the code does not state unilateral or bilateral, it is assumed that the procedure is bilateral.

5. _____ Laparoscopic repair of a hernia performed at the same time as the orchiopexy would be reported with two repair codes, one indicating the hernia repair and one for the orchiopexy.

## Fill in the Blank

**Instructions:** Fill in the blanks in the statements that follow.

6. The distal end of the penis is also known as the _____.

7. The erectile tissue of the penis is called the _____.

8. The structure that is located below the urinary bladder and on the upper end of the urethra is the _____.

9. The germ cell secretion of the testicles is called _____.

10. An elective procedure used to remove the foreskin completely from the glans penis is called _____.

# Coding Assignments

**Instructions:** Using the CPT manual, assign the correct code to the following procedures.

1. Vasovasostomy _____

2. Exposure of prostate for insertion of a radioactive substance _____

3. Destruction of a lesion on the penis using cryosurgery _____

4. Repair of hypospadias—fistula stricture—by simple closure method _____

5. Removal of all components of an inflatable penile prosthesis—no replacement _____

6. Lysis of post-circumcision adhesions _____

7. Needle biopsy of testis _____

8. Corpora cavernosa—saphenous vein shunt—unilateral _____

9. Radical orchiectomy with abdominal exploration _____

10. Puncture aspiration of hydrocele, tunica vaginalis—no medication was injected _____

11. Scrotoplasty, simple _____

12. Excision of varicocele of spermatic veins _____

13. Exploration for undescended testis with abdominal exploration _____

14. Insertion of testicular prosthesis _____

15. Urethroplasty for second-stage hypospadias repair—2.5 cm _____

16. Deep I&D of the shaft of the penis _____

17. Plastic surgery on the penis following a car accident _____

18. Surgical reduction of torsion of testis with fixation of contralateral testis _____

19. Needle biopsy of epididymis _____

20. Excision of spermatocele without epididymectomy _____

21. Partial amputation of penis _____

22. Excision of spermatocele with epididymectomy _____

23. Incisional biopsy of testis _____

24. Scrotal resection _____

25. Unilateral excision of hydrocele of spermatic cord _____

26. Laser destruction of three lesions on penis _____

27. Irrigation of corpora cavernosa for priapism _____

28. Excision of bilateral hydrocele _____

29. Fixation of contralateral testis _____

30. Foreskin manipulation including lysis of preputial adhesions and stretching _____

# Case Studies

**Instructions:** Review each case and indicate the correct code(s).

## Case 1

**Procedure:** Circumcision

This 23-hour-old male was brought to the operating room and prepped and draped in the usual fashion for a circumcision. General anesthesia was administered. An incision was made in the preputial foreskin at the coronal sulcus and extended. The foreskin was retracted, and a second incision was made on the mucous part of the foreskin. The skin was dissected with sharp dissection. After this, electrocoagulating current was used to obtain hemostasis, and the frenum was approximated with sutures. The skin was then closed with 3-0 chromic catgut sutures. Blood loss was minimal. The newborn was taken to the recovery room in good condition.

**CPT code(s):** _____

# Case 2

**Preoperative and postoperative diagnosis:** Left hydrocele

**Procedure:** Hydrocelectomy

This 39-year-old male was brought to the operating room and prepared and draped in the usual fashion. General anesthesia was administered, and the patient was placed in the lithotomy position. On the left scrotum, a 3.4-cm incision was made. A hydrocele was visualized, and by dissection, it was freed and removed through the incision site. After removing the hydrocele, sutures were used to close the site. A drain was placed and the wound was closed in layers. The patient was returned to the recovery suite in satisfactory condition. Blood loss was minimal.

CPT code(s): _____

# Case 3

**Preoperative diagnosis:** Prostate tumor

**Postoperative diagnosis:** Same

**Anesthesia:** Conscious sedation

**Procedure performed:** Needle biopsy of the prostate

**Procedure:** Moderate sedation was administered, and all precautions were taken and documented on the surgical flow sheet. Verification of the questionable site using transabdominal and prostate ultrasound was performed. The biopsy needle was inserted into the skin of the perineum. The biopsy needle was guided to the area of the prostate in question, and the sheath was advanced over the needle and twisted to obtain the sample. This procedure was repeated two more times to be sure that we had adequate sampling. All samples were sent to pathology for testing.

CPT code(s): _____

# Case 4

**Preoperative diagnosis:** Undescended testis on the right

**Postoperative diagnosis:** Undescended testis on the right

**Anesthesia:** General endotracheal

**Indications:** This seven-year-old male presents with a right inguinal testis, which is palpable to the brim of the scrotum.

**Procedure:** The patient was brought to the operating suite, and general endotracheal anesthesia was administered. The patient was prepped and draped in a sterile fashion. 5 cc of 0.5% Marcaine was injected as an ilioinguinal nerve block on the right side.

A transverse groin incision was made on the right, midway between the distal iliac spine and the pubic tubercle. Dissection was carried down, and the ilioinguinal nerve was identified and preserved. The tunica vaginalis was opened, and the testis appeared normal. Movement went up the cord approximately 2 cm, where a small hernia sac was identified and taken down. Once the hernia sac was repaired, there was adequate room for the testis to be brought down into the scrotum. The inguinal incision was irrigated with normal saline, and closure, using continuous 4-0 Monocryl, was performed. Steri-Strips were applied, and the patient was returned to the recovery room. Patient tolerated the procedure well.

**CPT code(s):** _____

# Case 5

**Indications for procedure:** This is an elective procedure being done at the request of the patient. This is a 37-year-old male who presents with his wife today for elective vasectomy. All risks, benefits, and techniques were discussed with both husband and wife. We discussed the possibility of reversal if he so chooses in the future; however, he was adamant that this would not be the case.

**Procedure:** The patient's penis was taped out of the way, and the scrotum was then prepped and draped in the usual sterile fashion. Lidocaine was then injected into the skin along the median raphe. After the Lidocaine numbed the area, blunt dissection was used to divide the subcutaneous tissue. The left side was addressed first. The vas clamp was used to elevate the vas, which was injected with local anesthesia. An incision was made using cautery, at which time blunt dissection was used to isolate the vas. The vas was elevated more, clamped proximally and distally where the segment was then removed and sent for pathology. Each end was then ligated with 3-0 silk sutures, and the remaining exposed mucosa was cauterized. Exactly the same procedure was performed on the right side.

The skin was rinsed with saline, and the midline incision was then closed with interrupted 4-0 Vicryl sutures. The skin was sealed with Histoacryl glue. The patient tolerated the procedure well and left the procedure room in good condition.

**CPT code(s):** _____

# Case 6

**Indications:** This is a 53-year-old male who presents today for simple destruction of two lesions that appear to be molluscum contagiosum on the shaft of the penis. The risks, benefits, and methods of destruction were discussed in detail with this patient. The patient has elected for surgical excision of the lesions.

**Procedure:** The patient was brought to the surgical suite in the supine position. The genital area, including the penile shaft, was prepped and draped in sterile fashion. The area was anesthetized using 1% Lidocaine. The first lesion, which was 0.3 cm, was removed using a scalpel. This lesion was located on the underside of the shaft. Once the lesion was removed and sent to pathology, two sutures were placed to close the area. The second lesion, located on the lateral aspect of the penis, was removed in a similar fashion. This lesion was 0.2 cm and was also sent to pathology. This area was also closed using two sutures. Pathology confirmed the diagnosis of molluscum contagiosum.

CPT code(s): _____

# Case 7

**Indications:** This is a 75-year-old male who presents today for a laparoscopic orchiectomy on the left side due to a small precancerous lesion found in the testicle.

**Procedure:** Under general anesthesia, a trocar is inserted at the umbilicus into the retroperitoneal space, and the abdominal cavity is insufflated. Additional trocars are placed on either side of the abdomen. The left testicle is identified and lifted up from the scrotum. All nerves and vessels in the area are relocated until the testicle is freed. The testicle, once freed, is removed through the retroperitoneal space. No damage to any nerves or vessels is noted. The scrotum is then packed and flushed with normal saline. The patient has opted not to undergo prosthetic surgery at this time. The scrotum is then closed carefully in layers. The trocars are removed, and the incision is closed in layers using 3-0 Vicryl. The patient tolerated the procedure well.

CPT code(s): _____

## Case 8

**Preoperative and postoperative diagnosis:** Deep abscess on penis

**Procedural Notes:**

After local anesthesia was injected into the penal area, an incision was made. The incision was carried down from the skin into the deeper layers where the abscessed cavity was found. The abscessed area was drained, and a drain was left in place to promote further drainage. The patient tolerated the procedure well, with minimal blood loss.

CPT code(s): _____

## Case 9

**Preoperative diagnosis:** Lesion on penis

**Postoperative diagnosis:** Pending pathology report

**Procedure:** Biopsy

After anesthetizing the penis, a small incision was made to remove a small portion of a lesion that was on the left side of the penis. The wound did not require closure. The removed tissue was sent to pathology for examination.

CPT code(s): _____

## Case 10

**Preoperative and Postoperative diagnosis:** Post-circumcision adhesions

**Anesthesia:** General

**Procedure:** Lysis of adhesions

The patient was prepped and draped in the usual fashion, and general anesthesia was administered. The foreskin was retracted, and the adhesions were released and the glans was cleansed. The area was examined and no fibrous rings were noted. The defect area was closed using three interrupted sutures. The patient tolerated the procedure and was sent to the recovery room in stable condition.

CPT code(s): _____

# Female Genital System

## Chapter Outline

Introduction

Guidelines Related to the National
   Correct Coding Initiative (NCCI)

Abbreviations Associated with the Female
   Genital System

Vulva, Perineum, and Introitus (56405–56821)

Procedures Completed on the Vagina
   (57000–57426)

Procedures Completed on the Cervix Uteri
   (57452–57800)

Procedures Completed on the Corpus Uteri
   (58100–58540)

Laparoscopy and Hysteroscopy (58541–58579
   and 58674)

Procedures Completed on the Oviduct and
   Ovary (58600–58960)

In Vitro Fertilization (58970–58976) and Other
   Procedures (58999)

Summary

Internet Links

Chapter Review

Coding Assignments

Case Studies

## Learning Objectives

### At the conclusion of this chapter, you should be able to:

1. Define key terms related to coding procedures on the female genital system.
2. Define abbreviations associated with the female genital system.
3. Describe the basic anatomy and functions of the female genital system.
4. Define common procedures completed on the female genital system.
5. Apply specific coding guidelines for the female genital system.
6. Select CPT codes for procedures completed on the female genital system.
7. Identify and code procedures for the female genital system from case studies.

## Key Terms

| | | | |
|---|---|---|---|
| abdominal hysterectomy | colpocentesis | colposcopy | endometrium |
| Bartholin's glands | colpocleisis | colpotomy | enterocele |
| cerclage | colpopexy | conization | fallopian tubes |
| cervix uteri | colporrhaphy | corpus uteri | fulguration |

| | | | |
|---|---|---|---|
| hymen | myomectomy | perineum | vaginectomy |
| hymenectomy | omentectomy | pudendum | vestibular glands |
| hysterectomy | oophorectomy | salpingo-oophorectomy | vulva |
| hysteroscope | ovaries | sling procedures | vulvectomy |
| introitus | paravaginal | trachelectomy | |
| in vitro fertilization | Pereyra procedure | vagina | |

# Introduction

Procedures performed on the female genital system may be performed endoscopically, laparoscopically, or as open procedures. The structures of the female genital system include the vulva, perineum, introitus, vagina, cervix uteri, corpus uteri, and ovaries. Accessory organs include the uterus and fallopian tubes.

Terminology and knowledge of anatomy are essential when you are choosing a code that accurately reflects the service performed. Internal and external genitalia of the female body are involved in the reproductive process. Hormones play a large role in the female system because the female reproductive system needs to be able to sustain a developing fetus during pregnancy. Figure 14-1 illustrates the female reproductive system.

**FIGURE 14-1** Organs of the Female Reproductive System

# Guidelines Related to the National Correct Coding Initiative (NCCI)

Perform the following steps to obtain the most current coding guideline information related to this chapter online.

1. Log on to *https://www.cms.gov/medicare-medicaid-coordination/national-correct-coding-initiative-ncci /ncci-medicare/medicare-ncci-policy-manual*.

2. Scroll to the section titled "View Manual by Chapter."

3. Click "Chapter 7" for guidelines specific to the female genital system.

# Abbreviations Associated with the Female Genital System

The following are some of the most common abbreviations associated with the female genital system:

| Abbreviations | Definitions |
| --- | --- |
| AB | abortion |
| CIN | cervical intra-epithelial neoplasia |
| CIS | carcinoma in situ |
| Cx | cervix |
| D&C | dilatation and curettage |
| ECC | endocervical curettage |
| EMB | endometrial biopsy |
| GIFT | gamete intrafallopian transfer |
| GYN | gynecology |
| IUD | intrauterine device |
| IVF | in vitro fertilization |
| LEEP | loop electrosurgical excision procedure |
| LLETZ | large-loop excision of the transformation zone |
| Pap smear | Papanicolaou smear |
| PID | pelvic inflammatory disease |
| PMS | premenstrual syndrome |
| SAB | spontaneous abortion |
| TAB | therapeutic abortion |
| TAH-BSO | total abdominal hysterectomy with bilateral salpingo-oophorectomy |
| ZIFT | zygote intrafallopian transfer |

# Vulva, Perineum, and Introitus (56405–56821)

The **vulva** is an inclusive term used to describe the external genitalia of the female body. The vulva may also be referred to as **pudendum**. The structures that make up the vulva are the mons pubis, labia majora, clitoris, labia minora, vestibule, urinary meatus, vaginal orifice, Bartholin's glands, and perineum. Figure 14-2 illustrates the structures that make up the vulva.

The **perineum** is the diamond-shaped area of skin between the upper area of the vaginal orifice and the anus. The purpose of the perineum is to support pelvic structures. The term **introitus** refers to an opening or space.

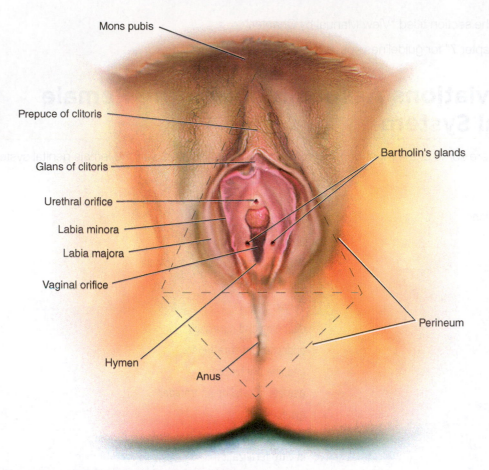

**FIGURE 14-2** Female External Genitalia

This code range begins with incision codes and then moves to destruction codes; see Table 14-1.

**TABLE 14-1** Incision and Destruction Codes (56405–56515)

| Code(s) | Description |
|---|---|
| 56405–56442 | Incision and drainage codes are coded from this range. The incision and drainage of an abscess of the vulva, perineal, or **Bartholin's glands** would be coded from this range. Bartholin's glands, illustrated in Figure 14-2, are glands that secrete lubricating mucous in the vagina. Bartholin's glands may also be referred to as the **vestibular glands**. |
| 56501 and 56515 | Destructions of lesion(s) of vulva, differentiated as simple or extensive, are coded from this code range. Attention to detail is necessary when coding destructions. As stated in the instructional notations that follow code 56515, if a destruction of a Skene's gland cyst or abscess or a cautery destruction of a urethral caruncle is performed, this code range would not be referenced.

For an extensive destruction code to be used, multiple lesions or complicated lesion removal need to be performed. The procedure note would need to be referenced for supporting documentation. |

The next code range is used to report excision procedures (see Table 14-2). The approach used to perform the procedure is important to understand when coding excisions.

**TABLE 14-2** Excision Codes (56605–56740)

| Code(s) | Description |
|---|---|
| 56605 and 56606 | A biopsy of the vulva or perineum is coded from this code set. Biopsy of one lesion is reported using code 56605, and 56606 is used to report a biopsy of each additional lesion after the first one. Code 56606 is an add-on code and should be used only in conjunction with 56605. Note that code 56606 is for each separate additional lesion that is biopsied. |

*(continues)*

**TABLE 14-2** (continued)

| Code(s) | Description |
|---|---|
| 56620–56640 | Vulvectomy procedures are reported with these codes. A **vulvectomy** is the removal of all or part of the vulva. The extent of the excision determines the code selection. To determine the code that best reflects the service rendered, you must understand the extent of the excision:<br>• Simple: The excision of skin and superficial subcutaneous tissue.<br>• Radical: More extensive than simple, with removal of deep subcutaneous tissue.<br>• Partial: <80% of vulvar area<br>• Complete: >80% of vulvar area |
| 56700 | **Hymenectomy** is a procedure in which the hymen is excised. The **hymen** is a membrane that covers the external opening of the vagina. Code 56700 is used to report a partial hymenectomy or a revision of the hymenal ring. |
| 56740 | Excision of Bartholin's gland or cyst is reported by using this code. It should be noted that in the CPT manual, there are numerous instructional notations that appear under this code. These instruct the coder to use other codes for excisions of Skene's gland, urethral caruncle, and so on. Reference the notes for more information. |

> **EXAMPLE:** Dr. Gaius completed a biopsy of three lesions of the vulva. The CPT codes to use for this case is code 56605, to report the first lesion, code 56606 to report the second lesion and code 56606 to report the third lesion. Therefore three codes are used. Code 56605 reports 1 lesion and code 56606 is used to report each separate additional lesion after the first. Review the full code descriptions in the CPT manual.

Codes 56800–56810 report repairs. This code range includes plastic repair of the introitus (code 56800), clitoroplasty for intersex state (code 56805), and perineoplasty for nonobstetrical injury that is completed as a separate procedure (code 56810). The operative note should be reviewed carefully before a code is assigned. Coders should note the instructional notation below code 56810.

Codes 56820 and 56821 report endoscopic procedures performed on the vulva. A **colposcopy** is a procedure in which a scope is used to view the vaginal and cervical area. The two codes would not be reported together, as 56821 includes a colposcopy with biopsy(s). The coder also needs to keep in mind that if a diagnostic colposcopy is performed to assess the area prior to a surgical procedure, the colposcopy should not be separately reported.

## Exercise 14.1—Check Your Understanding

### Code Range 56405–56821

Indicate whether each statement is true (T) or false (F).

1. _____ One lesion excised from the vulva is reported using code 56606. Code 56610 is used to report a biopsy of each additional lesion of the vulva after the first one.

2. _____ The hymen is a membrane that covers the external opening of the vagina.

3. _____ Vulva repair is reported using codes 56800–56810.

4. _____ If a destruction of a cyst, abscess, or a cautery destruction of a urethral caruncle is performed, the code set used to report this service is 56700–56740.

5. _____ Procedures performed on the female genital system may be performed endoscopically, laparoscopically, or open.

6. _____ A complete radical vulvectomy is reported using code 56633.

7. _____ A partial vulvectomy procedure is the removal of greater than 80% of the vulvar area.

8. _____ A simple vulvectomy procedure is the removal of the skin and superficial subcutaneous tissue.

9. _____ A radical procedure, as it relates to the vulvectomy codes, is defined as the removal of less than 80% of the vulvar area.

10. _____ A colposcopy of the vulva with biopsy is reported using CPT code 56821.

# Procedures Completed on the Vagina (57000–57426)

The **vagina** is a fibromuscular structure that connects with the external genitalia and ascends in a tubelike structure to the cervix uteri. The vagina has several functions as a passageway in the female body. The vagina is a passageway for the penis during sexual intercourse. It is also a passageway for menstrual flow and is part of the birth canal, through which the baby passes during a vaginal birth.

An understanding of terminology helps when you are reading the operative reports. When you see the prefix *colp/o* or the prefix *vagin/o*, realize that this is a term relating to the vagina.

Incision procedures are listed first in this subcategory. Codes 57000–57023 are used to report open surgical procedures of the vagina. Colpotomy and colpocentesis are both reported using codes from this code range. A **colpotomy** is a procedure using an open approach, by which an incision is made in the vagina. A **colpocentesis** is the aspiration of fluid through the vaginal wall into a syringe.

Destruction of vaginal lesions using cryosurgery, laser surgery, or electrosurgery is reported using codes 57061 and 57065.

Excision codes are reported with CPT codes 57100–57135. Table 14-3 outlines the excision code range.

**TABLE 14-3** Excision (57100–57135)

| Code(s) | Description |
| --- | --- |
| 57100 and 57105 | Biopsy of vaginal mucosa, either simple or extensive, is reported with these codes. |
| 57106–57109 | Vaginectomy, partial with removal of vaginal wall, is reported with this range of codes. **Vaginectomy** is a procedure in which the vagina is excised. In this code range, only partial removal is performed. |
| 57110–57111 | Codes 57110–57111 are used to report vaginectomy, the complete removal of the vaginal wall. The codes in this range are differentiated by additional procedures that are completed with the complete vaginectomy. |
| 57120 | Colpocleisis procedures are reported with this code. **Colpocleisis** is a surgical closure of the vagina. |
| | The operative report may state that a Le Fort–type procedure was performed. This procedure is reported using this code. |
| 57130 and 57135 | Excision of vaginal septum, a cyst, or a tumor is reported with this range of codes. |

Introduction codes are reported using the 57150–57180 code range. This code range includes the fitting and insertion of a pessary device, a diaphragm, or a cervical cap. The introduction of hemostatic agents for nonobstetrical vaginal hemorrhage is reported using code 57180.

Repairs of the vagina are reported using the 57200–57335 code range (see Table 14-4). The codes in this code range for repair procedures are determined based on the type of repair and the approach.

**EXAMPLE:** Dr. Troas completed a repair of an enterocele via a vaginal approach as a separate procedure. The procedure is the repair of the enterocele and the approach is vaginal. In the CPT index reference the term "Enterocele," then "Repair," then "Vaginal Approach." Codes 57268 and 57556 appear. Review the descriptions of the codes in the CPT manual and select code 57268 as the repair was completed as a separate procedure.

**TABLE 14-4** Repair (57200–57335)

| Code(s) | Description |
| --- | --- |
| 57200–57265 | Colporrhaphy procedures are reported with this range of codes. **Colporrhaphy** is the surgical repair of the vagina. |
| 57267 | This is an add-on code for insertion of mesh or other prosthesis for repair of pelvic floor defect. This code should not be used alone but needs to be used in conjunction with codes 45560, 57240–57265, and 57285. |
| 57268 and 57270 | Repair of **enterocele**—code assignment depends on the surgical approach. *Enterocele* is another term for small bowel prolapse. |

(continues)

**TABLE 14-4** (*continued*)

| Code(s) | Description |
|---|---|
| 57280–57283 | Colpopexy procedures are reported from this code range. **Colpopexy** is a procedure in which the vagina is sutured to the abdominal wall. Surgical approach determines code selection. |
| 57284 and 57285 | **Paravaginal** defect repair is reported using these codes. *Paravaginal* refers to the area around the vagina. Code 57284 is used to report an open abdominal approach, while code 57285 is used to report a vaginal approach. These procedures help restore normal anatomical positions of the vagina, bladder, and urethra. |
| 57287 and 57288 | These codes report **sling procedures**. Slings are used to help correct urinary-stress incontinence. These procedure codes are used to report the initial repair, removal, or revision of the sling. |
| 57289 | A **Pereyra procedure**, including anterior colporrhaphy, is reported with this code. This is a procedure in which sutures are laced through the Pereyra ligature carrier, and the urethrovesical junction is raised. |
| 57291–57296 | Construction or revision of a vagina is reported with this range of codes. Distinction is made by whether the revision is completed with or without a graft and by the approach that is used. |
| 57300–57335 | Codes 57300 to 57330 report the closure of fistulas in the vaginal area. A fistula is an abnormal passage. Code 57335 reports a vaginoplasty for intersex state. |

Manipulation of the vagina includes dilation, examination, and removal of a foreign body with manipulation. The code range for reporting these services is 57400–57415. If removal of the impacted vaginal foreign body is not performed with anesthesia, this code range should not be used; the procedure should be reported using an evaluation and management code. When you are reporting vaginal approach procedures, dilation of the vagina (57400) should not be reported separately, as it is a routine part of the surgical field encountered.

Endoscopic and laparoscopic procedures of the vagina are reported using CPT codes 57420–57426. Code 57420 reports a colposcopy of the entire vagina with the cervix, if the cervix is present. Code 57421 reports a colposcopy of the entire vagina with the cervix, if present, with biopsy(s) of the vagina/cervix. Reference the CPT manual following code 57421 for instructional notations that relate to these two codes. Code 57423 reports a laparoscopic repair of a paravaginal defect. Code 57423 is not to be reported with the codes that are listed in the CPT manual following code 57423. A surgical laparoscopic colpopexy is reported with code 57425, while a laparoscopic revision of a prosthetic vaginal graft is reported with code 57426. When reading operative or procedural notes it is essential that coders identify the approach, such as the use of a laparscope, to ensure that proper code selection occurs.

## Exercise 14.2—Check Your Understanding

### Vocabulary

Fill in the blanks in the statements that follow.

1. A procedure in which the vagina is sutured to the abdominal wall is called _____.

2. The vagina is a(n) _____ for the penis during intercourse, for menstrual flow, and for a baby to travel through during the birth process.

3. Enterocele is another term for _____.

4. The aspiration of fluid through the vaginal wall into a syringe is called a(n) _____.

5. Repairs of the vagina are reported using the _____ code range.

6. A surgical repair of the vagina is called a(n) _____.

7. A biopsy of the vaginal mucosa would be reported using the _____ code range.

8. Paravaginal defect repairs are reported using the _____ code range.

9. The structure that connects with the external genitalia and ascends to the corpus uteri is the _____.

10. Procedures that are used to help correct urinary stress incontinence are called _____ procedures.

# Procedures Completed on the Cervix Uteri (57452–57800)

The **cervix uteri** lies between the ostium uteri and the isthmus. A colposcope is used to view the cervix and portions of the vagina. Biopsies are reported using selected codes from code range 57452–57461. The code selection for biopsies is based on the technique used to perform the biopsy or biopsies. Figure 14-3 illustrates the uterus and other structures.

Excision codes are reported using code range 57500–57558 (see Table 14-5). These procedures are performed as open procedures rather than by using a scope.

**FIGURE 14-3**  Female Reproductive System Organs

**TABLE 14-5**  Excision (57500–57558)

| Code(s) | Description |
| --- | --- |
| 57500 | Biopsy, single or multiple, or local excision of lesion, with or without fulguration (separate procedure), are reported with this code. **Fulguration** is the use of an electric current to destroy living tissue, usually to control bleeding. |
| 57505 | This code reports endocervical curettage (not done as part of a dilation and curettage). The opening of the cervix into the uterine cavity is scraped. |
| 57510–57513 | Cautery of the cervix is reported with this range of codes. The codes are differentiated based on cautery technique. |
| 57520 and 57522 | Conization of the cervix is reported with this code range. **Conization** is a procedure performed on the cervix to surgically cut a cone-shaped portion of tissue for examination. |
| 57530 and 57531 | Trachelectomy procedures are reported with these codes. A **trachelectomy** is the removal of the cervix uteri. |
| 57540–57556 | Excision of cervical stump—code selection depends on approach and other repairs performed at the same time. |
| 57558 | This code is used to report the dilation and curettage of a cervical stump. |

Repair codes (57700–57720), along with the manipulation code (57800), finish this range of codes. Found in the repair code section is code 57700—Cerclage of uterine cervix, nonobstetrical. **Cerclage** is a technique of encircling the cervix uteri with a wire, ligature, or loop. It should be noted here that this is *not* the correct code to be used when an obstetrician is performing the procedure to prevent a spontaneous abortion. When you are reporting vaginal approach procedures, dilation of the cervix (57800) should not be reported separately, as it is a routine part of the surgical field encountered.

# Procedures Completed on the Corpus Uteri (58100–58540)

The **corpus uteri** is the area of structures that begins at the fundus of the uterine cavity and moves down to encompass the cervical canal or the external os.

There is an extensive list of excision services reported from this range of codes. Understanding terminology is important in assigning the proper code. Table 14-6 describes the codes found in code range 58100–58294.

**TABLE 14-6** Corpus Uteri Excision Procedures (58100–58294)

| Code(s) | Description |
|---|---|
| 58100 and 58110 | This range of codes reports endometrial sampling. The **endometrium** is the innermost layer of the uterus. |
| 58120 | Dilation and curettage, diagnostic and/or therapeutic (nonobstetrical), is reported with this code. |
| 58140–58146 | This range of codes reports myomectomy procedures. A **myomectomy** is a procedure in which uterine fibroid tumors are removed from the wall of the uterus. The procedure is performed when the objective is to preserve the uterus, which would not be possible if a hysterectomy were performed. |
| 58150–58240 | Abdominal hysterectomy procedures are reported with these codes. A **hysterectomy** is a procedure in which the uterus is removed. The type of hysterectomy performed depends on whether just the uterus is removed or whether the cervix, fallopian tubes, and/or ovaries are also removed. The term **abdominal hysterectomy** refers to a hysterectomy that is performed through an incision made in the abdomen. |
| 58260–58294 | Vaginal hysterectomy procedures are reported using this range of codes. The approach for reporting these procedures is the vagina instead of the abdomen. The extent of the surgery, along with the weight of the uterus, will determine code selection. |

Introduction procedures are reported with code set 58300–58356. This includes insertion and removal of intrauterine devices (IUDs), insertion of Heyman capsules for clinical brachytherapy, and endometrial ablation. Careful attention to the procedure notes and the verbiage within CPT will determine code assignment.

Repair codes are reported using code range 58400–58540. Hysterorrhaphy and hysteroplasty are found in this code range.

## Exercise 14.3—Check Your Understanding

**Vocabulary**

Fill in the blank with the correct term(s) to complete each statement.

1. The term for the removal of the cervix uteri is _____.

2. The area of structures that begins at the fundus of the uterine cavity and moves down to encompass the cervical canal or the external os is the _____.

3. The term used for the technique of encircling the cervix uteri with a wire, ligature, or loop is _____.

4. Insertion of an IUD is reported with code _____.

5. The removal of uterine fibroid tumors from the wall of the uterus is reported using code range _____.

*(continues)*

## Exercise 14.3 (*continued*)

6. The innermost layer of the uterus is the _____.

7. A term for the procedure in which uterine fibroid tumors are removed from the wall of the uterus is _____.

8. The code range used to report the cautery of the cervix is _____.

9. A procedure in which the uterus is removed is known as a(n) _____.

10. The term used for a procedure in which a cold knife is used to surgically cut a cone-shaped portion of tissue from the cervix is a _____ procedure.

# Laparoscopy and Hysteroscopy (58541–58579 and 58674)

Many gynecological procedures are performed using a laparoscope. As explained in earlier chapters, diagnostic laparoscopic procedures are included in surgical laparoscopic procedures and should not be billed separately.

A **hysteroscope** can be a fiber-optic-type scope or a rigid-type scope. It can be used for diagnostic and surgical procedures. Like the laparoscopic procedure, the diagnostic hysteroscopic procedure is included in the surgical procedure and should not be billed separately. Table 14-7 summarizes the laparoscopic and hysteroscopic procedures.

**TABLE 14-7** Laparoscopic and Hysteroscopic Procedures (58541–58579)

| Code(s) | Description |
|---------|-------------|
| 58541–58554 | Laparoscopic procedures are reported with this range of codes. These procedure codes include excision of myomas, the uterus (hysterectomy), fallopian tube(s), and ovary(ies). The weight in grams is a factor in coding from this code range. |
| 58555–58565 | Hysteroscopic procedures are reported with these codes. These procedure codes include diagnostic hysteroscopy, biopsy samplings, resection, ablation, and removal of impacted foreign bodies. |
| 58570–58573 | This code range reports surgical laparoscopy with total hysterectomy. The codes are differentiated by the weight of the uterus in grams, along with how extensive the procedure was. |
| 58578 | This code is used to report an unlisted laparoscopy procedure, uterus. |
| 58579 | Unlisted hysteroscopy procedure, uterus. |

Code 58674 is an out of sequence code that is listed first in the CPT manual after the heading entitled Laparoscopy/Hysteroscopy and before the code 58541. Code 58674 reports a surgical laparoscopy completed for an ablation of uterine fibroid(s) and includes intraoperative ultrasound guidance and monitoring, radiofrequency.

# Procedures Completed on the Oviduct and Ovary (58600–58960)

This range of codes is divided into oviduct and ovary. This code range includes procedures performed on the fallopian tubes and ovaries. The **fallopian tubes** are bilateral tubes that open at one end in the uterus and at the other end into the peritoneal cavity.

The **ovaries** are also referred to as female gonads and function in producing eggs, which are released during ovulation. The ovaries also produce the female hormones estrogen and progesterone.

Understanding word parts are essential when you are trying to select the correct code assignment. Being able to apply this knowledge will help you in understanding and translating an operative note and is key to choosing the correct code. Table 14-8 lists prefixes that coders will encounter in operative documentation.

**TABLE 14-8** Prefixes

| Combining Form | Meaning |
|---|---|
| hyster/o, metr/o | Uterus |
| men/o | Menstruation |
| o/o, ov/o | Egg, ovum |
| oophor/o, ovari/o | Ovary |
| salping/o | Fallopian tubes |

The coding for this section begins with incision codes. Incision codes for the oviduct/ovary area begin with the ligation or transection of the fallopian tube. The approach can be either vaginal or abdominal, but there needs to be a determination as to whether the procedure was done at the time of a cesarean delivery. The code set 58600–58611 should be referenced for reporting these services. The codes apply equally for both unilateral and bilateral procedures. This would mean that if the procedure was performed on one side or both sides, code selection would be the same, and the quantity would always be one.

If open occlusion of the fallopian tubes is performed, code 58615 would be used to report this service. If the occlusion is done laparoscopically, code 58671 would be used to report the service.

Laparoscopic procedures on the ovaries and oviduct are reported with code set 58660–58679. The procedure codes listed here are surgical laparoscopic procedures and include lysis of adhesions, fulguration or excision of lesions, occlusion of oviducts, and salpingostomy. Excisional procedures reported with code 58700 (reports salpingectomy, complete or partial, unilateral or bilateral) and code 58720 (reports salpingo-oophorectomy, complete or partial, unilateral or bilateral) are separate procedure codes that are not completed via a scope.

The repair codes for fallopian tubes are reported using code range 58740–58770. The repairs are done as open procedures. The coder would reference the laparoscopic section of codes for procedures done through the scope. Open procedures performed on the ovaries begin with incision codes (58800–58822) for the drainage of an ovarian abscess or cyst. The transposition of the ovary is reported using code 58825.

The ovary excision services are reported using code set 58900–58960. Table 14-9 lists the codes for code range 58900–58960.

**TABLE 14-9** Ovary Excisions (58900–58960)

| Code(s) | Description |
|---|---|
| 58900 | Biopsy of ovary, unilateral or bilateral (separate procedure), is reported with this code. |
| 58920 | This code reports wedge resection or bisection of ovary, unilateral or bilateral.<br><br>In this procedure, the surgeon makes a very small, pie-shaped (or wedge) incision into the ovaries. This wedge is taken to reduce the size of the ovaries. |
| 58925 | Ovarian cystectomy, unilateral or bilateral, is reported with this code. This procedure code is used to report the removal of ovarian cysts. |
| 58940–58943 | **Oophorectomy**—a partial or total removal of the ovary, unilateral or bilateral, is reported with these codes. |
| 58950–58952 | Resection of ovarian, tubal, or primary peritoneal malignancy with bilateral salpingo-oophorectomy and omentectomy.<br><br>Through abdominal incision, the malignancy is surgically removed, along with any affected structures. A **salpingo-oophorectomy** refers to fallopian tubes and ovaries. An **omentectomy** is the removal of part of the omentum. |

*(continues)*

**TABLE 14-9** (continued)

| Code(s) | Description |
|---|---|
| 58953–58956 | These codes report bilateral salpingo-oophorectomy. Code selection is based on the reason for the surgery. Coders should note the instructional notation that appears after code 58956. |
| 58957 and 58958 | Code 58957 reports a resection or tumor debulking of a recurrent ovarian, tubal, primary peritoneal, uterine malignancy with omentectomy, if performed. Code 58958 reports the same procedure as code 58957 with the addition of a pelvic lymphadenectomy and limited para-aortic lymphadenectomy being completed. |
| 58960 | Laparotomy, for staging or restaging of ovarian, tubal, or primary peritoneal malignancy (second look), with or without omentectomy, peritoneal washing, biopsy of abdominal and pelvic peritoneum, diaphragmatic assessment with pelvic and limited para-aortic lymphadenectomy. |

# In Vitro Fertilization (58970–58976) and Other Procedures (58999)

In vitro fertilization is a process in which a mature egg is exposed to sperm in a laboratory setting. The ova are then implanted into the uterus.

The procedure codes are used to report the retrieval of the egg, the placement of the fertilized egg into the uterus, the gamete intrafallopian transfer (GIFT) procedure, and finally the zygote intrafallopian transfer (ZIFT) procedure.

The last code, code 58999, in this section of the CPT manual is used to report an unlisted procedure for the female genital system (nonobstetrical).

# Summary

- Procedures performed on the female genital system may be performed endoscopically, laparoscopically, or as an open approach.
- Terminology and knowledge of anatomy are essential for choosing a code that accurately reflects the service performed.
- Multiple structures of the female genital system are coded from this subsection of the surgery chapter of CPT.
- *Vulva* is an inclusive term used to describe the external genitalia of the female body.
- The vagina is a fibromuscular structure that connects with the external genitalia and ascends in a tubelike structure to the cervix uteri.
- The cervix uteri lies between the ostium uteri and the isthmus.
- The corpus uteri is the area of structures that begins at the fundus of the uterine cavity and moves down to encompass the cervical canal or the external os.
- The fallopian tubes are bilateral tubes that open on one end in the uterus and open at the other end into the peritoneal cavity.
- The ovaries are also referred to as *female gonads* and function in producing eggs, which are released during ovulation.
- The ovaries produce the female hormones estrogen and progesterone.

# Internet Links

To learn more about procedures completed on the female genital system, visit *http://www.acog.org* and *http://www.reproductive.org*.

# Chapter Review

## True/False

**Instructions:** Indicate whether the following statements are true (T) or false (F).

1. _____ If open occlusion of the fallopian tubes is performed, code 58627 should be used to report this service.

2. _____ A colpocentesis is the aspiration of fluid through the vaginal wall into a syringe.

3. _____ Code 56606 is an add-on code and should be used only in conjunction with 56605.

4. _____ Endoscopic and open procedures of the vagina are reported using CPT codes 57420–57425.

5. _____ When you are reporting vaginal approach procedures, dilation of the cervix (57800) should be reported separately, as it is a routine part of the surgical field encountered.

## Fill in the Blank

**Instructions:** Fill in the blanks in the statements that follow.

6. The term _____ refers to an opening or space.

7. The use of an electric current to destroy living tissue, usually used to control bleeding, is known as a(n) _____.

8. A(n) _____ is an abnormal passage.

9. The surgical closure of the vagina is a(n) _____.

10. Another term for small bowel prolapse is _____.

# Coding Assignments

**Instructions:** Using the CPT manual, assign the correct code to the following procedures.

1. Radical partial vulvectomy
_____

2. Simple biopsy of the vaginal mucosa
_____

3. Colposcopy of vulva with biopsy
_____

4. Sling procedure for stress incontinence
_____

5. Electrosurgery for extensive destruction of vulva lesions _____

6. Simple hymenotomy _____

7. Colpotomy with exploration
_____

8. Thermal cautery of cervix
_____

9. Plastic repair of urethrocele
_____

10. Closure of rectovaginal fistula using the abdominal approach _____

11. Pelvic examination under general anesthesia
_____

12. Pereyra procedure, including anterior colporrhaphy
_____

13. Vaginal hysterectomy with total vaginectomy
_____

14. Total abdominal hysterectomy with removal of tubes and ovaries _____

15. Lysis of adhesions of ovaries, laparoscopic procedure _____

16. Drainage of ovarian abscess using open vaginal approach _____

17. Follicle puncture for oocyte retrieval
_____

18. Bilateral salpingo-oophorectomy with omentectomy, total abdominal hysterectomy, and radical dissection for debulking
_____

19. Wedge resection of right ovary
_____

20. Tubotubal anastomosis
_____

21. Electrosurgery destruction of vulva lesion
_____

22. Revision of hymenal ring
_____

23. Laser ablation for cautery of cervix
_____

24. Pelvic floor repair following excision of a cervical stump via the abdominal approach
_____

25. Vaginal transection of fallopian tubes
_____

26. Excision of Bartholin's cyst
_____

27. Nonobstetrical perineoplasty
_____

28. I&D of vaginal hematoma due to spontaneous bleeding. The patient is not pregnant.
_____

29. Vaginal repair of enterocele
_____

30. Cervical cap fitting with discussion of instructions for use _____

# Case Studies

**Instructions:** Review each case and indicate the correct code(s).

## Case 1

**Preoperative diagnosis:** Vaginal pain

**Postoperative diagnosis:** Vaginal cyst, pathology pending

The patient was brought to the operating suite and prepped and draped in the usual fashion. After general anesthesia, a speculum was inserted into the vagina. There was one 3-cm cyst on the vagina. Using a $CO_2$ laser set, the cyst was excised by the laser, and part of the cyst was sent to pathology for further review. Bleeding of the site was controlled, and the patient tolerated the procedure and was sent to the recovery area in satisfactory condition.

**CPT code(s):** _____

## Case 2

**Preoperative diagnosis:** Pelvic pain preventing pelvic exam

**Postoperative diagnosis:** Vulvar adhesions

The patient was placed under general anesthesia and placed in the supine lithotomy position. Examination of the pelvis revealed multiple adhesions in the vulvar area. The vagina and cervix were examined and found to be normal. The patient tolerated the procedure and was sent to recovery. Additional therapeutic procedures will be discussed with the patient.

**CPT code(s):** _____

## Case 3

**Preoperative diagnosis:** Vaginal stricture

**Postoperative diagnosis:** Vaginal stricture

**Procedure:** Repair of introitus

The patient was brought to the operating room and prepped and draped in the usual fashion. General anesthesia was given, and the surgical site was cleansed. Three V-shaped incisions were made in the area of the vaginal stricture. Because of the amount of scar tissue present, the tissue was excised. To obtain hemostasis, the mucosa was sewn with sutures, thus repairing the area. The patient tolerated the procedure with minimal blood loss.

**CPT code(s):** _____

## Case 4

**Preoperative and postoperative diagnosis:** Heavy menstrual bleeding

**Procedure:** Thermal endometrial ablation

This 53-year-old female patient was brought to the operating room and was prepped and draped for surgery. The patient has been experiencing extensive menstrual bleeding and has elected to undergo an ablation at this time. The patient was placed in the dorsal lithotomy position under general anesthesia. A resectoscope was inserted, and an endometrial ablation was completed, removing tissue and coagulating the area via a fulguration current. Hemostasis was obtained with minimal blood loss. The patient was found to be in satisfactory condition and was sent to the recovery room.

**CPT code(s):** _____

# Case 5

**Preoperative and postoperative diagnosis:** Uterine fibroids

**Procedure:** Total abdominal hysterectomy with BSO

**Anesthesia:** General

This 59-year-old female patient was taken to the operating room and prepped and draped for surgery. The abdomen was opened and explored. A retractor was placed, and the operative field was prepared. Division of the round ligaments occurred, and an incision was made in the anterior peritoneum. The posterior peritoneum was incised, and the uterine vessels were grasped and sutured. Clamps were placed, and the vagina was entered anteriorly while the cervix was excised in toto. The vaginal cuff was sutured with sutures, and the cuff was then sutured. Hemostasis was obtained. Closure of the fascia and fatty layers was completed. The skin was closed with staples. There was marginal blood loss, and the patient tolerated the procedure and was sent to the recovery room in stable condition. Tissue samples were sent to pathology.

**CPT code(s):** _____

# Case 6

**Preoperative diagnosis:** Cervical lesion

**Postoperative diagnosis:** Squamous intraepithelial lesion of the cervix

**Indications for procedure:** This is a 27-year-old female who presented for her annual Pap and pelvic examination. The results of the Pap smear identified an abnormality. The follow-up Pap confirmed the abnormality, and an ultrasound was performed, after which surgery was scheduled to get a definitive diagnosis.

**Procedure:** The patient was placed in the supine position and administered general anesthesia. She was placed in cane stirrups and then prepped and draped in the usual fashion, although her vaginal vault was not prepped in any way. A coated speculum was inserted, and the cervix was exposed. It was painted with Lugol, and the entire active cervix was nonstaining with the clearly defined margins where the stain began to pick up. Approximately 6 cc of Lidocaine with 1% epinephrine was then injected into the cervix. A large loop wire was then used to excise the anterior cervical lesion. Conization of the cervical 4.5-cm lesion was performed. All specimens were sent to pathology at this time. Hemostasis was achieved using cautery and then Monsel. All instruments were removed and accounted for. The patient was sent to the recovery room in good, stable condition.

**CPT code(s):** _____

# Case 7

**Preoperative and postoperative diagnosis:** Perineal abscess

**Procedural Notes:**

After local anesthesia was injected into the perineal area, the area was examined and the abscessed area was visualized between the vulva and the anus. An incision was made into the abscess, and purulent contents were drained. The abscessed cavity was examined and flushed with an antibiotic wash, and the site was packed with medicated gauze. The patient tolerated the procedure and was given discharge instructions and is to follow up in two weeks.

CPT code(s): _____

# Case 8

**Preoperative diagnosis:** Polymenorrhea

**Postoperative diagnosis:** Benign endometrial polyp

**Anesthesia:** General

**Indication for procedure:**

This 49-year-old female has been experiencing polymenorrhea and menorrhagia for the past eight months. Diagnostic examination is necessary to rule out any pathology.

**Procedural Notes:**

The patient was brought to the operating suite, and general anesthesia was given. The patient was then prepped and draped in the usual fashion while in the dorsal lithotomy position. A speculum was placed, and a tenaculum was used to grasp the cervix, which was dilated to 7 mm. The hysteroscope was placed through the vagina and into the cervical os to visualize the uterine cavity. An endometrial polyp was visualized, and a polypectomy was completed. A small amount of uterine contents were removed via sharp curettage. Specimens were sent to pathology. The tenaculum was taken off the cervix and the scope was withdrawn. The patient was sent to the recovery area in satisfactory condition.

CPT code(s): _____

## Chapter Outline

Introduction
Guidelines Related to the National Correct
   Coding Initiative (NCCI)
Abbreviations Associated with Maternity Care
   and Delivery
Antepartum and Fetal Invasive Services
   (59000–59350)
Vaginal Delivery, Antepartum and Postpartum
   Care (59400–59430), and Cesarean Delivery
   (59510–59525)

Delivery after Previous Cesarean
   Delivery (59610–59622)
Abortion and Other Procedures
   (59812–59899)
Summary
Internet Links
Chapter Review
Coding Assignments
Case Studies

## Learning Objectives

### At the conclusion of this chapter, you should be able to:

1. Define key terms related to coding maternity care and delivery procedures.
2. Define abbreviations associated with maternity care and delivery procedures.
3. Define common maternity care and delivery services and procedures.
4. Apply specific coding guidelines for maternity care and delivery.
5. Select CPT codes for maternity care and delivery procedures.
6. Identify and code procedures for maternity care and delivery from case studies.

## Key Terms

abortion
amniocentesis
amnioscopy
antepartum

cesarean section
  delivery
chorionic villus
cordocentesis
curettage

ectopic
  pregnancy
embryo
episiotomy
hydatidiform mole

hysterorrhaphy
incomplete abortion
legally induced abortion
missed abortion

| multifetal pregnancy reduction (MPR) | oligohydramnios | spontaneous abortion | vaginal birth after cesarean (VBAC) |
|---|---|---|---|
| obstetrics | perinatal period | | |
| | septic abortion | | |

# Introduction

The procedure codes used to report obstetric care begin with code 59000 and end with code 59899. This chapter contains information on procedure codes relating to maternity care and delivery, also known as obstetrics. **Obstetrics** is the specialty that treats women during pregnancy, childbirth, and the period of time immediately following childbirth. During the second week through the eighth week of pregnancy, the embryo grows and develops into a fetus. The **embryo** is referred to as the *fetus* from nine weeks until birth, usually at 40 weeks. The period immediately following the birth up to 28 days after birth is considered the **perinatal period**.

# Guidelines Related to the National Correct Coding Initiative (NCCI)

Perform the following steps to obtain the most current coding guideline information related to this chapter online.

1. Log on to *https://www.cms.gov/medicare-medicaid-coordination/national-correct-coding-initiative-ncci/ncci-medicare/medicare-ncci-policy-manual.*
2. Scroll to the section titled "View Manual by Chapter."
3. Click "Chapter 7" for guidelines specific to maternity care and delivery.

# Abbreviations Associated with Maternity Care and Delivery

The following abbreviations are most commonly used in relation to maternity care and delivery:

| Abbreviations | Definitions |
|---|---|
| CPD | cephalopelvic disproportion |
| C-section | cesarean section |
| DUB | dysfunctional uterine bleeding |
| EDB | expected date of birth |
| EDC | estimated date of confinement |
| EDD | estimated date of delivery |
| FHR | fetal heart rate |
| FHT | fetal heart tones |
| G | gravida |
| L&D | labor and delivery |
| LMP | last menstrual period |
| multip | multipara |

*(continues)*

| | |
|---|---|
| (continued) | |
| NB | newborn |
| OB | obstetrics |
| PIH | pregnancy-induced hypertension |
| SAB | spontaneous abortion |
| SVD | spontaneous vaginal delivery |

# Antepartum and Fetal Invasive Services (59000-59350)

Antepartum care is the care rendered during the time prior to childbirth. Antepartum care is usually reported with a "no charge" visit code for a normal pregnancy check because this period of time is part of the global period reimbursed at the time of delivery. Those services rendered during the antepartum period that are unrelated to the pregnancy or childbirth would be reported with an Evaluation and Management (E/M) code.

**EXAMPLE:** Sara is 22 weeks pregnant and has presented today with an earache. After a brief and problem-focused examination, it was determined that she had otitis media, and an antibiotic was ordered. She is seen by a provider as an established patient.

Due to the fact that Sara's visit was totally unrelated to her pregnancy, her visit would be coded with an Evaluation and Management code from the 99211–99215 code set. The diagnosis code would clearly indicate that the visit was unrelated to the pregnancy. Normal prenatal care would include visits once a month for up to 28 weeks. A high-risk pregnancy may require more frequent visits. From 29 weeks through 36 weeks, biweekly visits would be considered normal. From 37 weeks until delivery, weekly visits are the norm. Table 15-1 identifies the CPT codes related to antepartum and fetal invasive services. In a CPT manual, review the extensive information that is found prior to code 59000 that follows the heading Maternity Care and Delivery. These notes explain services that are included in antepartum care, delivery services and postpartum care, and services that are not included in these specific types of care.

**TABLE 15-1** Antepartum and Fetal Invasive Services (59000–59076)

| Code(s) | Description |
|---|---|
| 59000 and 59001 | Amniocentesis—diagnostic and therapeutic procedures are reported using code 59000 for a diagnostic amniocentesis and code 59001 for a therapeutic amniocentesis completed for amniotic fluid reduction (includes ultrasound guidance). An amniocentesis is a procedure in which a needle is inserted into the amniotic sac to withdraw fluid for examination. Figure 15-1 illustrates an amniocentesis and preparation of a specimen for analysis. |
| 59012 | Cordocentesis (intrauterine), any method—cordocentesis is a procedure in which an amniocentesis needle is inserted into the umbilical vessel to obtain blood from the fetus. The procedure is not done until the second or third trimester. |
| 59015 | This code reports chorionic villus sampling, any method—chorionic villus is the medical term for the placenta. |
| 59020 and 59025 | These codes report fetal stress testing. The codes in this series are used to report stress or nonstress testing of the fetus. The fetal heart rate and the contractions are monitored. Contractions may or may not be present during testing. |
| 59030 | This code reports fetal scalp blood sampling. This procedure is performed in some cases as a way of determining fetal distress. |

(continues)

**TABLE 15-1** (*continued*)

| Code(s) | Description |
|---------|-------------|
| 59050 and 59051 | Fetal monitoring during labor by consulting physician (i.e., nonattending physician) with written report and supervision and interpretation is reported with this series of codes. This service is *not* reported by the attending physician, as the service is not separately reportable when the physician is getting reimbursed for global services. |
| 59070 | This code reports transabdominal amnioinfusion, including ultrasound guidance. This procedure is performed in cases where there is less than sufficient amniotic fluid present, or **oligohydramnios**, is diagnosed. |
| 59072 | Fetal umbilical cord occlusion, including ultrasound guidance, is reported by using this code. This is a procedure that may need to be done in cases of multiple gestation. One of the fetuses may be getting too much fluid while the other is not getting enough, and the exchange of blood between the fetuses needs to be stopped in an effort to save both fetuses. |
| 59074 | Fetal fluid drainage (e.g., vesicocentesis, thoracocentesis, paracentesis), including ultrasound guidance, is reported with this code. |
| 59076 | This code reports fetal shunt placement, including ultrasound guidance. |

**FIGURE 15-1** Amniocentesis and Preparation of Specimen for Amniotic Fluid Analysis

Many of these procedures are performed with scopes. **Amnioscopy** is a scope procedure used to view the fetus in the amniotic sac. A fetoscope or laparoamnioscope may also be used.

The excision procedures are reported with the 59100–59160 code set. These procedures may be reported if there is an abnormal pregnancy and the pregnancy needs to be terminated. Terminology is key and is explained in Table 15-2, which also notes the codes for excisions.

**TABLE 15-2** Excision Codes (59100–59160)

| Code(s) | Description |
|---------|-------------|
| 59100 | This code reports a hysterotomy, abdominal (e.g., for hydatidiform mole, abortion). For accurate code assignment review the instructional notations that follow the code.<br><br>A **hydatidiform mole** is a grapelike grouping of cysts that is really the ova that cannot develop properly. |
| 59120–59140 | Surgical treatment of ectopic pregnancy; tubal or ovarian, requiring salpingectomy and/or oophorectomy, an abdominal or a vaginal approach is reported with this range of codes. An **ectopic pregnancy** is a pregnancy that occurs outside the uterus. Code assignment is based on the extent of the procedure performed. |
| 59150 and 59151 | This range of codes reports laparoscopic treatment of ectopic pregnancy. Code assignment is based on the extent of the procedure performed. |
| 59160 | This code reports a curettage, postpartum. A **curettage** is a surgical scraping; in this case, the endometrial lining of the uterus would be scraped after childbirth. |

Antepartum introduction and repair codes are reported using codes from the 59200–59350 code range. Prior to inducing labor, the physician may need to insert a cervical dilator to chemically stimulate the cervical canal to dilate. Insertion of the cervical dilator would be reported using code 59200.

Codes 59300 to 59350 report repairs. An episiotomy or vaginal repair completed by a provider other than the attending provider is reported with code 59300. An **episiotomy** is an incision made at the vaginal opening to prevent tearing during delivery. A vaginal or abdominal cerclage of the cervix during pregnancy is completed when the cervix appears to be incompetent or unable to hold the pregnancy and needs reinforcement until it is time to deliver the baby. This procedure is reported using code 59320 for vaginal cerclage or code 59325 for an abdominal cerclage. This repair section of the CPT manual, is also used to report the repair of an obstetrical ruptured uterus. A repair of a ruptured uterus is referred to as a **hysterorrhaphy**.

EXAMPLE: A patient presents with an obstetrical ruptured uterus. Dr. Phoenica completes a hysterorrhaphy to treat the rupture. In the CPT manual index reference the term "Hysterorrhaphy" and note that two codes appear, codes 58520 and 59350. Reference the code descriptions in the CPT manual and note that code 58520 reports a nonobstetrical hysterorrhaphy and code 59350 reports an obstetrical hysterorrhaphy. Therefore, code 59350 is used for this case.

## Exercise 15.1—Check Your Understanding

**Coding Assignments and terms that relate to maternity care and delivery**

Indicate whether the following statements are true (T) or false (F).

1. _____ Antepartum introduction and repair are reported using codes from the 59200–59350 code range.

2. _____ Normal maternity care includes monthly visits up to 36 weeks of gestation.

3. _____ Services unrelated to pregnancy should be reported using the Evaluation and Management codes.

4. _____ *Chorionic villus* is another term for *placenta*.

5. _____ Obstetrics is the specialty that deals with women during pregnancy, childbirth, and the period immediately following childbirth.

6. _____ The embryo is referred to as the fetus from the first six weeks of pregnancy until birth.

7. _____ Vesicocentesis is reported using 59012.

8. _____ Code 59076 is used to report fetal shunt placement, including ultrasound guidance.

9. _____ Code 59030 would be used to report fetal monitoring during labor.

10. _____ Code 59325 is used to report a hysterorrhaphy of a ruptured uterus.

# Vaginal Delivery, Antepartum and Postpartum Care (59400–59430), and Cesarean Delivery (59510–59525)

Codes found in this code range report antepartum care, delivery of the fetus, and postpartum care. Delivery services include any workup performed relative to the admission and management of labor.

Delivery services also include management of a vaginal or cesarean section delivery. A **cesarean section delivery** is a delivery in which there is a surgical procedure (incision) performed through the abdominal wall to extract the fetus. Postpartum services include hospital care and office visits from immediately following birth to six weeks. It should be noted that if your provider renders only part of the care to the mother, the services should not be billed as global and should be broken out to accurately reflect the portion of the services provided.

> **EXAMPLE:** Dr. Carter monitored Mrs. Black's antepartum care for the first five months, which included four visits. Mrs. Black then relocated to another town.

In this example, Dr. Carter would report code 59425 for antepartum care only.

Services such as fetal monitoring during labor, delivery of the placenta, and episiotomy are included in most delivery services and should not be coded separately. Ultrasound, amniocentesis, and other visits for conditions unrelated to the pregnancy are separately billable. Table 15-3 identifies the codes found in code range 59400 to 59430.

**TABLE 15-3** Vaginal Delivery, Antepartum Care, and Postpartum Care (59400–59430)

| Code(s) | Description |
| --- | --- |
| 59400 | Routine obstetric care, including antepartum care, vaginal delivery (with or without episiotomy and/or forceps), and postpartum care, is reported by this code. Figure 15-2 illustrates the stages of labor and a vaginal delivery. |
| 59409 and 59410 | These codes are used to report vaginal delivery. Review these codes in the CPT manual for the specific descriptions of the codes and note the procedures that are included or not included in the code descriptions. |
| 59412 | This code reports external cephalic version, with or without tocolysis. This procedure is performed when a fetus is presenting breech instead of head down. The fetus is turned within the uterus to a cephalic presenting position. |
| 59414 | Delivery of placenta is reported with this code. This is a separate procedure code. |
| 59425 and 59426 | These codes report antepartum care only, four visits or more. Fewer than four visits would be reported with an Evaluation and Management code. |
| 59430 | Postpartum care only—the physician reporting this code would not have performed any of the antepartum care or the delivery. These services would be reported by another physician. This is a separate procedure code. |

Table 15-4 identifies the codes that are used to report delivery by cesarean section and associated services.

**TABLE 15-4** Cesarean Delivery Services (59510–59525)

| Code(s) | Description |
| --- | --- |
| 59510 | Routine obstetric care, including antepartum care, cesarean delivery, and postpartum care. |
| 59514 and 59515 | Cesarean delivery only is reported with code 59514 while a cesarean delivery including postpartum care is reported with code 59515. |
| 59525 | Subtotal or total hysterectomy after cesarean delivery. Since this is an add-on code, the primary procedure code must be reported first, with this code to follow. This code must be used in conjunction with codes 59510, 59514, 59515, 59618, 59620, and 59622. |

(1) Position of the fetus before labor

Placenta    Urinary bladder    Pubic bone

Urethra
Vagina
Cervix
Rectum

Partially dilated cervix

(2) First stage of labor, cervical dilation

(3) Second stage of labor, fetal delivery

(4) Third stage of labor, delivery of placenta

Placenta    Uterus    Umbilical cord

**FIGURE 15-2** The Stages of Labor

# Delivery after Previous Cesarean Delivery (59610–59622)

As explained earlier in this chapter, a cesarean delivery is the delivery of a fetus through a surgical incision. Some cesarean deliveries are planned; some are emergency.

The 59610–59614 code range is used to report services rendered to patients who successfully complete a vaginal delivery after a previous cesarean section. The services may also be referred to as **vaginal birth after cesarean (VBAC)**. If the attempt at a vaginal birth is unsuccessful, codes 59618–59622 would be used instead.

## Exercise 15.2—Check Your Understanding

**Code Range 59000–59622 and terms related to maternity care and delivery**

Fill in the blanks in the statements that follow.

1. A delivery in which there is a surgical procedure (incision) performed through the abdominal wall to extract the fetus is called a(n) _____.

2. A hysterectomy performed after a cesarean delivery is reported using CPT add-on code _____.

3. Delivery of the placenta is reported using CPT code _____.

*(continues)*

## Exercise 15.2 *(continued)*

4. Routine obstetric care, including antepartum care, vaginal delivery, and postpartum care, is reported using code _____.

5. Services that include hospital care and office visits from immediately following birth to six weeks are _____ services.

6. Code range _____ would be referenced when a patient who had a previous cesarean delivery has a successful vaginal delivery.

7. A procedure in which an amniocentesis needle is inserted into the umbilical vessel to obtain blood from the fetus is a(n) _____.

8. CPT code _____ would be used to report fetal fluid drainage. This code includes ultrasound guidance.

9. The condition in which there is less than sufficient amniotic fluid present is called _____.

10. The abbreviation EDC means _____.

# Abortion and Other Procedures (59812–59899)

**Abortion** is a term used to indicate that a pregnancy was ended prior to the time that a fetus reached a viable age (i.e., being able to survive outside the uterus). There are several types of abortion, and an understanding of the terms used will aid in correctly coding the service rendered.

A **missed abortion** refers to a fetus that has died before the completion of 22 weeks of gestation, with retention of the dead fetus or products of conception up to four weeks after demise. An **incomplete abortion** indicates that all products of conception have not been expelled from the uterus. A **legally induced abortion** can be elective or therapeutic, and is performed by medical personnel working within the law. A **septic abortion** is one in which fever and infection are present and the endometrium around the uterus is inflamed. This infection can be life threatening to the mother as well as to the fetus. A **spontaneous abortion** is the complete or incomplete expulsion of the products of conception before a pregnancy goes beyond 22 weeks of gestation. Table 15-5 identifies the codes used to report these services.

Another procedure that may be reported from this code set is **multifetal pregnancy reduction (MPR)**. MPR is a procedure in which one or more fetuses are removed from the uterus in order to increase the chances of the survival of the strongest one. Removal of cerclage suture under anesthesia, uterine evacuation for hydatidiform mole, and unlisted maternity and delivery codes are all found in the 59866–59899 code range.

**TABLE 15-5** Abortion Services (59812–59857)

| Code(s) | Description |
|---|---|
| 59812 | Treatment of incomplete abortion, any trimester, completed surgically—the physician would evacuate any products of conception. |
| 59820 and 59821 | Treatment of missed abortion, completed surgically—based on trimester. |
| 59830 | Treatment of septic abortion, completed surgically. |
| 59840–59857 | Induced abortion—code selection is based on the technique used, as well as whether there was any other procedure performed at the same time. |

# Summary

- An understanding of the global package for obstetric care is necessary to select the proper codes for services rendered.
- An understanding of terminology is important to proper code assignment.
- Complications that typically would not be part of the regular maternity care should be coded separately using Evaluation and Management codes.

- Cesarean section deliveries can be either planned or emergency.
- VBAC deliveries are those in which a vaginal birth is successfully performed following a cesarean section during a prior pregnancy.
- Abortion treatment can be elective or for treatment following a spontaneous, incomplete, or missed abortion.
- An understanding of the different types of abortion is essential for proper code assignment.

# Internet Links

To learn more about pregnancy, childbirth, and postpartum care, visit Dr. Donnica's Women's Health site at **http://www.drdonnica.com** and the American Congress of Obstetricians and Gynecologists at **http://www.acog.org**.

# Chapter Review

## True/False

**Instructions:** Indicate whether the following statements are true (T) or false (F).

1. _____ Antepartum care is the care rendered during the time prior to childbirth.

2. _____ A spontaneous abortion can be elective or therapeutic, and is induced by medical personnel working within the law.

3. _____ Services such as fetal monitoring during labor, delivery of the placenta, and episiotomy are not included in most delivery services and should be coded separately.

4. _____ During the second week through the eighth week of pregnancy, the embryo grows and develops into a fetus.

5. _____ Delivery services include any workup performed relative to the admission and management of labor, as well as ultrasounds performed before the mother goes home from the hospital.

## Fill in the Blank

**Instructions:** Fill in the blanks in the following sentences.

6. The procedure codes used to report obstetric care begin with _____ and go through _____.

7. The acronym VBAC stands for _____.

8. Another term for placenta is a(n) _____.

9. Services that include hospital care and office visits immediately following birth, up to six weeks are called _____ services.

10. A procedure in which one or more fetuses are removed from the uterus in order to increase the chances of the survival of the strongest one is a(n) _____.

# Coding Assignments

**Instructions:** Using the CPT manual, assign the correct code to the following procedures.

1. Fetal nonstress test _____

2. Hysterorrhaphy of ruptured uterus _____

3. Laparoscopic treatment of ectopic pregnancy with salpingectomy _____

4. Vaginal delivery only, with episiotomy _____

5. Treatment of incomplete abortion, second trimester, completed surgically _____

6. Uterine evacuation and curettage for hydatidiform mole _____

7. Induced abortion by dilation and evacuation _____

8. Routine obstetric care, including antepartum care, vaginal delivery, and postpartum care after previous cesarean delivery _____

9. Removal of cerclage suture under general anesthesia _____

10. Multifetal pregnancy reduction _____

11. Fetal shunt placement, including ultrasound guidance _____

12. Antepartum chorionic villus sampling, any method _____

13. Hysterotomy, abdominal _____

14. Transabdominal amnioinfusion, including ultrasound guidance _____

15. Insertion of cervical dilator during obstetric care _____

16. Cerclage of cervix, during pregnancy, vaginal _____

17. Diagnostic amniocentesis _____

18. Routine obstetric care, including antepartum care, cesarean delivery, and postpartum care _____

19. External cephalic version, with tocolysis _____

20. Cesarean delivery only, following attempted vaginal delivery after previous cesarean delivery, including postpartum care _____

21. C-section delivery only _____

22. Antepartum care, five visits, prior to vaginal delivery _____

23. Postpartum care, following previous vaginal delivery _____

24. Surgical treatment of missed abortion, first trimester _____

25. Postpartum curettage _____

# Case Studies

**Instructions:** Review each case and indicate the correct code(s).

## Case 1

Woman presents in active labor and is admitted for delivery at 41 weeks gestation. Dr. Martin is the covering OB and has never seen the patient until today. Upon check of the cervix, dilation is at 10, and baby is ready to deliver. No type of anesthesia has been given. The fetal monitor is showing a strong, viable fetus. After several pushes, the head appears, and the baby is suctioned immediately. A healthy male child is delivered at 10:08 p.m. Apgar score is 8. Placenta

*(continues)*

*(continued)*

is delivered, no forceps, no episiotomy. Mother and child are doing well. Dr. Martin will not be completing the postpartum care.

CPT code(s): _____

## Case 2

A 28-year-old female presents to the emergency room with severe abdominal pain. Upon examination, it is determined that the patient is pregnant, but it is an ectopic pregnancy. The tube is unruptured at this time, so the decision is made to do a laparoscopic resection of the ectopic pregnancy. Laparoscopic technique is used to get to the site. When the area is found, an incision is made in the tube using an electrosurgical technique. Using forceps, the trophoblastic tissue is removed, bleeding is controlled, and the procedure is finished in the usual manner.

CPT code(s): _____

## Case 3

**Office Note**

**Diagnosis:** Pregnancy at 30 weeks

This 29-year-old patient is 30 weeks pregnant and has been seen by me since she was eight weeks pregnant. She is moving out of town and is going to be seen by Dr. Nicon in Atlanta, Georgia. Her prenatal records will be sent. At this time, her pregnancy is normal with no complications. She has been seen seven times by me.

**Note to billing staff:** Please bill patient's insurance at this time.

CPT code(s): _____

## Case 4

**Office Note**

**Diagnosis:** Normal pregnancy and vaginal delivery

Mrs. Smith delivered a 6-pound, 10-ounce baby girl on 1/10/XX at 1:23 a.m. This is her final postpartum visit. See OB flow sheet for physical findings and record of the antepartum care visits that I completed during her pregnancy.

**Note to billing staff:** Please bill patient's insurance at this time.

CPT code(s): _____

## Case 5

**Office Note**

**Diagnosis:** Normal pregnancy followed by attempted vaginal delivery after previous C-section delivery

Mrs. Williams delivered an 8-pound, 12-ounce baby boy on 4/15/XX at 11:11 a.m. via C-section after attempting to deliver the child vaginally. This is her final postpartum visit. See OB flow sheet for physical findings and antepartum visit record.

**Note to billing staff:** Please bill patient's insurance at this time.

CPT code(s): _____

## Case 6

This is a 24-year-old female who has been in active labor for the past 17 hours. The hope was that the labor would progress to a vaginal delivery, but the baby has now turned and is breech. After close observation of the baby through monitoring, the decision was made to perform the cesarean section. I have never seen this patient; she is here visiting from out of town. She is three weeks prior to her due date.

A low transverse abdominal incision was made with a sharp scalpel. The incision was carried through the subcutaneous tissue and the superficial fascia where the incision extended bilaterally. Fascia was grasped with Kocher clamps and undermined with sharp and blunt dissection using Mayo scissors.

Forceps were used to grasp the preperitoneal fascia, which was incised with Metzenbaum scissors until the peritoneal cavity was entered, and the incision extended superiorly and inferiorly.

The Mezenbaum was used to incise a low uterine segment after the bladder was moved to safety with a bladder retractor. Inferior to the peritoneum was then undermined and the bladder retractor replaced in the flap. The low uterine segment was then incised with a sharp scalpel until the intrauterine cavity was entered. The infant was guided to the incision and delivered from the uterus with fundal pressure. The legs were delivered by flexion of the knees, and arms were delivered by rotation of the body. Then the head was delivered. The baby scored 7 on Apgar at 1 minute, and 9 at 5 minutes. Closure of the abdominal incision on the mother was made in layers. Mother and baby were sent to recovery in good condition.

CPT code(s): _____

## Case 7

**Preoperative diagnosis:** Hydatidform mole

**Postoperative diagnosis:** Same

**Indications for surgery:** This is a 23-year-old female who presented thinking she might be miscarrying. Her last menstrual cycle was eight weeks ago. She has noted some abdominal pain and now some bleeding. After a pregnancy test, a brief pelvic exam, and ultrasound study, it was determined that she is not pregnant but suffering from a hydatidform mole. The patient is bleeding quite heavily at this time, and there was identification of a hydatid cyst.

**Procedure:** The patient was taken to the operating room where general anesthesia was administered. She was prepped and draped in the normal sterile fashion, then placed in the dorsal lithotomy position. A weighted speculum was placed in the posterior vagina, and a Deaver retractor was placed anteriorly. At this time, a single-tooth tenaculum was placed in the anterior cervix for retraction. The cervix was then dilated with Hanks dilators to 25 French. A #7 suction curette was inserted without incident. The suction machine appeared to evacuate all cysts, but a curette was manually used with gentle scraping to be sure that all cysts were removed. The curette was gently removed. All instruments were accounted for, and the patient left the operating room in good condition.

**CPT code(s):** _____

## Case 8

**Preoperative and postoperative diagnosis:** Incomplete spontaneous abortion

**Procedure:** Treatment of incomplete abortion

This 16-week-pregnant patient was brought to the operating suite and prepped and draped in the usual fashion. A speculum was placed to view the cervix. The cervix was grasped with a tenaculum, and a dilator was inserted into the endocervix. A cannula was passed into the uterus, and a suction machine was used to evacuate the contents by rotating the cannula. To ensure that the uterus was emptied of all contents, a sharp curette was used to scrape the uterine wall. The patient tolerated the procedure and was sent to the recovery area in satisfactory condition.

**CPT code(s):** _____

# Endocrine System

## Chapter Outline

Introduction

Guidelines Related to the National Correct
   Coding Initiative (NCCI)

Abbreviations Associated with the
   Endocrine System

Thyroid Gland (60000–60300)

Parathyroid, Thymus, Adrenal Glands,
   Pancreas, and Carotid Body (60500–60605)

Laparoscopy and Other Procedures
   (60650–60699)

Summary

Internet Links

Chapter Review

Coding Assignments

Case Studies

## Learning Objectives

### At the conclusion of this chapter, you should be able to:

1. Define key terms related to coding procedures on the endocrine system.
2. Define abbreviations associated with the endocrine system.
3. Describe the basic anatomy and functions of the endocrine system.
4. Define common procedures completed on the endocrine system.
5. Apply specific coding guidelines for the endocrine system.
6. Select CPT codes for procedures completed on the endocrine system.
7. Identify and code procedures for the endocrine system from case studies.

## Key Terms

| | | | |
|---|---|---|---|
| adrenal glands | hormones | pancreas | thymus gland |
| endocrine system | hypothyroidism | parathyroid | thyroid gland |

## Introduction

The **endocrine system** consists of several different internal groups of glands and structures that produce or secrete hormones. **Hormones** are chemical substances produced by the body to keep organs and tissues functioning properly. When structures of the endocrine system are not functioning properly and the hormones are not released as they should be, illness occurs that may require intervention by a physician. The main function of the endocrine system is to keep the body in balance and working properly.

Some of the major structures of the endocrine system and their locations are noted in Figure 16-1. The hormones and their functions are summarized in Table 16-1.

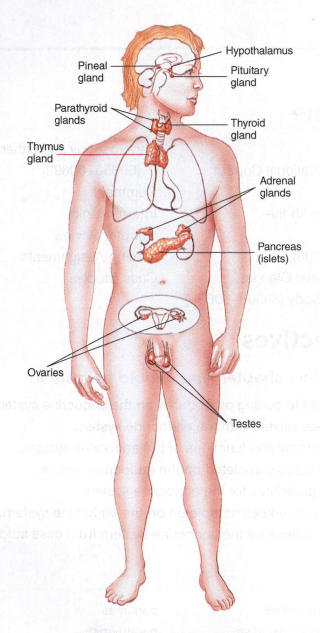

**Endocrine system** Pituitary, thyroid, parathyroid, thymus, adrenal, and pineal glands, as well as portions of the hypothalamus, pancreas, liver, kidneys, skin, digestive tract, ovaries, testes, and placenta. Also included are hormonal secretions from each gland.

**FIGURE 16-1** Endocrine System

**TABLE 16-1** Hormones and Functions

| Hormone | Functions |
|---|---|
| Adrenocorticotropic hormone (ACTH) | Stimulates the growth and secretions of the adrenal cortex. |
| Aldosterone | Aids in regulating the levels of salt and water in the body. |
| Androgens | Influence sex-related characteristics. |
| Antidiuretic hormone (ADH) | Helps control blood pressure by reducing the amount of water that is excreted. |
| Calcitonin | Works with the parathyroid hormone to regulate calcium levels in the blood and tissues. |
| Cortisol | Regulates the metabolism of carbohydrates, fats, and proteins in the body. Also has an anti-inflammatory action. |
| Epinephrine | Stimulates the sympathetic nervous system. |
| Estrogen | Develops and maintains the female secondary sex characteristics and regulates the menstrual cycle. |
| Follicle-stimulating hormone (FSH) | In the female, stimulates the secretion of estrogen and the growth of ova (eggs). In the male, stimulates the production of sperm. |
| Glucagon | Increases the level of glucose in the bloodstream. |
| Growth hormone (GH) | Regulates the growth of bone, muscle, and other body tissues. |
| Human chorionic gonadotropin (HCG) | Stimulates the secretion of the hormones required to maintain pregnancy. |
| Insulin (In) | Regulates the transport of glucose to body cells and stimulates the conversion of excess glucose to glycogen for storage. |
| Lactogenic hormone (LTH) | Stimulates and maintains the secretion of breast milk. |
| Luteinizing hormone (LH) | In the female, stimulates ovulation. In the male, stimulates testosterone secretion. |
| Melatonin | Influences the sleep–wakefulness cycles. |
| Norepinephrine | Stimulates the sympathetic nervous system. |
| Oxytocin (OXT) | Stimulates uterine contractions during childbirth. Causes milk to flow from the mammary glands after birth. |
| Parathyroid hormone (PTH) | Works with calcitonin to regulate calcium levels in the blood and tissues. |
| Progesterone | Completes preparation of the uterus for possible pregnancy. |
| Testosterone | Stimulates the development of male secondary sex characteristics. |
| Thymosin | Plays an important role in the immune system. |
| Thyroid hormones (T4 and T3) | Regulates the rate of metabolism. |
| Thyroid-stimulating hormone (TSH) | Stimulates the secretion of hormones by the thyroid gland. |

# Guidelines Related to the National Correct Coding Initiative (NCCI)

Perform the following steps to obtain the most current coding guideline information related to this chapter online.

1. Log on to *https://www.cms.gov/medicare-medicaid-coordination/national-correct-coding-initiative-ncci/ncci-medicare/medicare-ncci-policy-manual*.
2. Scroll to the section titled "View Manual by Chapter."
3. Click "Chapter 8" for guidelines specific to the endocrine system.

# Abbreviations Associated with the Endocrine System

The following abbreviations are most commonly used in relation to the endocrine system:

| Abbreviations | Descriptions |
|---|---|
| ADH | antidiuretic hormone |
| ALD | aldosterone |
| DI | diabetes insipidus |
| DM | diabetes mellitus |
| FA | fructosamine test |
| FBS | fasting blood sugar |
| GD | Grave's disease |
| HG | hypoglycemia |
| IDDM | insulin-dependent diabetes mellitus |
| NIDDM | non-insulin-dependent diabetes mellitus |
| TSH | thyroid-stimulating hormone |

# Thyroid Gland (60000–60300)

Understanding structures of the endocrine system and their particular function in this system will help determine code selection. The **thyroid gland** secretes hormones that regulate growth and metabolism. The thyroid gland is an organ located in the neck with a lobe on either side of the larynx and the trachea. The two lobes are connected by the isthmus. Sometimes the thyroid is not as active as it should be, and a condition known as **hypothyroidism** occurs. The procedure coding for the thyroid gland contains incision, excision, and removal codes. These codes are summarized in Table 16-2.

**EXAMPLE:** Dr. Halick is completing a percutaneous core needle biopsy of the thyroid to rule out cancer. This would be coded with code 60100 since a core needle is being used percutaneously to complete the biopsy. In the CPT manual index reference the term "Biopsy" and then "Thyroid" to locate the code. Remember to always review the full code description found in the CPT manual.

**TABLE 16-2**  Thyroid Gland (60000–60300)

| Code(s) | Description |
|---|---|
| 60000 | This code is used to report the incision and drainage of a thyroglossal duct cyst that is infected. A thyroglossal cyst is also known as a *thyrolingual cysts*. |
| 60100 | This code is used to report a biopsy of the thyroid completed via a percutaneous core needle. It should be noted that the CPT manual contains instructional notations that pertain to the assignment of this code when imaging guidance is performed with this procedure, as well as notations that pertain to fine needle aspiration and evaluation of the fine needle aspirate. |
| 60200 | Excision of cyst or adenoma of thyroid, or transection of isthmus is reported by use of this code. |
| 60210 and 60212 | To report a partial thyroid lobectomy, this range of codes is used. The codes are differentiated by accompanying procedures. |
| 60220 and 60225 | Total thyroid lobectomy, unilateral, is reported with these codes, which are differentiated by accompanying procedures. |
| 60240 | This code is used to report a thyroidectomy, total or complete. |

(continues)

**TABLE 16-2** (*continued*)

| Code(s) | Description |
|---|---|
| 60252 and 60254 | Thyroidectomy, total or subtotal for malignancy, is reported with these codes, which are differentiated by limited neck dissection and radical neck dissection. |
| 60260 | Thyroidectomy, removal of all remaining thyroid tissue following previous removal of a portion of thyroid, is reported with this code which is used for the unilateral procedure. For a bilateral procedure, report code 60260 with a modifier of 50. |
| 60270 and 60271 | Thyroidectomy, including substernal thyroid, is reported with these codes, which are differentiated by a sternal split or transthoracic approach and a cervical approach. |
| 60280 and 60281 | Excision of thyroglossal duct cyst or sinus is reported with these codes. Before code assignment can occur, the coder must be able to determine whether this is a recurrent procedure. |
| 60300 | This code is used to report aspiration and/or injection of a thyroid cyst. It should be noted that there are notations following the code that affect code selection. |

# Parathyroid, Thymus, Adrenal Glands, Pancreas, and Carotid Body (60500–60605)

The **parathyroid** is located along the posterior of the thyroid. There are two parathyroids on each lobe of the thyroid. The parathyroid is another structure that secretes hormones that regulate serum calcium levels. Another structure that should be mentioned is the **pancreas**. The pancreas functions in both the digestive and the endocrine system. In the endocrine system, the pancreas secretes insulin, which is a hormone that regulates blood sugar levels. When the pancreas is not functioning properly, or in some cases not functioning at all, the patient is diagnosed with diabetes mellitus.

The **thymus gland** is located in the middle of the chest, just underneath the sternum. The function of the thymus is to secrete thymosin, which is a hormone that the bone marrow needs to produce T cells that work with the immune system.

The **adrenal glands** sit atop the kidneys. Their function is to regulate electrolytes and help in the metabolism of glucose and adrenaline, which plays an important role in heart and lung function. Procedures that are completed on the parathyroid, thymus, adrenal glands, pancreas, and carotid body are assigned to code range 60500–60605 and are summarized in Table 16-3.

**EXAMPLE:** A total thymectomy via a transcervical approach was performed by Dr. Troas. This was performed as a separate procedure. Code 60520 would be used for this case. Note that code 60520 reports a total or a partial thymectomy.

**TABLE 16-3** Parathyroid, Thymus, Adrenal Glands, Pancreas, and Carotid Body (60500–60605)

| Code(s) | Description |
|---|---|
| 60500–60505 | Parathyroidectomy or exploration of parathyroid(s) is assigned to these codes. The codes are divided according to whether the procedure was initially completed, completed for reexploration, or with mediastinal exploration, sternal split, or transthoracic approach. |
| 60512 | This code reports a parathyroid autotransplantation and is an add-on code that is listed separately, in addition to the code for the primary procedure completed. Code 60512 can be used with codes 60500, 60502, 60505, 60212, 60225, 60240, 60252, 60254, 60260, 60270, and 60271. |
| 60520–60522 | A thymectomy, partial or total, is reported with these codes. All of these codes are separate procedure codes. The codes are differentiated by the approach. |
| 60540 and 60545 | An adrenalectomy, partial or complete, or exploration of adrenal gland with or without biopsy, transabdominal, lumbar or dorsal, is assigned to these codes. Code 60540 is a separate procedure code. It should be noted that there are numerous instructional notations that appear in the CPT manual in regard to these codes. Review these instructional notations in the CPT manual. |
| 60600 and 60605 | Codes 60600 and 60605 are used to report the excision of a carotid body tumor. The codes are differentiated by whether there was also an excision of a carotid artery. |

# Laparoscopy and Other Procedures (60650–60699)

There are two codes that are used to report laparoscopic procedures completed on the endocrine system. Code 60650 is used to report a surgical laparoscopy:

- With adrenalectomy, partial or complete. During this procedure, a laparoscope is used to view or remove the adrenal gland.
- The exploration of an adrenal gland with or without biopsy, transabdominal, lumbar, or dorsal.

Code 60659 is the second laparoscopic procedure code. This code is used to report any other laparoscopic procedure that is completed on the endocrine system.

The final code in the endocrine system section is code 60699, which is used to report any unlisted procedure not found in this subsection.

# Summary

- The endocrine system consists of several different internal groups of glands and structures that produce or secrete hormones.
- Procedures completed on the endocrine system are assigned to CPT codes 60000–60699.
- The thyroid gland secretes hormones that regulate growth and metabolism.
- The parathyroid, located along the posterior of the thyroid, is another structure that secretes hormones that regulate serum calcium levels.
- The thymus gland is located in the middle of the chest, just underneath the sternum, and secretes thymosin.
- The function of the adrenal glands is to regulate electrolytes, help in the metabolism of glucose and adrenaline.

# Internet Links

To learn more about the endocrine system and procedures completed on this system, visit the sites below and search on procedures discussed in this chapter:

- *http://www.medterms.com*
- *http://www.endocrine.org*
- *http://www.mayoclinic.com*

# Chapter Review

## Fill in the Blank

**Instructions:** Fill in the blanks in the statements that follow.

1. Chemical substances produced by the body to keep organs and tissues functioning properly are known as

   _____.

2. The gland that sits atop the kidneys is called the _____.

3. In the endocrine system, the pancreas secretes a hormone that regulates blood sugar levels. This hormone is called _____.

4. The function of the thymus is to secrete a hormone that the bone marrow needs to produce T cells that work with the immune system. This hormone is called _____.

5. Code 60500 is used to report an exploration of the parathyroid(s) or a(n) _____.

## True/False

**Instructions:** Indicate whether the following statements are true (T) or false (F).

6. _____ Cortisol stimulates uterine contractions during childbirth.

7. _____ Norepinephrine stimulates the somatic nervous system.

8. _____ The thymus gland sits in the middle of the chest just under the sternum.

9. _____ The code used to report a complete thyroidectomy is 60240.

10. _____ A parathyroid autotransplantation is reported using 60300.

# Coding Assignments

**Instructions:** Using the CPT manual, assign the correct code to each of the following procedures.

1. Excision of a carotid body tumor without excision of the carotid artery _____

2. Transcervical partial thymectomy _____

3. Complete thyroidectomy _____

4. Aspiration of thyroid cyst _____

5. Excision of thyroid cyst _____

6. Excision of thyroglossal duct cyst _____

7. Dorsal complete adrenalectomy _____

8. Exploration of parathyroid with transthoracic mediastinal exploration _____

9. Total unilateral thyroid lobectomy _____

10. Sternal split thyroidectomy, including substernal thyroid _____

11. Laparoscopic partial adrenalectomy _____

12. Total thyroidectomy with radical dissection of neck to treat malignancy _____

13. Partial thymectomy with radical mediastinal dissection, sternal split approach _____

14. Unilateral thyroidectomy following previous removal of a portion of the thyroid _____

15. Partial unilateral thyroid lobectomy with isthmusectomy _____

# Case Studies

**Instructions:** Review each case and indicate the correct code(s).

## Case 1

Patient presents with pain and swelling in the neck area, abnormal TSH, and other symptoms of an abnormally functioning thyroid. After examination, the physician is unclear as to what the problem is and sends the patient to a surgeon.

*(continues)*

(*continued*)

The surgeon reviews tests, finds an area of swelling, and suspects a tumor. A biopsy is performed, and a stat pathology report confirms that there is a malignant mass forming on the thyroid. A complete thyroidectomy is performed, leaving the parathyroid glands intact. The wound is closed, and the patient tolerates the procedure well.

**CPT code(s):** _____

# Case 2

Patient presents, after study, with a mass on the thyroid. It was determined that a biopsy of the thyroid should be completed. The thyroid was located by palpation. A large, hollow percutaneous core needle was passed through the skin into the thyroid. The needle was used to remove the tissue. The tissue was sent to pathology for examination. The patient tolerated the procedure well and was sent to the recovery area.

**CPT code(s):** _____

# Case 3

**Preoperative diagnosis:** Small mass on left adrenal

**Postoperative diagnosis:** 5-cm malignant neoplasm, left adrenal

**Procedure:** Adrenalectomy, left

Patient was prepped and draped in the usual sterile fashion. A 5-mm, 30-degree scope was used in conjunction with two more 5-mm ports and one 11-mm port. Spleen, colon, and pancreas were all carefully checked and showed no signs of disease. The adrenal was identified, and all vessels leading to the adrenal were taken down carefully and without incident using a Harmonic scalpel. The mass was identified. The left adrenal was carefully dissected and dropped easily into the bag, which was removed through the 11-mm port site. The kidney was examined, and no sign of disease was noted, so we left the area. The port sites were closed, and the patient was taken to the recovery area in good condition.

**CPT code(s):** _____

# Case 4

**Preoperative diagnosis:** Hyperparathyroidism, primary

**Postoperative diagnosis:** Same

**Procedure performed:** Parathyroidectomy, left side

**Procedure:** The patient was prepped and draped in the usual sterile fashion. We proceeded with a transverse collar incision on the left. Dissection went through the subcutaneous tissue until the platysma muscles were identified. A subplatysma flap was created, and strap muscles were divided along the midline. The thyroid gland was identified and slightly rotated into position so that the parathyroid on the left was easily identified. The parathyroid was enlarged and somewhat calcified. This calcification allowed for easy removal of the parathyroid without damage to the thyroid gland itself. The surrounding structures were left in good condition, and the neck wound was closed in a layered fashion. The patient left the surgical suite in excellent condition and was taken to recovery.

CPT code(s): _____

# Case 5

**Preoperative diagnosis:** Right thyroid nodule

**Postoperative diagnosis:** Same

**Procedure:** Right thyroid lobectomy

**Procedure performed:** This 42-year-old female was placed supine on the operating table. General anesthesia was induced, after which the neck was prepped and draped with Betadine. A transverse incision was made in the skin fold on the right side of the neck, and was carried down through the skin and subcutaneous tissues. The platysma and strap muscles were divided, and subplatysmal flaps were then raised. The 4.5-cm thyroid nodule was encountered posteriorly on the nerve. It was then necessary to ligate the inferior thyroid artery and vein, the middle thyroid vein, and the superior thyroid artery and vein. The gland was then rotated medially for better access to the nodule. A Harmonic scalpel was used to remove the nodule encompassing the right lobe, which was sent for pathology. The pathology came back as a benign colloid goiter. The left side of the thyroid as well as the parathyroids were left intact. The strap muscles were closed with 3-0 Vicryl, as was the platysma. The skin was then closed with subcuticular 4-0 Vicryl, Benzoin, Steri-Strips, and dressings were applied.

The patient left the operating room in good condition for the recovery room.

CPT code(s): _____

## Case 6

**Preoperative diagnosis:** Thyroglossal duct cyst

**Postoperative diagnosis:** Same

**Anesthesia:** General

**Procedural Notes:**

This 34-year-old male patient was placed in the supine position. He was then placed under general anesthesia, and his neck was prepped and draped in the usual fashion and then flexed for the procedure. The skin around the cyst was circumferentially incised, and the cyst and duct were dissected free to the level of the hyoid bone. The midpoint of the hyoid bone was then excised. A 3-0 plain catgut triple-strand suture was then used to ligate the thyroglossal duct. Iris scissors were used to remove the cyst, and hemostasis was obtained. The wound site was closed in layers. No significant blood loss occurred. The patient was in stable condition and sent to the recovery area.

**CPT code(s):** _____

# Nervous System

## Chapter Outline

Introduction

Guidelines Related to the National
Correct Coding Initiative (NCCI)

Abbreviations Associated with the
Nervous System

Anatomy of the Nervous
System

Procedures Completed on the Nervous System
(61000–64999)

Summary

Internet Links

Chapter Review

Coding Assignments

Case Studies

## Learning Objectives

### At the conclusion of this chapter, you should be able to:

1. Define key terms related to coding procedures on the nervous system.
2. Define abbreviations associated with the nervous system.
3. Describe the basic anatomy of the nervous system.
4. Define common procedures completed on the nervous system.
5. Apply the specific coding guidelines for the nervous system.
6. Select CPT codes for procedures completed on the nervous system.
7. Identify and code procedures for the nervous system from case studies.

## Key Terms

arachnoid mater

autonomic nervous
system

brain

brain stem

burr hole
procedures

central nervous system

cerebellum

cerebral cortex

cerebrum

craniectomy

craniotomy

diencephalon

dura mater

endovascular therapy

meninges

mesencephalon

midbrain

peripheral nervous
system

pia mater

somatic nervous system

spinal nerves

trephine

# Introduction

The nervous system is composed of the brain, spinal cord, and peripheral nerves. Within CPT, procedures that are completed on these structures, as well as the skull, meninges, extracranial nerves, and autonomic nervous system, are assigned to codes in the 61000–64999 code range.

# Guidelines Related to the National Correct Coding Initiative (NCCI)

The student will need to perform the following steps to obtain the most current coding guideline information related to this chapter online:

1. Log on to *https://www.cms.gov/medicare-medicaid-coordination/national-correct-coding-initiative-ncci /ncci-medicare/medicare-ncci-policy-manual*.
2. Scroll to the section titled "View Manual by Chapter."
3. Click "Chapter 8" for guidelines specific to the nervous system.

# Abbreviations Associated with the Nervous System

These abbreviations are the more common abbreviations used for the nervous system:

| Abbreviations | Definitions |
|---|---|
| ANS | autonomic nervous system |
| CNS | central nervous system |
| CSF | cerebral spinal fluid |
| CT | computed tomography |
| EEG | electroencephalogram |
| EMG | electromyogram |
| ICP | intracranial pressure |
| LP | lumbar puncture |
| PNS | peripheral nervous system |
| TENS | transcutaneous electrical nerve stimulation |

# Anatomy of the Nervous System

The structures that comprise the nervous system are responsible for the communication and control of the body. The nervous system is divided into two systems: the **central nervous system**, which comprises the brain and spinal cord, and the **peripheral nervous system**, which comprises the nerves that connect the body organs to the central nervous system.

The peripheral nervous system is divided into two systems:

- **Somatic nervous system**, which connects the central nervous system to the skin and skeletal muscles via the cranial and spinal nerves.
- **Autonomic nervous system**, which connects the central nervous system to the visceral organs via the cranial and spinal nerves.

Figure 17-1 illustrates the central nervous system and the peripheral nervous system.

The **brain** has more than 100 billion neurons that are connected by means of electrochemical pulses, and it is responsible for all physical and mental functions of the body. The protective tissue that covers the brain and

Cerebrum

Cerebellum

Cranial nerve

Phrenic nerve

Spinal cord

Radial nerve

Median nerve

Ulnar nerve

Iliohypogastric nerve

Ilioinguinal nerve

Sacral plexus

Sciatic nerve

Tibial nerve

Superficial peroneal nerve

Deep peroneal nerve

Brain

Spinal cord

Central nervous system (CNS)

Peripheral nerves + Sensory receptors

Peripheral nervous system (PNS)

sensations

stimulus

peripheral nerve

sensory receptors

**FIGURE 17-1** The Peripheral Nervous System Connects the Central Nervous System to the Structures of the Body

**FIGURE 17-2** Meninges and Related Structures

spinal cord is the **meninges**. The outermost layer of the meninges is the **dura mater**, the middle layer of the meninges is the **arachnoid mater**, and the innermost layer is the **pia mater**. Figure 17-2 illustrates the meninges and related structures.

The brain is composed of the following areas:

- **Cerebral cortex**—consists of a layer of neurons on the surface of the brain. The cerebral cortex is made up of gray matter.

- **Cerebrum**—the largest part of the brain, which is separated by depressions and grooves and is divided into separate hemispheres by a groove called the *longitudinal fissure.* Each hemisphere is divided into four lobes. Each lobe has a different functional distinction. Figure 17-3 illustrates the lobes and functions of the cerebrum, brain stem, and cerebellum.

- **Cerebellum**—the second-largest part of the brain, separated from the cerebrum by the transverse fissure and the tentorium cerebelli. This part of the brain coordinates skeletal muscle movements and learning new motor skills. Injury to the cerebellum may affect coordination and balance depending on the severity of the trauma.

- **Diencephalon**—this structure is located between the cerebrum and the midbrain. The primary structures found in this area include the thalamus, hypothalamus, posterior pituitary gland, and pineal gland.

- **Brain stem**—connects the diencephalon to the spinal cord. Structures of the brain stem include the medulla oblongata, pons, and midbrain. The **midbrain**, also known as the **mesencephalon**, is located between the diencephlon and the pons. Figure 17-4 illustrates the brain stem.

The spinal cord is a column of nervous tissue that runs within the vertebral canal of the vertebra. The spinal cord's function is to conduct impulses to and from the brain and to serve as a reflex center for the body. The spinal cord is surrounded by the meninges and cerebral spinal fluid. When cross-sectioned, the spinal cord reveals areas of both white and gray matter. Figure 17-5 illustrates the white and gray matter of the spinal cord.

There are 31 pairs of **spinal nerves** located in the spinal area. Most spinal nerves are named for the corresponding vertebrae. Figure 17-6 illustrates the spinal cord and the spinal nerves.

There are 12 pairs of cranial nerves that originate from underneath the brain. The cranial nerves are named for the area or function that they serve and are identified by Roman numerals. Figure 17-7 identifies the Roman numerals and names used for each cranial nerve.

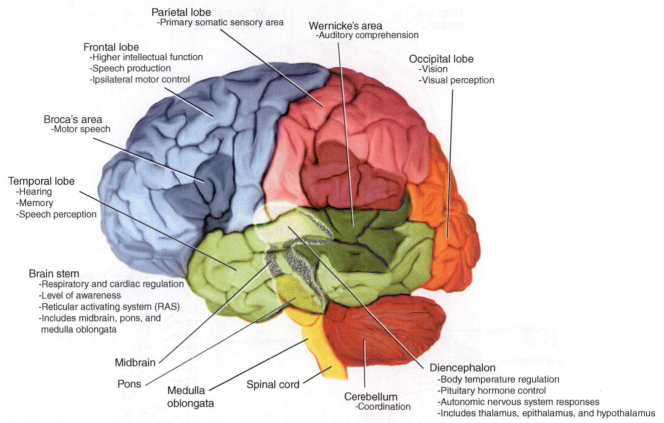

Parietal lobe
-Primary somatic sensory area

Wernicke's area
-Auditory comprehension

Frontal lobe
-Higher intellectual function
-Speech production
-Ipsilateral motor control

Occipital lobe
-Vision
-Visual perception

Broca's area
-Motor speech

Temporal lobe
-Hearing
-Memory
-Speech perception

Brain stem
-Respiratory and cardiac regulation
-Level of awareness
-Reticular activating system (RAS)
-Includes midbrain, pons, and
  medulla oblongata

Midbrain

Pons

Medulla
oblongata

Spinal cord

Cerebellum
-Coordination

Diencephalon
-Body temperature regulation
-Pituitary hormone control
-Autonomic nervous system responses
-Includes thalamus, epithalamus, and hypothalamus

**FIGURE 17-3** Functions of the Cerebrum, Brain Stem, and Cerebellum

Thalamus
Diencephalon

Third ventricle

Pineal body

Mid brain

Cerebral peduncle

Trochlear nerve

Superior

Cerebellar
peduncles

Middle

Pons

Inferior

Medulla

**FIGURE 17-4** The Brain Stem

**FIGURE 17-5**  Cross-Section of the Spinal Cord

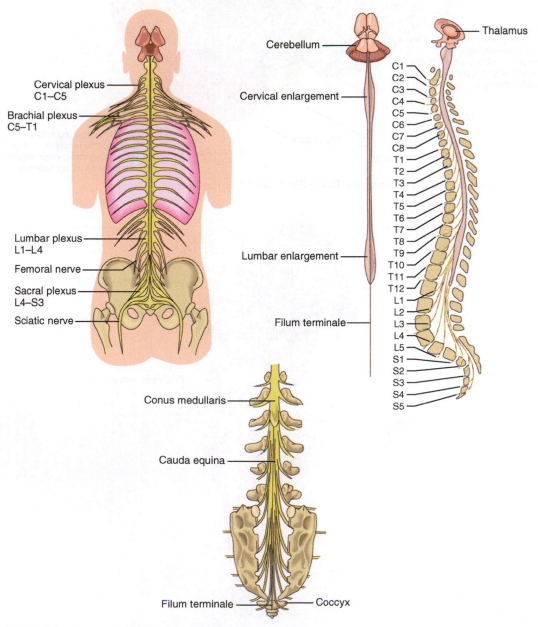

**FIGURE 17-6**  The Spinal Cord and Nerves

**FIGURE 17-7**  Cranial Nerves Are Identified by Roman Numerals and Are Named for the Area or Function They Serve

# Procedures Completed on the Nervous System (61000–64999)

The codes for the nervous system are divided into three areas:

- Skull, meninges, and brain—code range 61000–62258
- Spine and spinal cord—code range 62263–63746
- Extracranial nerves, peripheral nerves, and autonomic nervous system—code range 64400–64999

## Skull, Meninges, and Brain (61000–62258)

This first range of codes, codes 61000–62258, is divided into the following:

- Injection, drainage, or aspiration
- Twist drill, burr holes, or trephine
- Craniectomy or craniotomy
- Surgery of skull base
  - Approach procedures—anatomical area involved
  - Definitive procedures—i.e., biopsy, resection, repair, etc.
  - Repair and/or reconstruction of surgical defects of skull base—reported if certain procedures are performed as outlined in CPT
- Endovascular therapy
- Surgery for aneurysm, arteriovenous malformation, or vascular disease

- Stereotaxis
- Stereotactic Radiosurgery (Cranial)
- Neurostimulators (intracranial)
- Repair
- Neuroendoscopy
- Cerebrospinal fluid (CSF) shunt

Prior to the description of these codes, there are three instructional notations that relate to injection procedures and should be referenced by the coder.

## Injections, Drainage, or Aspiration Procedures (61000–61070)

Injections, drainage, or aspiration procedures completed on the skull, meninges, and brain are reported with codes 61000–61070. Codes 61000 and 61001 are used to report a subdural tap through fontanelle, or suture, unilateral or bilateral, for an infant. These codes are differentiated by whether the tap was an initial or subsequent tap. Taps are usually performed when the infant is suffering from hydrocephalus or has a diagnosis of meningitis.

Codes 61020 and 61026 are used to report ventricular puncture through a previous burr hole, fontanelle, suture, or implanted ventricular catheter/reservoir. These codes are differentiated by whether an injection occurred. Codes 61050 and 61055 are used to report cisternal or lateral cervical puncture and are differentiated by whether injections occurred with the procedure. The final code in this section is assigned for puncture for shunt tubing or a reservoir for an aspiration or injection procedure, code 61070. This procedure may be performed to evaluate the function of the tubing or reservoir. The coder is instructed to reference code 75809 for radiological intervention if necessary.

## Twist Drill, Burr Hole(s), or Trephine (61105–61253)

Codes 61105 to 61108 are used to report a twist drill hole for punctures. Code 61105 reports a twist drill hole for subdural or ventricular puncture. Codes 61107 and 61108 report twist drill hole(s) for subdural, intracerebral or ventricular punctures and are differentiated by the accompanying procedures that are completed.

Burr hole(s) procedures are reported with codes 61120–61253. During **burr hole procedures**, the physician drills a burr hole in the cranium to complete the procedure, which could include a biopsy of a brain or intracranial lesion, drainage of a brain abscess or cyst, tapping of an abscess or cyst, drainage of a hematoma, and other brain or intracranial procedures. A **trephine** is a surgical instrument that is used to cut a cylindrical shape. This, at times, is used for cutting holes in bone. Figure 17-8 illustrates the creation of burr holes.

**FIGURE 17-8** Burr Holes

## Craniectomy or Craniotomy (61304–61576)

A **craniectomy** is completed to remove a skull bone, while a **craniotomy** involves simply making an incision into the skull without removal of bone. Codes 61304 to 61576 are used to report these procedures. CPT codes 61304 or 61305 should not be reported separately when there is a more extensive craniectomy or craniotomy procedure being performed in the same operative session. The codes are differentiated according to the reason for the craniectomy or craniotomy. For example, code 61314 is used to report a craniectomy or craniotomy for the evacuation of a hematoma, while code 61321 is used to report a craniectomy or craniotomy for the drainage of an intracranial abscess located in the infratenorial region. To become familiar with this range of codes, complete the following exercise.

### Exercise 17.1—Check Your Understanding

Code Range 61000–61576

Complete the description of each code listed. The first one is completed for you.

| Code | Description | Code | Description |
|------|-------------|------|-------------|
| 1. 61557 | Craniotomy for craniosynostosis; bifrontal bone flap | 5. 61570 | _____ |
|  |  | 6. 61105 | _____ |
|  |  | 7. 61333 | _____ |
| 2. 61533 | _____ | 8. 61517 | _____ |
| 3. 61550 | _____ | 9. 61501 | _____ |
| 4. 61558 | _____ | 10. 61566 | _____ |

## Surgery of Skull Base (61580–61619)

Codes 61580 to 61619 are used to report procedures that are completed on the base of the skull. These are extensive procedures that typically involve more than one surgeon. The procedure can have three components: the approach, the definitive procedure, and repair or reconstruction. At times, one physician may complete more than one component. When this occurs, the physician should report the codes and add a modifier of 51 to the secondary and/or additional procedure.

> **EXAMPLE:** Dr. Yousaf completed the craniofacial approach to the anterior cranial fossa and used code 61580 to report this portion of the procedure. He completed the definitive procedure, an extradural excision of a neoplastic lesion, and reported code 61600-51.

When different surgeons perform different components, each surgeon reports the code for the component that he or she completed.

> **EXAMPLE:** Dr. Yousaf completed the craniofacial approach to the anterior cranial fossa and reported code 61580.
>
> Dr. Jones completed the definitive procedure, an extradural excision of a neoplastic lesion, and reported code 61600.

The repair codes 61618 and 61619 are reported separately when extensive dural grafting, cranioplasty, local or regional myocutaneous pedicle flaps, or extensive skin grafts are required.

## Endovascular Therapy (61623–61651)

Code range 61623 to 61651 is used to report endovascular therapy. **Endovascular therapy** is completed within the vascular system of the head or neck for a specific purpose, such as to control bleeding, destroy a tumor, achieve hemostasis for a bleeding aneurysm, control blood flow during intracranial or extracranial procedures, and for other reasons. These codes are differentiated by the type of endovascular therapy, such as balloon angioplasty or balloon dilation. Some of the codes are further differentiated according to the location or the number of vessels on which the procedure was completed. Codes 61650, and 61651 report cerebral endovascular therapeutic interventions in any intracranial artery. Code 61651 is an add-on code. Review and follow the instructional notations that appear in the CPT manual after the code description prior to reporting these codes.

## Surgery for Aneurysm, Arteriovenous Malformation, or Vascular Disease (61680–61711)

To report surgery for aneurysm, arteriovenous malformation, or vascular disease, codes 61680 through 61711 should be used. To reference these codes in the Alphabetical Index of the CPT manual, the following terms should be located:

- Aneurysm repair, then carotid artery
- Aneurysm repair, then intracranial artery
- Arteriovenous malformation, then cranial repair
- Vascular malformation, then cerebral repair

Codes 61680 to 61692 are used to report surgery of intracranial arteriovenous malformation. For these procedures, the surgeon is resecting an arteriovenous malformation in the brain. To select a code from this range, the coder must determine the tumor location and the complexity of accessing the tumor, simple or complex. Documentation should justify the selection of the codes that describe the procedure completed as complex.

> **EXAMPLE:** Dr. Frankowski performed a craniotomy after angiography located a tumor of the blood vessels. The infratentorial area where the vessels were located was extremely difficult to access. The vessels feeding the tumor took time to ligate. The tumor was removed, bleeding was controlled, and the bone flap was secured.

This procedure is reported using CPT code 61686.

## Stereotaxis (61720–61791)

Stereotactic procedures completed on the brain are reported with codes 61720 to 61791. During stereotactic procedures, a computed tomography (CT) or magnetic resonance imaging (MRI) scan is used to scan the brain to locate the area of the brain in which the procedure will be performed. Burr holes are then used to access the brain to insert a needle, electrodes, catheters, or probes. This range of codes is differentiated by the procedure performed and the reason for the procedure.

## Stereotactic Radiosurgery (Cranial) (61796–61800)

This range of codes is used to report a procedure that uses externally generated ionizing radiation to eradicate specific targets in the head. No surgical incision is necessary. These codes would be reported by the neurosurgeon. The oncologist would report the appropriate 70000 codes for treatment delivery and management. Extensive instructional notes are present in the CPT manual.

## Neurostimulators, Intracranial (61850–61888)

Codes 61850 to 61888 are used to report procedures that involve both simple and complex neurostimulators. The codes are differentiated by the type of approach (twist drill, burr hole or craniotomy, craniectomy, and so on) and the type of neurostimulator placed. This range also contains codes for the insertion, replacement, revision, and removal of neurostimulators. There are coding guidelines located at the beginning of this code range that must be read and followed for proper code assignment.

## Repairs (62000–62148)

Repairs completed on the skull and skull vault are reported with codes 62000–62148. Terms to reference in the Alphabetical Index of the CPT manual include:

- Craniotomy, then encephalocele
- Repair, then encephalocele

- Cranioplasty
- Cranioplasty, then encephalocele
- Cranioplasty, then defect
- Cranioplasty, then autograft
- Cranioplasty, then bone graft

## Neuroendoscopy (62160–62165)

Neuroendoscopy procedures are reported with codes 62160 to 62165. A diagnostic neuroendoscopy is included in a surgical neuroendoscopy. The codes are differentiated by the reason for the neuroendoscopy, which may include:

- Dissection of adhesions
- Fenestration of septum pellucidum
- Excision of cyst
- Excision of tumor

## Cerebrospinal Fluid (CSF) Shunt (62180–62258)

Procedures that involve cerebrospinal fluid shunts are reported with codes 62180 to 62258. Cerebrospinal fluid shunts are placed to drain cerebrospinal fluid away from the brain. Figure 17-9 illustrates a cerebrospinal fluid shunt. This range of codes also reports replacement, irrigation, and removal of CSF shunts.

# Spine and Spinal Cord (62263–63746)

Procedures completed on the spine and spinal cord are reported with codes 62263 to 63746. In the CPT manual prior to code 62263 there are extensive instructional notations for the coder to review before assigning codes

**FIGURE 17-9** CSF Shunt

from this section of the manual. Locate and read the instructional notations found in the CPT manual. The codes are divided into the following areas:

- Injection, drainage, or aspiration (including codes for myelography via lumbar injection)—codes 62263 to 62329.
- Catheter implantation—codes 62350 to 62355.
- Reservoir/pump implantation—codes 62360 to 62370.
- Endoscopic decompression of neural elements and/or excision of herniated intervertebral discs—code 62380. Review the definitions that are found in the CPT manual prior to code 62380 before assigning this code.
- Posterior extradural laminotomy or laminectomy for exploration/decompression of neural elements or excision of herniated intervertebral discs—codes 63001 to 63053. Review the definitions that are found in the CPT manual prior to code 63001 before assigning codes from this range of codes.
- Transpedicular or costovertebral approach for posterolateral extradural exploration/decompression—codes 63055 to 63066.
- Anterior or anterolateral approach for extradural exploration/decompression—codes 63075 to 63091. Review the instructional notations that are found in the CPT manual prior to code 63075 before assigning codes from this range.
- Lateral extracavitary approach for extradural exploration/decompression—codes 63101 to 63103.
- Incision—codes 63170 to 63200.
- Excision by laminectomy of lesion other than herniated disc—codes 63250 to 63295.
- Excision, anterior or anterolateral approach, intraspinal lesion—codes 63300 to 63308. Review the instructional notations found in the CPT manual prior to code 63300 before assigning codes from this range of codes.
- Stereotaxis—codes 63600 to 63610.
- Stereotactic radiosurgery (spinal)—codes 63620 and 63621. Review the instructional notations that are found in the CPT manual prior to code 63620 before assigning codes in this range of codes.
- Neurostimulators (spinal)—codes 63650 to 63688. Review the instructional notations that are found in the CPT manual prior to code 63650 before assigning codes in this range of codes.
- Repair—codes 63700 to 63710.
- Shunt, spinal CSF—codes 63740 to 63746.

Many of these procedures are completed not only on the brain but also on the spine and spinal cord. Prior to code 62263, an extensive instructional note appears that instructs the coder in the use of codes 62263 to 62329 for catheter-based treatments. There are also references to the 70000 codes for radiological services that might be used in conjunction with this code range. Throughout this section of CPT, there are numerous instructional notes that should be referenced prior to code assignment.

Codes 62350–62351, catheter implantation, and codes 62360–62362, reservoir/pump implantation, are used to report the placement of a catheter or pump to allow for medication instillation into the spinal area.

Exploration and/or decompression of the spinal cord and nerve roots are reported with codes 63001–63053 and are differentiated by the type of approach and segment of the spinal area in which the procedure occurred.

Codes 63055 to 63066 are used to report a transpedicular or costovertebral approach for posterolateral extradural exploration and/or decompression, while codes 63075 to 63091 report an anterior or anterolateral approach for extradural exploration and/or decompression.

Procedures involving placement, revision, removal, and replacement of neurostimulators in the spinal cord area are reported with codes 63650 to 63688. Because neurostimulators are also placed in the brain, it is important for the coder to read the operative report carefully to determine the site of the neurostimulator. Codes 63700 to 63710 report repairs on the spinal cord. Shunt procedures involving cerebral spinal fluid, such as creation of shunts, and replacement and removals of shunt systems are reported with codes 63740, 63741, 63744, and 63746.

## Extracranial Nerves, Peripheral Nerves, and Autonomic Nervous System (64400–64999)

Procedures completed on the extracranial nerves, peripheral nerves, and autonomic nervous system are reported with codes 64400 to 64999. This range of codes is divided into the following areas:

- Introduction/injection of anesthetic agent (nerve block), diagnostic or therapeutic—code range 64400 to 64530. This section of codes is differentiated by procedures completed on the somatic nerves and procedures completed on the autonomic nerves. Codes 64461, 64462, and 64463 are contained within this range of codes but are resequenced codes. These codes report thoracic paravertebral blocks and codes 64461 and 64462 are differentiated by the number of injection sites, while code 64463 reports a continuous infusion by a catheter. They include imaging guidance when performed.
- Neurostimulators (peripheral nerves)—code range 64553 to 64595. This section is used to report the implantation of neurostimulator electrodes and is differentiated by the type of procedure completed and by the nerve on which the procedure was completed.
- Destruction by neurolytic agent (e.g., chemical, thermal, electrical, or radiofrequency, chemodenervation)—code range 64600 to 64681. This section of codes is differentiated by the destruction of somatic nerves and sympathetic nerves.
- Neuroplasty (exploration, neurolysis, or nerve decompression)—code range 64702 to 64727. These codes are differentiated by the anatomical site of the nerve (e.g., digit, arm, or leg).
- Transection or avulsion—code range 64732 to 64772. These codes are organized according to the nerve location.
- Excision—code range 64774 to 64823. Division of codes in this range is organized according to somatic nerves and sympathetic nerves.
- Neurorrhaphy—code range 64831 to 64876. These codes are used to report the suturing of nerves and are differentiated by the nerve sutured.
- Neurorrhaphy with nerve graft, vein graft, or conduit—code range 64885 to 64913. These codes are used to report nerve grafts and are differentiated by the site and the length of the graft.

When coding procedures that are completed on the nerves, the coder must identify the specific nerve on which the procedure was completed. Coding in this area can be complex, so coders are cautioned to read every detail of medical documentation pertaining to the procedure and all guidelines associated wtih the particular section of this chapter being referenced.

# Summary

- The central nervous system is composed of the brain and spinal cord.
- The peripheral nervous system is composed of the nerves that connect body organs to the central nervous system.
- There are 31 pairs of spinal nerves located in the spinal area.
- A craniectomy is completed to remove a skull bone.
- A craniotomy involves making an incision into the skull.

# Internet Links

To learn more about the nervous system and procedures completed on the nervous system, visit **http://www.innerbody.com**.

To view information about nerve injections, visit **http://www.spineuniverse.com**.

To learn about multiple types of spinal surgeries, visit **https://www.spine-health.com/treatment /back-surgery/lumbar-spine-surgery**.

# Chapter Review

## Fill in the Blank

**Instructions:** Fill in the blanks in the statements that follow.

1. The diencephalon is connected to the spinal cord by the _____.

2. The outermost layer of the meninges is the _____.

3. The middle layer of the meninges is the _____.

4. The innermost layer of the meninges is the _____.

5. The procedure to remove the skull bone is called a _____.

## True/False

**Instructions:** Indicate whether the following statements are true (T) or false (F).

6. _____ The largest portion of the brain is the cerebellum.

7. _____ The temporal lobe is where the nerves related to hearing, memory, and speech perception are located.

8. _____ The brachial plexus extends from the C1 vertebrae to the T3 vertebrae.

9. _____ Stereotactic procedures completed on the brain are reported using codes 61720 to 61750.

10. _____ The mesencephalon is located between the midbrain and the cerebrum.

# Coding Assignments

**Instructions:** Using the CPT manual, assign the correct code to the following procedures.

1. Craniectomy for drainage of intracranial abscess, infratentorial _____

2. Craniotomy for repair of encephalocele at skull base _____

3. Intradural cervical laminectomy for excision of intraspinal lesion _____

4. Repair of cerebrospinal fluid leak not requiring a laminectomy _____

5. Repair of 6.3-cm myelomeningocele _____

6. Laminectomy for excision of an intraspinal intradural neoplasm in the sacral (intradural) area _____

7. Stereotactic stimulation of spinal cord, percutaneous, separate procedure not followed by other surgery _____

8. Ventriculocisternostomy _____

9. Replacement of ventricular catheter _____

10. Removal of prosthetic plate of skull _____

11. Burr hole with biopsy of brain _____

12. Subtemporal cranial decompression _____

13. Stereotactic implantation of depth electrodes into the cerebrum for the long-term monitoring of seizure activity _____

14. Percutaneous intracranial balloon angioplasty _____

15. Supratentorial exploratory craniotomy _____

16. Burr hole for aspiration of intracerebral cyst _____

17. Puncture of shunt tubing for injection procedure _____

18. Intracranial craniotomy for hypophysectomy of pituitary tumor _____

19. Craniectomy with excision of foreign body from brain _____

20. Epidural injection of clot patch _____

21. Transcranial decompression of orbit _____

22. Reduction of craniomegalic skull _____

23. Removal of spinal neurostimulator electrode percutaneous array _____

24. Injection of anesthetic agent into maxillary trigeminal nerve _____

25. Facial-spinal accessory nerve anastomosis _____

26. Infratentorial exploratory craniotomy _____

27. Craniotomy with elevation of bone flap for selective amygdalohippocampectomy _____

28. Simple extradural elevation of depressed skull fracture _____

29. Cranioplasty for 3.5 cm diameter skull defect _____

30. Suture of sciatic nerve _____

31. Burr hole for ventricular puncture _____

32. Craniectomy for craniosynostosis with single cranial suture _____

33. Simple supratentorial surgery for intracranial arteriovenous malformation _____

34. Repair of encephalocele of skull vault with cranioplasty _____

35. Removal and replacement of complete cerebrospinal fluid shunt system at same operative session _____

# Case Studies

**Instructions:** Review each case and indicate the correct code(s).

## Case 1

**Preoperative and postoperative diagnosis:** Lower back pain

**Procedure:** Injection of 6% phenol into L4

The patient was placed in the spinal tap position, and the lumbar area was sterilized. An epidural needle was advanced into the L4 space, 2% Lidocaine was injected, and an epidural catheter was placed; 1.5 cc of 6% phenol was injected into the space. The catheter was removed, and the wound site was dressed. The patient was sent to the recovery area.

CPT code(s): _____

## Case 2

**Indications for surgery:** This 27-year-old male, who was in a motor vehicle accident just prior to arrival, suffered a head injury.

**Procedure:** Right frontal burr hole placement of ventriculostomy

**Operation:** After shaving the frontal scalp, the area was prepped and draped. A curvilinear posterolateral concave incision was made in the right frontal scalp, exposing the periosteum. A twist drill burr hole was placed in the right frontal skull. The dura was then opened with a blade knife, as was the pia. A ventricular catheter was placed, and there was good flow of cerebrospinal fluid. This helped relieve the brain edema. A catheter was tunneled out. The scalp was then stitched up, and a sterile dressing was applied. The patient was returned to the recovery room in good condition.

CPT code(s): _____

## Case 3

This 79-year-old female had suffered from high-pressure cerebral spinal edema. To take care of this issue, the patient underwent a right cerebrospinal fluid shunt system placement. At this time, she is ready for the shunt system to be removed. The patient was taken to the operating room, and this procedure was performed without incident.

CPT code(s): _____

## Case 4

**Indications:** This patient is a 32-year-old female who presented with a chief complaint of left leg pain radiating from the midcalf to the heel. There is no history of injury, and the use of anti-inflammatory medications, though it offered relief at first, has now stopped working for this patient. She states she has no feeling on the plantar aspect of the left foot at night. She was misdiagnosed several times until recently, when we confirmed the diagnosis of a damaged posterior tibial nerve. Until we do surgery, the extent of the damage is unknown.

**Procedure:** After induction of general anesthesia, the patient's left leg was prepped and draped in the usual sterile fashion. A vertical incision was made over the medial malleous into the subcutaneous level. Identifying the lacinate ligament overlying the posterior tibial nerve, the ligament was dissected, revealing a slightly damaged posterior tibial nerve. The damaged area was sutured using two sutures. The ligament was then repaired, and layered closure was performed. The patient tolerated the procedure and was sent to recovery in good condition.

CPT code(s): _____

## Case 5

Stephen is a 22-year-old male suffering from cerebral palsy. He has been dealing with muscle spasms for the past two years, but they have gotten increasingly worse in his right arm. After a brief examination and discussion of risks and benefits, it was decided to try a Botox injection in the right arm to try and offer some relief.

**Procedure:** The right arm was swabbed with Betadine, and the Botox injection was administered into the brachioradialis muscle. The patient tolerated the procedure well.

CPT code(s): _____

## Case 6

**Preoperative diagnosis:** Herniated disc at the right C7

**Postoperative diagnosis:** Herniated disc at the right C7

**Procedure:** Foraminotomy

This patient was administered general anesthesia and moved into the prone position. The cervical area was prepped and draped in the usual sterile manner. A midline incision was made posteriorly over the C7 vertebra. The incision was carried down to the paravertebral muscles through the lamina to reach the spinal cord. A foraminotomy was carried out, giving exposure to the nerve at C7. Once this was completed, the area felt well decompressed. The wound was irrigated out. Some extra bone was removed, and the disc was tapped into place. The wound was irrigated and closed with 3-0 coated Vicryl and 4-0 Vicryl in the skin.

CPT code(s): _____

## Case 7

**Preoperative diagnosis:** Pain in left leg

**Postoperative diagnosis:** Same

**Procedural Notes:**

This 43-year-old male patient was placed in the supine position, and his lumbar area was sterilized. An injection of 1.5% Lidocaine was placed into the L2–L3 space, and an additional injection for infiltration was placed into the interspinous ligament. A total of 8 cc was injected. The epidural space was then injected with 12 cc of 0.5% Lidocaine and 80 mg of Aristocort. The needle was removed, and the wound was dressed. There were no complications noted.

CPT code(s): _____

## Case 8

**History of Present Illness:** Three days ago the patient was in an automobile accident. At that time he refused to come to the hospital. Today he was brought to the hospital via ambulance due to headache and blurred vision. CT scan was completed and shows brain edema.

**Physical:** Pupils are reactive and equal. A complete H&P was completed and documented at the time of admission. At this time there are no other changes noted from the admission H&P.

**Assessment and Plan:** Traumatic diffuse brain edema. Surgical intervention is needed at this time to reduce the trauma caused to the brain.

**Procedure:** The patient was brought to the operating room and was prepped and draped for the procedure. IV sedation was administered.  Sedation was obtained. A curvilinear posterolateral concave incision was made in the right frontal scalp. A right twist drill burr hole was completed in the right frontal skull. Using a #11 knife, the dura was opened and the placement of a ventricular catheter was completed. After the placement of the catheter a flow of blood-tinged cerebrospinal fluid was obtained and the edema was reduced. The catheter was secured in place with 3-0 silk sutures.  There was minimal blood loss. Scalp was closed in layers and a sterile dressing was applied. The patient was sent to the recovery area in stable condition.

**Pre and Post Operative Diagnosis:** Diffuse brain edema, due to trauma.

**Procedure:** Placement of ventricular catheter via Burr Hole.

CPT code(s): _____

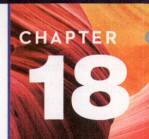

# Eye and Ocular Adnexa

## Chapter Outline

Introduction

Guidelines Related to the National
Correct Coding Initiative (NCCI)

Abbreviations Relating to the Eye and
Ocular Adnexa

Anatomy of the Eye

Procedures Completed on the Eyeball
(65091–65290)

Procedures Completed on the Anterior
Segment (65400–66999)

Procedures Completed on the Posterior
Segment (67005–67299)

Procedures Completed on the Ocular
Adnexa (67311–67999)

Procedures Completed on the
Conjunctiva (68020–68899)

Summary

Internet Links

Chapter Review

Coding Assignments

Case Studies

## Learning Objectives

### At the conclusion of this chapter, you should be able to:

1. Define key terms related to coding procedures on the eye and ocular adnexa.
2. Define abbreviations associated with the eye and ocular adnexa.
3. Describe the basic anatomy of the eye and ocular adnexa.
4. Define common procedures completed on the eye and ocular adnexa.
5. Apply coding guidelines for the eye and ocular adnexa.
6. Select CPT codes for procedures completed on the eye and ocular adnexa.
7. Identify and code procedures for the eye and ocular adnexa from case studies.

## Key Terms

| | | | |
|---|---|---|---|
| anterior chamber | ciliary body | evisceration | intracapsular extraction |
| aqueous humor | conjunctiva | exenteration | iris |
| chalazion | cornea | extracapsular extraction | lacrimal duct |
| choroid | enucleation | eyelashes | lacrimal gland |

| lens | optic nerve | retina | tarsorrhaphy |
| lower eyelid | orbital implants | sclera | upper eyelid |
| ocular implant | posterior chamber | scleral reinforcement | vitreous humor |
| optic disc | pupil | suspensory ligaments | |

# Introduction

The Eye and Ocular Adnexa subsection of the Surgery section of the CPT manual is used to code procedures completed on the eye and ocular adnexa. The eye is mostly contained in the bony orbit of the facial bones and is the structure that allows the transmission of images to the brain for vision to occur. When selecting codes for the eye and ocular adnexa, remember to read the code descriptions and notations that are present in the code manual carefully as there are many notations throughout this section that have an impact on code assignment.

# Guidelines Related to the National Correct Coding Initiative (NCCI)

The student will need to perform the following steps to obtain the most current coding guideline information related to this chapter online:

1. Log on to *https://www.cms.gov/medicare-medicaid-coordination/national-correct-coding-initiative-ncci /ncci-medicare/medicare-ncci-policy-manual*.
2. Scroll to the section titled "View Manual by Chapter."
3. Click "Chapter 8" for guidelines specific to the eye and ocular adnexa.

# Abbreviations Relating to the Eye and Ocular Adnexa

The following abbreviations are commonly used for the eye and ocular adnexa:                           .

| Abbreviations | Definitions |
|---|---|
| ARMD | age-related macular degeneration |
| ECCE | extracapsular cataract extraction |
| EOM | extraocular movement |
| ICCE | intracapsular cataract extraction |
| IOL | intraocular lens |
| IOP | intraocular pressure |
| LASIK | laser-assisted in situ keratomileusis |
| OD | right eye |
| Ophth | ophthalmology |
| OS | left eye |

*(continues)*

*(continued)*

| | |
|---|---|
| OU | both eyes |
| PERRLA | pupils equal, round, reactive to light and accommodation |
| PRK | photorefractive keratectomy |
| RK | radial keratotomy |
| VA | visual acuity |
| VF | visual field |

# Anatomy of the Eye

There are numerous parts of the eye. The white portion of the eye is known as the **sclera**. This fibrous membrane serves as a protective covering for the eye and maintains the shape of the eyeball. The **iris** is the colored portion of the eye. The **pupil** is in the center of the iris. The pupil controls the amount of light entering the eye. The **conjunctiva** is a colorless mucous membrane that lines the anterior part of the eye.

Tears are produced by the **lacrimal gland** and drain from the eye though the **lacrimal duct**. The lacrimal duct is located at the inner edge of the eye.

The eyes are covered by the **upper eyelid** and **lower eyelid**, which keep the surface of the eyeball lubricated and protected from particles. The **eyelashes** are located along the edge of the eyelids to protect the eye from foreign materials. These structures are identified in Figure 18-1.

**FIGURE 18-1** Front View of the Eye

The **cornea**, a transparent nonvascular structure, is located on the anterior portion of the sclera. The layer just beneath the sclera is the **choroid**, which contains capillaries that provide the blood supply and nutrients to the eye.

Posterior to the iris is the **lens**, which is a colorless structure that allows the eye to focus on images. The structures that are responsible for adjusting the lens are the **ciliary body** and muscle. Attached to the ciliary body and muscle are the **suspensory ligaments**, which attach to the lens and hold it in place.

The nerve cell layer of the eye is the **retina**, which changes light rays into nerve impulses. The impulses are transmitted to the brain by the **optic nerve**. On the optic nerve is a blind spot known as the **optic disc**, which is the point of entry for the artery that supplies blood to the retina.

There are two cavities that make up the interior of the eye, which are filled with a clear, watery fluid known as **aqueous humor**. The **anterior chamber** is located in front of the lens, and the **posterior chamber** is located behind the lens.

The posterior chamber is also filled with **vitreous humor**, a clear, jellylike substance that helps to shape the eye. Figure 18-2 illustrates a lateral cross-section of the eye, showing the relationships among the various structures of the eye.

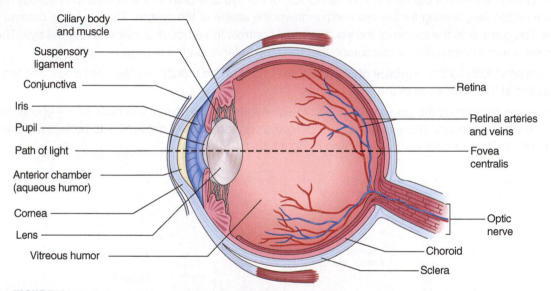

**FIGURE 18-2** Lateral Cross-Section of the Eye

# Procedures Completed on the Eyeball (65091–65290)

Code range 65091 to 65290 is used to report procedures completed on the eyeball. These codes are divided into the following sections:

- Removal of the eye
- Secondary implant procedures
- Removal of foreign body
- Repair of laceration

Code range 65091 to 65114 is used to report procedures that remove the eye or structures of the eye. To locate these procedures in the Alphabetical Index of the CPT manual, the coder would reference the following terms:

- Evisceration, then ocular contents. **Evisceration** means removal of an organ.
- Enucleation, then eye. **Enucleation** means to remove without cutting into the structure. Figure 18-3 illustrates an enucleation.
- Exenteration, then eye. **Exenteration** means the surgical removal of the contents of a cavity.

(A) Attachments of the globe are separated

(B) Optic nerve is transected

(C) Conjunctiva is approximated

**FIGURE 18-3** Enucleation

Codes in the 65091 to 65105 range, Evisceration of the Ocular Contents and Enucleation of the Eye, are differentiated by whether the procedure was performed with or without implants. Codes in the 65110–65114 range, exenteration of the orbit, are differentiated by whether the procedure occurred with the therapeutic removal of bone or with a muscle or myocutaneous flap.

Secondary implant procedures are performed both inside and outside of the muscular cone of the eye. An **ocular implant** is an implant performed inside the muscular cone and is reported with code range 65125–65175. The codes are differentiated according to the type of procedure, including modification of ocular implant, insertion of ocular implant secondary, reinsertion of ocular implant, and removal of ocular implant. Implants that are outside the muscle cone are known as **orbital implants**, and insertion and removal procedures are reported with codes 67550 and 67560. Be sure to look at the instructional notation following code 65175.

Code range 65205–65265 is used to report procedures completed to remove foreign bodies from the external eye or intraocular area. Codes 65205–65222 report procedures completed on the external eye, whereas codes 65235–65265 report intraocular foreign-body removal.

Repairs of lacerations of the conjunctiva and cornea are reported with code range 65270 to 65290. These codes are differentiated by the site of the repair, conjunctiva or cornea, and then by accompanying procedures. A unique feature of codes 65272 and 65273 is that the codes are differentiated by whether the patient was hospitalized.

# Procedures Completed on the Anterior Segment (65400–66999)

Code range 65400–66999 is used to report procedures completed on the anterior segment of the eye. This subsection is organized according to the structures found in the anterior segment: cornea, anterior chamber, anterior sclera, iris, ciliary body, and lens. The codes are then further organized according to the type of procedure completed: incision, excision, removal or destruction, or repair or revision. Table 18-1 summarizes some of the codes found in this section.

**TABLE 18-1** Anterior Segment (Selected Codes for Code Range 65400–66999)

| Codes | Description |
|---|---|
| 65710–65757 | This range is used to report keratoplasty, which is differentiated by whether or not the procedure was completed for aphakia or pseudophakia. During a keratoplasty, also known as a *corneal transplant*, the central part of the cornea is replaced with a graft. Figure 18-4 illustrates a corneal transplantation. |
| 65800–65880 | This range of codes is used to report incisional procedures completed on the anterior chamber. Procedures in this range include paracentesis of the anterior chamber of the eye, goniotomy, trabeculotomy, trabeculoplasty, and the severing of adhesions. |
| 65900–65930 | This range codes removals that occur in the anterior chamber. |
| 66020–66030 | This code range reports the injection of air, liquid, or medication into the anterior chamber of the eye. |
| 66130–66250 | Excisions and repairs or revisions completed on the anterior sclera are reported with this range of codes. It is important for the coder to read the operative report carefully to determine any accompanying procedures and the approach of the procedures, as codes are differentiated by this. For example code 66179 reports an aqueous shunt to extraocular equatorial plate reservoir, external approach without graft, while code 66180 reports the same procedure with the accompanying procedure of a graft placement. |
| 66500–66770 | This code range is used to report procedures completed on the iris and ciliary body. Procedures include incision, excision, repair, and destruction. When selecting codes for destructions, codes 66700–66770, the coder must be able to identify the method of destruction used, such as diathermy, cyclophotocoagulation, cryotherapy, laser, etc. |
| 66820–66991 | This code range is used to code procedures that are completed on the lens. The most common codes used in this section include codes for the removal of cataracts. These codes are differentiated by a number of factors that include whether the cataract was secondary; the type of cataract removal, extracapsular or intracapsular; and the removal of lens material according to the type of technique. Coders need to become familiar with the notation that appears in the CPT manual before the code 66830. This notation describes the procedures that are included as part of the code for the extraction of the lens. It should be noted that there are codes that are resequenced in this range of codes. |
| +66990 | This is an add-on code that is used to report the use of an ophthalmic endoscope. This code should be reported in addition to the code for the primary procedure that was completed. There is a notation immediately following this code description which lists the codes that this add-on code would apply to. |
| 66999 | This code reports an unlisted procedure of the anterior segment of the eye. |

**Extracapsular extraction** involves the removal of the lens without removing the posterior capsule. This would include codes 66840 to 66852, 66940, 66982, and 66984. Codes 66920, 66930, and 66983 are used to report the removal of the entire lens with the capsule, which is known as an **intracapsular extraction**. When a cataract is extracted and an intraocular lens prosthesis is inserted during the same operative session, codes 66982, 66983, and 66984 should be reported. Figure 18-5 illustrates an intracapsular and extracapsular cataract extraction.

(A) Trephination

(B) Placement of graft

(C) Graft sutured in position

**FIGURE 18-4** Corneal Transplant

Posterior
lens capsule

(A) Intracapsular: removal of the entire lens
    and lens capsule.

(B) Extracapsular: lens is removed with its anterior
    capsule, leaving posterior capsule intact.

**FIGURE 18-5** Types of Cataract Extractions

The exchange of an intraocular lens is reported by using code 66986, while the insertion of an intraocular lens after cataract removal is reported by the use of code 66985. The numerous notations found after code 66985 should be referenced.

Prior to completing cataract extraction, a preoperative evaluation needs to occur to determine whether there is justification for the procedure. Medicare has outlined requirements that must be met to justify the surgery, including the following.

There must be documentation of:

- Visual functional status
- Visual impairment
- Informed consent
- Preoperative ophthalmologic testing and medical assessment

It should also be noted that bilateral cataract extraction should not be performed on both eyes on the same day. This is to prevent bilateral vision loss if the procedures were to have complications.

## Exercise 18.1—Check Your Understanding

### Removal of Cataracts

Read the notation that appears in the CPT manual, under the heading of Removal, prior to code 66830. State yes if the procedure is included as part of the code for the extraction of the lens. State no if the procedure listed is not included as part of the code for the extraction of the lens.

1. Iridectomy _____
2. Repair of iris _____
3. Ciliary body destruction _____
4. Anterior capsulotomy _____
5. Subconjunctival injections _____

6. Posterior capsulotomy _____
7. Enzymatic zonulysis _____
8. Lateral canthotomy _____
9. Iridotomy _____
10. Viscoelastic agents _____

# Procedures Completed on the Posterior Segment (67005–67299)

Code range 67005 to 67299 is used to report procedures completed on the posterior segment of the eye. This code range is divided into the following sections:

- Vitreous
- Retina or Choroid
- Posterior Sclera
- Other Procedures

Codes that are reported using this range are summarized in Table 18-2.

**TABLE 18-2**  Posterior Segment (67005–67299)

| Codes | Description |
|---|---|
| 67005–67043 | This range of codes reports procedures completed on the vitreous. Code 67027 is used to report the implantation of an intravitreal drug-delivery system. During this procedure, an implant is placed in the vitreous that releases medication into the vitreous. Codes 67036–67043 are used to report mechanical vitrectomy completed by a pars plana approach. Before assigning codes 67036–67043, the coder needs to reference the operative report to ensure that the vitrectomy was mechanical. This is usually indicated in the operative report by the use of an ocutome, MicroVit, or daisy wheel probe. The coder will also need to note the extent of the procedure. The numerous notations that follow code 67043 should be referenced. |
| 67101–67121 | This code range is used to report repairs completed on the retina or choroid. Diathermy, cryotherapy, and photocoagulation are also methods used to reattach a retina. As instructed by the notation in the CPT manual, when more than one of these approaches are used during the same operative session, the principal modality used should be the therapy reported. Coders should read the operative report carefully and compare the CPT code descriptions to ensure proper code assignment, as many of these codes include multiple components. A detached retina can also be repaired by performing scleral buckling. In this procedure, the retinal breaks are identified and are treated with a cryoprobe, and then the breaks are supported with a scleral buckle. Code 67107 is used to report this procedure. Figure 18-6 illustrates scleral buckling. A complete repair of retinal detachments is reported using CPT code 67113. |
| 67141–67145 | Prophylaxis of retinal detachment is reported with these codes, which are differentiated according to the type of therapy used: cryotherapy and/or diathermy or photocoagulation. These procedures are often performed in repetitive sessions, and the codes are intended to include all of the sessions. Various payers have different reporting requirements for these codes. |
| 67208–67229 | Destructions of lesions of the retina or choroid, or extensive or progressive retinopathy, are reported with these codes. Codes are differentiated according to the type of therapy used to destroy the lesion or retinopathy, such as cryotherapy, diathermy, photocoagulation, radiation by implantation of source, or photodynamic therapy. These procedures are often performed in repetitive sessions, and the codes are intended to include the sessions. Various payers have different reporting requirements for these codes. |
| 67250–67255 | Repairs of the sclera, known as **scleral reinforcement**, are reported with these codes, which are differentiated by whether or not a graft was placed. |
| 67299 | This is the Unlisted Procedure code for procedures completed on the posterior segment of the eye. |

(A) Preparation of sclera for buckle          (B) Scleral buckle sutured in place

**FIGURE 18-6**  Scleral Buckling for Treatment of Retinal Detachment

# Procedures Completed on the Ocular Adnexa (67311–67999)

Code range 67311 to 67999 is used to report procedures completed on the ocular adnexa. The codes are grouped according to the following:

- Extraocular muscles
- Orbit
- Eyelids

There are six muscles that are arranged in pairs surrounding the eye. They are responsible for the ability of the eye to move. The pairs are as follows:

- Superior and inferior rectus
- Superior and inferior oblique
- Lateral and medial rectus

These muscles are illustrated in Figure 18-7. Coders must have an understanding of the muscles of the eye to select codes from code range 67311–67318, strabismus surgery, because specific muscles are identified in the descriptions of the codes. Strabismus surgery is completed to correct a deviation that occurs in one eye. These codes are for unilateral procedures. Code assignment is also based on the number of muscles on which surgery was performed.

Code range 67400–67599 is used to report procedures completed on the orbit that include exploration, excision, and decompression of the orbital area. Terms to reference in the Index of the CPT manual to locate codes in this section include:

- Orbitotomy
- Orbit, then implant
- Orbit contents, then aspiration

**FIGURE 18-7** Muscles of the Eye.

- Orbit transplant
- Optic nerve, then decompression

Procedures completed on the eyelids are assigned to codes 67700–67999. These codes are divided into the following sections:

- Incision
- Excision, Destruction
- **Tarsorrhaphy**, the entire or partial suturing of the eyelids together
- Repair (Brow, Ptosis, Blepharoptosis, Lid Retraction, Ectropion, and Entropion)
- Reconstruction
- Other Procedures

A common procedure that falls within this code range is an excision of a chalazion of the eyelid. A **chalazion** is a small tumor of the eyelid that is formed by retention of secretions of the meibomian gland. Codes 67800–67808 are assigned to report the excision, which are differentiated by the number of tumors removed, by the eyelids involved, whether general anesthesia was used, and whether hospitalization occurred.

Repairs completed on the eyelids are assigned to codes 67900–67924. Codes are differentiated according to the type of repair and the site of the repair. Reconstruction procedures completed on the eyelids fall into code range 67930–67975. Procedures in this range include suturing of a recent wound of the eyelid, removal of a foreign body embedded in the eyelid, canthoplasty, and reconstruction of the eyelid by full-thickness transfer of a skin flap. Code 67999 is for unlisted procedures completed on the eyelids.

# Procedures Completed on the Conjunctiva (68020–68899)

Code range 68020–68899 reports procedures completed on the conjunctiva, including procedures completed on the lacrimal system. Terms to reference in the Index of the CPT manual to locate codes from this section include:

- Conjunctivoplasty
- Conjunctiva, then the type of procedure, such as biopsy, incision and drainage, or lesion destruction
- Conjunctivorhinostomy
- Dacryocystorhinostomy
- Lacrimal duct, then the procedure
- Lacrimal gland, then the procedure
- Lacrimal punctum, then the procedure
- Lacrimal sac, then the procedure

# Summary

- The white portion of the eye is known as the *sclera*.
- The iris is the colored portion of the eye.
- The pupil is in the center of the iris.

- The cornea is located on the anterior portion of the sclera.
- The layer just beneath the sclera is the choroid.
- The structures that are responsible for adjusting the lens are the ciliary body and muscle.
- The anterior chamber is located in front of the lens, and the posterior chamber is located behind the lens.
- An ocular implant is placed inside the muscular cone, while an orbital implant is placed outside the muscle cone.
- There are six muscles that are arranged in pairs surrounding the eye.
- Extracapsular extraction involves the removal of the lens without removing the posterior capsule.
- The removal of the entire lens with the capsule is known as *intracapsular extraction*.
- When selecting codes for the eye and ocular adnexa, remember to read the code descriptions and notations that are present in the code manual carefully, as there are many notations throughout this section that have an impact on code assignment.

# Internet Links

To learn about conditions of the eye and procedures completed on the eye, visit ***http://www.medicinenet.com*** and search for the type of procedure, such as keratoplasty. Also visit ***http://www.allaboutvision.com*** and search for the name of the procedure, such as cataract surgery. Visit ***http://www.ascrs.org***, the website of the American Society of Cataract and Refractive Surgery.

# Chapter Review

## Fill in the Blank

**Instructions:** Fill in the blanks in the statements that follow.

1. Tears are produced by the _____.

2. Implants that are outside the muscle cone are known as _____.

3. Posterior to the iris is the _____, which is a colorless structure that allows the eye to focus on images.

4. To remove without cutting into the structure is called _____.

5. The posterior chamber is also filled with _____, a clear, jellylike substance that helps to shape the eye.

## True/False

**Instructions:** Indicate whether the following statements are true (T) or false (F).

6. _____ Code 67101 would be used to report a repair of retinal detachment by cryotherapy, including drainage of subretinal fluid.

7. _____ The retina is a transparent nonvascular structure located on the anterior portion of the sclera.

8. _____ The colored portion of the eyeball is called the *pupil*.

9. _____ Light rays are changed into nerve impulses, which travel to the brain via the optic nerve.

10. _____ Codes in the 65110–65114 code range are differentiated by whether a repair of the cornea or the conjunctiva was performed.

# Coding Assignments

**Instructions:** Using the CPT manual, assign the correct code to the following procedures.

1. Ciliary body destruction by diathermy _____

2. Diagnostic scraping of cornea for smear sample _____

3. Removal of blood clot from anterior segment of eye _____

4. Repair of conjunctival laceration, nonperforating laceration sclera, direct closure _____

5. Radial keratotomy _____

6. Reduction of overcorrection of ptosis _____

7. Exchange of intraocular lens _____

8. Canthotomy _____

9. Fine needle aspiration of orbital contents _____

10. Injection of medication into Tenon's capsule _____

11. Conjunctivoplasty with buccal mucous membrane graft _____

12. Probing of lacrimal canaliculi with irrigation _____

13. Plastic repair of canaliculi _____

14. Repair of retinal detachment by injection of air _____

15. Destruction of macular edema by diathermy _____

16. Scleral reinforcement with graft _____

17. Biopsy of conjunctiva _____

18. Subconjunctival injection _____

19. Partial dacryoadenectomy _____

20. Destruction of progressive retinopathy by cryotherapy _____

21. Canthoplasty _____

22. Fenestration of optic nerve sheath _____

23. Iridectomy with corneoscleral section for removal of one lesion _____

24. Diagnostic aspiration of aqueous via paracentesis of the anterior chamber of the eye _____

25. Repair of scleral staphyloma with graft _____

26. Keratoprosthesis _____

27. Corneal biopsy _____

28. Removal of epithelial downgrowth of the anterior chamber of the eye _____

29. Iridotomy by stab incision _____

30. Release of vitreous fluid pars plana approach _____

31. Intraocular removal of foreign body from anterior chamber of lens _____

32. Incision for corneal relaxing for correction of surgically induced astigmatism _____

33. McCannel suture _____

34. Repositioning of intraocular lens prosthesis via incision _____

35. Scleral reinforcement, no grafting completed _____

# Case Studies

**Instructions:** Review each case and indicate the correct code(s).

## Case 1

**Preoperative diagnosis:** Foreign object in right eye

**Postoperative diagnosis:** Same

**Procedure:** Removal of foreign body from right eye

The patient was brought to the operating suite, and 2% Lidocaine was injected into the right eye. A slit lamp was used to visualize the area. The object was embedded in the conjunctiva. A V-shaped incision was made to access the foreign object. The object was removed with the side of the beveled edge of an optic needle. An antibiotic was applied to the surface of the eye. The patient tolerated the procedure well and was sent to the recovery area.

**CPT code(s):** _____

## Case 2

**Postoperative diagnosis:** Lesion on left eye sclera

**Procedure:** Lesion excision

The patient was prepped and draped in the usual fashion and placed under general anesthesia. An incision was made in the left eye conjunctiva to visualize the lesion. The lesion was 0.5 cm and was removed with scleral scissors. Because of the small incision and the obtaining of hemostasis, sutures were not used to close the site. An antibiotic was used in the eye, and a 24-hour pressure patch was applied. The patient had no complications and was sent to the recovery room.

**CPT code(s):** _____

## Case 3

**Preoperative and postoperative diagnosis:** Nuclear cataract of left eye

**Procedure:** Cataract removal with lens implant of left eye

The patient's identification was verified, and a peribulbar block was administered into the left eye. The patient was then prepped and draped in the usual sterile fashion. The placement of a lid speculum occurred, and a paracentesis was made using a diamond blade.

*(continues)*

*(continued)*

Viscoelastic was used to fill the anterior chamber. A triplanar temporal clear-corneal incision was made. A 360-degree capsulorrhexis was completed, and the lens was then hydrated and removed in segments. An aspirator tip was then used to remove the remaining cortical material from the area. Viscoelastic was used to fill the bag, and the lens was then inserted into the bag. After this, the viscoelastic was removed, and the area was hydrated. A Kenalog injection was given. The patient tolerated the procedure with no complications or difficulties. Blood loss was minimal.

CPT code(s): _____

# Case 4

**Preoperative and postoperative diagnosis:** Obscuring vision after cataract, right eye

**Procedure:** YAG laser discission

The patient was brought into the laser room, and identification was determined. The patient was given Mydfrin 2.5% and Mydriacyl 1% in the right eye prior to the use of the laser at 900. Immediately prior to the use of the laser, Alcaine 0.5% was placed in the right eye. A laser was used to perform a capsulotomy of secondary membranous cataract tissue. The laser was started at 1000 and was finished at 1001. No complications were noted. Alphagan P 0.15% was placed in the patient's right eye following the use of the laser.

CPT code(s): _____

# Case 5

**Preoperative and postoperative diagnosis:** Hemorrhage of vitreous of the right eye and retinal detachment

**Procedure:** Trans pars plana vitrectomy and cryoretinopexy of right eye

**Anesthesia:** General

The patient was brought to the operating room and prepped and draped in a sterile fashion. General anesthesia was administered. A speculum was placed in the right eye, and an incision was made into the conjunctiva and Tenon's. Bleeding was present. A complete vitrectomy was performed using a pars plana approach. The patient's retina was then attached via cryoretinopexy. This area was closed and sealed with 6-0 interrupted Vicryl sutures. The conjunctiva and Tenon's were closed with 6-0 plain sutures. Antibiotics and additional topical medications were applied. The patient tolerated the procedure well and was sent to the recovery area in satisfactory condition.

CPT code(s): _____

## Case 6

**Preoperative diagnosis:** Retinal break

**Postoperative diagnosis:** Same

This 58-year-old male patient presents for a prophylaxis cryotherapy treatment of a retinal break of the right eye. Under conscious sedation, a speculum is used at the lateral aspect of the right eyeball, and the cryoprobe is used to seal the break on the lateral aspect of the right eyeball. The patient tolerated the procedure well and was sent home in good condition. He will return in three days for follow-up.

**CPT code(s):** _____

## Case 7

A 15-year-old female presented to the emergency room today complaining of "something in my eye." The irritation started just prior to arrival. She said that she was sitting outside reading when she felt a sensation around her right eye, and then the irritation was present. She tried flushing the eye, but it still feels like something is in there. The patient was lying supine, with her head slightly raised when I inspected the eye. There appears to be some trichiasis. Using a biomicroscope and forceps, several eyelashes were removed, which alleviated the problem. The patient left the emergency room in good condition.

**CPT code(s):** _____

## Case 8

**Preoperative diagnosis:** Chalazion of left upper eyelid

**Postoperative diagnosis:** Same

**Anesthesia:** General

**Procedural Notes:**

This three-year-old male patient was placed in the supine position, and general anesthesia was administered. A chalazion clamp was applied to the left upper eyelid to expose the posterior surface of the eyelid with the lid inverted. The chalazion was incised and purulent contents drained. To control hemostasis, the lid was cauterized. Garamycin ointment was applied to the left eye. The clamp was released. There were no complications, and the patient was sent to the recovery area.

**CPT code(s):** _____

# Auditory System and Operating Microscope

## Chapter Outline

Introduction

Guidelines Related to the National Correct Coding Initiative (NCCI)

Abbreviations Associated with the Auditory System

Anatomy of the Auditory System

Procedures Completed on the External Ear (69000–69399)

Procedures Completed on the Middle Ear (69420–69799)

Procedures Completed on the Inner Ear and the Temporal Bone, Middle Fossa Approach (69801–69979)

Operating Microscope

Summary

Internet Links

Chapter Review

Coding Assignments

Case Studies

## Learning Objectives

### At the conclusion of this chapter, you should be able to:

1. Define key terms related to coding procedures on the auditory system.
2. Define abbreviations associated with the auditory system.
3. Describe the basic anatomy and functions of the auditory system.
4. Define common procedures completed on the auditory system.
5. Apply the specific coding guidelines to this chapter.
6. Select CPT codes for procedures completed on the auditory system.
7. State the code used to report the use of an operating microscope.

## Key Terms

| | | | |
|---|---|---|---|
| auditory ossicles | cerumen | cochlear duct | external auditory canal |
| auditory tube | ceruminous glands | earlobe | external auditory meatus |
| auricle | cilia | endolymph | external ear |
| bony labyrinth | cochlea | eustachian tube | incus |

| | | | |
|---|---|---|---|
| labyrinth | oval window | semicircular ducts | tympanostomy |
| malleus | perilymph | stapes | utricle |
| membranous labyrinth | pharyngotympanic tube | tympanic cavity | vestibule |
| middle ear | pinna | tympanic membrane | |
| organ of Corti | saccule | tympanic neurectomy | |
| otoplasty | semicircular canals | tympanoplasty | |

# Introduction

The auditory system enables a person to hear and to maintain balance when the head and body move. The structures of the ear pick up sound waves for interpretation by the brain. The ear also plays a role in the maintenance of equilibrium by sending messages to the brain about the position and movement of the head.

# Guidelines Related to the National Correct Coding Initiative (NCCI)

Perform the following steps to obtain the most current coding guideline information related to this chapter online:

1. Log on to https://www.cms.gov/medicare-medicaid-coordination/national-correct-coding-initiative-ncci/ncci-medicare/medicare-ncci-policy-manual.
2. Scroll to the section titled "Review Manual by Chapter."
3. Click "Chapter 8" for guidelines specific to the auditory system.

# Abbreviations Associated with the Auditory System

The following abbreviations are used in reference to the auditory system:

| Abbreviations | Definitions |
|---|---|
| AD | right ear |
| AS | left ear |
| AU | both ears |
| BC | bone conduction |
| BOM | bilateral otitis media |
| dB | decibel |
| ENT | ears, nose, throat |
| Oto | otology |
| PE tube | pressure equalization tube |
| TM | tympanic membrane |

# Anatomy of the Auditory System

The structures that comprise the auditory system are divided into three regions: external ear, middle ear, and inner ear. Figure 19-1 illustrates the regions of the ear.

The **external ear** is the visible, outermost part of the ear and is not within the structure of the skull. There are two structures that make up the external ear: the auricle and the external auditory meatus. The **auricle**, also known as the **pinna**, is a flexible cartilaginous flap that has a bottom portion known as the **earlobe**. The auricle allows sound waves to enter the ear canal, which is known as the **external auditory canal** or the **external auditory meatus**. Along the external auditory canal, tiny hairs called **cilia** are present that aid in transmitting sound waves inward to other auditory structures. Also within the external auditory canal are sweat glands, called **ceruminous glands**, that secrete a honey-colored, thick, waxy substance known as earwax or **cerumen**. Cerumen helps to protect and lubricate the ear. In combination with the cilia, the cerumen helps to protect the eardrum from foreign objects. The eardrum, known as the **tympanic membrane**, separates the external ear from the middle ear. The tympanic membrane is a thin, semitransparent membrane, silvery gray in color, that transmits sound vibrations to the inner ear through the auditory ossicles.

The auditory ossicles are part of the **middle ear**. The middle ear, also known as the **tympanic cavity**, is found within the temporal bone and houses the auditory ossicles and the eustachian tube. The **auditory ossicles** consist of three small bones that transmit and amplify sound waves. The bones are named according to their shape:

- **Malleus**—shaped like a hammer
- **Incus**—shaped like an anvil
- **Stapes**—shaped like a stirrup

The tube that connects the bony structures of the middle ear to the pharynx is the **eustachian tube**. The eustachian tube is also known as the **auditory tube** or **pharyngotympanic tube**. The purpose of the eustachian tube is to equalize air pressure within the middle ear.

**FIGURE 19-1** External, Middle, and Inner Ear

The middle ear is separated from the inner ear by the **oval window**. Within the inner ear, also known as the **labyrinth**, are bony structures and membranous structures. The bony structures, called the **bony labyrinth**, consist of the following:

- **Vestibule**—the central portion of the inner ear. This structure contains the **utricle** and the **saccule**, which are membranous sacs that aid in maintaining balance.

- **Semicircular canals**—located behind the vestibule, these are three bony structures that are filled with fluid that also help to maintain balance. The **semicircular ducts** are also found in this area and aid in balance.

- **Cochlea**—a snail-shaped, bony structure that contains **endolymph** and **perilymph**, which are auditory fluids that transmit sound. The **organ of Corti**, also found in the cochlea, is the true organ of hearing. The **cochlear duct**, a membranous structure, is found in this area of the ear and aids in the hearing process. The tiny hair cells found in the organ of Corti are stimulated by the sound vibrations. These sound vibrations convert to nerve impulses and are carried to the brain.

The **membranous labyrinth** is a term that is used to describe the utricle, saccule, semicircular ducts, and cochlear ducts, because these structures are all membranous structures.

Figure 19-2 illustrates numerous structures found in the ear.

**FIGURE 19-2**  Structures of the Ear

# Procedures Completed on the External Ear (69000–69399)

The first subsection of codes, 69000–69399, is used to report procedures completed on the external ear. These codes are grouped as follows:

- Incision
- Excision
- Removal
- Repair
- Other Procedures

# Incision (69000–69090)

This range of codes is used to report drainages that are completed on the external ear and for ear piercing. Codes 69000 and 69005 are used to report the drainage of an abscess or hematoma of the external ear. For both of these procedures, a small incision is made in the skin to drain the contents of the abscess or hematoma. At times, it is necessary to insert a drainage tube and to pack the area. When the physician devotes an extensive amount of time to cleaning the area and the time is documented in the patient's record, it is appropriate to select code 69005, which denotes that the procedure was complicated. Often during this more complicated procedure, antibiotic eardrops are used, and a soft sponge is placed in the ear canal. Code 69020 is used to report the drainage of an abscess of the external auditory canal. At times, packing will occur to absorb abscess material and to promote healing. Ear piercing is reported by code 69090.

# Excision (69100–69155)

Code range 69100–69155 is used to report biopsies and excisions completed on the external ear. Table 19-1 summarizes codes 69100 to 69155.

**TABLE 19-1**  Code Range 69100–69155

| Codes | Description |
|---|---|
| 69100 and 69105 | These codes report biopsies of the external ear that are completed for diagnostic purposes. During these procedures, the physician uses an instrument to excise tissue. Code 69100 reports a biopsy on the external ear, while code 69105 reports a biopsy completed on the external auditory canal. If the incisional area is large, a suture closure may be necessary. Packing in the ear canal may be necessary for some biopsies completed in the ear canal. |
| 69110 and 69120 | Excisions completed on the external ear are reported with these codes. The codes are differentiated by the size of the area excised. Code 69110 reports a partial excision with a simple repair, while code 69120 reports a complete amputation. After the complete amputation, the site is typically closed during a second procedure that involves a skin flap or graft. |
| 69140 and 69145 | Excisions completed on the external auditory canals are reported with these codes. The approach for both of these procedures is to enter the ear canal through the external opening of the ear. The physician will then make an incision to remove the bony growth or the soft-tissue lesion. |
| 69150 and 69155 | These codes are used to report a radical excision of an external auditory canal lesion. During both of these procedures, the physician makes a postauricular incision to remove the lesion. Code 69150 is reported when the procedure is completed without neck dissection. When neck dissection occurs, thus removing the lymph nodes from the side of the neck of the procedure, code 69155 is reported. |

# Removal (69200–69222)

Code range 69200–69222 is used to report the removal of a foreign body or debridement of the mastoid cavity. Codes 69200 and 69205 report foreign body removal from the external auditory canal. These codes are differentiated by whether or not general anesthesia was used. Unilateral removal of impacted cerumen using irrigation/lavage is reported with code 69209. Unilateral removal of impacted cerumen requiring instrumentation is coded by reporting code 69210. There are numerous instructional notations that follow code 69210 that need to be reviewed prior to assigning code 69210. Locate these notations in the CPT manual and review them.

Codes 69220 and 69222 report debridement of the mastoid cavity. These procedures are completed for patients who have undergone a radical or modified radical mastoidectomy. Because of the extent of this procedure, the site has to be cleaned every three to six months. If the procedure is completed bilaterally, modifier 50 should be reported. When routine cleaning occurs, code 69220 is reported. If anesthesia is used or extensive cleaning occurs, code 69222 is reported.

# Repairs and Other Procedures (69300–69399)

Coders should read the notation that is present at the start of this subcategory. The notation instructs the coder to use code range 12011–14302 to report the suturing of a wound or injury of the external ear.

This code range, 69300–69320, is used to report only otoplasty and reconstructions of the external auditory canal. Code 69300 is used to report **otoplasty**, plastic surgery of the ear, for a protruding ear. Reconstructions of the external auditory canal are reported with codes 69310 and 69320. The codes are differentiated by whether the reconstruction occurred because of congenital atresia or for another reason. When selecting these codes, the coder must identify the diagnosis on the operative report to justify code selection.

# Procedures Completed on the Middle Ear (69420–69799)

The second subsection of codes, 69420–69799, is used to report procedures completed on the middle ear. These codes are divided into the following ranges:

- Incision—codes 69420 to 69450
- Excision—codes 69501 to 69554
- Repair—codes 69601 to 69676
- Osseointegrated Implants—codes 69714–69719, 69726, 69727
- Other Procedures—codes 69700 to 69799

## Incision (69420–69450)

Codes 69420–69421 include procedures that involve the eustachian tubes. These codes are used to report myringotomy that includes aspiration and/or eustachian tube inflation, with or without general anesthesia. Removal of a ventilating tube that is completed using general anesthesia is reported by using code 69424. Since this procedure is often performed bilaterally, the coder would need to add a modifier of 50 to report the bilateral procedure. After code 69424, an instructional notation appears in the CPT manual that lists codes that are not to be reported with code 69424.

**Tympanostomy** is an incision made into the tympanic membrane to create an opening in the membrane. This procedure is completed using local, topical, or general anesthesia and is reported with codes 69433 or 69436, depending on the type of anesthesia used. Modifier 50 is added for a bilateral procedure.

Code 69440 is used to report the exploration of the middle ear through a postauricular ear canal incision, and code 69450 is used to report a transcanal tympanolysis.

## Excision (69501–69554)

Code range 69501 to 69554 is used to report excisional procedures that are completed on the middle ear. To locate these procedures in the Index of the CPT manual, reference the following terms:

- Mastoidectomy, then the type of procedure: complete, revision, radical, simple, and so on
- Resection, then temporal bone
- Excision, then lesion, then middle ear or excision, then tumor, then middle ear

## Repair (69601–69676)

Repairs completed on the middle ear are coded with code range 69601–69676. These codes are summarized in Table 19-2.

**TABLE 19-2** Code Range 69601–69676

| Codes | Description |
|---|---|
| 69601–69604 | This range of codes reports revision mastoidectomy. The codes are differentiated by the intensity of the procedure performed: complete mastoidectomy, modified radical, radical, or the completion of a tympanoplasty. |
| 69610 | When a tympanic membrane repair is completed, this code is reported. This code may or may not include site preparation, and may or may not include the placement of a patch. |
| 69620 | This code is used to report myringoplasty. This is confined to the drumhead and donor site. |

*(continues)*

**TABLE 19-2** (continued)

| Codes | Description |
|---|---|
| 69631–69646 | These codes are used to report tympanoplasty, the surgical repair of the tympanic membrane. The codes are differentiated by the accompanying procedures that are completed with the tympanoplasty, such as mastoidectomy, antrotomy, etc. Coders must read the operative reports and carefully match the description of the procedure with the description found in CPT because many procedures are grouped into each code found in this section of CPT, thus elevating the need for multiple codes. |
| 69650–69662 | Procedures completed on the stapes are reported with this range of codes. Included are stapes mobilization, stapedectomy, and revisions of stapes. |
| 69666 and 69667 | Repair and revision of an oval window or round window fistula are reported with these codes. |
| 69670 | This is a separate procedure code that is used to report mastoid obliteration. |
| 69676 | This code reports a unilateral tympanic neurectomy, which is the removal of the Jacobson's nerve that is located in the middle ear. If the procedure is completed bilaterally, add modifier 50. |

## Osseointegrated Implants (69714–69719, 69726, 69727)

Codes 69714, 69716, 69717, 69719, 69726, and 69727 are used to report procedures that involve an osseointegrated implant device that is placed into the skull to treat hearing loss. Locate these codes in the CPT manual and review the instructional notations that appear prior to code 69714. Note that these codes are differentiated according to implantation, replacement and removal.

## Other Procedures (69700–69799)

Procedures reported using code range 69700–69799 include:

- Closure of postauricular fistula
- Surgical nasopharyngoscopy with dilation of eustachian tube
- Implantation or replacement of hearing devices and implants
- Removal and repair of devices and implants
- Decompression and suturing of facial nerves

Unlisted procedures completed on the middle ear are coded with code 69799.

## Exercise 19.1—Check Your Understanding

### Matching

Match Column 1 to the definition in Column 2.

| Column 1 | Column 2 |
|---|---|
| 1. 69210 | a. transcanal tympanolysis |
| 2. ceruminous glands | b. equalizes pressure in the middle ear |
| 3. endolymph | c. ears, nose, and throat |
| 4. 69450 | d. unilateral removal of impacted cerumen requiring instrumentation |
| 5. middle ear | e. sweat glands in the external auditory canal |
| 6. ENT | f. biopsy of external auditory canal |
| 7. AD | g. left ear |
| 8. AS | h. an auditory fluid that transmits sound |
| 9. auditory tube | i. right ear |
| 10. 69105 | j. contains the auditory ossicles |

# Procedures Completed on the Inner Ear and the Temporal Bone, Middle Fossa Approach (69801–69979)

Code range 69801–69979 is used to report procedures completed on the inner ear and the temporal bone. Figure 19-3 illustrates the structures that are found in the inner ear. These codes are divided into the following ranges of codes:

- Incision and/or destruction—code range 69801–69806. This range is used to report such procedures as labyrinthotomy, and endolymphatic sac operations without a shunt or with a shunt. The coder must read the notes found here for proper code assignment.

- Excision—code range 69905–69915. Labyrinthectomy and vestibular nerve section are reported with these codes. The coder must be able to identify the approach used for the labyrinthectomy to properly select a code.

- Introduction—code 69930. Implantation of a cochlear device is reported with this code. The procedure may or may not include a mastoidectomy.

- Temporal bone, middle fossa approach—code range 69950–69979. Procedures reported with this range of codes include vestibular nerve section, facial nerve decompression, decompression of auditory canal, and removal of tumor.

**FIGURE 19-3** Inner Ear Structures

# Operating Microscope

Following the codes for the auditory system, code 69990 appears in the CPT manual. This code reports the use of an operating microscope with any procedure completed in CPT, except for those codes in which the use of the operating microscope is included. Code 69990 is not reported when the operating microscope is used to magnify or enhance visualization. Code 69990 should not be reported with the codes that are listed in the instructional notation that appears in the CPT manual preceding the description of code 69990. This is an add-on code, so it must accompany another CPT code for the primary procedure.

# Summary

- The auditory system is divided into three regions: external ear, middle ear, and inner ear.
- The external ear is composed of the auricle, external auditory meatus, and tympanic membrane.
- The middle ear consists of the malleus, incus, and stapes.
- The inner ear consists of the bony labyrinth and membranous labyrinth.
- The eustachian tube is also known as the *auditory tube* or *pharyngotympanic tube*.

# Internet Links

To learn more about the auditory system and procedures completed on the auditory system, visit the following site:

- **http://www.vestibular.org** to reference information on surgical procedures completed on the ear. (Search for descriptions of various ear surgeries.)

# Chapter Review

## Fill in the Blank

**Instructions:** Fill in the blanks in the statements that follow.

1. The auditory canal is located in the _____ section of the ear.

2. The external ear and middle ear are separated by the _____.

3. The middle ear is separated from the inner ear by the _____.

4. The middle ear is also known as the _____.

5. An incision made into the tympanic membrane to create an opening in the membrane is known as a(n) _____.

6. Plastic surgery of the ear is called _____.

7. A bony structure found in the middle ear that is shaped like a hammer is the _____.

8. Excisions completed on the middle ear are reported with codes _____.

9. Code 69990 is used to report the use of a(n) _____.

10. The unlisted procedure code for procedures completed on the inner ear is _____.

# Coding Assignments

**Instructions:** Using the CPT manual, assign the correct code to each of the following procedures.

1. Endolymphatic sac operation with shunt placement _____

2. Mobilization of stapes _____

3. Complete mastoidectomy _____

4. Bilateral removal of impacted cerumen requiring instrumentation _____

5. Biopsy of right earlobe _____

6. Implantation of osseointegrated implant, skull with magnetic transcutaneous attachment to external speech processor. This was completed outside of the mastoid and there was a removal of 105 sq mm surface area of bone deep to the outer cranial cortex. _____

7. Ventilating tube removal under general anesthesia _____

8. Transcanal tympanolysis _____

9. Patch placed after site preparation with tympanic membrane repair _____

10. Ear canal incision with middle ear exploration _____

11. Excision of aural polyp _____

12. Labyrinthectomy with mastoidectomy _____

13. Revision of stapedotomy _____

14. Implantation of cochlear device with mastoidectomy _____

15. Meatoplasty, external auditory canal, due to extensive infection _____

16. External auditory canal excision of soft-tissue lesion _____

17. Debridement of the mastoidectomy cavity _____

18. Bilateral surgical nasopharyngoscopy with balloon dilation of eustachian tube _____

19. Inner ear fenestration revision operation _____

20. Tympanic neurectomy _____

21. Decompression of internal auditory canal _____

22. Myringotomy with aspiration and eustachian tube inflation _____

23. Transmastoid antrotomy _____

24. Repair of oval window fistula _____

25. Excision aural glomus tumor; transcanal _____

26. Closure postauricular fistula, mastoid _____

27. Removal of tumor of temporal bone _____

28. Repair of round window fistula, AD _____

29. Biopsy of external auditory canal, AS _____

30. Bilateral otoplasty of protruding ear with size reduction _____

# Case Studies

**Instructions:** Review each case and indicate the correct code(s).

## Case 1

**Preoperative and postoperative diagnosis:** Chronic otitis media in left ear

**Procedure:** Myringotomy with tube insertion

**Anesthesia:** General

The patient was prepared and draped in the usual fashion. After the induction of anesthesia, an incision was made in the left tympanic membrane. The cavity was found to contain a thick mucus material, which was removed. A tympanostomy tube was placed in the left ear. There were no complications noted, and the patient was sent to the recovery room in satisfactory condition.

**CPT code(s):** _____

## Case 2

**Preoperative and postoperative diagnosis:** Foreign object in right ear

**Procedure:** Foreign body removal

**Anesthesia:** General

This 3-year-old male was brought to the operating room and placed under general anesthesia for removal of a foreign body from his right ear. Under direct visualization, a forcep was used to remove a paper clip that was located in the external auditory canal. There was minimal bleeding in the canal, and no other complications were noted. The patient was sent to the recovery suite.

**CPT code(s):** _____

## Case 3

**Preoperative diagnosis:** Tinnitus

**Postoperative diagnosis:** Tinnitus

**Procedure:** Middle ear exploration through postauricular incision, right ear

**Anesthesia:** General

**Indications:** This is a 42-year-old male who has had ringing in his right ear for the past three weeks. Preliminary testing has not revealed any problems, so we will be performing an exploratory procedure on the middle ear.

**Procedure:** The anesthesiologist administered general endotracheal anesthesia without incident. A curved incision was made just past the postauricular crease. The middle ear canal was exposed after the eardrum was carefully lifted posteriorly. The ossicular chain mobility was tested, and no abnormalities were noted. The eardrum was gently repositioned, and the canal skin was also moved back into place. The ear canal was packed. The incision was then sutured with 4-0 Vicryl. The patient was returned to the recovery room in good condition.

**CPT code(s):** _____

## Case 4

**Preoperative diagnosis:** Labyrinthitis, worsening, left ear

**Postoperative diagnosis:** Labyrinthitis, worsening, left ear

**Procedure:** Labyrinthectomy with mastoidectomy, postauricular incision, left ear

**Anesthesia:** General endotracheal

(*continues*)

*(continued)*

**Indications:** This is a 72-year-old male who has had hearing loss in his left ear for the past three months. Preliminary testing has revealed worsening labyrinthitis of the lining of the labyrinth.

**Procedure:** The anesthesiologist administered general endotracheal anesthesia without incident. A curved incision was made just past the postauricular crease. Using the drill, the mastoid cavity was drilled out. The posterior ear canal wall looks to be sound and intact. There is a large area of inflammation found to be in the lining of the labyrinth moving into the posterior semicircular canals. Under microscopic guidance the horizontal, posterior, and superior semicircular canals were removed, along with the lining of the labyrinth. The eardrum was gently repositioned, and the canal skin was also moved back into place. The ear canal was packed. The incision was then sutured with 4-0 Vicryl. The patient was returned to the recovery room in good condition.

**CPT code(s):** _____

# Case 5

**Preoperative diagnosis:** Bilateral persistent T-tubes with small tympanic granuloma

**Postoperative diagnosis:** Same

**Operation:** Removal of bilateral T-tubes with bilateral patching of the eardrums.

**Indications for surgery:** Examination reveals persistent T-tubes in place over the anterior/inferior quadrant with a small amount of tympanic granuloma and no purulence or any granuloma inside the middle ear space. There was a moderate amount of tympanosclerosis over the eardrums bilaterally.

**Procedure:** Under general anesthesia, using a laryngeal mask, the ears were scrubbed and draped in the usual manner. Under operating microscope, the ear canals were cleaned, and the eardrums and tubes could be well visualized.

Tubes were removed, along with the small granuloma round them. The eardrums showed some tympanosclerosis bilaterally with no signs of chronic inflammation, granuloma, or any cholesteatoma in the middle ear space. There was drainage on either side.

The edges of the eardrum perforations were refreshed, and the perforation was covered with an EpiDisc. A small piece of Gelfoam was laid carefully over the EpiDisc graft, and the ear canals were filled with Bacitracin ointment.

The patient was awakened and left the operating room in good and stable condition.

**Blood loss:** less than 1 cc.

**CPT code(s):** _____

# Radiology

## Chapter Outline

Introduction

Guidelines Related to the National Correct
  Coding Initiative (NCCI)

Terminology Associated with Radiology

Abbreviations Associated with Radiology

Coding for Radiology

Diagnostic Radiology (70010–76499)

Diagnostic Ultrasound (76506–76999)

Radiologic Guidance (77001–77022)

Breast Mammography (77046–77067)

Bone/Joint Studies (77071–77092)

Radiation Oncology (77261–77799)

Nuclear Medicine (78012–79999)

Summary

Internet Links

Chapter Review

Coding Assignments

Case Studies

## Learning Objectives

### At the conclusion of this chapter, you should be able to:

1. Define key terms related to coding radiologic procedures.
2. Define abbreviations associated with radiologic procedures.
3. Define common radiologic procedures.
4. Select CPT codes for radiologic procedures as they relate to documentation requirements.
5. Identify and code procedures for radiology from case studies.

## Key Terms

abduction

adduction

A-mode technique

angiography

anteroposterior

aortography

arteriography

arthrography

axial

bone density test

brachytherapy

B-scan

cineradiography

complete study

computed axial
  tomography (CAT)

decubitus

Diagnostic Radiology

Doppler

dosimetry

dual photon
  absorptiometry

echocardiography

endovascular repair

eversion

extension

fluoroscopy

follow-up/repeat study

hyperthermia

inversion

isodose

lateral

limited study

lymphangiography

magnetic resonance
imaging (MRI)

mammography

M-mode technique

nuclear medicine

oblique

port

positron emission
tomography (PET)

posteroanterior

prone

proton beam treatment

pulmonary perfusion
imaging

radiologic technician

radiologist

radiology

radiopharmaceuticals

real-time scanning

scanning

simulation

supine

teletherapy

tomography

ultrasonography

uptake

venography

views

x-ray

# Introduction

**Radiology** is the study of x-rays, high-frequency sound waves, and high-strength magnetic fields, which sometimes includes the use of radioactive compounds, to diagnose and/or treat diseases or injuries. Radiology looks at internal structures of the body. A **radiologist** is a doctor whose specialty is radiology. The person who is specially trained to use the equipment that generates the pictures or studies is known as a **radiologic technician**.

# Guidelines Related to the National Correct Coding Initiative (NCCI)

Perform the following steps to obtain the most current coding guideline information related to this chapter online:

1. Log on to *https://www.cms.gov/medicare-medicaid-coordination/national-correct-coding-initiative-ncci/ncci-medicare/medicare-ncci-policy-manual*.
2. Scroll to the section titled "Review Manual by Chapter."
3. Click "Chapter 9" for guidelines specific to radiology.

# Terminology Associated with Radiology

An understanding of some of the terminology used in the positioning of a patient as the radiological procedure is performed aids the coder in selecting the appropriate code for the service provided.

| Term | Definition |
| --- | --- |
| **Abduction** | To move away from the body |
| **Adduction** | To move toward the axis of the body |
| **Anteroposterior** | From front to back |
| **Axial** | Referencing the axis of a structure or part of the body |
| **Decubitus** | Patient is on his or her back or stomach, which helps in localizing fluid |

*(continues)*

*(continued)*

| Term | Definition |
|------|-----------|
| Eversion | Turning outward |
| Extension | Movement that increases an angle of a joint |
| Inversion | Turning inward or turning inside out |
| Lateral | On the side |
| Oblique | Different angles |
| Posteroanterior | Back to front |
| Prone | Horizontal position but facedown |
| Supine | Lying on back |

## Exercise 20.1—Check Your Understanding

### Terminology

Using the terms listed in the preceding box, provide the position described by the example given.

1. Mr. Kasson was lying facedown on the examination table. _____
2. The small boy's ankle was turned inward. _____
3. Dr. Kelly wanted an x-ray view coming in from the side of Joey's arm. _____
4. Dr. Martin wanted Steven to have the scan done in a position that required him to lie on his back so that fluid would collect in the ankle. _____
5. When Tracy fell, her arm had to be moved away from her body to allow for a better view of her injury. _____

Radiology is not just about x-rays. The specialty of radiology includes CT or CAT scans, MRI, fluoroscopy, echocardiography, and mammography, just to name a few aspects. Because of the vast number of radiological tests that are available, we will define only a few; this list is by no means comprehensive.

| Term | Definition |
|------|-----------|
| Angiography | X-ray visualization of the heart and blood vessels after intravascular introduction of a contrast medium. |
| Arteriography | Radiologic visualization of arteries after the introduction of a contrast medium into the bloodstream or into a vessel. |
| Arthrography | Radiographic visualization of the inside of a joint using a contrast medium. |
| Cineradiography | A type of x-ray that films at a high speed in order to take a series of images of motion in an organ or system. This technique combines fluoroscopy, radiography, and the use of a camera to film images on a fluorescent screen. |

*(continues)*

*(continued)*

| Term | Definition |
|---|---|
| Computed axial tomography (CAT) | Cross-sectional images are produced after an ionizing radiational substance is administered. This is a noninvasive test, usually diagnostic. |
| Doppler | Frequency change in sound, light, or radio waves given off by a source as it moves toward or away from the observer. Often used in determining velocity of blood flow. |
| Echocardiography | Ultrasound is used to study the structures of the heart. |
| Fluoroscopy | Immediate serial images are produced using roentgen rays, which allow for examination of the function of a body part or organ. |
| Magnetic resonance imaging (MRI) | Radio frequency signals are used to examine the soft tissue and bony structures of the body without radiation. |
| Mammography | Radiographic examination of soft breast tissue for benign or malignant growths. |
| Positron emission tomography (PET) scan | Radioactive substances are administered that allow images of various body structures to be examined in color codes that indicate the degree and intensity of the metabolic process. |
| Scanning | A study that displays images of body areas by recording and displaying the images for evaluation. |
| Tomography | A detailed cross-section of tissue structures are produced. |
| Ultrasonography | Sound waves are passed over body structures to send a signal to a computer, which is then turned into a picture for examination. |
| X-ray | Electromagnetic waves are used to produce a picture of internal structures of the body. |

# Exercise 20.2—Check Your Understanding

## Vocabulary Understanding

Using the previous box of terms and definitions, match the term to the correct definition.

_____ 1. Tomography

_____ 2. Scanning

_____ 3. X-ray

_____ 4. Echocardiography

_____ 5. MRI

a. A study that displays images of body areas by recording and displaying the images for evaluation.

b. An ultrasound used to study the structures of the heart.

c. A detailed cross-section of tissue is produced.

d. Radio frequency signals used to examine the soft tissue and bony structures of the body without radiation.

e. Electromagnetic waves used to produce a picture of internal structures of the body.

# Abbreviations Associated with Radiology

| Abbreviations | Definitions |
|---|---|
| AP | anteroposterior |
| CAT | computed axial tomography |
| CT | computed tomography |
| CXR | chest x-ray |
| ECHO | echocardiogram |
| Fx | fracture |
| KUB | kidneys, ureters, and bladder |
| MRI | magnetic resonance imaging |
| PET | positron emission tomography |
| Rad | radiation absorbed dose |
| Rad Onc | radiation oncology |
| SPECT | single-photon emission computed tomography |
| u/s | ultrasound |

# Coding for Radiology

The radiology specialty is constantly changing, and the coding changes with it. The Radiology chapter of the CPT manual routinely has updates. The coder should review changes and updates frequently to keep up with information that may be critical for reimbursement to the provider.

Like other parts of the CPT manual, the codes in the Radiology chapter are arranged by anatomical site, starting with the head and neck and moving down the body, then by body system. CPT manual divides the chapter into sections that include the following:

- Diagnostic Radiology—e.g., magnetic resonance imaging (MRI) and interventional radiologic procedures
- Diagnostic Ultrasound—e.g., A-mode, B-scan
- Radiologic Guidance—e.g., fluoroscopic guidance
- Breast Mammography
- Bone and Joint Studies
- Radiation Oncology
- Nuclear Medicine—including diagnostic and therapeutic procedures

The CPT codes for the Radiology chapter begin with code 70010 and go through 79999. The radiologist may report services that fall outside this chapter of CPT, such as cardiac catheterizations. Likewise, physicians, surgeons, and other practitioners can select codes from within this chapter when they apply to the services they perform.

# Diagnostic Radiology (70010-76499)

**Diagnostic Radiology** is the section of the Radiology chapter that is used to report a procedure or service rendered during the assessment of a disease for a more definitive diagnosis, as well as its progression or remission.

This section of CPT refers to different **views**, or the position of the patient in relation to the camera or device used to take the pictures. Attention to the way the code reads and how the service is performed is very important.

> **EXAMPLE:** 70210 Radiologic examination, sinuses, paranasal, less than three views

Some codes also mention "with or without contrast." When a code refers to contrast, this means that the patient has been administered a substance that will enhance the image produced. There are different substances, as well as different ways to administer the substance.

> **EXAMPLE:**
> 70450    Computerized tomography, head or brain; without contrast material
> 70460    With contrast material(s)
> 70470    Without contrast material, followed by contrast material(s) and further sections

The codes in this subsection of CPT begin with diagnostic imaging codes for the head and neck and then move to the chest, spine, and pelvis, and then the upper and lower extremities. Following these sections, the code selection moves into the abdomen and gastrointestinal tract, urinary tract, gynecological and obstetrical areas, and then the heart and vascular procedures.

## Exercise 20.3—Check Your Understanding

### Understanding Radiology Coding

Using the CPT manual, code the following from the Diagnostic Radiology subsection of the Radiology chapter.

1. MRI of spinal canal, thoracic; with contrast _____

2. X-ray of the femur, one view _____

3. CT of the abdomen; without contrast material _____

4. Cholecystography, oral contrast _____

5. Urography, infusion, drip technique and/or bolus technique _____

6. Endoscopic catheterization of the biliary ductal system, radiological supervision and interpretation _____

7. Pelvimetry without placental localization _____

8. Diagnostic CT colonography including image postprocessing _____

9. CT of the lumbar spine with contrast material _____

10. Single view, frontal, chest x-ray _____

## Vascular Procedures (75600–75893)

The coding for vascular procedures is extremely difficult for coders because the knowledge of basic anatomy is not enough to code the services rendered correctly. Coding for procedures done on arteries is different than coding for procedures done on veins. Knowledge of the anatomy of a vascular family is essential, as is an understanding of where the surgeon is during each step of an op note. Table 20-1 notes the vascular procedure codes.

Contrast injections, roadmapping, venography, and angiography are services that would be included in the interventional procedure. Separately billable services are identified within the guidelines for this section, so the

CPT manual should be referenced for other services that may or may not be reported. It should also be noted that the radiological procedures are only one component of coding the services rendered. The movement of the catheter is also a service that needs to be reported. Codes from the 36000 code range should be referenced in addition to the codes from this subsection of the chapter.

**TABLE 20-1** Vascular Procedures (75600–75893)

| Codes | Description |
|---|---|
| 75600–75630 | **Aortography**—aorta and branches are injected with contrast material to visualize problems.<br>The site should be referenced to determine the correct code to report the service performed. |
| 75635 | Computed tomographic angiography, abdominal aorta, and bilateral iliofemoral lower extremity runoff. This code includes the imaging that is done prior to as well as following the administration of contrast. |
| 75705–75774 | Angiography—the site should be referenced to determine the correct code to report the service performed. Introduction of a catheter or injection procedures might be performed at the same time as the angiography. Additional code assignments might need to be reported depending on the documentation. |
| 75801–75807 | **Lymphangiography**—examination of the lymphatic system after contrast material has been injected.<br>The site for the procedure, as well as whether the procedure was done unilaterally or bilaterally, needs to be identified to determine the correct code to report the service performed. |
| 75809 | Shuntogram for investigation of previously placed indwelling nonvascular shunt (e.g., LeVeen shunt, ventriculoperitoneal shunt, indwelling infusion pump), radiological supervision and interpretation. |
| 75810 | Splenoportography, radiological supervision and interpretation.<br>The site should be referenced to determine the correct code to report the service performed. |
| 75820–75880 | **Venography**—x-ray image of the veins, also referred to as a *phlebography*. |
| 75885–75887 | Percutaneous transhepatic portography with or without hemodynamic evaluation, radiological supervision and interpretation.<br>This is a radiographic exam of the portal vein of the liver. |
| 75889–75891 | Hepatic venography, wedged or free, with or without hemodynamic evaluation, radiological supervision and interpretation. |
| 75893 | Venous sampling through catheter, with or without angiography (e.g., for parathyroid hormone, renin), radiological supervision and interpretation. |

## Exercise 20.4—Check Your Understanding

### Vascular Procedures

Using Table 20-1 and your CPT manual, select the correct CPT code.

1. Percutaneous transhepatic portography with hemodynamic evaluation, radiological supervision and interpretation _____.

2. Hepatic venography, wedged, without hemodynamic evaluation, supervision and interpretation _____.

3. Thoracic aortography injected with contrast material to perform a serialography, radiological supervision and interpretation _____.

4. Phlebography performed bilaterally on an extremity, radiological supervision and interpretation _____.

5. Splenoportography, radiological supervision and interpretation _____.

# Transcatheter Procedures (75894–75989)

Transcatheter procedures are addressed in the next subsection of this chapter. Table 20-2 notes the codes that fall within this code set.

**TABLE 20-2** Transcatheter Procedures (75894–75989)

| Code(s) | Description |
|---|---|
| 75894 | Transcatheter therapy—This procedure involves catheter placement for infusion to clinically obstruct blood flow to a clogged vessel or tumor, treat vascular malformations, or control hemorrhaging. |
| 75898 | Angiography through existing catheter for follow-up study for transcatheter therapy, embolization or infusion, other than for thrombolysis is reported with this code. |
| 75901–75902 | Mechanical removal of pericatheter obstructive material/intraluminal material from central venous device via separate venous access or device lumen, radiologic supervision and interpretation. The notes that appear following the codes in the CPT manual should be followed. |
| 75956–75959 | Endovascular repair—repair within the vessel. The site of the repair should be referenced to determine the correct code to report the service performed. |
| 75970 | This code reports transcatheter biopsy, radiological supervision and interpretation. Note the instructional notations that follow this code in the CPT manual. |
| 75984 | This code is used to report the changing of a percutaneous tube or drainage catheter with contrast monitoring. It includes the radiological supervision and interpretation. There are numerous notations that follow this code that should be read prior to code assignment. |
| 75989 | Radiological guidance (e.g., fluoroscopy, ultrasound, or computed tomography) for percutaneous drainage (e.g., abscess, specimen collection), with placement of catheter, radiological supervision and interpretation. |

## Exercise 20.5—Check Your Understanding

**Transcatheter Procedures**

Using Table 20-2 and your CPT manual, fill in the blanks in the sentences that follow.

1. To report angiography through existing catheter for follow-up study for transcatheter therapy, embolization or infusion, other than for thrombolysis, use code _____.
2. Repair within the vessel is also known as a(n) _____.
3. To report transcatheter therapy, embolization—any method—radiological supervision and interpretation use code _____.
4. To report radiological guidance for percutaneous drainage with placement of catheter and radiological supervision and interpretation, use code _____.
5. Transcatheter biopsy, radiological supervision and interpretation, would be coded using code _____.

# Other Procedures (76000–76499)

The last subsection in the Diagnostic Radiology section of this chapter of the CPT manual covers other procedures. Code 76000 reports a fluoroscopy (separate procedure) for up to 1 hour of physician or other qualified health care professional time. The instructional notation that follows code 76000 needs to be referenced to identify the codes that cannot be reported in conjunction with code 76000. Codes for other procedures performed at the same time as the fluoroscopy may be billed separately, but the NCCI or CPT should be consulted for any additional notes. Table 20-3 lists some of the codes found in code range 76000 to 76499.

**TABLE 20-3** Other Procedures

| Code(s) | Description |
|---------|-------------|
| 76098 | Radiological examination, surgical specimen<br>The surgeon will complete the operation once the specimen has been examined. |
| 76100 | Radiologic examination, single plane body section (e.g., tomography), other than with urography |
| 76120 | Cineradiography/videoradiography, except where specifically included |
| 76125 | Cineradiography/videocardiology to complement routine examination (list separately in addition to code for primary procedure). This is an add-on code. |
| 76145 | This code reports the evaluation of the radiation dose for a patient to assure the safe delivery of radiation that exceeds the institutional review threshold. The provider will evaluate the technical aspects of radiation given to the patient with a goal of achieving a desired diagnostic or therapeutic result. The completion of the report is included in this code as well as the evaluation. |

## Exercise 20.6—Check Your Understanding

**Other Procedures**

Using your CPT manual, code the following.

1. An unlisted fluoroscopic procedure _____.
2. Cineradiography _____.
3. Radiologic exam of child, looking for foreign body from nose to rectum _____.
4. Computed tomography, with a limited or localized follow up study _____.
5. An unlisted magnetic resonance procedure _____.

# Diagnostic Ultrasound (76506–76999)

This subsection of the chapter is organized by anatomical site, beginning with the head and neck and moving down the body to the extremities. If an ultrasound is performed to establish a diagnosis, the technique used and the extent of the study are what impact code selection.

> **EXAMPLE:** 76881 Ultrasound, complete joint (i.e., joint space and periarticular soft tissue structures) real-time with image documentation

The extent of the study indicates whether the study was complete, limited, or follow-up/repeat. A **complete study** is a study that encompasses the entire body area. A **limited study** is a partial scan or examination of a body area or quadrant. It also would be used to report a single-organ examination. **Follow-up/repeat study** is a study performed on an area that requires an additional completed, documented study or exam. Throughout this subsection of the CPT manual instructional notations appear that give direction for specific code ranges. For example locate code 76881. Prior to code 76881 an instructional notation appears that provides guidance on the reporting of codes 76881 and 76882. Review the notation as it also provides guidance on the documentation requirements that need to be recorded for codes that are reported in this subsection.

Different techniques that a coder might encounter in documentation include A-mode, B-scan, M-mode, real-time, and Doppler. Doppler studies have previously been explained. The **A-mode technique** is a one-dimensional measurement. **B-scan** is a two-dimensional image. The **M-mode technique** is a type of ultrasound technique that takes the measurements of the velocity and amplitude of moving echo-producing structures and allows for one-dimensional viewing. **Real-time scanning** provides a two-dimensional image of both structure and movement.

When reporting services from this subsection, the coder should verify that there is not only an image present in the medical record, but also a written report to accompany this image. Should the record be missing either of these pieces, the service cannot be reported.

---

### Exercise 20.7—Check Your Understanding

**Diagnostic Ultrasound (76506–76999)**

Using the CPT manual, locate the correct CPT code for the services provided.

1. Ultrasound, chest, real time, with image documentation _____
2. Ultrasound, transvaginal _____.
3. Fetal biophysical profile, without nonstress testing _____.
4. Ultrasound, infant hips, real time with imaging documentation; no manipulation _____.
5. Intraoperative ultrasonic guidance _____.

**Fill in the blanks in the following sentences, using the information in this text on diagnostic ultrasound.**

6. Supporting documentation must include a(n) _____ report along with a(n) _____ and must be found in the medical record.
7. The _____ is a one-dimensional measurement.
8. A(n) _____ is a partial scan or examination of a body area or quadrant.
9. This subsection of the chapter is organized by _____.
10. _____ provides a two-dimensional image of both structure and movement.

---

# Radiologic Guidance (77001–77022)

Codes 77001–77022 are used to report fluoroscopic guidance, computed tomography (CT) guidance, magnetic resonance guidance, and other radiologic guidance. Numerous instructional notations appear after the codes. These notations need to be read and followed. For example, code 77001 contains a notation that signals to the coder that code 77001 should not be used with code 77002 and other codes listed. Reference the CPT manual to locate this note. Some insurance payers are no longer paying these codes because they are considering them to be included in the main procedure.

# Breast Mammography (77046–77067)

Code range 77046–77067 reports mammography procedures. Reference this range of codes in the CPT coding manual and note the detail in the description of the codes. Some of the code descriptions state that the imaging is completed without contrast material as described in code 77046. Other code descriptions state that the procedure is completed without and with contrast materials. This type of description is seen in code 77048. Another common item to note is the use of the terms unilateral or bilateral. For example, code 77065 is used to report a unilateral mammography, whereas code 77066 is used to report a bilateral mammography. Also note the use of the terms diagnostic and screening. Screening procedures are completed when there are no signs of a disease process. Diagnostic procedures are completed when there are signs of a disease process such as when there is mass in a breast. Codes 77061 and 77062 report diagnostic digital breast tomosynthesis whereas code 77063 reports a screening digital breast tomosynthesis. Documentation needs to support a diagnostic or a screening procedure.

# Bone/Joint Studies (77071–77092)

Bone and joint studies are reported using codes 77071–77092. The codes are differentiated by the type of study, such as:

- Bone age studies
- Bone length studies
- Osseous survey
- Joint survey
- Bone mineral density study

Bone studies are found in the diagnostic radiology subsection of the chapter. A bone age study can be done to determine what the skeletal age is by comparing the x-ray of a wrist and hand to a standard equal to chronological age. Code 77072 should be referenced for this study.

Code 77073 is referenced to study the length of the long bones in the skeleton. There are usually four films included in this study, which would include views of the hip, leg, knee, and ankle.

Also found in this area of the Diagnostic Radiology codes are CT scans and dual energy x-ray absorptiometry (DXA) bone density tests. A **bone density test** is used to determine the presence of osteoporosis by looking at the mass or density of the bone.

Codes 77089–77092 are used to report imaging that is completed to determine the structural condition of the bone microarchitecture to obtain a trabecular bone score (TBS). Review the codes for the full code description and note that code 77089 is not to be reported with codes 77090, 77091, and 77092. Code 77089 is a comprehensive code whereas codes 77090, 77091, and 77092 denote only components that relate to code 77089.

# Radiation Oncology (77261–77799)

Oncology radiology is therapeutic, as opposed to diagnostic, in nature. The patient is typically undergoing treatment for a malignant neoplasm that may respond to radiation by eradicating or shrinking the neoplasm or obstruction, relieving pain. The codes in this chapter of CPT are for actual treatment and should not be used to report consultations or other evaluation and management services that occur between the radiation oncologist and the patient. Services that would be included in these codes are the actual clinical treatment, medical radiation, planning, and the delivery and management of the radiation services.

To determine the best course of treatment, clinical treatment planning comprises planning and simulation. The planning half of the services is reported using codes 77261–77263, which are noted in Table 20-4.

Simulation is the other half of the treatment planning. **Simulation** mimics the disease so that field settings for the size and location of ports to be used can be determined. These codes are reported only once per setup procedure (see Table 20-5). A dedicated simulator, a radiation therapy treatment unit, or a diagnostic x-ray machine can be used.

**TABLE 20-4** Radiation Oncology

| Code | Description |
| --- | --- |
| 77261 | Therapeutic radiology treatment planning; simple<br><br>A simple planning requires a single treatment area of interest encompassed in a single port or simple parallel opposed ports with simple or no blocking. A **port** is a point of entry for treatment. |
| 77262 | ; intermediate<br><br>The use of this code would require three or more converging ports and two separate treatment areas, multiple blocks or special time dose constraints. |
| 77263 | ; complex<br><br>Complex planning requires highly complex blocking, custom shielding blocks, tangential ports, special wedges or compensators, three or more separate treatment areas, rotational or special beam considerations, and combinations of therapeutic modalities. |

**TABLE 20-5** Additional Radiation Oncology Codes

| Code | Description |
| --- | --- |
| 77280 | Therapeutic radiology simulation-aided field setting; simple<br><br>Simple simulation is the simulation of a single treatment area. |
| 77285 | ; intermediate<br><br>Intermediate simulation involves the simulation of two separate treatment areas. |
| 77290 | ; complex<br><br>Complex simulation involves three or more treatment areas, or any number of treatment areas if any of the following are involved: particle, rotation or arc therapy, complex blocking, custom shielding blocks, brachytherapy simulation, hyperthermia probe verification, and any use of contrast materials. |
| 77295 | 3-dimensional radiotherapy plan, including dose-volume histograms<br><br>Some of the tests produce a three-dimensional image of a tumor or associated critical structures. This three-dimensional image is reported using this code. Documentation to report this code must include dose distribution and 3-D volume reconstruction. Add on code 77293 is used with this code and code 77301 to report respiratory motion management simulation in addition to the primary procedure code. |

The next section of the Radiation Oncology subsection is medical radiation physics, dosimetry, treatment devices, and special services. The code set is 77295–77370. In order to code from this section, the coder needs to understand some of the terms used. These are defined in the following box:

| Term | Definition |
| --- | --- |
| Brachytherapy | An internal radiation therapy that is used to treat tissue |
| **Dosimetry** | The scientific determination of the rate, amount, and dose of radiation to be administered |
| **Isodose** | Equal-intensity doses of radiation to more than one area |
| **Teletherapy** | An external radiation treatment where the machine delivers the radiation after being positioned a specified distance from the patient |

Radiation treatment delivery encompasses the radiation therapy, as well as the care of the patient throughout his or her treatment. Physician involvement needs to be documented and should include the patient's response to treatment, including any adverse effects. A nonphysician may deliver the treatment, but a physician does need to be involved in the other aspects of the patient's care, such as prescribing and approving the treatment plan.

Radiation and neutron beam treatment delivery codes begin with code 77401, radiation treatment delivery, superficial and/or ortho voltage, and go to 77425. These codes cover the delivery of the radiation and neutron beam treatment.

The next range of codes, 77427, radiation treatment management, five treatments, through code 77499, unlisted procedure, therapeutic radiology treatment management, is used to report radiation treatment management services. The coder should be aware of the instructional notation that follows the heading of Radiation Treatment Management, which is found before code 77427 in the CPT manual. Review the notation and the Radiation Management and Treatment Table that are located in the CPT manual. Locate code 77401 and review the codes that follow. It should be noted that there are out of sequence codes that appear in this subsection of CPT, codes 77385 to 77387 and codes 77424 and 77425.

Radiation treatment management is reported in units of five fractions or treatment sessions. Sessions are not time driven. Multiple treatment sessions on the same day are counted separately so long as there is a distinct break noted in therapy sessions, and the fractions being counted would typically be rendered on a separate date. Evaluation and Management (E/M) services related to treatment management should not be billed separately because they are also included in these services. Additional detailed information is found in the instructional note that appears under the heading Radiation Treatment Management.

The next sets of codes involve proton beam treatment delivery and hyperthermia treatments. **Proton beam treatment** delivery is reported using codes 77520–77525. Proton beam treatment is used to treat malignancies by using a high dose of radiation on tumors, but it does not exceed the radiation tolerance of normal healthy tissue. Areas this may apply to include the optic nerves and the spinal cord.

**Hyperthermia** is a treatment using heat, such as ultrasound, probes, and radiofrequencies, together with radiation therapy, to treat malignancies by speeding up cell metabolism. Speeding up cell metabolism makes the malignancy more vulnerable to the therapy. Hyperthermia treatment is reported using codes 77600–77620.

The radiation oncology subsection of the chapter finishes off with clinical **brachytherapy**. Brachytherapy involves the use of natural or artificial radio elements that are inserted into the body next to or inside the tumor. Treating cancer in this way allows for higher doses of radiation to a smaller, more focused area.

## Exercise 20.8—Check Your Understanding

### Radiation Oncology

Using information from the Radiation Oncology section, fill in the blanks with the correct term(s) to complete each of the statements that follow.

1. To determine the best course of treatment, clinical treatment planning comprises _____ and _____.

2. _____ is a treatment used to treat malignancies by using high doses of radiation on tumors, but it does not exceed the radiation tolerance of normal healthy tissue.

3. _____ is a term used to indicate equal-intensity doses of radiation to more than one area.

4. "A therapeutic radiology simulation-aided field setting; simple" is reported by code _____.

5. A treatment using heat is referred to as _____ treatment.

# Nuclear Medicine (78012-79999)

**Nuclear medicine** treats and diagnoses diseases using radioactive isotopes. The subsection on nuclear medicine is broken down by whether the procedure is diagnostic or therapeutic in nature. Then it moves on to classifying by body system. Diagnostic workups and follow-up care are not included in these services unless the code specifies that they are.

The endocrine system starts off the chapter. The code series begins with 78012 and goes through 78099. The codes in this section involve services rendered to organs of the endocrine system, such as the thyroid, parathyroid, and adrenal cortex. Imaging as well as uptake services are found here. An **uptake** looks at the amount and time that a substance takes to draw up or absorb. For example, code 78012—"Thyroid uptake; single or multiple quantitative measurement(s) (including stimulation, suppression, or discharge, when performed)"—measures the thyroid function by determining how much iodine the thyroid takes up and expresses in relation to the amount administered.

Hematopoietic, reticuloendothelial, and lymphatic system codes are next in the Nuclear Medicine section. This code series is 78102–78199. These radiological services are performed on the spleen, lymph nodes, blood, platelets, plasma, and bone marrow.

Nuclear Medicine for the gastrointestinal system are reported using codes 78201–78299. The liver, salivary glands, esophagus, and intestines are studied through imaging and function studies. These services are found in this subsection of the Radiology chapter.

The musculoskeletal system is reported using codes 78300–78399. Bone density studies, as well as joint imaging, are located in this part of the subsection. Dual photon absorptiometry is coded to 78351. **Dual photon absorptiometry** is a type of noninvasive bone density test in which low doses of radiation are beamed through the bone, and a computer evaluates the amount of radiation that was absorbed. The summary is interpreted by a physician.

Next is the cardiovascular system subsection, which contains codes that can be reported in addition to stress testing or other procedures as part of the overall service performed on the patient. The code range is 78414–78499. Blood pool imaging, myocardial imaging, venous thrombosis imaging, and cardiac shunt detection are all found in this subsection.

The respiratory system codes begin with 78579 and go through 78599. Pulmonary perfusion imaging is found in this code range. **Pulmonary perfusion imaging** is the imaging of localized radioactive particles and the proportional blood flow that maps lung perfusion. Radioactive macroaggregated albumin particles are injected, which allows a camera to take the images of particles that are too big to pass through pulmonary capillary beds.

Next, we move on to the Nervous System subsection, which includes brain imaging and imaging of cerebrospinal fluid. The codes used for reporting these services are 78600–78699.

The genitourinary system is the last system before the other procedures. The code series is 78700–78799 and includes urinary bladder residual study, kidney function study, and vascular flow studies of the kidneys and testicles.

The last subsection of the nuclear medicine heading is Other Procedures. Radiopharmaceuticals are located in this area of the chapter. **Radiopharmaceuticals** are drugs that are used in testing the cause of a problem by indicating the location, size, or function of organs, tissues, or vessels. Radioactive material aids in the determinations made with regard to the patient's condition. Also found in this subsection is tumor imaging.

The Therapeutic Procedures subsection, which contains the codes to finish the chapter, are reported with codes 79005–79999. This subsection is for radiopharmaceutical services rendered to patients orally, or by intravenous or intra-arterial particulate administration.

## Exercise 20.9—Check Your Understanding

**Nuclear Medicine**

Fill in the blanks in the statements that follow.

1. _____ is a type of noninvasive bone density test in which low doses of radiation are beamed through the bone, and a computer evaluates the amount that was absorbed.

2. Nuclear medicine codes for the nervous system are reported using codes _____.

3. A(n) _____ looks at the amount and time that a substance takes to draw up or absorb.

4. _____ are drugs that are used in testing the cause of a problem by the use of radioactive material.

5. Nuclear medicine codes for the cardiovascular system are reported using codes _____.

# Summary

- Radiology is the study of x-rays, high-frequency sound waves, and high-strength magnetic fields, which sometimes includes the use of radioactive compounds to diagnose and/or treat diseases or injuries.

- A radiologist is a doctor whose specialty is radiology.

- Radiology is divided into four sections:
  - Diagnostic Radiology
  - Diagnostic Ultrasound
  - Radiation Oncology
  - Nuclear Medicine

# Internet Links

To learn more about radiology and radiologic procedures, visit **http://www.acr.org**, the website for the American College of Radiology, and **http://www.radiologyinfo.org**. Also do a search on radiology at **http://www.mmcradiology.com/procedures/index.html**.

# Chapter Review

## Fill in the Blank

**Instructions:** Fill in the blanks in the statements that follow.

1. The study of x-rays, high-frequency sound waves, and high-strength magnetic fields, which sometimes include the use of radioactive compounds to diagnose and/or treat diseases or injuries is known as _____.

2. A physician whose specialty is radiology is a(n) _____.

3. A study that encompasses the entire body area is called a(n) _____.

4. A partial scan or examination of a body area or quadrant is called a(n) _____.

5. A type of noninvasive bone density test in which low doses of radiation are beamed through the bone, and a computer evaluates the amount of radiation that was absorbed, is known as _____.

6. When radioactive isotopes are used to treat and diagnose diseases, the field of medicine that is used is _____ medicine.

7. An internal radiation therapy that is used to treat tissue is known as_____.

8. Drugs that are used in testing the cause of a problem by indicating the location, size, or function of organs, tissues, or vessels are _____.

9. Proton beam treatment is used in treating malignancies by using a high dose of _____ on tumors.

10. A treatment that uses heat, such as ultrasound, probes, and radiofrequencies, together with radiation therapy to treat malignancies by speeding up cell metabolism, is called _____.

# Coding Assignments

**Instructions:** Using the CPT manual, assign the correct code to the following procedures.

1. Splenoportography, radiological supervision and interpretation only _____

2. X-ray of optic foramina _____

3. Two-view x-ray of cervical spine _____

4. Two-view x-ray of hand _____

5. Swallowing function with videoradiography _____

6. Real-time transvaginal ultrasound of pregnant uterus with image documentation _____

7. Thyroid imaging _____

8. Peptide acute venous thrombosis imaging _____

9. Parathyroid imaging _____

10. Gastric empty imaging _____

11. Radiopharmaceutical therapy by intra-arterial particulate administration _____

12. PET scan of the brain for metabolic evaluation _____

13. Proton treatment delivery, simple _____

14. Therapeutic radiology simulation-aided field setting, complex _____

15. Esophageal motility study, imaging _____

16. CT scan of the maxillofacial area without the use of contrast material _____

17. Two-view x-ray of the sacroiliac joint _____

18. Radiological exam of the upper GI tract with scout abdominal radiograph and delayed image, single barium contrast study _____

19. Shoulder x-ray, complete, three views _____

20. Perineogram _____

21. Liver and spleen imaging with vascular flow _____

22. Radiopharmaceutical therapy by intravenous administration _____

23. Dacryocystography, nasolacrimal duct, radiological supervision and interpretation _____

24. Magnetic resonance angiography, neck with contrast _____

25. Radiologic examination of the calcaneus, two views _____

26. Bilateral screening mammography including CAD _____

27. Diagnostic CT of thorax without contrast _____

28. Medical physics dose evaluation and report for radiation exposure that will exceed institutional review threshold _____

29. Intravenous urography with KUB and tomography _____

30. Unilateral X-ray of ribs, 2 views _____

31. X-ray of spine, one view, including entire cervical, thoracic, lumbar and sacral spine and skull _____

32. Low dose CT of thorax for lung cancer screening, no contrast _____

33. CT of thoracic spine with contrast _____

34. MRI of lumbar spinal canal and contents, no contrast _____

35. X-ray of sacroiliac joints, 4 views _____

# Case Studies

**Instructions:** Review each case and indicate the correct code(s).

## Case 1

**Patient:** Fernandiz, Jose

**MRN:** 58585858

**Indication:** Possible benign prostatic hypertrophy

**Procedure:** CT scan of the pelvis with contrast

After oral contrast medium was given, 7-mm helical sections were obtained. Nonionic IV contrast was administered in the right arm. The exam shows no pelvic mass or adenopathy. There is a small amount of ascites in the pelvic area. There was also enlargement of the prostate gland. There is no bowel dilation. The bowel wall appears normal. The venous structures are unremarkable.

**Impression:** Enlarged prostate gland. Small amount of pelvic ascites.

**CPT code(s):** _____

## Case 2

**Patient:** Latesen, Meg

**MRN:** 777444

(continues)

(*continued*)

**Indication:** Pleural effusion

**Procedure:** Ultrasound of the chest, real time with image documentation

Sonography of the right hemothorax demonstrates right pleural effusion. Magic marker was used on the dorsal surface of the skin at the site of the maximum depth of the pleural fluid.

**CPT code(s):** _____

# Case 3

**Patient:** Maki, Tu

**MRN:** 123456

**Indication:** Right leg pain, Rule out DVT

**Procedure:** CT of right leg
                CT of right leg with contrast

**Findings:** Free vascular flow of all veins, no DVT noted.

**CPT code(s):** _____

# Case 4

**Clinical indication:** Status postlumbar spine fusion

**Orders:** X-rays of spine (complete, lumbosacral, six views), flexion/extension

**Comparison:** Lateral and flexion/extension views, six, of the lumbar spine 8/22/XX

**Findings:** This patient is six months status post–L3-L4 discectomy and placement of an intervertebral disc spacer. The patient is also status post–posterior lumbar spin fusion from L3 to L5 with placement of bilateral pedicle screws, joined on each side by vertical rods. There is no evidence of hardware failure or complications on any of the views. Alignment is anatomical. L2–L5 are stable.

**Impression:** Status post L3–L4 discectomy and placement of an interbody disc spacer. Status post–L3–L5 posterior fusion. Alignment is anatomical, and there is no evidence of abnormal motion on these flexion/extension views. Degenerative changes are stable.

**CPT code(s):** _____

## Case 5

**CT scan of the head/brain w/o contrast**

**Diagnosis:** Mental status change.

**Technique:** Axial images were obtained from the skull base to the vertex. No intravenous contrast was administered for this test.

**Comparison study:** 3/15/XXXX

**Findings:** There has been no significant change in one month. There is no evidence of intracranial hemorrhage, large vessel infarction, or mass. There is mild small vessel ischemic disease. This is the same as the last scan. Mild ventriculomegaly is reidentified. The skull is unremarkable accept for atherosclerotic large vessel calcifications. These are unchanged from the last scan.

**Impression:** No evidence of acute intracranial abnormality.

**CPT code(s):** _____

## Case 6

**Technique:** Dual-energy x-ray absorptiometry was performed.

**Findings:** Lumbar levoscoliosis evident with some focally increased density seen at the right side of the L3–L4 junction, likely due to vertebral endplate sclerosis accompanying degenerative disc disease.

Bone mineral density of the lumbar spine is 1.156 g/sq cm with a T score of −0.2.

Bone mineral density of the left femoral neck is 0.754 g/sq cm with a T score of −2.0.

Femoral density of the right femoral neck is 0.818 g/sq cm with a T score of −1.6.

**Impression:** Osteopenia of right and left femoral necks with moderate fracture risks. Normal bone mineral density of the lumbar spine.

**CPT code(s):** _____

## Case 7

The patient is a normal, healthy 12-year-old male who fell while skateboarding. The patient states that he tried to break his fall by extending his left hand, at which time he experienced immediate pain and deformity. The patient's parents rushed him to

*(continues)*

(*continued*)

the emergency room, where complete views of the wrist were taken by radiology and interpreted by this physician. The findings are as follows:

**Findings:** Four views of the left wrist show a comminuted fracture of the distal radial metaphysic with angulations and displacement of the fracture fragments. Carpal bones are intact, as is the distal ulna.

At this time, we will be moving the patient to the operating suite, where a closed reduction with casting will be performed.

**CPT code(s):** _____

## Case 8

This 72-year-old female presents today with chest pain, coughing, and wheezing. She has no history of COPD or heart problems. After examination, it appears she has an upper respiratory infection, but she will be sent for a chest x-ray to rule out any other possibilities.

**Report:** Two views of the chest, frontal and lateral, are submitted for review. No prior studies are available for comparison.

**Findings:** The cardiac, mediastinal, and hilar shadows are grossly unremarkable. No focal infiltrate or effusions identified. The pulmonary vascularity is grossly normal. The visualized bones demonstrate no abnormalities at this time.

**Impression:** No active cardiopulmonary disease

**CPT code(s):** _____

## Case 9

**Patient:** Ralf Nieves

**MRN:** 1092847

**Indication:** Cough and fever times 15 days

**Radiological Report:**

**Procedure:** AP, DEC, LAT, OBL, PA views of chest taken

**Impression:** There are hypoinflative changes in both lungs.

**CPT code(s):** _____

# Case 10

**Patient:** Zach Grand

**Indications:** Back pain

**Procedure:** Patient was standing and an AP thoracolumbar junction 2 view x-ray of the thoracolumbar spine was taken.

**Impression:** Curvature of spine at L1–L2–L3.

CPT code(s): _____

# Pathology and Laboratory

## Chapter Outline

Introduction

Guidelines Related to the National Correct
Coding Initiative (NCCI)

Coding for Pathology and Laboratory Services

Abbreviations Associated with
Laboratory Coding

Sections

Drug Procedures

Summary

Internet Links

Chapter Review

Coding Assignments

## Learning Objectives

**At the conclusion of this chapter, you should be able to:**

1. Define key terms related to coding pathology and laboratory tests.
2. Define abbreviations common to lab testing.
3. Select CPT codes for pathology and laboratory tests.

## Key Terms

analyte

cervical intraepithelial
neoplasia (CIN)

coagulation

cytogenetic

cytopathology

hematology

immunology

microbiology

panel test

transfusion

## Introduction

The Pathology and Laboratory section of the CPT manual begins with panel test 80047 and continues through code 89398 and codes 0001U to 0354U. The codes in this section represent testing ordered by providers to rule out a disease or problem, as well as to provide a definitive diagnosis depending on test results and symptoms of the patient. Laboratory testing is also used to monitor a disease process or to measure various substances that might be in the body. Pathology and laboratory codes are more often assigned in an outpatient setting; they are not required for billing inpatient services. However, some hospitals capture the codes for inpatients to keep statistics on the number of tests completed.

In some instances, it is important for a coder to understand how the lab test is performed. Because laboratory services are constantly changing and improving, the coder may need to ask the physician or lab technician for clarification.

This chapter of the CPT manual is further divided into sections, which will be discussed in this chapter. Also addressed in this chapter are consultation codes used only by pathologists that reflect a service, not a test.

During March of 2020 the World Health Organization declared a pandemic due to SARS-CoV-2, commonly known as COVID-19. During 2020 medical professionals and scientists treated and developed testing for COVID-19. As the spread of the disease increased new testing was developed. This impacted the CPT coding manual especially the Pathology and Laboratory Section of CPT.

Since 2020 there has been additional codes added in CPT that relate to COVID-19. One of the best ways in which to become familiar with the COVID-19 codes found in the CPT manual is to reference the terms COVID-19 or SARS-CoV-2 (Severe Acute Respiratory Syndrome Coronavirus 2) in the index of the manual. By referencing the index you will see that there are entries for antibody detention, immunization administration, infectious agent detection, pathogen detection, public health emergency, and vaccines. These entries are also further defined.

To locate  information about the COVID-19 CPT codes reference https://www.ama-assn.org/practice -management/cpt/covid-19-cpt-coding-and-guidance. On this page you will find information that pertains to new codes for immunizations, Category I and Proprietary Laboratory Analyses (PLA), CPT® Assistant provides guidance for new codes, and other resources and tools.

This website and section should be reviewed on a regular basis by coders for the latest CPT codes and other information that relate to COVID-19.

# Guidelines Related to the National Correct Coding Initiative (NCCI)

Perform the following steps to obtain the most current coding guideline information related to this chapter online:

1. Log on to *https://www.cms.gov/medicare-medicaid-coordination/national-correct-coding-initiative-ncci /ncci-medicare/medicare-ncci-policy-manual.*
2. Scroll to the section titled "View Manual by Chapter."
3. Click "Chapter 10" for guidelines specific to pathology and laboratory services.

# Coding for Pathology and Laboratory Services

Coding for lab testing involves having an understanding of the test being ordered and then being able to assign the code that best reflects the service rendered. Each lab test ordered is assigned its own code unless the group of tests ordered falls under a panel test. A **panel test** is one CPT code that encompasses a group, or panel, of tests.

> **EXAMPLE:** Barb's doctor wanted her cholesterol and triglycerides checked, so he wrote an order for the following tests: serum cholesterol (82465), lipoprotein (83718), and triglycerides (84478).

Each of these tests has its own separate CPT code, but the group of them together can be billed as a lipid panel (80061), which encompasses all the tests requested. If billed separately, the services would be rejected as unbundled and would have to be recoded as a panel test.

Pathology and laboratory services billed together do not require modifier 51 to be used. Coders in an outpatient setting would use this chapter of CPT much more frequently than coders in an inpatient setting. Laboratory tests are itemized for patients in an inpatient setting, but in the outpatient setting, many offices perform their own tests.

The notes at the beginning of each section should be referenced to understand any guidelines specific to that particular section. The coder should read these and become familiar with any specifics before assigning a code.

# Abbreviations Associated with Laboratory Coding

| Abbreviations | Definitions |
|---|---|
| Barb | Barbiturate |
| Ca | Calcium |
| CBC | Complete blood count |
| CIN | Cervical intraepithelial neoplasia |
| FBS | Fasting blood sugar |
| Gu, gu | Guaiac |
| Hct | Hematocrit |
| Hgb | Hemoglobin |
| K | Potassium |
| Li | Lithium |
| Mg | Magnesium |
| mg | Milligram |
| O2 | Oxygen |
| RBC | Red blood count |
| U/A | Urinalysis |
| WBC | White blood count |

# Sections

The CPT manual divides Pathology and Laboratory into sections. Each section begins with the guidelines or notes that are specific to that section.

## Organ or Disease-Oriented Panel (80047–80081)

The panel tests have specific components that, when run together, comprise the panel.

**EXAMPLE:**

80051   Electrolyte panel

This panel must include the following:

Carbon dioxide (82374)

Chloride (82435)

Potassium (84132)

Sodium (84295)

In this example, the electrolyte panel is made up of four different lab tests that, when run together, make up the electrolyte panel.

If other tests need to be run on the same day and are not part of the panel, they are billed separately.

**EXAMPLE:** If an electrolyte panel was ordered, and the physician also requested a CBC, then the panel test 80051 would be coded for the electrolytes, and then the code 85027 would also be coded for the CBC that was also requested.

CPT guidelines located at the beginning of the panels indicate when certain panels or tests cannot be billed out together. The guidelines also instruct the coder that two or more panel tests that include or duplicate any of the same tests are not to be reported together.

**EXAMPLE:**

80048    Basic metabolic panel

   This panel must include the following:

   Calcium, total (82310)

   Carbon dioxide (bicarbonate) (82374)

   Chloride (82435)

   Creatinine (82565)

   Glucose (82947)

   Potassium (84132)

   Sodium (84295)

   Urea nitrogen (BUN) (84520)

(Do not use code 80048 in addition to 80053.)

A panel test (80048; basic metabolic panel, Calcium, total) and a comprehensive metabolic panel (80053) would not be billed together. If the coder read the tests included in code 80053, it would be evident that all tests listed in code 80048 are included in 80053, with the addition of albumin (82040), bilirubin, total (82247), phosphatase alkaline (84075), protein, total (84155), transferase, alanine amino (ALT) (SGPT) (84460), and transferase, aspartate amino (AST)(SGOT) (84450). Careful attention to the tests being ordered are necessary to assign the correct code or codes, and attention to any notes surrounding the code assignments is essential.

## Exercise 21.1—Check Your Understanding

### Panel Tests

Choose the correct panel test code for the following lab tests ordered.
1. Transferase, aspartate amino (AST)(SGOT), albumin, protein (total), transferase, alanine amino (ALT) (SGPT), bilirubin (total), bilirubin (direct), phosphate alkaline panel test _____
2. Albumin, glucose, potassium, creatinine, calcium, phosphate, sodium, carbon dioxide, chloride, BUN panel test _____
3. HDL cholesterol, cholesterol (serum, total), triglycerides panel test _____
4. Carbon dioxide, potassium, glucose, creatinine, sodium, BUN, calcium, chloride panel test _____
5. Potassium, sodium, creatinine, calcium, albumin, glucose, phosphatase alkaline, carbon dioxide, chloride, total bilirubin, total protein, alanine amino transferase, aspartate amino transferase, BUN, CBC, TSH, WBC panel test _____

# Drug Procedures

Procedures that relate to drug testing, or the presence of a substance within a patient's body, are divided into three subsections in the CPT manual:

- Drug Assay—This includes presumptive drug class screening, and definitive drug testing, which are tests used to identify possible use and non-use of specific drugs or drug classes.
- Therapeutic Drug Assay—These tests are completed to monitor clinical response to a known prescribed medication.
- Chemistry—These tests are completed to determine if a substance, such as amylase, chromium, creatine, and so on is present in the examination material specimen.

Each of these subsections listed above is discussed within this chapter of the book and appears within this chapter according to the code numbers for each subsection. They are not presented in the CPT manual in numerical order.

## Drug Assay (80305–80377 and 83992)

In the CPT manual following code 80076, the subsection of Drug Assay appears. Locate this subsection in your CPT manual. Here the definitions appear for the two major categories for drug testing in the Drug Assay subsection, which include:

- Presumptive Drug Class—These tests are completed to identify possible use or non-use of a drug or drug class.
- Definitive Drug Class—These tests are qualitative or quantitative and identify possible use or non-use of a drug.

Reference the subsection in the CPT manual and read the entire notations that appear for this subsection of the manual.

## Therapeutic Drug Assays (80143–80299)

Codes from the Therapeutic Drug Assays section reflect testing to monitor the patient's clinical response to a known, prescribed or over-the-counter medication. Whole blood, serum, plasma, or cerebrospinal fluid are used for quantitative testing. Locate code 80143 in the CPT coding manual and review the pages that follow this code. Note that there are numerous notations in this part of the coding manual. Also note that there are numerous codes that are not in numerical order. This is because the codes in this section list the drug tested in alphabetical order. As drugs are inserted into this code range it creates the nonsequential listing of the codes.

## Evocative/Suppression Testing (80400–80439)

Code range 80400–80439 contains panel tests that are used to confirm or rule out a diagnosis and reflect only the technical component of the testing. In the CPT manual, prior to code 80400, coders are instructed to reference Hydration, Therapeutic, Prophylactic, Diagnostic Injections and Infusions, and Chemotherapy and Other Highly Complex Drug or Highly Complex Biologic Agent Administration to report the adminstration of evocative or suppressive agents. The professional component, in which the provider administers the suppressive agent (codes from the Medicine chapter of the CPT manual), is used to report this administration. New coders should be sure to read the text information that appears in the CPT manual in this section.

Another notation that should be noted in this section is "× 2." This alerts the coder to the fact that the test is usually run twice and should not be billed with a quantity of 2.

## Pathology Clinical Consultations (80503–80506)

Codes 80503 to 80506 report Pathology Clinical Consultations. These codes denote that a service has been performed by a pathologist, at the request of another physician or other qualified health care professional, to provide additional medical interpretive judgement regardless if the services occur at the same or another institution. Codes 80503 to 80506 are reported when a specific request is made and the pathologist provides interpretive judgment. A pathologist can also provide a Pathology Clinical Consultation when it is mandated by a federal or state regulation.

Locate code 80503 in the CPT manual and read the information that precedes the code and appears after the heading "Pathology Clinical Consultations". These instructional notes in the CPT manual are extensive and provide information that outlines the proper use and documentation needed to bill codes 80503 to 80506. Please note that in regards to code selection, these codes can be reported using either the total time (as defined in the codes' descriptions) or the level of medical decision making (as defined within the codes' descriptions). The codes' descriptions state the total time spent on the date of the consultation and also state components that relate to the complexity of the problem, review of the history and physical, and the level of medical decision making. For example: code 80503 reports 5 to 20 minutes of total time or reports a service that is for a clinical problem with a limited review of the patient's history and medical records, and medical decision making that is straightforward.

## Urinalysis (81000–81099)

The Urinalysis section of CPT contains codes for various tests on urine. The coder needs to know how the test was run to properly code in this section. The dipstick or tablet is frequently used in the office, but a microscope or an automated test may also be performed.

## Molecular Pathology (81105–81408 and 81479)

This subsection is used to report medical laboratory procedures that are completed to analyze nucleic acid to detect variants in genes. The codes are differentiated based on the specific gene being analyzed. The name of the genes are described as per the gene names approved by the Human Genome Organization (HUGO). Extensive notations appear in the CPT manual prior to code 81170 that apply to the assignment of these codes. They state that these codes include all analytical services performed. Procedures that are performed prior to cell lysis should be reported separately. Read the notations to review these notes and the definitions that apply to these codes.

## Genomic Sequencing Procedures and Other Molecular Multianalyte Assays (81410–81471)

Genomic sequencing procedures and other molecular multianalyte assays are DNA or RNA sequence analysis methods that allow for the analysis of the human genome. This analysis helps to determine the patient's DNA or RNA makeup, which can have medical significance or be useful in the medical management of the patient's case.

## Multianalyte Assays with Algorithmic Analyses (81490–81599)

Codes 81490 to 81599 report multianalyte assays with algorithmic analyses. The results from the completed assays are analyzed using algorithmic analysis and patient information (if available), and then are scored with a numerical value or probability that is typically unique to a single clinical laboratory or manufacturer. These tests analyze if a patient is at risk for a disease. It should be noted that individual payers may or may not pay for these tests.

## Chemistry (82009–84999)

Unless otherwise stated, tests in the Chemistry section are considered quantitative. The sources or specimens can be blood, stool, urine, or blood serum. If the code does not specify a source, any code can be used for any of the sources. Each source is considered a separate specimen, so if the exact same test is run on urine and blood, the coder would use one code for the urine and the exact same code for the blood. The coder may encounter the term **analyte**, which refers to the substance being tested.

## Hematology and Coagulation (85002–85999)

**Hematology** is the study of blood. **Coagulation** is the clotting of blood. The Hematology and Coagulation section contains codes for blood testing such as clotting factors, blood counts, and platelets.

# Immunology (86000–86849)

As the name implies, **immunology** is the study of the immune system. The tests in the Immunology section include testing for allergies and sensitivity to a substance, such as antibodies. Because of the coronavirus disease (COVID-19) pandemic, new codes were added to the CPT coding manual. Code 86328 was added to report an immunoassay for the COVID-19 antibody. This code is reported when the single-step method is used such as a reagent strip. When you reference this code in the CPT manual you will see an instructional notation that refers you to code 86769 when the testing uses a multiple-step method. As the scientific community learns more about COVID-19 additional COVID-19 testing methods will be used and the codes will be updated.

Tissue-typing procedures are also found in this section. Cross-matching for transplant patients would be found in this section as well.

# Transfusion Medicine (86850–86999)

**Transfusion** is the direct introduction of whole blood or blood components into the bloodstream. Code range 86850–86999 includes codes for antibody screens, antibody identification, and blood typing. Other procedures, such as volume reduction of blood or blood products and leukocyte transfusion, are also coded from this section.

# Microbiology (87003–87999)

**Microbiology** is the study of microorganisms, which involves the identification of organisms. The technique for obtaining the specimen is very important here, as some descriptions in this section are similar to those described in the Immunology section. Using a CPT manual reference codes 87426 and 87428. These codes are used to report infectious agent antigen detection by a qualitative or semiqualitative immunoassay technique for detecting COVID-19 or COVID-19 and influenza virus types A and B. Code 87426 reports testing for COVID-19 while code 87428 reports the testing for COVID-19, influenza A and influenza B. Review the codes in the CPT manual for the full code descriptions.

# Anatomic Pathology (88000–88099)

The Anatomic Pathology section is what physicians use to bill their services for autopsies and postmortem examinations.

# Cytopathology (88104–88199)

**Cytopathology** is the study of cells, especially in the disease process. Codes from this section include Pap smears and cervical screenings.

Codes 88142–88143 may be referred to as "thin prep" codes. The collection of the specimen may be done by aspiration of vaginal fluid, or by cervical or endocervical scraping.

Codes 88150–88153 are used when any method other than the Bethesda system is used to evaluate the specimen. This is where a coder may see designations of **cervical intraepithelial neoplasia (CIN)** of CIN 1, CIN 2, and CIN 3. In this system, 1 designates mild dysplasia and 3 designates severe dysplasia.

# Cytogenetic Studies (88230–88299)

**Cytogenetic** studies address heredity or genes at the cellular level. A chromosome study is coded to the Cytogenetic Studies section of the CPT manual.

# Surgical Pathology (88300–88399)

The Surgical Pathology section of the CPT manual contains codes that would be used for gross examination of a specimen. Gross examination involves the collection of a specimen that is bigger than a cell. Microscopic examination may or may not be necessary for the pathologist to determine a diagnosis. The six levels of gross or microscopic examination are identified using codes 88300–88309.

# In Vivo (e.g., Transcutaneous) Laboratory Procedures (88720–88749)

Codes in the range 88720–88749 are used to report in vivo procedures.

## Other Procedures and Reproductive Medicine Procedures (89049–89398)

Code range 89049–89240 reports procedures that include cell count of miscellaneous body fluids, fat stain, gastric intubation, aspiration, and fractional collections. Codes 89250 to 89398 report reproductive medicine procedures that include the preparation of an embryo for transfer, cryopreservation of embryos, and semen analysis to name a few.

## Proprietary Laboratory Analyses (0001U–0354U)

This subsection includes codes that describe proprietary clinical laboratory analyses. The analyses can be provided by a single laboratory or licensed or marketed to multiple providing laboratories. The laboratories must be cleared or approved by the Food and Drug Administration.

Reference the extensive instructional notation that appears after the heading of Proprietary Laboratory Analyses and before the code 0001U.

# Summary

- Codes from this chapter represent testing done to assist in diagnosing as well as ruling out various diseases.
- Laboratory testing is constantly changing and improving, so the coder needs to be aware of changes and also have references that will aid in understanding and choosing codes from this section.
- Unlike other chapters in the CPT manual, coding guidelines for this chapter are typically found at the beginning of each section. Careful attention to these notes is necessary.
- The coder may encounter abbreviations within provider notes that will need clarification in order to locate a proper code.
- Attention to detail is essential for performing correct coding in this chapter.

# Internet Links

To learn about laboratory tests, visit **http://www.labtestsonline.org**.

To review information on tests, visit **https://dlmp.uw.edu/** and click the "Diagnostic" tab to learn about various laboratory tests.

# Chapter Review

## True/False

**Instructions:** Indicate whether the following statements are true (T) or false (F).

1. _____ Code 89190 is used to report a nasal smear for eosinophils.

2. _____ The abbreviation for magnesium is mg.

3. _____ Pathology codes are broken into panel tests.

4. _____ Code 80055 reports an obstetric panel.

5. _____ Code 80048 reports an electrolyte panel.

## Fill in the Blank

**Instructions:** Fill in the blanks in the statements that follow.

6. One CPT code that encompasses a group of tests is called a(n) _____.

7. A substance being tested is also known as a(n) _____.

8. The direct introduction of whole blood into the bloodstream is _____.

9. The most severe of the cervical intraepithelial neoplasia designations is _____.

10. The abbreviation WBC stands for _____.

# Coding Assignments

**Instructions:** Using the CPT manual, assign the correct code to each of the following.

1. Semen analysis for presence of sperm, including Huhner test _____

2. Lymphocytotoxicity assay, visual crossmatch, with titration _____

3. ANA titer _____

4. Lipase, chemistry test _____

5. Renal function panel _____

6. Aldosterone suppression evaluation panel _____

7. Protein analysis of tissue by Western blot, with interpretation and report _____

8. Level VI Surgical pathology, gross and microscopic examination _____

9. Chromosome analysis; count five cells, one karyotpe, with banding _____

10. Compatibility test; incubation technique _____

11. Obstetric panel _____

12. Lithium assay _____

13. Calcium, total _____

14. CBC, automated _____

15. Clot retraction _____

16. Pinworm microbiology examination _____

17. Immune complex assay _____

18. Thrombomodulin _____

19. TSH _____

20. Lipid panel _____

21. Flow cytometry DNA analysis _____

22. Rh(D) blood typing _____

23. RBC antibody screen _____

24. Phospholipid platelet neutralization _____

25. Cold agglutinin screen _____

26. Amikacin therapeutic drug assay _____

27. Pathology clinical consultation for a high complexity clinical problem. Pathologist completed a comprehensive review of the patient's history and a comprehensive review of the patient's medical record. A high level of medical decision making was completed because of the complexity of the case. _____

28. Urine pregnancy test, by visual color comparison methods _____

29. Aldolase chemistry _____

30. Serum cholinesterase chemistry _____

31. Definitive drug testing for Fentanyl _____

32. Therapeutic Drug Assay for Acetaminophen _____

33. MPL gene analysis, common variants _____

34. COVID-19 single step antibody detection immunoassay _____

35. Deoxyribonuclease antibody detection _____

## CHAPTER 22

# Medicine

## Chapter Outline

Introduction

Guidelines Related to the National Correct Coding Initiative (NCCI)

Immune Globulins (90281–90399)

Immunization Administration for Vaccines and Toxoids (90460–90474) and (0001A–0112A)

Vaccines and Toxoids (90476–90756) and (91300–91311)

Psychiatry (90785–90899)

Biofeedback (90901–90913)

Dialysis (90935–90999)

Gastroenterology (91010–91299)

Ophthalmology (92002–92499)

Special Otorhinolaryngologic Services (92502–92700)

Cardiovascular (92920–93799)

Noninvasive Vascular Diagnostic Studies (93880–93998)

Pulmonary (94002–94799)

Allergy and Clinical Immunology (95004–95199)

Endocrinology (95249–95251)

Neurology and Neuromuscular Procedures (95700–96020)

Medical Genetics and Genetic Counseling Services (96040) and Adaptive Behavior Services (97151–97158)

Central Nervous System Assessments and Tests (96105–96146), Health Behavior Assessment and Intervention (96156–96171), and Behavior Management Services (96202–96203)

Hydration, Therapeutic, Prophylactic, Diagnostic Injections and Infusions, and Chemotherapy and Other Highly Complex Drug or Highly Complex Biologic Agent Administration (96360–96549)

Photodynamic Therapy (96567–96574)

Special Dermatological Procedures (96900–96999)

Physical Medicine and Rehabilitation (97010–97799)

Additional Procedures (97802–99607)

Summary

Internet Links

Chapter Review

Coding Assignments

Case Studies

## Learning Objectives

### At the conclusion of this chapter, you should be able to:

1. Define key terms related to coding from the Medicine section of the CPT manual.
2. Define procedures that are found in the Medicine section of the CPT manual.

3. Identify the method of administration for common vaccines and toxoids.

4. Select CPT codes for services that are found in the Medicine section of the CPT manual.

5. Identify and code procedures for medicine from case studies.

# Key Terms

| | | | |
|---|---|---|---|
| biofeedback | immune globulin | peripheral arterial disease (PAD) rehabilitation | psychoanalysis |
| gonioscope | narcosynthesis | | refractor |
| hemodialysis | ophthalmologist | peritoneal dialysis | serial tonometry |
| hemoperfusion | ophthalmology | psychiatrist | spirometry testing |
| hypnotherapy | optometrist | psychiatry | vaccine |

# Introduction

The Medicine section of the CPT manual is found after the Pathology and Laboratory section. The code range in this section begins with code 90281 and goes through code 99607. A wide variety of services are found in the Medicine section. Locate the Medicine Guidelines that appear at the start of the Medicine Section. The guidelines provide information that is relevant to the Medicine Section of CPT. Review the guidelines and note the definitions and other items. Make special note of the definition of the terms foreign body and implant. These definitions, as defined in the CPT manual, have an impact on code selection. The subsections found in this section of CPT are as follows:

- Immune Globulins, Serum or Recombinant Products
- Immunization Administration for Vaccines/Toxoids
- Vaccines/Toxoids
- Psychiatry
- Biofeedback
- Dialysis
- Gastroenterology
- Ophthalmology
- Special Otorhinolaryngologic Services
- Cardiovascular
- Noninvasive Vascular Diagnostic Studies
- Pulmonary
- Allergy and Clinical Immunology
- Endocrinology
- Neurology and Neuromuscular Procedures
- Medical Genetics and Genetic Counseling Services
- Adaptive Behavior Services
- Central Nervous System Assessments/Tests
- Health and Behavior Assessment/Intervention
- Behavior Management Services
- Hydration, Therapeutic, Prophylactic, Diagnostic Injections and Infusions, and Chemotherapy and Other Highly Complex Drug or Highly Complex Biologic Agent Administration

- Photodynamic Therapy
- Special Dermatological Procedures
- Physical Medicine and Rehabilitation
- Medical Nutrition Therapy
- Acupuncture
- Osteopathic Manipulative Treatment
- Chiropractic Manipulative Treatment
- Education and Training for Patient Self-Management
- Non–Face-to-Face Nonphysician Services
- Special Services, Procedures, and Reports
- Qualifying Circumstances for Anesthesia
- Moderate (Conscious) Sedation
- Other Services and Procedures
- Home Health Procedures/Services
- Medication Therapy Management Services

# Guidelines Related to the National Correct Coding Initiative (NCCI)

Perform the following steps to obtain the most current coding guideline information related to this chapter online:

1. Log on to *https://www.cms.gov/medicare-medicaid-coordination/national-correct-coding-initiative-ncci /ncci-medicare/medicare-ncci-policy-manual*.
2. Scroll to the section titled "View Manual by Chapter."
3. Click "Chapter 11" for guidelines specific to the Medicine, Evaluation, and Management Services section.

# Immune Globulins (90281–90399)

An **immune globulin** functions as an antibody for a short period of time. This type of passive immunity occurs as the immune globulin circulates through the body. The basic structure determines the type of immunoglobulin function.

The code range is 90281–90399. Botulism immune globulin, hepatitis B immune globulin, rabies immune globulin, and varicella-zoster immune globulin are all coded from this code range. Most of these immune globulin products are administered intramuscularly, but the coder would need to read the code and determine whether the route of administration listed is reflected accurately in the code selection. The codes in this range are reported in addition to administration codes and are modifier 51 exempt.

# Immunization Administration for Vaccines and Toxoids (90460–90474) and (0001A–0112A)

The codes in the range 90460–90474 report services provided by a physician when counseling the patient and/or family on any adverse effects related to immunization during administration of a vaccine. These codes are reported separately in addition to the code for the vaccine or toxoid supply. Table 22-1 provides the codes and descriptions.

**TABLE 22-1** Immunization Administration for Vaccines/Toxoids

| Codes | Description |
|---|---|
| 90460–90461 | Immunization administration through 18 years of age. The route of administration (i.e., intramuscular, intradermal, subcutaneous, or percutaneous) does not matter. These two codes are used *only* when the physician or another qualified health-care professional (i.e., nurse) provides face-to-face counseling to the patient or family during administration of the vaccine.<br><br>Code 90461 is an add-on code and is reported with 90460 for each additional vaccine or vaccine component given.<br><br>EXAMPLE<br><br>Mary received an MMR vaccine. The physician provided counseling to her mother just prior to the injection being given by the nurse. The following codes were reported:<br><br>90707—"Measles, mumps, and rubella virus vaccine (MMR), live, for subcutaneous use"<br><br>90460—"Immunization administration—first vaccine (measles)"<br><br>90461 × 2—"Each additional vaccine/toxoid component (mumps, rubella)" |
| 90471–90472 | These administration codes are reported for immunization administration for patients over the age of 18 or administration of a vaccine that is not accompanied by face-to-face physician or qualified health-care professional counseling. The route of administration (i.e., intramuscular, intradermal, subcutaneous, or percutaneous) does not matter. |
| 90473–90474 | Immunization administration by intranasal or oral route; each vaccine (single or combination vaccine/toxoid) |
| 0001A–0112A | This code range is used to report the administration of COVID-19 vaccines. The codes are organized according to the specific vaccine product and the dose. Codes 0001A to 0112A report the administration of the vaccine and codes 91300 to 91311 report the vaccine product only. Two codes are used when a COVID vaccine is given. A code from 0001A to 0112A, to report the administration, and a code from 91300 to 91311, to report the vaccine product. Locate Appendix Q in the CPT manual. The table that is presented in Appendix Q outlines the vaccine code, vaccine administration codes, vaccine manufacturer, vaccine name(s), NDC 10/NDC 11 Labeler Product ID (Vial) and the Dosing Interval. |

# Vaccines and Toxoids (90476–90756) and (91300–91311)

A **vaccine** is a dead microorganism that is administered for prevention or treatment of a disease. A toxoid is the actual bacterial exotoxin that has lost its toxic effect but kept its ability to produce antibodies. A live vaccine is one that was prepared from live microorganisms but has been thinned down and that has kept the immunogenic properties.

Adenovirus vaccines, hepatitis A and B vaccines, influenza virus vaccines, and rabies vaccines are all found in code range 90476–90749. Also found in this code range are childhood immunizations such as the diphtheria, tetanus toxoids, and pertussis vaccine; measles, mumps, and rubella (MMR) vaccine; and poliovirus vaccine. The 90476–90749 codes identify vaccine products only and would require an additional code assignment for their administration. Codes 91300–91311 report the vaccine product only for COVID-19. Locate these codes in the CPT manual and note the instructional notations that appear after each code. The notation directs the coder in assigning the administration code to be used with the listed vaccine product code. For example: Code 91300, vaccine product code, would be used with administration code 0001A, for the first dose, or code 0002A for the second dose.  As boosters are administered and new vaccine products are developed expect to see additional administration and vaccine product codes that relate to COVID-19.

## Exercise 22.1—Check Your Understanding

**Vaccines and Administrations**

Assign the correct CPT code to each of the following vaccines, and indicate the method of administration (i.e., subcutaneous, intramuscular, or intradermal).

1. Tdap for a 14-year-old _____
2. Typhoid vaccine, live _____
3. MMRV, live vaccine _____
4. HepA, pediatric/adolescent dosage 3 dose schedule _____
5. DTaP-Hib-IPV _____
6. Varicella virus vaccine live for subcutaneous use _____
7. Adenovirus type 4 live oral use _____
8. HepA, adult dosage _____
9. Anthrax _____
10. Yellow fever vaccine, live, for subcutaneous use _____

# Psychiatry (90785–90899)

**Psychiatry** is the branch of medicine that treats mental disorders, which include emotional and behavioral disorders. A **psychiatrist** is a medical doctor who administers treatment for patients with mental, emotional, and behavioral disorders. A similar mental disorder can manifest itself in different levels of severity in different patients.

Psychiatry codes found in the 90785–90853 code range are illustrated in Table 22-2.

Other psychiatric services or procedures are found in code range 90863–90899. This code range encompasses codes that fall outside the other subcategories noted. Table 22-3 notes other psychiatric service codes.

**TABLE 22-2** Psychiatry Codes (90785–90853)

| Code(s) | Description |
|---------|-------------|
| 90785 | This is an add-on code that is reported with codes 90791, 90792, 90832, 90833, 90834, 90836, 90837, 90838, and 90853. This code reports interactive complexity when delivering the primary service. For example, the use of play equipment or other devices during the session. Coders must read the instructional notations that appear before code 90785 for a complete listing of factors that indicate the use of this code. |
| 90791–90792 | Psychiatric diagnostic evaluations are reported with these codes. Code 90791 reports a psychiatric diagnostic evaluation, while code 90792 reports a psychiatric diagnostic evaluation with medical services. Extensive notations prior to these codes should be read and understood by the coder prior to code assignment. |
| 90832–90838 | This code range reports psychotherapy, which is treatment of mental illnesses and behavioral disturbances through therapeutic communication. The codes are time based and are differentiated by the lengths of time of the therapy and whether an evaluation and management service occurred with the therapy. Codes 90833, 90836, and 90838 are add-on codes that are used with the appropriate Evaluation and Management (E/M) codes to denote that E/M services and psychotherapy occurred on the same date by the same provider. Following each of these add-on codes, notations appear in the CPT manual that will assist the coder in code selection. Also, coders should read the extensive notations that appear prior to code 90832 regarding the assignment of codes from this section. |
| 90839–90840 | These codes are time based and are used to report psychotherapy for crisis situations. Prior to code 90839, an extensive notation appears that instructs the coder how to report these codes. The coder should report the total face-to-face time even if the time is not continuous. |
| 90845 | **Psychoanalysis**—a form of psychotherapy in which the patient's unconscious thoughts are recognized and analyzed<br><br>Different techniques might be used for this type of psychotherapy. |

(continues)

**TABLE 22-2** (continued)

| Code(s) | Description |
|---|---|
| 90846–90847 | Family psychotherapy<br>This procedure may or may not be done with the patient present. |
| 90849 | Multiple family group psychotherapy |
| 90853 | Group psychotherapy (other than a multiple-family group)<br>This might be a session in which more than one patient participates. The patients involved may or may not have the same problem. This code selection is not a correct choice if the group is made up of the patient and family members. |

**TABLE 22-3** Other Psychiatric Services (90863–90899)

| Code(s) | Description |
|---|---|
| 90863 | Pharmacologic management, including prescription, and review of medication, when performed with psychotherapy services. This is an add-on code that is reported with codes 90832, 90834, or 90837. |
| 90865 | Narcosynthesis for psychiatric diagnostic and therapeutic purposes (e.g., sodium amobarbital [amytal] interview)<br>**Narcosynthesis** is a form of psychiatry that involves the administering of an intravenous drug that allows the patient to release thoughts that might be suppressed or repressed. |
| 90867–90869 | Therapeutic repetitive transcranial magnetic stimulation treatment delivery management. Each code is reported once per session. |
| 90870 | Electroconvulsive therapy (includes necessary monitoring)<br>This type of therapy is used to treat patients with chronic or profound depression when all other forms of treatment have been unsuccessful. |
| 90875–90876 | Individual psychophysiological therapy incorporating biofeedback training by any modality (face-to-face with the patient) with psychotherapy (e.g., insight-oriented, behavior modifying, or supportive psychotherapy)<br>Code choice is determined by the approximate time spent with the patient; time must appear in the documentation. |
| 90880 | **Hypnotherapy** is a type of psychotherapy that alters the state of consciousness to heighten awareness and opens the patient up to suggestions that may alter the patient's thoughts or behavior. |
| 90882 | Environmental intervention for medical management purposes on psychiatric patient's behalf with agencies, employers, or institutions |
| 90885 | Psychiatric evaluation of hospital records, other psychiatric reports, psychometric and/or projective tests, and other accumulated data for medical diagnostic purposes |
| 90887 | Interpretation or explanation of results of psychiatric or other medical examinations and procedures, or other accumulated data to family or other responsible persons, or advising them how to assist patient |
| 90889 | Preparation of report of patient's psychiatric status, history, treatment, or progress (other than for legal or consultative purposes) for other individuals, agencies, or insurance carriers |
| 90899 | Unlisted psychiatric service or procedure |

## Exercise 22.2—Check Your Understanding

**Psychiatry (Code Range 90785–90899)**

Indicate whether the following statements are true (T) or false (F).

1. _____ Family psychotherapy without the patient present is reported using CPT code 90847.
2. _____ Code 90839 reports 60 minutes of psychotherapy for crisis.
3. _____ Code 90845 is used for the management of the patient's medications.
4. _____ Electroconvulsive therapy and monitoring is reported with code 90870.
5. _____ Code 90885 is described as an environmental intervention for medical management purposes on the psychiatric patient's behalf with agencies, employers, or institutions.

# Biofeedback (90901-90913)

**Biofeedback** deals with involuntary physiological responses and teaches the patient how to consciously manage these responses. The physiological responses that can be treated using biofeedback include high blood pressure and incontinence. The code selected is determined by the modality. Biofeedback may or may not be covered by a particular payer. This should be discussed with the patient prior to treatment.

# Dialysis (90935-90999)

The Dialysis subsection is divided into four components in the CPT manual: Hemodialysis, Miscellaneous Dialysis Procedures, End-Stage Renal Disease Services (ESRD), and Other Dialysis Procedures.

## Hemodialysis (90935-90940)

**Hemodialysis** removes waste from the blood but involves a continuous movement of blood from the body to a hemodialyzer for filtering, and then the clean blood is returned to the patient's bloodstream. Figure 22-1 illustrates the hemodialysis machine and process. Table 22-4 lists the codes used for reporting hemodialysis services.

This code range includes all evaluation and management services related to the patient's renal disease on the day of the hemodialysis procedure.

To vein

From artery

**FIGURE 22-1** Hemodialysis

**TABLE 22-4** Hemodialysis (90935-90940)

| Code | Description |
|---|---|
| 90935 | Hemodialysis procedure with single provider evaluation<br>The catheter would have already been placed in an artery or vein. This code would be used to report a single treatment that includes the physician evaluation. |
| 90937 | Hemodialysis procedure requiring repeated evaluations, with or without substantial revision of dialysis prescription<br>The catheter would have already been placed in an artery or vein. This code would be used to report services provided by the physician during the patient's hemodialysis treatment. |
| 90940 | Hemodialysis access flow study to determine blood flow in grafts and arteriovenous fistulae by an indicator method |

# Miscellaneous Dialysis Procedures (90945–90947) and Other Dialysis Procedures (90989–90999)

The procedures found in the 90945–90947 and 90989–90999 code ranges are used to report services that are not found in the other code ranges for dialysis procedures, such as peritoneal dialysis, hemofiltration, and other continuous renal replacement therapies. **Peritoneal dialysis** is another form of cleaning the waste from the bloodstream, but instead of a machine to filter the blood, the peritoneal membrane is used as the filter. Figure 22-2 illustrates peritoneal dialysis.

Also found in this code range are procedure codes that report dialysis training and hemoperfusion. **Hemoperfusion** is a way for toxins to be removed from the blood in which the physician perfuses the blood through activated charcoal or resin and then transfuses the blood back into the patient.

Fresh dialysate solution

Peritoneal cavity

Tenchkoff peritoneal catheter

Adapter

Used dialysate solution

**FIGURE 22-2** Peritoneal Dialysis

# End-Stage Renal Disease Services (90951–90970)

Code range 90951–90970 is used to report end-stage renal disease services. Codes 90951–90966 are reported once per month. Codes 90967–90970 are for services lasting less than a full month and are billed per day. The codes are differentiated by age-specific services and place of service—outpatient, home, or inpatient setting.

## Exercise 22.3—Check Your Understanding

**Dialysis Services**

Assign the correct code for each of the following.

1. Monitoring and nutrition assessment for the month of May, for a 15-year-old ESRD patient _____

2. Dialysis training, patient, including helper where applicable—completed course _____

3. Hemodialysis access flow study to determine blood flow in grafts and arteriovenous fistulae by an indicator method _____

4. ESRD services for 35-year-old ESRD patient for five days of the month; the rest of the month, he was in the hospital (code only for the outpatient setting) _____

5. Hemoperfusion _____

# Gastroenterology (91010–91299)

The services reported in the Gastroenterology code range are for diagnostic procedures performed on the gastrointestinal system. If Evaluation and Management (E/M) services were performed at the same time, these services would be reported separately. The surgical section for procedures of the digestive tract should be referenced before codes from this code range are used.

Procedures of the esophagus are reported first, including intubation and gastroesophageal reflux tests. Gastric intubation, gastric aspiration or lavage, and gastric saline load testing are also reported from this code range.

Gastric physiology is reported using codes 91132 and 91133. These codes report electrical activity generated by the stomach, which enables physicians to detect abnormalities of the stomach.

# Ophthalmology (92002–92499)

**Ophthalmology** is the study of diseases and disorders of the eye. An **ophthalmologist** is a medical doctor who specializes in treatment of these diseases and disorders. An ophthalmologist is able to prescribe medication as part of the treatment plan, as well as conduct tests and issue prescriptions for corrective lenses. An **optometrist** is not a medical doctor and cannot prescribe medication but is able to prescribe corrective lenses.

The codes in the Ophthalmology subsection of the Medicine section of the CPT manual are services reported by an ophthalmologist. General ophthalmological services are divided into new patient and established patient services. The services report the medical examination and evaluation with initiation of treatment. The levels of service reported are intermediate and comprehensive. The code selection is determined by whether the patient is new or established, and whether the service was intermediate or comprehensive.

Intermediate levels of service (codes 92002 and 92012) include patient history, general medical observation, and external examination. Ophthalmoscopy is included, as is biomicroscopy, mydriasis, and tonometry. Initiation of a plan of care is also included in these service codes.

Comprehensive levels of service (codes 92004 and 92014) include all of the same services that are reported in the intermediate service codes, in addition to gross visual field testing and basic sensorimotor examination.

Special ophthalmological services (code range 92015–92145) include refractor testing. A **refractor** is a machine that contains a large series of lenses that are changed quickly during an examination as the patient views an eye chart. Also included in this code range is code 92020 for gonioscopy. A **gonioscope** is a type of scope that examines the eye for signs of glaucoma. Table 22-5 summarizes some of these services.

**TABLE 22-5** Specialized Services (92015–92287)

| Code(s) | Description |
|---|---|
| 92065 and 92066 | Orthoptic training |
| | These codes are used when the patient needs to be trained to perform exercises to correct ocular problems related to the ocular muscles. Review the CPT manual and note that these codes are differentiated by whether a physician or other qualified health care professional performed the service or if another person performed the service under the supervision of a physician or other qualified health care professional. |
| 92081–92083 | Visual field examination, unilateral or bilateral, with interpretation and report. Code selection is based on the extent of the examination. |
| 92100 | Serial tonometry (separate procedure) with multiple measurements of intraocular pressure over an extended time period with interpretation and report, same day (e.g., diurnal curve or medical treatment of acute elevation of intraocular pressure) |
| | **Serial tonometry** is a procedure that measures pressure over the course of the day. There are multiple pressure checks that record the significant peaks within a 24-hour period. |
| 92132–92134 | These codes report scanning computerized ophthalmic diagnostic imaging (e.g., scanning laser) with interpretation and report, unilateral or bilateral. |
| 92136 | Ophthalmic biometry by partial coherence interferometry with intraocular lens power calculation is reported with this code. |
| 92145 | This code reports a corneal hysteresis determination, by air impulse stimulation, unilateral or bilateral, with interpretation and report. During corneal hysteresis a measurement is taken that determines the eye(s) response to application and removal of air impulse stimulation thus measuring the biomechanic properties of the cornea. This test can determine ocular abnormalities and eyes that are at risk for diseases. The most common reason to complete this test is for the diagnosis and monitoring of glaucoma. However this test is also completed to identify other corneal pathology or for pre-refractive surgery risk assessment |

## Other Specialized Services

Opthalmoscopy procedures (code range 92201–92260) are billed separately only if they are not part of a general ophthalmologic service. Fluorescein and fundus procedures are found in this code range.

Other specialized services (code range 92265–92499) include electroretinography, color-vision examination, and fitting of contact lenses. Codes for fitting of spectacles or prosthesis services are located in the 92340–92371 code range and should be reviewed carefully before codes are assigned.

# Special Otorhinolaryngologic Services (92502–92700)

The Special Otorhinolaryngologic Services subsection reports special diagnostic services typically performed by an ear, nose, and throat (ENT) specialist. Screening tests, such as speech evaluations and hearing tests, are found in this code range.

# Cardiovascular (92920–93799)

The Cardiovascular subsection of the Medicine section includes codes used to report diagnostic and therapeutic services. Codes 92920–92944, as well as other codes in the cardiovascular subsection of the Medicine section, are out of numerical sequence in the CPT manual.

The therapeutic services reported here include such procedures as stent placements, percutaneous transluminal coronary angioplasty (PTCA), and percutaneous transluminal coronary arthrectomy.

- Coronary therapeutic services and procedures are reported with codes 92920–92979, which includes percutaneous transluminal coronary procedures. Attention to documentation is necessary in order to assign the proper codes from this code range. Coders should also note the codes in this range that are add-on codes.
- Cardiopulmonary resuscitation is reported using code 92950.

- Cardiography and cardiovascular monitoring services are reported using code range 93000–93278. Electrocardiograms, cardiovascular stress tests, and Holter monitoring are found in this code range. Some codes in this code range differentiate the technical and professional components. Per the guidelines, an order must be present in the patient's record in addition to the separate written reports. Orders and reports must be authenticated by the provider. Attention to the service the physician actually provides is key in code assignment.

- Implantable insertable, and wearable cardiac device evaluations are reported with codes 93264–93298. These services are diagnostic procedures used to assess device therapy and cardiovascular physiologic data.

- Echocardiography services are reported using codes from the 93303–93356 code range. Documentation is important in billing these services. If the clinically relevant findings are not documented, the service cannot be reported. The documentation must include quantitative measurements, and any abnormalities need to be described.

- Cardiac catheterization is used to view the heart and associated structures, such as great vessels and coronary arteries. It is an invasive procedure and may or may not be performed with other services. Introduction, positioning, gauging pressure, and obtaining samples are included in the codes. When coding cardiac catheterizations, the coder must determine whether the catheterization is being performed for congenital heart disease or other reasons. Extensive detailed guidelines must be followed for proper code assignment. The codes used to report cardiac catheterization services are 93451–93583. It should be noted that endomyocardial biopsy services and repair of a septal defect should be reported from this code range. Locate code 93451 in a CPT manual and prior to this code there is a heading entitled Cardiac Catheterization. Read all of the information between the heading and code 93451.

- Transcatheter closure of a paravalvular leak is reported with code range 93590–93592. Code 93590 reports the percutaneous transcatheter closure of a paravalvular leak for the initial occlusion device of a mitral valve. Code 93591 reports the percutaneous transcatheter closure of a paravalvular leak for the initial occlusion device of an aortic valve. Code 93592 is an add-on code used to report each additional occlusion device and is to be reported in conjunction with 93590 or 93591.

- Cardiac Catheterization for Congenital Heart Defects is reported with codes 93593–93598. Locate code 93593 in the CPT manual and read the extensive instructional notation that appears prior to the code. The notations outline relevant information pertaining to right and left heart catheterization for congenital heart defects and catheter placement and injection procedures.

- Intracardiac electrophysiological procedures and studies are reported using codes from the 93600–93662 code range. The services in this code range report the evaluation of the electrical conduction system of the heart.

- **Peripheral arterial disease (PAD) rehabilitation** is reported using code 93668. The PAD rehabilitation codes refer to patient-monitored exercise until symptoms of the disease lessen and are reported "per session." The exercise session lasts anywhere from 45 to 60 minutes. The patient's claudication threshold is monitored, tracking any symptoms.

- Other cardiac and vascular studies are reported using codes 93701–93799. Electronic analysis of pacemakers and thermograms, as well as determining venous pressure are services that are coded from this code range.

# Noninvasive Vascular Diagnostic Studies (93880–93998)

Code range 93880–93998 covers supervision of patient care, as well as studies and interpretation for noninvasive vascular diagnostic studies. The patient record needs to include documentation of the vascular study, as well as the interpretation and bidirectional vascular flow or imaging when performed. A handheld screening device does not constitute enough work to report these codes for payment and would be considered part of the physical exam related to the vascular system.

- Cerebrovascular arterial studies are reported using codes 93880–93895.
- Extremity arterial studies (including digits) are reported using codes 93922–93931.
- Extremity venous studies (including digits) are reported using codes 93970 and 93971.
- Visceral and penile vascular studies are reported using codes 93975–93981.
- Extremity arterial–venous studies are reported using code 93985–93990.

# Pulmonary (94002-94799)

Pulmonary codes are used to report both diagnostic and therapeutic procedures and services. The coder needs to be aware that these codes include laboratory services as well as physician services, and the codes should not be reported separately. The interpretation of results is also bundled into the codes reported.

**Spirometry testing** measures lung capacity and is reported using codes 94010-94070.

Bronchospasm evaluations and vital capacity testing are also found in the Pulmonary subsection of the Medicine section. Breathing response testing and aerosol inhalation treatments are found in this code range. It should be noted that referencing documentation is essential to correct code selection. This section is used for code selection when a code from the Respiratory subsection in the Surgery section has been referenced and a better code has not been found.

Codes 94625 and 94626 report outpatient pulmonary rehabilitation services completed by a physician or other qualified health care professional. Code 94625 reports the services without continuous oximetry monitoring and code 94626 reports the services with continuous oximetry monitoring. Note that these codes are reported per session. Review the full descriptions of the codes in the CPT manual and note the instructional notation following code 94626 regarding codes that are not reported in conjunction with these codes.

# Allergy and Clinical Immunology (95004-95199)

Code selection from the Allergy and Clinical Immunology code range is based on the patient's history, physical findings, and clinical judgment of the physician or provider of the service. The code description may refer to the number of tests performed. For reimbursement purposes as well as accurate reporting, the quantity should reflect the correct number of tests performed. Allergy testing and immunotherapy does not include any additional evaluation and management services, which means they should be reported separately if applicable.

- Allergy testing is reported using code set 95004-95070. The technique used in testing could be scratch, puncture, prick, or intradermal, and it should be noted in the documentation.
- Ingestion challenge testing is reported using codes 95076 and 95079. During this testing, a patient is given food, a drug, or another substance to ingest, and is then monitored for an allergic reaction. Code 95076 reports the first 120 minutes of testing, and code 95079 reports each additional 60 minutes of testing. The notation in the CPT manual prior to code 95076 states that if testing time is less than 61 minutes, an Evaluation and Management (E/M) code should be reported if appropriate.
- Allergen immunotherapy is reported using code set 95115-95199. Allergenic extracts are administered at specific intervals until therapy levels are reached. The number of injections should be noted, as this will steer code selection.

# Endocrinology (95249-95251)

Two codes are found in the Endocrinology subsection that are used to report continuous glucose monitoring of interstitial tissue fluid via a subcutaneous sensor for up to 72 hours. The codes for physician interpretation and report are also found here. When reporting these codes, do not add code 99091. These codes are reported no more than once per month.

# Neurology and Neuromuscular Procedures (95700-96020)

Code range 95700 to 96020 is used to report neurology and neuromuscular procedures. It should be noted that codes are out of numerical order. This range of codes is divided into the following sections:

- Sleep Testing—code range 95800-95811 and codes 95782 and 95783. This range of codes is used to report sleep studies and polysomnography to diagnose sleep disorders. Sleep studies are differentiated from polysomnography studies in the selection of codes from this range. Polysomnography studies include the recording of sleep and sleep staging.
- Routine Electroencephalography (EEG)—code range 95812-95830. These codes are differentiated by the monitoring time. Extended EEG includes reporting times longer than 40 minutes.

Routine EEG includes 20 to 40 minutes of monitoring time. Code 95829 is used to report an electrocorticogram completed at surgery.

- Electrocorticography—codes 95829 and 95836. These are out of sequence codes that report the recording of an EEG. Code 95829 reports an electrocorticogram at surgery (separate procedure) while code 95836 reports the recording of the electrocorticogram from an implanted brain neurostimular pulse generator/transmitter. Code 95836 includes the recording and interpretation, and written report up to 30 days. Prior to assigning code 95836, the coder should review the instructional notations that follow the code for further coding guidance.

- Range of Motion Testing—code range 95851–95857. This range of codes is used to report muscle and range of motion testing. The codes are differentiated according to the location of the muscle testing (e.g., extremity versus hand).

- Electromyography and Nerve Conduction Tests—code range 95860–95913. This range of codes is differentiated by the location of the testing. For example, code 95860 reports a needle electromyography of one extremity with or without related paraspinal areas, and code 95865 reports needle electromyography of the larynx.

- Intraoperative Neurophysiology—codes 95940 and 95941. These codes report intraoperative neurophysiology monitoring. These codes are add-on codes. Code 95940 requires that the provider is in attendance and reports each 15 minutes of attendance. Code 95941 reports the monitoring from outside the operating room or the monitoring of more than one case while in the operating room, and it reports an hour of time.

- Autonomic Function Tests—code range 95919–95924. These codes report the testing of autonomic nervous system functions and is differentiated according to the nerve that is tested.

- Evoked Potentials and Reflex Tests—code range 95925–95939. This group of codes reports studies completed to obtain information about the functioning of the nerves being tested.

- Special EEG Tests—code range 95954–95967. This code range is used to report special EEG tests that are completed to monitor the brain's electrical activity. Please note that there are numerous codes that are out of sequence.

- Neurostimulators, Analysis—Programming—code range 95970–95984. This range of codes is used to report the testing of neurostimulators. The codes are differentiated by the type of neurostimulator that is analyzed.

- Motion Analysis—code range 96000–96004. A patient's movement is analyzed by the completion of motion analysis.

- Functional Brain Mapping—code 96020. This includes neurofunctional testing selection and administration during noninvasive brain testing.

# Medical Genetics and Genetic Counseling Services (96040) and Adaptive Behavior Services (97151–97158)

Medical Genetics and Genetic Counseling Services are reported with code 96040. An extensive notation appears in the CPT manual in front of code 96040. This code is reported for each 30-minute face-to-face service with the patient or family. The time spent must be face-to-face time with the patient. Code range 97151 to 97158 are out of sequence codes that report Adaptive Behavior Assessments (codes 97151 and 97152) and Adaptive Behavior Treatment (codes 97153 to 97158). The CPT manual contains extensive instructional notations for this range of codes. In the CPT manual, review the instructional notations that apply to this range of codes.

# Central Nervous System Assessments and Tests (96105–96146), Health Behavior Assessment and Intervention (96156–96171), and Behavior Management Services (96202–96203)

Central nervous system assessments and tests (e.g., neurocognitive, mental status, and speech testing) are reported with code range 96105–96146. Included in this range are codes for psychological testing, assessment of aphasia, developmental testing, and neurobehavioral and neuropsychological testing. Following the completion of the tests, a report is typically generated. The codes require that the time reported to support the code selection is face-to-face time.

Health behavior assessment and intervention is reported with code range 96156–96171. This range is used to report assessments that are completed to identify the various psychological, behavioral, emotional, cognitive, and social factors that have an effect on the patient's physical health problems, and the prevention, treatment, or management of the physical health problems. The codes are differentiated by assessments versus interventions. The assessments are divided into initial assessments and reassessments. The intervention codes identify interventions completed for individuals, groups, or families. Code 96160 reports the administration of a patient-focused health risk assessment instrument with scoring and documentation for each standardized instrument. Code 96161 reports the administration of a care-giver focused health risk assessment instrument for the benefit of the patient, with scoring and documentation for each standardized instrument.

Codes 96202 and 96203 report Behavior Management Services. Locate these codes in a CPT manual and note that the selection of these codes are based on time. Review the definitions and notes prior to code 96202 that define behavior modification.

# Hydration, Therapeutic, Prophylactic, Diagnostic Injections and Infusions, and Chemotherapy and Other Highly Complex Drug or Highly Complex Biologic Agent Administration (96360–96549)

Codes in the 96360–96549 range are used to report the following services:

- Hydration (codes 96360–96361). These codes indicate that prepackaged fluids and electrolytes were administered through an intravenous (IV) infusion. The nurse usually starts these under the orders of a physician, who supervises the service. No special monitoring is required, and the patient is usually at little risk. These codes require that start and stop times be documented for accurate code assignment, as well as to support the service reported. These codes are not intended to be reported by the physician in the facility setting.

- Therapeutic, Prophylactic, and Diagnostic Injections and Infusions (excludes Chemotherapy and Other Highly Complex Drug, or Highly Complex Biologic Agent Administration) (code range 96365–96379). These codes are used to report IV infusions or injections for the administration of substances or drugs for reasons other than hydration. The person administering the treatment usually needs some type of training. The physician usually supervises the administration or performs the service, but in some instances, the physician assesses the patient and writes the order, which allows another qualified person to administer the drug or drugs. Constant presence of a qualified health-care professional is necessary, and time must be documented.

- Chemotherapy and Other Highly Complex Drug or Highly Complex Biologic Agent Administration (code range 96401–96549). This range of codes is divided into the following sections:

  - Injection and Intravenous Infusion Chemotherapy and Other Highly Complex Drug or Highly Complex Biologic Agent Administration—code range 96401–96417. This range is used to report chemotherapy administration by various techniques that include subcutaneous or intramuscular, intralesional, push technique, and intravenous infusion.

  - Intra-arterial Chemotherapy and Other Highly Complex Drug or Highly Complex Biologic Agent Administration—code range 96420–96425. Intra-arterial chemotherapy administration is coded to this range, which is differentiated by the technique, the length of time of the administration, or the use of a portable or implantable pump.

  - Other Injection and Infusion Services—code range 96440–96549. All other types of chemotherapy administration are reported with these codes. The refilling and maintenance of portable pumps, irrigation of devices, and other injections are also reported with this range.

It should be noted that extensive notes in the CPT manual apply to this range of codes.

# Photodynamic Therapy (96567–96574)

Code range 96567–96571 is used to report photodynamic therapy. During this type of therapy, the physician applies a photosensitizing agent to treat lesions. It should be noted that some of the codes are reported according to the length of time of the treatment. Medical documentation should be reviewed to ensure that the times that are reported by the codes can be substantiated.

# Special Dermatological Procedures (96900–96999)

Code range 96900–96999 is used to report special dermatological procedures. Procedures in this range include actinotherapy, examination of hair, photochemotherapy, and laser treatment for skin disease. Laser treatment codes are divided further according to the total area involved in the treatment.

# Physical Medicine and Rehabilitation (97010–97799)

Physical Medicine and Rehabilitation is divided into the following areas:

- Physical Therapy Evaluations—code range 97161–97164. These codes are out of sequence codes when presented in the CPT manual. Codes 97161 to 97163 report physical therapy evaluations ranging from low to high complexity. Code 97164 reports the re-evaluation of a physical therapy established plan of care. Prior to assigning these codes coders need to review the instructional notations and definitions that apply to these codes which appear before the code descriptions. Review these codes in the CPT manual.

- Occupational Therapy Evaluations—code range 97165–97168. These codes are out of sequence codes when presented in the CPT manual. Codes 97165 to 97167 report occupational therapy evaluations ranging from low to high complexity. Code 97168 reports the re-evaluation of an occupational therapy established plan of care. In the CPT manual, prior to the listing of these codes, instructional notations and definitions are listed that pertain to these codes. Review these instructional notations and definitions in the CPT manual.

- Athletic Training Evaluations—code range 97169–97172. These codes are out of sequence codes when presented in the CPT manual. Codes 97169 to 97171 report athletic training evaluations ranging from low to high complexity. Code 97172 reports the re-evaluation of an athletic training established plan of care. Prior to assigning these codes coders need to review the instructional notations and definitions that appear in the CPT manual prior to the listing of these codes. Locate and review these in the CPT manual.

- Modalities—supervised—code range 97010–97028. This includes any physical agent that is used for therapy, including application of hot or cold packs, traction, electrical stimulation, vasopneumatic devices, paraffin baths, whirlpool, diathermy, infrared, and ultraviolet. These services do not require constant one-on-one contact between patient and provider.

- Modalities—constant attendance—code range 97032–97039. To report this range of codes, the provider must be one on one with the patient; thus, the term *constant attendance*.

- Therapeutic Procedures—code range 97110–97546. These codes also require the physician or therapist to be in direct contact with the patient. The codes are differentiated by the therapeutic procedure that is completed. Some of the codes are reported for each 15 minutes of therapy. If time is associated with the code chosen, it must be supported in the documentation.

- Active Wound Care Management—code range 97597–97610. To report these codes, the provider must be in direct contact with the patient. These procedures are completed to promote healing or to remove devitalized and/or necrotic tissue. The coder should know the total surface area in square centimeters to appropriately capture all services.

- Tests and Measurements—code range 97750–97755. Physical performance tests or measurements and assistive technology assessments are reported with these codes. Each code represents 15-minute intervals.

- Orthotic Management and Prosthetic Management—code range 97760–97763. Orthotic management, prosthetic management, and checkout for established patients are reported with this range of codes.

Because most codes in this range are time-based codes, documentation of time in and time out is required by most insurance carriers.

# Additional Procedures (97802–99607)

The code range 97802–99607 reports the following procedures:

- Medical Nutrition Therapy—code range 97802–97804
- Acupuncture—code range 97810–97814
- Osteopathic Manipulative Treatment—code range 98925–98929
- Chiropractic Manipulative Treatment—code range 98940–98943
- Education and Training for Patient Self-Management—code range 98960–98962
- Non-Face-to-Face Nonphysician Services—code range 98966–98972, 98975–98978, and 98980–98981. This range of codes is expanding as more and more services are being offered to patients as a non-face-to-face service. Telephone Services, Qualified Nonphysician Health Care Professional Online Digital Assessment and Management Service, Remote Therapeutic Monitoring Services, and Remote Therapeutic Monitoring Treatment Management Services are reported in this code range. Review the codes and the instructional notations that appear for the codes in the CPT manual.
- Special Services, Procedures, and Reports—code range 99000–99082
- Qualifying Circumstances for Anesthesia—code range 99100–99140
- Moderate (Conscious) Sedation—code range 99151–99157
- Other Services and Procedures—code range 99170–99199
- Medication Therapy Management Services—code range 99605–99607

# Summary

- The Medicine section follows the Pathology and Laboratory section.
- There are many sections within the Medicine section.
- Diagnostic and therapeutic procedures are found in the Medicine section.
- Some codes break out the professional and technical components.
- Some codes in the Medicine section are time based.
- Code range 98966–98981 reports non-face-to-face nonphysician services.

# Internet Links

For more information on some of the topics related to psychiatry covered in this chapter, visit **http://www.aapb.org**. To learn about procedures, navigate to **https://www.nlm.nih.gov/index.html** and search for procedures discussed in this chapter.

# Chapter Review

## True/False

**Instructions:** Indicate whether the following statements are true (T) or false (F).

1. _____ The code range for medical nutrition therapy is 97802–97804.

2. _____ The Cardiovascular subsection of the Medicine section includes codes used to report diagnostic and therapeutic services.

3. _____ Cardiopulmonary resuscitation is reported using code 92990.

4. _____ The physiological responses that cannot be treated using biofeedback include high blood pressure and incontinence.

5. _____ An optometrist is not a medical doctor but can prescribe medication and corrective lenses.

## Fill in the Blank

**Instructions:** Fill in the blanks in the statements that follow.

6. The process of taking waste from the blood when the kidneys are not functioning properly to allow the body to do this on its own is called _____.

7. A form of psychiatry that involves the administering of an intravenous drug that allows the patient to release thoughts that might be suppressed or repressed is called _____.

8. A type of scope that examines the eye for signs of glaucoma is called _____.

9. Lung capacity can be measured by _____ testing.

10. Peripheral artery disease (PAD) rehabilitation is reported using code _____.

# Coding Assignments

**Instructions:** For each of the following procedures, select the appropriate CPT code.

1. 15 minutes of upper-extremity prosthetic training initial encounter _____

2. Home visit for intramuscular injections _____

3. Photo tests _____

4. Determination of venous pressure _____

5. Cardiopulmonary resuscitation _____

6. Diagnostic analysis of cochlear implant with programming for 4-year-old patient _____

7. Binaural electroacoustic evaluation for hearing aid _____

8. Live yellow fever vaccine, for a 22-year-old (no counseling), subcutaneous use _____

9. Family psychotherapy with patient present _____

10. 16-year-old, end-stage renal disease service, one day of service _____

11. Duodenal motility study _____

12. Re-evaluation of an occupational therapy established plan of care. (Assume that the documentation meets all of the components for this code.) _____

13. Select picture audiometry _____

14. Auditory rehabilitation for postlingual hearing loss _____

15. Left heart catheterization by transseptal puncture through intact septum _____

16. Initiation and management of continuous positive airway pressure ventilation _____

17. Vestibular evoked myogenic potential testing, cervical, with interpretation and report _____

18. Ergonovine provocation test _____

19. Monaural hearing aid check _____

20. Hypnotherapy _____

21. Anorectal manometry _____

22. Electro-oculography with interpretation and report _____

23. Tone-decay test _____

24. Filtered speech test _____

25. Complete transcranial Doppler study of the intracranial arteries _____

# Case Studies

**Instructions:** Review each case and indicate the correct code(s).

## Case 1

This is an 80-year-old male who has been suffering for the past eight weeks with a nonhealing ulcer on the lateral aspect of the right calf. The ulcer does look better today, having gone from 6 cm to 4.3 cm. It is still oozing, and there is some necrosis around the lower edge of the wound. I debrided the wound with a scalpel into the dermal layer of all devitalized tissue. Bacitracin was applied, and the wound was dressed. The patient was given instructions on how to care for the wound until he presents again in two weeks.

**CPT code(s):** _____

## Case 2

This is a 32-year-old, Type 2 diabetic female. She was diagnosed approximately two weeks ago and now presents for an initial assessment and intervention for medical nutrition therapy. She does not want to have to take insulin, so her doctor agreed that, with some nutrition counseling and exercise, she may be able to avoid it. We spent 30 minutes discussing the American Diabetic Association diet plan and how to implement it. We also discussed exercise and how to work it into her schedule. She will follow up with me in two weeks to see how things are progressing. If she has any problems before then, she will call this office.

**CPT code(s):** _____

## Case 3

Marcus is a 2-year-old child who presents here with his mother. He is running a fever of 101 and is very lethargic for a 2-year-old. He is not eating or drinking, and mom said he has vomited each time he tries. She did get a few drops of water into him prior to this visit, but nothing else. He has not had a wet diaper in the past six hours. An IV of D5-1/2 normal saline + 30 mEq KCl was started. We performed the IV therapy for one hour, after which Marcus was acting much improved. His temp was down to 98. We gave him a popsicle, which he kept down. Mom was instructed to let us know if he does not have a wet diaper over the next few hours or if his condition worsens.

**CPT code(s):** _____

# HCPCS Codes

## Chapter Outline

Introduction

Certificate of Medical Necessity for
    DME Items and Advance Beneficiary Notice

Organization and Use of HCPCS
    Level II Codes

HCPCS Sections

Appendices

Summary

Internet Links

Chapter Review

Coding Assignments

Case Studies

## Learning Objectives

### At the conclusion of this chapter, you should be able to:

1. Define key terms related to HCPCS coding.
2. Identify who publishes HCPCS Level II codes and when updates are made.
3. Select HCPCS Level II codes.
4. Summarize the contents included in each of the HCPCS Level II appendices.

*Note:* A Level II HCPCS manual is needed to work through this chapter.

## Key Terms

Advance Beneficiary
    Notice (ABN)

advanced life support
    (ALS)

basic life support (BLS)

Certificate of Medical
    Necessity (CMN)

durable medical
    equipment (DME)

durable medical
    equipment,
    prosthetics, orthotics,

and supplies
    (DMEPOS)

enteral

Healthcare Common
    Procedure Coding
    System (HCPCS)

Level II codes

National Drug Codes
    (NDCs)

parenteral

## Introduction

The **Healthcare Common Procedure Coding System** is referred to with the acronym **HCPCS**, which is pronounced "hicpics." HCPCS consists of CPT codes, Level I and National Codes, and Level II codes. The **Level II codes** are published annually by the Centers for Medicare & Medicaid Services (CMS) at the same time the Level I codes or CPT codes are published. The American Medical Association (AMA) maintains the Level I codes, whereas CMS maintains Level II codes (ever since a 2003 mandate by the Secretary of the Department of Health and Human Services). Level II codes report **durable medical equipment (DME)**, such as wheelchairs, crutches, and bandages. These codes are also used to report prosthetics, medications, orthotics, temporary Medicare codes, provider services that are not found in CPT, and temporary National Codes. Because the CPT codes do not cover all services provided, HCPCS codes allow for more accurate reporting of services rendered during a patient encounter. The coder may see DME noted as **DMEPOS (durable medical equipment, prosthetics, orthotics, and supplies)**.

HCPCS codes are alphanumeric, comprising one letter followed by four numbers.

> **EXAMPLE:**
> J0207          Injection, amifostine, 500 mg

The alpha character indicates the section where the code is found. In our example, the *J* indicates this code is found in the section that identifies HCPCS drugs administered by means other than oral.

Level II codes are a standardized coding system that is accepted by Medicare, Medicaid, workers' compensation insurance, and most commercial and private insurances to most accurately reflect the supplies provided to patients at the time of a service. Some payers may not accept certain codes from the HCPCS coding system, but prior to billing a service, the coder may check fee schedules or contact the payer directly to see if the code will be recognized.

Medical record documentation needs to support the medical necessity for billing of items reported with HCPCS Level II codes. The clinical notes need to be clear as to why a DME or DMEPOS is necessary, and a signed and dated order must be provided.

> **EXAMPLE:** Dr. Martin had been treating Sylvia for the past two years for pain and swelling occurring with arthritis. Today she was given a 20 mg injection of methylprednisolone acetate. This visit is for the first injection.

In this instance, Dr. Martin would report J1020 to reflect the injection of the 20 mg of methylprednisolone acetate. The reason for the injection was clearly noted in an effort to support the medical necessity for the injection. Of note is the fact that these codes are *not* used on the inpatient side for facility billing. These services would be included in the reimbursement paid to the facility based on the diagnosis, not on services rendered.

# Certificate of Medical Necessity for DME Items and Advance Beneficiary Notice

A **Certificate of Medical Necessity (CMN)** clearly explains why a physician feels that a patient needs the DME item or service. This certificate should be filed in the patient's medical record for certain supplies. Although a CMN may be kept on file, this alone cannot justify the medical necessity for the DME. The CMN can be used in addition to clinical documentation substantiating the service or item rendered. If a DME supplier is audited by Medicare, the original CMN may be requested. Although a faxed copy to the supplier is enough to support the issuance of a supply, there is an understanding that an original CMN is kept on file at the provider's office.

If there is no clinical documentation to support the medical necessity of a service rendered, the provider cannot bill the patient directly unless the provider of the service could not have known that the service would not be paid by Medicare or if the provider had the patient sign an **Advance Beneficiary Notice (ABN)**. An ABN is written notice to the patient that states the patient was made aware of the exact procedure being considered, the dollar amount associated with the procedure, and the possibility that Medicare would not pay for this service. All payers have their own guidelines for payment of the HCPCS codes. Medicare publishes noncovered HCPCS Level II codes in the HCPCS manual.

# Organization and Use of HCPCS Level II Codes

HCPCS Level II codes are organized into the following sections:

- A codes—Transportation Services Including Ambulance, Medical and Surgical Supplies
- B codes—Enteral and Parenteral Therapy
- C codes—Outpatient PPS
- E codes—Durable Medical Equipment
- G codes—Procedures/Professional Services (Temporary)
- H codes—Alcohol and Drug Abuse Treatment Services
- J codes—Drugs Administered Other Than Oral Method and Chemotherapy Drugs
- K codes—Temporary Codes, for use by Durable Medical Equipment Administrative Contractors
- L codes—Orthotic and Prosthetic Procedures and Devices
- M codes—Medical Services
- P codes—Pathology and Laboratory Services
- Q codes—Q Codes (Temporary)
- R codes—Diagnostic Radiology Services
- S codes—Temporary National Codes (Non-Medicare)
- T codes—National T Codes Established for State Medicaid Agencies
- U codes—Other
- V codes—Vision Services and Hearing Services

The HCPCS Level II manual is arranged by code number. Though services are grouped together, the index is set up by the name of the medical or surgical supply, the orthotic or prosthetic, or the service provided. The index may also be referenced by the brand name or the generic name of a drug. In some instances, the actual body part that requires the supply may also be referenced.

> **EXAMPLE:**
> Cervical
>
> collar, L0120, L0130, L0140, L0150, L0170
>
> halo, L0810–L0830
>
> head harness/halter, E0942
>
> helmet, A8000–A8004
>
> orthotic, L0180–L0200
>
> traction equipment, not requiring frame, E0855

The symbols used in the HCPCS Level II code manual are similar to those in the CPT manual. A black circle (●) preceding a code indicates a new code, and a black triangle (▲) indicates revised terminology or rules.

Each of the publishers of HCPCS Level II code manuals has its own color coding, symbols, and level-of-coverage instructions. You will need to read the introduction to your particular manual to be sure you are getting the greatest benefits from it.

Steps in code selection for HCPCS are the same as the steps in locating any other CPT code. The coder first needs to identify the service or procedure performed. The term referenced may be a supply, a route of administration, a body part, or a procedure. After identifying the term necessary to locate the code, the coder references the index. A code is selected and then located in the manual. Check the exact verbiage associated with the code selected. All instructional notations should be reviewed. If necessary, refer to the appendices and identify any modifiers that might need to be applied. After making these references, select and assign a code to the service.

> **EXAMPLE:** The diagnostic statement reads, "Issue a drainable ostomy pouch for use on barrier with locking flange (2-piece system)." The coder follows these steps:
> 1. Turn to the index and look under the term *ostomy*.
> 2. Locate the terms listed under the main term.
> 3. Locate the term *pouch*, and follow indentations under *pouch* to the term *drainable*.
> 4. Find codes A4412 and A4413 and A5056 and A5057.
> 5. Locate these codes in the A code section of the code manual.

When the coder reviews the verbiage associated with A4412 and A4413, he or she finds that these codes do not include the term *locking flange*. However, further review of this code section brings the coder to A4426—Ostomy pouch, drainable; for use on barrier with locking flange (2-piece system), each.

## Exercise 23.1—Finding a HCPCS Code

**Underline the main term that would be referenced in the index to find the correct HCPCS code.**

Then assign the proper HCPCS code.

1. Single-vision lenticular lens _____
2. Aluminum crutches _____
3. Food supplement _____
4. Indwelling port _____
5. Breast pump manual _____
6. Wound cleanser _____
7. Elbow splint _____
8. Urine sensitivity study _____
9. Vascular closure device _____
10. Diabetic shoe inlay _____

The coder should be sure that a HCPCS Level I code is not available before assigning a HCPCS Level II code. The coder needs to read the selected code carefully because some codes indicate "each" or "per," so the quantity reported may need to be more than 1. Hospitals and offices can lose revenue if the proper amounts are not reported.

> **EXAMPLE:** Stuart needed new handgrips for his walker. Two hand grips were dispensed. The code reported was A4636 × 2.

The A4636 code reads, "Replacement, handgrip, cane, crutch, or walker, each." The word *each* indicates that for each replacement handgrip given, the code may be reported separately, so the quantity would be 2. Reimbursement is lost if the quantity is reported incorrectly.

## Exercise 23.2—Learning HCPCS

**Locate the correct code for the statement given.**

1. Implantable neurostimulator adaptor
   _____

2. Static finger splint _____

3. Dry pressure mattress _____

4. Urinary incontinence repair device without sling graft _____

5. Seat attachment for walker
   _____

6. Clubfoot wedge _____

7. Prolotherapy _____

8. Mental health assessment by nonphysician
   _____

# HCPCS Sections

After the index, the sections of the manual begin with the A codes. A codes are used to report transportation services; medical and surgical supplies; and administrative, miscellaneous, and investigational services. It should be noted that there are large gaps in the numbering system for HCPCS Level II codes. The reason for these gaps in numbering is that there is room for growth within a code set, allowing new items to be used by providers.

## A Codes—Transportation Services Including Ambulance, Medical and Surgical Supplies

The transportation services are reported using A0021–A0999 and include wheelchair van services, taxi transportation, and ambulance emergency transportation. Also reported using A codes are ground mileage, nonemergency transportation, and air transportation. Some of the codes mention "ancillary" in the code description.

> **EXAMPLE:**
> A0200        Nonemergency transportation: ancillary lodging, escort

The ancillary service codes are used to report additional expenses incurred during travel, such as lodging, tolls, and meals. Some of the codes in this section contain abbreviations such as ALS and BLS. **ALS** is used to denote **advanced life support**, **BLS** is used to indicate **basic life support**.

Ambulance services require identification of point of pickup and point of destination. These points of origin and destination are indicated by the use of specific modifiers, which are noted within HCPCS. The arrangement modifiers are placed after the code for the service being rendered. The QM modifier "Ambulance service provided under arrangement by a provider of services," or the QN modifier "Ambulance service furnished directly by a provider of services," would be appropriate. The modifiers describing the origin and destination are listed second.

The Medical and Surgical Supplies section of the A codes comprises the A4201–A9999 code range. The coder should query the local Medicare or primary insurance carrier to verify payment of services rendered or items dispensed that would be coded from this code range. Some items or services, though found here to have a specific code, are considered bundled into other services and are not reported separately.

## Exercise 23.3—A Codes

Select the proper A code for the item or service described.

1. Mileage for an ALS patient who needed to be transported 3 miles _____

2. Ostomy irrigation bag _____

3. Blood pressure monitor _____

4. One fistula cannulation kit for hemodialysis _____

5. Nonelastic, below-the-knee compression wrap, right and left _____

6. One sterile eye pad _____

7. One pint of Betadine solution _____

8. Replacement battery for patient-owned ventilator _____

# B Codes—Enteral and Parental Therapy

The next section in the HCPCS Level II manual is Enteral and Parenteral Therapy. This chapter is broken down into the enteral formulae and enteral medical supplies, parenteral nutritional solutions and supplies, and enteral and parenteral pumps. The term **enteral** refers to a route of administration involving the gastrointestinal tract. **Parenteral** refers to a route of administration *not* involving the gastrointestinal tract. Some of the pump codes found in this section of HCPCS require the use of an MS modifier, which reads, "Six months' maintenance and servicing fee for reasonable and necessary parts and labor which are not covered under any manufacturer or supplier warranty." Coders should check with local carriers to see if the use of this modifier is appropriate in their area.

# C Codes—HCPCS Outpatient PPS

C codes are used to report services that may be used by the outpatient prospective payment system (OPPS) and are not to be used to report any other services. These codes are used for technical services only and may be reported by non-OPPS hospitals; Critical Access Hospitals; Indian Health Service Hospitals; hospitals located in Guam, Saipan, American Samoa, and the Virgin Islands; and Maryland waiver hospitals at their discretion. CMS updates the C codes quarterly. These codes can only be reported for facility (technical) services.

## Exercise 23.4—HCPCS B and C Codes

Select the correct B or C code for each of the following services or items.

1. Catheter for hemodialysis patient receiving short-term infusion _____

2. Enteral nutrition infusion pump with alarm _____

3. Nasogastric tubing with stylet _____

4. Transluminal atherectomy rotational catheter _____

5. Clevidipine butyrate injection, 1 mg _____

6. Parenteral nutrition solution; amino acid, 3.5%—home mix _____

7. NOC for enteral supplies _____

8. Ureteral catheter _____

# D Codes—Dental Procedures

Dental procedures and services begin with D0000 and go through D9999. This range of codes is copyrighted and modified by the American Dental Association (ADA), not by the national panel responsible for the other HCPCS codes.

The D codes are used for reporting oral evaluations, x-rays, laboratory testing, preventive services, restorative services, and prosthetics. There are also codes included for surgical procedures and orthodontics. The coder should refer to a CPT manual for codes that may be more appropriate for the setting in which the service was performed. D codes are not currently found in the HCPCS manual. The ADA holds the copyright on these codes and has instructed CMS to remove them. D codes are available in other resources.

# E Codes—Durable Medical Equipment

E codes are used to report durable medical equipment such as walkers, canes, crutches, respiratory equipment, and pacemakers. A good deal of the equipment used for patients with respiratory disorders is found in this code range. The documentation surrounding the billing of these codes must support the medical necessity of the supply being reported. If the medical necessity is not clear, the service may be denied.

# G Codes—Temporary Procedures/Professional Services

G codes are used to report professional procedures and services that have not been assigned a CPT code but would typically be services found in the CPT manual. These national codes are assigned by CMS on a temporary basis.

> **EXAMPLE:**
>   **G0156**      Services of home health/hospice aide in home health or hospice settings, each 15 minutes

The services provided by a home health aide are not found within CPT, so the services are reported using code G0156. Should a better code become available within CPT, the CPT code would be the code reported instead of the G code. The G codes may or may not be paid by insurances. The coder should check with the carrier before the service is rendered.

## Exercise 23.5—E and G Codes

**Match the code in the first column with the correct description in the second column.**

1. E0310 _____
2. E0190 _____
3. G0252 _____
4. E2610 _____
5. E0160 _____
6. G0390 _____
7. E1310 _____
8. G0379 _____
9. G0106 _____
10. E0607 _____

a. Wheelchair seat cushion
b. Home blood glucose monitor
c. Direct admission of patient for observation
d. Barium enema, for colorectal cancer screening
e. Full-length bed rails
f. Built-in whirlpool
g. Trauma response team
h. Portable sitz bath equipment with commode
i. Decubitus care pillow
j. PET imaging of breast

# H Codes—Behavioral Health and/or Substance Abuse Treatment Services

H codes are not recognized by Medicare but are used by Medicaid agencies that are state mandated for reporting mental health services, including behavioral health. Drug and alcohol treatment services are included in this code range.

# J Codes—Drugs Administered Other Than Oral Method

J codes are used to report drugs that would typically not be self-administered. J codes can be found by referencing the following terms: *chemotherapy, inhalation,* or *IV solution*. Appendix 1—Table of Drugs can also be used to locate the proper J code. Most of the codes in this chapter are noted by generic names, but the brand names are listed under the code description in some cases.

> **EXAMPLE:**
> J0300        Injection, amobarbital, up to 125 mg
> **Use this code for Amytal.**

Some payers require the submission of **National Drug Codes (NDCs)** when you report medications using J codes. An NDC number is an 11-digit number that identifies the manufacturer, the product, and the package size. The NDC number can be found on the box, bottle, or other part of the packaging. The NDC numbers can also be found online. It is extremely important that the correct information is reported.

## Exercise 23.6—J Codes

**Identify the correct J code for the description given.**

1. NebuPent Route INH
2. Hydrocortisone sodium succinate
3. Dacarbazine, 200 mg
4. Levalbuterol (compounded) administered through a nebulizer, 0.5 mg
5. Trilone, 5 mg injection
6. 1 mg injection of busulfan
7. Amifostine injection, 500 mg
8. Maxipime injection, 500 mg

# K Codes—Temporary Codes Assigned to DME Regional Carriers

Next are the temporary K codes that are used to report DME wheelchairs and accessories to DME regional carriers instead of to Medicare. The K codes include wheelchairs and wheelchair accessories and quality measures.

# L Codes—Orthotic and Prosthetic Procedures and Devices

Orthotic and prosthetic procedures and devices are reported with L codes. L codes include orthotic devices, halo procedures, and scoliosis procedures. The use of orthotic treatment of scoliosis requires continual adjustments.

When you are coding from this section of HCPCS, it is important to read any notations that might be associated with the codes you are looking at because some codes are classified as "base" codes. Base codes report basic procedures and can be modified by adding codes from the "Additions" section. For example, the procedures in the L6000–L6590 range are considered base procedures and can be modified by adding procedure codes from section L6600–L6698.

---

## Exercise 23.7—K and L Codes

**Select the code that best identifies the supply rendered or service performed.**

1. Rancho hip action, hip orthotic, custom fabricated _____

2. Group 5, single-power wheelchair for child weighing 85 lb _____

3. One replacement battery for external infusion pump owned by the patient; silver oxide, 1.5 volts _____

4. Transmitting coil for a cochlear implant _____

5. Hallux prosthetic implant _____

6. Cervical, collar, molded to patient model _____

7. Above-knee, molded-socket, single-axis constant friction, knee, shin, SACH foot _____

8. Hallux implant _____

---

# M Codes—Medical Services and Quality Measures

The M codes are used to report cellular therapy, prolotherapy, intravenous (IV) chelation therapy, fabric wrapping of an abdominal aneurysm and quality measures.

# P Codes—Pathology and Laboratory Services

Pathology and laboratory services are currently reported using P codes. This code range is used to report chemistry and toxicology tests, pathology screening tests, microbiology, and miscellaneous pathology and laboratory services. This section is also where the coder will find the codes for transfusions and infusions.

# Q Codes—Temporary Codes

Q codes are temporary codes used to report various supplies, drugs, and biologicals in instances where no permanent code has been assigned.

# R Codes—Diagnostic Radiology Services

Radiology services are currently reported using R codes. There are very few R codes at this time. The R codes are used to report the transportation of electrocardiogram (EKG) equipment and/or portable x-ray equipment.

# S Codes—Temporary National Codes

S codes are non-Medicare codes. These codes are temporary codes that are utilized by Blue Cross/Blue Shield Association (BCBSA) and also the Health Insurance Association of America (HIAA). The codes are used to report supplies, drugs, and services when there are no National Codes.

Along with BCBSA and other private payers, Medicaid also recognizes some S codes. The Medicaid fee schedule should be referenced to identify the S codes that are recognized by Medicaid.

# T Codes—Temporary National Codes Established for State Medicaid Agencies

T codes are used by Medicaid state agencies. Like the S codes, T codes are not recognized by Medicare but are recognized by some private payers. Some of the services found in this code range include respite care, sign language or interpretive services, and nursing care in the home. As with the S codes, query the payers as to whether they will pay a service reported by the T code before you bill the code.

# U Codes—Other

U codes are used to report other codes that are not found in HCPCS. Currently the U codes contain codes that relate to COVID-19 diagnostic panels and infectious agent detection. Reference a HCPCS Level II coding manual for the specific codes.

# V Codes—Vision Services and Hearing Services

HCPCS also contains V codes. The V codes within HCPCS are used to report services that are related to the senses. Vision services are first, followed by services related to hearing, and then speech and language pathology services. This is the last section before the appendices.

# Appendices

The appendices of HCPCS contain a great deal of information and are used very frequently. Appendix 1, Table of Drugs, is referenced for medications. Appendix 1 is a four-column table. The first column of drug names is listed in alphabetic order by brand name and generic name. The second column notes the unit dose, the third column identifies the route of administration, and the last column indicates the HCPCS code used to identify the medication. These sample columns are illustrated in Table 23-1.

**TABLE 23-1** HCPCS Appendix 1 Table Columns

| Drug Name | Unit Per | Route | Code |
|-----------|----------|-------|------|
| Adalimumab | 20 mg | SC | J0135 |
| Adasuve | 1 mg | INH | J2062 |
| Adcetris | 1 mg | IV | J9042 |
| Adenocard | 1 mg | IV | J1053 |

Appendix 2 identifies modifiers used with HCPCS codes. HCPCS Level II code modifiers are used in the same manner as HCPCS Level I codes. Modifiers are used to enhance or further identify a service code. The modifiers could be alpha or alphanumeric.

**EXAMPLE:** The podiatrist performed a trimming of dystrophic nails on the first three toes of the left foot.

The doctor would report a G0127 for the nail trimming and use modifiers to identify the toes treated. The modifiers begin with TA for the great toe, left foot; T1, for the second digit, left foot; and T2 for the third digit.

Appendix 3 in the CPT manual lists abbreviations and acronyms used in HCPCS descriptors. Appendix 4 in the CPT manual is entitled Internet-only Manuals. It identifies the listing of the CMS Web-based system program instruction and provides a very brief description of sections of the CMS manual. This appendix is quite long but does contain good information. Appendix 5 contains new, changed, deleted, and reinstated HCPCS codes. This appendix is used as a quick reference for yearly coding changes. The last appendix is Appendix 6, which is a quick reference for place of service and types of service.

## Exercise 23.8—Understanding the Drug Table

Using Appendix 1 in the HCPCS manual, locate the drug noted and complete the table.

| Drug Name | Unit Per | Route | Code |
|---|---|---|---|
| Alemtuzumab | | | |
| Cancidas | | | |
| Enbrel | | | |
| Gastromark | | | |
| Fertinex | | | |
| Nubain | | | |
| Wehdryl | | | |
| Medidex | | | |
| Panitumumab | | | |

# Summary

- Level II HCPCS codes are published annually by the Centers for Medicare & Medicaid Services (CMS).
- Level II codes are used to report prosthetics, medications, orthotics, temporary Medicare codes, provider services that are not found in CPT, and temporary National Codes.
- A Certificate of Medical Necessity (CMN) can be used in addition to the clinical documentation to substantiate a service rendered.
- Level II codes are organized into the following sections:
  - A codes—Transportation Services Including Ambulance, Medical and Surgical Supplies
  - B codes—Enteral and Parenteral Therapy
  - C codes—Outpatient PPS
  - E codes—Durable Medical Equipment
  - G codes—Procedures/Professional Services
  - H codes—Alcohol and Drug Abuse Treatment Services
  - J codes—Drugs Administered By Other Than Oral Method including Chemotherapy
  - K codes—Temporary Codes, for use by Durable Medical Equipment Administrative Contractors
  - L codes—Orthotic and Prosthetic Procedures and Devices
  - M codes—Medical Services
  - P codes—Pathology and Laboratory Services
  - Q codes—Temporary Codes
  - R codes—Diagnostic Radiology Services
  - S codes—Temporary National Codes (Non-Medicare)
  - T codes—National T Codes Established for State Medicaid Agencies
  - U codes—Other
  - V codes—Vision Services and Hearing Services

# Internet Links

Internet references can be found at the following locations:

**http://www.cms.hhs.gov/MedHCPCSGenInfo/**

**http://www.nd.gov/eforms/doc/sfn00526.pdf** (This is a copy of the Certificate of Medical Necessity.)

# Chapter Review

## Fill in the Blank

**Instructions:** Complete the following statements.

1. HCPCS Level II codes are published _____ by _____ .
   (when)                                    (who)

2. A document clearly explains why the physician feels the patient needs durable medical equipment or a service, and it must be filed in the patient's medical record for certain supplies. This document is known as a certificate of _____ necessity.

3. HCPCS codes that are used to report transportation services are _____ codes.

4. A written notice to the patient that identifies a provided service that might not be covered by CMS is known as a(n) _____ .

5. A postural drainage board is reported with code _____ .

## True/False

**Instructions:** Indicate whether the following statements are true (T) or false (F).

6. _____ Appendix 2 identifies modifiers used with category 1 and category 2 codes.

7. _____ The route of administration involving the gastrointestinal tract is called the parenteral.

8. _____ When coding for ambulance services, the point of pickup and the destination must both be identified.

9. _____ Level I codes are published by the CMS.

10. _____ Codes related to the senses, such as speech and hearing, are located in the Q code series.

# Coding Assignments

**Instructions:** Assign the correct HCPCS Level II code for each of the following statements.

1. Instruction in initial use of insulin pump

   _____

2. Pelvic sling _____

3. Abdominal aneurysm wrap

   _____

4. Hearing aid battery _____

5. Oxygen stand _____

6. Foot drop splint, prefabricated

   _____

7. Colorectal cancer screening, screening sigmoidoscopy barium enema _____

8. Adult, fiberglass short arm cast

   _____

9. Durable humidifier for extensive supplemental humidification during IPPB treatment

   _____

10. Full-length bedrails _____

11. Dual-chamber, rate-responsive pacemaker _____

12. Durr-Fillauer semi-rigid cervical collar _____

13. CPAP mask _____

14. Heel holder, with ankle strap _____

15. Levine stomach tube _____

16. Food thickener (3 oz) _____

17. Community psychiatric supportive treatment, as needed _____

18. DonJoy knee immobilizer _____

19. Lobar lung transplantation _____

20. 50 mg of Phenergan _____

21. Pelvic belt _____

22. Inversion/eversion correction device _____

23. Annual depression screening, 15 minutes _____

24. Benesch boot, pair, child _____

25. 1 mg of Pertuzumab _____

26. Replacement tubing for breast pump _____

27. Embolization protective system _____

28. Fixed height folding walker _____

29. Portable Sitz type bath _____

30. Cervical overdoor traction equipment _____

# Case Studies

Instructions: Review each case and indicate the correct code(s).

## Case 1

Sally Smith presented today for a follow-up visit after eye surgery. The wound was examined, and no complications were noted. An occlusive eye patch was placed on her left eye. She was instructed to return in eight weeks.

**Note to billing:** Visit was postoperative care; bill for supply used.

**HCPCS code(s):** _____

## Case 2

Michelle presented to her doctor's office with a complaint of amenorrhea. A pregnancy test showed that she was pregnant. The doctor gave her prenatal vitamins and told her he would see her in four weeks.

The patient will be charged only for the prenatal vitamins because her pregnancy will fall into a global service.

**HCPCS code(s):** _____

## Case 3

**DME Delivery Bill**

**Patient:** Harry Westin

**Age:** 73 years old

**Site of Delivery:** Patient's home

**Item Delivered:** Full-length bedside rails

HCPCS code(s): _____

## Case 4

**Orthotics Invoice**

**Name:** Mary Jump     DOB: 1/10/57

**Diagnosis:** Left foot arch deformity

**Arch support supplied:** Premolded longitudinal left foot arch support, removable

HCPCS code(s): _____

## Case 5

**Hemodialysis Clinic Note**

Ralf Past will be traveling out of town and will be performing his dialysis on his own with the assistance of his wife, who is a nurse. He was given a portable compact travel hemodialyzer system.

HCPCS code(s): _____

## Case 6

Sandra was suffering with shoulder pain, which started about six weeks ago, getting progressively worse. Most movement is painful, and the patient states that she is unable to lift anything over her head. We discussed several options. Sandra agreed that the injection would be the best option. 80 mg of Cortimex was injected into the shoulder joint for bursitis.

HCPCS code(s): _____

# Billing Forms (CMS-1500 and UB-04)

**FIGURE A1-1** The CMS-1500 Form

**FIGURE A1-2**  The UB-04 Form, Also Known as the CMS-1450 Form

**FIGURE A2-1** Supine Position

**FIGURE A2-2** Trendelenburg Position

**FIGURE A2-3** Reverse Trendelenburg Position

**FIGURE A2-4** Fowler's Position

**FIGURE A2-5** Sitting Position

**FIGURE A2-6** Lithotomy Position

**FIGURE A2-7** Prone Position

**FIGURE A2-8** Kraske Position

**FIGURE A2-9** Right Lateral Position

**FIGURE A2-10** Right Kidney Position

(A) Regions

(B) Quadrants

**FIGURE A3-1** Abdominopelvic Divisions

# 2023 Anesthesia Code Base Units

| Code | 2023 Base Unit | Code | 2023 Base Unit | Code | 2023 Base Unit | Code | 2023 Base Unit |
|---|---|---|---|---|---|---|---|
| 00100 | 5 | 00218 | 13 | 00537 | 10 | 00731 | 5 |
| 00102 | 6 | 00220 | 10 | 00539 | 18 | 00732 | 6 |
| 00103 | 5 | 00222 | 6 | 00540 | 12 | 00750 | 4 |
| 00104 | 4 | 00300 | 5 | 00541 | 15 | 00752 | 6 |
| 00120 | 5 | 00320 | 6 | 00542 | 15 | 00754 | 7 |
| 00124 | 4 | 00322 | 3 | 00546 | 15 | 00756 | 7 |
| 00126 | 4 | 00326 | 7 | 00548 | 17 | 00770 | 15 |
| 00140 | 5 | 00350 | 10 | 00550 | 10 | 00790 | 7 |
| 00142 | 4 | 00352 | 5 | 00560 | 15 | 00792 | 13 |
| 00144 | 6 | 00400 | 3 | 00561 | 25 | 00794 | 8 |
| 00145 | 6 | 00402 | 5 | 00562 | 20 | 00796 | 30 |
| 00147 | 4 | 00404 | 5 | 00563 | 25 | 00797 | 11 |
| 00148 | 4 | 00406 | 13 | 00566 | 25 | 00800 | 4 |
| 00160 | 5 | 00410 | 4 | 00567 | 18 | 00802 | 5 |
| 00162 | 7 | 00450 | 5 | 00580 | 20 | 00811 | 4 |
| 00164 | 4 | 00454 | 3 | 00600 | 10 | 00812 | 3 |
| 00170 | 5 | 00470 | 6 | 00604 | 13 | 00813 | 5 |
| 00172 | 6 | 00472 | 10 | 00620 | 10 | 00820 | 5 |
| 00174 | 6 | 00474 | 13 | 00625 | 13 | 00830 | 4 |
| 00176 | 7 | 00500 | 15 | 00626 | 15 | 00832 | 6 |
| 00190 | 5 | 00520 | 6 | 00630 | 8 | 00834 | 5 |
| 00192 | 7 | 00522 | 4 | 00632 | 7 | 00836 | 6 |
| 00210 | 11 | 00524 | 4 | 00635 | 4 | 00840 | 6 |
| 00211 | 10 | 00528 | 8 | 00640 | 3 | 00842 | 4 |
| 00212 | 5 | 00529 | 11 | 00670 | 13 | 00844 | 7 |
| 00214 | 9 | 00530 | 4 | 00700 | 4 | 00846 | 8 |
| 00215 | 9 | 00532 | 4 | 00702 | 4 | 00848 | 8 |
| 00216 | 15 | 00534 | 7 | 00730 | 5 | 00851 | 6 |

(*continues*)

(*continued*)

| Code | 2023 Base Unit | Code | 2023 Base Unit | Code | 2023 Base Unit | Code | 2023 Base Unit |
|------|------|------|------|------|------|------|------|
| 00860 | 6 | 00948 | 4 | 01402 | 7 | 01680 | 3 |
| 00862 | 7 | 00950 | 5 | 01404 | 5 | 01710 | 3 |
| 00864 | 8 | 00952 | 4 | 01420 | 3 | 01712 | 5 |
| 00865 | 7 | 01112 | 5 | 01430 | 3 | 01714 | 5 |
| 00866 | 10 | 01120 | 6 | 01432 | 6 | 01716 | 5 |
| 00868 | 10 | 01130 | 3 | 01440 | 8 | 01730 | 3 |
| 00870 | 5 | 01140 | 15 | 01442 | 8 | 01732 | 3 |
| 00872 | 7 | 01150 | 10 | 01444 | 8 | 01740 | 4 |
| 00873 | 5 | 01160 | 4 | 01462 | 3 | 01742 | 5 |
| 00880 | 15 | 01170 | 8 | 01464 | 3 | 01744 | 5 |
| 00882 | 10 | 01173 | 12 | 01470 | 3 | 01756 | 6 |
| 00902 | 5 | 01200 | 4 | 01472 | 5 | 01758 | 5 |
| 00904 | 7 | 01202 | 4 | 01474 | 5 | 01760 | 7 |
| 00906 | 4 | 01210 | 6 | 01480 | 3 | 01770 | 6 |
| 00908 | 6 | 01212 | 10 | 01482 | 4 | 01772 | 6 |
| 00910 | 3 | 01214 | 8 | 01484 | 4 | 01780 | 3 |
| 00912 | 5 | 01215 | 10 | 01486 | 7 | 01782 | 4 |
| 00914 | 5 | 01220 | 4 | 01490 | 3 | 01810 | 3 |
| 00916 | 5 | 01230 | 6 | 01500 | 8 | 01820 | 3 |
| 00918 | 5 | 01232 | 5 | 01502 | 6 | 01829 | 3 |
| 00920 | 3 | 01234 | 8 | 01520 | 3 | 01830 | 3 |
| 00921 | 3 | 01250 | 4 | 01522 | 5 | 01832 | 6 |
| 00922 | 6 | 01260 | 3 | 01610 | 5 | 01840 | 6 |
| 00924 | 4 | 01270 | 8 | 01620 | 4 | 01842 | 6 |
| 00926 | 4 | 01272 | 4 | 01622 | 4 | 01844 | 6 |
| 00928 | 6 | 01274 | 6 | 01630 | 5 | 01850 | 3 |
| 00930 | 4 | 01320 | 4 | 01634 | 9 | 01852 | 4 |
| 00932 | 4 | 01340 | 4 | 01636 | 15 | 01860 | 3 |
| 00934 | 6 | 01360 | 5 | 01638 | 10 | 01916 | 5 |
| 00936 | 8 | 01380 | 3 | 01650 | 6 | 01920 | 7 |
| 00938 | 4 | 01382 | 3 | 01652 | 10 | 01922 | 7 |
| 00940 | 3 | 01390 | 3 | 01654 | 8 | 01924 | 5 |
| 00942 | 4 | 01392 | 4 | 01656 | 10 | 01925 | 7 |
| 00944 | 6 | 01400 | 4 | 01670 | 4 | 01926 | 8 |

(*continues*)

*(continued)*

| Code | 2023 Base Unit | Code | 2023 Base Unit | Code | 2023 Base Unit | Code | 2023 Base Unit |
|------|----------------|------|----------------|------|----------------|------|----------------|
| 01930 | 5 | 01940 | 4 | 01960 | 5 | 01968 | 2 |
| 01931 | 7 | 01941 | 5 | 01961 | 7 | 01969 | 5 |
| 01932 | 6 | 01942 | 5 | 01962 | 8 | 01990 | 7 |
| 01933 | 7 | 01951 | 3 | 01963 | 8 | 01991 | 3 |
| 01937 | 4 | 01952 | 5 | 01965 | 4 | 01992 | 5 |
| 01938 | 4 | 01953 | 1 | 01966 | 4 | 01996 | 3 |
| 01939 | 4 | 01958 | 5 | 01967 | 5 | 01999 | 0 |

# APPENDIX
# V
# Locality-Adjusted Anesthesia Conversion Factors as a Result of the CY 2023 Final Rule

| Contractor | Locality | Locality Name | 2023 Work GPCI | 2023 PE GPCI | 2023 MP GPCI | National Anes CF of 20.6097 |
|---|---|---|---|---|---|---|
| 10112 | 00 | ALABAMA | 1.000 | 0.878 | 0.748 | 19.88 |
| 02102 | 01 | ALASKA* | 1.500 | 1.100 | 0.603 | 28.42 |
| 03102 | 00 | ARIZONA | 1.000 | 0.963 | 0.855 | 20.30 |
| 07102 | 13 | ARKANSAS | 1.000 | 0.853 | 0.492 | 19.47 |
| 01112 | 54 | BAKERSFIELD | 1.027 | 1.079 | 0.694 | 20.92 |
| 01112 | 55 | CHICO | 1.021 | 1.079 | 0.579 | 20.67 |
| 01182 | 71 | EL CENTRO | 1.021 | 1.079 | 0.595 | 20.69 |
| 01112 | 56 | FRESNO | 1.021 | 1.079 | 0.579 | 20.67 |
| 01112 | 57 | HANFORD-CORCORAN | 1.021 | 1.079 | 0.579 | 20.67 |
| 01182 | 18 | LOS ANGELES-LONG BEACH-ANAHEIM (LOS ANGELES CNTY) | 1.045 | 1.185 | 0.724 | 21.60 |
| 01182 | 26 | LOS ANGELES-LONG BEACH-ANAHEIM (ORANGE CNTY) | 1.045 | 1.185 | 0.724 | 21.60 |
| 01112 | 58 | MADERA | 1.021 | 1.079 | 0.579 | 20.67 |
| 01112 | 59 | MERCED | 1.021 | 1.079 | 0.579 | 20.67 |
| 01112 | 60 | MODESTO | 1.021 | 1.079 | 0.579 | 20.67 |
| 01112 | 51 | NAPA | 1.051 | 1.265 | 0.513 | 21.69 |
| 01112 | 07 | SAN FRANCISCO-OAKLAND-BERKELEY (ALAMEDA/CONTRA COSTA CNTY) | 1.082 | 1.374 | 0.452 | 22.48 |
| 01182 | 17 | OXNARD-THOUSAND OAKS-VENTURA | 1.027 | 1.181 | 0.689 | 21.25 |
| 01112 | 61 | REDDING | 1.021 | 1.079 | 0.579 | 20.67 |
| 01112 | 62 | RIVERSIDE-SAN BERNARDINO-ONTARIO | 1.021 | 1.079 | 0.924 | 21.11 |
| 01112 | 63 | SACRAMENTO-ROSEVILLE-FOLSOM | 1.036 | 1.119 | 0.579 | 21.05 |
| 01112 | 64 | SALINAS | 1.050 | 1.149 | 0.579 | 21.37 |
| 01182 | 72 | SAN DIEGO-CHULA VISTA-CARLSBAD | 1.032 | 1.176 | 0.596 | 21.20 |

*(continues)*

(*continued*)

| Contractor | Locality | Locality Name | 2023 Work GPCI | 2023 PE GPCI | 2023 MP GPCI | National Anes CF of 20.6097 |
|---|---|---|---|---|---|---|
| 01112 | 05 | SAN FRANCISCO-OAKLAND-BERKELEY (SAN FRANCISCO CNTY) | 1.082 | 1.374 | 0.452 | 22.48 |
| 01112 | 52 | SAN FRANCISCO-OAKLAND-BERKELEY (MARIN CNTY) | 1.082 | 1.374 | 0.487 | 22.52 |
| 01112 | 65 | SAN JOSE-SUNNYVALE-SANTA CLARA (SAN BENITO CNTY) | 1.098 | 1.409 | 0.579 | 23.01 |
| 01182 | 73 | SAN LUIS OBISPO-PASO ROBLES | 1.021 | 1.111 | 0.579 | 20.78 |
| 01112 | 06 | SAN FRANCISCO-OAKLAND-BERKELEY (SAN MATEO CNTY) | 1.082 | 1.374 | 0.452 | 22.48 |
| 01112 | 09 | SAN JOSE-SUNNYVALE-SANTA CLARA (SANTA CLARA CNTY) | 1.098 | 1.409 | 0.417 | 22.80 |
| 01112 | 66 | SANTA CRUZ-WATSONVILLE | 1.031 | 1.207 | 0.579 | 21.26 |
| 01182 | 74 | SANTA MARIA-SANTA BARBARA | 1.031 | 1.175 | 0.579 | 21.15 |
| 01112 | 67 | SANTA ROSA-PETALUMA | 1.036 | 1.205 | 0.579 | 21.34 |
| 01112 | 68 | STOCKTON | 1.021 | 1.079 | 0.579 | 20.67 |
| 01112 | 53 | VALLEJO | 1.051 | 1.265 | 0.487 | 21.66 |
| 01112 | 69 | VISALIA | 1.021 | 1.079 | 0.579 | 20.67 |
| 01112 | 70 | YUBA CITY | 1.021 | 1.079 | 0.579 | 20.67 |
| 01112 | 75 | REST OF CALIFORNIA | 1.021 | 1.079 | 0.579 | 20.67 |
| 04112 | 01 | COLORADO | 1.005 | 1.050 | 0.797 | 20.60 |
| 13102 | 00 | CONNECTICUT | 1.030 | 1.102 | 1.070 | 21.52 |
| 12202 | 01 | DC + MD/VA SUBURBS | 1.056 | 1.214 | 1.231 | 22.52 |
| 12102 | 01 | DELAWARE | 1.007 | 1.007 | 0.938 | 20.67 |
| 09102 | 03 | FORT LAUDERDALE | 1.000 | 0.999 | 1.815 | 21.65 |
| 09102 | 04 | MIAMI | 1.000 | 1.025 | 2.564 | 22.69 |
| 09102 | 99 | REST OF FLORIDA | 1.000 | 0.940 | 1.451 | 20.98 |
| 10212 | 01 | ATLANTA | 1.000 | 0.998 | 1.016 | 20.62 |
| 10212 | 99 | REST OF GEORGIA | 1.000 | 0.881 | 1.015 | 20.23 |
| 01212 | 01 | HAWAII, GUAM | 1.003 | 1.146 | 0.618 | 20.66 |
| 02202 | 00 | IDAHO | 1.000 | 0.893 | 0.439 | 19.53 |
| 06102 | 16 | CHICAGO | 1.009 | 1.033 | 1.945 | 22.07 |
| 06102 | 12 | EAST ST. LOUIS | 1.000 | 0.930 | 1.723 | 21.30 |
| 06102 | 15 | SUBURBAN CHICAGO | 1.007 | 1.055 | 1.530 | 21.58 |

(*continues*)

*(continued)*

| Contractor | Locality | Locality Name | 2023 Work GPCI | 2023 PE GPCI | 2023 MP GPCI | National Anes CF of 20.6097 |
|---|---|---|---|---|---|---|
| 06102 | 99 | REST OF ILLINOIS | 1.000 | 0.912 | 1.282 | 20.67 |
| 08102 | 00 | INDIANA | 1.000 | 0.911 | 0.475 | 19.64 |
| 05102 | 00 | IOWA | 1.000 | 0.910 | 0.441 | 19.59 |
| 05202 | 00 | KANSAS | 1.000 | 0.907 | 0.499 | 19.66 |
| 15102 | 00 | KENTUCKY | 1.000 | 0.873 | 0.870 | 20.02 |
| 07202 | 01 | NEW ORLEANS | 1.000 | 0.931 | 1.342 | 20.81 |
| 07202 | 99 | REST OF LOUISIANA | 1.000 | 0.876 | 1.144 | 20.38 |
| 14112 | 03 | SOUTHERN MAINE | 1.000 | 1.005 | 0.654 | 20.18 |
| 14112 | 99 | REST OF MAINE | 1.000 | 0.905 | 0.651 | 19.84 |
| 12302 | 01 | BALTIMORE/SURR. CNTYS | 1.024 | 1.087 | 1.311 | 21.68 |
| 12302 | 99 | REST OF MARYLAND | 1.011 | 1.027 | 1.022 | 20.90 |
| 14212 | 01 | METROPOLITAN BOSTON | 1.045 | 1.200 | 0.868 | 21.83 |
| 14212 | 99 | REST OF MASSACHUSETTS | 1.022 | 1.061 | 0.819 | 20.93 |
| 08202 | 01 | DETROIT | 1.000 | 0.992 | 1.670 | 21.44 |
| 08202 | 99 | REST OF MICHIGAN | 1.000 | 0.911 | 1.076 | 20.41 |
| 06202 | 00 | MINNESOTA | 1.000 | 1.019 | 0.326 | 19.81 |
| 07302 | 00 | MISSISSIPPI | 1.000 | 0.847 | 0.720 | 19.74 |
| 05302 | 02 | METROPOLITAN KANSAS CITY | 1.000 | 0.952 | 0.941 | 20.37 |
| 05302 | 01 | METROPOLITAN ST. LOUIS | 1.000 | 0.964 | 0.941 | 20.41 |
| 05302 | 99 | REST OF MISSOURI | 1.000 | 0.855 | 0.901 | 20.00 |
| 03202 | 01 | MONTANA** | 1.000 | 1.000 | 0.978 | 20.58 |
| 05402 | 00 | NEBRASKA | 1.000 | 0.913 | 0.269 | 19.38 |
| 01312 | 00 | NEVADA** | 1.000 | 1.000 | 1.098 | 20.73 |
| 14312 | 40 | NEW HAMPSHIRE | 1.000 | 1.036 | 0.907 | 20.61 |
| 12402 | 01 | NORTHERN NJ | 1.056 | 1.186 | 0.996 | 22.12 |
| 12402 | 99 | REST OF NEW JERSEY | 1.039 | 1.124 | 1.014 | 21.67 |
| 04212 | 05 | NEW MEXICO | 1.000 | 0.902 | 1.169 | 20.50 |
| 13202 | 01 | MANHATTAN | 1.061 | 1.184 | 1.843 | 23.28 |
| 13202 | 02 | NYC SUBURBS/LONG ISLAND | 1.056 | 1.212 | 2.307 | 23.89 |
| 13202 | 03 | POUGHKPSIE/N NYC SUBURBS | 1.036 | 1.105 | 1.458 | 22.12 |
| 13292 | 04 | QUEENS | 1.061 | 1.212 | 2.061 | 23.65 |
| 13282 | 99 | REST OF NEW YORK | 1.000 | 0.952 | 0.742 | 20.12 |
| 11502 | 00 | NORTH CAROLINA | 1.000 | 0.927 | 0.742 | 20.03 |
| 03302 | 01 | NORTH DAKOTA** | 1.000 | 1.000 | 0.474 | 19.94 |

*(continues)*

(*continued*)

| Contractor | Locality | Locality Name | 2023 Work GPCI | 2023 PE GPCI | 2023 MP GPCI | National Anes CF of 20.6097 |
|---|---|---|---|---|---|---|
| 15202 | 00 | OHIO | 1.000 | 0.912 | 1.063 | 20.39 |
| 04312 | 00 | OKLAHOMA | 1.000 | 0.886 | 0.798 | 19.97 |
| 02302 | 01 | PORTLAND | 1.018 | 1.083 | 0.612 | 20.68 |
| 02302 | 99 | REST OF OREGON | 1.000 | 0.966 | 0.589 | 19.97 |
| 12502 | 01 | METROPOLITAN PHILADELPHIA | 1.023 | 1.068 | 1.188 | 21.45 |
| 12502 | 99 | REST OF PENNSYLVANIA | 1.000 | 0.933 | 0.906 | 20.26 |
| 09202 | 20 | PUERTO RICO | 1.000 | 1.000 | 1.000 | 20.61 |
| 14412 | 01 | RHODE ISLAND | 1.023 | 1.044 | 0.915 | 21.02 |
| 11202 | 01 | SOUTH CAROLINA | 1.000 | 0.908 | 0.756 | 19.99 |
| 03402 | 02 | SOUTH DAKOTA** | 1.000 | 1.000 | 0.364 | 19.80 |
| 10312 | 35 | TENNESSEE | 1.000 | 0.894 | 0.518 | 19.64 |
| 04412 | 31 | AUSTIN | 1.000 | 1.053 | 0.727 | 20.44 |
| 04412 | 20 | BEAUMONT | 1.000 | 0.924 | 0.749 | 20.03 |
| 04412 | 09 | BRAZORIA | 1.023 | 1.014 | 0.673 | 20.61 |
| 04412 | 11 | DALLAS | 1.017 | 1.017 | 0.711 | 20.57 |
| 04412 | 28 | FORT WORTH | 1.013 | 0.996 | 0.721 | 20.45 |
| 04412 | 15 | GALVESTON | 1.023 | 1.013 | 0.703 | 20.64 |
| 04412 | 18 | HOUSTON | 1.023 | 1.016 | 1.154 | 21.23 |
| 04412 | 99 | REST OF TEXAS | 1.000 | 0.950 | 0.759 | 20.13 |
| 03502 | 09 | UTAH | 1.000 | 0.926 | 0.865 | 20.19 |
| 14512 | 50 | VERMONT | 1.000 | 0.997 | 0.543 | 20.02 |
| 11302 | 00 | VIRGINIA | 1.000 | 0.990 | 0.826 | 20.35 |
| 09202 | 50 | VIRGIN ISLANDS | 1.000 | 1.000 | 1.000 | 20.61 |
| 02402 | 02 | SEATTLE (KING CNTY) | 1.039 | 1.207 | 0.815 | 21.69 |
| 02402 | 99 | REST OF WASHINGTON | 1.003 | 1.027 | 0.773 | 20.46 |
| 11402 | 16 | WEST VIRGINIA | 1.000 | 0.860 | 1.266 | 20.48 |
| 06302 | 00 | WISCONSIN | 1.000 | 0.950 | 0.314 | 19.57 |
| 03602 | 21 | WYOMING** | 1.000 | 1.000 | 0.790 | 20.34 |

These case studies provide additional coding practice.

## Case 1

**Preoperative Diagnosis:** Recurrent acute otitis media.

**Postoperative Diagnosis:** Recurrent acute right otitis media and left acute otitis media, right serous otitis media.

**Operation Performed:** Bilateral myringotomy with PE tube placement.

**Anesthesia:** General.

**Indications:** This is a 21-month-old female with a history of recurrent acute otitis media and at this time she presents for bilateral PE tube placement.

**Details of Procedure:** The patient was taken to OR and underwent uneventful induction of anesthesia. The right ear was examined first. Small amount of cerumen was cleaned. There were obvious air-fluid levels and a diffuse mild negative pressure with mild retraction of pars tensa.

The radial incision was made just anterior to the 6 o'clock position and a #5 suction was used to aspirate thick mucous. We utilized Cipro ophthalmic drops to help mobilize the thick mucous. When that was evacuated, a Reuter-Bobbin tube was placed. It was blue, Medronic style, and had a 1.14 mm inner diameter. This was kept in place with a Rosen pick in usual manner and Cipro drops were placed.

Next the left ear was explored. The left ear was bulging and very thickened and hyperemic. There was a full mucoid effusion there. A radial incision was made and a turbid mucopus came forward from the incision. She was aspirated with #5 suction. The middle ear cleft was well defined. The ear drum remained quite thickened. I was able to uneventfully place a Reuter-Bobbin tube there which was of a 1.14 mm inner diameter.

Ciprofloxacin ophthalmic drops were placed, and then suctioned out, irrigated again, and suctioned again. It looked like lumen of the tube was clear and there was no ongoing bleeding. We put more Cipro drops in and awakened the patient uneventfully having tolerated bilateral tube placement well.

I prescribed Cefzil p.o. for 7 days at 150 mg p.o. b.i.d. and Ciprodex drops for three days b.i.d. I asked the mother to put the Ciprodex in the left ear three times today.

*(continues)*

(*continued*)

The patient tolerated the procedure well and I will see her back in the office in approximately 10 days. I will consider getting an audiogram update on her when I review the chart at the post-op visit.

**ICD-10-CM Code(s):** _____

**CPT Code(s):** _____

# Case 2

**Date of Surgery:** 10/3/XXXX

**Preoperative Diagnosis:** NUCLEAR CATARACT OD

**Postoperative Diagnosis:** Same as above

**Procedure:** Cataract Removal Lens Implant OD

**Anesthsia:** Topical

**Surgeon:** Samantha Friends

In the preoperative area the anesthesia department applied a topical anesthesia of 2% Xylocaine gel to the patient's right eye.

In the operating room the patient's right eye was prepared and draped in the usual manner. A Barraquer wire speculum was placed between the lids. Ocucoat was applied to the cornea. A side port incision was made at 12 o'clock. Healon 5 was instilled into the anterior part of the anterior chamber. A bent needle with balance salt solution was then placed into the anterior chamber and used to deepen the anterior chamber between the lens and the Healon 5, and was used to produce a continuous circular capsulorhexis. A 1.1 mm diamond incision was made at the limbus about 2 mm long temporally. The side port incision was then superiorly increased to 1.1 mm. Hydrodissection of the nucleus was done with a Ryecroft cannula on a syringe containing l/3 cc of unpreserved 1% Xylocaine, after clearing a path to the incision. After the fluid wave was completed, the lens was rotated 180 degrees and flipped within the capsular bag. Healon 5 was then placed between the lens and the cornea, the cornea incision temporally and superiorly. An irrigating Bechert nucleus rotator was placed through the superior incision and the Phaco tip was placed through the temporal incision. The lens was emulsified within the capsular bag. An irrigating hand piece with an irrigating solution containing epinephrine, Vancomycin, and Gentamycin was then placed through the superior incision, and an aspiration hand piece through the temporal incision. This was used to remove the cortical remnants and polish the capsule. Healon 5 was then placed into the anterior chamber to plug up the capsulorhexis. Balance salt solution was then placed below this into the capsular bag to deepen the capsular bag. A 2.8 mm diamond keratome was used to

(*continues*)

*(continued)*

enlarge the 1.1 mm temporal corneal limbal incision. A + 17.0 diopter AMO lens was carefully inspected, irrigated, and loaded into the unfolder and placed through the incision and the leading haptic, placed into the capsular bag followed by the optic and then the trailing haptic. The irrigation aspiration hand pieces were then used to remove the viscoelastic. The lens was carefully inspected and was in good position. The incisions were hydrated with balance salt solution. The anterior chamber was restored to its normal depth with irrigating solution. The incision was checked for leakage. The conjunctiva and cornea were flushed with a Betadine solution. The speculum was removed. Blood loss was minimal. The patient left the operating room in good condition. There were no complications of surgery.

ICD-10-CM Code(s): _____

CPT Code(s): _____

# Case 3

**Preoperative Diagnosis:**
1. Pregnancy, term, undelivered.
2. Fetal intolerance to labor.

**Postoperative Diagnosis:**
1. Pregnancy, term, delivered (living female infant).
2. Fetal intolerance to labor.
3. Thick green amniotic fluid (3 + meconium).

**Name Of Procedure:**
1. Primary cesarean section (low transverse).

**Operative Findings:** The uterus, tubes, and ovaries had a normal appearance.

Time and date of delivery: 1631 hours, 12/12/94 Weight at birth: 7 lb. 5 oz.

Apgar scores were 8 at one minute and 9 at five minutes. ESTIMATED BLOOD LOSS: 600 cc.

**Operative Procedure:** The patient was prepped and draped under spinal block anesthesia. A Foley catheter was in place. She was in the supine position. A Pfannenstiel incision was made and carried down to the rectus fascia. The bladder was incised transversely, and undermined cephalad and caudad. With sharp and blunt dissection, the rectus and pyramidalis muscles were separated in the midline. The peritoneum was entered, and the defect was extended under direct vision, avoiding the bladder reflection. The uterine incision was made transversely at the cervical area above the bladder reflection, and extended bilaterally using bandage scissors. Thick, green amniotic fluid was noted on entering the uterine cavity. The vertex was delivered from a left occiput posterior presentation. The upper respiratory tracts were suctioned before delivery of the shoulder, torso, and breech, without complication.

*(continues)*

(*continued*)

The cord was doubly clamped, cut, and the infant was handed to Dr. Hawa who attended the delivery. The placenta was manually removed. The uterus was exteriorized. The uterine cavity was cleaned. The uterine incisions were approximated using tfl chromic suture continuously, interlocking. Further suturing was necessary for hemostasis. The uterus was placed back in the abdomen. The wound was irrigated using saline solution. The peritoneum was closed using a 4-0 chromic suture continuously. The rectus fascia was closed using a #0 Vicryl continuously. The subcutaneous tissues were approximated using a 3-0 chromic suture continuously. The skin was approximated using staples.

The patient tolerated the procedure well and was returned to the Recovery Room in good condition. The estimated blood loss was 600 cc. No blood was replaced.

**ICD-10-CM Code(s):** _____

**CPT Code(s):** _____

# Case 4

**Preprocedure Diagnosis:** Rule out upper GI pathology and colonic pathology.

**Postprocedure Diagnosis:** Colonic polyp as well as submucosal deformity of the duodenal bulb with active bleeding.

**Procedure Performed:** Colonoscopy with polypectomy and panendoscopy with bicap therapy.

**Physician:** Micelle Cousins, M.D.

**Anesthesia:** Demerol 25 mg IV, Versed 1 mg IV.

**Indications:** The patient is a 78-year-old male with a history of anemia and lung carcinoma.

Recent upper GI series revealed some deformity of the duodenal bulb.

Complete history and physical is as per consultation note.

**Procedure:**

**Colonoscopy:** The colonoscope was advanced into the cecum. The ileocecal valve was well visualized and within normal limits. Just distal to the cecal valve there was a villous-appearing polyp measuring at approximately 2 × 1 cm. This was resected almost completely and retained for analysis. There are multiple large diverticula in the left colon without active bleeding. There are no other inflammatory changes and/or polyps throughout the colon.

**Upper Endoscopy:** The endoscope was advanced under direct vision of the esophagus. This appeared unremarkable. The scope was then advanced into the gastric lumen and, again, this revealed no significant abnormalities. Upon entering the duodenal bulb very carefully,

(*continues*)

*(continued)*

there was evidence of recent bleeding with a focal coagulant of blood in the bulb. On closer inspection, with washing of the catheter revealed a submucosal prominence with active bleeding was revealed. A bicap probe was used to coagulate this area and stop the blood loss. No ulceration was seen at this site. This appeared to be a submucosal process. The remaining portion of the duodenum was unremarkable.

**Impression:**

1. Large polyp in the right colon, most likely villous adenoma.
2. Multiple large diverticula.
3. Submucosal process in the duodenal bulb with secondary active blood loss.
4. Status post bicap therapy to this lesion.

**Recommendation:**

1. We will place patient on Carafate 1 gm q.i.d. over the next 10 days for this site of the bicap therapy.
2. Obtain a CT scan of the abdomen to rule out extrinsic pathology accounting for this tuberance into the lumen in the bulb. With his history of lung carcinoma this needs to be ruled out for other extrinsic pathology.
3. Will see the patient back in the office in two weeks.

Follow-up: Hematocrit on the current iron therapy.

**ICD-10-CM Code(s):** _____

**CPT Code(s):** _____

# Case 5

**Preoperative Diagnosis:** End stage renal disease.

**Postoperative Diagnosis:** Same.

**Operation:** Left radial cephalic arteriovenous fistula.

**Wound Classification:** clean.

**Operative Procedure:**

Under satisfactory monitored anesthesia care, the left arm was prepped with Betadine, draped in a sterile fashion. 1% Xylocaine was used for local anesthesia. An incision was made halfway between the radial artery and the cephalic vein. The cephalic vein was mobilized. The vein was on the small side but I still felt it was worth a try to use it for an AV fistula. The radial artery was in excellent condition. The patient was given Heparin, the radial artery was controlled, arteriotomy was made in the radial artery, and the end of the vein was sutured to the side of the artery with running 7-0 Prolene suture. After appropriate flushing, clamps

*(continues)*

*(continued)*

were released, reestablishing flow through the fistula. Technically the anastomosis appeared to be good. The patient was given Protamine, the wound was closed with running Vicryl in the subcutaneous tissue and 5-0 Monosoft in the skin. Dry sterile dressing was applied. Sponge and needle count was correct. The patient was sent to the day surgery area in satisfactory condition.

**ICD-10-CM Code(s):** _____

**CPT Code(s):** _____

# Case 6

**Preoperative Diagnosis:** Urinary retention.
**Postoperative Diagnosis:** Same.
**Operation Performed:** Cystoscopy transurethral prostatectomy and bladder neck incision.
**Anesthesia:** General.
**Blood Loss:** 100 CC.
**Drain In Place:** A 22-French 3-way Foley catheter with 40 cc in balloon.

**Procedure:** With the patient in the dorsal lithotomy position under general anesthesia, he was prepped and draped in a routine sterile manner for a cystoscopy. A 23.5 cystoscope was introduced into the bladder under direct vision. There was noted to be a trabeculated bladder with catheter reaction and an obstructing 2.5-cm prostate. At that point, the scope was removed and the 24-French Teflon resectoscope sheath was placed after lubricating it with K-Y jelly and Vaseline. Using a cutting current of 170 and a coagulation current of 70, the procedure was performed.

A groove was cut from the bladder neck to the verumontanum. The left lobe was then resected posteriorly to anteriorly and a similar resection was performed on the right. Additional tissue was removed circumferentially from the apex. Hemostasis was accomplished. The chips were irrigated out of the bladder. There was still tightness of the bladder neck, so bladder neck incisions were made with a Collings knife, which opened up the bladder neck. The bladder was filled, the scope removed, and a 22-French 3-way Foley catheter was inserted, placed on moderate traction on the left leg after inflating it to 40 cc. The catheter irrigated well and the patient was taken to recovery in good condition.

**ICD-10-CM Code(s):** _____

**CPT Code(s):** _____

# Case 7

**Preoperative Diagnosis:** Mass

**Postoperative Diagnosis:** Intracellular neoplasm

**Procedure:** Biopsy with excision of vulvar area

This 49-year-old patient has been seen by me for the last six weeks. She has had biopsies of lesions that extend from the clitoris on the left. The pathology report taken on 12/31/XX confirmed condyloma and dysplasia that extends to the lateral margins. A pap smear was obtained and the pathology was found to be negative.

Today the patient presents for an excisional biopsy.

## Procedure:

The patient was placed in the dorsal lithotomy position and the vagina was prepped and draped in the usual sterile fashion. The condylomatous changes were easily demarcated. The area was prepped with Betadine and 10 cc of 1% Xylocaine. In an elliptical fashion the entire lesion was excised with an addition of a 6 mm margin on both sides. Bleeding was controlled and the skin edges were closed with a continuous locked suture of 4-0 Vicryl. The patient tolerated the procedure and was sent to the recovery area in stable condition. The tissue was sent to pathology for analysis.

**ICD-10-CM Code(s):** _____

**CPT Code(s):** _____

# Case 8

**Preoperative Diagnosis:** Missed abortion.

**Postoperative Diagnosis:** Same.

**Operation:** Suction Uterine Curettage.

**Operative Findings:**

The uterus was about ten weeks' size, soft; both adnexae were negative. The tissue removed was consistent with the products of conception.

**Operative Procedure:**

The patient was placed in the supine position on the operating table. General anesthesia was given by Dr. Tinst. The patient was then placed in the lithotomy position. The vagina, perineum, and abdomen were prepped and draped in the usual fashion. An examination under anesthesia was carried out, which revealed a uterus of ten to eleven weeks' size. The adnexae were negative for masses. The cervix was closed. A weighted speculum was placed. The cervix was visualized and the anterior lip of the cervix was grasped with a single-tooth tenaculum.

(continues)

(*continued*)

The cervix was dilated until adequate dilation was achieved. Using a 12-mm size suction curette tip, the uterine cavity was emptied of its contents. Confirmation of the completeness of the uterine curettage was done with a sharp curette and no further tissue was obtained.

**Estimated Blood Loss:** The estimated blood loss was approximately 500 ml.

The tenaculum was then removed and the anterior lip of the cervix was inspected. Adequate hemostasis was present at the tenaculum application site. At the conclusion of the procedure, the uterus was firmly contracted. During the procedure, a dilute solution of Pitocin was infused. The patient was also given Methergine, 0.2 mg, intramuscularly. The patient tolerated the procedure well and left for the Recovery Room in satisfactory condition.

**ICD-10-CM Code(s):** _____

**CPT Code(s):** _____

# Case 9

**Preoperative Diagnosis:** Abdominal aortic aneurysm.

**Postoperative Diagnosis:** Same.

**Operation Performed:** Abdominal aortic aneurysm repair, retroperitoneal approach.

**Anesthesia:** General endotracheal with epidural.

**Indications for Procedure:** The patient is a 51-year-old white male who was found to have an abdominal aortic aneurysm by physical exam. He has some history of glucose intolerance but is otherwise healthy.

He is here for elective aneurysm repair.

**Procedure:** The patient was taken to the operating room and placed on the table in the supine position and Anesthetized with general endotracheal anesthesia without difficulty. A Foley catheter was inserted and then the patient was positioned with his shoulders in the right lateral decubitus position and his hips as flat as possible to open up the space between his left iliac crest and his left costal margin. The table was also reverse flexed to help open up this space.

We made an incision from the tip of the 11th rib extending medially toward the lateral border of the rectus. We used the knife and then Bovie cautery to go through the subcutaneous tissues, and then through the external and internal oblique muscles and the transversalis muscle. We stayed extraperitoneally and bluntly dissected in this plane, lifting both the kidney and the ureter up with peritoneal cavity, and keeping the retroperitoneal fat down along the psoas muscle. We used the Omni retractor for retraction once we had dissected out this plane. The patient was fairly thin and we were able to easily identify two lumbar veins and the left renal vein. We tied the lumbar vein and retracted the left renal vein superiorly. We were also able to identify the left renal artery and it appeared to have two branches that came off fairly close to the takeoff of the main artery.

(*continues*)

(*continued*)

We carefully dissected out the neck of the aneurysm and were able to get completely around it with a finger. We chose a gently curved clamp for the aortic clamp. We then worked our way distally. We were able to identify the left iliac artery very easily. It came up almost directly to the left. We cleared it off circumferentially and planned to place a clamp on this. The right iliac artery we could palpate, but we were not able to dissect out. We planned on using a balloon catheter to occlude this.

We then gave the patient 5,000 units of heparin intravenously and after three minutes we clamped the aorta and the left iliac artery and opened the aneurysm with the 11 blade. Once we had the aneurysm open, we palpated for the orifice of the right iliac artery and placed in the 9 French balloon occlusion catheter down the artery and pulled back gently as the balloon was inflated to occlude the artery. Once we had hemostatic control, we removed other clots, thrombi, and plaque from inside of the aneurysm and used 2-0 silk sutures to suture ligate any backbleeding from the lumbar arteries. We did not see the IMA, but on the patient's preoperative angiogram, all the branches of the IMA, the celiac, and the SMA were opened and visualized. With the aneurysm open, we T'd off the ends to prepare the sewing rings and then chose a #20-mm Hemashield graft for the graft. Because the proximal aorta was somewhat still dilated, we used 2-0 Tycron pledgeted sutures to do an interrupted mattress anastomosis. We completed the anastomosis and slowly released the clamp. It was apparent that there were a few gaps between the sutures. We used about three or four more 2-0 Tycron sutures in order to gain control and finally we had a hemostatic anastomosis.

When we were satisfied with this anastomosis, after placing a clamp on the graft itself, we removed the clamp on the proximal aorta and then stretched the graft to choose the length to do the distal anastomosis. We cut off the graft and then the distal anastomosis with a running 3-0 Prolene suture. We started posteriorly with a mattress stitch and worked our way around from either side. When we were finished, we flushed back the left iliac artery, and then reclamped it and flushed back the right. We removed the balloon occlusion catheter from the right and completed sewing the anastomosis. We then removed the left iliac clamp. We then gradually released the clamp from the graft to open perfusion to the legs. We did this slowly and anesthesia kept up with the volume. The patient's blood pressure did not drop below 100 for more than 20 seconds and was easily resuscitated back up to blood pressures in the 110–120 range. He continued to make urine throughout the case.

Once the clamp was off, we checked again for hemostasis. There was another lumbar which we had to oversew with a 2-0 silk, and we removed more plaque and identified more small branches which required oversewing. We used 2-0 chromic suture to oversew the edge of the aneurysm wall itself, which was oozing slightly. We packed for five minutes and checked again. When we were satisfied with the hemostasis, we removed all the retractors and began to close. We closed the incision in layers of 2-0 Vicryl suture starting with transversalis, then the internal oblique, and then the external oblique. We then irrigated between layers and

(*continues*)

(*continued*)

closed the skin with staples. There was approximately 1,500 cc of blood loss and 1,200 cc of Cell Saver, 3 L of LR, 1,000 cc of Hespan, and 500 cc of 5% albumin was given during the case. The patient was taken to the recovery room where he was extubated. He tolerated the procedure well. He will keep his Foley catheter.

**ICD-10-CM Code(s):** _____

**CPT Code(s):** _____

# Case 10

**Preoperative Diagnosis:** Chronic osteomyelitis, left second toe.

**Postoperative Diagnosis:** Chronic osteomyelitis, left second toe.

**Operation Performed:** Amputation of distal phalanx, left second toe.

**Anesthesia:** Local with sedation.

**Procedure:** In the supine position, the left foot was prepped with Betadine scrub and was washed and draped in a sterile fashion; 0.5% Xylocaine with 0.5% Marcaine was infiltrated in the dermis of the left second toe, approximately 6 cc was used.

A posterior flap incision was made through the dermis and subcutaneous fat down to bone circumferentially. The bone was cut at the DIP joint with bone cutters, and the articular surface of the proximal phalanx was debrided with rongeurs. Bleeding was good at the tissue level and the tissue appeared quite viable. No purulent material was seen and good healthy bone remained. The area was cauterized in several places and closed with interrupted 4-0 nylon suture; ¼-inch Steri-strips with benzoin were also applied, and sterile dressing was placed.

The patient was taken to the recovery room in good condition. Estimated blood loss approximately 2 cc. Needle and sponge counts correct times two.

**ICD-10-CM Code(s):** _____

**CPT Code(s):** _____

# Case 11

**Preoperative Diagnosis:** Bilateral hydroceles

**Postoperative Diagnosis:** Bilateral hydroceles

**Operation Performed:** Bilateral Hydrocelectomy

**Anesthesia:** General

**Clinical History:** This is a 2-year-old boy with an obvious hydrocele. The left cord was thickened.

**Operative Findings:** Bilateral communicating hydroceles.

**Procedure:** With the patient under general anesthesia, the abdomen and groin were prepped and draped in a sterile manner. A transverse incision was made over the right inguinal canal. The external oblique fascia was opened in the direction of its fibers through the external ring. The cord was brought up into the wound and the cord was explored. The hydrocele was identified and separated from the vas and vessels. It was clamped and divided and traced proximally to the internal ring where it was twisted and triply ligated with 2-0 Ethibond sutures. The distal sac was subtotally excised down to the testicle using electrocautery. The external oblique fascia was closed with interrupted 4-0 Vicryl sutures. Scarpa's fascia was closed with interrupted 4-0 Vicryl sutures and the skin was closed with interrupted 5-0 Vicryl in a subcuticular fashion and reinforced with Mastisol and Steri-strips. The left side was explored through a similar incision. The external oblique fascia was identified, and the cord was seen and explored. A small communicating hydrocele was identified, separated from the vas and vessels, and was traced proximally to the internal ring where it was triply ligated with 3-0 Ethibond suture. The distal hydrocele was then taken down to the testicle and removed. The external oblique fascia was closed with interrupted 3-0 Vicryl sutures, the Scarpa's fascia was closed with interrupted 4-0 Vicryl sutures, and the skin was closed with interrupted 5-0 Vicryl in a subcuticular fashion and reinforced with Mastisol and Steri-strips. Blood loss was minimal. There were no operative complications. The child tolerated the procedure well.

**ICD-10-CM Code(s):** _____

**CPT Code(s):** _____

# Case 12

**Preoperative Diagnosis:** Status post left distal radius and ulna fractures with gradually worsening apex volar angulation of the radius fracture.

**Postoperative Diagnosis:** Same

**Operation:** Closed manipulation or closed osteoclasis, left distal radius fracture and application of a long-arm fiberglass cast.

**Wound Classification:** Clean

**Operative Indications:** The indications can be reviewed on my admission History & Physical exam note.

**Operative Procedure:**

This is a eight-year-old child, right-hand dominant, admitted to Outpatient Surgery at the Sunny View Hospital by me today, 6/4/XX. There being no medical or anesthetic contraindications to surgery, the patient was brought to the operating room. General mask anesthesia was administered per anesthesiologist.

With the patient appropriately anesthetized, I simply manipulated the distal radius. It was largely healed, but I was able to change the apex volar angulation for more than 30 degrees to approximately 10–15 degrees. I really could not move the fracture any further.

Intraoperative radiographs documented the improvement in the apex volar angulation and a long arm, well-padded fiberglass case was applied with elbow flexion at 90 degrees; the forearm in neutral rotation; the carpus in neutral rotation; and the index, little digit metacarpophalangeal joints were left free to allow full, passive and active flexion.

Three-point fixation molds were applied about that distal forearm carpus and proximal hand area.

At the conclusion of the closed manipulation, or osteoclasis, and application of the cast, the patient was simply awakened and brought to the Recovery Room where she arrived in stable condition. The patient tolerated the procedure well.

The patient did not receive fluids perioperatively. It was a closed procedure, hence, no blood loss. There were no pathologic specimens.

**ICD-10-CM Code(s):** _____

**CPT Code(s):** _____

# Case 13

**Preoperative Diagnosis:** Lipoma of right posterior shoulder/axilla

**Postoperative Diagnosis:** Same, pending pathology

**Operation Performed:** Excision of Lipoma of Right Posterior Shoulder/Axilla

**Anesthesia:** Local with intravenous sedation and monitoring

**Description:** With the patient in left lateral decubitus position, the right shoulder and axilla were prepared with Betadine, and draped with sterile drapes. There is a bulging mass at the posterior axillary fold. Margins of this were delineated, 1% xylocaine with epinephrine was infiltrated in the skin over the mass and at the periphery and deep to it. Later, supplementary doses were administered.

A 13 cm long incision was made obliquely from superior posterior to anterior inferior, ending at the posterior axilla. It was carried through the skin and superficial subcutaneous tissue. A multi-lobular fatty mass was encountered. It is invading the surrounding tissue and is partitioned at the periphery in multi-septal fashion. At the posterior aspect of the muscle, the surface is flat and it is the only area which has some sort of delineating capsule. Anteriorly there is a 2.5 × 3.5 cm single bulge extending in the axilla itself. This was dissected out without injuring any of the vessels. The entire lesion is about 11 × 9 cm in size. Multiple bleeders were coagulated. A Jackson Pratt drain was inserted anteriorly/inferiorly through a separate stab incision and secured with #2 silk.

A multilayer repair with interrupted 4-0 and 5-0 polysorb sutures to the subcutaneous tissue and skin, and 5-0 nylon to the superficial skin was performed. A dressing with Xeroflo, dressing sponges, and Hypafix was applied. Blood loss was minimal. Prior to the conclusion of the procedure 10 cc of 0.25% Marcaine was infiltrated in the skin and surrounding tissue for postoperative comfort.

**Pathology**

**Tissue:**

A) LIPOMA, RT POSTERIOR SHOULDER

**Clinical Diagnosis And History:** Lipoma, Rt Posterior Shoulder

Gross Description:

Specimen received in formalin labeled, "lipoma right shoulder" is a lobulated partially encapsulated tan to pink-red 9.5 × 6.0 × 2.5 cm portion of fibroadipose tissue. Sectioning shows a homogeneous yellow-tan lobulated and fatty cut surface. Representative sections are submitted (4 blocks).

**Diagnosis:**

MATURE FAT, CONSISTENT WITH LIPOMA, RIGHT POSTERIOR SHOULDER

ICD-10-CM Code(s): _____

CPT Code(s): _____

# Case 14

**Preoperative Diagnosis:** Right testicular torsion

**Postoperative Diagnosis:** Torsion of right testicular appendix

**Operation Performed:** Exploration of right testicle with excision of right testicular appendix.

**Operative Note:** With the patient under satisfactory general anesthesia, the scrotum was prepped and draped in the usual sterile manner. An incision was made in the hemi-scrotum, and the testicle was extruded through the incision. The appendix testis was cross clamped and excised. The base was tied with a simple 3-0 Chromic tie. The testicle was fixed in the scrotum with 1 suture of 4-0 Chromic suture extending through the tunica albuginea and into the scrotum. The testicle was returned to the scrotum. The incision was closed with interrupted 4-0 Chromic suture. Neosporin was applied to the incision. The patient was discharged to the Recovery Room in good condition.

**ICD-10-CM Code(s):** _____

**CPT Code(s):** _____

# Case 15

**Preoperative Diagnosis:** Right middle finger extensor contracture.

**Postoperative Diagnosis:** Same

**Operative Procedure:** Right middle finger extensor tenolysis and partial collateral ligament incision metacarpophalangeal joint.

**Indications for Procedure:** This is a 25-year-old right dominant painter, who complains of right middle finger pain at the MP joint. He originally underwent a bone grafting of a giant cell tumor in the metacarpal approximately two years ago. Since then, he has had considerable discomfort in the MP joint, with difficulty extending and flexing the finger. He has had extensive therapy without relief of his symptoms.

His physical examination shows flexion to approximately 75 degrees, without full active extension.

**Procedure:** After adequate median, dorsal, radial, and ulnar sensory nerve blocks with Lidocaine 2% and Marcaine 0.5%, equal volumes, 20 cc total, the right upper extremity was prepped and draped in the usual sterile fashion. The arm was exsanguinated and forearm tourniquet inflated to 250 mm of mercury.

A pre-existing longitudinal surgical scar over the MP joint was extended proximally the distance of 1 cm. This dissection was carried down through the skin and subcutaneous tissues. An extensive amount of scar tissue was encountered just above the sagittal bends. This was resected, and sent to pathology.

*(continues)*

*(continued)*

The extensor tendon was then identified, firmly adherent to the sagittal band. Tenolysis was begun at this level, which was slightly proximal to the MP joint. A combination of blunt and sharp dissection was used. Primarily scissors were used to free up the sagittal band in the tunnel through which the tendon could pass. At the completion of the tenolysis, the MP joint could be passively and fully extended by placing pressure on the tendon. Passive flexion was achievable to approximately 80 degrees. It was felt to be improved, but not completely resolved.

It was, therefore, elected to perform a partial resection of the collateral ligament. Sharp dissection was placed through the sagittal bands, down to the capsule. A mini-arthrotomy measuring about 4 mm, was extended over the insertion of the collateral ligament, and using a #69 beaver blade, they were resected. The flexion was then improved to approximately 90 degrees. Hyperflexion to 100 degrees was not achievable with this procedure. However, it was felt to be sufficient so that he would have a functional range of motion and a good grip.

The wound was thoroughly irrigated. The tourniquet was released, and hemostasis was achieved after five minutes of digital pressure. The skin was reapproximated with Ethilon 4-0 suture, using the horizontal mattress technique. A light dressing with Coban was applied. The patient tolerated the procedure well, and was taken to the recovery room in stable condition.

**ICD-10-CM Code(s):** _____

**CPT Code(s):** _____

# Case 16

**Preoperative Diagnosis:** Anal fissure, class 4 hemorrhoids.

**Postoperative Diagnosis:** Same.

**Operation Performed:** Hemorrhoidectomy and sphincterotomy, left lateral.

**Procedure:** The patient was put in the prone position on the Wilson frame, the buttocks were spread with tape, the perianal area was prepped and draped in normal sterile fashion with 2% lidocaine with Epinephrine being placed in the anal canal. Left lateral, right anterior and right posterior hemorrhoidectomy was performed in the same fashion by making an incision on each side of the lead, lifting the hemorrhoidal tissue off the internal and external sphincter, undermining the mucosa and anoderm then reapproximating with 3-0 chromic suture. The left lateral had some growth-like structure that looked as if they were large papilloma, pathology is pending. A margin was obtained on that lead around the internal sphincter partially, small amount to treat the posterior anal fissure, which had been quite bothersome. All three leads were checked and found to have adequate hemostasis, a dressing was placed after 0.75% Marcaine was placed in the wounds.

**ICD-10-CM Code(s):** _____

**CPT Code(s):** _____

# Case 17

**Diagnosis:** Displaced subcapital fracture right hip

**Postoperative Diagnosis:** Same as above

**Operation:** Modular Austin Moore femoral head replacement right hip

**Wound Classification:** Clean

**Anesthesia:** Spinal

**Operative Procedure:**

In the laminar flow operating room spinal anesthesia was induced. The patient was positioned supine with a rolled sheet under the right hip, which was scrubbed and prepped with Betadine and sterilely draped. A lateral incision was made with an anterolateral approach to the hip used. Homan retractors were used for exposure. The anterior capsule was exposed and excised. The femoral neck was trimmed with an oscillating power saw to the appropriate level and angle, and the bone fragments and femoral head removed from the acetabulum. This measured exactly 55 mm and a 55 mm femoral head trial prosthesis was found to fit very well within the acetabulum. The remainder of the capsule was excised and the short rotators released at their insertion on the greater trochanter. The leg was then adducted and externally rotated, and the proximal femur was exposed with Homan retractors. The medullary canal was initially opened with a mortis and chisel and a blunt tipped tapered reamer, followed by progressive sizes of rasps to a size large, which provided an excellent press fit. A size large Zimmer modular Austin Moore stem was then inserted into the femur and impacted so that the collar was the calcar, and a 55 mm module chrome cobalt femoral was head placed on the stem. The hip was irrigated well to remove any bone debris or chips within the acetabulum, which was checked carefully, both manually and visually, and the hip reduced. There was excellent stability and motion. Two Hemovac drains were brought out anteriorly through separate stab wounds. The incision was closed using interrupted Vicryl for the deeper tissues and staples for the skin. A dry sterile dressing was applied. The patient tolerated the procedure well and was taken to the recovery room in satisfactory condition.

ICD-10-CM Code(s): _____

CPT Code(s): _____

## Case 18

**Indications for Procedure:** A 70-old male with a recently discovered left hilar mass, probable left upper lobe and lingula. No clinical symptoms except a long history of COPD. Has not smoked in 12 years. Bronchoscopy to be done for evaluation.

**Pre-Procedure Diagnosis:** Rule out carcinoma of left lung

**Post-Procedure Diagnosis:** Same

**Anesthesia:** Topical Cetacaine and Cyclaine

**Procedure Performed:** Flexible Bronchoscopy

**Findings:** After induction of satisfactory anesthesia, the flexible bronchoscope was introduced. There were normal appearing cords, which moved normally. The carina was midline and sharp. The entire right side was examined, and was within normal limits. On the left side, there were some bronchitic changes in the left upper lobe region, no question of narrowing, and there was no sign of any tumor. Washings were obtained from the entire left side including the left upper lobe for cytology and culture. The bronchoscope was removed. The patient tolerated the procedure well and went to the Recovery Room in satisfactory condition.

**ICD-10-CM Code(s):** _____

**CPT Code(s):** _____

## Case 19

Left Stereotactic Breast Biopsy

**Indications:** This patient had a prior comparison bilateral mammogram performed at the hospital last week, which demonstrated a mass in the posterior aspect of the left breast. This was suspicious for malignancy. A core biopsy was requested.

Using the stereotactic prone core biopsy device, multiple core samples were obtained through the area of mammographic abnormality.

The patient tolerated the procedure without incident.

Biopsy showed poorly differentiating infiltrating ductal carcinoma, grade III.

**Impression:** Positive core biopsy for malignancy in the left breast.

**ICD-10-CM Code(s):** _____

**CPT Code(s):** _____

# Case 20

**Preoperative Diagnosis:** Urinary retention

**Postoperative Diagnosis:** Same

**Operation Performed:** Suprapubic punch cystotomy

**Operative Note:** With the patient in the supine position, the lower abdomen was prepped and draped in the usual sterile manner. 10 cc of 1% Xylocaine with Epinephrine were instilled into an area two fingerbreadths above the pubic symphysis. A small transverse skin incision was made and a Campbell suprapubic punch trocar was inserted into the bladder. An 18 French Foley catheter was inserted, inflated and secured at skin level. Sterile dressings were applied. The patient was discharged to his room in good condition.

ICD-10-CM Code(s): _____

CPT Code(s): _____

# GLOSSARY

## A

**abdomen**   the area of the body that lies between the thorax and the pelvis

**abdominal hysterectomy**   the removal of the uterus performed through an incision made in the abdomen

**abduction**   to move away from the body

**abortion**   the term used to indicate that a pregnancy was ended prior to the time that a fetus reached a viable age and could survive outside the uterus

**acellular dermal replacement**   replacing skin with a skin substitute that is composed of porous lattice fibers and a synthetic substance

**add-on code symbol (+)**   used within CPT to list procedures that are completed in addition to the primary procedure or service performed

**adduction**   to move toward the axis of the body

**adenoids**   one of three sets of tonsils; also referred to as the *nasopharyngeal tonsils*

**adjacent tissue transfer**   a procedure in which healthy tissue is manipulated or rearranged from a site close to or next to an area that is open due to disease or injury

**adrenal gland**   a gland that sits atop the kidney; regulates electrolytes and helps in the metabolism of glucose and adrenaline

**Advance Beneficiary Notice (ABN)**   a written notice that is signed by a patient to document that the patient has been made aware that a procedure or service to be completed may not be payable through Medicare

**advance life support (ALS)**   specialized life support services and/or supplies that are used when treating a patient

**alimentary canal**   another name for the digestive tract

**allogenic bone marrow transplants**   procedures in which cells are taken from a donor and transplanted to a patient needing the cells

**allotransplantation**   a type of transplant that occurs between like species

**alternative laboratory platform testing**   modifier 92

**alveolus**   socket where the tooth sits

**amniocentesis**   a procedure in which fluid is withdrawn from the amniotic sac

**amnioscopy**   a scope procedure used to view the fetus in the amniotic sac

**A-mode technique**   a radiological technique that takes a one-dimensional measurement

**analyte**   a substance being tested

**anastomosis**   the process of surgically connecting two structures that are usually hollow, tubular parts

**anesthesia**   loss of sensation

**anesthesiologist**   a physician who is qualified to administer anesthesia and is board certified

**aneurysm**   an area in the artery that becomes weakened

**angiography**   imaging of the vessels

**angioplasty**   a procedure in which a balloon is inflated in the vessel to push and flatten plaque against the vessel wall

**angioscopy**   a procedure in which a fiber-optic scope is used to see within a noncoronary vessel

**anomaly**   an abnormality or deviation from the norm in a structure

**anoscopy**   an endoscopic procedure performed on the anus

**antepartum**   the time period prior to childbirth

**anterior chamber**   a chamber located in front of the lens of the eye

**anterior mediastinotomy**   a mediastinotomy completed from the front of the body

**anteroposterior**   front to back

**anus**   the most distal structure of the digestive system

**aortic valve**   sits between the aorta and the left ventricle and is one of the main valves of the heart

**aortography**   a test in which contrast material is injected to visualize problems with the aorta and its branches

**appendix**   a small, twisted, tubelike structure located at the blind end of the cecum

**aqueous humor**   clear, watery fluid that fills the interior of the eye

**arachnoid mater**   the middle layer of the meninges

**arteries**   vessels that move oxygen-rich blood from the heart to the rest of the body (with the exception of the pulmonary vein)

**arteriography**   imaging of the arteries

**arthrodesis**   surgical repair or reconstruction fixation of a joint

**arthrography**   x-ray of the inside of a joint

**arthroplasty**   plastic surgery of a joint

**arthroscope**   a scope used to view the joints

**arthroscopy**   the examination of the interior of a joint by using an arthroscope

**arthrotomy**   surgical incision of a joint

**arytenoidectomy**   surgical excision of the arytenoid cartilage

**ascending colon**   the part of the colon that begins at the ileocecal junction; at the undersurface of the liver, it becomes the transverse colon

**aspiration**   the surgical removal of fluid from the body

**assistant surgeon**   modifier 80

**assistant surgeon (when qualified resident surgeon not available)**   modifier 82

**atria**   the upper chambers of the heart that receive blood from the veins

**atrioventricular node (AV node)**   sometimes referred to as the *AV node;* directs the impulses to the ventricles, causing them to contract

**auditory ossicles**   three small bones that transmit and amplify sound waves

**auditory tube**   also called the *eustachian tube;* connects the bony structure of the middle ear to the pharynx

**augmentation**   the surgical increase of the size of a structure

**auricle**   a flexible cartilaginous flap that has a bottom portion known as the *earlobe*

**autogenous graft**   a type of graft in which tissue is taken from one part of a person's body and put on another part of the same person's body

**autograft**   surgical transplantation of a person's own tissue

**autologous bone marrow transplants**   transplants for which cells are cultivated from patient's own marrow

**autonomic nervous system**   connects the central nervous system to the visceral organs via the cranial and spinal nerves

**axial**   an axis of a structure or part of the body

**axillary lymph nodes**   nodes located in the armpit

## B

**backbench work**   the physician's preparation of a donor organ

**balanced anesthesia**   anesthesia delivered by a combination of inhalation, injection, and instillation

**bariatric surgery**   a type of operative procedure using bands and port insertion; performed as a treatment of morbid obesity

**Bartholin's glands**   glands that secrete lubricating mucous in the vagina; also referred to as the *vestibular glands*

**base unit**   reflects the usual services attached to anesthesia and the value of the work associated with the anesthesia services provided; also called *basic value* or *relative value*

**base unit value**   reflects the usual services attached to anesthesia and the value of the work associated with the anesthesia services; also called *basic value* or *relative value*

**basic life support (BLS)**   services that are provided for life support that include, but are not limited to, the control of bleeding, immobilization of fractures, treatment of shock, delivering of babies, and cardiopulmonary resuscitation

**basic value**   reflects the usual services attached to anesthesia and the value of the work associated with the anesthesia services provided; also called *relative value*

**benign lesion**   a lesion whose cell growth is abnormal but not life threatening

**Bier blocks**   injections of an anesthetic agent into the arm below the elbow, or in the leg below the knee

**bilateral procedure**   modifier 50

**biliary tract**   organs and ducts that are involved in the processing and movement of bile into the duodenum

**biofeedback**   measurements of physiological responses and patient instruction on how to control these responses

**biopsy**   removal of tissue for pathological examination

**block**   see *block anesthesia*

**block anesthesia**   a type of regional anesthesia in which anesthetic is injected along a major nerve tract, interrupting the nerve conductivity

**bone density test**   a test used to determine the presence of osteoporosis by looking at the mass or density of the bone

**bony labyrinth**   a maze of bony structures within the inner ear

**brachytherapy**   an internal radiation therapy that is used to treat tissue

**brain**   the organ responsible for all physical and mental functions of the body

**brain stem**   a structure that connects the diencephalons to the spinal cord

**bronchi**   large air passages in the lung through which air is inhaled and exhaled

**bronchoscopy**   an examination of the bronchi using a flexible endoscope

**B-scan**   a two-dimensional radiological image

**bullet symbol**   denotes a new code that has been added since the previous edition of CPT

**bundled**   a term indicating that preoperative, postoperative, and the service itself are included in the price the physician receives for the procedure

**bundle of His**   the conduction fibers that cause the contractions of the heart

**burn**   an injury to the body tissue that is a result of heat, flame, sun, chemicals, radiation, and/or electricity

**burr hole procedures**   procedures in which the physician drills a burr hole in the cranium. The acts could include a biopsy of the brain or intracranial lesion, drainage of brain abscess or cyst, tapping of abscess or cyst, drainage of hematoma, and other brain or intracranial procedures

## C

**cardiac pacemaker**   a device used to correct and manage heart dysrhythmias

**cardiovascular system**   the system that pumps blood through the body via the heart and blood vessels

**care plan oversight**   services coordinated for a patient over a 30-day period for the purpose of assessment or care decisions

**cartilage**   thin sheets of fibrous connective tissue

**case management**   physician supervision and coordination of direct care received by a patient as part of an interdisciplinary team

**casts**   fiberglass, plaster, or plastic rigid dressing used to immobilize an area to prevent movement

**Category I**   codes from the main sections of CPT

**Category II**   tracking codes; not mandatory

**Category III**   codes for collection of statistical data

**central nervous system**   the system composed of the brain and spinal cord

**central venous access (CVA) device**   a catheter classified as such if the tip ends in the subclavian, brachiocephalic, right atrium, or superior or inferior vena cava

**cerclage**   a technique of encircling the cervix uteri with a wire, ligature, or loop

**cerebellum**   the second-largest part of the brain, which coordinates skeletal muscle movements and the learning of new motor skills

**cerebral cortex**   consists of a layer of neurons on the surface of the brain

**cerebrum**   the largest part of the brain, which is separated by depressions and grooves and is divided into separate hemispheres by a groove called the *longitudinal fissure*

**Certificate of Medical Necessity (CMN)**   a document that clearly explains why a physician feels a patient needs the durable medical equipment (DME) item or service; should be filed in the patient's medical record for certain supplies

**certified registered nurse anesthetist (CRNA)**   a registered nurse with 36 months of additional training in anesthesiology who is certified to administer anesthesia

**cerumen**   wax in the ear

**ceruminous glands**   canal sweat glands that secrete cerumen

**cervical intraepithelial neoplasia (CIN)** the Bethesda System used to evaluate the specimen

**cervical lymph nodes** nodes located in the neck area

**cervical mediastinotomy** a mediastinotomy completed from the front of the body

**cervix uteri** the area between the ostium uteri and the isthmus

**cesarean section delivery** a delivery in which there is a surgical procedure (incision) performed through the abdominal wall to extract the fetus

**chalazion** a small tumor of the eyelid that is formed by the retention of secretions of the meibomian gland

**cheiloplasty** repair of the lips

**chemical pleurodesis** a process where a chemical is placed into the pleural space to cause inflammation; this reduces effusion of the area

**chief complaint** the reason for the patient encounter

**choanal atresia** a narrowing or blockage of the nasal airway by tissue; a congenital condition

**chorionic villus** the medical term for the placenta

**choroid** the layer just beneath the sclera that provides the blood supply and nutrients to the eye

**cilia** an external auditory canal with tiny hairs that help in transmitting sound waves

**ciliary body** the muscles that are responsible for adjusting the lens of the eye

**cineradiography** a type of x-ray that films at a high speed to take a series of images of motion in an organ or system

**circumcision** a procedure in which the foreskin is completely removed from the glans penis

**class findings** reflect the clinical findings of patients with severe peripheral involvement

**clean-contaminated wound** a wound with a low infection rate; involves a minor break in surgical technique, but no inflammation is present

**clean wound** a wound with a very low infection rate; involves no inflammation or break in sterile technique

**closed reduction** manual application of force to realign an injured area

**closed treatment** where a fracture site is not surgically exposed or open

**coagulation** clotting of blood

**cochlea** a snail-shaped, bony structure that contains auditory fluids that transmit sound

**cochlear duct** a membranous structure that aids in the hearing process

**colonoscopy** an endoscope is used to examine the entire colon, from the rectum to the cecum

**colpocentesis** the aspiration of fluid through the vaginal wall into a syringe

**colpocleisis** a surgical closure of the vagina

**colpopexy** a procedure in which the vagina is sutured to the abdominal wall

**colporrhaphy** the surgical repair of the vagina

**colposcopy** a procedure in which a scope is used to view the vaginal and cervical area

**colpotomy** a procedure by which an incision is made in the vagina

**combined hemorrhoid (mixed hemorrhoid)** found in both the superior vein and outside the external sphincter; usually dilated

**complete PFSH** the review of at least two areas of the past, family, or social history

**complete replacement** replacement of the whole vessel device through the same access site

**complete study** a study that encompasses the entire body area

**complex repair** repair that involves reconstruction, skin grafting, stents, retention sutures, or time-consuming techniques in addition to a layered closure

**computed axial tomography (CT, CAT)** a procedure in which cross-sectional images are produced after an ionizing radiational substance is administered

**conduction anesthesia** a type of regional anesthesia in which anesthetic is injected along a major nerve tract, interrupting the nerve conductivity

**conization** a procedure performed on the cervix in which a cold knife is used to cut a cone-shaped portion of tissue surgically for examination

**conjunctiva** a colorless mucous membrane that lines the anterior part of the eye

**conscious sedation** a method of anesthetizing the patient that causes a controlled state of depressed consciousness; also called *moderate sedation*

**consultation** a request to render an opinion or expertise by another provider or appropriate source

**contaminated wound** a major break in surgical technique; acute nonpurulent inflammation is present

**cordocentesis** a procedure in which an amniocentesis needle is inserted into the umbilical vessel to obtain blood from the fetus

**cornea** a transparent nonvascular structure located on the anterior portion of the sclera

**coronary artery bypass grafts (CABG)** types of grafts performed on the heart using veins, arteries, or a combination of veins and arteries

**corpora cavernosa** the erectile tissue of the penis

**corpus uteri** the area of structures that begins at the fundus of the uterine cavity and moves down to encompass the cervical canal or the external os

**CPT modifier** a two-digit code that is appended to the CPT code to indicate that a service or procedure has been altered for some reason, but that the main definition of the code has not changed

**craniectomy** a procedure to remove the skull bone

**craniotomy** an incision into the skull without removal of bone

**critical care** care for a patient who requires constant attention by the provider because of situations related to his or her medical condition, whose illness or injury would put the patient at high risk

**cryosurgical ablation of prostate** a surgical procedure used for ablation of the prostate

**curettage** the process of removing tissue by scraping

**Current Procedural Terminology (CPT)** a coding system developed by the American Medical Association (AMA)

**cystostomy** an incision is made in the midline and carried through until the bladder is incised and then a tube is inserted and sutured in place.

**cystotomy** an incision that is made into the bladder

**cystourethroscopy** examination of the posterior urethra and the urinary bladder with a cystoscope.

**cytogenetic** studies of heredity or genes at the cellular level

**cytopathology** the study of cells, especially in the disease process

**D**

**debridement** a type of cleansing

**decision for surgery** modifier 57

**decubitus** the position of a patient on his or her back or stomach, which helps in localizing fluid

**decubitus ulcer** an ulcer resulting from continuous pressure in an area that eventually breaks down, causing a sore

**deep biopsy** the removal of nodes located below the muscle tissue

**deep removal** see *deep biopsy*

**defect site** an area that will receive tissue; also called a *recipient site*

**dermal autograph** a skin graft taken from a patient's own body that involves the dermal tissue.

**dermatome** an instrument that cuts slices of skin; the thickness is determined by the surgeon

**dermis** a thick layer of tissue located directly below the epidermis

**descending colon** the part of the colon that moves down the left side of the abdomen to the sigmoid colon

**destruction** a procedure that totally destroys or removes something

**diagnostic arthroscope** a scope used to view the joints of the body for diagnostic purposes

**diagnostic endoscope** a scope used to view the body internally for diagnostic purposes

**diagnostic nasal endoscopy** the inspection of the entire nasal cavity, the meatus, the turbinates, and the sphenoethmoid recess

**diagnostic procedures** done to determine a diagnosis and establish a care plan

**Diagnostic Radiology** the section of the Radiology chapter used to report a procedure or service rendered when assessing a disease for a more definitive diagnosis, as well as its progression or remission

**diaphragm** a dome-shaped muscle that separates the thorax from the abdomen

**diencephalon** the structure located between the cerebrum and the midbrain

**digestive system** this system performs the functions that take in and break down food for nutrient absorption and elimination of waste products

**dilation** a procedure performed when an expansion or stretching is necessary

**direct inguinal hernia** an inguinal hernia that protrudes into the abdominal wall by the Hesselbach triangle

**direct laryngoscopy** direct viewing of the larynx and adjacent structures by use of a laryngoscope

**dirty and infected wound** nonsterile conditions in which infection and inflammation are present and a foreign body may be present; also known as an infected wound

**discontinued out-patient hospital/ambulatory surgery center (ASC) procedure after administration of anesthesia** modifier 74

**discontinued out-patient hospital/ambulatory surgery center (ASC) procedure prior to the administration of anesthesia** modifier 73

**discontinued procedure** modifier 53

**dislocation** displacement of bone from the normal anatomical position

**distinct procedural service** modifier 59

**donor site** the area that provides the tissue used to make the repair

**Doppler** frequency change in sound, light, or radio waves given off by a source as it moves toward or away from the observer

**dosimetry** the scientific determination of the rate, amount, and dose of radiation to be administered

**drainage procedures** procedures completed to remove a fluid from an area

**dual-chamber system** a pacemaker system that has two electrodes, one in the atrium and one in the ventricle

**dual photon absorptiometry** a type of noninvasive bone density test in which low doses of radiation are beamed through the bone, and a computer evaluates the amount of radiation that was absorbed

**duodenotomy** making an incision into the duodenum

**durable medical equipment** medical equipment that is used in a patient's home repeatedly for a specific medical purpose

**durable medical equipment, prosthetics, orthotics, and supplies (DMEPOS)** medical equipment, prosthetics, orthotics, and supplies that are repeatedly used by patients for a specific medical purpose

**dura mater** the outermost layer of the meninges

**dynamic splint** a splint that allows limited mobility

**E**

**earlobe** the bottom portion of the external ear

**echocardiography** an ultrasound that is used to study structures of the heart

**ectopic pregnancy** a pregnancy that occurs outside the uterus

**electrodes** devices attached to the pulse generator in a cardiac pacemaker

**elements of examination** system or body areas that are examined

**embryo** the fetus from 9 weeks until birth, usually at 40 weeks

**emergency department (ED)** an organized hospital-based facility for the provision of unscheduled episodic services to patients who present for immediate medical attention

**endarterectomy** a procedure used to remove plaque deposits from blood vessels

**endocardium** the innermost lining of the heart

**endocrine system** internal glands and structures that produce or secrete hormones

**endolymph** an auditory fluid that transmits sound

**endometrium** the innermost layer of the uterus

**endoscope** an instrument used to visualize an internal body organ or cavity

**endoscopic procedure** a procedure involving the insertion of a flexible or rigid instrument called an *endoscope*, which is used to view internal structures

**endoscopic retrograde cholangiopancreatography (ERCP)** an endoscopic procedure that combines a retrograde cholangiography and a transhepatic cholangiography

**endotracheal intubation** the insertion of an endotracheal tube into the trachea to keep it open

**endovascular repair** repair within the vessel

**endovascular therapy**    a specific procedure to control bleeding, destroy a tumor, achieve hemostasis for a bleeding aneurysm, control blood flow during intracranial or extracranial procedures, and other reasons

**enteral**    route of administration involving the gastrointestinal tract

**enterocele**    another term for a vaginal hernia

**enteroenterostomy**    a procedure used to report the surgical anastomosis of two parts of the intestine with the creation of an opening between the two areas

**enterolysis**    freeing of intestinal adhesions

**enterotomy**    a procedure in which an incision is made into the intestines

**enucleation**    removal without cutting into a structure

**epicardium**    the inner layer of the double-walled sac around the heart; also known as *visceral pericardium*

**epidermal autograft**    an autograft that involves the epidermis

**epidermis**    the outermost layer of the skin

**epididymis**    a tubular structure that is found at the posterior border of a testis and that carries sperm to the *vas deferens*

**epidural anesthesia**    the injection of an anesthetic agent into the epidural space above the dura mater that contains the spinal nerves and cerebrospinal fluid

**epidural blocks**    the injection of an anesthetic agent into the epidural space above the dura mater that contains the spinal nerves and cerebrospinal fluid

**epiglottidectomy**    a surgical excision of the epiglottis

**episiotomy**    an incision made at the vaginal opening to prevent tearing during childbirth

**escharotomy**    the removal of necrosed tissue of severely burned skin

**esophagogastroduodenoscopy procedure (EGD)**    a procedure in which a scope is used to view the esophagus and the upper portion of the gastrointestinal tract, including the stomach, upper duodenum, and/or jejunum

**esophagus**    a muscular structure that moves food from the pharynx to the stomach

**established patient**    a patient who has received professional services from a physician or another physician of the same specialty within the past three years in the same group setting

**ethmoidectomy**    the partial or total removal of the ethmoid bone or ethmoid cells within the ethmoid sinus

**ethmoid sinuses**    sinuses located between the eyes

**eustachian tube**    a tube that connects the bony structures of the middle ear to the pharynx

**Evaluation and Management (E/M)**    codes that reflect the evaluation by a provider and also the management portion of the patient's care

**eversion**    turning outward

**evisceration**    the removal of an organ

**excision**    the surgical removal of a structure

**exenteration**    the surgical removal of the contents of a cavity

**exostosis**    a benign bony growth that projects from the surface of a bone

**extension**    movement that increases an angle of a joint

**extensive nasal polyp excision**    a procedure in which a polyp's shape or thickness or the number of polyps present may require more skill and effort for removal

**external auditory canal**    ear canal

**external auditory meatus**    ear canal

**external ear**    the outermost part of the ear that is visible, outside the structure of the skull

**external fixation**    the placement of pins through soft tissue into bone to hold an external appliance in place

**external hemorrhoid**    a type of hemorrhoid found outside the external sphincter

**external sphincter**    a sphincter that controls the release of urine from the bladder

**extracapsular extraction**    extraction that involves the removal of the lens without removing the posterior capsule

**extraperiosteal pneumonolysis**    the separation of the surface of the lung from the inside surface of the chest cavity

**eyelashes**    hairs that work with the upper and lower eyelids to protect the eye from foreign material

# F

**face-to-face time**    the provider's time with the patient during an examination

**fallopian tubes**    bilateral tubes that open at one end in the uterus and at the other end in the peritoneal cavity

**family history**    information regarding immediate family members who suffer from a chronic or acute illness, which would affect care of the patient either during current or future encounters

**fascia**    a sheet of fibrous tissue

**fasciectomy**    removal of fasciae

**fine needle aspiration**    an aspiration in which a very fine needle is inserted into a site to withdraw fluid

**first-degree burn**    the least severe kind of burn

**fixation**    the process of suturing; fastening a structure in place

**flash symbol**    indicates codes for vaccines that are pending FDA approval

**flexible bronchoscope**    a scope inserted through the nose or mouth

**fluoroscopy**    the use of a scope to produce immediate serial images using roentgen rays, which allow for examination of the function of a body part or organ

**follow-up/repeat study**    a study performed on an area that requires an additional completed, documented study or exam

**forbidden symbol**    indicates that a code is exempt from the use of modifier -51 but has not been designated as CPT add-on procedures or services.

**foreskin**    loose skin covering the glans penis; also referred to as *prepuce*

**free graft**    a freeing of tissue from its original site

**frenum**    a connection

**frontal sinuses**    sinuses located within the frontal bone, behind the eyebrows

**frontal sinusotomy**    a procedure that involves incisions made into the frontal sinuses

**fulguration**   the use of an electric current to destroy living tissue

**full-thickness graft**   a surgical transplantation that involves the epidermis and dermis of the donor site

## G

**gastric bypass surgery**   division of the small bowel with anastomosis to the proximal stomach to bypass the major portion of the stomach

**gastrotomy**   a procedure that involves surgical incisions into the stomach

**general anesthesia**   anesthesia that affects the whole body, causing a loss of consciousness

**genioplasty**   plastic surgery of the chin

**glans penis**   the distal end of the penis

**global days**   preoperative services, postoperative services, and the procedure; also called the *global package* or *surgical package*

**global package**   preoperative services, postoperative services, and the procedure; also called the *global days* or *surgical package*

**glossectomy**   partial or complete removal of the tongue

**gonioscope**   a type of scope that examines the eye for signs of glaucoma

**graft**   a section of tissue that is moved from one site to another in an effort to heal or repair a defect

**guidelines**   items that are necessary to appropriately interpret and report the procedures and services contained in a section

## H

**habilitative services**   modifier 96

**Healthcare Common Procedure Coding System (HCPCS)**   a coding classification system that consists of CPT (Level I codes) and National Codes (Level II codes)

**heart**   the major organ of the circulatory system

**hematology**   the study of blood

**hematoma**   the collection of blood in a particular space or organ

**hematopoietic progenitor cell (HPC) boost**   a procedure in which the patient receives an infusion of hematopoietic progenitor cells from a donor.

**hemilaryngectomy**   partial removal of the larynx

**hemodialysis**   a process that removes waste from the blood but involves a continuous movement of blood from the body to a hemodialyzer for filtering; clean blood is returned to the patient's bloodstream

**hemoperfusion**   a way for toxins to be removed from the blood by perfusing the blood through activated charcoal or resin; the blood is transfused back into the patient

**hemorrhoid**   an enlarged varicose vein in or near the anus

**hernia**   a protrusion or bulge

**heterodermic graft**   a type of graft in which tissue from a different species is used for repair

**hiatal hernia**   a type of hernia that pushes the stomach upward into the mediastinal cavity through the diaphragm

**hip arthroplasty**   plastic surgery to repair the hip

**history**   contains the chief complaint; history of present illness (HPI); review of systems; and past, family, and social history (PFSH)

**history of present illness (HPI)**   a chronological description of the patient's present illness

**hollow circle symbol**   indicates a reinstated or recycled code in CPT

**homograft**   a graft involving tissue from an individual of the same species; also known as a *homologous graft*

**homologous graft**   a graft involving tissue from an individual of the same species; also known as a *homograft*

**horizontal triangles symbol**   indicates new or revised text in the CPT manual

**hormones**   chemical substances produced by the body to keep organs and tissues functioning properly

**hydatidiform mole**   a grape-like grouping of cysts that are really the ova and cannot properly develop

**hymen**   the membrane that covers the external opening of the vagina

**hymenectomy**   a procedure in which the hymen is excised

**hyperkeratotic**   an overgrowth of skin

**hyperthermia**   a treatment using heat, such as ultrasound probes, and radiofrequencies together with radiation therapy to treat malignancies by speeding up cell metabolism

**hypnotherapy**   a type of psychotherapy that alters the state of consciousness to heightened awareness and opens the patient up to suggestions that may alter his or her thoughts or behavior

**hypospadias**   repair of the penis when it is abnormally curved or when the ureter opening is not properly located, affecting the flow of urine out of the body

**hypothyroidism**   a condition that results in an underactive thyroid gland

**hysterectomy**   a procedure in which the uterus is removed

**hysterorrhaphy**   repair of the uterus

**hysteroscope**   a fiber-optic–type scope that can be used for surgical or diagnostic procedures in the uterus

## I

**imaging guidance**   a radiologic procedure that assists the physician in locating the area to be addressed

**imbrication of the diaphragm**   a transthoracic or transabdominal incision to draw back abdominal organs

**immune globulin**   functions as an antibody for a short period of time

**immunology**   study of the immune system

**incision**   a surgical cut made in skin or flesh

**incisional hernia**   a type of hernia that has developed through a surgical scar or scar tissue

**incision and drainage (I&D)**   surgically cutting over an area to be drained and then withdrawing or draining the fluid

**incomplete abortion**   an abortion in which all products of conception have not been expelled from the uterus

**increased procedural services**   modifier 22

**incus**   a bone of the ear shaped like an anvil

**indirect inguinal hernia**   a sac that extends through the inguinal ring and into the inguinal canal

**indirect laryngoscopy**   viewing of larynx by using a laryngeal mirror that is placed in the back of the throat while a second mirror is held outside the mouth

**informational modifier** a statistical modifier; used for informational purposes

**inguinal hernia** bulging at the inguinal opening

**inguinal lymph nodes** nodes in the upper femoral triangle of the thigh

**inhalation** when a substance is moved through the respiratory and/or circulatory systems

**initial rhinoplasty** the surgical repair of the nose; also known as *primary rhinoplasty*

**injection** a substance administered directly into the bloodstream, subcutaneous tissue, or intramuscular

**insertion** to place a device or substance within the body or body part; a catheter placed in a newly established venous access

**instillation** introduction into a body cavity that has a mucous membrane

**integumentary system** considered the largest body system, it protects the internal parts of the body; also called the *skin*

**intermediate repair** a procedure where laceration is fixed in layers; wound layers do not go deeper than non-muscle fascia

**internal fixation** pins or plate internally placed into bone to hold the fracture; also known as *open reduction internal fixation (ORIF)*

**internal hemorrhoid** a type of hemorrhoid located in the superior vein

**intestine** a membranous tube that begins at the pyloric opening of the stomach and ends at the anus

**intracapsular extraction** removal of the entire lens of the eye with a capsule

**intranasal biopsy** a biopsy that is completed within the nasal cavity

**intraspinal anesthesia** injection of an anesthetic agent within the spinal column

**introitus** an opening or space

**inversion** turning inward or inside out

**in vitro fertilization** a process in which a mature egg is exposed to sperm in a laboratory setting; ova are then implanted into the uterus

**iris** the colored portion of the eye

**island flap** a flap repair made using subcutaneous tissue with nutrient vessels

**isodose** equal-intensity doses of radiation to more than one area

# K

**kidneys** organs that remove waste products from the blood and regulate the volume and composition of the blood by allowing the reabsorption of water and other substances into the bloodstream

**knee arthroplasty** surgical repair of the knee

# L

**labyrinth** bony and membranous structures within the inner ear that form a maze

**lacrimal duct** the duct that tears drain through

**lacrimal gland** the gland that produces tears

**laparoscopy** a procedure that views interior structures of the abdomen

**large intestine** an organ that begins with the cecum and moves to the colon, rectum, and anus

**laryngectomy** surgical removal of the larynx

**larynx** the voice organ that connects the pharynx with the trachea

**lateral** on the side

**lateral nasal wall reconstruction** repair of the lateral aspect of the nasal wall

**Le Fort fracture** bilateral fracture of the maxilla

**legally induced abortion** an abortion induced by medical personnel working within the law; can be elective or therapeutic

**lens** a colorless structure that allows the eye to focus on images

**Level I codes** CPT codes that are designated as level I within the Healthcare Common Procedure Coding System (HCPCS)

**Level I (CPT) modifiers** two-digit numeric codes that are appended to a level I (CPT) code to indicate that a service or procedure has been altered, but the main definition of the code has not changed

**Level II codes** codes published annually by Medicare and used to bill for services and procedures; also referred to as National Codes

**Level II (HCPCS/National) modifiers** alphanumeric characters that are used to modify a Level II code

**ligaments** bands of connective tissue that bind the joints together and connect the articular bones and cartilages to allow movement

**ligation** the act of tying off; in vessel procedures, the division and stripping of vessels

**limited study** a partial scan or examination of a body area or quadrant

**lingual** referring to the tongue

**lingual tonsils** one of three sets of tonsils that are located at the base of the tongue on the posterior surface

**liver** the organ that filters red blood cells, stores essential vitamins, and contains enzymes that break down poisons and produce bile, which helps break down fats

**local anesthesia** when an anesthetic agent is applied topically to the skin or injected subcutaneously

**local autograft** a procedure in which one incision is used to harvest a graft from a patient who is the recipient and donor

**low birth weight (LBW)** description of an infant with a present body weight of 1,500–2,500 grams

**lower eyelid** the bottom eyelid; works with the upper eyelid to keep the surface of the eyeball lubricated and protected from particles

**lungs** the pair of organs that are located in the thorax and constitute the main organ of the respiratory system

**lymphadenitis** having an enlarged or inflamed lymph node

**lymphangiography** examination of the lymphatic system after contrast material has been injected

**lymphangiotomy** an incision made into a lymph node

**lymphatic channels** vessels that transport fluid away from the tissues of the body toward the thoracic cavity

**lymphatic vessels** see *lymphatic channels*

**lymph glands (nodes)** located at various areas along the lymphatic vessels; collections of lymphatic tissue

**lymph nodes (glands)** collection of lymphatic tissue

## M

**magnetic resonance imaging (MRI)**  imaging where radio frequency signals are used to examine the soft tissue and bony structures of the body without radiation

**malignant lesion**  lesion that has abnormal, cancerous cell growth

**malleus**  one of the auditory ossicles; shaped like a hammer

**mammary ductogram**  the study done on the mammary duct to the mammary gland

**mandated services**  modifier 32

**manipulation**  reduction of a dislocation or fracture

**mastectomy**  the excision of the breast or breast tissue

**mastotomy**  a surgical incision of the breast

**maxillary sinuses**  sinuses located below the eye and lateral to the nasal cavity

**maxillary sinusotomy**  an incision made into the maxillary sinus

**maxillectomy**  removal of the maxillary sinus

**Meckel's diverticulum**  a form of diverticulum of the ileum

**mediastinoscope**  a scope inserted into sternum area to visually examine the mediastinum, trachea, and major vessels found in this area

**mediastinotomy**  a procedure in which an incision is made to open the mediastinum

**mediastinum**  the space in the thoracic cavity between the lungs

**membranous labyrinth**  structures within the ear that include the utricle, saccule, semicircular ducts, and cochlear ducts

**meninges**  protective tissue that covers the brain and spinal cord

**mesencephalon**  a structure located between the diencephalon and the pons; also known as the *midbrain*

**mesentery**  the membranous attachment of an organ to the body wall

**metastasis**  when a malignant growth or tumor spreads from one part of the body into another

**microbiology**  the study of microorganisms

**microlaryngoscopy**  the use of an operating microscope on the larynx

**midbrain**  a structure located between the diencephalons and the pons; also known as the *mesencephalon*

**middle ear**  a structure found within the temporal bone; houses the auditory ossicles and eustachian tube

**minimum assistant surgeon**  modifier 81

**missed abortion**  a fetus that has died before completion of 22 weeks of gestation, with retention of the dead fetus or products of conception up to 4 weeks after demise

**mitral valve**  the valve between the left atrium and left ventricle

**mixed hemorrhoids**  see *combined hemorrhoid*

**M-mode technique**  an ultrasound technique that takes the measurement of the velocity and amplitude of moving echo-producing structures and allows for one-dimensional viewing

**moderate sedation**  a method of anesthetizing the patient that causes a controlled state of depressed consciousness; also called conscious sedation

**modifier 22**  increased procedural services

**modifier 23**  unusual use of general anesthesia

**modifier 24**  unrelated E/M service, same physician, during postoperative period

**modifier 25**  significant, separately identifiable E/M service by the same physician on the same day of the procedure or other service

**modifier 26**  professional component; physician reports only the professional component of a service rendered

**modifier 27**  multiple outpatient hospital E/M encounters on the same date

**modifier 32**  mandated services; required or mandated by a peer review organization; insurance company; governmental, legislative, or regulatory agency

**modifier 33**  preventive service

**modifier 47**  anesthesia by surgeon when regional or general anesthesia is provided by the same physician or surgeon who is performing the procedure or service

**modifier 50**  bilateral procedure

**modifier 51**  multiple procedures; additional procedure(s) or service(s) would be reported with this modifier; not used by facilities

**modifier 52**  reduced services; procedure is partially reduced or eliminated at the physician's discretion

**modifier 53**  discontinued procedure; termination of a surgical or diagnostic procedure because of extenuating circumstances that threaten the well-being of the patient

**modifier 54**  surgical care only

**modifier 55**  postoperative management only

**modifier 56**  preoperative management only

**modifier 57**  decision for surgery

**modifier 58**  staged or related procedure or service by the same physician during the postoperative period

**modifier 59**  distinct procedural service

**modifier 62**  two surgeons; two primary surgeons work together to perform distinct parts of a single reportable procedure

**modifier 63**  procedure performed on infants less than 4 kilograms

**modifier 66**  surgical team; several physicians of different specialties, other highly skilled and specially trained personnel, and various types of complex equipment during the operative procedure

**modifier 73**  discontinued outpatient hospital/ASC procedure prior to the administration of anesthesia

**modifier 74**  discontinued outpatient hospital/ASC procedure after administration of anesthesia

**modifier 76**  repeat procedure by same physician

**modifier 77**  repeat procedure by another physician; basic procedure or service performed by another physician had to be repeated

**modifier 78**  return to the operating room for a related procedure during the postoperative period

**modifier 79**  unrelated procedure or service by the same physician during the postoperative period

**modifier 80**  assistant surgeon

**modifier 81**  minimum assistant surgeon; second surgeon for a short period of time but not throughout the whole procedure

**modifier 82**  assistant surgeon when a qualified resident surgeon is not available in a teaching facility; used in a teaching-hospital residency program

**modifier 90**  references outside laboratory; laboratory procedures are performed by a party other than the treating or reporting physician

**modifier 91**   repeat clinical diagnostic laboratory test

**modifier 92**   alternative laboratory platform testing

**modifier 95**   synchronous telemedicine service rendered via a real-time interactive audio and video telecommunications system

**modifier 96**   habilitative services

**modifier 97**   rehabilitative services

**modifier 99**   indicates that multiple modifiers are needed for an individual CPT code

**modifying units**   determined by physical conditions and qualifying circumstances that affect the administration of anesthesia

**Mohs micrographic surgery**   a type of chemosurgery

**morselized allograft**   a procedure in which small pieces of bone are harvested to form the graft from a source other than the patient

**morselized autograft**   the harvesting of small pieces of the patient's own bone through a separate incision

**multifetal pregnancy reduction (MPR)**   a procedure in which one or more fetuses are removed from the uterus to increase the chances of survival of the strongest one or ones

**multiple modifiers**   modifier 99

**multiple outpatient hospital E/M encounters on the same date**   modifier 27

**multiple procedure**   modifier 51

**muscle**   tissue that is composed of fibers and cells that cause movement and are able to contract

**myocardium**   the middle layer of the heart

**myomectomy**   a procedure in which uterine fibroid tumors are removed from the wall of the uterus

# N

**narcosynthesis**   a form of psychiatry that involves the administering of an intravenous drug that allows the patient to release thoughts that might be suppressed or repressed

**nasal polyps**   growths in the nasal cavity that are commonly associated with rhinitis

**nasal vestibular stenosis**   narrowing of the nasal vestibule

**nasopharyngeal tonsils**   one of three sets of tonsils that are also referred to as the adenoids

**nasopharynx**   the part of the pharynx that is located posterior to the nasal cavity

**National Codes**   codes published annually by Medicare and used to bill for services and procedures; also referred to as *Level II codes*

**National Correct Coding Initiative (NCCI)**   an initiative implemented to standardize proper coding and payment for Medicare Part B claims

**National Drug Code (NDC)**   an 11-digit number that identifies the manufacturer, the product, and the package size of a drug

**nephrectomy**   an excision completed on a kidney

**nephrolithotomy**   removal of a kidney stone by making an incision into the kidney

**nephrorrhaphy**   suturing of the kidney

**nephrotomy**   an incision made into the kidney so the physician can explore the interior

**new patient**   a patient who has not received professional services within the past three years from a physician or another physician of the same specialty who belongs to the same group practice

**nonselective placement**   where a catheter is functioning in the vessel punctured and does not go into any other vessel

**nuclear medicine**   medicine that treats and diagnoses diseases using radioactive isotopes

**number symbol**   indicates codes that are out of numerical sequence

# O

**oblique**   different angles

**obstetrics**   the specialty that deals with women during pregnancy, childbirth, and the time immediately following childbirth

**ocular implant**   an implant performed inside the muscular cone

**oligohydramnios**   when there is insufficient amniotic fluid present

**omentectomy**   removal of the omentum

**omentum**   the part of the peritoneum that connects the stomach to other structures of the abdomen

**oophorectomy**   a partial or total removal of the ovary, unilateral or bilateral

**open colectomy**   excision of all or part of the colon by making an incision into the area

**open drainage of a perirenal abscess**   a procedure in which an incision is made into the area, the site is irrigated, and drain tubes are placed

**open drainage of a renal abscess**   a procedure in which an incision is made into the area, the site is irrigated, and drain tubes are placed

**open reduction**   a procedure in which a site is surgically opened to realign the area

**open reduction internal fixation (ORIF)**   a procedure in which pins or a plate is internally placed into bone to hold the fracture; also known as *internal fixation*

**open treatment**   a procedure in which a fracture site is surgically exposed and visualized

**open-tube bronchoscope**   a scope inserted through the mouth; also referred to as a *rigid bronchoscope*

**ophthalmologist**   a doctor who specializes in the treatment of diseases and disorders of the eye

**ophthalmology**   the study of diseases and disorders of the eye

**optic disc**   a blind spot on the optic nerve

**optic nerve**   the nerve through which impulses are sent to the brain

**optometrist**   a healthcare professional who prescribes corrective lenses

**orbital implants**   implants that are outside the muscle cone

**orchiopexy**   a surgical fixation of the testis in the scrotal sac

**organ of Corti**   the true organ of hearing

**ostectomy**   a procedure in which bone is removed

**osteoclasis**   the process of creating a surgical fracture of a bone to correct a deformity

**osteoectomy**   a procedure in which bone is removed

**osteoplasty**   surgical repair or reconstruction completed on bone tissue

**osteotomy**   sawing or cutting of a bone

**otoplasty**   plastic surgery of the ear

**oval window** a structure that separates the middle ear from the inner ear

**ovaries** structures referred to as *female gonads;* they function in producing eggs, which are released during ovulation

# P

**pacing cardioverter-defibrillator** a device that emits defibrillating shocks that stimulate the heart and treat ventricular fibrillation or ventricular tachycardia

**palate** roof of the mouth

**palatine tonsils** one of three sets of tonsils that come off the soft palate

**palatoplasty** repair of the roof of the mouth

**pancreas** an organ that secretes juices necessary for digestion and to regulate blood sugar levels

**panel test** a group of tests reported by one CPT code

**parathyroid** a structure on the posterior of the thyroid that secretes hormones that regulate serum calcium levels

**paravaginal** the area around the vagina

**parenteral** a route of administration not involving the gastrointestinal tract

**parietal pericardium** the outermost layer of the heart

**parotid glands** one of three sets of salivary glands that are located in front of each ear

**partial laryngectomy** the partial removal of the larynx; also known as a *hemilaryngectomy*

**partial nephrectomy** removal of part of the kidney

**partial replacement** replacement of a catheter component, but not the whole device, during a vessel procedure

**past, family and/or social history (PFSH)** components of a patient's history that affect the level of history selected for an Evaluation and Management (E/M) code

**past history** any past medical information that may affect the medical decision-making process

**pedicle flap** a flap of skin that hangs on a stem of skin that contains blood vessels

**penis** the male organ through which the urethra passes to allow urine to be expelled from the body as part of the urinary system; also a part of the reproductive system as the male organ that delivers spermatozoa to the female reproductive tract

**percutaneous skeletal fixation** a fracture treatment in which a fracture site is neither open nor closed and fixation is placed across the fracture site

**percutaneous ventricular assist device (pVAD)** a mechanical pump that assists a weakened heart in injecting blood to the body.

**Pereyra procedure** a procedure in which sutures are laced through a Pereya ligature carrier and the urethrovesical junction is raised up

**pericardial fluid** fluid that prevents the two layers of the pericardial sac from rubbing against each other.

**pericardial sac** a double-walled sac composed of membranous tissue that surrounds the heart

**pericardiocentesis** a procedure in which the physician removes fluid from the pericardial space by insertion of a fine needle to aspirate the fluid

**pericardium** a double-walled sac that encloses the heart

**peridural anesthesia** injection of an anesthetic agent into the epidural space above the dura mater that contains the spinal nerves and cerebrospinal fluid

**perilymph** an auditory fluid that transmits sound

**perinatal period** the period of time immediately following birth up to 28 days after birth

**perineum** the diamond-shaped area of skin between the upper area of the vaginal orifice and the anus

**peripheral arterial disease (PAD) rehabilitation** a process comprising patient-monitored exercise until symptoms of the arterial disease lessen

**peripheral nervous system** a system composed of the nerves that connect the body organs to the central nervous system

**peritoneal dialysis** a form of cleaning waste from the bloodstream; instead of a machine to filter the blood, the peritoneal membrane is used as the filter

**peritoneum** the membranous lining of the abdomen

**pertinent PFSH** review of the history related to the problem identified in the history of present illness (HPI)

**Peyronie's disease** a condition in which the corpora cavernosa becomes hardened

**pharyngeal flap** an incision made through the soft palate to the posterior pharyngeal wall and advanced to the muscle to create a flap

**pharyngolaryngectomy** a surgical excision of the hypopharynx and larynx

**pharyngoplasty** plastic surgery or a reconstructive operation on the pharynx

**pharyngostomy** a procedure in which an artificial opening is made into the pharynx

**pharyngotympanic tube** a tube within the middle ear that equalizes air pressure; also known as the *eustachian tube*

**pharynx** the tubular structure that extends from the base of the skull to the esophagus

**physical status modifiers** modifiers used to describe the patient's health status

**pia mater** the innermost layer of tissue surrounding the brain

**pilonidal cyst** a closed sac, located in the sacrococcygeal area, which contains epithelial tissue with hair nested within the sac

**pinch graft** surgical transplantation of a small amount of autograft tissue

**pinna** the flexible cartilaginous flap that is located at the base of the ear, known as the *earlobe*

**place of service (POS)** the location in which the service is performed, such as the home, office, hospital, or skilled nursing facility

**pleurectomy** surgical removal of the pleura

**pneumonectomy** removal of a lung

**pneumothorax** an accumulation of air or gas in the pleural cavity

**port** an area where a treatment beam will enter the skin and focus on a malignant area

**positron emission tomography (PET) scan** a scan in which radioactive substances are administered that allow images of various body structures to be examined in color codes that indicate the degree and intensity of the metabolic process

**postanesthesia recovery period** the period of time following the completion of surgery, in which anesthesia was administered by an anesthesiologist or other professional administering anesthesia, until the patient is released to the surgeon or to another physician.

**posterior chamber**   a chamber located behind the lens of the eye

**posteroanterior**   back to front

**postoperative management only**   modifier 55

**preoperative management only**   modifier 56

**prepuce**   loose skin covering the glans penis; also referred to as *foreskin*

**preventive medicine service**   a service in which a patient presents for a well visit or a physical examination

**pricing modifier**   an increase or decrease of the fee for the service provided

**primary rhinoplasty**   a surgical repair of the nose; also known as *initial rhinoplasty*

**procedure performed on infants less than 4 kg**   modifier 63

**proctosigmoidoscopy**   examination of the rectum with scope advancement into the sigmoid colon

**professional component**   modifier 26

**prohibitory symbol**   Indicates that a code is exempt from modifier -51 and also has not been denoted as a CPT add-on code

**prolapsed hemorrhoid**   a hemorrhoid that has descended past the anal sphincter

**prone**   horizontal position, facedown

**proprietary laboratory analyses (PLA) tests symbol**   this symbol is used to denote duplicate proprietary laboratory analyses tests.

**prostate gland**   a gland that secretes fluid that is part of the semen and aids in the motility of sperm

**proton beam treatment**   a technique used in treating malignancies by using higher doses of radiation on tumors; at the same time, it does not exceed the radiation tolerance of normal healthy tissue

**psychiatric residential treatment center**   a facility that provides 24-hour care, which includes a therapeutically planned and professionally staffed group living and learning environment

**psychiatrist**   a medical doctor who administers treatment for patients with mental, emotional, or behavioral disorders

**psychiatry**   the branch of medicine that deals with mental disorders

**psychoanalysis**   a form of psychotherapy in which the patient's unconscious thoughts are recognized and analyzed

**pudendum**   an inclusive term used to describe the external genitalia of the female body; also referred to as the *vulva*

**pulmonary perfusion imaging**   imaging of localized radioactive particles and the proportional blood flow that maps the lung perfusion

**pulmonary valve**   a valve that sits between the pulmonary artery and right ventricle

**pulse generator**   a part of a pacemaker that controls the heart rate, the energy output, and the pacing modes

**pupil**   a structure located in the center of the iris

**pyeloplasty**   the plastic surgery completed on the renal pelvis of the kidney

**pyelotomy**   an incision made into the renal pelvis

**pyloromyotomy**   the cutting of the pyloric muscle

**qualifying circumstances**   conditions that are unusual or out of the ordinary and affect the administration of anesthesia

# R

**radical lymphadenectomy**   a procedure in which lymph nodes are dissected and removed in addition to tissue under the skin

**radiologic technician**   a person who is specially trained to use equipment that generates pictures or studies taking during radiological testing

**radiologist**   a doctor whose specialty is radiology

**radiology**   the study of x-rays, high-frequency sound waves, and high-strength magnetic fields in an effort to treat or diagnose disease or injury

**radiopharmaceuticals**   drugs used in testing the cause of a problem by indicating location, size, or function of organs, tissues, or vessels

**real-time scanning**   scanning that provides a two-dimensional image of both structure and movement

**recipient site**   the area that will receive a graft; also known as the *defect site*

**reconstruction**   surgical rebuilding of a structure

**rectum**   distal end of the large intestine

**reduced services**   modifier 52

**reduction**   an attempt to realign a bone or joint

**reference (outside) laboratory**   modifier 90

**referral**   a patient transfer to a specialist for treatment of a condition

**refractor**   a machine that contains a large series of lenses that are changed quickly during an examination as the patient views an eye chart

**regional anesthesia**   anesthesia in which a particular body area or region is anesthetized

**rehabilitative services**   modifier 97

**relative value**   a value that reflects the usual services attached to anesthesia and the work associated with the anesthesia services provided; also called *basic value*

**Relative Value Guide (RVG)**   a guide that contains the basic value of each of the anesthesia services and additional codes that act as supplements to the regular CPT codes, along with narratives

**removal**   to take out an entire structure, lesion, or device

**renal endoscopic procedures**   procedures performed on the kidneys using a scope

**repair**   surgical closure of an area that may have been injured as a result of trauma or that was surgically created; procedure involves fixing, not replacing

**repeat clinical diagnostic laboratory test**   modifier 91

**repeat procedure by another physician**   modifier 77

**repeat procedure by same physician**   modifier 76

**retina**   the nerve cell layer of the eye that changes light rays into nerve impulses

**review of systems (ROS)**   an inventory of body systems that is obtained from the patient to identify signs and/or symptoms that the patient may be experiencing

**revision rhinoplasty** minor, intermediate, or major revisions of the nose; also known as *secondary rhinoplasty*

**rhinectomy** removal of the nose

**rhinophyma** a rosacea condition of the skin of the nose. The skin appears red, swollen, distorted with sebaceous hyperplasia

**rhinoplasty** surgical repair of the nose

**rhinotomy** a surgical procedure in which an incision is made along one side of the nose

**rigid bronchoscope** referred to as an *open-tube broncho-scope;* inserted through the mouth

# S

**saccule** like the utricle, this membranous sac aids in maintaining balance

**salivary glands** glands that secrete saliva that contains enzymes that aid in digestion

**salpingo-oophorectomy** removal of the fallopian tubes and ovaries

**scalpel** a small, pointed surgical knife

**scanning** a study that displays certain body areas for evaluation

**sclera** the white portion of the eye

**scleral reinforcement** repairs of the sclera

**scrotum** a structure that encloses, protects, and supports the testicles

**secondary rhinoplasty** minor, intermediate, or major revisions of the nose; also known as *revision rhinoplasty*

**second-degree burn** a partial-thickness burn that forms blisters

**selective placement** the placement of a catheter that moves into one of the great vessels off the aorta, not including the vessel puncture for access

**semicircular canals** canals located behind the vestibule; three bony structures that are filled with fluid that help to maintain balance

**semicircular ducts** ducts located behind the vestibule that help to maintain balance

**seminal vesicle** part of the ejaculatory duct posterior to the urinary bladder

**septic abortion** an abortion in which fever and infection are present

**septoplasty** rhinoplasty that includes major septal repair

**serial tonometry** a procedure that measures pressure over the course of the day

**serous pericardium** the outermost layer of the pericardial sac

**shaft** the proximal end of the penis

**shaving** removal of a lesion from the epidermal or dermal layer without incision or slicing into the subcutaneous level of the skin

**sigmoid colon** the descending colon moves down the left side of the abdomen to the sigmoid colon, which then connects to the rectum

**sigmoidoscopy** a procedure in which the endoscope is moved all the way through the rectum and sigmoid colon and may even advance slightly into the descending colon

**significant, separately identifiable E/M service by the same physician on the same day of the procedure or other service** modifier 25

**simple nasal polyp excision** a procedure in which a polyp's shape allows it to be removed easily

**simple repair** a repair in which there is a single-layer closure, where laceration does not go any deeper than the subcutaneous tissue

**simulation** in radiology, it mimics the disease so that field settings for size and location of ports to be used can be determined

**single-chamber system** a pacemaker system that has one electrode in either the atrium or the ventricle

**sinoatrial node (SA node)** a node that sends impulses across the heart, causing contractions and pushing blood into the ventricles

**sinogram** a diagnostic procedure on the sinus tract

**sinus** a cavity that is located in the skull, close to the paranasal area

**skeletal traction** the application of force to a limb using felt that is applied to the skin

**skin tags** small lesions that can be brownish or flesh colored and are raised away from the body

**skin traction** the application of a pull on an affected body structure; straps are attached to the skin surrounding the structure

**sling procedures** procedures using slings to correct urinary stress incontinence

**small intestine** a structure that begins at the pyloric sphincter and moves through the duodenum, jejunum, ileum, and ileocecal sphincter

**SOAP note** a provider note that contains a subjective, objective, assessment, and plan

**social history** part of the history of past illness (HPI) that records a patient's marital status, use of tobacco, alcohol, and drugs, and other social factors that would influence the care of the patient

**somatic nervous system** a system that connects the central nervous system to the skin and skeletal muscles via the cranial and spinal nerves

**sperm** a germ cell secretion of the testicles

**spermatic cord** a covering around the nerves and vessels that encloses the seminal duct

**sphenoid sinuses** sinuses located directly behind the nose at the center of the skull

**sphenoid sinusotomy** incisions made into the sphenoid sinus

**spinal anesthesia** injection of an anesthetic agent into the spinal area

**spinal nerves** 31 pairs of nerves located in the spinal area

**spirometry testing** testing that measures lung capacity

**spleen** an organ that filters blood; the largest organ of the lymphatic system

**splenectomy** surgical removal of the spleen

**splenorrhaphy** repair of the spleen

**split-thickness autograft** a skin graft taken from a patient's own body that contains only part of the dermal layer.

**split-thickness graft** a graft in which the tissue is about half or more of the thickness of the skin

**spontaneous abortion** the complete or incomplete expulsion of products of conception before a pregnancy goes beyond 22 weeks of gestation

**spreader grafting** repair of the lateral nasal wall

**staged or related procedure or service by the same physician during the postoperative period** modifier 58

**staged procedure**   a second procedure that was planned as part of the main procedure

**Standby Services**   a type of prolonged services in which a physician requests that another physician stand by in the event that the services of the second physician are needed.

**stapes**   one of the auditory ossicles, shaped like a stirrup

**star symbol**   denotes codes that may be used to report synchronous (real-time) telemedicine services when modifier -95 is appended to the code

**static splint**   a splint used to prohibit mobility

**statistical modifier**   an informational modifier; used for informational purposes

**stoma**   a surgical opening between a part of the intestine and the outside surface of the abdomen

**stomach**   a pouchlike structure that aids in the breakdown and digestion of food

**strangulated hemorrhoid**   a hemorrhoid in which the anal sphincter causes blood supply to be occluded

**strangulated hernia**   a hernia that develops gangrene because the sac is tightly constricted

**strapping**   taping to bind, protect, or immobilize an anatomical structure

**structural allograft**   a procedure in which a large segment of bone is harvested from a donor source, other than the patient, and is placed into the interspace of the spine

**structural autograft**   spine surgery involving a bicortical or tricortical graft that is harvested through a separate incision

**subarachnoid anesthesia**   injection of an anesthetic agent into the spinal area

**subcutaneous**   the layer of skin that makes the connection to the muscle surface

**sublingual**   relating to the area under the tongue

**sublingual gland**   one of three sets of salivary glands that contain enzymes, which aid in digestion; located under the tongue

**submandibular gland**   one of three sets of salivary glands, which contain enzymes that aid in digestion; located on the floor of the mouth

**submandibular lymph nodes**   nodes located under the mandible or lower jaw

**superficial biopsy**   the removal of lymph nodes located close to the surface of the skin and subcutaneous tissue

**superficial removal**   see *superficial biopsy*

**supine**   a sitting position

**surgical arthroscopy**   a procedure that surgically treats an injury or condition of abnormality of a joint

**surgical care only**   modifier 54

**surgical endoscopy**   a procedure that surgically treats an injury or condition of an internal body organ or cavity

**surgical nasal endoscopy**   a procedure in which a nasal endoscope is used to complete a surgical procedure

**surgical package**   preoperative services, postoperative services, and the procedure; also called the *global package* or *global days*

**surgical team**   modifier 66

**suspensory ligaments**   ligaments that hold the lens of the eye in place

**symphysiotomy for horseshoe kidney**   correction of a condition of abnormal union of the kidneys

**synechia**   an adhesion of the iris to either the cornea or lens

**synovectomy**   removal of the synovial membrane of a joint

# T

**tarsorrhaphy**   the entire or partial suturing of the eyelids

**teletherapy**   an external radiation treatment in which the machine delivers the radiation after being positioned a specified distance from the patient

**tendon**   dense fibrous band of connective tissue that attaches muscles to bones

**testes**   glands located in the scrotal sac that produce sperm and are referred to as the *testicles*

**therapeutic procedures**   part of the care plan; procedures used as treatment for a diagnosis that has already been rendered

**third-degree burn**   a burn that goes to the subcutaneous layer or further

**thoracoscopy**   the examination of the pleura, lungs, and mediastinum using an endoscope to visualize the area

**thoracostomy**   an incision made into the chest wall

**thoracotomy**   a surgical opening into the thoracic cavity

**thromboendarterectomy**   a surgical incision that is made into an artery to remove a thrombus or plaque and the arterial lining

**thrombosed hemorrhoid**   a hemorrhoid that contains a blood clot and is extremely painful

**thymus gland**   a gland that functions to secrete thymosin, which is a hormone the bone marrow needs to produce T cells that work with the immune system

**thyroid gland**   a gland that secretes hormones that regulate growth and metabolism

**time unit**   anesthesia time or time spent providing anesthesia services

**tissue-cultured epidermal autograft**   a graft where tissue is harvested in a split tissue autograft and then cultured tissue is grafted back to the donor

**tomography**   a radiological procedure in which a detailed cross section of tissue structure is produced

**tonsils**   structures considered the first line of defense for the respiratory system

**trachea**   a tube-shaped structure in the neck that extends from the larynx to the bronchi

**trachelectomy**   removal of cervix uteri

**tracheostomy**   an incision made into the trachea

**transfusion**   the introduction directly into the bloodstream of whole blood or blood components

**transthoracic mediastinotomy**   a mediastinotomy performed through the fourth intercostal space

**transverse colon**   the part of the colon that moves in a horizontal direction, and at the splenic flexure, makes a downward turn to the descending colon

**trephine**   a surgical instrument used to cut a cylindrical shape; at times, used for cutting holes in bone

**triangle symbol**   denotes that a code has been revised from the previous edition of CPT with a substantial change in the description of procedure or service

**tricuspid valve**   the valve between the right atrium and right ventricle

**tube pericardiostomy**   a procedure in which fluid is drained from the pericardial space by placing a long needle into the pericardial space and then exchanging the needle for an indwelling catheter

**tunica vaginalis**   the membranous sac within the scrotum that covers the sides and front of the testis and epididymis

**two surgeons**   modifier 62

**tympanic cavity**   the cavity in the temporal bone that houses the auditory ossicles and eustachian tube

**tympanic membrane**   the part of the eardrum that separates the external ear from the middle ear

**tympanic neurectomy**   removal of the Jacobson's nerve located in the middle ear

**tympanoplasty**   surgical repair of the tympanic membrane

**tympanostomy**   an incision made into the tympanic membrane to create an opening

# U

**ulcerated hemorrhoid**   a hemorrhoid that is inflamed and may have necrotic changes in surrounding tissue

**ulcers**   erosions of the skin in which tissue becomes inflamed and then lost

**ultrasonography**   a radiological procedure in which sound waves are passed over body structures to send a signal to a computer that is then turned into a picture for examination

**unbundling**   a coder's selection of more than one code for a procedure when only one code should have been selected

**unplanned return to the operating room for a related procedure during the postoperative period**   modifier 78

**unrelated E/M service by the same physician during postoperative period**   modifier 24

**unrelated procedure or service by the same physician during the postoperative period**   modifier 79

**unusual anesthesia**   modifier 23

**upper eyelid**   a structure that works with the lower eyelid to keep the surface of the eyeball lubricated and protected from particles

**uptake**   the amount and time a substance takes to draw up or absorb

**ureterectomy**   removal of a ureter

**ureters**   structures that move urine from the kidneys into the urinary bladder

**urethra**   a mucous membrane–lined tube that leads the urine from the bladder to be excreted from the body

**urinary bladder**   a structure that serves as a temporary reservoir for urine

**urodynamics**   the study of the holding and storage of urine in the bladder, motion and rate of the movement of the urine, and analysis of how the bladder empties

**utricles**   along with the saccule, these are membranous sacs that aid in maintaining balance

**uvula**   a small, cone-shaped mass of flesh that hangs in the posterior border of the soft palate

# V

**vaccine**   a dead microorganism that is administered for prevention or treatment of a disease

**vagina**   a fibromuscular structure that connects with the external genitalia and ascends in a tubelike structure to the cervix uteri

**vaginal birth after cesarean (VBAC)**   an attempt at vaginal delivery after a previous cesarean section

**vaginectomy**   a procedure in which the vagina is excised

**vagotomy**   the surgical cutting of the vagus nerve with the intent of reducing acid secretions in the stomach

**vas deferens**   a tube that starts at the epididymis and goes over the top of the urinary bladder and allows sperm to move outside the system

**vasectomy**   excision of the *vas deferens* to prevent sperm from moving out of the system; renders a man sterile

**veins**   vessels that move deoxygenated blood back to the heart (with the exception of the pulmonary veins)

**venography**   x-ray image of the veins; also referred to as a *phlebography*

**venous access device**   a device or catheter that allows for access to the venous system

**ventral hernia**   a type of hernia that protrudes through an abdominal scar where the abdominal wall is protected only by scar tissue

**ventricles**   the lower chambers of the heart that send blood to the arteries

**vermilion**   a pinkish border of the lips

**very low birth weight (VLBW)**   infant weight less than 1,500 grams

**vessels**   structures that move fluid throughout the body

**vestibular glands**   glands that secrete lubricating mucous in the vagina; also referred to as *Bartholin's glands*

**vestibule**   the central portion of the inner ear

**vestibule of the mouth**   mucosal tissue and submucosal tissue of the lips and cheeks

**V-excision**   removal of tissue using a V-shaped incision

**views**   positions of the patient in relation to the camera or device taking pictures

**visceral pericardium**   the inner layer of the double-walled sac of the heart; also known as the *epicardium*

**vitreous humor**   a clear, jellylike substance that helps to shape the eye

**vulva**   external genitalia of the female body; also referred to as the *pudendum*

**vulvectomy**   removal of all or part of the vulva

# W

**wedge excision**   an excision shaped like a wedge

**wound exploration**   examination that determines the extent of the injury and includes surgical examination of a wound area

# X

**xenograft**   a graft made up of nonhuman material

**x-ray**   electromagnetic waves that are used to produce a picture of internal structures of the body

# INDEX

## A

A codes, 453
A-mode technique, 410
abbreviations
  anesthesia, 86
  auditory system, 390
  cardiovascular system, 195–196
  digestive system, 247
  endocrine system, 348
  eye and ocular adnexa, 374–375
  female genital system, 317
  integumentary system, 107
  male genital system, 303
  maternal care and delivery, 333–334
  musculoskeletal system, 138–139
  nervous system, 356
  pathology and laboratory, 423–424
  respiratory system, 168–169
  urinary system, 281
abdomen, 271–272
abdominal aorta, 211, 282
abdominal aortic aneurysm, 212–214
abdominal cerclage, 336
abdominal hysterectomy, 323
abdominal quadrants, 466
abdominopelvic divisions, 466
abdominopelvic regions, 466
abdominoperiperineal resection, 263
abducens nerve, 361
abduction, 402
ABN (advance beneficiary notice), 450
abortion, 339
accessory nerve, 361
accessory sinuses, 175–177
  anatomical diagram, 176
  endoscopy, 177
  excision, 177
  four pair of sinuses, 175
  incision, 176–177
acellular dermal replacement, 123–124
Achilles tendon, 145
acoustic nerve, 361
acromion, 142
active wound care management, 445
acupuncture, 446

add-on codes (App. D)
  description of, 8
  symbol for, 4
additions, deletions, revisions (App. B), 8
adduction, 402
adductor longus, 143
adductor magnus, 145
adenoids, 252
adjacent tissue transfer or rearrangement, 119–120
adnexa, ocular. See eye and ocular adnexa
adrenal glands, 282, 346, 349
adrenalectomy, 349–350
adrenocorticotropic hormone (ACTH), 347
advance beneficiary notice (ABN), 450
advance care planning, 42, 77
advanced life support (ALS), 453
advancement, 120
aerosol inhalation treatments, 442
aldosterone, 347
alimentary canal, 245. See also digestive system
allergy and clinical immunology, 442
allogenic bone marrow transplant, 229
allotransplantation, 268
alphabetical clinical topics listing (App. H), 9
alphanumeric modifiers, 30–35
ALS (advanced life support), 453
alternative laboratory platform testing, 28
alveolectomy, 250
alveolus (alveoli), 181, 250
ambulance origin and destination modifiers, 35
ambulance services, 453
ambulatory surgery center hospital outpatient use, 18
American Medical Association (AMA), 1–2
amniocentesis, 334–335
amnioscopy, 335
amniotic fluid analysis, 335
anal canal, 261

anastomosis, 262, 270
anatomic pathology, 428
anconeus, 145
androgens, 347
anesthesia, 85–99
  abbreviations, 86
  how administered?, 87
  anesthesia by surgeon (modifier), 21
  anesthetic administered by physician, 93–94
  balanced, 87
  billing concerns, 94
  bundled service, 93
  calculating anesthesia charges, 90–93
  conduction, 87
  general, 87
  local, 87
  locality-adjusted conversion factors, 470–473
  locating procedure codes, 88–89
  moderate or conscious sedation, 94
  modifiers, 89–90, 92
  NCCI, 86
  physical status modifiers, 90, 92
  regional, 87
  2022 anesthesia code base units, 467–469
  types of, 87
  unusual anesthesia (modifier), 19
anesthesia by surgeon, 21
anesthesiologist, 87
aneurysm
  definition of, 212
  repair of, 215, 364
  ruptured, 215
angiography, 403, 407
angioplasty, 204
angioscopy, 215
ankle, 156
anomaly, 206
anoplasty, 267
antepartum and fetal invasive services, 334–336
anterior chamber, 376
anterior mediastinotomy, 240
anteroposterior, 402

antidiuretic hormone (ADH), 347
anus, 246, 261, 266–268, 316, 318
aorta, 211
aortic semilunar valve, 198
aortic valve, 204
aortograph, 407
aponeurosis, 143
appendices, 8–9
appendix, 258, 265
aqueous humor, 376
arachnoid mater, 358
arachnoid villi, 358
arrector pili muscle, 108
arterial and arteriovenous procedures, 217–220
arterial and intraosseous codes, 217
arterial catheterization, 217
arterial circulation, 211
arterial puncture, 217
arterial transposition, 216
arteries and veins, 210–217
arteriography, 403
arteriovenous fistula repair, 215
arteriovenous malformation, 364
arthrodesis, 140, 157
arthrography, 403
arthroplasty, 140, 152–153
arthroscope, 159
arthroscopy, 140, 159–160
arthrotomy, 140
artificial heart, 207, 209
artificial intelligence taxonomy for medical services and procedures (App. S), 9
arytenoid cartilage, 178
arytenoidectomy, 179
ascending colon, 258, 260–261
aspiration, 109
assistant surgeon, 27–28
athletic training evaluations, 445
atria, 196
atrioventricular (AV) node, 196
auditory ossicles, 391
auditory system, 389–400
  abbreviations, 390
  anatomy, 391–392
  external ear, 391–394
auditory tube, 391
augmentation, 152
auricle, 391
autogenic bone marrow transplant, 229
autogenous graft, 120

autograft, 121–123
autologous bone marrow transplant, 229
autonomic function test, 443
autonomic nervous system, 357, 367
AV (atrioventricular) node, 196
axial, 402
axillary lymph nodes, 230–231
axillary lymphadenectomy, 233

## B

B codes, 454
B-scan, 410
backbench work, 186, 208, 286
balanced anesthesia, 87
balloon angioplasty, 363
balloon dilation, 363
bariatric surgery, 259
Bartholin's glands, 318
basal cell carcinoma, 114
base unit, 91
base unit value, 91
basic life and/or disability evaluation services, 75
basic life support (BLS), 453
basic value, 91
bedsore, 126
behavior management services, 443–444
behavioral health services, 456
benign lesions, 114
biceps brachii, 143
biceps femoris, 145
bicuspid valve, 198, 204
Bier blocks, 87
bilateral procedure, 21
bilateral salpingo-oophorectomy, 326
biliary tract, 268–270
biofeedback, 436
biopsy
  bone marrow, 229
  deep, 231
  definition of, 113
  esophageal, 254
  fine needle aspiration, 109–110
  intranasal, 172
  perineal, 318
  superficial, 231
  vulvar, 319
bladder, 282–283, 290–294
block, 87

block anesthesia, 87
blood-derived peripheral stem cell transplantation, 229
blood flow of normal heart, 198
blood vessel repair, 215
BLS (basic life support), 453
bone density test, 411
bone marrow
  aspiration of, 229
  biopsy of, 229
  transplants of, 229
bone/joint studies, 411
bony labyrinth, 392
brachial plexus, 360
brachioradialis, 145
brachytherapy, 323, 412–413
brain, 357–359, 361–365
brain stem, 358–359
breast mammography, 404, 410–411
breast surgery, 129–130
breathing response testing, 442
Broca's area, 359
bronchi. See trachea and bronchi
bronchial thermoplasty, 182
bronchioles, 181
bronchoscope, 182
bronchoscopy, 181
bronchospasm evaluations, 442
bronchus (bronchi), 170, 181. See also trachea and bronchi
bullet symbol, 3–4
bundle of His, 196
bundled, 93
burns, 126–127
burr holes, 362
bypass graft, 216

## C

C codes, 454
calcaneus, 141–142, 156
calcitonin, 347
cancerous lesions, 128
cardiac assist, 209–210
cardiac catheterization, 441
cardiac notch, 170, 239
cardiac orifice, 258
cardiac pacemaker, 198
cardiac tumor, 198–199
cardiac valve procedures, 203–204
cardiography, 441
cardiopulmonary bypass, 199

cardiovascular examination, 55

cardiovascular system, 194–225

abbreviations, 195–196

abdominal aortic aneurysm, 212–214

adjuvant technique codes, 216

anatomy, 196–198

aneurysm and associated occlusive disease, 215

angioplasty, 204

angioscopy, 215

arterial and arteriovenous procedures, 217–220

arterial and intraosseous codes, 217

arterial circulation, 211

arterial transposition, 216

arteries and veins, 210–217

arteriovenous fistula repair, 215

artificial heart, 207, 209

blood flow of normal heart, 198

blood vessel repair, 215

bypass graft, 216

cardiac assist, 209–210

cardiac tumor, 199

cardiac valve procedures, 203–204

composite graft, 216

congenital cardiac anomalies, 206

coronary artery anomalies, 204–205

coronary artery bypass graft procedures, 205–207

dialysis circuit, 218

electrophysiologic operative procedures, 202–203

embolectomy, 210

endarterectomy, 204

endoscopy, 203, 219

endovascular revascularization, 219

excision, 216–217

exploration, 216–217

extracorporeal life support, 209

extracorporeal membrane oxygenation, 209

fenestrated endovascular graft, 213

heart and associated structures, 197

heart anomalies, 206

heart/lung transplantation, 207–209

implantable defibrillator, 199–202

implantable hemodynamic monitor, 203

intravascular ultrasound services, 219

ligation and other procedures, 220

medicine section of CPT, 440–441

NCCI, 195

pacemaker, 199–202

pacing cardioverter-defibrillator, 200–201

pericardiocentesis, 198

physical examination, 55

portal decompression procedures, 218

pseudoaneurysm, 215

repair, 216–217

revision, 216–217

subcutaneous cardiac rhythm monitors, 203

thrombectomy, 210

thromboendarterectomy, 215

transcatheter procedures, 218

transmyocardial laser revascularization, 198–199

vascular embolization and occlusion, 219

vascular injection procedures, 217

venous circulation, 212

venous grafting for coronary artery bypass, 205

venous reconstruction, 211

wounds of heart and great vessels, 203

care management services, 42, 76–77

care plan oversight services, 42, 72–73

carotid body tumor, 349

carpals, 141–142, 156

cartilage, 140

case management, 72, 42

cast removals or repairs, 158

casts and strapping, 157–158

CAT (computed axial tomography), 404

cataract extractions, 378–379

Category I codes, 10

Category I proprietary laboratory analyses (PLA) tests symbol, 5

Category II codes, 10

Category III codes, 10

cauda equina, 360

cecostomy, 264

cecum, 246, 258, 261

celiac trunk, 211

central nervous system (CNS)

assessment of, 443–444

description of, 356

central venous access device (CVA) device, 217

cerclage, 322, 336

cerebellar peduncle, 359

cerebellum, 357–360

cerebral cortex, 358

cerebral embolic protection devices, 203

cerebrospinal fluid (CSF) shunt, 365–366

cerebrum, 357–358

certificate of medical necessity (CMN), 450

certified registered nurse anesthetist (CRNA), 87

cerumen, 391, 393

ceruminous gland, 391

cervical canal, 322

cervical intraepithelial neoplasia (CIN), 428

cervical lymph nodes, 230–231

cervical mediastinotomy, 240

cervical plexus, 360

cervical vertebrae, 141–142

cervix, 316

cervix uteri, 322–323

cesarean section delivery, 336

chalazion, 383

Chamberlain approach, 240

cheiloplasty, 248

chemical cauterization of granulation tissue, 128

chemical pleurodesis, 185

chemotherapy, 444

chest examination, 55

chief complaint (CC), 52

childbirth. See maternal care and delivery

chiropractic manipulative treatment, 446

choanal atresia, 174

choledochostomy, 268

choledochotomy, 268

chorionic villus sampling, 334

choroid, 376

cicatricial, 114

cilia, 391

ciliary body, 376

CIN (cervical intraepithelial neoplasia), 428

cineradiography, 403, 409

circulatory system, 227. See also cardiovascular system; hemic and lymphatic systems

circumcision, 305

class findings, 112

clavicle, 141–142

clean-contaminated wound, 118

clean wound, 118

cleft lip, 248
clinical examples (App. C), 8
clinical immunology, 442
clitoris, 316
clitoroplasty, 319
Cloquet's node, 233
closed reduction, 154
closed treatment, 140
CMN (certificate of medical necessity), 450
CMS-1450 form, 463
CMS-1500 form, 16, 463
CNS (central nervous system), 356
coagulation, 427
coccyx, 141–142
cochlea, 392, 396
cochlear duct, 392, 396
cochlear nerve, 396
cognitive assessment and care plan services, 42
colectomy, 263
colon, 265–266
colon resection options, 263
colonoscopy, 264, 266
coloproctostomy, 262
colostomy, 264
colpocentesis, 320
colpocleisis, 320
colpopexy, 321
colporrhaphy, 320
colposcope, 322
colposcopy, 319
colpotomy, 320
combined hemorrhoids, 266
common bile duct, 258
complete replacement, of catheter, 217
complete study, 409
complex repair, 117–118
composite graft, 216
comprehensive examination, 57
computed axial tomography (CAT), 404
computed tomographic angiography, 407
conduction anesthesia, 87
congenital, 114
congenital cardiac anomalies, 206
conization, 322
conjunctiva, 375–376, 383
conjunctivoplasty, 383
conjunctivorhinostomy, 383
conscious sedation, 9, 94
consultations (clinical pathology), 426–427

consultations, 61–63
contaminated wound, 118
continent ileostomy, 264
contraceptive capsules, 117
conus medullaris, 360
conversion table, 108
cordocentesis, 334
cornea, 376
corneal transplant, 378
corniculate cartilage, 178
coronary artery anomalies, 204–205
coronary artery bypass graft procedures, 205–207
coronavirus disease (COVID-19)
    codes for, 423, 428
    vaccine (App. Q), 9
corpora cavernosa, 305
corpus uteri, 323
correct coding edits, 105
cortisol, 347
COVID-19
    codes for, 423
    vaccine (App. Q), 9
Cowper's glands, 304
CPT. See current procedural terminology (CPT)
CPT modifier, 15. See also modifiers
cranial nerves, 357–358, 361
craniectomy, 363
cranioplasty, 365
craniotomy, 363–364
cricothyroid ligament, 178
cricothyroid muscles, 178
cricotracheal ligament, 178
crista ampullaris, 396
critical care services, 42, 64–68
    inpatient neonatal and pediatric, 67–68
    pediatric critical care patient transport, 65–66
CRNA (certified registered nurse anesthetist), 87
cryosurgical ablation of the prostate, 308
cryotherapy, 381
CSF (cerebrospinal fluid) shunt, 365
cubital nodes, 230
cuneiform cartilage, 178
curettage, 150, 336
current procedural terminology (CPT), 1–13
    appendices, 8–9
    guidelines, 7–8

historical overview, 2
index, 8
introduction, 3
sections, subsections, categories, 6–7
structure and design of, 2–9
symbols, 3–6
update notifications, 2
cuticle, 115
CVA device, 217
cyclophotocoagulation, 378
cyst, 110, 114
cystectomy, 292
cystic, 114
cystic duct, 246, 258
cystoplasty, 292
cystorrhaphy, 293
cystostomy, 291
cystotomy, 292
cystourethroplasty, 292
cystourethroscopy, 293–294
cytogenetic studies, 428
cytopathology, 428

**D**

D codes, 455
dacryocystorhinostomy, 383
debridement
    defined, 140
    integumentary system, 110–111, 119
    of mastoid cavity, 393
decubitus, 402
decubitus ulcer, 126
deep biopsy, 231
deep peroneal nerve, 357
deep removal, 231
defect site, 120
delivery/birthing room attendance and resuscitation services, 42, 76
deltoid, 143, 145
dental procedures, 455
dentoalveolar structures, 250
Dermabond, 117
dermatome, 111
dermis, 107–108
descending colon, 260–261
destruction
    anus, 268
    dentoalveolar structures, 250
    extracranial nerves, 367
    inner ear, 396
    integumentary system, 127–129
    lungs and pleura, 184–185

destruction (*continued*)
  nose, 174–175
  palate and uvula, 251
  vulva, 318
detailed examination, 58
diabetes mellitus, 110
diagnostic procedures, 102
  bone marrow aspiration, 229
  bone marrow biopsy, 229
  endoscopy/arthroscopy, 159
  esophagoscopy, 254
  nasal endoscopy, 177
  radiology, 405–409
  ultrasound, 409–410
dialysis, 437–438
dialysis circuit, 218
diaphragm, 170, 181, 197, 238–241,
  246
diaphragmatic hernia, 240
diathermy, 378, 381
diencephalon, 358–359
digestive system, 244–279
  abbreviations, 247
  abdomen, 271–272
  adenoids, 252
  anatomy, 246, 248
  anus, 266–268
  appendix, 265
  bariatric surgery, 259
  biliary tract, 268–270
  colon, 265–266
  dentoalveolar structures, 250
  esophagus, 253–257
  functions, 245
  hemorrhoids, 266–267
  hernia, 271–272
  intestines, 260–265
  lips, 247–249
  liver, 268
  Meckel's diverticulum, 265
  mesentery, 265
  mouth, 248–250
  NCCI, 246
  omentum, 271
  oral cavity, 248
  palate and uvula, 251
  pancreas, 270–271
  peritoneum, 271
  pharynx, 252–253
  rectum, 265–266
  salivary glands and ducts, 251–252
  stomach, 257–259

tongue and floor of mouth, 249–250
tonsils, 252–253
digital medicine-services taxonomy
  (App. R), 9
dilation
  esophagus, 256–257
  rectum, 266
dilation and curettage, 323
direct inguinal hernia, 271
direct laryngoscopy, 179
dirty and infected wound, 119
discontinued procedure, 22–23
  after administration of anesthesia, 26
  prior to administration of anesthesia,
  26
dislocation, 140, 154
distal phalanx, 156
distinct procedural service, 24–25
DME (durable medical equipment), 30,
  455
DME regional carriers, 456
DMEPOS (durable medical equipment,
  prosthetics, orthotics, and supplies),
  450
donor enterectomy, 262
donor site, 120
Doppler, 404
dosimetry, 412
double pedicle flaps, 120
drainage procedure, 171
drug assay, 426
drug delivery implant system, 117
drug-induced sleep endoscopy, 253
drug testing, 426
dual-chamber system, 200
dual photon absorptiometry, 414
ductus deferens, 307
duodenotomy, 262
duodenum, 246, 258
dura mater, 358
durable medical equipment (DME), 30,
  455
dynamic splint, 157

**E**

E codes, 455
ear, 391–392, 396. *See also* auditory
  system
ear, nose and throat (ENT), 55, 440
earlobe, 391
earwax, 391
EBUS (endobronchial ultrasound), 182

echocardiography, 404, 441
ECLS (extracorporeal life support),
  209
ECMO (extracorporeal membrane
  oxygenation), 209
ectopic pregnancy, 336
EEG (electroencephalography), 442–443
EGD (esophagogastroduodenoscopy)
  procedures, 255–256
ejaculatory duct, 304
electrocardiogram, 440
electrocautery needle, 115
electroconvulsive therapy (shock
  therapy), 436
electrocorticography, 443
electrode, 200
electroejaculation, 308
electroencephalography (EEG), 442–443
electromyography, 443
electrophysiologic operative
  procedures, 202–203
elements of examination, 55–57
E/M codes. *See* evaluation and
  management (E/M)
embolectomy, 210
embryo, 333
emergency department services, 42,
  63–64
empyemectomy, 184
end-stage renal disease services, 438
endarterectomy, 204
endobronchial ultrasound (EBUS), 182
endocardium, 196–198
endocrine system, 345–354
  abbreviations, 348
  adrenal glands, 349
  anatomical diagram, 346
  carotid body tumor, 349
  hormones, 345, 347
  laparoscopy, 350
  medicine section of CPT, 442
  NCCI, 347
  pancreas, 349
  parathyroid, 349
  thymus gland, 349
  thyroid gland, 348–349
endolymph, 392, 396
endometrial ablation, 323
endometrium, 322
endoscope, 159
endoscopic retrograde
  cholangiopancreatography (ERCP),
  256

endoscopic/laparoscopic procedures, 269
endoscopy
    accessory sinuses, 177
    anus, 267
    biliary tract, 269
    bladder, 293
    brain, 365
    cardiovascular system, 203, 219
    coronary artery anomalies, 204–205
    drug-induced sleep, 253
    esophagus, 254–256
    intestines, 264
    kidneys, 288
    larynx, 179–180
    musculoskeletal system, 159–160
    trachea and bronchi, 181–182
    ureter, 290
    vagina, 321
endotracheal intubation, 179
endovascular repair, 408
endovascular revascularization, 219
endovascular therapy, 363–364
ENT (ear, nose and throat), 55, 440
enteral and parenteral therapy, 454
enterectomy, 262
enterocele, 320
enterocystoplasty, 293
enteroenterostomy, 262
enterolysis, 262
enterostomy, 263–264
enterotomy, 262
enucleation, 376–377
epicardium, 196–197
epidermal autograft, 122
epidermis, 107–108
epididymis, 304–305
epidural anesthesia, 87
epidural block, 87
epiglottidectomy, 179
epiglottis, 169, 178, 181, 253
epinephrine, 347
episiotomy, 336
ERCP (endoscopic retrograde cholangiopancreatography), 256
escharotomy, 127
esophageal dilation, 257
esophagectomy, 254
esophagogastric fundoplasty, 256
esophagogastroduodenoscopy (EGD) procedures, 255–256
esophagogastrostomy, 256

esophagojejunostomy, 256
esophagomyotomy, 256
esophagostomy, 256
esophagus, 169, 246, 253–258
established patient
    defined, 45
    vs. new patient, 43
estrogen, 324, 347
ethmoid sinus, 175–176
ethmoidectomy, 177
eustachian tube, 391
evaluation and management (E/M), 40–84
    advance care planning, 77
    care management services, 76–77
    cognitive assessment and care plan services, 42
    consultations, 61–63
    critical care services, 64–68
    delivery/birthing room attendance and resuscitation services, 76
    documentation guidelines, 41
    emergency department services, 63–64
    established patient. See established patient
    home or residence services, 70–73
    hospital inpatient and observation care services coding, 59–61
    levels of service. See levels of service for E/M codes
    location of service provided, 45–47
    new patient. See new patient
    newborn care, 75–76
    non-face-to-face services, 75
    nursing facility services, 68–70
    office or other outpatient services, 47–51
    overview (categories and code ranges), 42
    place of service (POS) codes, 45–47
    preventive medicine services, 73–75
    prolonged service time, 51
    psychiatric collaborative care management services, 42
    special evaluation and management services, 75
    transitional care management services, 77
eversion, 403
evisceration, 376
evocative/suppression testing, 426
evoked potentials and reflex tests, 443
examination, 54–58

    comprehensive, 57
    detailed, 58
    general multisystem, 55–57
    single-organ, 54
excision
    abnormal pregnancy, 335–336
    accessory sinuses, 177
    anus, 267
    benign lesions, 114
    biliary tract, 269
    bladder, 292
    breast, 129
    cardiovascular system, 216–217
    cervix uteri, 322
    corpus uteri, 323
    dentoalveolar structures, 250
    esophagus, 254
    external ear, 393
    extracranial nerves, 367
    inner ear, 396
    integumentary system, 114
    intestines, 262
    kidneys, 284–285
    larynx, 178–179
    lungs and pleura, 184–185
    lymph nodes, 231
    malignant lesions, 114
    middle ear, 394
    musculoskeletal system, 142, 150
    nose, 171–172
    oviduct/ovary, 325–326
    pancreas, 270
    prostate, 308
    salivary glands, 251
    spine and spinal cord, 365–367
    spleen, 227
    stomach, 258–259
    tongue and floor of mouth, 250
    ureter, 289–290
    urethra, 295
    vagina, 320
    vulva, 319
excision codes, 322
exenteration, 376
exostosis, 140
exploration, cardiovascular system, 216–217
extension, 403
extensive nasal polyp excision, 172
extensive retroperitoneal transabdominal lymphadenectomy, 233
extensor carpi muscles, 143

extensor carpi radialis longus, 145
extensor carpi ulnaris, 145
extensor digitorum communis, 145
external anal sphincter, 261
external auditory canal, 391
external auditory meatus, 391
external ear, 391–394
external fixation, 154
external hemorrhoids, 266
external oblique, 143
external sphincter, 282
extracapsular extraction, 378–379
extracorporal shock wave lithotripsy, 288
extracorporeal life support (ECLS), 209
extracorporeal membrane oxygenation (ECMO), 209
extracranial nerves, 367
extraperiosteal pneumonolysis, 186
extrapleural thoracoplasty, 186
eye and ocular adnexa, 373–388
    abbreviations, 374–375
    anatomy, 375–376
    anterior segment, 378–380
    cataract extractions, 378–379
    conjunctiva, 383
    enucleation, 376–377
    extracapsular/intracapsular extraction, 378–379
    eye examination, 55
    eyeball, 376–378
    eyelids, 375, 383
    HCPCS level II codes, 458
    muscles of the eye, 382
    NCCI, 374
    ocular adnexa, 382–383
    ocular/orbital implants, 377
    ophthalmic endoscope, 378
    posterior segment, 380–381
    retinal detachment, 381
    scleral buckling, 381
    strabismus surgery, 382
eyeball, 376–378
eyelashes, 375
eyelids, 375, 383

**F**

facial nerve, 361, 395
fallopian tubes, 316, 322, 324
falx cerebri, 358
family history, 52
fascia, 140

fasciectomy, 150
female external genitalia, 318
female genital system, 315–331
    abbreviations, 317
    cervix uteri, 322–323
    corpus uteri, 323
    female external genitalia, 318
    hysteroscopy, 324
    laparoscopy, 324
    NCCI, 316–317
    organs of female reproductive system, 316
    oviduct and ovaries, 324–326
    vagina, 320–321
    in vitro fertilization, 326
    vulva and perineum, 317–319
female gonads, 324
femoral neck fracture, 155
femoral nerve, 360
femoropopliteal vein segment, 205
femur, 141–142, 156
femur fracture, 155
fenestrated endovascular graft, 213
fetal fluid drainage, 335
fetal invasive services, 334–336
fetal scalp blood sampling, 334
fetal umbilical cord occlusion, 335
fiber-optic bronchoscopy, 181
fibrous, 114
fibrous pericardium, 196
fibula, 141–142
filum terminale, 360
fimbriae, 322
fine needle aspiration, 109
fine needle aspiration biopsy, 109–110
fingernails, 115
first-degree burn, 126
fixation devices, 154–155
flap-type repairs, 125–126
flash symbol, 5
flexible bronchoscope, 182
flexible esophagoscope, 254
flexor carpi muscles, 143
flexor carpi ulnaris, 145
fluoroscopy, 404
follicle-stimulating hormone (FSH), 347
follow-up/repeat study, 409
foot, 156
foot care, 111–112
forbidden or prohibitory symbol, 5
foreign body

cardiovascular system, 218
    definition of, 104–105
    ear, 393
    nose, 172
foreskin, 304
fovea centralis, 376
Fowler's position, 465
fracture/dislocation, 154–155
free graft, 120
free skin graft, 120
frenoplasty, 250
frenum, 249
frontal lobe, 359
frontal sinus, 169, 175–176
frontal sinusotomy, 177
fulguration, 322
full thickness graft, 124
functional brain mapping, 443

**G**

G codes, 455
gallbladder, 246, 258
gamete intrafallopian transfer (GIFT), 326
gamete intrafallopian transfer (GIFT) procedure, 326
gastrectomy, 258
gastric bypass surgery, 259
gastrocnemius, 143, 145
gastroenterology, 439
gastrointestinal examination, 56
gastrojejunostomy, 271
general anesthesia, 87
general behavioral health integration care management, 42
general multisystem examination, 55–57
genetic counseling services, 443
genetic testing code modifiers (App I), 9
genioplasty, 152
genital system. *See* female genital system; male genital system
genitourinary examination, 56
genomic sequencing procedures, 427
GIFT (gamete intrafallopian transfer), 326
gingiva, 248
gingivectomy, 250
gingivoplasty, 250
glans penis, 304
global days, 103
global package, 102

glossectomy, 250
glossopharyngeal nerve, 361
glucagon, 347
gluteus maximus, 145
gluteus medius, 145
gonioscope, 439
goniotomy, 378
gracilis, 145
graft, 121–125, 146–147
growth, 114
growth hormone (GH), 347
guidelines, 7–8
gynecomastia, 130

## H

H codes, 456
habilitative services, 29
hamstring muscles, 145
hand, 156
hard palate, 248
HCPCS level I codes, 10. *See also* current procedural terminology (CPT)
HCPCS level II codes, 11, 449–462
  A codes, 453
  ambulance services, 453
  appendices, 458
  B codes, 454
  background information, 449–450
  behavioral health services, 456
  C codes, 454
  D codes, 455
  dental procedures, 455
  diagnostic radiology services, 457
  DME regional carriers, 456
  drugs administered other than oral method, 456
  durable medical equipment (DME), 455
  E codes, 455
  enteral and parenteral therapy, 454
  G codes, 455
  H codes, 456
  index, 451–452
  J codes, 456
  K codes, 456
  L codes, 456–457
  level II modifiers, 15, 30–35, 90
  M codes, 457
  medical and surgical supplies, 453
  medical services and quality services, 457
  orthotic and prosthetic procedures and devices, 456–457
  outpatient prospective payment section (OPPS), 454
  overview (organization of level II codes into sections), 451
  P codes, 457
  pathology and laboratory services, 457
  Q codes, 457
  R codes, 457
  S codes, 457
  substance abuse treatment services, 456
  symbols, 451
  temporary codes, 457
  temporary national codes, 457–458
  temporary procedures (professional services), 455
  transportation services, 453
  use of, 451–452
  V codes, 458
  vision services and hearing services, 458
HCPCS level II modifiers, 15, 30–35, 90
health behavior assessment, 444
Health Insurance Claims Form (CMS-1500 form), 463
Healthcare Common Procedure Coding System (HCPCS), 10–11, 449. *See also* HCPCS level I codes; HCPCS level II codes
hearing. *See* auditory system
hearing devices, 395
heart and associated structures, 197
heart anomalies, 206
heart/lung transplantation, 207–209
hematology, 427
hematoma, 115
hematopoietic progenitor cell (HPC) boost, 229
hemic and lymphatic systems, 226–237
  anatomy, 227–228
  lymph nodes and lymphatic channels, 227, 230–233. *See also* lymph nodes and lymphatic channels
  NCCI, 227
  spleen, 227–229
  transplantation and post-transplantation cellular infusions, 229
hemicolectomy, 263
hemilaryngectomy, 179
hemodialysis, 437
hemodialysis access, 218
hemoperfusion, 438
hemorrhoidectomy, 267
hemorrhoids, 266–267
hepatic duct, 246
hepatic venography, 407
hepaticostomy, 268
hepaticotomy, 268
hernia, 240, 271–272
hernioplasty, 271
herniorrhaphy, 271
herniotomy, 271
heterodermic graft, 120
Heyman capsules, 323
hiatal hernia, 271
hip arthroplasty, 152
hip fracture, 155
history, 51–54
  chief complaint (CC), 52
  history of the present illness (HPI), 52
  past, family, and/or social history (PFSH), 52
  review of systems (ROS), 52
  selecting a type of, 53–54
  SOAP note, 53
hollow circle symbol, 5
Holter monitoring, 440
home or residence services, 42, 70–73
  care plan oversight services, 72–73
  case management, 72
  established patients, 71
  new patients, 71
  prolonged services, 71–72
homograft, 120
homologous graft, 120
horizontal triangles symbol, 4
hormones, 345, 347
horseshoe kidney, 287
hospital inpatient and observation care services, 42
hospital inpatient and observation care services coding, 59–61
hospital outpatient services, 18
HPC (hematopoietic progenitor cell) boost, 229
human chorionic gonadotropin (HCG), 347
humerus, 141–142
hydatidiform mole, 336
hydration, 444
hymen, 318

hymenectomy, 319
hyoid bone, 170, 178
hyperkeratotic, 111
hyperthermia, 413
hypnotherapy, 436
hypoglossal nerve, 361
hypospadias, 305
hypothalamus, 346
hypothyroidism, 348
hysterectomy, 323
hysteroplasty, 323
hysterorrhaphy, 323, 336
hysteroscope, 324
hysteroscopy, 324
hysterotomy, 336

## I

I&D (incision and drainage), 110
ICF (intermediate care facilities), 68
ileocecal sphincter, 261
ileoscopy, 264
ileostomy, 262, 264
ileum, 258, 261
iliac artery exposure, 214
iliac nodes, 230
iliohypogastric nerve, 357
ilioinguinal nerve, 357
ilium, 141–142
imaging guidance, 104, 109, 143
imbrication of the diaphragm, 241
immune globulins, 433
immunization, 433–434
immunology, 428, 442
implant(s)
    definition of, 104–105
    drug delivery, 117
    musculoskeletal system, 146–147
    ocular/orbital, 377
    osseointegrated, 395
implantable contraceptive capsules,
    117
implantable defibrillator, 199–202
implantable hemodynamic monitor, 203
in vitro fertilization, 326
in vivo laboratory procedures, 428
incision
    accessory sinuses, 176–177
    anus, 267
    bladder, 291
    breast, 129
    external ear, 393

inner ear, 396
intestines, 262
kidneys, 284
lungs and pleura, 183–184
lymph nodes, 231
middle ear, 394
musculoskeletal system, 149
nose, 171
oviduct/ovary, 325
palate and uvula, 251
pancreas, 270
prostate, 308
spine and spinal cord, 366
stomach, 257
tongue and floor of mouth, 249–250
trachea and bronchi, 181
ureter, 289–290
urethra, 295
vulva, 318
incision and drainage (I&D), 110, 149
incisional biopsy, 113
incisional hernia, 271
incisions, 270
incomplete abortion, 339
increased procedural services, 19
incus, 391
index, 8
indirect inguinal hernia, 271
indirect laryngoscopy, 179
induced abortion, 339
infected wound, 119
inferior lobe, 170, 239
inferior vena cava, 198, 282
inflammatory, 114
informational modifiers, 16–17
infraspinatus, 145
infundibulum, 322
inguinal hernia, 271
inguinal lymph nodes, 230–231
inhalation, 87
initial hospital or observation care,
    59
initial rhinoplasty, 174
injection, 87
inner ear, 391, 396
inpatient neonatal intensive care
    services, 42
instillation, 87
insulin, 270, 347
integumentary system, 106–130
    abbreviations, 107
    acellular dermal replacement, 123

adjacent tissue transfer or
    rearrangement, 119–120
anatomy, 107–108
breast surgery, 129–130
burns, 126–127
class findings, 112
debridement, 110–111, 119
decubitus ulcer, 126
destruction, 127–129
excision, 114
fine needle aspiration biopsy, 109–110
flap-type repairs, 125–126
foot care, 111–112
functions, 107
grafts, 121–125
incision and drainage (I&D), 110
introduction and removal, 110,
    116–117
mastectomy procedures, 130
measurements (conversion table), 108
Mohs micrographic surgery, 128
nails, 115–116
NCCI, 106
other procedures, 126, 129
paring and cutting, 111
pilonidal cyst, 116
pressure ulcer, 126
repair, 117–119
routine foot care, 111–112
shaving, 114
skin examination, 56
skin replacement surgery/skin
    substitutes, 120–126
skin tags, 113–114
special dermatological procedures,
    445
surgical preparation, 120–121
tattooing, 116
wound classification, 118–119
intercostals, 143
intermediate care facilities (ICF), 68
intermediate repair, 117
internal anal sphincter, 261
internal fixation, 154
internal hemorrhoids, 266
internal oblique, 143
intersex surgery, 308
intervascular cannulation for
    extracorporeal circulation, 218
intestinal plication, 264
intestines, 260–265
intracapsular extraction, 378–379

intracranial neurostimulators, 364
intranasal biopsy, 172
intraoperative neurophysiology, 443
intraspinal anesthesia, 87
intrauterine devices (IUDs), 323
intravascular ultrasound services, 219
introduction
    antepartum and fetal invasive services, 336
    biliary tract, 268–269
    bladder, 292
    breast, 129
    corpus uteri, 323
    extracranial nerves, 367
    inner ear, 396
    integumentary system, 116–117
    kidneys, 287
    larynx, 178–179
    lungs and pleura, 184–185
    lymph nodes, 233
    musculoskeletal system, 143–144, 150–151
    nose, 172
    pancreas, 271
    penis, 305
    spleen, 229
    stomach, 259
    trachea and bronchi, 182–183
    ureter, 289–290
introitus, 317
inversion, 403
iris, 375–376
ischium, 141
island flap, 251
isodose, 412

**J**

J codes, 456
jejunostomy, 262, 264
jejunum, 258

**K**

K codes, 456
keratoplasty, 378
kidney, harvesting of, 286
kidneys, 282, 284–289
knee arthroplasty, 152
Kock procedure, 264
Kraske position, 465

**L**

L codes, 456–457
labia majora, 316, 318
labia minora, 316, 318
labor, stages of, 338
laboratory modifiers
    alternative laboratory platform testing, 28
    reference (outside) laboratory, 28
    repeat clinical diagnostic laboratory test, 28
laboratory services. See pathology and laboratory
labyrinth, 392
labyrinthectomy, 396
labyrinthotomy, 396
lacrimal duct, 375
lacrimal gland, 375
lactogenic hormone (LTH), 347
laminectomy, 366
laminotomy, 366
laparoscopy
    appendectomy, 265
    biliary tract, 269
    bladder, 293
    cholecystectomy, 269–270
    ectopic pregnancy, 336
    endocrine system, 350
    esophagus, 256
    female genital system, 324
    hernia repair, 272
    intestines, 262–263
    kidneys, 287
    liver, 268
    lymph nodes, 232
    oviduct/ovary, 325
    prostate, 308
    rectum, 266
    spleen, 229
    stomach, 259
    ureter, 290
    vagina, 321
laparotomy, 326
large intestine, 260–261
laryngeal prominence, 178
laryngectomy, 170, 179
laryngopharynx, 169, 181
laryngoscopy, 179
laryngotomy, 179
larynx, 178–181
    defined, 170

    endoscopy, 179–180
    excision, 178–179
    introduction, 178–179
    other procedures, 180
    repair, 180
lateral, 403
lateral malleolus, 156
lateral nasal wall reconstruction, 174
latissimus dorsi, 145
LBW (low birth weight), 67
LCD (local coverage determinations), 112
Le Fort I fracture, 152–153
Le Fort II fracture, 152
Le Fort III fracture, 152
left colectomy, 263
left hemicolectomy, 263
left hilum, 170
left primary bronchus, 170
legally induced abortion, 339
lens, 376
Level I codes, 10. See also current procedural terminology (CPT)
Level I modifiers, 15, 19–30. See also modifiers
Level II codes, 11. See also HCPCS level II codes
Level II modifiers, 15, 30–35, 90
levels of service for E/M codes, 51–58
    examination, 54–58
    history, 51–54
ligaments, 140
ligation
    arterial and arteriovenous procedures, 220
    esophagus, 256
limited lymphadenectomy for staging, 232
limited study, 409
lingual, 249, 253
lingual tonsil, 169, 252
lining of the heart, 196
lip shave, 247
lips, 246–249
lithotomy position, 465
liver, 246, 258, 268
lobectomy, 348
local allograft, 147
local anesthesia, 87
local coverage determinations (LCD), 112
long term care facilities (LTCF), 68

longitudinal fissure, 358
low birth weight (LBW), 67
low-weight infants, 25
lower arm, 156
lower eyelid, 375
LTCF (long term care facilities), 68
lumbar nerves, 360
lumbar plexus, 360
lumbar vertebrae, 141
lungs and pleura, 170, 183–187
  definition of, 171
  destruction, 184–185
  excision, 184–185
  incision, 183–184
  introduction, 184–185
  removal, 184–185
  repair, 186
  resection, 184–185
  stereotactic radiation therapy, 185
  surgical collapse therapy, 186–187
  thoracoplasty, 186–187
  thoracoscopy, 185
  transplantation of, 186
  video-assisted thoracic surgery
    (VATS), 185
lunula, 115
luteinizing hormone (LH), 347
lymph glands, 227
lymph nodes and lymphatic channels,
  227–228, 230–233
  anatomy, 230
  excision, 231
  introduction and other procedures,
    233
  laparoscopy, 232
  limited lymphadenectomy for staging,
    232
  major concentrations of lymph nodes,
    231
  radical lymphadenectomy, 232–233
lymphadenitis, 231
lymphangiography, 407
lymphangiotomy, 231
lymphatic channels, 227
lymphatic examination, 56
lymphatic system. *See* hemic and
  lymphatic systems
lymphatic vessels, 227–228

## M

M codes, 457
M-mode technique, 410

magnetic resonance imaging (MRI),
  404
male genital system, 302–314
  abbreviations, 303
  anatomical diagram, 304
  epididymis, 305
  intersex surgery, 308
  NCCI, 303
  penis, 304–305
  prostate, 307–308
  reproductive system procedures, 308
  scrotum, 307
  seminal vesicles, 307
  spermatic cord, 307
  testis (testes), 305–306
  tunica vaginalis, 305
  vas deferens, 307
malignant lesions, 114
malleus, 391–392
mammary plexus, 230
mammography, 404, 410–411
mandated services, 21
manipulation, 140, 154
  cervix uteri, 322
  esophagus, 256
  penis, 305
  rectum, 266
  urethra, 295
  vagina, 321
manipulative treatment, 446
marsupialization
  pancreatic cyst, 271
  sublingual salivary cyst, 251
masseter, 143
mastectomy, 129
mastectomy procedures, 130
mastoid cavity debridement, 393
mastoidectomy, 394
maternal care and delivery, 332–344
  abbreviations, 333–334
  abortion, 339
  amniocentesis, 334–335
  amniotic fluid analysis, 335
  antepartum and fetal invasive
    services, 334–336
  cesarean section delivery, 337
  chorionic villus sampling, 334
  cordocentesis, 334
  fetal fluid drainage, 335
  fetal scalp blood sampling, 334
  fetal umbilical cord occlusion, 335
  labor, stages of, 338

multifetal pregnancy reduction (MPR),
  339
NCCI, 333
oligohydramnios, 335
vaginal birth after cesarean (VBAC),
  338
vaginal delivery, antepartum care, and
  postpartum care, 337
maxillary sinus, 175–176
maxillary sinusotomy, 176
maxillectomy, 177
Meckel's diverticulum, 265
medial malleolus, 156
median nerve, 357
mediastinoscopy, 240
mediastinotomy, 240
mediastinum, 170, 181, 238–240
medical and surgical supplies, 453
medical decision making, 48–49
  types, 49
medical genetics and genetic
  counseling services, 443
medical nutrition therapy, 446
Medicare
  local coverage determinations (LCD),
    112
  routine foot care, 111
  surgical packages, 103
medicine section, 431–448
  allergy and clinical immunology, 442
  behavior management services,
    443–444
  biofeedback, 436
  cardiovascular, 440–441
  central nervous system assessments,
    443–444
  chemotherapy, 444
  dialysis, 437–438
  end-stage renal disease services, 438
  endocrinology, 442
  gastroenterology, 439
  health behavior assessment, 444
  hemodialysis, 437
  hydration, 444
  immune globulins, 433
  immunization, 433–434
  medical genetics and genetic
    counseling services, 443
  NCCI, 433
  neurology and neuromuscular
    procedures, 442–443
  noninvasive vascular diagnostic
    studies, 441

ophthalmology, 439–440

overview (subsections), 432–433

photodynamic therapy, 445

physical medicine and rehabilitation, 445–446

psychiatry, 435–436

pulmonary, 442

special dermatological procedures, 445

special otorhinolaryngologic services, 440

therapeutic, prophylactic and diagnostic injections, 444

vaccines and toxoids, 9, 433–434

medulla oblongata, 359

Meissner's corpuscles, 260

melanoma of the skin, 114

melatonin, 347

membranous ampulla, 396

membranous labyrinth, 392

meninges, 358, 361–365

mesencephalon, 358

mesentery, 258, 260, 265

metacarpals, 141–142, 156

metastasis, 114

metatarsals, 141, 156

metric conversion table, 108

microbiology, 428

microscope, operating, 396

midbrain, 358–359

middle ear, 391, 394–395

middle lobe, 170, 239

middle phalanx, 156

minimum assistant surgeon, 27–28

minimum data set (MDS), 68

missed abortion, 339

mitral valve, 198, 204

mixed hemorrhoids, 266

moderate (conscious) sedation, 9

moderate sedation, 9, 94

modifiers

  alphanumeric, 30–35

  alternative laboratory platform testing, 28

  ambulance origin and destination, 35

  ambulatory surgery center hospital outpatient use, 18

  anesthesia by surgeon, 21

  anesthesia, generally, 89–90

  assistant surgeon (qualified surgeon not available), 28

  assistant surgeon, 27

  bilateral procedure, 21

  decision for surgery, 23–24

  definition of, 15

  discontinued procedure, 22–23

  discontinued procedure after administration of anesthesia, 26

  discontinued procedure prior to administration of anesthesia, 26

  distinct procedural service, 24–25

  genetic testing, 9

  habilitative services, 29

  hospital outpatient services, 18

  increased procedural services, 19

  informational, 16–17

  level I, 19–30

  level II, 30–35, 90

  mandated services, 21

  minimum assistant surgeon, 27–28

  multiple, 17, 30

  multiple procedures, 22

  outpatient hospital E/M encounters, 20–21

  physician services, 16–17

  postoperative management only, 23

  preoperative management only, 23

  preventive services, 21

  pricing, 16

  procedure on infants less than 4 kg, 25

  professional component, 20

  purposes of, 15–16

  Q, 112

  reduced services, 22

  reference (outside) laboratory, 28

  rehabilitative services, 30

  repeat clinical diagnostic laboratory test, 28

  repeat procedure by another physician, 26

  repeat procedure by same physician, 26

  separately identifiable E/M service by same physician, 20

  staged or related procedure by same physician, 24

  statistical, 16–17

  surgical care only, 23

  surgical team, 25

  telemedicine services, 29

  two surgeons, 25

  unplanned return to operating/procedure room by same physician, 27

  unrelated E/M service by same physician, 19–20

  unrelated procedure by same physician during postoperative period, 27

  unrelated service by same physician, 19–20

  unusual anesthesia, 19

  uses, 16–17

  X, 24–25

modifying unit, 91

Mohs micrographic surgery, 128

molecular multianalyte assays, 427

molecular pathology, 427

mons pubis, 318

morselized allograft, 146–147

motion analysis, 443

mouth, 248–250

MPR (multifetal pregnancy reduction), 339

MRI (magnetic resonance imaging), 404

mucosectomy, 262

multianalyte assays with algorithmic analyses, 427

multifetal pregnancy reduction (MPR), 339

multiple procedures, 22

muscles, 140, 143, 145. See also musculoskeletal system

muscularis externa, 260

musculoskeletal examination, 56

musculoskeletal system, 137–166

  abbreviations, 138–139

  anatomy (figures), 141–143, 145, 156

  ankle and foot, medial view, 156

  arm, wrist, and hand, dorsal view, 156

  arthrodesis, 157

  arthroplasty, 152–153

  augmentation, 152

  casts and strapping, 157–158

  codes arranged by body site, 148

  endoscopy, 159–160

  excision, 142, 150

  femur, medial view, 156

  fracture/dislocation, 154–156

  genioplasty, 152

  grafts or implants, 146–147

  incision, 149

  introduction or removal, 143–144, 150–151

  muscles, 143, 145

  NCCI, 138

  other procedures, 147

musculoskeletal system, (*continued*)
  physical examination, 56
  repair, revision, and reconstruction, 151–152
  replantation, 144–146
  splints, 157
  terminology (definitions), 140
  wound exploration, 141
mutually exclusive codes, 105
mutually exclusive edits, 105
myenteric plexus, 260
myocardium, 196–198
myomectomy, 323
myometrium, 322
myringoplasty, 394
myringotomy, 394

**N**

nails, 115–116
narcosynthesis, 436
nasal cavity, 169
nasal polyp, 172
nasal procedures, 171–175
  destruction and other procedures, 174–175
  excision, 171–172
  incision, 171
  introduction, 172
  removal of foreign body, 172
  repair, 173–174
nasal septal perforations, 174
nasal vestibular stenosis, 174
nasopharyngeal hemorrhage, 253
nasopharyngeal tonsils, 252
nasopharyngoscopy, 395
nasopharynx, 169, 181, 252
national codes, 11. *See also* HCPCS level II codes
National Correct Coding Initiative (NCCI)
  anesthesia, 86
  auditory system, 390
  cardiovascular system, 195
  correct coding edits, 105
  diaphragm, 239
  digestive system, 246
  endocrine system, 347
  eye and ocular adnexa, 374
  female genital system, 316–317
  hemic and lymphatic systems, 227
  integumentary system, 106
  male genital system, 303
  maternal care and delivery, 333

mediastinum, 239
medicine section, 433
musculoskeletal system, 138
mutually exclusive codes, 105
mutually exclusive edits, 105
nervous system, 356
pathology and laboratory, 423
purpose, 105
radiology, 402
respiratory system, 168
urinary system, 281
NCCI. *See* National Correct Coding Initiative (NCCI)
near-total esophagectomy, 254
neck examination, 55
neoplasm, 114
nephrectomy, 284–286
nephrolithotomy, 284
nephrorrhaphy, 287
nephrotomy, 284
nerve conduction test, 443
nervous system, 355–372
  abbreviations, 356
  anatomy, 356–361
  aneurysm repair, 364
  arteriovenous malformation, 364
  autonomic nervous system, 357, 367
  brain, 358–359
  brain stem, 359
  burr holes, 362
  central nervous system, 356, 443–444
  cerebrospinal fluid shunt, 365
  cranial nerves, 360–361
  craniectomy or craniotomy, 363
  endovascular therapy, 363–364
  extracranial nerves, 367
  NCCI, 356
  neurology and neuromuscular procedures, 442–443
  neurostimulators, 364
  peripheral nerves, 367
  peripheral nervous system, 356
  repairs to skull and skull vault, 364–365
  skull, meninges, and brain, 361–365
  spinal cord and nerves, 360
  spine and spinal cord, 365–367
  stereotactic radiosurgery, 364
  stereotaxis, 364
  surgery of skull base, 363
  trephine, 362
  twist drill hole, 362

vascular disease, 364
neurologic examination, 56
neurology and neuromuscular procedures, 442–443
neuroplasty, 367
neurorrhaphy, 367
neurostimulators, 364, 366–367, 443
new patient
  defined, 44
  vs. established patients, 43
  same-specialty consideration, 44
  same vs. different group practice considerations, 44
  three-year consideration, 44
newborn care, 75–76
newborn care services, 42
non-face-to-face physician services, 42
non-face-to-face services, 75
noninvasive vascular diagnostic studies, 441
nonmalignant tumors, 114
nonselective placement, of catheter, 217
norepinephrine, 347
nose, 181. *See also* nasal procedures
nuclear medicine, 414
number symbol, 4
nursing facility services, 42, 68–70

**O**

oblique, 403
observation discharge codes, 61
obstetrics, 333. *See also* maternal care and delivery
occipital lobe, 359
occipitalis, 145
occlusive disease, 215
occupational therapy evaluations, 445
ocular adnexa. *See* eye and ocular adnexa
ocular implants, 377
oculomotor nerve, 361
office or other outpatient services, 42, 47–51
olfactory nerve, 361
oligohydramnios, 335
omentectomy, 325
omentum, 271
oophorectomy, 325
open colectomy, 262
open cystostomy, 291

open drainage
  of perirenal abscess, 284
  of renal abscess, 284
open iliac artery exposure, 214
open reduction, 154
open reduction internal fixation (ORIF), 154
open treatment, 140
open-tube bronchoscope, 182
operating microscope, 396
operculectomy, 250
ophthalmic endoscope, 378
ophthalmologist, 439
ophthalmology, 439–440
OPPS (outpatient prospective payment section), 454
optic disc, 376
optic nerve, 361, 376
optometrist, 439
oral cavity, 246, 248
orbicularis oculi, 143
orbicularis oris, 143
orbital implants, 377
orbitotomy, 382
orchiopexy, 305
organ of Corti, 392
organ or disease-oriented panel, 424–425
ORIF (open reduction internal fixation), 154
oropharyngeal hemorrhage, 253
oropharynx, 169, 181
orthotic management, 445, 456–457
osseointegrated implants, 395
ostectomy, 126, 140
osteoclasis, 140
osteoectomy, 150
osteopathic manipulative treatment, 446
osteoplasty, 140
osteotomy, 140
otoplasty, 394
otorhinolaryngologic services, 440
outpatient hospital E/M encounters, 20–21
outpatient prospective payment section (OPPS), 454
outpatient services, 18
oval window, 392, 396
ovary, 316, 322, 324–326, 346
ovary excision services, 325
oviduct and ovaries, 324–326
oxytocin (OXT), 347

**P**

P codes, 457
pacemaker, 199–202
pacing cardioverter-defibrillator, 200–201
packing, 268
PAD (peripheral arterial disease) rehabilitation, 441
palate, 251
palatine tonsil, 169, 252–253
palatoplasty, 251
pancreas, 228, 246, 258, 270–271, 346, 349
pancreaticojejunostomy, 271
pancreatorrhaphy, 271
panel test, 423–424
papillocystic carcinoma, 114
paracentesis, 335
paraesophageal hiatal hernia, 256
paranasal sinus, 181
parathyroid autotransplantation, 349
parathyroid glands, 346, 349
parathyroid hormone (PTH), 347
parathyroidectomy, 349
paravaginal defect repair, 321
parietal lobe, 359
parietal pericardium, 196–197
parietal pleura, 170, 239
paring and cutting, 111
parotid gland, 246, 251
partial esophagectomy, 254
partial laryngectomy, 179
partial nephrectomy, 285
partial replacement, of catheter, 217
partial thyroid lobectomy, 348
past, family, and social history (PFSH), 52
past history, 52
patella, 141
pathology and laboratory, 422–430
  abbreviations, 424
  anatomic pathology, 428
  chemistry, 427
  coagulation, 427
  consultations (clinical pathology), 426–427
  COVID-19, 423
  cytogenetic studies, 428
  cytopathology, 428
  drug assay, 426
  drug testing, 426
  evocative/suppression testing, 426
  genomic sequencing procedures, 427
  HCPCS level II codes, 457
  hematology, 427
  immunology, 428
  in vivo laboratory procedures, 428
  microbiology, 428
  molecular multianalyte assays, 427
  molecular pathology, 427
  multianalyte assays with algorithmic analyses, 427
  NCCI, 423
  organ or disease-oriented panel, 424–425
  panel test, 423–424
  proprietary laboratory analyses, 429
  reproductive medicine procedures, 429
  surgical pathology, 428
  therapeutic drug assay, 426
  transfusion medicine, 428
  urinalysis, 427
pectoralis major, 143
pediatric and neonatal critical care services, 42
pedicle flap, 120
pelvic lymphadenectomy, 233
penis, 304–305
percutaneous cholecystostomy, 268
percutaneous nephrostolithotomy, 284
percutaneous pleural drainage, 185
percutaneous skeletal fixation, 140
percutaneous transhepatic portography, 407
percutaneous ventricular assist device (pVAD), 209
Pereyra procedure, 321
pericardial cavity, 197
pericardial fluid, 196
pericardial sac, 196
pericardiectomy, 198–199
pericardiocentesis, 198
pericardiotomy, 198
pericardium, 196–198
peridural anesthesia, 87
perilymph, 392
perimetrium, 322
perinatal period, 333
perineoplasty, 319
perineum, 317–319
periosteum, 358
peripheral arterial disease (PAD) rehabilitation, 441

peripheral nerves, 367

peripheral nervous system (PNS), 356

peripheral vascular disease, 110

peritoneal dialysis, 438

peritoneum, 271

peroneus longus, 143, 145

peroral endoscopic myotomy (POEM), 257

PET (positron emission tomography) scan, 404

Peyer's patches, 228

Peyronie's disease, 305

phalanges, 141–142, 156

pharyngeal flap, 251

pharyngeal tonsil, 169

pharyngoesophageal repair, 253

pharyngolaryngectomy, 179

pharyngoplasty, 253

pharyngostomy, 253

pharyngotympanic tube, 391

pharynx, 171, 246, 248, 252–253

phlebography, 407

photocoagulation, 381

photodynamic therapy, 445

phrenic nerve, 357

physical examination. See examination

physical medicine and rehabilitation, 445–446

physical status modifiers, 90, 92

physical therapy evaluations, 445

physician services, 16–17

pia mater, 358

pilonidal cyst, 110, 116

pinch graft, 122

pineal gland, 346

pinna, 391

pituitary gland, 346

PLA test codes, 5

place of service (POS) codes, 45–47

plantaris, 145

pleura. See lungs and pleura

pleurectomy, 184

pneumonectomy, 184

PNS (peripheral nervous system), 356

polyp, 172

polysomnography studies, 442

pons, 359

popliteal nodes, 230

port, 412

POS (place of service) codes, 45–47

positron emission tomography (PET) scan, 404

postanesthesia recovery period, 91

postauricular ear canal incision, 394

posterior chamber, 376

posteroanterior, 403

postoperative management only, 23

pregnancy, childbirth, and perinatal period. See maternal care and delivery

preoperative management only, 23

prepuce, 304

pressure ulcer, 126

preventive medicine services, 42, 73–75

  counseling risk factor reduction and behavioral change intervention, 74–75

  established patient, 74

  new patient, 73

preventive services, 21

pricing modifiers, 16

primary rhinoplasty, 174

proctectomy, 266

proctoplasty, 266

proctosigmoidoscopy, 266

product pending FDA approval (App. K), 9

professional component, 20

progesterone, 324, 347

prolapsed hemorrhoid, 267

prolonged service time, 51

prone, 403

prone position, 465

proprietary laboratory analyses (PLA), 5, 429

prostate gland, 282, 294, 304, 307–308

prostatectomy, 308

prosthetic management, 445, 456–457

proton beam treatment, 413

protopexy, 266

proximal phalanx, 156

pseudoaneurysm, 215

psychiatric collaborative care management services, 42

psychiatric examination, 57

psychiatric residential treatment center, 68

psychiatrist, 435

psychiatry, 435–436

psychoanalysis, 435

pterygomaxillary fossa surgery, 176

pudendum, 317

pulmonary codes, 442

pulmonary perfusion imaging, 414

pulmonary semilunar valve, 198, 204

pulmonary veins, 198

pulse generator, 199

punch biopsy, 113

pupil, 375–376

pVAD (percutaneous ventricular assist device), 209

pyeloplasty, 287

pyelostolithotomy, 284

pyelotomy, 284

pyloric sphincter, 258

pyloromyotomy, 257

pyloroplasty, 256

**Q**

Q codes, 457

Q modifiers, 112

QM modifier, 453

QN modifier, 453

quadriceps femoris, 143

qualifying circumstances, 91–92

**R**

R codes, 457

radial nerve, 357

radiation oncology, 411–413

radical lymphadenectomy, 232–233

radical resection of lymph nodes, 232–233

radiologic guidance, 410

radiologic technician, 402

radiological tests (definitions), 403–404

  therapeutic radiology simulation, 412

  transcatheter procedures, 408

  vascular procedures, 406–407

radiologist, 402

radiology, 401–421

  bone/joint studies, 411

  breast mammography, 410–411

  defined, 402

  diagnostic, 405–409

  diagnostic ultrasound, 409–410

  HCPCS level II codes, 457

  NCCI, 402

  nuclear medicine, 414

  positioning of patient (terminology), 402–403

radiopharmaceuticals, 414

radius, 141–142, 156

range of motion testing, 443

real-time scanning, 410

recipient renal allotransplantation, 286
recipient site, 120
reconstruction
  breast, 130
  eyelids, 383
  Le Fort I fracture, 152–153
  musculoskeletal system, 151–152
  nose, 174
rectum, 246, 261, 265–266, 304, 316
rectus abdominis, 143
rectus femoris, 143
reduced services, 22
reduction, 154
reference (outside) laboratory, 28
referral, 63
refractor, 439
regional anesthesia, 87
rehabilitative services, 30
relative value, 91
relative value guide (RVG), 91
removal
  bladder, 291
  cardiovascular system, 217
  foreign body. See foreign body
  integumentary system, 110
  lungs and pleura, 184–185
  musculoskeletal system, 143–144,
    150–151
renal endoscopic procedures, 288
renal transplantation, 286
renumbered CPT codes—citations
    crosswalk (App. M), 9
repair
  antepartum and fetal invasive
    services, 336
  anus, 267
  bladder, 292–293
  breast, 130
  cardiovascular system, 216–217
  cervix uteri, 322
  conjunctiva/cornea, 378
  corpus uteri, 323
  esophagus, 256
  external ear, 393
  eyelids, 383
  fallopian tubes, 325
  integumentary system, 110, 117–119
  intestines, 264
  kidneys, 287
  larynx, 180
  liver, 268
  lungs and pleura, 186

middle ear, 394
musculoskeletal system, 151–152
neuroendoscopy, 365
nose, 173–174
palate and uvula, 251
penis, 305
pharynx, 253
rectum, 266
retina/choroid, 381
salivary glands, 252
sclera, 381
skull and skull vault, 364–365
spine and spinal cord, 366
spleen, 228
tongue and floor of mouth, 250
trachea and bronchi, 182–183
ureter, 290
urethra, 295
vagina, 320–321
repair codes, 323
repeat clinical diagnostic laboratory
    test, 28
repeat procedure by another physician,
    26
repeat procedure by same physician, 26
replantation
  arm, 144
  digit, 145–146
  foot, 145
  forearm, 145
  hand, 145
  thumb, 145
reporting more than one procedure/
    service, 104
reproductive medicine procedures, 429
reproductive systems. See female
    genital system; male genital system
resection, lungs and pleura, 184–185
resequenced CPT codes (App. N), 9
resident assessment instrument (RAI), 68
resident assessment protocol (RAP), 68
respiratory examination, 55
respiratory system, 167–193
  abbreviations, 168–169
  accessory sinuses, 175–177
  anatomical diagrams, 169–170
  larynx, 178–180
  lungs and pleura, 183–187
  nasal procedures, 171–175
  NCCI, 168
  physical examination, 55
  terminology (definitions), 170–171

trachea and bronchi, 180–183
retina, 376
retinal detachment, 381
reverse Trendelenburg position, 465
review of systems (ROS), 52
revision
  cardiovascular system, 216–217
  of colostomy, 264
  of ileostomy, 264
  mastoidectomy, 394
  musculoskeletal system, 151–152
  rhinoplasty, 174
rhinectomy, 172
rhinophyma, 172
rhinoplasty, 173
rhinotomy, 172
rhombic flaps, 120
ribs, 141–142
right colectomy, 263
right hemicolectomy, 263
right hilum, 170
right kidney position, 465
right lateral position, 465
right primary bronchus, 170
rigid bronchoscope, 182
rigid esophagoscopy, 254
roof of the mouth, 251
Ross-Konno procedure, 204
rotation, 120
routine foot care, 111–112
ruptured aneurysm, 215
RVG (relative value guide), 91

## S

S codes, 457
SA (sinoatrial) node, 196
saccule, 392, 396
sacral plexus, 357, 360
sacrum, 141–142
salivary glands and ducts, 251–252
salpingectomy, 325–326
salpingo-oophorectomy, 325–326
same physician
  repeat procedure, 26
  separately identifiable E/M service, 20
  staged or related procedure, 24
  unplanned return to operating/
    procedure room, 27
  unrelated procedure, during
    postoperative period, 27
  unrelated service, 19–20

saphenous vein, 205

SARS-CoV-2 (Severe Acute Respiratory Syndrome Coronavirus 2). *See* COVID-19

sartorius, 143

scalpel, 111

scapula, 141–142

Schede-type thoracoplasty, 186

sciatic nerve, 357, 360

sclera, 375–376

scleral buckling, 381

scleral reinforcement, 381

scrotum, 307

sebaceous gland, 108

second-degree burn, 127

secondary rhinoplasty, 174

selective placement, of catheter, 217

semicircular canals, 392

semicircular ducts, 392

semimembranosus, 145

seminal duct, 307

seminal vesicles, 304, 307

semitendinosus, 145

sentinel lymph nodes, 233

separate procedure, 104

separately identifiable E/M service by same physician, 20

septal or other intranasal dermatoplasty, 174

septic abortion, 339

septoplasty, 174

septum, 198

serial tonometry, 440

serous pericardium, 196

serratus anterior, 143

severe acute respiratory syndrome coronavirus 2 (SARS-CoV-2) (App. Q), 9

shaving, 114

shock therapy (electroconvulsive therapy), 436

shunt insertion, 218

shuntogram, 407

sialolithotomy, 251

sigmoid colon, 260

sigmoidoscopy, 266

simple mastectomy, 130

simple nasal polyp excision, 172

simple nephrectomy, 286

simple repair, 117

simulation, 411

single-chamber system, 200

single-organ examinations, 54

sinoatrial node (SA node), 196

sinogram, 143

sinuses, 171, 175–176. *See also* accessory sinuses

sinusotomy, 176–177

sitting position, 465

skeletal traction, 140

Skene's gland, 318

skilled nursing facilities (SNF), 68

skin, 107. *See also* integumentary system

skin examination, 56

skin flap, 120

skin replacement surgery/skin substitutes, 120–126

skin substitute graft, 124

skin tags, 113–114

skin traction, 140

skull, 141–142, 361–365

sleep endoscopy, drug-induced, 253

sleep testing, 442

sling procedures, 321

small intestinal endoscopy, 264

small intestine, 260

SNF (skilled nursing facilities), 68

SOAP note, 52

social history, 52

soft palate, 248

soleus, 143, 145

somatic nervous system, 357

special evaluation and management services, 42, 75

special otorhinolaryngologic services, 440

special reports, 104

sperm, 307

spermatic cord, 307

spermatozoa, 304

sphenoid sinus, 169, 175–176

sphenoid sinusotomy, 176

sphincteroplasty, 267–268

spinal anesthesia, 87

spinal cord, 357–361, 365–367

spinal nerves, 358, 360

spinal neurostimulators, 366

spine, 365–367

spirometry testing, 442

spleen, 227–229, 258

splenectomy, 227–228

splenic hilum, 228

splenius capitis, 145

splenocolic ligament, 228

splenophrenic ligament, 228

splenoportography, 407

splenorrhaphy, 228

splints, 157

split-skin graft, 120

split-thickness autograft, 122

split-thickness graft, 120

spontaneous abortion, 339

spreader grafting, 174

squamous cell carcinoma, 114

staged or related procedure by same physician, 24

standby services, 72

stapes, 391

star symbol, 5–6

static splint, 157

statistical modifiers, 16–17

stem cell transplantation, 229

stereotactic radiation therapy, 185

stereotactic radiosurgery, 364, 366

stereotaxis, 364, 366

sternocleidomastoid, 143, 145

sternum, 141, 197

stoma, 264

stomach, 228, 246, 257–259

strabismus surgery, 382

strangulated hemorrhoid, 267

strangulated hernia, 271

strapping, 157

structural allograft, 147

subarachnoid anesthesia, 87

subarachnoid space, 358

subcutaneous, 107

subcutaneous cardiac rhythm monitors, 203

subcutaneous fatty tissue, 108

subcutaneous mastectomy, 130

subdural space, 358

sublingual, 249

sublingual gland, 246, 251

submandibular gland, 246, 251

submandibular lymph nodes, 231

submucosal plexus, 260

subsequent hospital inpatient or observation care visits, 59–60

substance abuse treatment services, 456

subungual hematoma, 115

superficial biopsy, 231

superficial inguinofemoral lymphadenectomy, 233

superficial peroneal nerve, 357

superficial removal, 231

superior lobe, 170, 239
superior sagittal sinus, 358
superior vena cava, 198, 212
supine, 403, 465
supplied materials, 104
surgery of skull base, 363
surgery section
    body systems, 102
    follow-up care, 104
    foreign body, 104–105
    imaging guidance, 104
    implant, 104–105
    reporting more than one procedure/
        service, 104
    separate procedure, 104
    services, 102
    special reports, 104
    supplied materials, 104
    surgical destruction, 104
    surgical package, 102–104
    topics covered, 101
    unlisted service or procedure, 104
surgical care only, 23
surgical collapse therapy, 186–187
surgical destruction, 104. See also
    destruction
surgical endoscopy/arthroscopy, 159
surgical nasal endoscopy, 177
surgical pathology, 428
surgical positions, 465
surgical team, 25
surgical wound classification, 118–119
suspensory ligaments, 376
sweat pore, 108
symbols, 3–6
symphysiotomy, 287
symphysis pubis, 316
synchronous real-time interactive audio-
    only telemedicine services (App. T), 9
synchronous telemedicine services, 9,
    29
    rendered via telephone, 29
synechia, 174
synovectomy, 150

**T**

T3, 347
T4, 347
talus, 156
tangential biopsy, 113
tarsals, 141, 156
tarsorrhaphy, 383

TAS (transcatheter atrial septostomy),
    206
tattooing, 116
teeth, 246, 248
telemedicine services, 9, 29
teletherapy, 412
temporal bone, middle fossa approach,
    396
temporal lobe, 359
temporalis, 143
tendon, 140
teres major, 145
testicle, 304
testis (testes), 305–306, 346
testosterone, 347
thalamus, 359–360
therapeutic drug assay, 426
therapeutic pneumothorax, 187
therapeutic procedures, 102
therapeutic, prophylactic and diagnostic
    injections, 444
therapeutic radiology simulation, 412
third-degree burn, 127
thoracic cavity, 141
thoracic duct, 230
thoracocentesis, 335
thoracoplasty, 186–187
thoracoscopy, 185
thoracostomy, 184
thoracotomy, 184
thrombectomy, 210, 218
thromboendarterectomy, 215
thrombosed hemorrhoid, 267
thymectomy, 349
thymosin, 347
thymus gland, 228, 346, 349
thyrohyoid ligament, 178
thyrohyoid membrane, 178
thyroid cartilage, 170, 178
thyroid gland, 197, 346, 348–349
thyroid hormones, 347
thyroid-stimulating hormone (TSH), 347
thyroidectomy, 348–349
thyrolingual cyst, 348
tibia, 141–142, 156
tibial nerve, 357
tibialis anterior, 143
time unit, 91
TIS (transcatheter intracardiac shunt),
    206
tissue-cultured epidermal autograft, 123
tissue expanders, 117

tissue-typing procedures, 428
TMVR (transcatheter mitral valve repair),
    204
toenails, 115
tomography, 404
tongue, 246, 248–250, 253
tongue base suspension, 250
tonsils, 228, 248, 252–253
total esophagectomy, 254
total hip replacement, 153
total knee replacement, 153
total thyroid lobectomy, 348
toxoids, 434
trabeculoplasty, 378
trabeculotomy, 378
trachea and bronchi, 169–170, 180–183,
    197, 239
    anatomical diagram, 181
    bronchial thermoplasty, 182
    definition of, 171
    endoscopy, 181–182
    incision, 181
    introduction, 182–183
    repair, 182–183
tracheal cartilages, 169, 178
trachelectomy, 322
tracheostomy, 250
transcanal tympanolysis, 394
transcatheter atrial septostomy (TAS),
    206
transcatheter intracardiac shunt (TIS),
    206
transcatheter mitral valve repair (TMVR),
    204
transcatheter procedures, 218, 408
transduodenal sphincterotomy, 268
transfusion medicine, 428
transitional care management services,
    42, 77
transmyocardial laser revascularization,
    198–199
transplantation
    bone marrow transplants, 229
    heart/lung, 207–209
    kidneys, 286
    liver, 268
    lungs, 186
    pancreas, 271
    parathyroid, 349
    stem cells, 229
transportation services, 453
transthoracic mediastinotomy,
    240

transurethral surgery, 294
transverse colectomy, 263
transverse colon, 260–261
transversus abdominis, 143
trapezius, 145
trephine, 362
triangle symbol, 3
triceps brachii, 145
triceps lateral head, 143
tricuspid valve, 198
trigeminal nerve, 361
trochanter, 156
trochlear nerve, 359, 361
tumor, 114
tunica vaginalis, 305
twist drill hole, 362
two surgeons, 25
tympanic cavity, 391
tympanic membrane, 391
tympanic neurectomy, 395
tympanoplasty, 395
tympanostomy, 394

## U

UB-04 form, 464
ulcer, 126
ulcerated hemorrhoid, 267
ulna, 141–142, 156
ulnar nerve, 357
ultrasonography, 404
unbundling, 106
unplanned return to operating/procedure
    room by same physician, 27
unrelated E/M service by same
    physician, 19–20
unrelated procedure by same physician
    during postoperative period, 27
unrelated service by same physician,
    19–20
unusual anesthesia, 19
update notifications, 2
upper eyelid, 375
upper gastrointestinal endoscopy, 255
uptake, 414
ureter, 282, 289–290
ureteral orifices, 282
ureterectomy, 285
ureteroenterostomy, 290
ureterolithotomy, 289
ureterolysis, 290
ureteroneocystostomy, 290

ureteroplasty, 290
ureteropyelostomy, 290
ureterosigmoidostomy, 290
ureterostomy, 290
ureterotomy, 289
urethra, 282, 295, 304, 316
urethral meatus, 282
urethral orifice, 316, 318
urethropexy, 293
urinalysis, 427
urinary bladder, 282–283, 290–294, 304,
    316
urinary system, 280–301
    abbreviations, 281
    anatomy, 282
    bladder, 282–283, 290–294
    kidneys, 284–289
    NCCI, 281
    release of urine process, 283
    renal transplantation, 286
    transurethral surgery, 294
    ureter, 289–290
    urethra, 295
    urodynamics, 292
    vesical neck and prostate, 294
urodynamics, 292
uterus, 316
utricle, 392, 396
uvula, 248, 251

## V

V codes, 458
V-excision, 247
vaccines and toxoids, 9, 433–434
vagina, 316, 320–322
vaginal birth after cesarean (VBAC),
    338
vaginal cerclage, 336
vaginal delivery, antepartum care, and
    postpartum care, 337
vaginal hysterectomy, 323
vaginal orifice, 316, 318
vaginectomy, 320
vagotomy, 259
vagus nerve, 361
valve replacement, 204
valvotomy, 204
valvuloplasty, 204
vas deferens, 304, 307
vascular diagnostic studies
    (noninvasive), 441

vascular disease, 364
vascular embolization and occlusion,
    219
vascular families (App. L), 9
vascular injection procedures, 217
vasectomy, 307
vasotomy, 307
vasovasorrhaphy, 307
vasovasostomy, 307
vastus lateralis, 143, 145
vastus medialis, 143
VATS (video-assisted thoracic surgery),
    185
VBAC (vaginal birth after cesarean), 338
veins, 210–217
venipuncture, 217
venography, 407
venous access device, 217
venous circulation, 212
venous grafting for coronary artery
    bypass, 205
venous reconstruction, 211
ventral hernia, 271
ventricles, 196
ventricular fold, 178
vermiform appendix, 246, 261
vermilion, 247
vermilionectomy, 247
vertebral column, 141–142
very low birth weight (VLBW), 67
vesical neck and prostate, 294
vesicocentesis, 335
vessels, 210
vestibular glands, 318
vestibular nerve, 396
vestibule
    of ear, 392, 396
    of mouth, 249
video-assisted thoracic surgery (VATS),
    185
videoradiography, 409
views, 406
visceral pericardium, 196–197
visceral pleura, 170, 239
vision. See eye and ocular adnexa
vitrectomy, 381
vitreous humor, 376
VLBW (very low birth weight), 67
vocal cords, 169, 178
vulva and perineum, 317–319
vulvectomy, 319
VY-plasty, 120

## W

W-plasty, 120
wearable cardiac devices, 441
wedge excision, 116
Wernicke's area, 359
work-related or medical disability
    evaluation services, 75
wound(s)
  classification of, 118–119
  exploration of, 141
  of heart and great vessels, 203

wound care management, 445
wrist, 156

## X

X modifiers, 24–25
x-ray, 404
xenograft, 125

## Z

Z-plasty, 120
ZIFT (zygote intrafallopian transfer),
    326
zygote intrafallopian transfer (ZIFT),
    326

**W**

W-plasty, 120
wearable cardiac devices, 441
wedge excision, 116
Wernicke's area, 550
work-related or medical disaster
  evaluation services, 73
wound(s)
  classification of, 116–118
  exploration of, 141
  of heart and great vessels, 205
wound care management, 445
wrist, 150

**X**

X modifiers, 24–26
x-ray, 101
xenograft, 425

**Z**

Z-plasty, 120
ZIFT (zygote intrafallopian transfer), 320
zygote intrafallopian transfer (ZIFT), 320